Praise for Simon Sebag Montefiore's

Young Stalin

"It's a dark and terrifying story, and there could be no better guide than Montefiore. He has uncovered a mind-blowing amount of material from archives in Russia and Georgia. . . . The ultimate effect of *Young Stalin* is to create a haunting, meticulous and compelling story of a man well worth trying to understand."   —*Los Angeles Times Book Review*

"A prodigious researcher. . . . Montefiore has found new archival sources, interviewed survivors and visited the haunts and homes of the great dictator. . . . [He] enfolds even what is familiar about Stalin in a vivid narrative rich with new details and sensational revelations."
                                        —*The Washington Post Book World*

"Montefiore relates [Stalin's youth] with flair, writing in a style that is best described as propulsive. Yet *Young Stalin*'s greatest strength is the remarkable new material Montefiore has uncovered."
                                        —*San Francisco Chronicle*

"[A] fine biography. . . . Montefiore's portrait of Stalin in his childhood and youth is an extraordinarily detailed portrait of one of the twentieth century's trilogy of monsters."   —*Financial Times*

"A masterpiece of detail. . . . In Montefiore's hands we see a terrible evil born."   —*The Times* (London)

SIMON SEBAG MONTEFIORE

Young Stalin

Simon Sebag Montefiore is a historian and writer. His study of Josef Stalin in power, *Stalin: The Court of the Red Tsar*, won the History Book of the Year Prize at the British Book Awards. *Potemkin: Catherine the Great's Imperial Partner* was shortlisted for the Samuel Johnson, Duff Cooper, and Marsh Biography Prizes. Montefiore's books are worldwide bestsellers, published in thirty-four languages. His next history will be *Jerusalem: The Biography,* and he is the author of a novel, *Sashenka.* Born in 1965, Montefiore attended Cambridge University and is a Fellow of the Royal Society of Literature. He lives in London with his wife, the novelist Santa Montefiore, and their two children.

www.simonsebagmontefiore.com

Young Stalin

SIMON SEBAG MONTEFIORE

VINTAGE BOOKS
A DIVISION OF RANDOM HOUSE, INC.
NEW YORK

FIRST VINTAGE BOOKS EDITION, OCTOBER 2008

Copyright © 2007 by Simon Sebag Montefiore

All rights reserved. Published in the United States by Vintage Books, a division of Random House, Inc., New York. Originally published in Great Britain by Weidenfeld and Nicholson, the Orion Publishing Group Ltd., London, and subsequently in hardcover in the United States by Alfred A. Knopf, a division of Random House, Inc., New York, in 2007.

Vintage and colophon are registered trademarks of Random House, Inc.

The Library of Congress has cataloged the Knopf edition as follows:
Montefiore, Sebag.
Young Stalin / Simon Sebag Montefiore.
p. cm.
Includes bibliographical references and index.
1. Stalin, Joseph, 1879–1953.   2. Heads of state—Soviet Union—Biography.   I. Title.
DK268.S8M574 2007
947.084'2092—dc22
[B] 2007029220

Vintage ISBN: 978-1-4000-9613-8

Author photograph © Ian Jones
Book design by Soonyoung Kwon

www.vintagebooks.com

Printed in the United States of America
10 9 8 7 6 5 4 3 2 1

To my darling son,
Sasha

Contents

Illustrations

Alexander Davidov[17]
Lidia Pereprygina[17]
Bolshevik exiles photographed at Monastyrskoe in the summer of 1915[1]
Vera Shveitzer[14]
KGB boss Serov's memo to Khrushchev in 1956, about the investigation
  into Stalin's affair with thirteen-year-old Lidia Pereprygina[12]
Taurida Palace[3]
Soldiers in St. Petersburg, February–March 1917[3]

1917–1918

Lenin addresses the crowds from Kseshinskaya's palace in St. Petersburg,
  July 1917[3]
July Days coup[3]
Nadya Alliluyeva[1]
Stalin's bedroom in the Alliluyev apartment[3]
Lenin[1]
Smolny and new Soviet government, 1917[3]
The first meeting of the new government[15]
Lenin's orders to his guards on access to his office[15]
Stalin[5]
Alexandra Kollontai and Pavel Dybenko ca. 1917[5]
Stalin, ca. 1917[5]

The author and publishers offer their thanks to the following for their
kind permission to reproduce images:

1. David King Collection
2. Stalin House Museum, Gori
3. Author's collection
4. Davrichewy Family Collection
5. RIA Novosti
6. Khariton Akhvlediani State Museum, Batumi
7. Georgian Filial Institute of Marxism-Leninism (GF IML)
8. Mirrorpix
9. Getty
10. Roger Viollet / Topfoto
11. Azerbaijan International Magazine
12. RGASPI
13. Lisa Train
14. Dr. Piers Vitebsky
15. Smolny Institute Museum

16. Achinsk Regional Museum (ARM)
17. *The Sunday Times* (London)
18. Egnatashvili Family Collection

While every effort has been made to trace copyright holders, if any have been inadvertently overlooked, the publishers will be happy to acknowledge them in future editions.

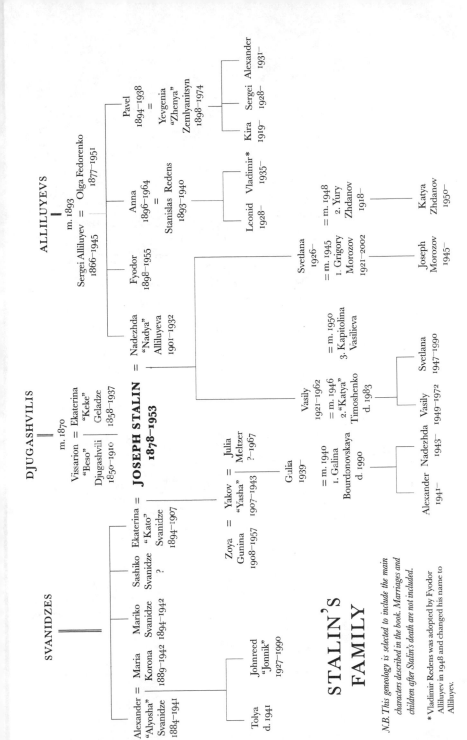

STALIN'S FAMILY

SVANIDZES

Alexander "Alyosha" Svanidze 1884–1941 = Maria Korona 1889–1942
Mariko Svanidze 1894–1942
Sashiko Svanidze ?
Ekaterina "Kato" Svanidze 1894–1907 = JOSEPH STALIN

Tolya d. 1941
Johnreed "Jonnik" 1927–1990

Zoya Gunina 1908–1957 = Yakov "Yasha" 1907–1943 = Julia Meltzer ?–1967
Gulia 1939–

DJUGASHVILIS

m. 1870
Vissarion "Beso" Djugashvili 1850–1910 = Ekaterina "Keke" Geladze 1858–1937

JOSEPH STALIN 1878–1953

ALLILUYEVS

m. 1893
Sergei Alliluyev 1866–1945 = Olga Fedorenko 1877–1951

Pavel 1894–1938 = Yevgenia "Zhenya" Zemlyanitsyn 1898–1974
Anna 1896–1964 = Stanislas Redens 1893–1940
Fyodor 1898–1955
Nadezhda "Nadya" Alliluyeva 1901–1932

Kira 1919–   Sergei 1928–   Alexander 1931–
Leonid 1928–   Vladimir* 1935–

JOSEPH STALIN = Nadezhda "Nadya" Alliluyeva

Vasily 1921–1962
= m. 1940 1. Galina Bourdonovskaya d. 1990
= m. 1946 2. "Katya" Timoshenko d. 1983
= m. 1950 3. Kapitolina Vasilieva

Svetlana 1926–
= m. 1945 1. Grigory Morozov 1921–2002
= m. 1948 2. Yury Zhdanov 1918–

Alexander 1941–   Nadezhda 1943–   Vasily 1949–1972   Svetlana 1947–1990

Joseph Morozov 1945–   Katya Zhdanov 1950–

N.B. This genealogy is selected to include the main characters described in the book. Marriages and children described after Stalin's death are not included.

* Vladimir Redens was adopted by Fyodor Alliluyev in 1948 and changed his name to Alliluyev.

The Russian Empire, 1878–1917

BARENTS SEA

Solvychegodsk

River Yenisei

Kureika
Monastyrskoe
Kostino

Perm

Narym

Achinsk
S I B E R I A
Novosibirsk
Krasnoyarsk
Novaya
Uda

MPIRE

Omsk

RAL
SEA

///// Western border of the Russian
Empire before 1914

++++ Rail trip taken by Stalin
in March 1917

0   1,000 miles
0   1,500 km

Gori   St. Petersburg

Gori   Moscow

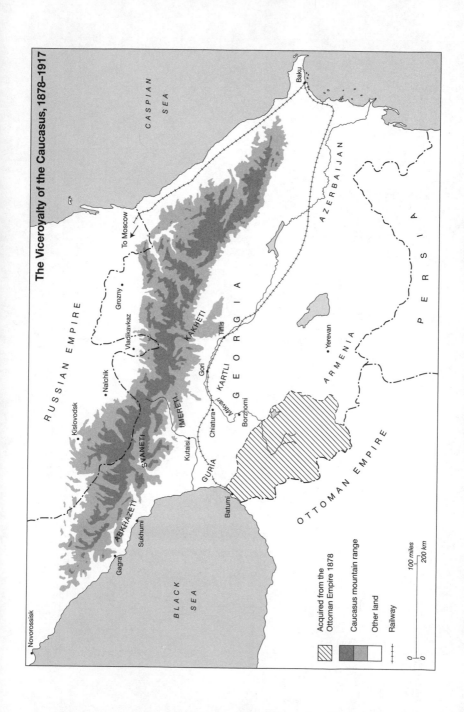

The Viceroyalty of the Caucasus, 1878–1917

CASPIAN SEA

Baku

RUSSIAN EMPIRE

To Moscow

Grozny

Vladikavkaz

Nalchik

Kislovodsk

KAKHETI

SWANETI

IMERETI

Tiflis

Gori

KARTLI

GEORGIA

Mtkvari

Chiatura

Borzhomi

Kutaisi

GURIA

ABKHAZETI

Sukhumi

Gagra

Batumi

AZERBAIJAN

PERSIA

Yerevan

ARMENIA

OTTOMAN EMPIRE

Novorossisk

BLACK SEA

Acquired from the
Ottoman Empire 1878

Caucasus mountain range

Other land

Railway

100 miles

200 km

0

0

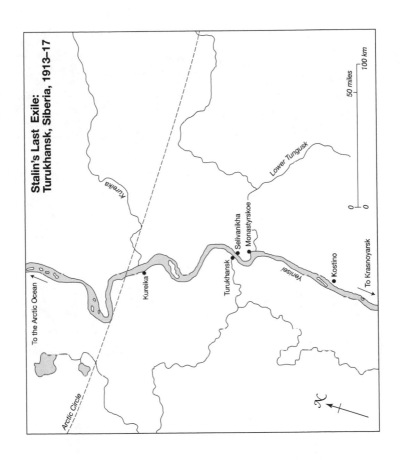

Stalin's Last Exile:
Turukhansk, Siberia, 1913–17

Kureika

To the Arctic Ocean

Arctic Circle

Kureika

Turukhansk

Selivanikha

Monastyrskoe

Lower Tungusk

Yenisei

Kostino

To Krasnoyarsk

0

0

50 miles

100 km

N

Introduction

"All young people are the same," said Stalin, "so why write . . . about the young Stalin?" Yet he was wrong: he was always different. His youth was dramatic, adventurous and exceptional. When in old age he reflected on the mysteries of his early years, he seemed to change his mind. "There are," he mused, "no secrets that won't be revealed for everyone later." For me as a historian unveiling his clandestine life up to his emergence as one of Lenin's top henchmen in the new Soviet government, he was right about the secrets: many of them can now be revealed.

There are few works on early Stalin (compared to many on young Hitler), but this is because there seemed to be so little material. In fact, this is not so. A wealth of vivid new material that brings to life his childhood and his career as revolutionary, gangster, poet, trainee priest, husband and prolific lover, abandoning women and illegitimate children in his wake, lay hidden in the newly opened archives, especially those of often-neglected Georgia.

Stalin's early life may have been shadowy but it was every bit as extraordinary as, and even more turbulent than, those of Lenin and Trotsky—and it equipped him (and damaged him) for the triumphs, tragedies and predations of supreme power.

Stalin's pre-revolutionary achievements and crimes were much greater than we knew. For the first time, we can document his role in the bank robberies, protection-rackets, extortion, arson, piracy, murder—the political gangsterism—that impressed Lenin and trained Stalin in the very skills that would prove invaluable in the political jungle of the Soviet Union. But we can also show that he was much more than a gangster godfather: he was also a political organizer, enforcer and master at infiltrating the Tsarist security services. In contrast to Zinoviev, Kamenev or Bukharin, whose reputations as great politicians are ironically founded on their destruction in the Terror, he was not afraid to take physical risks. But he also impressed Lenin as an independent and thoughtful politician, and as a vigorous editor and journalist, who was never afraid to confront and contradict the older man. Stalin's success was at least partly due to his unusual combination of education (thanks to the seminary) and street violence; he was that rare combination: both "intellectual" and killer. No wonder in 1917 Lenin turned to Stalin as the ideal lieutenant for his violent, beleaguered Revolution.

This book is the result of almost ten years of research on Stalin in twenty-three cities and nine countries, mainly in the newly opened archives of Moscow, Tbilisi and Batumi, but also in St. Petersburg, Baku, Vologda, Siberia, Berlin, Stockholm, London, Paris, Tampere, Helsinki, Cracow, Vienna and Stanford, California.

Young Stalin is written to be read on its own. This is a study of Stalin's life before power, up to his arrival in government in October 1917, whereas my last book, *Stalin: The Court of the Red Tsar*, covers Stalin in power up to his death in March 1953. Both are intimate histories of the man and politician but also of his milieu. I hope they will together form an introduction to the most elusive and fascinating of twentieth-century titans, showing the development and early maturity of the ultimate politician. What missing empathy in Stalin's upbringing allowed him to kill so easily, but equally what quality equipped him so well for political life? Were the cobbler's son of 1878, the idealistic seminarist of 1898, the brigand of 1907 and the forgotten Siberian hunter of 1914 destined to become the fanatical Marxist mass-murderer of the 1930s or the conqueror of Berlin in 1945?

My two books are not meant to form an exhaustive narrative history covering every political, ideological, economic, military, international and personal aspect of Stalin's life. That has already been superbly done, in different eras, by two scholars—Robert Conquest, the founding maestro of Stalinist history, with his *Stalin: Breaker of Nations* and, more recently, Robert Service, with his *Stalin: A Biography*—and I do not think I could improve on their broader works.

I make no apology that my two books are tightly focused on the intimate and secret, political and personal lives of Stalin and the small circle that ultimately came to create and rule the Soviet Union until the 1960s. Ideology must be our foundation as it was for the Bolsheviks, but the new archives show that the personalities and patronage of a minuscule oligarchy were the essence of politics under Lenin and Stalin, as they were under the Romanov emperors—and just as they are today under the "managed democracy" of twenty-first-century Russia.

Stalin's prolonged youth has always been a mystery, in many senses. Before 1917, he cultivated the mystique of obscurity but also specialized in the "black work" of underground revolution, which was, by its nature, secretive, violent and indispensible—but disreputable.

Once in power, Stalin's campaign to succeed Lenin required a legitimate heroic career which he did not possess because of his experience in what he called "the dirty business" of politics: this could not be told, either because it was too gangsterish for a great, paternalistic statesman or because it was too Georgian for a Russian leader. His solution was a clumsy but all-embracing cult of personality that invented, distorted and concealed the truth. Ironically this self-promotion was so grotesque that it fanned sparks, sometimes innocent ones, which flared up into colossal anti-Stalin conspiracy-theories. It was easy for his political opponents, and later for us historians, to believe that it was *all* invented and that he had done nothing much at all—particularly since few historians had researched in the Caucasus where so much of his early career took place. An anti-cult, as erroneous as the cult itself, grew up around these conspiracy-theories.

The most intriguing rumour remains: was Stalin a double-agent for the Tsar's secret police? The dictator's most infamous secret policemen, Nikolai Yezhov and Lavrenti Beria, secretly sought such evidence to use against Stalin in case he turned against them—as indeed he did. It is significant that neither of them, with the absolute researching power of the NKVD behind them, ever found that "smoking gun."

Yet there is a deeper mystery too: every historian has quoted Trotsky's claim that Stalin was a provincial "mediocrity" and Sukhanov's that he was just a "grey blur" in 1917. Most historians followed Trotsky's line that Stalin was so greyly mediocre that he failed to perform in 1905 and 1917, becoming, in Robert Slusser's words, "The Man Who Missed the Revolution."

Yet, if this was so, how did the "mediocrity" seize power, outwit talented politicians such as Lenin, Bukharin and Trotsky himself, and coordinate his programme of industrialization, the savage war on the peasantry and the ghoulish Great Terror? How did the "blur" become the homicidal but super-effective world statesman who helped create and industrialize the USSR, outplayed Churchill and Roosevelt, organized Stalingrad, and defeated Hitler? It is as if the pre-1917 mediocrity and the twentieth-century colossus cannot be the same man. So how did one become the other?

They are in fact absolutely the same man. It is clear from hostile and friendly witnesses alike that Stalin was always exceptional, even from childhood. We have relied on Trotsky's unrecognizably prejudiced portrait for too long. The truth was different. Trotsky's view tells us more about his own vanity, snobbery and lack of political skills than about the early Stalin. So the first aim of this work is to reveal the true record of Stalin's rise, as unblemished as possible by either the Stalinist cult or the anti-Stalin conspiracy-theory industry.

There is a tradition of biographies dealing with the early careers of great statesmen. Winston Churchill wrote of his own youth and there have been many works on his early career. The same goes for many other historical titans, such as both presidential Roosevelts. Young Hitler has become an industry, though no work comes close to the outstanding first volume of Ian Kershaw's *Hitler 1889–1936: Hubris*.

On Stalin, in a field of thousands of books, there have been just two serious Western works on his pre-1917 years: the excellent political-psychological *Stalin as Revolutionary* by Robert Tucker (1974), written long before the new archives were opened; and a Cold War work of anti-Stalin conspiracy-theory by Edward Ellis Smith (1967), who argues that Stalin was a Tsarist agent. There have been more in Russia, mainly journalistic sensationalism. However, the outstanding work is Alexander Ostrovsky's magisterial, indefatigable *Kto stoyal za spinoi Stalina?* (Who Was Behind Stalin?) (2002). My own work is indebted to all three.

So much of the inexplicable about the Soviet experience—the hatred of the peasantry for example, the secrecy and paranoia, the murderous witch hunt of the Great Terror, the placing of the Party above family and life itself, the suspicion of the USSR's own espionage that led to the success of Hitler's 1941 surprise attack—was the result of the underground life, the *konspiratsia* of the Okhrana and the revolutionaries, and also the Caucasian values and style of Stalin. And not just of Stalin.

By 1917, Stalin knew many of the characters who would form the Soviet elite and his court in the years of supreme power. The violence and clannishness of the Caucasians, men like Stalin, Ordzhonikidze and Shaumian, played a special role in the formation of the USSR at least as great as the contributions of the Latvians, Poles, Jews and perhaps even Russians. They were the essence of the "Committeemen," who formed the heart of the Bolshevik Party and were likely to support Stalin against intellectuals, Jews, émigrés and particularly the brilliant, haughty Trotsky. Such types took to the brutality of the Civil War (and to the liquidation of the peasantry, and to the Terror) because, like Stalin, indeed alongside him, they had been raised in the same streets, had shared gang warfare, clan rivalries, and ethnic slaughter, and had embraced the same culture of violence. My approach avoids much of the psycho-history that has both obscured and over-simplified our understanding of Stalin and Hitler. As I hope this book shows, Stalin was formed by much more than a miserable childhood, just as the USSR was formed by much more than Marxist ideology.

Yet the formation of Stalin's character is particularly important because the nature of his rule was so personal. Furthermore, Lenin and Stalin created the idiosyncratic Soviet system in the image of their ruthless little circle of conspirators before the Revolution. Indeed much of the tragedy of Leninism-Stalinism is comprehensible only if one realizes that the Bolsheviks continued to behave in the same clandestine style whether they formed the government of the world's greatest empire in the Kremlin or an obscure little cabal in the backroom of a Tiflis tavern.

It seems that Russia today—dominated by, and accustomed to, autocracy and empire, and lacking strong civic institutions especially after the shattering of its society by the Bolshevik Terror—is destined to be ruled by self-promoting cliques for some time yet. On a wider plane the murky world of terrorism is more relevant than ever today: terrorist organizations, whether Bolshevik at the beginning of the twentieth century or Jihadi at the start of the twenty-first, have much in common.

In 1917, Stalin had known Lenin for twelve years and many of the others for over twenty. So this is not just a biography but the chronicle of their milieu, a pre-history of the USSR itself, a study of the subterranean worm and the silent chrysalis before it hatched the steel-winged butterfly.[1]

List of Characters

THE SCHOOLMASTERS

Simon Gogchilidze, Stalin's singing teacher and patron at the Gori Church School

Prince David Abashidze, Father Dmitri, "Black Spot," priestly pedant at the Tiflis Seminary and Stalin's hated persecutor

THE GIRLS

Natalia "Natasha" Kirtava, landlady and girlfriend in Batumi

Alvasi Talakvadze, protégée and girlfriend in Baku

Ludmilla Stal, Bolshevik activist and girlfriend in Baku and St. Petersburg

Stefania Petrovskaya, Odessan noblewoman, exile, mistress and fiancée in Solvychegodsk and Baku

Pelageya "Polia" Onufrieva, "Glamourpuss," schoolgirl mistress in Vologda

Serafima Khoroshenina, mistress and partner in Solvychegodsk

Maria Kuzakova, landlady and mistress in Solvychegodsk, mother of Constantine

Tatiana "Tania" Slavatinskaya, married Bolshevik and mistress

Valentina Lobova, Bolshevik fixer and probable mistress

Lidia Pereprygina, thirteen-year-old orphan seduced by Stalin in Turukhansk and mother of two children by him, fiancée

COMRADES, ENEMIES AND RIVALS—TIFLIS AND BAKU

Lado Ketskhoveli, Gori priest's son, Stalin's Bolshevik mentor and hero

Prince Alexander "Sasha" Tsulukidze, rich aristocrat, Stalin's Bolshevik mentor and hero

Mikha Tskhakaya, founder of Georgian SDs (Social-Democrats), early Bolshevik, Stalin's patron

Philip Makharadze, Bolshevik and Stalin's sometime ally

Budu "the Barrel" Mdivani, actor and Bolshevik terrorist, Stalin's ally

Abel Yenukidze, early Bolshevik, friend of Alliluyevs, Svanidzes and Stalin

Silibistro "Silva" Jibladze, ex-seminarist, Menshevik firebrand

Lev Rosenblum, "Kamenev," well-off Tiflis engineer's son, moderate Bolshevik

Mikhail "Misha" Kalinin, peasant, butler, early Bolshevik in Tiflis

Suren Spandarian, son of well-off Armenian editor, Bolshevik, womanizer, Stalin's best friend

Stepan Shaumian, well-off Armenian Bolshevik, Stalin's ally and rival
Grigory "Sergo" Ordzhonikidze, poor nobleman, nurse, Bolshevik hard
    man, Stalin's longtime ally
Sergo Kavtaradze, young henchman of Stalin in western Georgia, Baku,
    St. Petersburg

WIVES AND IN-LAWS
Alexander "Alyosha" Svanidze, seminarist, Stalin friend, early Bolshevik
    and later brother-in-law
Alexandra "Sashiko" Svanidze, sister of above and Stalin friend
Mikheil Monoselidze, Sashiko's husband and Bolshevik ally of Stalin
Maria "Mariko" Svanidze, sister of Sashiko and Alyosha
Ekaterina "Kato" Svanidze Djugashvili, youngest of family, Stalin's first
    wife and mother of
Yakov "Yasha" or "Laddie" Djugashvili, Stalin's son
Sergei Alliluyev, railway and electrical manager, early Bolshevik, Stalin
    ally in Tiflis, Baku and St. Petersburg
Olga Alliluyeva, wife of Sergei, early Stalin friend, possibly mistress,
    later mother-in-law
Pavel Alliluyev, son of Olga
Anna Alliluyeva, daughter of Olga
Fyodor "Fedya" Alliluyev, son of Olga
Nadezhda "Nadya" Alliluyeva, daughter of Sergei and Olga, Stalin's
    second wife

GANGSTERS, MASTERMINDS AND FIXERS
Kamo, Simon "Senko" Ter-Petrossian, Stalin's friend, protégé, then bank
    robber and hitman
Kote Tsintsadze, Stalin's hitman and brigand in western Georgia and
    later bank-robbery chief
Leonid Krasin, Lenin's master of bomb-making, money-laundering,
    bank robberies and elite contacts, later fell out with Lenin
Meyer Wallach, "Maxim Litvinov," Bolshevik arms-dealer and money-
    launderer
Andrei Vyshinsky, well-off Odessa pharmacist's son, brought up in Baku,
    Stalin's enforcer and later Menshevik

THE TITAN OF MARXISM
Georgi Plekhanov, father of Russian Social-Democracy

THE BOLSHEVIKS

Vladimir Illich Ulyanov, "Lenin," or "Illich" to his intimates, Russian SD leader and founder of Bolsheviks

Nadezhda Krupskaya, his wife and assistant

Grigory Radomyslsky, "Zinoviev," Jewish milkman's son, Lenin's sidekick in Cracow, then ally of Kamenev

Roman Malinovsky, burglar, rapist and Okhrana spy, Bolshevik leader in the Imperial Duma

Yakov Sverdlov, Jewish Bolshevik leader and Stalin's roommate in exile

Lev Bronstein, "Trotsky," leader, orator and writer, independent Marxist, Menshevik Chairman of the Petersburg Soviet in 1905, joined Bolsheviks in 1917

Felix Dzerzhinsky, Polish nobleman, veteran revolutionary, joined Bolsheviks in 1917

Elena Stasova, "Absolute" and "Zelma," noblewoman and Bolshevik activist

Klimenti Voroshilov, Lugansk lathe-turner, Bolshevik friend of Stalin, roommate in Stockholm

Vyacheslav Scriabin, "Molotov," young Bolshevik and founder with Stalin of *Pravda*

THE MENSHEVIKS

Yuli Tsederbaum, "Martov," Lenin's friend then bitter enemy, founder of Mensheviks

Noe Jordania, founder of Georgian Social-Democracy and leader of Georgian Mensheviks

Nikolai "Karlo" Chkheidze, moderate Menshevik in Batumi and later in St. Petersburg

Isidore Ramishvili, Menshevik enemy of Stalin

Said Devdariani, Seminary friend then political enemy and Menshevik

Noe Ramishvili, tough Menshevik enemy of Stalin

Minadora Ordzhonikidze Toroshelidze, Menshevik friend of Stalin and wife of Bolshevik ally Malakia Toroshelidze

David Sagirashvili, Georgian Menshevik and memoirist

Grigol Uratadze, Georgian Menshevik and memoirist

Razhden Arsenidze, Georgian Menshevik and memoirist

Khariton Chavichvili, Menshevik memoirist

Note

STALIN

Stalin did not start to use his renowned name until 1912: it only became his surname after October 1917. His real name was Josef Vissarionovich Djugashvili. His mother, friends and comrades called him "Soso" even after 1917. He published poems as "Soselo." He increasingly called himself "Koba," but he used many names in the course of his secret life.

For the sake of clarity, "Stalin" and "Soso" are used throughout the book.

NAMES AND TRANSLITERATIONS
I have followed the same principles as I did in my other books on Russia. Wherever possible, I have tried to use the most recognizable, best-known and most easily transliterated versions of the Georgian and Russian names. Of course, this leads to many inconsistencies—for example, I call the Georgian Menshevik leader Noe Jordania, not Zhordania, and use Jibladze, not Djibladze, yet I feel I must spell Stalin's real name Djugashvili because it is so well known by that spelling. I use the French spellings of Davrichewy and Chavichvili (instead of Davrishashvili and Shavishvili) because their memoirs are published under these names. I apologize to the many linguists who may be appalled by this.

DATES
Dates are given in the Old Style Julian Calendar, used in Russia, which ran thirteen days behind the New Style Gregorian Calendar used in the

West. When describing events in the West, both dates are given. The Soviet government switched to the New Style Calendar at midnight on 31 January 1918 with the next day declared 14 February.

MONEY

In early-twentieth-century rates, 10 roubles = £1. The simplest way to convert this into today's money is to multiply by five to get pounds sterling and by ten to get U.S. dollars. A couple of examples: as a labourer in the Rothschild refineries in Batumi, young Stalin received 1.70 roubles per day, or 620 per annum ($6,000 or £3,000 per annum today). Tsar Nicholas II paid himself a personal allowance of 250,000 roubles a year while the bodyguard of the Tsarevich Alexei was paid a salary of 120 roubles a year ($1,200 or £600 per annum today). Yet these numbers are meaningless: the figures give little idea of real buying power and value. For example, Nicholas II was probably the richest man in the world, certainly in Russia. Yet his entire personal wealth of land, jewels, palaces, art and mineral deposits were calculated in 1917 as being worth 14 million roubles which, transferred into today's money, is a mere $140 million or £70 million— clearly an absurdly small figure.

TITLES

There are not always equivalents of Tsarist titles and ranks but I have tried to use as close an equivalent as possible. For the Russian autocrats, I use "Tsar" and "Emperor" interchangeably. Tsar Peter the Great crowned himself "Emperor" in 1721. The title of the ruler of the Caucasus varied. Grand Duke Mikhail Nikolaievich, son and brother of emperors, was the viceroy. His successor, Prince Grigory Golitsyn, in office during Stalin's seminary days, had the lesser rank of governor-general. His successor Count Illarion Vorontsov-Dashkov would again be viceroy in 1905–16.

DISTANCES/WEIGHTS
10 versts = 6.63 miles
1 pud = 36 lb.

Young Stalin

Prologue

The Bank Robbery

At 10:30 a.m. on the sultry morning of Wednesday, 26 June 1907, in the seething central square of Tiflis, a dashing moustachioed cavalry captain in boots and jodhpurs, wielding a big Circassian sabre, performed tricks on horseback, joking with two pretty, well-dressed Georgian girls who twirled gaudy parasols—while fingering Mauser pistols hidden in their dresses.

Raffish young men in bright peasant blouses and wide sailor-style trousers waited on the street corners, cradling secreted revolvers and grenades. At the louche Tilipuchuri Tavern on the square, a crew of heavily armed gangsters took over the cellar bar, gaily inviting passers-by to join them for drinks. All of them were waiting to carry out the first exploit by Josef Djugashvili, aged twenty-nine, later known as Stalin, to win the attention of the world.[1]

Few outside the gang knew of the plan that day for a criminal-terrorist "spectacular," but Stalin had worked on it for months. One man who did know the broad plan was Vladimir Lenin, the leader of the Bolshevik Party,* hiding in a villa in Kuokola, Finland, far to the north. Days

---

* In 1903, the Russian Social-Democratic Workers Party, founded in 1898, split into two factions, the Bolsheviks under Lenin and the Mensheviks under Martov, who fought one another but remained part of the same party until 1912 when they formally divided, never

earlier, in Berlin, and then in London, Lenin had secretly met with Stalin to order the big heist, even though their Social-Democratic Party had just strictly banned all "expropriations," the euphemism for bank robberies. But Stalin's operations, heists and killings, always conducted with meticulous attention to detail and secrecy, had made him the "main financier of the Bolshevik Centre."[2]

The events that day would make headlines all over the globe, literally shake Tiflis to its foundations, and further shatter the fragmented Social-Democrats into warring factions: that day would both make Stalin's career and almost ruin it—a watershed in his life.

In Yerevan Square, the twenty brigands who formed the core of Stalin's gang, known as "the Outfit," took up positions as their lookouts peered down Golovinsky Prospect, Tiflis's elegant main street, past the white Italianate splendour of the Viceroy's Palace. They awaited the clatter of a stagecoach and its squadron of galloping Cossacks. The army captain with the Circassian sabre caracoled on his horse before dismounting to stroll the fashionable boulevard.

Every street corner was guarded by a Cossack or policeman: the authorities were ready. Something had been expected since January. The informers and agents of the Tsar's secret police, the Okhrana, and his uniformed political police, the Gendarmes, delivered copious reports about the clandestine plots and feuds of the gangs of revolutionaries and criminals. In the misty twilight of this underground, the worlds of bandit and terrorist had merged and it was hard to tell tricks from truth. But there had been "chatter" about a "spectacular"—as today's intelligence experts would put it—for months.

On that dazzling steamy morning, the Oriental colour of Tiflis (now Tbilisi, the capital of the Republic of Georgia) hardly seemed to belong to the same world as the Tsar's capital, St. Petersburg, a thousand miles away. The older streets, without running water or electricity, wound up the slopes of Mtatsminda, Holy Mountain, until they were impossibly steep, full of crookedly picturesque houses weighed down with balconies, entwined with old vines. Tiflis was a big village where everyone knew everyone else.

Just behind the military headquarters, on genteel Freilinskaya Street, a stone's throw from the square, lived Stalin's wife, a pretty young Geor-

---

to reunite. Lenin organized and led a secret three-man cabal called the Bolshevik Centre to raise money using bank robbery and organized crime rackets.

gian dressmaker named Kato Svanidze, and their newborn son, Yakov. Theirs was a true love match: despite his black moods, Stalin was devoted to Kato, who admired and shared his revolutionary fervour. As she sunned herself and the baby on her balcony, her husband was about to give her, and Tiflis itself, an unholy shock.

This intimate city was the capital of the Caucasus, the Tsar's wild, mountainous viceroyalty between the Black and the Caspian Seas, a turbulent region of fierce and feuding peoples. Golovinsky Prospect seemed Parisian in its elegance. White neo-classical theatres, a Moorish-style opera house, grand hotels and the palaces of Georgian princes and Armenian oil barons lined the street, but, as one passed the military headquarters, Yerevan Square opened up into an Asiatic potpourri.

Exotically dressed hawkers and stalls offered spicy Georgian *lobio* beans and hot *khachapuri* cheesecake. Water-carriers, street-traders, pickpockets and porters delivered to or stole from the Armenian and Persian Bazaars, the alleyways of which more resembled a Levantine souk than a European city. Caravans of camels and donkeys, loaded with silks and spices from Persia and Turkestan, fruit and wineskins from the lush Georgian countryside, ambled through the gates of the Caravanserai. Its young waiters and errand boys served its clientele of guests and diners, carrying in the bags, unharnessing the camels—and watching the square. Now we know from the newly opened Georgian archives that Stalin, Faginlike, used the Caravanserai boys as a prepubescent revolutionary streetintelligence and courier service. Meanwhile in one of the Caravanserai's cavernous backrooms, the chief gangsters gave their gunmen a pep talk, rehearsing the plan one last time. Stalin himself was there that morning.

The two pretty teenage girls with twirling umbrellas and loaded revolvers, Patsia Goldava and Anneta Sulakvelidze, "brown-haired, svelte, with black eyes that expressed youth," casually sashayed across the square to stand outside the military headquarters, where they flirted with Russian officers, Gendarmes in smart blue uniforms, and bowlegged Cossacks.

Tiflis was—and still is—a languid town of strollers and boulevardiers who frequently stop to drink wine at the many open-air taverns: if the showy, excitable Georgians resemble any other European people, it is the Italians. Georgians and other Caucasian men, in traditional *chokha*—their skirted long coats lined down the chest with bullet pouches—swaggered down the streets, singing loudly. Georgian women in black head scarves, and the wives of Russian officers in European fashions, promenaded through the gates of the Pushkin Gardens, buying ices and sherbet along-

side Persians and Armenians, Chechens, Abkhaz and Mountain Jews, in a
fancy-dress jamboree of hats and costumes.

Gangs of street urchins—*kintos*—furtively scanned the crowds for
scams. Teenage trainee priests, in long white surplices, were escorted by
their berobed bearded priest-teachers from the pillared white seminary
across the street, where Stalin had almost qualified as a priest nine years
earlier. This un-Slavic, un-Russian and ferociously Caucasian kaleidoscope of East and West was the world that nurtured Stalin.

Checking the time, the girls Anneta and Patsia parted, taking up new
positions on either side of the square. On Palace Street, the dubious clientele of the notorious Tilipuchuri Tavern—princes, pimps, informers and
pickpockets—were already drinking Georgian wine and Armenian
brandy, not far from the plutocratic grandeur of Prince Sumbatov's palace.

Just then David Sagirashvili, another revolutionary who knew Stalin
and some of the gangsters, visited a friend who owned a shop above the
tavern and was invited in by the cheerful brigand at the doorway, Bachua
Kupriashvili, who "immediately offered me a chair and a glass of red wine,
according to the Georgian custom." David drank the wine and was about
to leave when the gunman suggested "with exquisite politeness" that he
stay inside and "sample more snacks and wine." David realized that "they
were letting people *into* the restaurant but would not let them *out*. Armed
individuals stood at the door."

Spotting the convoy galloping down the boulevard, Patsia Goldava,
the slim brunette on lookout, sped round the corner to the Pushkin Gardens where she waved her newspaper to Stepko Intskirveli, waiting by the
gate.

"We're off!" he muttered.

Stepko nodded at Anneta Sulakvelidze, who was across the street just
outside the Tilipuchuri, where she made a sign summoning the others
from the bar. The gunmen in the doorway beckoned them. "At a given
signal" Sagirashvili saw the brigands in the tavern put down their drinks,
cock their pistols and head out, spreading across the square—thin, consumptive young men in wide trousers who had barely eaten for weeks.
Some were gangsters, some desperadoes and some, typically for Georgia,
were poverty-stricken princes from roofless, wall-less castles in the
provinces. If their deeds were criminal, they cared nothing for money:
they were devoted to Lenin, the Party and their puppet-master in Tiflis,
Stalin.

"The functions of each of us had been planned in advance," remembered a third girl in the gang, Alexandra Darakhvelidze, just nineteen, a friend of Anneta, and already veteran of a spree of heists and shootouts.

The gangsters each covered the square's policemen—the *gorodovoi*, known in the streets as *pharaoh*s. Two gunmen marked the Cossacks outside the City Hall; the rest made their way to the corner of Velyaminov Street and the Armenian Bazaar, not far from the State Bank itself. Alexandra Darakhvelidze, in her unpublished memoirs, recalled guarding one of the street corners with two gunmen.

Now Bachua Kupriashvili, nonchalantly pretending to read a newspaper, spotted in the distance the cloud of dust thrown up by the horses' hooves. They were coming! Bachua rolled up his newspaper, poised . . .

The cavalry captain with the flashing sabre, who had been promenading the square, now warned passers-by to stay out of it, but when no one paid any attention he jumped back onto his fine horse. He was no officer but the ideal of the Georgian *beau sabreur* and outlaw, half-knight, half-bandit. This was Kamo, aged twenty-five, boss of the Outfit and, as Stalin put it, "a master of disguise" who could pass for a rich prince or a peasant laundrywoman. He moved stiffly, his half-blind left eye squinting and rolling: one of his own bombs had exploded in his face just weeks before. He was still recuperating.

Kamo "was completely enthralled" by Stalin, who had converted him to Marxism. They had grown up together in the violent town of Gori forty-five miles away. He was a bank robber of ingenious audacity, a Houdini of prison-escapes, a credulous simpleton—and a half-insane practitioner of psychopathic violence. Intensely, eerily tranquil with a weird "lustreless face" and a blank gaze, he was keen to serve his master, often begging Stalin: "Let me kill him for you!" No deed of macabre horror or courageous flamboyance was beyond him: he later plunged his hand into a man's chest and cut out his heart.

Throughout his life, Stalin's detached magnetism would attract, and win the devotion of, amoral, unbounded psychopaths. His boyhood henchman Kamo and these gangsters were the first in a long line. "Those young men followed Stalin selflessly . . . Their admiration for him allowed him to impose on them his iron discipline."[3] Kamo often visited Stalin's home, where he had earlier borrowed Kato's father's sabre, explaining that he was "going to play an officer of the Cossacks."[4] Even Lenin, that fastidious lawyer, raised as a nobleman, was fascinated by the daredevil Kamo, whom he called his "Caucasian bandit." "Kamo," mused Stalin in old age, "was a truly amazing person."[5]

"Captain" Kamo turned his horse towards the boulevard and trotted audaciously right past the advancing convoy, coming the other way. Once the shooting started, he boasted, the whole thing "would be over in three minutes."

The Cossacks galloped into Yerevan Square, two in front, two behind and another alongside the two carriages. Through the dust, the gangsters could make out that the stagecoach contained two men in frockcoats—the State Bank's cashier Kurdyumov and accountant Golovnya—and two soldiers with rifles cocked, while a second phaeton was packed with police and soldiers. In the thunder of hooves, it took just seconds for the carriages and horsemen to cross the square ready to turn into Sololaki Street, where stood the new State Bank: the statues of lions and gods over its door represented the surging prosperity of Russian capitalism.*

Bachua lowered his newspaper, giving the sign, then tossed it aside, reaching for his weapons. The gangsters drew out what they nicknamed their "apples"—powerful grenades which had been smuggled into Tiflis by the girls Anneta and Alexandra, hidden inside a big sofa.

The gunmen and the girls stepped forward, pulled the fuses and tossed four grenades which exploded under the carriages with a deafening noise and an infernal force that disembowelled horses and tore men to pieces, spattering the cobbles with innards and blood. The brigands drew their Mauser and Browning pistols and opened fire on the Cossacks and police around the square who, caught totally unawares, fell wounded or ran for cover. More than ten bombs exploded. Witnesses thought they rained from every direction, even the rooftops: it was later said that Stalin had thrown the first bomb from the roof of Prince Sumbatov's mansion.

The bank's carriages stopped. Screaming passers-by scrambled for cover. Some thought it was an earthquake: was Holy Mountain falling on to the city? "No one could tell if the terrible shooting was the boom of cannons or explosion of bombs," reported the Georgian newspaper *Isari* (Arrow). "The sound caused panic everywhere . . . almost across the whole city, people started running. Carriages and carts were galloping

---

* The distances in this urban village are tiny. The seminary, Stalin's family home, the Viceroy's Palace and the bank are all about two minutes' walk from the site of the bank robbery. Most of the buildings in Yerevan (later Beria, then Lenin, now Freedom) Square that feature here remain standing: the Tilipuchuri Tavern (now empty of any princes or brigands), the seminary (now a museum), the City Hall, the HQ of the Caucasus Command, the State Bank and the Viceroy's Palace (where Stalin's mother lived for so long) are all unchanged. The Caravanserai, Pushkin Gardens, Adelkhanov Shoe Warehouse (where Stalin had worked) and the bazaars are gone.

away . . ." Chimneys had toppled from buildings; every pane of glass was shattered as far as the Viceroy's Palace.

Kato Svanidze was standing on her nearby balcony tending Stalin's baby with her family, "when all of a sudden we heard the sound of bombs," recalled her sister, Sashiko. "Terrified, we rushed into the house." Outside, amid the yellow smoke and the wild chaos, among the bodies of horses and mutilated limbs of men, something had gone wrong.

One horse attached to the front carriage twitched, then jerked back to life. Just as the gangsters ran to seize the money-bags in the back of the carriage, the horse reared up out of the mayhem and bolted down the hill towards the Soldiers Bazaar, disappearing with the money that Stalin had promised Lenin for the Revolution.[6]

During the ensuing century, Stalin's role that day was suspected yet unprovable. But now the archives in Moscow and Tbilisi show how he masterminded the operation and groomed his "inside-men" within the Bank over many months. The unpublished memoirs of his sister-in-law Sashiko Svanidze, in the Georgian archives, record Stalin openly acknowledging that he presided over the operation.* A century after the heist, it is now possible to reveal the truth.

Stalin revelled in the "dirty business of politics," the conspiratorial drama of revolution. When he was dictator of Soviet Russia, he referred enigmatically, even nostalgically, to those games of "Cossacks and bandits"—*kazaki i razboyniki*, the Russian version of "cops and robbers"— but never gave details that might undermine his credentials as a statesman.[7]

The Stalin of 1907 was a small, wiry, mysterious man of many aliases, usually dressed in a red satin shirt, grey coat and his trademark black fedora. Sometimes he favoured a traditional Georgian *chokha*, and he liked to sport a white Caucasian hood, draped dashingly over his shoulder. Always on the move, often on the run, he used the many uniforms of Tsarist society as his disguises, and frequently escaped manhunts by dressing in drag.

---

* Stalin would not have thanked the Svanidzes for their frankness. They were close family for thirty years. His sister-in-law Sashiko, who left this memoir in 1934, died of cancer in 1936—or she might have shared the fate of her sister Mariko, her brother Alyosha and his wife. Sashiko Svanidze's memoirs are used here for the first time. Some of the bank robbers, such as Kamo, Bachua Kupriashvili and Alexandra Darakhvelidze, left unpublished, if incomplete, memoirs, also used here for the first time.

Attractive to women, often singing Georgian melodies and declaiming poetry, he was charismatic and humorous, yet profoundly morose, an odd Georgian with a northern coldness. His "burning" eyes were honey-flecked when friendly, yellow when angry. He had not yet settled on the moustache and hair *en brosse* of his prime: he sometimes grew a full beard and long hair, still with the auburn tinge of his youth, now darkening. Freckled and pockmarked, he walked fast but crookedly, and held his left arm stiffly, after a spate of childhood accidents and illnesses.

Indefatigable in action, he bubbled with ideas and ingenuity. Inspired by a hunger for learning and an instinct to teach, he feverishly studied novels and history, but his love of letters was always overwhelmed by his drive to command and dominate, to vanquish enemies and avenge slights. Patient, calm and modest, he could also be vainglorious, pushy and thin-skinned, with outbursts of viciousness just a short fuse away.

Immersed in the honour and loyalty culture of Georgia, he was the gritty realist, the sarcastic cynic and the pitiless cutthroat *par excellence*: it was he who had created the Bolshevik bank-robbery and assassination Outfit, which he controlled from afar like a Mafia don. He cultivated the coarseness of a peasant, a trait which alienated comrades but usefully concealed his subtle gifts from snobbish rivals.

Happily married to Kato, he had chosen a heartless wandering existence that, he believed, liberated him from normal morality or responsibility, free from love itself. Yet while he wrote about the megalomania of others, he had no self-knowledge about his own drive for power. He relished his own secrecy. When he knocked on the doors of friends and they asked who was there, he would answer with mock-portentousness: "The Man in Grey."

One of the first professional revolutionaries, the underground was his natural habitat, through which he moved with elusively feline grace—and menace. A born extremist and conspirator, the Man in Grey was a true believer, "a Marxist fanatic from his youth." The violent rites of Stalin's secret planet of Caucasian conspiracy would later flower into the idiosyncratic ruling culture of the Soviet Union itself.[8]

"Stalin had opened the era of the hold-up," wrote one of his fellow bank-robbery masterminds, his hometown friend Josef Davrichewy.[9] Stalin, we used to believe, organized operations but never took part personally. This may have been true that day in 1907, but we know now that Stalin himself, usually armed with his Mauser, was more directly involved in other robberies.[10]

He always kept his eyes skinned for the spectacular prize and knew that the best bank robberies are usually inside jobs. On this occasion, he had two "inside-men." First, he patiently groomed a useful bank clerk. Then he bumped into a school friend who happened to work for the banking mail office. Stalin cultivated him for months until he proffered the tip that a huge sum of money—perhaps as much as a million roubles—would arrive in Tiflis on 13 June 1907.

This key "inside-man" afterwards revealed that he had helped set up this colossal heist only because he was such an admirer of Stalin's romantic poetry. Only in Georgia could Stalin the poet enable Stalin the gangster.[11]

The runaway horse with the carriage and its booty bolted across the square. Some of the gangsters panicked, but three gunmen moved with astonishing speed. Bachua Kupriashvili kept his head and sprinted towards the horse. He was too close for his own safety, but he tossed another "apple" under its belly, tearing out its intestines and blowing off its legs. Thrown into the air, Bachua fell stunned to the cobbles.

The carriage careened to a halt. Bachua was out of action but Datiko Chibriashvili jumped onto the coach and pulled out the sacks of money. Gripping the money-bags, he staggered through the smoke towards Velyaminov Street. But the gang was in disarray. Datiko could not run far holding the weight of the banknotes: he must hand them over—but to whom?

The drifting smoke parted to reveal carnage worthy of a small battle-field. Screams and shots still rent the air as blood spread across cobbles strewn with body parts. Cossacks and soldiers started to peep out, reaching for their weapons. Reinforcements were on their way from across the city. "All the comrades," wrote Bachua Kupriashvili, "were up to the mark—except three who had weak nerves and ran off." Yet Datiko found himself momentarily almost alone. He hesitated, lost. The success of the plan hung by a thread.

Did Stalin really throw the first bomb from the roof of Prince Sumbatov's house? Another source, P. A. Pavlenko, one of the dictator's pet writers, claimed that Stalin had attacked the carriage himself and been wounded by a bomb fragment. But this seems unlikely.[12] Stalin usually "held himself apart" from everyone else in all matters for security reasons and because he always regarded himself as special.[13]

In the 1920s, according to Georgian sources, Kamo would drunkenly claim that Stalin had taken no active part but had watched the robbery, a report confirmed by another, questionable source connected to the police, who wrote that Stalin "observed the ruthless bloodshed, smoking a cigarette, from the courtyard of a mansion" on Golovinsky Prospect. Perhaps the "mansion" was indeed Prince Sumbatov's.[14] The boulevard's milkbars,* taverns, cobblers, hairdressers and haberdashers crawled with Okhrana informers. Most likely, Stalin, the clandestine master who specialized in sudden appearances and vanishings, was out of the way before the shooting started. Indeed the most informed source puts him in the railway station that mid-morning.[15]

Here he could keep in easy contact with his network of porters and urchins on Yerevan Square. If these artful dodgers brought bad news, he would jump on a train and disappear.

Just as the robbery was about to collapse, "Captain" Kamo rode into the square driving his own phaeton, reins in one hand and firing his Mauser with the other. Furious that the plan had failed, cursing at the top of his voice "like a real captain," he whirled his carriage round and round, effectively retaking possession of the square. Then he galloped up to Datiko, leaned down and, aided by one of the gun girls, heaved the sacks of money into the phaeton. He turned the carriage precipitously and galloped back up the boulevard right past the Viceroy's Palace, which was buzzing like a beehive as troops massed, Cossacks saddled up and orders for reinforcements were despatched.

Kamo noticed a police phaeton cantering along in the opposite direction bearing A. G. Balabansky, the deputy police chief. "The money's safe. Run to the square," shouted Kamo. Balabansky headed for the square. Only the next day did Balabansky realize his mistake. He committed suicide.

Kamo rode straight to Vtoraya Goncharnaya Street and into the yard of a joiner's shop behind a house owned by an old lady named Barbara "Babe" Bochoridze. Here, with Babe's son Mikha, Stalin had spent many nights over the years. Here the robbery had been planned. It was an address well known to the local police, but the gangsters had suborned at least one Gendarme officer, Captain Zubov, who was later indicted for taking bribes—and even helping to hide the spoils. Kamo, exhausted,

---

* The popular cafés of the day.

delivered the money, changed out of his uniform and poured a bucket of water over his sweltering head.

The shock waves of Stalin's spectacular reverberated around the world. In London the *Daily Mirror* announced RAIN OF BOMBS: REVOLUTIONARIES HURL DESTRUCTION AMONG LARGE CROWDS OF PEOPLE: "About ten bombs were hurled today, one after another, in the square in the centre of town, thronged with people. The bombs exploded with terrific force, many being killed . . ." *The Times* just called it TIFLIS BOMB OUTRAGE; *Le Temps* in Paris was more laconic: CATASTROPHE!

Tiflis was in uproar. The usually genial viceroy of the Caucasus, Count Vorontsov-Dashkov, ranted about the "insolence of the terrorists." The "administration and army are mobilized," announced *Isari*. "Police and patrols launched searches across the city. Many have been arrested . . ." St. Petersburg was outraged. The security forces were ordered to find the money and the robbers. A special detective and his team were despatched to head the investigation. Roads were closed; Yerevan Square was surrounded, while Cossacks and Gendarmes rounded up the usual suspects. Every informer, every double-agent was tapped for information and duly delivered a farrago of versions, none of them actually fingering the real culprits.

Twenty thousand roubles had been left in the carriage. A surviving carriage driver, who thought he had got lucky, pocketed another 9,500 roubles but was arrested with it later: he knew nothing about the Stalin and Kamo gang. A jabbering woman gave herself up as one of the bank robbers but turned out to be insane.

No one could guess how many robbers there had been: witnesses thought there were up to fifty gangsters raining bombs from the roofs, if not from Holy Mountain. No one actually saw Kamo take the banknotes. The Okhrana heard stories from all over Russia that the robbery was, variously, arranged by the state itself, by Polish socialists, by Anarchists from Rostov, by Armenian Dashnaks, or by the Socialist-Revolutionaries.

None of the gangsters was caught. Even Kupriashvili regained consciousness just in time to hobble away. In the chaotic aftermath, they scarpered in every direction, melting into the crowds. One, Eliso Lominadze, who had been covering a street-corner with Alexandra, slipped into a teachers' conference, stole a teacher's uniform and then nonchalantly wandered back to the square to admire his handiwork. "Everyone survived it," said Alexandra Darakhvelidze, dictating her memoirs in 1959, by then the only member of the ill-fated gang still alive.

Fifty lay wounded in the square. The bodies of three Cossacks, the bank officials and some innocent passers-by lay in pieces. The censored newspapers kept casualties low but the Okhrana's archives reveal that around forty were killed. Dressing-stations for the wounded were set up in nearby shops. Twenty-four seriously wounded were taken to hospital. An hour later, passers-by saw the funereal progress of a ghoulish carriage carrying the dead and their body-parts down Golovinsky, like the giblets from an abattoir.[16]

The State Bank itself was unsure if it had lost 250,000 roubles or 341,000, or somewhere between the two figures—but it was certainly an impressive sum worth about £1.7 million (U.S. $3.4 million) in today's money though its effective buying power was much higher.

Bochoridze and his wife, Maro, another of the female bank robbers, sewed the money into a mattress. Svelte Mauser-toting Patsia Goldava then called porters, perhaps some of Stalin's urchins, and supervised its removal to another safe house across the river Kura. The mattress was then placed on the couch of the director of the Tiflis Meteorological Observatory, where Stalin had lived and worked after leaving the seminary. It was Stalin's last job before he plunged into the conspiratorial underground, indeed his last real employment before he joined Lenin's Soviet government in October 1917. Later the director of this weather-centre admitted he had never known what riches lay under his head.

Stalin himself, many sources claim, helped stow the cash in the observatory. If this sounds like a myth, it is plausible: it transpires that he often handled stolen funds, riding shotgun across the mountains with saddle-bags full of cash from bank robberies and piracy.

Surprisingly, that night Stalin felt safe enough to go home to Kato and boast of his exploit to his family—his boys had done it.[17] Well might he boast. The money was safe in the weatherman's mattress and would soon be on its way to Lenin. No one suspected Stalin or even Kamo. The booty would be smuggled abroad, some of it even laundered through the Credit Lyonnais. The police of a dozen nations would pursue cash and gangsters for months, in vain.

For a couple of days after the heist, Stalin, it is said, unsuspected of any connection to the robbery, was secure enough to drink insouciantly in riverside taverns, but not for long. He suddenly told his wife that they were leaving at once to start a new life in Baku, the oil-boom city on the other side of the Caucasus.

"The devil knows," reflected *Novoye Vremya* (the Tiflis *New Times*), "how this uniquely audacious robbery was carried out." Stalin had pulled off the perfect crime.

The Tiflis bank robbery turned out to be far from perfect. Indeed it became a poisoned chalice. Afterwards, Stalin never lived in Tiflis or Georgia again. The fate of Kamo would be insanely bizarre. The quest for the cash—some of which, it turned out, was in marked notes—would be tangled, but even these astonishing twists were far from the end of the matter for Stalin. The heist's success was almost a disaster for him. The robbery's global notoriety became a powerful weapon against Lenin, and against Stalin personally.

The gangsters fell out over the spoils. Lenin and his comrades fought for possession of the cash like rats in a cage. His enemies spent the next three years launching three separate Party investigations hoping to ruin him. Stalin, *persona non grata* in Georgia, tainted by the brazen flouting of Party rules and this reckless carnage, was expelled from the Party by the Tiflis Committee. This was a blot that could have derailed his bid to succeed Lenin and spoiled his ambition to become a Russian statesman and a supreme pontiff of Marxism. It was so sensitive that even in 1918 Stalin launched an extraordinary libel case to suppress the story.* His career as gangster godfather, audacious bank robber, killer, pirate and arsonist, though whispered at home and much enjoyed by critics abroad, remained hidden until the twenty-first century.

In another sense, the Tiflis spectacular was the making of him. Stalin had now proved himself, not only as a gifted politician but also as a ruthless man of action, to the one patron who really counted. Lenin decided that Stalin was "exactly the kind of person I need."

Stalin, his wife and baby vanished from Tiflis two days later—but it was far from his last heist. There were new worlds to conquer—Baku, the

---

* In the 1920s, before he was dictator, Stalin went to remarkable lengths to conceal his role in the expropriations. In 1923–24, his chief gangster, Kote Tsintsadze, by then in opposition to Stalin, published his memoirs in a small Georgian journal. They were republished in 1927 but afterwards the pages involving Stalin's part in assassinations and robberies were removed, a process continuing in the 1930s under Beria. Today, they are extremely hard to find.

greatest oil city in the world, St. Petersburg the capital, and vast Russia herself. Indeed Stalin, the Georgian child raised rough on the violent, clannish streets of a turbulent town that was the bank-robbery capital of the Empire, now stepped, for the first time, onto the Russian stage. He never looked back.

Yet he was on the eve of a personal tragedy which helped transform this murderous egomaniac into the supreme politician for whom no prize, no challenge and no cost in human life would be too great to realize his personal ambitions and his utopian dreams.[18]

PART ONE

Morning

The rose's bud had blossomed out
Reaching out to touch the violet
The lily was waking up
And bending its head in the breeze

High in the clouds the lark
Was singing a chirruping hymn
While the joyful nightingale
With a gentle voice was saying —

"Be full of blossom, oh lovely land
Rejoice Iverians' country
And you oh Georgian, by studying
Bring joy to your motherland."

—SOSELO (Josef Stalin)

Keke's Miracle: Soso

On 17 May 1872, a handsome young cobbler, the very model of a chivalrous Georgian man, Vissarion "Beso" Djugashvili, aged twenty-two, married Ekaterina "Keke" Geladze, seventeen, an attractive freckled girl with auburn hair, at the Uspensky Church in the small Georgian town of Gori.[1]

A matchmaker had visited Keke's house to tell her about the suit of Beso the cobbler: he was a respected artisan in Baramov's small workshop, quite a catch. "Beso," says Keke in newly discovered memoirs,* "was considered a very popular young man among my friends and they were all dreaming of marrying him. My friends nearly burst with jealousy. Beso was an enviable groom, a true *karachogheli* [Georgian knight], with beautiful moustaches, very well dressed—and with the special sophistication of a town-dweller." Nor was Keke in any doubt that she herself was some-

---

* The memoirs have lain in the Georgian Communist Party archive, forgotten for seventy years. They were never used in the Stalinist cult. It seems Stalin neither read them nor knew they existed because, as far as this author can learn, they were not sent to Stalin's Moscow archives. He did not want his mother's views published. When Keke was interviewed *Hello!* magazine style in 1935 in the Soviet press, Stalin furiously reprimanded the Politburo: "I ask you to forbid the Philistine riffraff that has penetrated our press from publishing any more 'interviews' with my mother and all other crass publicity. I ask you to spare me from the importunate sensationalism of these scoundrels!" Keke, always strong-willed and unimpressed with her son's power, must have recorded them secretly and in defiance of him on 23–27 August 1935, shortly before her death.

thing of a catch too: "Among my female friends, I became the desired and beautiful girl." Indeed, "slender, chestnut-haired with big eyes," she was said to be "very pretty."

The wedding, according to tradition, took place just after sunset; Georgian social life, writes one historian, was "as ritualised as English Victorian behaviour." The marriage was celebrated with the rambunctious festivity of the wild town of Gori. "It was," Keke remembers, "hugely glamorous." The male guests were true *karachogheli*, "cheerful, daring and generous," wearing their splendid black *chokha*s, "broad-shouldered with slim waists." The chief of Beso's two best men was Yakov "Koba" Egnatashvili, a strapping wrestler, wealthy merchant and local hero who, as Keke puts it, "always tried to assist us in the creation of our family."

The groom and his friends gathered for toasts at his home, before parading through the streets to collect Keke and her family. The garlanded couple then rode to church together in a colourfully decorated wedding phaeton, bells tingling, ribbons fluttering. In the church, the choir gathered in the gallery; below them, men and women stood separately among the flickering candles. The singers burst into their elevating and harmonic Georgian melodies accompanied by a *zurna*, a Georgian wind instrument like a Berber pipe.

The bride entered with her bridesmaids, who were careful not to tread on the train, a special augur of bad luck. Father Khakhanov, an Armenian, conducted the ceremony, Father Kasradze recorded the marriage, and Father Christopher Charkviani, a family friend, sang so finely that Yakov Egnatashvili "generously tipped him 10 roubles," no mean sum. Afterwards, Beso's friends headed the traditional singing and dancing procession through the streets, playing *duduki*, long pipes, to the *supra*, a Georgian feast presided over by a *tamada*, a joke-telling and wisdom-imparting toastmaster.

The service and singing had been in the unique Georgian language—not Russian because Georgia was only a recent addition to the Romanov Empire. For a thousand years, ruled by scions of the Bagrationi dynasty, the Kingdom of Sakartvelo (Georgia to Westerners, Gruzia to Russians) was an independent Christian bulwark of knightly valour against the Islamic Mongol, Timurid, Ottoman and Persian Empires. Its apogee was the twelfth-century empire of Queen Tamara, made timeless by the national epic, *The Knight in the Panther Skin* by Rustaveli. Over the centuries, the kingdom splintered into bickering principalities. In 1801 and 1810, the Tsars Paul and Alexander I annexed principalities to their empire. The Russians had only finished the military conquest of the Caucasus with the surrender of Imam Shamyl and his Chechen warriors in 1859 after a thirty-year war—and Adjaria, the last slice of Georgia, was gained in 1878. Even the most aristocratic Georgians, who served at the courts of the Emperor in St. Petersburg or of the viceroy in Tiflis, dreamed of independence. Hence Keke's pride in following Georgian traditions of manhood and marriage.

Beso, mused Keke, "*appeared* to be a good family man . . . He believed in God and always went to church." The parents of both bride and groom had been serfs of local princes, freed in the 1860s by the Tsar-Liberator, Alexander II. Beso's grandfather Zaza was an Ossetian* from the village of Geri, north of Gori.[2] Zaza, like Stalin, his great-grandson, became a Georgian rebel: in 1804, he joined the uprising of Prince Elizbar Eristavi against Russia. Afterwards, he was settled with other "baptized Ossetians" in the village of Didi-Lilo, nine miles from Tiflis, as a serf of Prince Badur Machabeli. Zaza's son Vano tended the Prince's vineyards and had two sons: Giorgi, who was murdered by bandits, and Beso, who got a job in Tiflis in the shoe factory of G. G. Adelkhanov but was headhunted by the Armenian Josef Baramov to make boots for the Russian garrison in Gori.[3] There young Beso noticed the "fascinating, neatly dressed girl with chestnut hair and beautiful eyes."

Keke was also new to Gori, daughter of Glakho Geladze, a peasant serf of the local grandee, Prince Amilakhvari. Her father worked as a potter nearby before becoming the gardener for a wealthy Armenian, Zakhar Gambarov, who owned fine gardens at Gambareuli, on Gori's outskirts. As her father died young, Keke was raised by her mother's family. She remembered the excitement of moving to unruly Gori: "What a happy journey it was! Gori was festively decorated, crowds of people swelled like

---

* The Ossetians were a semi-pagan mountain people who lived on the northern borders of Georgia proper, some becoming assimilated Georgians though most remain proudly separate: in 1991–93, South Ossetians fought the Georgians and are now autonomous. When Stalin's dying father was admitted to hospital, significantly he was still registered as Ossetian. Stalin's enemies, from Trotsky to the poet Mandelstam in his famous poem, relished calling him an "Ossete" because Georgians regarded Ossetians as barbarous, crude and, in the early nineteenth century, non-Christian. Djugashvili certainly sounds as if it has an Ossetian root: it means "son of Djuga" in Georgian. Stalin's mother says Beso told her the name was based on the Georgian *djogi*, or "herd," root because they were herdsmen and were driven out of Geri by marauding Ossetians. The real relevance is lost because, by the time of Stalin's birth, the Djugashvilis were totally Georgianized. Stalin himself wrote about this: "What is to be done with the Ossetians . . . becoming assimilated by the Georgians?"

the sea. A military parade dazzled our eyes. Music blared. *Sazandari* [a band of four percussion and wind instruments], and sweet *duduki* played, and everyone sang."[4]

Her young husband was a thin dark figure with black eyebrows and moustaches, always sporting a black Circassian coat, tightly belted, a peaked cap and baggy trousers tucked into high boots. "Unusual, peculiar and morose," but also "clever and proud," Beso was able to speak four languages (Georgian, Russian, Turkish and Armenian) and quote the *Knight in the Panther Skin.*[5]

The Djugashvilis prospered. Many houses in Gori were so poor they were made of mud and dug out of the earth. But for the wife of the busy cobbler Beso there was no fear of such poverty. "Our family happiness," declared Keke, "was limitless."

Beso "left Baramov to open his own workshop," backed by his friends, especially his patron Egnatashvili, who bought him the "machine-tools." Keke was soon pregnant. "Many married couples would envy our family happiness." Indeed, her marriage to the desired Beso still caused jealousy among her contemporaries: "Evil tongues didn't stop even after the marriage." It is interesting that Keke stresses this gossip: perhaps someone else had expected to marry Beso. Whether or not Keke stole him from another fiancée, "evil tongues," later citing the best man Egnatashvili, the priest Charkviani, Gori's police officer Damian Davrichewy and a host of celebrities and aristocrats, started wagging early in the marriage.

Just over nine months after the wedding, on 14 February 1875, "our happiness was marked by the birth of our son. Yakov Egnatashvili helped us so very much." Egnatashvili stood godfather and "Beso laid on a grand christening. Beso was almost mad with happiness." But two months later the little boy, named Mikheil, died. "Our happiness turned to sorrow. Beso started to drink from grief." Keke fell pregnant again. A second son, Giorgi, was born on 24 December 1876. Again Egnatashvili stood godfather, again unluckily. The baby died of measles on 19 June 1877.

"Our happiness was shattered." Beso was manic with grief and blamed "the icon of Geri," the shrine of his home village. The couple had appealed to the icon for the life of their child. Keke's mother, Melania, started visiting fortune-tellers. Beso kept drinking. The icon of St. George was brought into the house. They climbed the Gorijvari mountain, towering over the town, to pray in the church that stood beside the medieval fortress. Keke fell pregnant for the third time and swore that, if the child survived, she would go on pilgrimage to Geri to thank God for the miracle of St. George. On 6 December 1878, she gave birth to a third son.[6]*

"We sped up the christening so he wouldn't die unchristened." Keke cared for him in the poky two-room one-storey cottage that contained little except a samovar, bed, divan, table and kerosene lamp. A small trunk held almost all the family's belongings. Spiral stairs led down to the musky cellar with three niches, one for Beso's tools, one for Keke's sewing-kit and one for the fire. There Keke tended the baby's cot. The family lived on the basic Georgian fare: *lobio* beans, *badridjani* aubergine and thick *lavashi* bread. Only rarely did they eat *mtsvadi*, Georgian shashlik.

On 17 December the baby was christened Josef, known as Soso—the boy who would become Stalin. Soso was "weak, fragile, thin," said his mother. "If there was a bug, he was sure to catch it first." The second and third toes of his left foot were webbed.

Beso decided not to ask the family's benefactor Egnatashvili to be godfather. "Yakov's hand was unlucky," said Beso, but even if the merchant missed the church formalities, Stalin and his mother always called him "godfather Yakov."

Keke's mother reminded Beso that they had sworn to take a pilgrimage to the church at Geri if the baby lived. "Just let the child survive," answered Beso, "and I'll crawl to Geri on my knees with the child on my shoulders!" But he delayed it until the child caught another chill which shocked him into prayer: they travelled to Geri, "facing much hardship on the way, donated a sheep, and ordered a thanksgiving service there." But the Geri priests were conducting an exorcism, holding a little girl over a precipice to drive out evil spirits. Keke's baby "was horrified and screamed," and they returned to Gori where little Stalin "shuddered and raved even in his sleep"—but he lived and became his mother's beloved treasure.

---

* Stalin later invented much about his life: his official birthday was 21 December 1879, over a year later, an invented date. He generally stuck to 6 December 1878 until an interview in 1920 with a Swedish newspaper. In 1925, he ordered his secretary Tovstukha to formalize the 1879 date. There are several explanations, including his desire to re-create himself. Most likely, he moved the date later to avoid conscription. As for the house where he was born, this is the hovel that now stands alone on Gori's Stalin Boulevard, surrounded by the Grecian temple built during the 1930s by Stalin's Caucasian viceroy and later secret police chief, Lavrenti Beria, next to the cathedral-like Stalin Museum. The Djugashvilis did not live there long.

"Keke didn't have enough milk," so her son also shared the breasts of the wives of Tsikhatatrishvili (his formal godfather) and Egnatashvili. "At first the baby didn't accept my mother's milk," says Alexander Tsikhata-trishvili, "but gradually he liked it providing he covered his eyes so he couldn't see my mother." Sharing the milk of the Egnatashvili children made them "like milk brothers with Soso," says Galina Djugashvili, Stalin's granddaughter.

Soso started to speak early. He loved flowers and music, especially when Keke's brothers Gio and Sandala played the *duduki* pipes. The Georgians love to sing and Stalin never lost his enjoyment of the haunting Georgian melodies.* In later life, he remembered hearing the "Georgian men singing on their way to market."[7]

Beso's little business was flourishing—he took on apprentices and as many as ten employees. One of the apprentices, Dato Gasitashvili, who loved Soso and helped bring him up, recalled Beso's prosperity: "He lived better than anyone else of our profession. They always had butter in their house." There were later whispers about this prosperity, embarrassing for a proletarian hero. "I'm not the son of a worker," Stalin admitted. "My father had a shoe workshop, employing apprentices, an exploiter. We didn't live badly." It was during this happy time that Keke became friends with Maria and Arshak Ter-Petrossian, a wealthy Armenian military contractor, whose son Simon would become infamous as the bank robber Kamo.[8]

Keke adored her child and "in old age, I still can see his first steps, a vision that burns like a candle." She and her mother taught him to walk by exploiting his love of flowers: Keke would hold out a camomile, and Soso ran to grasp it. When she took Soso to a wedding, he noticed a flower in the bride's veil and grabbed it. Keke told him off but godfather Egnatashvili lovingly "kissed the child and caressed him, saying, 'If even now you want to steal the bride, God knows what you'll do when you're older.'"

Soso's survival seemed miraculous to the grateful mother. "How happy we were, how we laughed!" reminisces Keke. Her reverence must have instilled in Soso a sense of specialness: the Freudian dictum that the mother's devotion made him feel like a conqueror was undoubtedly true.

---

* Stalin the dictator became a keen gardener, growing lemons, tomatoes and, above all, roses and mimosas. His favourite Georgian songs were "Fly Away Black Swallow" and "Suliko."

"Soselo," as she lovingly called him, grew up super-sensitive but also displayed a masterful confidence from an early age.

Yet at the height of Beso's success there was a shadow: his clients paid him partly in wine, which was so plentiful in Georgia that many workers received alcohol instead of cash. Furthermore, he did some business in the corner of a friend's *dukhan* (tavern), which encouraged him to drink too much. Beso befriended a drinking partner, a Russian political exile named Poka, possibly a *narodnik* populist or a radical connected to the People's Will, the terrorists who were at that time repeatedly attempting to assassinate Emperor Alexander II. So Stalin grew up knowing a Russian revolutionary. "My son made friends with him," says Keke, "and Poka bought him a canary." But the Russian was a hopeless alcoholic who lived in rags. One winter, he was found dead in the snow.

Beso found he "could not stop drinking. A good family man was destroyed," declares Keke. The booze started to ruin the business: "His hands began shaking and he couldn't sew shoes. The business was only kept going by his apprentices."

Learning nothing from Poka's demise, Beso acquired a new boon drinking companion in the priest Charkviani. Provincial Georgia was priest-ridden, but these men of God enjoyed their worldly pleasures. Once church services were over, the priests spent much of their time drinking wine in Gori's taverns until they were blind drunk. As an old man, Stalin remembered: "As soon as Father Charkviani finished his service, he dropped in and the two men hurried to the *dukhan*."* They returned home leaning on each other, hugging and "singing out of tune," totally sozzled.

"You're a good bloke, Beso, even for a shoemaker," drawled the priest.

"You're a priest, but what a priest, I love you!" wheezed Beso. The two drunks would embrace. Keke begged Father Charkviani not to take Beso drinking. Keke and her mother beseeched Beso to stop. So did Egnatashvili, but that did not help—probably because of the rumours already spreading around town.[9]

Perhaps these were the same "evil tongues" Keke mentioned at the wedding because Josef Davrichewy, the son of Gori's police chief, claims in his memoirs that "the birth was gossiped about in the neighbourhood—

---

* These Georgian inns "provide nothing but unfurnished and dirty rooms, bread (with cheese), tea, wine and at best eggs and poultry," warns German travel-book publisher Karl Baedeker. "Those who wish for meat must buy a whole sheep (4–5 roubles) or suckling pig (2–3 roubles)."

that the real father of the child was Koba Egnatashvili ... or my own father Damian Davrichewy." This could not have helped Beso, whom Davrichewy calls "a manically jealous runt," already sinking into alcoholism.[10]

In the course of 1883, Beso became "touchy and very careless," getting into drunken fights and earning the nickname "Crazy Beso."

Paternity suits develop proportional to the power and fame of the child. Once Stalin became Soviet dictator, his rumoured fathers included the celebrated Central Asian explorer Nikolai Przhevalsky, who resembled the adult Stalin and passed through Gori, and even the future Emperor Alexander III himself, who had visited Tiflis, supposedly staying at a palace where Keke toiled as a maid. But the explorer was a homosexual who was not near Georgia when Stalin was conceived, while Keke was not in Tiflis at the same time as the Tsarevich.

Leaving aside these absurdities, who was Stalin's real father? Egnatashvili was indeed the patron of the family, comforter of the wife and sponsor of the son. He was married with children, lived affluently, owned several flourishing taverns and was a prosperous wine-dealer in a country that virtually floated on wine. More than that, this strapping athlete with the waxed moustaches was a champion wrestler in a town that worshipped fighters. As already noted, Keke herself writes that he "always tried to assist us in the creation of our family," an unfortunate but perhaps revealing turn of phrase. It seems unlikely she meant it literally—or was she trying to tell us something?

Davrichewy the police chief, who helped Keke when she complained about her husband's unruly drinking, was another potential father: "As far I know, Soso was the natural son of Davrichewy," testified Davrichewy's friend Jourouli, the town's mayor. "Everyone in Gori knew about his affair with Soso's pretty mother."

Stalin himself once said his father was really a priest, which brings us to the third candidate, Father Charkviani. Egnatashvili, Davrichewy and Charkviani were all married, but in Georgia's macho culture, men were almost expected to keep mistresses, like their Italian brethren. Gori's priests were notoriously debauched. All three were prominent local men who enjoyed rescuing a pretty young wife in trouble.[11]

As for Keke herself, it has always been hard to match the pious old lady in her black nunnish headdress of the 1930s with the irrepressible young woman of the 1880s. Her piety is not in doubt, but religious observance has never ruled out sins of the flesh. She certainly took pride in being "the desired and beautiful girl" and there is evidence that she was much more worldly than she appeared. As an old lady, Keke supposedly encouraged Nina Beria, wife of Lavrenti, Stalin's Caucasian viceroy, to take lovers and talked very spicily about sexual matters: "When I was young, I cleaned house for people and when I met a good-looking boy, I didn't waste the opportunity." The Berias are hostile witnesses, but there is a hint of earthy mischief even in Keke's memoirs. In her garden, she recounts, her mother managed to attract Soso with a flower, at which Keke jovially pulled out her breasts and showed them to the toddler, who ignored the flower and dived for the breasts. But the drunken Russian exile Poka was spying on them and burst out laughing, so "I buttoned up my dress."[12]

Stalin, in his elliptical, mendacious way, encouraged these stories. When he chatted in his last years to a Georgian protégé, Mgeladze, he gave him "the impression that he was Egnatashvili's illegitimate son" and seemed to deny he was Beso's. At a reception in 1934, he specifically said, "My father was a priest." But, in Beso's absence, all three paternal candidates helped bring him up: he lived with the Charkvianis, was protected by the Davrichewys and spent half his time at the Egnatashvilis' so he surely felt filial fondness for them. There was another reason for the priest rumour: the church school accepted only the children of clergy, so his mother says he was passed off as the son of a priest.[13]

Stalin remained ambiguous about Crazy Beso: he despised him, but he also showed pride and sympathy too. They had some happy moments. Beso told Soso stories of Georgia's heroic outlaws who "fought against the rich, stole from princes to help peasants." At hard-drinking dinners, Stalin the dictator boasted to Khrushchev and other magnates that he had inherited his father's head for alcohol. His father had fed him wine off his fingertips in his cot, and he insisted on doing the same with his own children, much to the fury of his wife, Nadya. Later he wrote touchingly about an anonymous shoemaker with a small workshop, ruined by cruel capitalism. "The wings of his dreams," he wrote, were "clipped." He once bragged that "my father could make two pairs of shoes in a single day" and, even as dictator, liked to call himself a shoemaker too. He later used the name Besoshvili—Son of Beso—as an alias, and his closest Gori friends called him "Beso."[14]

Weighing up all these stories, it is most likely that Stalin was the son of Beso despite the drunkard's rantings about Soso as a "bastard." A married woman was always expected to be respectable, but it is hardly outrageous if the pretty young Keke, a semi-widow, did become the mistress of Egnatashvili when her marriage disintegrated. In her memoirs, Egnatashvili appears as often as her husband, and is remembered much more fondly. She does say that he was so kind and helpful to her that it caused a certain "awkwardness." Some of the Egnatashvili family claim there was a "genetic" connection with Stalin. However, Egnatashvili's grandson, Guram Ratishvili, puts it best: "We simply do not know if he was Stalin's father, but we *do* know that the merchant became the boy's substitute father."[15]

Rumours of bastardy, like those of Ossetian origins, were another way of diminishing the tyrant Stalin, widely hated in Georgia, which he conquered and repressed in the 1920s. It is true that great men of humble origins are often said to be the sons of other men. Yet sometimes they really are the offspring of their official fathers.

"When he was young," testified a school friend, David Papitashvili, Stalin "closely resembled his father." As he got older, says Alexander Tsikhatatrishvili, "he looked more and more like his father and when he grew his moustache, they looked identical."[16]

By the time Soso was five, Crazy Beso was an alcoholic tormented by paranoia and prone to violence. "Day by day," said Keke, "it got worse."

2

Crazy Beso

Soso suffered bitterly, terrified of the drunk Beso. "My Soso was a very sensitive child," reports Keke. "As soon as he heard the sound of his father's singing *balaam-balaam* from the street, he'd immediately run to me asking if he could go and wait at our neighbours until his father fell asleep."

Crazy Beso now spent so much on drink that he even had to sell his belt—and, explained Stalin later, "a Georgian has to be in desperate straits to sell his belt."' The more she despised Beso, the more Keke spoiled Soso: "I always wrapped him up warmly with his woollen scarf. He for his part loved me very much too. When he saw the drunken father, his eyes filled with tears, his lips turned blue and he cuddled me and begged me to hide him."

Beso was violent to both Keke and Soso. A son was the pride of a Georgian man, but perhaps Soso had come to represent a husband's greatest humiliation if the evil tongues were right after all. Once Beso threw Stalin so hard to the floor that there was blood in the child's urine for days. "Undeserved beatings made the boy as hard and heartless as the father himself," believed his schoolmate Josef Iremashvili, who published his memoirs. It was through his father "that he learned to hate people." Young Davrichewy recalls how Keke "surrounded him with maternal love and defended him against all-comers," while Beso treated him "like a dog, beating him for nothing."

When Soso hid, Beso searched the house screaming, "Where is Keke's little bastard? Hiding under the bed?" Keke fought back. Once, Soso arrived at Davrichewy's house with his face covered in blood, crying: "Help! Come quickly! He's killing my mother!" The officer ran round to the Djugashvilis to find Beso strangling Keke.

This took a toll on the four-year-old. His mother remembered how Soso would take stubborn offence at his father. He first learned violence at home: he once threw a knife at Beso to defend Keke. He grew up pugnacious and truculent, so hard to control that Keke herself, who adored him, needed physical discipline to govern her unruly treasure.

"The fist which had subdued the father was applied to the upbringing of the son," said a Jewish lady who knew the family. "She used to thrash him," says Stalin's daughter, Svetlana. When Stalin visited Keke for the last time, in the 1930s, he asked her why she had beaten him so much. "It didn't do you any harm," she replied. But that is open to question. Psychiatrists believe that violence always damages children, and it certainly did not instil love and sympathy. Many children abused by alcoholic fathers repeat the behaviour to become child- or wife-beaters themselves, but few become murderous tyrants.* Besides, this was far from the only culture of violence which helped form Stalin.

He himself believed in the redemptive effect and practical use of violence. When the Tsar's Cossacks used their *nagaika* whips on demonstrators, he wrote, "the whiplash renders us great service." In later life, he believed in violence as both the holy scythe of History and as a useful management tool, encouraging his henchmen to "smash people in the face as a means of checking up on them." Yet he admitted that he "wept a lot" during his "terrible childhood."

The family lost the home which was Stalin's birthplace and became

---

* For what it is worth, Adolf Hitler was beaten by his drunken father, Alois. Stalin did not become a wife- or child-beater, although he was a destructive husband and father. He was at least partly to blame for the early deaths of both his wives. He abandoned his illegitimate children, ignored his son Yakov for almost fifteen years and then bullied him. Of the children of his second marriage, he both overpromoted and crushed his son Vasily. He sometimes smacked him but then the dictator's son developed into a spoiled and unmanageable little tyrant himself. Vasily became a hopeless alcoholic, the condition perhaps inherited from Beso. Stalin was loving to his daughter, Svetlana, until she became independent: he once slapped her as a teenager—but only when she was having an affair with a married womanizer in his forties. For the story of his second marriage and the fate of his children, see this author's *Stalin: The Court of the Red Tsar*.

wanderers. They had at least nine different homes, depressing rented rooms, in the next ten years, hardly a stable upbringing.[2] Now Keke and the child went to live with one of her brothers, but Beso promised to improve and brought her back. As he "could not stop the drinking," however, she moved in with the priest, Father Charkviani.

Keke could see the effect on her little Soso: "He became very reserved, frequently sat alone and didn't go out to play with other children any more. He said he wanted to learn to read. I wanted to send him to school but Beso was against it." He wanted Stalin to learn shoemaking. In 1884, Beso had just begun to teach him the craft when Soso fell desperately ill.

Smallpox was raging in Gori that year. Keke could "hear weeping in every household." Her dearest supporter Yakov Egnatashvili lost "three of his wonderful children all in one day. The poor man almost went mad with grief." Two sons and a daughter survived. The death of children was something else Keke shared with "godfather Yakov." She nursed her stricken Soso. By the third day, he was deliriously feverish. The young Stalin had inherited both his mother's freckles and her auburn hair: now he was marked for life on his face and hands by the pox. One of his nicknames—and an Okhrana code name for him—would be "Chopura" (the Pockmarked). But he survived. The mother was exultant, but at this moment her life again lurched towards disaster. Beso left her.

"Look after the child," he said, offering no help in paying for the family's food. Beso, said Stalin, demanded that Keke take in laundry and send *him* the money. "How many nights did I spend in tears!" Keke remembers. "I didn't dare cry in the child's presence for it worried him so much." Stalin "used to embrace me, peering fearfully into my face and say, 'Mummy, don't cry or I'll cry too.' So I'd control myself, laugh and kiss him. Then he'd ask again for a book."

It was now, alone with a child, and with no support, that Keke became determined to send Soso to school, the first of either family to study. In her dreams, "I always wanted him to become a bishop because when a bishop visited from Tiflis, I couldn't tear my eyes off him in admiration." When Beso staggered back into her life again, he banned any such plan: "Over my dead body, Soso be educated!" They started to fight and "only the sound of my child crying separated us."

Beso's alcoholism undoubtedly made him pathologically jealous, but the rumours of infidelity and the wiles of a wife who overthrew his God-given power as a Georgian male, turning the town against him, must have contributed to his breakdown. Keke's misery was indeed well known: Egnatashvili, Father Charkviani and the police chief Davrichewy did their bit to help her. Even Dato, the kind apprentice in Beso's shop, reminded Stalin during the Second World War how he used to cuddle and protect him. On one occasion in the streets a Russian called the puny Soso a "locust." Dato punched him and was arrested. But the judge laughed and the family protector, Egnatashvili, "paid for a feast for that Russian man."

Keke's life was falling apart. The business was failing, and even Dato left to set up his own cobbler's shop.* "When I was ten," Stalin recounted in 1938, "my father lost everything and became a proletarian. He swore all the time about his bad luck," but, he joked, "he became a proletarian so his ruin was my advantage! When I was ten, I wasn't happy he'd lost everything!"

Davrichewy employed Keke to do housework. She became the laundress for the Egnatashvilis: she was always in their house, where Soso would often have his dinner. It is clear from Keke's memoirs that Egnatashvili loved Soso, as did his wife, Mariam, who gave them baskets of food. If there had not been an earlier affair with Egnatashvili, there surely was now. "The family survived only with his help," says Keke. "He always helped us and he had his own family . . . and to tell the truth, I felt uneasy."

The priest also supported her plan to educate Soso and she asked the Charkvianis to let their teenage sons teach him Russian with their younger children. She sensed that Soso was gifted. The teenage boys were teaching their younger sister, who could not answer their questions—but young Stalin could. Stalin boasted as an old man that he had learned to read and write faster than the older children: he ended up teaching the teenagers. "It had to be top secret," says Father Charkviani's son Kote, "because Uncle Beso was getting worse daily, threatening, 'Don't ruin my son or else!' He'd drag Soso by the ear to the workshop, but as soon as his father went out, Soso joined us, we locked the door and studied." The Davrichewys let him share their son's lessons too.

Such was the charm of Keke and the horror of Beso that everyone wanted to help her. Now she had to inveigle Soso into Gori's excellent church school so that he could become a bishop. She made several

---

* Dato was still a cobbler fifty years later, in 1940, when Stalin ordered one of the Egnatashvilis to invite him to Moscow for a reunion. See Epilogue.

attempts. But the school was taking only the children of priests. Father Charkviani solved this problem by saying that Soso's father was a deacon, but this appears in none of the documents. One wonders if he actually whispered to the school authorities that he himself or some other sinful priest was the natural father. Was it this chicanery that made Stalin claim that his father was a priest?

Soso sat the examination—prayers, reading, arithmetic and Russian— and his performance was so outstanding that the church school accepted him into the second grade. "My happiness was endless," said Keke, but Beso, who could no longer work, "was infuriated."[3]

Crazy Beso smashed the windows of Egnatashvili's tavern. When Keke grumbled to Davrichewy, Beso attacked the policeman, stabbing him in the street with a cobbler's tool. Ironically, Mayor Jourouli presented this as proof that the policeman was Soso's father. But Davrichewy did not arrest Crazy Beso. According to his son, the police officer's wound was minor, and he had had some sort of relationship with the "very pretty" Keke: he always "took a special interest in Soso." Davrichewy merely ordered Beso to leave Gori, whereupon he took a job at the Adelkhanov Shoe Factory in Tiflis where he had started out. Sometimes Beso missed his son and sent Keke money, asking for a reconciliation. Keke agreed occasionally, but it never worked.

Stalin's father had lost the respect due to him as a man, let alone as a *karachogeli*. In the honour-and-shame society of Georgia, this was a sort of death. "He was a half-man now," said Keke, and this pushed him over the edge. For the moment, he was gone, but he was never far away.[4]

Keke got a proper job at the atelier of the Kulijanav sisters, who had just opened a lady's couture shop in Gori. Keke worked there for seventeen years. Now that she earned her own money, she tried to "make sure my child's heart didn't wither with sorrow—I gave him everything necessary."

She brought him up to be the Georgian knight, an ideal he transferred to himself as a knight of the working class. "A strong person," he wrote to her in her old age, "must always be valiant." He believed that he resembled Keke more than Beso. Stalin "loved her," said his daughter, Svetlana, "and he loved to talk about her though she beat him mercilessly. All the love Father had was for me and he told me it was because I looked like his mother." Yet he began to pull away from Keke.

Stalin "did not love his mother," claims Beria's son; others, mainly Georgians, swear he called her "whore." But these were often stories to dehumanize Stalin told by his enemies. Psychiatrists suggest he was confused by Keke's combination of virgin and whore, which may have made him suspicious of sexual women later in life.

Was he shocked by Keke's earthiness? Did he disapprove of her male protectors? Certainly he became prudish later, but so do many people as they get older. All we know for sure is that he was raised in a rigid, hypocritical and macho culture—yet his sexual morals as a young revolutionary were easygoing, almost liberated.

Soso was "devoted to only one person—his mother," according to Iremashvili, who knew them both well—and is a hostile witness. But the more likely reason for the growing distance between them was her sarcastic outspokenness—she "never hesitated to voice her opinion on everything," reports Beria's son—and her domineering drive to control his life. Her love—just as his would be for his own children and friends—was suffocating and severe. Mother and son were rather similar, and there lay the problem.

Yet in his own way he appreciated her intense love. During the Second World War, he laughed fondly about Keke mollycoddling him, telling Marshal Zhukov that she "never let him out of her sight until he was six."[5]

In late 1888, at the age of ten, Soso triumphantly enrolled at the Gori Church School,* a handsome two-storey redbrick building near the new station. Poor as she was, Keke was determined that her Soso would not stand out for his poverty among the well-off sons of priests. On the contrary, he would be positively the best-dressed pupil in the whole school of 150 boys.

So it turned out: many of the schoolboys remembered Stalin's first day decades later. "I saw among the schoolchildren an unknown boy wearing a long *arkhalukhi* [formal Georgian coat] down to his knees, new boots with high legs, a tight wide leather belt and a black peak-cap with a lacquered visor shining in the sun," recalled Vano Ketskhoveli, soon a friend. "This very short person, quite thin, was wearing tight trousers and boots and a pleated shirt with a scarf" and a "red chintz schoolbag." Vano was amazed: "No one else was dressed like that in the whole class, the whole

---

* The school still stands in Gori and was being renovated in 2006: until Khrushchev's denunciation of Stalin in 1956 it bore the inscription HERE IN THE FORMER CHURCH SCHOOL THE GREAT STALIN STUDIED FROM 1 SEPTEMBER 1888 TO JULY 1894.

school. Schoolboys surrounded him" in fascination. The poorest boy was outfitted the best, the Fauntleroy of Gori. Who had paid for these beautiful clothes? Priests, tavern owners and police officers had surely played their part.

Stalin's suffering had made him tough, for all his pretty clothes. "We avoided him out of fear," says Iremashvili, "but we were interested in him" because there was something peculiarly "unchildish" and "excessively passionate" about him. He was an odd child: when he was happy, "he'd express his satisfaction in the most peculiar way. He'd snap his fingers, yell loudly and jump around on one leg!"* Whether written within the oppressive cult of personality when Stalin was dictator or in vicious opposition to him, all memoirs of his childhood agree that Stalin, even aged ten, exerted a singular magnetism.[6]

Somewhere around this time, perhaps just as he started school, he had another close brush with death. "I sent him out to school healthy in the morning," says Keke, "and they bore him home unconscious in the afternoon." He had been hit in the street by a phaeton. The boys enjoyed playing "chicken," grabbing the axles of galloping carriages. Perhaps this was how Stalin was hurt. Once again the poor mother was "mad with fear" but the doctors treated him for free—or Egnatashvili was quietly paying the bills. Keke, her son said later, also called in a village quack who doubled as the local barber.

The accident gave him yet another reason, on top of the webbed foot, pockmarks and rumours of bastardy, for vigilance and inferiority, for being different. It permanently damaged his left arm, which meant he could never be the beau ideal of the Georgian warrior—he later said it prevented him dancing properly, but he still managed to fight.† On the other

---

* This is one of the reminiscences of Peter Kapanadze, Stalin's close friend with whom he maintained friendly contact. Kapanadze's very complimentary memoirs were published in the 1930s but this was one of the details that were left out of the official version—it appears in the archival original.

† This damaged left arm is variously blamed on a sledge accident, a birth defect, a childhood infection, a wrestling injury, a fight over a woman in Chiatura, a carriage accident and a beating from his father, all (except the birth defect) suggested by Stalin himself. There is much confusion about Stalin's accident probably because there were in fact *two* accidents: there was this, less serious accident when he had just started school (according to Keke) or aged six (according to later health reports), which probably damaged the arm, an injury that became more noticeable in old age. Then, not long afterwards, there was a much graver accident in which he was seriously hurt and for which he needed treatment in Tiflis: this damaged his legs. In her memoirs Keke, aged eighty, seems to have merged them together.

hand it would save him from conscription and probable death in the trenches of the First World War. Yet Keke was worried about how it would affect the future bishop. "When you're a priest, sonny," she asked him, "how will you hold the chalice?"

"Never mind, Mummy!" replied Soso. "Before I'm a priest, my arm will heal so that I'll be able to hold up the whole church!"[7]

Playing chicken was not the only danger in the streets of Gori, which were notoriously out of the control of the Tsarist authorities. Henceforth, even though he would swiftly become the best scholar at his school, young Stalin lived a Jekyll and Hyde existence—choirboy-cum-streetfighter, half–overdressed mummy's boy, half-urchin.

"There was hardly a day," says Father Charkviani's son, Kote, when "someone had not beaten him up, sent him home crying—or when he hadn't beaten up someone else."[8] Gori was that sort of town.

3

Brawlers, Wrestlers and Choirboys

L ittle Stalin now spent his spare time, away from Keke, on the streets of Gori, a liberated and violent place dominated by drinking, prayer and brawling.

Soso had every reason to escape from a home which was always dark and poor. "Day after day, Keke sat at her rickety sewing-machine." There was nothing but "two wooden couches, a couple of stools, a lamp and a simple table covered in textbooks," says a frequent visitor, Stalin's singing-master Simon Gogchilidze. The tiny room was "always clean and tidy" but Stalin's bed was made of planks: "As he got taller, his mother added a plank to make the bed longer." But Soso now defied his mother. "If you knew how haughty and proud he is!" she grumbled.[1]

He was a typical Goreli, for the denizen of Gori was notorious throughout Georgia as a *matrabazi*, a boastful, violent scallywag. Gori was one of the last towns to practise the "picturesque and savage custom" of free-for-all town brawls with special rules but no-holds-barred violence. The boozing, praying and fighting were all interconnected, with drunken priests acting as referees. The saloon-bars of Gori were incorrigible stews of violence and crime.[2]

The Russian and Georgian administrators had tried to ban this dubious sport that originated as military training at a time when medieval Georgia was constantly at war. Despite the presence of a Russian barracks, the *pristav*—local police chief—Davrichewy and his few policemen could hardly cope: no one could quell Gori's irrepressible lawlessness. It was no wonder too that, during the punch-ups, horses bolted and phaetons knocked down youngsters on the streets. Psychological historians attribute much of Stalin's development to his drunken father, but this streetfighting culture was just as formative.

Gori, wrote the visiting writer Maxim Gorky, "has a picturesque and original wildness all of its own. The sultry sky, the noisy turbulent waters of the Kura, the mountains in the near distance with their cave city, and farther away the Caucasus with its snows that never melt."

Gori's yellow, turreted fortress was probably built by Queen Tamara in the twelfth century. When her empire fragmented, Gori became the capital of one of the Georgian principalities.* It was a stop on the route from Central Asia. Camels still passed through on their way to Tiflis, but the opening of the railway to the Black Sea in 1871 downgraded this once proud town into a chaotic provincial backwater with grand connections and a specially riotous tradition. With just one proper street (then Tsar Street, now Stalin Street) and one square, children played, amid ambling oxen, in winding alleys half flooded by open drains. There were just 7,000 Gorelis, half of them Georgians like the Djugashvilis, half of them Armenians, like Kamo's family: the Armenians provided the entrepreneurs. There were just eighteen Jews. Much more important was Gori's division into two main neighbourhoods because these were the teams in the town brawls: the Russian Quarter and the Fortress Quarter.

Town brawls, wrestling tournaments and schoolboy gang-warfare were the three Goreli fighting traditions. At festivals, Christmas or Shrovetide before Lent, both quarters fielded a parade led by transvestites or actors riding as "carnival kings" on camels and donkeys, surrounded by pipe-

---

* Hence it was surrounded by the estates of semi-royals like the Princes Bagration-Mukhransky and grandees such as Prince Amilakhvari. The Georgian nobility was enormous—6 percent of the population—but impoverished and therefore much less isolated than in Russia proper. The viceroy of the Caucasus, Grand Duke Mikhail Niko-laievich, brother of Alexander II, built his Gothic Likani Palace nearby at Borzhomi, where these Romanovs summered until the Revolution. When Stalin rose to power, he showed little interest in returning to Gori, but spent the first holiday after the Civil War with his young pregnant wife, Nadya Alliluyeva, at the Likani Palace. It is significant too that, as his health deteriorated, he took his last Georgian holiday in 1951 at Likani. It was and is a beautiful sanctuary, but it must also have symbolized the success of a local boy made good. It is now the summer residence of the Georgian President.

players and singers in fancy dress. At the Keenoba carnival to celebrate Georgia's 1634 victory over Persia, one actor played the Georgian Tsar, another the Persian Shah—who was soon pelted with fruit, then doused in water.

The males in each family, from children upwards, also paraded, drinking wine and singing until night fell, when the real fun began. This "assault of free boxing"—the sport of *krivi*—was a "mass duel with rules": boys of three wrestled other three-year-olds, then children fought together, then teenagers and finally the men threw themselves into "an incredible battle," by which time the town was completely out of control, a state that lasted into the following day—even at school, where classes fought classes. Shops were often pillaged.[3]

Gori's favourite sport was the wrestling of champions, which resembled somewhat the biblical story of Goliath. It was a great leveller. Tournaments—*tschidooba*—took place in specially erected rings to the accompaniment of an orchestra of *zurnas*. Rich princes, like local landowner Prince Amilakhvari, and merchants, even villages, fielded their own champions, regarded with such esteem that they were addressed by the title *palavani*. Stalin's godfather, Egnatashvili, was himself one of three champion brothers. Now he was older, and rich, Palavani Egnatashvili fielded his own champions. Even in old age, Stalin was still boasting about his godfather's pugilistic triumphs:

> Those Egnatashvilis were such famed wrestlers they were known through the whole of Kartli, but the first and strongest of them was Yakov.
>
> Prince Amilakhvari had a bodyguard who was a Chechen giant. When he challenged the Gori champions, he beat everyone. So the Gorelis went to Yakov Egnatashvili, who said: "Let him fight my brother Kika; if he beats Kika, let him fight my brother Simon; if he beats him, I'll fight him." But Kika beat the Chechen Goliath.
>
> Once some bandits swaggered into town during a religious fête, wearing sheepskin hats and daggers.

They drank at the Egnatashvili tavern, then refused to pay. "We children," recalled Stalin, watched in amazement as Kika Egnatashvili "smashed one of them, knocked him down, grabbed a dagger from the other's scabbard and hit that one with the blunt end. The third one paid his bill."[4]

The church schoolboys joined in the semi-casual bare-knuckle fighting on Gori Cathedral Street. On threat of the detention cell and ultimately expulsion, the schoolboys were absolutely banned from these vicious scrummages, "but Soso still took part." Besides, his maths and geography teacher, Iluridze, loved to watch his boys in streetfights, yelling, "GO! Go! Well done!" and barely noticing if he was himself hit in the process or spattered with blood.[5]

"Little Stalin boxed and wrestled with a certain success," agrees Davrichewy.* His singing teacher observed him setting up wrestling matches, but once he hurt his already fragile arm. "It started as a wrestling match then turned into real boxing," recounts the master, "and they beat each other up." Soso's arm swelled up painfully and made it harder to fight by the rules.

His friend Iremashvili fought Stalin in the schoolyard. The bout was declared a draw, but as Iremashvili turned away Stalin ambushed him from behind, hurling him onto the grass. When he fearlessly took on stronger fighters, Soso was beaten within an inch of his life and Keke had to rescue him, running to the police chief crying, "My God, they've killed my son." But Stalin remained the most sartorially immaculate streetfighter in his year: "Sometimes his mother even dressed him in a big white collar that, as soon as her back was turned, he would take it off and put in his pocket."

The boys' real energies were reserved for gang-warfare. "The kids of our hometown were organized into gangs based on the streets or quarter where they lived. These bands were in constant warfare"—though they were melting-pots too. "Gori's kids were educated together in the street without distinction of religion, nationality or fortune." A ragamuffin like Stalin played in the streets with the son of Prince Amilakhvari—a famous general—who tried to teach him to swim. The children, armed with knives, bows and arrows, or catapults, led a blissfully free if wild existence: they swam in the river, they sang their favourite songs, pillaged apples

---

*Even the old Stalin prided himself as a macho wrestler: when he met Marshal Tito after the Second World War, the handsome Yugoslav somehow made Stalin feel older and weaker. He suddenly lifted Tito off the ground, boasting, "There's still strength in me." The Yugoslavs were appalled and bewildered, but here was his last display of Gori wrestling.

from Prince Amilakhvari's orchard, mischievously ranging across the countryside. Once Stalin set the Prince's orchards alight.

"Soso was very naughty," his younger friend Giorgi Elisabedashvili recalls, "always running through the streets. He loved his catapult and homemade bow. Once a herdsman was bringing his herd home, when Soso jumped out and catapulted a cow in the head. The ox went crazy, the herd stampeded and the herdsman chased Soso who disappeared," already elusive.* "He used to slip through my hands like a fish," wrote another school friend, "and it was no use trying to catch him." Soso once terrorized a shopkeeper by igniting some explosive cartridges that destroyed his shop. "His mother had to hear a lot of cursing about her son."

Soso loved to lead his band on the steep climb up to Gorijvari—the mountain on which the "castle of high yellow walls" stood—where they sang, fought, debated religion and admired the views: "He loved the beauties of nature." Six miles away, there was Uplis-Tsikhe, the "city of caves," such a hard climb that initially Stalin failed to reach the top. He practised tirelessly, says Iremashvili, until he could make it.

He was ruthless to other children, but protective of his vassals. When he learned to swim (though he never swam well due to his arm), he pushed a small child who could not swim into the fast Kura waters. The boy protested that he had almost drowned. "Yes, but when you got into trouble, you had to learn to swim," answered Soso. Yet when his pals were attacked by another gang, Soso "bombarded them with stones until they withdrew." A friend was being soundly thrashed when Soso appeared and shouted, "Hey, why are you standing there like a donkey? Use your fists!" He beat off the enemy.

Stalin constantly defied lads "older and stronger than himself," says young Josef Davrichewy. He was already chippy. He was too clumsy to master the Georgian *lekuri* dance, so he promptly deadlegged the boy who danced it most gracefully.

He displayed the will to power that remained with him until his last days. "Soso belonged to his local gang but he often crossed to the opposing band because he refused to obey his own gangleader," who grumbled that the boy Stalin "undermined my authority and tried to dethrone me." Iremashvili thought that "all people who, through greater age or strength,

---

* These stories by Giorgi Elisabedashvili and his cousin Sandro of the vicious little urchin abusing and almost ruining the livelihood of an industrious workingman or streetfighting are found in the archives, but naturally they never appeared in Stalin's biographies and remain unpublished.

dominated others seemed like his father: he developed a vengeful feeling against everyone positioned above himself." As soon as he was out of his mother's control, Stalin, even as a child, had to be the leader.

Somehow, the alternate bullying and crack-up of his father, the passionate adoration of his mother and his own natural intelligence and hauteur, created such a strong conviction that he was always right and must be obeyed that his infectious confidence won him followers. One follower was the son of one of his mother's Armenian friends—Simon "Senko" Ter-Petrossian, later Kamo. The wealthy father, who had made a fortune supplying the army during Alexander II's conquests of the Khiva and Bokhara Khanates, angrily asked his daughter "what on earth we saw in that penniless good-for-nothing Stalin. Aren't there any decent people in Gori?" Not many, it seems.

Soso "could be a good friend as long as one bowed to his dictatorial will," opines Iremashvili. When a boy sneaked on Kote Charkviani for eating communion bread, Stalin, in a puerile reenactment of his future purges, "cursed his life, called him an informer, a spy, made him hated by the other boys, then he even beat him black and blue. Soso was a devoted friend."

Stalin showed poetical enthusiasm for the mountains and skies but rarely compassion for people. The police officer's son remembers him at this time as the "very image of his mother." He was deeply calm and cautious but "when anger took over, he became brutal, swore and pushed things to extremes." With less to lose than others, with sparser emotional attachments, Stalin became a natural extremist.[6]

The streetfighting was legitimate not just because Goreli parents joined in the annual brawls and bet on the wrestling-bouts but because the boys were playing the Georgian bandit-heroes who fought the Russians in the nearby mountains. But now the schoolboys found themselves persecuted by the Russian Empire even at school.

The bovine Emperor Alexander III orchestrated a conservative backlash against the soft, liberal policies of his murdered father that would unite most Georgians against his Empire. The Tsar decreed that Georgians had to learn and study in Russian*—hence Stalin's Russian lessons with the Charkvianis.

---

* This foolish decree not only started Stalin on the road to rebellion but also ensured that his Russian, despite the strong Georgian accent which he never lost, was of a high enough standard that he could plausibly rule the Russian Imperium.

When he enrolled at the school in September 1890, Stalin shared the hatred of the new Russian rules. The boys were not even allowed to speak Georgian to each other. Unable to speak Russian very well, "our mouths had been locked in this prison for children," says Iremashvili. "We loved our native country and mother tongue . . . They considered us Georgians to be an inferior culture into whom the blessing of Russian civilization had to be beaten." Speaking Georgian in class was punished by "having to stand in a corner or holding a long piece of wood for a whole morning or being locked in a detention cell without food or water and in complete darkness until late evening."

The Russian teachers* were brutal pedants in Russian uniforms—tunics with gold buttons and peaked caps—who disdained the Georgian language. But one teacher was beloved—the singing master Simon Gogchilidze, a kindly dandy who always wore the latest fashions: spats, winged collars and a buttonhole. The schoolgirls were in love with him and even wrote songs about him. His favourite choirboy was Stalin, whom he tried to help in every way: "In two years, he learned music and began to help the conductor. There were a lot of solos and Soso always sang them . . ." It was not just his "beautiful, sweet high voice," writes the romantic teacher, but his "grand style of performance." Stalin was often hired to sing at weddings: "People would turn up just to watch him sing, saying, 'Let's go see how the Djugashvili boy amazes everyone with that voice.' " When Stalin "appeared for the solo in the pulpit wearing his surplice and sang in his wondrous alto, it delighted everyone!"

During these first school years, Stalin was so devout that he barely missed a mass. "He not only performed the rites but always reminded us of their significance," says a schoolfellow, A. Chelidze. Another, Suliashvili, remembers Stalin and two other boys in church, "wearing their surplices, kneeling, faces raised, singing Vespers with angelic voices while the other boys prostrated themselves filled with an ecstasy not of this world." He was the "best reader of Psalms" in church. Others were only permitted to read after being tutored by Soso himself. The grateful school presented him with David's Book of Psalms inscribed "To Josef Djugashvili . . . for excellent progress, behaviour and excellent recitation and singing of the Psalter."

Soso also painted well and showed a taste for acting that would

---

* School Inspector Butyrsky was typical—a dwarfish, rotund martinet with red moustaches. When he heard Georgian spoken, he shouted: "Don't speak that language!"

remain with him. He appeared in a satirical vaudeville that mocked Shakespeare: "Soso's expression made the audience burst into laughter!" He was already starting to write poetry: "He wrote verses instead of letters to his friends."*

He was also the school's most outstanding pupil in class. "He was a very clever boy," said the singing teacher. "Nobody remembers him scoring anything less than 5s [A grades]." Soso "spent his spare time reading books." He "often carried volumes stuck into the belt of his trousers" and liked to help less intelligent children with their work. "He never missed a class or arrived late and aimed always to be first in everything," says his classmate Petre Aadamshvili—whom he advised: "Improve yourself. Don't be lazy or you'll lose in life."

Even the Georgia-phobe teachers were impressed with Stalin's knowledge. School Inspector Butyrsky used to excuse himself from social events saying he had to go home to study because "if I'm not prepared [for tomorrow's class], there's a pupil named Djugashvili who's sure to catch me out!"† Stalin was such a goody-goody that when he was on class duty he marked down anyone who was late or tried to cheat. The other boys even nicknamed him "the Gendarme."

Yet the class pet was never deferential. When the school went on an expedition and one of the boys let Inspector Butyrsky ride over a stream on his back, Stalin sneered: "What are you, a donkey? I'd never let God himself ride on my back, let alone some school inspector." When the beloved Gogchilidze tried to persuade him to perform a song he did not like, Soso did not turn up on the day.

Lavrov, the most hated teacher and a persecutor of all things Georgian, appointed Stalin his "assistant," a decision he soon regretted. When Lavrov tried to force his "assistant" to inform on anyone speaking Georgian, Stalin acted. Backed up by some tough eighteen-year-olds, he lured

---

* As a politician, Stalin was the consummate actor. Those magnates who knew him well in power felt he was often acting: Khrushchev called him a "man of faces"; Kaganovich remarked that there were four or five different versions of Stalin; Mikoyan and Molotov both sensed at various times that Stalin was just playacting. As for the drawing, the only relic of this was his habit of sketching wolves during long meetings.

† All his life Stalin demanded that his subordinates be as prepared as he was: his deputy in the 1930s, Lazar Kaganovich, said he would prepare for meetings with Stalin like a schoolboy. In the archives there is a handwritten note from Stalin to his comrade Sergo Ordzhonikidze from the 1930s when they were the two most powerful Soviet leaders: "Sergo, tomorrow meeting on bank reform. Are you prepared? Necessary to be prepared." During the Second World War, he tore to shreds anyone who was not fully prepared.

the teacher into an empty classroom and threatened to kill him. Lavrov became much more compliant.

At the end of the fourth year, Stalin decided that his choir should pose for a portrait. The singing master heard him "dividing the tasks—one boy was to gather money, another to book the photographer and when we gathered [Stalin] arrived with a bunch of flowers, ordering the boys to put them in their buttonholes and arranging them for the photograph."

Yet there was always a shadow over Soso: Crazy Beso arrived drunk and seized him from the church school, demanding he become a cobbler. Keke appealed to her protectors: "I raised the entire world, my brothers, godfather Egnatashvili, the teacher . . ." and Beso "returned my son to me." But Beso repeatedly "burst into the school drunkenly to grab Soso by force." Henceforth, Soso had to be smuggled into school literally under the coat of Keke's brothers while "everyone helped and hid the child, telling the infuriated Beso that Soso wasn't even at the school."

The schoolboy Stalin, like the politician he became, was a bundle of contradictions: "Soso Djugashvili," Iremashvili sums up, "was the best but also the naughtiest pupil." Stalin's childhood had already been a triumph over misfortune. But just as he was prospering at school, he again faced a series of terrible blows that almost destroyed him.[7]

4

A Hanging in Gori

On 6 January 1890, the choirboys, shepherded by singing teacher Gogchilidze, were trooping out of church after the Epiphany Day blessing for Gori's Russian garrison. "No one noticed a runaway phaeton," recalled Gogchilidze, which galloped straight into the crowd. Stalin, now twelve, was just crossing the road when the carriage "hurtled towards him, a pole hit his cheek, knocking him off his feet, [the wheels] running over his legs. The crowd stood round him and picked up the child who had lost consciousness and we carried him away." The coachman was arrested and later sentenced to a month in jail, but poor Keke again had her bloodied child borne home. When he came round, he saw his desperate mother. "Don't worry, Mummy, I'm all right," he said pluckily. "I'm not going to die."[1]

The injuries were so grave that Soso was taken to hospital in Tiflis, the capital, missing school for months. His legs were seriously damaged. Years later at the seminary, he complained of "sore legs" and, even when he recovered, he walked in the heavy, sideways gait that won him another nickname. Already the Pockmarked (Chopura), he became the Loper (Geza). More than ever, he must have yearned to prove his strength yet also enjoyed the confidence of overcoming such adversity.

The accident brought Beso out of the shadows with a vengeance—the cobbler probably visited the boy in Tiflis. Keke had to let him know that the child was so ill. But Beso could not resist an opportunity to reimpose himself on his defiant family. As soon as Soso had recovered in Tiflis, his father kidnapped the boy and enrolled him as an apprentice cobbler at the Adelkhanov Shoe Factory, where he himself worked.

"You want my son to be a bishop? Over my dead body, he'll be educated!" he shouted at Keke. "I'm a shoemaker and my son will be one too."

Beso and his son now toiled with the eighty-strong Adelkhanov workforce for long hours and low wages in a half-flooded cellar lit by kerosene lamps amid the almost faecal reek of tanning leather. The stink made grown men vomit. Even the Tsarist authorities were worried about the number of child workers in Adelkhanov's grim rectangular factory. Living with his father in a room in the Avlabar workers' district and walking into work over the bridge past the Metekhi Fortress-Prison, Soso had to carry shoes from the factory to the shop-warehouse in the bazaar off Yerevan Square. Apart from the short spell in his father's Gori workshop, this was to be Stalin's only experience of a worker's existence during a life devoted to the proletariat. If Beso had succeeded, there would have been no Stalin, for he would have remained uneducated. Stalin owed his political success to his unusual combination of street brutality and classical education.

"The whole school missed Soso," recalled the singing master, "no one more than Keke." Once again, Keke flew into action, mobilizing all her allies. That formidable and good-looking woman arrived in Tiflis backed by the teachers at the school, Father Charkviani and Egnatashvili, who all tried to prevail over Beso. Even the Exarch of the Georgian Orthodox Church heard of the case and offered to find Soso a place as a chorister in Tiflis, but Keke was determined. Beso raged. The boy was consulted. He wanted to study at the church school in Gori. The priests returned him to Keke. Beso swore never to give another kopeck to his family, cutting them out of his life.

"Time passed," says Keke. "Beso's voice was heard no more. Nobody told me if he was dead or alive. I was even happy that, without him, I alone put the family on a firm footing again." But Beso would rear up again in Stalin's life—before disappearing forever.[2]

Stalin returned to the school where he again excelled as "the best pupil" (his mother's proud words). Without Beso's help, Keke could not pay the school bills. She worked herself ever harder, canvassing her patrons and finding new ones: she started to clean and launder for the decent chairman of the school board, Vasily Beliaev, with a wage of ten roubles a month. Egnatashvili and Davrichewy contributed more. The school itself, mobilized no doubt by Chairman Beliaev, Keke's protectors and the devoted singing master, not only reinstated Soso but offered a scholarship of three roubles, thirty kopecks too.

Perhaps the trauma of the accident, the kidnapping and the harsh existence at the factory drained Soso. Just after Beso released him, the boy fell seriously ill with pneumonia. His mother "almost lost him but again Soso escaped death," reports his singing master. This time, the school doubled the scholarship to seven roubles. Even when he was ill and feverish, his proud Keke reported that he raved, "Mother, let me go to school or teacher Iluridze will give me bad marks . . ."

For over a year, it had been one crisis after another. Now Stalin celebrated his return to school by taking to his studies with renewed enthusiasm. Yet he was becoming ever more rebellious. "He was punished almost on a daily basis," says Iremashvili, who sang with him in the choir trio. Soso arranged a protest against the hated inspector Butyrsky that almost led to a riot: "This was the first rebellion instigated by Soso."

His mother had to move into miserable rooms on Sobornaya Street, an "old, small and dirty house" with a roof that let in the wind and rain. "The room," recalls Iremashvili, "was in eternal twilight. The musty air, thick with the smell of rain, wet clothes and cooking, could not escape from it"—but Stalin could. He had even more reason to stay out with his gang in the streets and up Gorijvari Mountain.

While still the finest choirboy at the church school, Stalin started to show an interest in the plight of the poor and to doubt his faith. He became close friends with three priests' sons—the brothers Lado and Vano Ketskhoveli, who were to play a vital role in his future life, and Mikheil Davitashvili,* who, like Stalin, walked with a limp. The elder Ketskhoveli brother, Lado, soon entered the Tiflis Seminary and brought back news of how he had led a protest and strike that led to his being sent down. Stalin was inspired by these new friends and their books, but he still saw the priesthood as his vocation to help the poor. Now, however, he aspired to politics for the first time. Under Lado Ketskhoveli's charismatic

---

* The singing teacher was not the only master who helped Stalin. Davitashvili's older cousin Zakhary was another inspiring teacher of Russian literature, and years later Keke wrote, "I remember how you distinguished my son Soso and he told me many times that it was you who helped him grow fond of studying and it was thanks to you, he learned Russian so well."

influence, he declared he wanted to be a local administrator with the power to improve conditions.

He talked about books all the time. If he coveted a volume, he was happy to steal it from another schoolboy and run home with it. When he was about thirteen, Lado Ketskhoveli took him to a little bookshop in Gori where he paid a five kopeck subscription and borrowed a book that was probably Darwin's *Origin of Species*. Stalin read it all night, forgetting to sleep, until Keke found him.

"Time to go to bed," she said. "Go to sleep—dawn is breaking."

"I loved the book so much, Mummy, I couldn't stop reading . . ." As his reading intensified, his piety wavered.

One day Soso and some friends, including Grisha Glurjidze, lay on the grass in town talking about the injustice of there being rich and poor when he amazed all of them by suddenly saying: "God's not unjust, he doesn't actually exist. We've been deceived. If God existed, he'd have made the world more just."

"Soso! How can you say such things?" exclaimed Grisha.

"I'll lend you a book and you'll see." He presented Glurjidze with a copy of Darwin.

Soso's dreams of handing down justice merged with the stories of popular bandit-heroes and the resurgent Georgian nationalism. He revered the poems of the Georgian nationalist Prince Raphael Eristavi, memorizing his masterpiece *Khevsur's Motherland*. "That wonderful poem," Stalin enthused in old age. The schoolboy was now writing his own romantic poems. All the boys hung around Stalin's place avidly discussing these forbidden ideas and works.[3]

By now, Stalin had fallen in love, another human moment that was cut out of the official memoirs and never published. His passion was for Father Charkviani's daughter: he and his mother had rented rooms from the family. "In the third form, he fell in love with the Charkviani girl," says Giorgi Elisabedashvili. "He used to tell me about this emotion and laugh at himself for the fact that he was carried away with the sentiment." When she was learning Russian, "I often dropped by and took an interest in these lessons," Stalin reminisced fifty years later. "Once when the pupil was in trouble, I gave her a hand . . ." We do not know whether the priest's daughter returned his love, but the two of them had always been close in childhood as her brother Kote noticed: "He began to play dolls with my sister. He'd drive her to tears, but after a moment they'd reconcile and sit together with their books as real friends . . ."[4]

One event—the "most remarkable occasion in Gori in the late nineteenth century"—made a deep impression on Stalin. On 13 February 1892, the teachers of the church school ordered all their pupils to attend a gruesome *mise-en-scène* that they hoped "would arouse fear and respect in the boys": a hanging.

Three gallows were erected on a sunny winter's day on the banks of the Kura River beneath the mountain fortress. Many of the Gorelis came to watch and the uniforms of the church school pupils were visible in the crowd. But the boys were "deeply depressed by the execution."

The condemned men had stolen a cow and, in the ensuing pursuit, had killed a policeman. But the boys learned that the criminals were actually just three "peasants who had been so oppressed by landowners that they escaped into the forest," petty Robin Hoods, attacking only local squires and helping other peasants. Stalin and Peter Kapanadze wondered how it could be right to kill the bandits given that the priests taught them the Mosaic commandment: "Thou shalt not kill." The two schoolboys were especially appalled to see a priest standing at the gallows with a big cross.

The boys were fascinated. "Soso Djugashvili, me and four other schoolboys climbed a tree and watched the terrifying show from there," remembers one of the group, Grigory Razmadze. (Yet the police chief Davrichewy banned his own son from attending.) Another spectator whom Stalin would later befriend and promote was Maxim Gorky, then a journalist, soon to be Russia's most celebrated writer.

The Gorelis sympathized with these brave Caucasian bandits—two of them Ossetians, one an Imeretian. The executions were a Russian show of strength; young Davrichewy called the condemned men "holy martyrs." The crowd became menacing; double ranks of Russian soldiers encircled the square. The drums began to beat. "The authorities in uniforms lingered around the scaffold," wrote Gorky in his article. "Their dreary and severe faces looked strange and hostile." They had reason to be nervous.

The three bandits in leg irons were marched onto the scaffold. One was separated from the others—he had been reprieved. The priest offered the two condemned men his blessings; one accepted and one refused. Both asked for a smoke and a sip of water. Sandro Khubuluri was silent, but the handsome and strong "ringleader," Tato Jioshvili, smiled and joked valiantly before the admiring crowd. He leaned on the railings of the gallows and, noticed Gorky, "chatted to people who had come to see him die." The crowd threw stones at the hangman, who was masked and clad completely in scarlet. He placed the condemned on stools and tightened the nooses around their necks. Sandro just twirled his moustache and readjusted the noose. The time had come.

The hangman kicked away the stools. As so often with Tsarist repression, it was inept: Sandro's rope broke. The crowd gasped. The scarlet hangman replaced him on the stool, placed a new noose round his neck and hanged him again. Tato also took a while to die.

The townsfolk and the schoolboys hurried away. Stalin and his school friends discussed what would happen to the souls of the executed: would they go to hellfire? Stalin settled their doubts. "No," he said. "They've been executed and it would be unjust to punish them again." The boys thought this made sense. The hanging is often cited as an event that stimulated Stalin's murderous nature, but all we know is that the boys sympathized with these Georgian outlaws, and disdained their Russian oppressors. If anything, the spectacle helped make Stalin a rebel, not a murderer.[5]

It was time to move on from Gori: Soso was about to graduate from the church school. Keke often sat at the head of his bed at dawn silently admiring her brilliant slumbering child. "My Soso had grown up," she says, but they still spent much time together. "We'd hardly ever been separated. He was always beside me." Even when he had been ill, "he used to read sitting next to me. His only other entertainment was walking along the river or up Mount Gorijvari."

Yet now she realized that to fulfil her dreams she had to let him go even though "he couldn't survive without me and I without him but his thirst for learning forced him to leave me." This thirst was indeed something that never left him.* Naturally, after the church school, he had to go to the best religious educational establishment in the southern Empire: the Tiflis Seminary. In July 1893, aged fifteen, he passed his exams with flying colours. All his teachers, especially Simon Gogchilidze, recommended him to the seminary—but there was a problem.

"One day Soso came home" to his mother "with tears in his eyes."

---

* Even as a septuagenarian dictator and conqueror of Berlin, he kept studying. "Look at me," he said in about 1950, "I'm old and I'm still studying." His library books are all carefully marked with his notes and marginalia. It was the thoughtful and diligent autodidactic fervour, well concealed under the crude manners of a brutal peasant, that his opponents such as Trotsky ignored at their peril.

"What's the matter, son?" asked Keke.

Soso explained that the strike and closure of the seminary in Tiflis, orchestrated partly by his radical friend Lado Ketskhoveli, meant "he could lose a year because there were no new entrants that summer who were not priests' sons."

"I comforted my son," Keke says, "and then I dressed up," probably in her best headdress, and called on Soso's teachers and patrons, who promised to help. The singing master offered to take Soso himself and enrol him in teacher-training college. But, for Keke, it had to be the best and it had to be the priesthood: that meant the seminary.

Keke set out for Tiflis with her son. Soso was excited but on the forty-five-mile train ride, he suddenly began to cry.

"Mummy," sobbed Stalin, "what if, when we arrive in the city, Father finds me and forces me to become a shoemaker? I want to study. I'd rather kill myself than become a cobbler."

"I kissed him," reminisces Keke, "and wiped away his tears."

"Nobody will stop you studying," she reassured him, "nobody is going to take you away from me."

Soso was impressed by Tiflis, the "throbbing bustle of the big city," though both the Djugashvilis were "terrified that Beso would appear," says Keke. "But we didn't meet Beso."

The indomitable Keke rented a room, and searched out her one well-connected relative in the capital, who was the tenant of an even better-connected priest with a resourceful wife.

"Please help this woman," the relative told the priest's wife, "and it will be as good a work as building a whole church."* The priest's wife appealed to more clergymen who spoke to the seminary and won Stalin the right to sit the entrance exam. That was all his mother wanted because "I knew he'd glorify me." Indeed he did "glorify" her, but the cost for a non-priest's son boarding at the seminary was 140 roubles a year, a sum Keke had no hope of raising on her own. Davrichewy, surely at Keke's bidding, persuaded a well-known aristocrat, Princess Baratov, to help too. With Keke frantically pulling strings, Soso applied for a scholarship and was accepted as a half-boarder, which meant he still had to pay a considerable sum—forty roubles a year—and buy the surplice uniform. Keke did not mind: the "happiest mother in the world" returned to Gori and started

---

* This was ironic given the number of beautiful and ancient churches that Stalin would later demolish and the number of priests he would execute.

to sew to raise the money. Egnatashvili and Davrichewy contributed to his fees.

"A month later," says Keke, "I saw Soso in the uniform of the seminarist and I cried so much out of happiness. I grieved very much too . . ." Having enrolled around 15 August 1894, Soso entered the seminary boarding-school and the wider world of the capital of the Caucasus.

The lame, pockmarked, web-toed boy, humiliatingly beaten and deserted by his father, adored but beaten some more by his single mother, haunted by bastardy, surviving accident and disease, had overcome the odds.

It is hard to exaggerate what a vital moment this was. Without the seminary, without the mother's determination, Soso would have missed the classical, if stifling, education that equipped the cobbler's son to become Lenin's successor.

"He wrote to me that he would save me from poverty soon," recalls his mother, the first of a lifetime of dutiful but distant letters from her beloved son. "When he sent me letters, I pressed them to my heart, slept with them and kissed them."

"Everyone at the school congratulated me," adds Keke, "but only Simon Gogchilidze looked wistful: 'The School seems somehow deserted,' he said.* 'Who'll sing in the choir now?' "[6]

---

* Stalin never forgot his singing teacher. When he wrote to Keke from exile or the underground, he would often send his regards to Simon Gogchilidze. Keke would show Gogchilidze the message but keep her hand over the rest of the letter: "You can read the passage about *you*," she said, "but there's no need for you to read the rest and know where my son is now."

5

The Poet and the Priesthood

The boy of sixteen from Gori, accustomed to the freedom of fighting in the streets or climbing Gorijvari, now found himself locked for virtually every hour of the day in an institution that more resembled the most repressive nineteenth-century English public-school than a religious academy: the dormitories, the bullying boys, the rife buggery, the cruel sanctimonious teachers and the hours in the detention cells made it a Caucasian version of *Tom Brown's Schooldays*.

Stalin arrived with a group from Gori, including Josef Iremashvili and Peter Kapanadze. These provincial boys, few of them as poor as Soso, found themselves among the "arrogant sons of wealthy parents.* We felt like the chosen few," wrote Iremashvili, because the seminary was "the source of Georgian intellectual life, with its historical grounds in a seemingly perfect civilisation."

Soso and the other 600 trainee priests lived in a four-storey neo-

---

* The seminarists were mainly gentry, poorer nobility and priests' sons, not the very richest—but much better off than Stalin. The Gori police chief's son Davrichewy and other better-off boys like Stalin's future comrade Kamenev attended the Tiflis Boys' Gymnasium. The affluent Egnatashvili boys, Vaso and Sasha, were sent to a gymnasium in Moscow. During the Stalin years, the seminary bore the plaque: THE GREAT STALIN— LEADER OF THE VKP(B) AND PROLETARIAT OF THE WORLD—LIVED AND STUDIED IN THE EX-THEOLOGICAL SEMINARY FROM 1 SEPTEMBER 1894 TO 29 MAY 1899 LEADING ILLEGAL WORKERS' CIRCLES IN TBILISI.

classical seminary with noble white pillars. On the top floor, he shared a dormitory of twenty or thirty beds. The other floors contained a chapel, classrooms and a refectory. In a day strictly divided by ringing bells, Soso was awoken every morning at 7 a.m., donned his surplice uniform, then proceeded to prayers in chapel followed by tea and classes. The pupil on duty read another prayer. There were lessons until two. At three he had lunch, then an hour and a half off before call-over at five, after which he was banned from going out again. After evening prayers, supper was at eight, followed by more classes then yet more prayers and lights-out at 10 p.m. At weekends the church services were interminable, "three or four hours on the same spot, shifting from one leg to the other, under the tireless penetrating eyes of the monks." But the boys were allowed out between 3 and 5 p.m.

The Empire's seminaries were "notorious for the savagery of their customs, medieval pedagoguery, and law of the fist," comments Trotsky. "All the vices banned by the Holy Scriptures flourished in this hotbed of piety." This seminary, nicknamed the Stone Sack, was worse than most: "utterly joyless," reported one pupil. "Droningly boring—we felt we were in prison."

When Stalin arrived, its twenty-three teachers were led by a lugubrious trinity: the rector, Archimandrite Serafim; his deputy, Inspector Germogen; and, the most hated of all, Father Dmitri, the only Georgian of the three, who had been born Prince David Abashidze. Soon promoted to inspector, this Abashidze was a fat swarthy pedant—"God's submissive, lowly slave, the Tsar's servant," in his own words.

The monks were determined to squeeze any hint of Georgianness out of their proudly Georgian boys. Georgian literature was totally banned, but then so were all Russian authors published since Pushkin, including Tolstoy, Dostoevsky and Turgenev. Two inspectors were deployed full-time in "constant unremitting supervision." Punishments and bad marks were all recorded in the school journal. Soon being sent down—the "wolf's ticket"—became a badge of honour.

Father Abashidze ran a circle of sneaks among the boys and spent much of Stalin's schooldays creeping on tiptoe around the seminary or conducting melodramatic dormitory raids in order to catch the boys reading forbidden books, abusing themselves or uttering naughty words. Stalin, who was an acute coiner of nicknames, soon dubbed this grotesque priest "the Black Spot." Initially terrifying, this man was ultimately comical in a way only the craziest pedagogic sticklers can be.

Stalin had heard all about the famous seminary rebellions from his mentor, Lado. A few years earlier, in 1885, a pupil had beaten up the rector for saying "Georgian was a dogs' language." The next year, the rector was murdered with a Georgian *khanjali* sword—a fate that even the most brutal English headmaster had managed to avoid.

The seminary was to pull off the singular achievement of supplying the Russian Revolution with some of its most ruthless radicals. "No secular school," wrote another seminarist, Stalin's comrade Philip Makharadze, "produced as many atheists as the Tiflis Seminary." The Stone Sack literally became a boarding-school for revolutionaries.

Stalin was initially "calm, attentive, modest and bashful," remembers one schoolmate, while another noticed the once swaggering Goreli gang leader turn "pensive and secluded, the love of games and fun of childhood gone." The moody teenage Soso was taking stock—and becoming a self-conscious romantic poet—but he was also studying seriously, passing his first grade with an "excellent" mark and coming eighth out of the whole year. In 1894–95, he won straight 5s (A grades) for Georgian singing and language and scores like 4, 5, 4, 5 in scripture. He was a model student, earning an "excellent 5" for behaviour.

As a scholarship boy in "pitiful" circumstances, Soso constantly had to beg the rector "on my knees" for further help with the fees.* Stalin earned more pocket-money (five roubles, he recalled later) by singing in the choir. He was "the first tenor of the right wing of the choir"—the key choirboy—and often performed in the Opera House.

Keke accompanied him to Tiflis and stayed for a few weeks to help him settle. She took a job sewing and serving food at the seminary—surely an embarrassment to Stalin, and perhaps another reason for his initial reticence. Mission accomplished, she returned to Gori. Henceforth, throughout his periods of exile, up until her death forty years on, Stalin wrote to her with dutiful regularity (especially when he needed money or clothes) but with growing detachment. He would never really return to

---

* "To Archimandrite Serafim, Very Reverend Rector of the Tiflis Orthodox Seminary from 2nd Grade student Josef Djugashvili: Your Reverence knows all about the pitiful circumstances of my mother who takes care of me. My father has not provided for me in three years. This is his way of punishing me for continuing my studies against his wishes . . . It is for this reason I am applying to Your Reverence for the second time. I beg you on my knees to help me and accept me on full public expense. Josef Djugashvili 25 August 1895."

the mother whose remarkable drive and sharp tongue he had himself inherited, yet whom he found unbearable.[1]

Somehow Beso, lurking in Tiflis, discovered Soso as a potential source of wine-money: he went to see Stalin's rector and demand his son back: "Make him leave because I need someone to take care of me!" Stalin was "unmoved," wanting to alleviate "the hardship of Beso and people like him," but repelled by the man himself.

"Once," recalled Stalin, "the nightwatchmen came in and told me that my father was outside." The boy hurried downstairs and "saw him standing there. He didn't even ask about me but just said briskly: 'Young man, sir, you've totally forgotten your father, haven't you? I'm leaving to work in another town.' "

"How would I have any money to help you?" replied Stalin.

"Shut up!" shouted Beso. "Give me at least 3 roubles and don't be as mean as your mother!"

"Don't yell!" replied Soso. "This is my boarding-school. If you don't leave now, I'll call the watchmen and they'll make you go."

The "threat worked," recounted Stalin. "Father slunk away into the streets, muttering something."[2]

In the holidays, Soso returned to Gori to see the doting Keke. Even though he "was starting to grow a beard, he still nestled up to me like a five-year-old." But he spent most of his time staying with his lame, well-off friend Mikha Davitashvili in his village, Tsromi. When he returned for the next term, Stalin did even better, winning another "excellent" and moving up to number five in his year. And he started to work on his verse.

At the end of term, Soso took his poems to the offices of the famous newspaper *Iveria* (Georgia), where he was received by the country's greatest poet, Prince Ilya Chavchavadze, a romantic nationalist who believed in an agrarian Georgia ruled by an enlightened aristocracy.

The Prince was sufficiently impressed to show the teenager's work to his editors. He admired Stalin's verse, choosing five poems to publish—quite an achievement. Prince Chavchavadze called Stalin the "young man with the burning eyes." He was admired in Georgia as a poet before he was known as a revolutionary.[3]

6

The "Young Man with the Burning Eyes"

Georgia regarded herself as an oppressed kingdom of knights and poets. The poems in *Iveria,* published under Stalin's nickname "Soselo," were widely read and became minor Georgian classics, appearing in anthologies of the best Georgian poetry before anyone had heard of "Stalin." *Deda Ena,* a children's anthology of Georgian verse, produced between 1912 and the 1960s, included Stalin's first poem—"Morning" in its 1916 edition. It remained in subsequent editions, sometimes ascribed to Stalin, sometimes not, up to the days of Brezhnev.

Stalin's singing, now that he was an adolescent tenor, was said to be good enough for him to go professional. As a poet he showed a certain talent in another craft which might have provided an alternative to politics and bloodletting. "One might even find reasons not purely political for regretting Stalin's switch from poetry to revolution," believes Professor Donald Rayfield, who translated the poems into English. Their romantic imagery was derivative but their beauty lay in the delicacy and purity of rhythm and language.

The scans and rhymes of his poem "Morning" work perfectly, but it was his sensitive and precocious fusion of Persian, Byzantine and Georgian imagery that won plaudits. "No wonder," reflects Rayfield, "the doyen of Georgian letters and politics, Ilya Chavchavadze, was willing to print this poem and at least four others."

Soselo's next poem, a crazed ode "To the Moon," reveals more of the poet. A violent, tragically depressed outcast, in a world of glaciers and divine providence, is drawn to the sacred moonlight. In his third poem, Stalin explores the "contrast between violence in man and nature and the gentleness of birds, music and singers."

The fourth is the most revealing. Stalin imagines a prophet not honoured in his own country, a wandering poet poisoned by his own people. Now seventeen, Stalin already envisions a "paranoiac" world where "great prophets could only expect conspiracy and murder." If any of Stalin's poems "contained an *avis au lecteur*," writes Rayfield, "it is this one."

Dedicated to Georgia's beloved poet* Prince Raphael Eristavi, Stalin's fifth poem was, with "Morning," his most admired. It was this that inspired Stalin's State Bank "inside man" to give him the tip-off for the Yerevan Square bank robbery and it was good enough to be included in Prince Eristavi's jubilee volume in 1899. Its heroic sage requires both the harp and the sickle.

The last poem, "Old Ninika," which appeared in the socialist weekly *Kvali* (Plough), affectionately describes an old hero who "dreams or tells his children's children of the past," perhaps a vision of an idealized Georgian like old Stalin himself, who ended up sitting on his Black Sea verandah regaling youngsters with his adventures.

Stalin's early verses explain his obsessional, destructive interest in literature as dictator as well as his reverence for—and jealousy of—brilliant poets such as Osip Mandelstam and Boris Pasternak. The words and influence of this "Kremlin crag-dweller" and "peasant-slayer" on literature were, as Mandelstam wrote in his famously scabrous poem denouncing

---

* Stalin was immersed in Georgian poetry: he loved Eristavi; Chavchavadze was "a great writer with a huge role in the freedom movement of Georgia"; and he enthused about Akaki Tsereteli: "My generation learned the poems of Tsereteli by heart and with joy . . . beautiful, emotional and musical, he's rightly called the nightingale of Georgia." But, looking back, Stalin also measured these poets politically, saying Tsereteli wrote "beautiful poems but ideologically primitive and parochial." Stalin was not the only poetical future Bolshevik: at exactly the same time, at his school in Odessa, young Leon Bronstein, the future Trotsky and near contemporary, was also writing poems. Trotsky far outstripped Stalin as a writer but not as a poet. If any of Stalin's colleagues had dedicated a poem to a prince, it would have been used against them in the Terror. In 1949, for Stalin's official seventieth birthday, the Politburo magnate Beria secretly commissioned the best poetical translators, including Boris Pasternak and Arseni Tarkovsky, to create a Russian edition of the poems. They were not told the author of the poems but one of the poets thought "this work is worthy of the Stalin Prize first rank," though perhaps they had guessed the identity of the young versifier. In the midst of the project, they received the stern order, clearly from Stalin himself, to stop the work.

Stalin, "leaden," his "fat fingers . . . greasy as maggots." But, ironically, the swaggering brute rightly notorious for his oafish philistinism concealed a classically educated man of letters with surprising knowledge. Stalin never ceased caring about poetry. Mandelstam was right when he said, "In Russia, poetry is really valued, here they kill for it."

The ex–romantic poet despised and destroyed modernism but promoted his distorted version of romanticism, Socialist Realism. He knew Nekrasov and Pushkin by heart, read Goethe and Shakespeare in translation, and could recite Walt Whitman. He talked endlessly about the Georgian poets of his childhood, and he himself helped edit a Russian translation of Rustaveli's *Knight in the Panther Skin,* delicately translating some of the couplets himself and asking modestly: "Will they do?"

Stalin respected artistic talent, generally preferring to kill Party hacks instead of brilliant poets. Hence on Mandelstam's arrest Stalin ordered, "Isolate but preserve." He would preserve most of his geniuses, such as Shostakovich, Bulgakov and Eisenstein, sometimes telephoning and encouraging them, at other times denouncing and impoverishing them. When he called Pasternak in one of his telephonic lightning-strikes from Olympus, he asked about Mandelstam: "He's a genius, isn't he?" Mandelstam's tragedy was sealed not only by his suicidal decision to mock Stalin in verse—the medium of the dictator's own childhood dreams—but also by Pasternak's failure to assert that his colleague was indeed a genius. Mandelstam was not sentenced to death, but nor was he preserved, perishing on the dystopian road to Gulag hell. But Stalin did preserve Pasternak: "Leave that cloud-dweller in peace."

The seminary's priest-poet of seventeen never publicly acknowledged his poems, but he later told a friend, "I lost interest in writing poetry because it requires one's entire attention—a hell of a lot of patience. And in those days I was like quicksilver"—the quicksilver of revolution and conspiracy that was now flashing through the youth of Tiflis and into the seminary.[1]

When he stood on the white steps of the Stone Sack, Soso could see the bustling but dangerous Persian and Armenian Bazaars around Yerevan Square, "a network of narrow lanes and alleys" with "open workshops of goldsmiths and armourers; stalls of pastry cooks and bakers with flat loaves baked in huge clay ovens . . . cobblers displaying gaudy slippers . . . and wine-merchants' shops where the wine is kept in sheep or buffalo skins with the fur inside."* Golovinsky Boulevard was almost Parisian; the rest more resembled "Lima or Bombay."

"The streets," reports Baedeker,

> are generally steep and so narrow that two carriages cannot pass, the houses, mostly adorned with balconies, perched one above the other on the mountainside like steps of a staircase. From sunrise to sunset, the streets are crowded with a motley throng of men and animals . . . the Georgian dealers in vegetables with large wooden trays on their heads, the Persians in long caftans and high black fur caps, often with red-dyed hair and fingernails; the Tartar *saids* and *mullahs* in flowing raiment with green and white turbans; the representatives of mountain tribes in picturesque *cherkeskas* and shaggy fur caps . . . Mohammedan women in veils . . . and horses carrying waterskins with gaily clad attendants.

A city of hot sulphur springs (and famous bathhouses), it was built right on the slopes of Holy Mountain and on the banks of the Kura River beneath the round-spired Georgian church and sombre towers of the fortress-prison of Metekhi, which Iremashvili called the "Bastille of Tiflis." High, up cobbled lanes on Holy Mountain, stood the white marble church (where Keke today lies buried among poets and princes), radiant and pristine.

Tiflis was a city of 160,000—30 percent Russians, 30 percent Armenians and 26 per cent Georgians, with the rest a smattering of Jews, Persians and Tartars. There were six Armenian newspapers, five Russian and four Georgian. Tiflis's workers mainly laboured in the railway depot and small workshops; its rich and powerful were Armenian tycoons, Georgian princes, and Russian bureaucrats and generals who converged on the court of the Emperor's viceroy. Its water-carriers were from Racha, in the

---

* "A hasty visit, especially if ladies are of the party," suggests Baedeker, "is best made by carriage . . . Public safety is on a somewhat unstable footing; it is well to avoid travelling alone or the exhibition of much money (for permission to carry a revolver see earlier). It is advisable to keep a sharp lookout on one's belongings as natives are not averse from picking up unconsidered trifles." Baedeker adds that even a letter of introduction from the viceroy or to local princes are of limited use in "surmounting difficulties that arise: these can be successfully met only by a resolute bearing"—and probably with the help of the revolver mentioned earlier.

west, its stonemasons Greek, its tailors Jewish, its bathkeepers Persian. It was like "a porridge of people and beasts, sheepskin hats and shaved heads, fezzes and peaked caps . . . horses and mules, camels, and dogs . . . All shout, bang, laugh, swear, jostle, sing . . . in the burning air."

This cosmopolitan imperial city of theatres, hotels, caravanserai, bazaars and brothels already vibrated with Georgian nationalism and international Marxism, which were seeping dangerously into the closed cloisters of the seminary.[2]

Soso and another boy, Said Devdariani, were moved out of their dormitory into a smaller room "because of our poor health." Devdariani was older, already a member of a secret circle at which the boys gathered to read forbidden socialist literature. "I suggested he join," says Devdariani, "and he was delighted—he agreed." There Stalin met up with his friends from Gori, Iremashvili and Davitashvili.

At first the books were hardly incendiary works of Marxist conspiracy but the sort of harmless books banned by the seminary. The boys joined a forbidden book club called the Cheap Library and started to get other books from a bookshop run by a former *narodnik*. "Remember the little bookshop," the owner of this small bookshop, Imedashvili, later wrote to the supreme Stalin. "How we thought and whispered there about great unanswerable questions!" Stalin discovered the novels of Victor Hugo, especially *1793*, whose hero Cimourdain, the revolutionary-priest, would become one of his prototypes.* But Hugo was strictly forbidden by the monks.

At night, Black Spot patrolled the corridors, constantly checking that the lights were out and that there was no reading—or other self-indulgent vices. As soon as he was gone, the boys lit candles and started reading again. Soso, typically, "overdid it and hardly slept at all, looking bleary-eyed and ill. When he started coughing," Iremashvili "took the book out of his hand and blew out the candle."

Inspector Father Germogen caught Stalin with Hugo's *1793* and ordered that "he be punished with a prolonged stay in the punishment cell." Then he was found with yet more Hugo by another snooping priest: "It emerges Djugashvili subscribes to Cheap Library and reads books

---

* Hugo's hero Cimourdain had "never been seen to weep . . . [he had an] inaccessible and frigid virtue. A just but awful man. There are no half-measures for a revolutionary-priest [who] must be infamous and sublime. Cimourdain was sublime . . . rugged, inhospitably repellent . . . pure but gloomy."

1878–1904

Stalin, the merciless, paranoid dictator in training. Here is the supreme secret operator, vigilant arch-conspirator, consummate politician, mastermind of criminal and political violence, Marxist fanatic in a fedora, stiff collar and silk cravat. A police mug shot from 1912.

Already a charismatic leader, the schoolboy Soso Djugashvili, the future Stalin, about ten years old. Smaller than his contemporaries, overcoming a series of illnesses and accidents to become an outstanding student and star choirboy, he suggested the taking of this photograph, ordered the photographer, arranged the sitting and placed himself in his favourite commanding position: back centre.

Soso became a streetfighter, gang leader and charismatic manipulator in the rough streets of Gori, one of the most violent towns in the Tsar's empire: Religious holidays were celebrated with organized brawls involving the entire population, from toddlers to greybeards. Stalin's birthplace is the house is on the left.

Left: Dubious parent—the official image of "Crazy Beso" Djugashvili, cobbler, alcoholic, wife- and child-beater. Stalin refused to confirm this was his father. Jealousy drove Beso mad. *Right:* Keke Djugashvili, Stalin's remarkable mother, in old age. In youth she was pretty and intelligent, but forceful, sarcastic and outspoken—like her son. Powerful men protected her from Beso.

Stalin's real father? Koba Egnatashvili, a wrestler and rich innkeeper, was a local hero who loved, funded and protected Soso.

Stalin's half brothers? Soso grew up with the dashing Egnatashvilis, including another wrestler and entrepreneur, Sasha, whom he later promoted to Kremlin courtier, NKVD General and trusted food taster. Sasha was nicknamed "the Rabbit."

Gori police chief Damian Davrichewy so flirted with Keke that Beso tried to kill him. His son, Josef *(left)*, was Stalin's childhood friend and claimed to be his half brother. He and Stalin became the most notorious (and successful) bank robbers and terrorists in the Caucasus.

Below left: His mother's delight. In 1893, Soso Djugashvili, scholar and chief chorister, studied for the priesthood at the Tiflis seminary, which resembled a Victorian English public school run by priests. Adolescent Soso (late 1890s, *below right*) soon caused havoc in the seminary (*above,* in his priestly robes, back row, second from left) by embracing Marxism and running an outrageous duel of wits with the priest he nicknamed "the Black Spot."

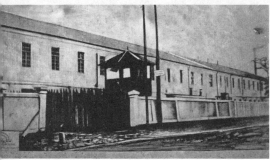

Batumi, 1902: "I got a job with the Rothschilds!" crowed
Stalin. Next day, the Rothschild refinery *(above)* was on fire
(top: a similar blaze at another refinery). Stalin, aged
twenty-four, unleashed mayhem in the oil port of Batumi:
He ordered his first killings of traitors, embarked on love
affairs, provoked a massacre and printed his writings with
the help of a friendly Muslim highwayman, Hashimi
Smirba *(right).*

Above: On his first arrest, Stalin dominated the prison, killing enemies and defying the authorities. In Kutaisi Prison, the long-haired Marxist arranged this photograph before his comrades were sent to Siberian exile, placing himself centre top (number 4). *Below left:* In Novaya Uda, his first exile, he caroused with his criminal friends—and prepared to escape. *Bottom left and right:* Kutaisi Prison—outside and Stalin's cell.

Even as an obscure penniless revolutionary, Stalin was never without a string of girlfriends: married, unmarried, young, old, peasants, intellectuals and noblewomen. One of the first was a beautiful married woman, Natasha Kirtava *(top left)*, but he was furious when she refused to move in with him. Half Gypsy Olga Alliluyeva *(top right)*, wife of Stalin's Bolshevik comrade Sergei, was notoriously promiscuous and probably had an affair with Stalin, to whom she remained devoted. Olga was also his future mother-in-law—seen below with her children, Pavel, Fyodor, Anna—and Nadya.

there. Today I have confiscated *Toilers of the Sea* by V. Hugo. I had already issued him with a warning in connection with the book *1793* by V. Hugo. Signed: Assistant Inspector: V. Murakhovsky."

Young Stalin was even more influenced by Russian writers who caused a sensation among radical youth: the poems of Nikolai Nekrasov and the novel by Chernyshevsky, *What Is to Be Done?* Its hero, Rakhmetov, became Stalin's prototype for the steely ascetic revolutionary. Like Rakhmetov, Stalin came to regard himself as "a special man."

Soon Stalin was caught reading another forbidden book "on the school stairs" for which he received, "on the Rector's order, a prolonged stay in the punishment cell and severe reprimand." He "worshipped Zola," his favourite of the Parisian's novels being *Germinal*. He read Schiller, Maupassant, Balzac and Thackeray's *Vanity Fair* in translation, Plato in the original Greek, Russian and French history—and he distributed these books to the other boys. He adored Gogol, Saltykov-Shchedrin and Chekhov, whose works he memorized and "could recite by heart." He admired Tolstoy "but was bored by his Christianity," later in life scrawling "ha-ha-ha!" beside Tolstoyan musings on redemption and salvation. He marked up heavily a copy of Dostoevsky's masterpiece on revolutionary conspiracy and betrayal, *The Devils*. These volumes were smuggled in, strapped under the surplices of the seminarists. Stalin later joked that he had to "expropriate"—steal—some of these books from the bookshop for the sake of the Revolution.[3]

Hugo was not the only writer who changed Stalin's life: another novelist changed his name. He read Alexander Kazbegi's forbidden novel *The Patricide*, which starred a classic Caucasian bandit-hero called Koba. "What impressed me and Soso," writes Iremashvili, "were the works of Georgian literature which glorified the Georgians' struggle for freedom." In the novel, Koba fights against the Russians, sacrificing everything for his wife and country, then visiting a terrible vengeance on his enemies.

"Koba became Soso's God and gave his life meaning," says Iremashvili. "He wished to become Koba. He called himself 'Koba' and insisted we call him that. His face shone with pride and pleasure when we called him 'Koba.' "The name meant a lot to Stalin—the vengeance of the Caucasus mountain peoples, the ruthlessness of the bandit, the obsession with loyalty and betrayal, and the sacrifice of person and family for a cause. It was a name he already loved: his "substitute father" Egnatashvili's first name was Koba, short for Yakov. "Koba" became a favourite *nom de révolution* and nickname. But his intimates still called him Soso.[4]

His poems were already appearing in the newspapers but at seventeen, in the autumn of 1896, Stalin started to lose interest in priestly studies and even in poetry. In his year, he slipped from fifth to sixteenth.

In hushed voices after lights-out, keeping a lookout for the dreaded Black Spot, the boys vigorously debated the great questions of existence. In his seventies, the dictator was still chuckling about these arguments. "I became an atheist in the first year," he said, which led to arguments with other boys such as his pious friend Simon Natroshvili. But, after some thought, Natroshvili "came to see me and admitted his mistake." Stalin was delighted until Simon continued: "If God exists, hell exists too. There's always a blazing hellfire. To keep the hellfires burning, who can provide enough logs? They would have to be endless and how can endless logs exist?" Stalin remembered, "I burst out laughing! I thought Simon had reached his conclusions by philosophical reasoning but actually he became an atheist for fear that there weren't enough logs for hell!"

Now Soso moved beyond mere sympathy towards outright rebellion. Just at this time, his uncle Sandala, Keke's brother, was killed by the police. Stalin never mentioned this but it must have played its part.

Stalin was "like quicksilver," moving from French novelists to Marx himself: the boys paid five kopecks to borrow *Das Kapital* for a fortnight.[5] He tried to study German so that he could read Marx and Engels in the original, and English too—he had a copy of *The Fight of the English Workers for Liberty*. This was the start of a lifelong effort to learn foreign languages, especially German and English.*

Stalin and Iremashvili were soon creeping out of the seminary, under cover of darkness, to attend their first meetings with real railway workers at little hovels built into the Holy Mountain. This first spark of conspiracy lit a fire that was never extinguished.

Stalin became bored by the worthy educational discussions of Devdariani's seminary club: he wanted to push the circle towards more

---

* These young Marxists would copy out Marx by hand and distribute the manuscripts. When his Gori friend Kote Khakhanashvili came home with some Marx volumes, Stalin borrowed them but then refused to return them: "Why do you need them? They're being passed through many hands and people are learning from them." He also purloined a German-language textbook. Yet his English and German studies never led to fluency: even in the early 1930s he was asking his wife, Nadya, to send him an English textbook to study on holiday.

aggressive action. Devdariani resisted, so Stalin launched a campaign against him and started to create his own group.[6]

The two remained friendly enough for him to stay in Devdariani's village for the Christmas holidays of 1896. Perhaps Stalin, always a master of "dosage" and soon to be a skilful abuser of hospitality, delayed the final rift so that he had somewhere to stay for the holidays. On the way, the boys visited Keke, who lived in a "little hut," where Devdariani noticed legions of bedbugs.

"It's my fault, son, that we eat without wine," said Keke over supper.

"Mine too," said Stalin.

"I hope the bedbugs let you sleep?" Keke asked Devdariani.

"I didn't notice any such thing," lied Devdariani tactfully.

"Oh he felt them all right," Stalin said to his poor mother. "He was wriggling his legs all night." Keke noticed how Soso "avoided me, he tried to speak as little as possible."

On his return to the seminary in 1897, Stalin broke with Devdariani. "Major and not altogether harmless feuds . . . were usually stirred up by Koba," says Iremashvili, who remained with Devdariani. "Koba thought it natural to be the leader and never tolerated any criticism. Two parties formed—one for Koba, and one against." It was a pattern to be repeated throughout his life. He found a tougher mentor, meeting up again with the inspiring Lado Ketskhoveli from Gori, who had been expelled from both the Tiflis and Kiev Seminaries, arrested and now released. Soso respected no one like Lado.

His mentor introduced his younger friend to the fiery black-eyed Silibistro "Silva" Jibladze, the legendary seminarist who had beaten up the rector. Jibladze and an elegant nobleman named Noe Jordania had, with some others, founded a Georgian socialist party, the Third Group (Mesame Dasi), in 1892. Now these Marxists reassembled in Tiflis, taking over the *Kvali* newspaper and starting to sow revolution among the workers. Jibladze took the teenager to the apartment of Vano Sturua, who recalls that "Jibladze brought an unknown youngster."

Eager to contribute, Stalin called on the group's forceful leader, Noe Jordania, just returned from exile, at *Kvali*, which had published his last poem. Jordania, tall, with "a graceful and handsome face, black beard . . . and aristocratic habits and demeanour," patronizingly suggested that Soso should study more. "I'll think it over," replied the truculent youth. Now he had an enemy to fight. He wrote a letter criticizing Jordania and *Kvali*. They refused to publish it, whereupon Stalin insulted the editorial staff for "sitting in there for days without expressing a decent opinion!"

Lado was also frustrated with Jordania's gentility and it must have been he who introduced Stalin to the mainly Russian workers' circles that were just starting to mushroom among the many small workshops of Tiflis. They met secretly at the German cemetery, at a little house beside a mill, and near the Arsenal. Stalin suggested they rent a room on Holy Mountain, "where we used to gather twice a week after dinner before call-over. It cost 5 roubles that we took from pocket-money our parents sent." Stalin started to keep a "handwritten journal in Georgian about their discussions" which was passed from hand to hand among his followers in the seminary.[7]

He was already crossing the line from rebellious schoolboy to a revolutionary who was, for the first time, of interest to the secret police. When another Marxist activist named Sergei Alliluyev, a skilled railway worker and Stalin's future father-in-law, was arrested, he was interrogated by the Gendarme captain Lavrov, who asked him: "Know any Georgian seminarists?"[8]

The romantic poet was becoming the "convinced fanatic" with a "quasi-mystical faith" to which he devoted his life and from which he never wavered. But what did he really believe?

Let him explain in his own words. Stalin's Marxism meant that "the revolutionary proletariat alone is destined by History to liberate mankind and bring the world happiness," but humanity would undergo great "trial and suffering and change" before it achieved "scientifically proven socialism." The heart of this providential progress was "the class struggle: Marxism *is* the masses whose liberation is the catalyst for the freedom of the individual."

This creed was, says Stalin, "not only a theory of socialism: it's an entire worldview, a philosophical system"—like a scientifically proven religion—of which these young revolutionaries were part. "I had the feeling," explained Trotsky, "I was joining a great chain as a tiny link." Trotsky, like Stalin, believed that "the lasting thing is gained through combat." Blood, death, conflict were essential: "Many storms, many torrents of blood," in Stalin's own words, would mark "the struggle to end oppression."

There was one big difference between Stalin and Trotsky then: Stalin was a Georgian. He never lost his pride in Georgia as a nation and a culture. The little nations of the Caucasus all found it hard to embrace real internationalist Marxism because their own repression made them also dream of independence. Young Stalin believed in a blend of Marxism and Georgian nationalism, almost opposed to internationalist Marxism.

Soso, poring over his Marxist texts, was rude and truculent to the priests, but he was not yet in open revolt as other seminarists were, before and after him. His own propaganda later exaggerated the precocity of his becoming a revolutionary, but he was far from the first of his generation to become the real thing. So far he was a schoolboy radical just dipping his toes into revolutionary waters.[9]

7

Battle of the Dormitories:
Soso versus Father "Black Spot"

By early 1897, Stalin was at war with the Black Spot. The school journal records that he was caught thirteen times reading banned works and had received nine warnings.

"Suddenly inquisitor Abashidze," says Iremashvili, started launching raids on their footlockers and even their dirty laundry baskets. The maniacal "Black Spot" Abashidze became obsessed with catching Stalin reading his forbidden books. At prayers, the boys had the Bible open on their desks and read Marx or Plekhanov, the sage of Russian Marxism, on their knees. In the courtyard stood a huge pile of firewood in which Stalin and Iremashvili would hide the banned works and where they would sit and read them. Abashidze waited for this and then sprang out to catch them, but they managed to drop the books into the logs: "We were locked up in the detention cell at once, sitting late into the evening in darkness without food, but hunger made us rebellious so we banged on the doors until the monk brought us something to eat."[1]

When it was time for the holidays, Stalin went to stay with a younger friend, the priest's son Giorgi Elisabedashvili, in his village (anything rather than spend time with his mother). The priest hired Stalin as a tutor to get Giorgi ready for the seminary's entrance examinations. He always had a strong pedagogic instinct, but he was more interested in converting the boy to Marxism. Arriving on the back of a cart perched atop a pile of illegal books, the two made mischief in the countryside, laughing at peasants, whom Stalin "mimicked perfectly." When they visited an old church, Stalin encouraged his pupil to pull down an old icon, smash it and urinate on it.

"Not afraid of God?" asked Stalin. "Good for you!"

Stalin's pupil failed his exams. Father Elisabedashvili angrily blamed the tutor. But the boy got in on a second attempt—and later became one of Stalin's Bolsheviks.[2]

Back at the seminary, Stalin was in constant trouble: in the school journal, the priests recorded that he was rude, "failed to bow" to a teacher and was "confined to the cell for 5 hours." He declined to cut his hair, growing it rebelliously long. Challenged by the Black Spot, he refused to cut it. He laughed and chatted in prayers, left Vespers early, was late for the Hymn of the Virgin, and pranced out of mass. He must have spent much of his time in the punishment cell. In December 1898, he turned twenty, much too old for boarding-school, and a year older than anyone else (because of time wasted recovering from his accidents). Small wonder he was frustrated.

He had outgrown the seminary. Seminarists were meant to kiss one another, like brothers, thrice whenever they met, but now, embroiled in factional struggles with Devdariani and devoted to Marxism, he distrusted this chivalrous humbug. "Such embracing is merely a mask. I'm not a Pharisee," he said, refusing to embrace. The obsession with masked traitors never left him.

There were frenzied searches for the atheists' *Life of Christ* by Renan, which Stalin proudly owned. His bedside table was repeatedly raided by the prince-monk-inquisitor—who found nothing. One of the boys cleverly hid the book under the rector's own pillow. Stalin remembered how the boys would be summoned into call-over and then come out to find that all their footlockers had been ransacked.

Soso was losing interest in his studies. By the start of his fifth grade he was twentieth out of twenty-three, scoring mainly 3s where he used to score 5s. He wrote to Rector Serafim blaming his bad studies on illness, but he still had to resit some of his exams.

Meanwhile Black Spot "watched us ever more vigilantly" and the other boys were encouraged to inform on the rebels. But Stalin was getting more daring and defiant by the week. When he and his allies started reading funny verses from his copybook, the sneaks reported it to Abashidze, who crept up and listened. He burst into the room and grabbed the journal. Stalin tried to snatch it back. Priest and teenager scuffled but the Black Spot won, frog-marching Stalin back to his flat where he "forced these unclean souls to douse their subversive writings" with paraffin. Then he set fire to the papers.

Finally Abashidze intensified his spying on Stalin: "At 9 p.m., the Inspector noticed in the dining-room a group of pupils around Dju-gashvili who was reading them something. On approach, Djugashvili tried to hide the notes and only after insistence did he reveal he was reading unauthorized books. Signed: D. Abashidze."

Stalin's mother heard "the evil talk that he had become a rebel." Being Keke, she dressed up and took the train to Tiflis to save the day—but for the first time "he got angry with me. He shouted that it wasn't my business. I said, 'My son, you're my only child, don't kill me—but how will you be able to defeat Emperor Nicholas II? Leave that to those who have brothers and sisters.'" Soso soothed and hugged her, telling her that he was not a rebel. "It was his first lie," remembers Keke sadly.

She was not the only concerned parent. Stalin was still seeing his ne'er-do-well father, probably unbeknown to Keke.* Accompanied by his mother's cousin Anna Geladze, Stalin visited Beso, who liked to present him with lovingly sewn boots. "I should mention," adds Anna, "that Soso had liked wearing boots ever since childhood." The dictator in jackboots was not just a militaristic pose but an unspoken tribute to his father and to the beautiful leather boots he made with his own hands.

Perhaps his maturity had alleviated his fear of Beso, his Marxism softening his intolerance. Beso, now working humbly in a clothing-repair shop, came to "love his child doubly, talking about him all the time," says Kote Charkviani. "Soso and I used to visit him. He didn't raise his voice to Soso"—but he did mutter: "I hear he's now rebelling against Nicholas II. As if he's ever going to overthrow him!"

The war between the Black Spot and Stalin was hotting up. The seminary journal reports that Stalin declared himself an atheist, stalked out of

---

* Most historians repeat the assertion that Stalin never saw Beso much after 1890, but a reading of several sources in the archive, as well as Candide Charkviani's memoirs, show he saw his alcoholic father much later.

prayers, chatted in class, was late for tea and refused to doff his hat to monks. He had eleven more warnings.

Their confrontations were increasingly farcical as the boys lost all respect for their inquisitor. Some of Soso's buddies were chatting in Yerevan Square's Pushkin Gardens when a boy ran out and reported that Stalin's footlocker was being raided (again) by Father Abashidze. They sprinted back into the seminary just in time to see the inspector force open Stalin's trunk and find some forbidden works. Abashidze grabbed them and was triumphantly bearing his prize up the stairs when one of the group, Vaso Kelbakiani, charged and rammed the monk, almost loosening his grip on the books. But Black Spot held on valiantly. The boys jumped on him and knocked the volumes out of his hands. Stalin himself ran up, seized the books and took to his heels. He was banned from visiting town, and Kelbakiani was expelled. Yet ironically Soso's schoolwork seemed to improve—he received "very good" 4s for most subjects and a 5 for logic. Even now he still enjoyed his history lessons. Indeed he so liked his history teacher, Nikolai Makhatadze, the only seminary teacher he admired, that he later took the trouble to save his life.*

Meanwhile, the Black Spot had lost control of Stalin but could not restrain his own obsessive pursuit of this malcontent. They were getting closer to the breaking point. The monk crept up on him and peeked at him reading yet another forbidden book. He then pounced, taking the book from him, but Stalin simply wrenched it out of his hands, to the amazement of the other boys. He then went on reading it. Abashidze was shocked. "Don't you know who I am?" he shouted.

Stalin rubbed his eyes and said, "I see the Black Spot and nothing else." He had crossed the line.

The Black Spot must have longed for someone to rid him of this turbulent trainee-priest. It was almost the end of term. Stalin earned a last reprimand on 7 April for not greeting a teacher and the school broke up two days later. He never returned. In May 1899, the journal simply noted, "Expelled . . . for non-appearance at examinations." As always with Stalin, things were not quite so simple.[3]

---

* In September 1931, his old history teacher, lingering in the dungeons of the Metekhi Fortress-Prison of Tiflis, managed to get an appeal to his old pupil, now the Soviet dictator. Stalin wrote thus to Beria, his Caucasian viceroy: "Nikolai Dmitrievich Makhatadze aged 73 finds himself in Metekhi Prison . . . I have known him since the Seminary and I do not think he can present a danger to Soviet power. I ask you to free the old man and let me know the result."

. . .

"I was expelled for Marxist propaganda," Stalin boasted mendaciously later, but the Black Spot may have been investigating something spicier than just horseplay in the chapel or even Marxist meetings in the town.

The boys with more pocket-money than Stalin used to hire rooms on Holy Mountain, purportedly to hold meetings of their liberal reading circle, but being teenage boys and Georgians, who prided themselves on their amours, it is likely there were parties there too, wine—and girls. The priests, especially Inspector Black Spot, also patrolled the town, like English public-school masters, to catch their boys in theatres, taverns or brothels.

When he was not studying, Stalin could drink and flirt too. He may have got into more serious trouble in the holidays in Gori. Was it his love for the Charkviani girl? He never forgot her, talking about her in old age. Years later, he also remembered another girl from Gori, Lisa Akopova. In 1926, he actually tried to find out what had become of her, which suggests they were close. This encouraged her to send him a letter: "I swear that the attention you show us by asking about us makes me very happy . . . I was always your inseparable friend in fortune and misfortune . . . If you've not forgotten . . . you were courted by your pretty neighbour Lisa." This was daring stuff for the 1920s but not half as daring as another letter Stalin received in 1938.

A woman wrote to Stalin about her niece, Praskovia Mikhailovskaya—Pasha, for short—who was allegedly fathered by Stalin himself in 1899. "If you remember your youth, you cannot forget. You certainly remember a small dark-eyed girl named Pasha." The letter claims that Stalin's mother had taken an interest in the child, who herself remembered Keke. Pasha's mother told her that her father "had devoted himself to saving the nation and had been exiled." Pasha grew up into a "tall svelte dark-eyed Georgian beauty," became a typist, and got married, but her mother and husband both died, leaving her destitute. She disappeared into 1930s Moscow.

The letter may be the sort of crazed correspondence attracted by politicians, except for the fact that Stalin, who did not keep much in his personal archive, filed the letter. The mention of his mother rings true, for Keke surely would have helped her beloved Soso in a situation that can hardly have been unknown among the young Casanovas of Georgia. Besides, only someone telling the truth—or a lunatic with a death wish—would have dared to write such a letter to Stalin at the height of the Great Terror. Had Stalin no history of abandoned mistresses and children, one would dismiss this. But henceforth he rarely seems to have been without a girlfriend, and he had no compunction in abandoning fiancées, wives and children. We will never know, but in terms of character and timing, it is plausible.[4]

If such an event was discovered by Father Abashidze or if Keke feared that the seminary was likely to find out, it might explain her role in his leaving. Soso spent the Easter of 1899 at home in Gori, claiming to be sick with chronic pneumonia. Perhaps he really was ill. "I took him out of school," Keke asserted. "He didn't want to leave." But she must have been bitterly disappointed.

Soso certainly exaggerated the glamour of his expulsion. He was not thrown out for being a revolutionary, and he maintained polite relations with the seminary afterwards. Some biographies claim that he was expelled for missing his exams, but this was forgivable if he was ill. Indeed the Church bent over backwards to accommodate him, letting him off repaying his scholarship (480 roubles) for five years; they even offered him a chance to resit the finals and a teaching job.

The truth is that Father Abashidze had found a soft way of getting rid of his tormentor. "I didn't graduate," Stalin told his Gendarme interrogators in 1910, "because in 1899, absolutely unexpectedly, I was invoiced 25 roubles to proceed with my education . . . I was expelled for not paying this." The Black Spot cunningly raised the school fees. Stalin did not try to pay them. He just left. Stalin's friend Abel Yenukidze, another ex-seminarist who met him at this time, puts it best: "He flew out of the Seminary." But not without controversy.

He confided to his Gori friend Davrichewy that he had been expelled after being denounced, which he said was "a blow." Afterwards, twenty others were expelled for revolutionary activities. Soso's enemies later claimed that he betrayed his fellow Marxists to the rector. It was said that later in prison he confessed, justifying his treachery by saying he was turning them into revolutionaries: they did indeed become the core of his followers. Stalin was capable of this sort of sophistry and betrayal, but would he have been accepted into the Marxist underground if this had been widely known? Even Trotsky thinks the story absurd. More likely, this was his sardonic answer to an accusation, but it fed the suspicion that he would later become an Okhrana spy. Anyhow, many seminarists were expelled every year.

Soso the autodidactic bibliophile "expropriated" the books he still kept from the seminary library. They tried to bill him eighteen roubles and another fifteen in autumn 1900, but by then he was underground, forever beyond the reach of the seminary. The Church was never repaid and Black Spot never got his books back.*

Stalin did not qualify as a priest, but the boarding-school educated him classically—and influenced him enormously. Black Spot had, perversely, turned Stalin into an atheist Marxist and taught him exactly the repressive tactics—"surveillance, spying, invasion of inner life, violation of feelings," in Stalin's own words—that he would re-create in his Soviet police state.

Stalin remained fascinated with priests throughout his life and when he met other seminarists or the sons of priests he would often question them carefully. "Priests teach one to understand people," he reflected. Furthermore he always used the catechismic language of religion. His Bolshevism aped Christ's religion with its cults, saints and icons: "The working-class," he blasphemously wrote on being hailed as the Leader in 1929, "gave birth to me and raised me in its own image and likeness."

The other irony of the seminary was its effect on foreigners such as Franklin Roosevelt, whose secretary recorded that the President—after being thoroughly charmed by Stalin at the 1943 Teheran Conference—was "intrigued that Stalin had been destined for the priesthood."

The old God remained a presence in his atheist consciousness. At one of their meetings during the Second World War, he forgave Winston Churchill's anti-Bolshevism, saying, "All that is in the past and the past belongs to God." He told U.S. envoy Averell Harriman, "Only God can forgive." Friends such as Kapanadze became priests, yet Stalin kept in generous contact. He and his grandees sang church hymns during their drunken Bolshevik dinners. He fused Orthodoxy and Marxism by half joking: "Only the saints are infallible. The Lord God can be accused of creating the poor." But Stalin's actions always speak loudest: the dictator mercilessly suppressed the Church and murdered and deported priests—

---

* George Gurdjieff, the spiritualist author of *Meetings with Remarkable Men,* charlatan to some, hierophant magus to others, claimed to have attended the seminary with Stalin, who, he said, stayed with his family in Tiflis. But Gurdjieff, of Armenian origins, was a fantasist: born in 1866, he was twelve years older than Stalin and there is no evidence he attended the seminary at all. Stalin boarded at the seminary during the term. Gurdjieff also claims a "Prince Nijeradze" as a companion: "Nizheradze" was an alias later used by Stalin in Baku. But there is no evidence that any of Gurdjieff's claims are true. During his reign, Stalin persecuted spiritualists and specifically "Gurdjieffites," who were often shot.

until 1943, when he restored the Patriarchate, but only as a wartime gesture to harness old Russian patriotism.*

Perhaps he revealed his real view of God when he sent his protégé Alexei Kosygin (future Premier under Brezhnev) a gift of fish after the Second World War with this handwritten note: "Comrade Kosygin, here are some presents for you from God! I am the executor of his will! J. Stalin." In some way, as the supreme pontiff of the science of History, the Tiflis seminarist really did regard himself as the executor of God's will.[5]

"Do you suppose," FDR mused several times, "it made some kind of difference in Stalin? Doesn't that explain part of the sympathetic quality in his nature that we all feel?" Perhaps it was the "priesthood" that had taught Stalin "the way a Christian gentleman should behave."

This most un-Christian of gentlemen had moved far from Christianity. Even moderate, noble socialists like Jordania now irritated him and Lado. "They're conducting cultural and educational activities among workers without training them to be revolutionaries," Soso complained. He denounced Jordania to his friends, explaining that he had discovered the works of a brilliant new radical named "Tulin," one of the aliases of Vladimir Ulyanov, who would become Lenin.

"If there'd been no Lenin," said Stalin in old age, "I'd have stayed a choirboy and seminarian." Now he told his friends about this far-off radical. "I must meet him at all costs!" he declared, about to commit himself absolutely to life as a Marxist revolutionary. But he had more immediate problems. Keke "got so angry with him" for leaving the seminary that Soso had to hide a few days in the Gambareuli Gardens, outside Gori, where his friends brought him food. He returned to Tiflis but he soon argued with his roommates, who were supporters of Jordania. He moved out. He had fought with his seminarist friends, then with his roommates, and now he would confront the older radicals of Tiflis. Wherever this rude and arrogant boy went, there was trouble.[6]

* On 4 September 1943, the exiled Russian Patriarch Sergei and two Metropolitans were summoned for a bizarre nocturnal Kremlin chat at which Stalin revealed that he had decided to restore the Patriarchate, churches and seminaries. Sergei thought perhaps it was too early for seminaries. Stalin replied, "Seminaries are better," but mused disingenuously, "Why don't you have any cadres? Where have they disappeared to?" Instead of replying that his "cadres" had been systematically liquidated by Stalin, Sergei tactfully joked: "One of the reasons is that we train a person for priesthood and he becomes a Marshal of the Soviet Union." Stalin then reminisced about the seminary until 3 a.m. "Your Grace," he concluded, wishing the priests good night, "that's all I can do for you now."

8

The Weatherman: Parties and Princes

Soso needed a job and a home. He became a weatherman. Unlikely as it sounds, the life of a meteorologist at the Tiflis Meteorological Observatory was a most convenient cover for a young revolutionary. His friend from Gori, Vano Ketskhoveli, younger brother of Lado, was already working there when in October 1899 Stalin arrived to share his small room beneath the observatory's tower.* As a "probationer-observer," he was on duty only three times a week from 6:30 a.m. until 10 p.m., checking temperatures and barometers hourly, in return for twenty roubles a month. On night duty, he worked from 8:30 p.m. to 8:30 a.m., but then he had the whole day off for revolutionary work. In late 1899, Lado, eagerly assisted by Soso, started to organize a strike, one of the first full-scale radical mobilizations of workers in Georgia.

On New Year's Day, Lado managed to paralyse the city when the drivers of its Belgian-owned trams stopped work. The secret police were observing Lado and his revolutionary weathermen. In the first weeks of 1900, the police turned up at the observatory, arrested Stalin and carted

---

* The observatory still stands, though it is as rundown as every institution in Georgia. Stalin's room remains, with a few of his supposed possessions and the old plaque: THE GREAT STALIN—LEADER OF VKPB AND WORLD PROLETARIAT—LIVED AND WORKED HERE, THE TIFLIS METEOROLOGICAL OBSERVATORY, FROM 28 DECEMBER 1899 TO 21 MARCH 1901, LEADING ILLEGAL SOCIAL-DEMOCRATIC WORKERS' CIRCLES.

him off to the Metekhi Fortress. The arrest, Stalin's first of many, was officially because Beso had not paid his local taxes in his native village, Didi-Lilo[1]—though probably this was a cryptic warning from the Gendarmes.

Stalin had no money, but his better-off friends (led by Davitashvili) banded together and settled the bill. This can hardly have added to Soso's paternal affections, yet Beso did visit him at the observatory several times.

When Keke heard that Beso had once again descended on her son, the redoubtable mother headed into Tiflis on a rescue mission. She insisted on staying in Soso's room.[2]

Once Stalin was released—and the interfering Keke had gone home—he returned to encouraging the workers to strike across the city: the railway workshops were the hub of this agitation. He spent much time around the railway depot, "a long stone building with large latticed windows, the deafening roar of clanks and knocks, the puffing and huffing of locomotives." Initially, his comrades assigned him two clandestine groups of railway workers—so-called circles—to supervise. "I was a complete greenhorn, a total beginner."[3]

Stalin lived and dressed the part, wearing what Trotsky called the "generally recognized sign of a revolutionary, especially in the provinces": a beard; long, almost hippyish hair; and a black satin Russian blouse with a red tie. And he revelled in his scruffiness. "You never saw him in anything," says Iremashvili, "but that dirty blouse and unpolished shoes."[4]

Soso energetically lectured and agitated at his circles. "Why are we poor?" he asked these small gatherings in workers' digs. "Why are we disenfranchised? How can our life be changed?" His answer was Marxism and the Russian Social-Democratic Workers Party (the SDs).[5]

The workers listened reverently to this young preacher—and it was no coincidence that many revolutionaries were seminarists and the workers, often pious ex-peasants. Some later nicknamed Soso "the Priest." "It's a holy struggle," explained the Tiflis agitator Mikhail Kalinin. Trotsky, agitating in another city, remembered that many of the workers thought the movement resembled "the early Christians" and had to be taught that they should be atheists.

"If the word 'committee' has a tedious twang nowadays, then the very words 'committee' and 'party' . . . charmed young ears like a seductive melody," wrote Trotsky. "These were the days of those aged 18–30. Anyone who joined knew prison and exile awaited him—it was a matter of honour to hold out as long as possible."

Soso, who also believed in the sanctity of the cause, soon achieved his first success.[6]

On 1 May 1900, Soso organized a secretive and seminal mass meeting with his characteristically meticulous security. May Day—the Maievka—was the Christmas Day of socialism. The secret police tried to arrest Lado, who scarpered to Baku, the oil city on the Caspian Sea. Stalin stepped into his shoes.

The evening before, instructions and passwords were distributed. At night, 500 workers and activists headed into the hills outside Tiflis to be met by lantern-waving picket-leaders who confided new passwords and routes. At the meeting, they sang "The Marseillaise." Stalin and the other speakers then clambered onto some rocks: there Soso gave his first big speech, vigorously encouraging strike action while Jordania and the Mesame Dasi opposed it.

Soso and his radicals won. The railroad depots struck, as did Adelkhanov's Shoe Factory, where Beso still worked.

"Why are you coming here?" he asked Soso, resenting his son's visit.

"To address these fellows," replied Soso.

"Why aren't you learning a trade?" It was their last recorded contact: Beso failed to cling to his job and became one of the flotsam and jetsam of vagrant desperadoes, borne away on a tide of alcoholism, poverty and despair.

For the first time, the secret police mentioned Soso Djugashvili—along with the much older Victor Kurnatovsky, who knew Lenin himself, and Silva Jibladze, the legendary rector-beater—as a leader in their reports. Stalin had made his mark.[7]

The secret police were circling, but life in Tiflis was still sleepy, charming, idyllic with its balmy nights and busy street cafés. The revolutionaries enjoyed an almost undergraduate existence. "Their evenings were filled with loud arguments, reading and prolonged conversations interspersed with guitar playing and singing," recalls Anna Alliluyeva, daughter of Sergei, the skilled electrician and Marxist agitator who operated alongside Stalin at the Tiflis railway depot. Tiflis was an intimate town where news travelled fast from one vine-entwined verandah to another on "the balcony telegraph."

Stalin was just beginning, but already he divided his comrades into heroes, followers and enemies. First he found a new mentor, Prince

Alexander "Sasha" Tsulukidze, a "tall handsome young man" dressed beautifully in Western suits, a friend of his other hero, Lado. Both hailed from classes above that of Stalin: Lado was a priest's son but the Red Prince's father was one of Georgia's richest aristocrats; the family of his mother, Princess Olympiada Shervashidze, had ruled Abkhazia.* Stalin praised the "astonishing, outstanding talents" of Lado and Prince Sasha, both of them beyond his jealousy because they were long dead. Stalin had only one real hero: himself. In a lifetime of defiant, self-reliant egotism, Lado, Prince Sasha and Lenin were the only others who came close. He was, he said, their "disciple."[8]

Stalin already had his own little court among the radical boys expelled from the seminary: another forty were sent down in 1901, including the icon-urinator (Stalin's ex-pupil) Elisabedashvili and his friend Alexander "Alyosha" Svanidze, who rented a flat in Sololaki Street, just above Yerevan Square. There Stalin gave lessons, preparing a reading list of 300 books for his circle. "He didn't just read books," said Elisabedashvili, "he *ate* them." Debonair with noble connections and three pretty sisters, Alyosha Svanidze would become Stalin's brother-in-law and intimate until the Terror. But Stalin did not meet the sisters for a while.

The other pupil, just arrived from Gori, was the semi-psychotic Simon Ter-Petrossian, aged nineteen, soon to be known as "Kamo," who had also spent his childhood joining in streetfights, "stealing fruit and my favourite activity—boxing!" He hung around Svanidze's flat "in order to learn something," but he wanted to be an army officer. His tyrannical father ranted at him for spending time with Stalin, "that penniless good-for-nothing." But "when my father went bankrupt in 1901," says Ter-Petrossian, he lost his power over the boy. "Stalin was my tutor. He taught me literature and gave me books . . . I really liked Zola's *Germinal*!" Stalin "drew him like a magnet."

Stalin was not the most patient teacher, however. When Ter-Petrossian struggled with Russian and Marxism, Stalin ordered another

---

* In Russia, the mercantile and middle classes, who had no access to political power, often sympathized with the revolutionaries, but in Georgia they could also count on local patriotism—and a web of family clans reaching the highest nobility. The Shervashidzes managed to be top Petersburg courtiers while on their Abkhazian estates enjoying links to the revolutionaries. Prince Giorgi Shervashidze was Chancellor of the Court of the Dowager Empress Maria Fyodorovna, Alexander III's widow and Nicholas II's mother. After the Revolution and until the 1930s, the Shervashidzes who remained in the USSR were protected by the local Bolshevik leader and Stalin courtier Nestor Lakoba.

of his acolytes, Vardoyan, to teach him. "Soso lay reading a book while I taught Kamo Russian grammar," remembers Vardoyan, "but Kamo had limited mental abilities and kept saying *kamo* instead of *komu* [to whom]." Stalin "lost his temper and jumped up but then laughed, '*Komu* not *kamo*! Try and remember it, *bicho* [boy]!' Afterwards, Soso, always an avid coiner of nicknames for his courtiers, nicknamed Ter-Petrossian 'Kamo,' which stuck for his whole life," says Vardoyan. If Kamo struggled with the language, he was intoxicated with Marxism, and "enthralled" by Stalin. "For now, just *read more!*" Stalin instructed him. "You might just manage to become an officer, but it would be better if you gave it up, and engaged in something else . . ." Stalin, like Dr. Frankenstein, groomed Kamo to become his enforcer and cutthroat.

"Soso was a philosophical conspirator from the start. We learned conspiracy from him," says Vardoyan. "I was addicted to his way of talking and laughing, his mannerisms. I found myself imitating him against my will so my friends called me 'Soso's gramophone.' "⁹

Yet Soso was never the carefree Georgian. Even then, "He was a very unusual and mysterious man," explains David Sagirashvili, a young socialist who met him at this time and noticed him "walking the streets of Tiflis, thin, pockmarked and carelessly dressed, burdened with a big stack of books."

Stalin attended a wild party given by Alyosha Svanidze. They were drinking cocktails of melon juice and brandy, and got wildly drunk. Yet Soso lay on a sofa on the verandah reading silently, making notes. So they started to look for him: "Where is he?"

"Soso's reading," replied Alyosha Svanidze.

"What are you reading?" his friends asked mockingly.

"Napoleon Bonaparte's *Memoirs*," Soso replied. "It's amazing what mistakes he made. I'm making a note of them!" The intoxicated gentry had hysterics at this autodidactic cobbler's son whom they now nicknamed the "Kunkula" (Staggerer), for his hasty and awkward gait.¹⁰ But the serious revolutionaries, such as Stalin, Lado and Prince Sasha, were not wasting their time on cocktails.

Georgia was in a revolutionary "ferment of ideas." These passionate young idealists "returned late at night with friends," recounts Anna Alliluyeva. "They sit down at the table, someone opens a book, starts to read aloud." They were all reading one thing—Lenin's new newspaper *Iskra* (Spark), which propagated the vision of a party led by a tiny militant elite.

This new model of a revolutionary electrified young hotheads like Stalin, who no longer aspired to be the gentleman-amateur enthusing broad groups of workers but resolved to be the brutal professional, leader of a ruthless sect. Always happiest in vigorous campaigns against internal as well as external foes, Soso, still only aged twenty-two, was determined to break Jordania and Jibladze, and bend the Tiflis Party to his own will.

"He spoke with cruelty," reports Razhden Arsenidze, a moderate Marxist who admitted that Stalin "radiated energy, his words imbued with a raw power and singlemindedness. Frequently sarcastic, his cruel witticisms were often as extreme as the lash of a whip." When his "outraged" listeners protested, he "apologized, explaining that it was the language of the proletariat," who "talked bluntly but always told the truth."

The secret police and the workers regarded this ex-seminarist as an "intellectual," but to the bewildered moderates he was "a muddled young comrade" launching a "hostile and disruptive agitation against the leaderships of the SD organization in Tiflis." They openly mocked Soso as "ignorant and obnoxious," according to Davrichewy. Jibladze grumbled that "we gave him circles to agitate against the state and instead he agitated against us."[11]

Stalin, his mentors and followers still met "on the banks of the Kura sitting under scented acacias drinking cheap wine, served by the kioskkeeper." But the success of Stalin's strikes had concentrated police minds. The secret police decided to crush the movement before it could organize its 1901 May Day riot. The Gendarmes, analysing their intelligence on the revolutionary "leader" Stalin, immediately spotted his talent for conspiracy: "an intellectual who leads a group of railway workers. External observation revealed he behaves very cautiously, always keeps looking behind him when walking." He was always hard to catch.[12]

Overnight on 21–22 March 1901, the secret police, the Okhrana, swooped down on the leaders, Kurnatovsky and Makharadze.* They surrounded the weather observatory to catch Stalin, who was returning on the tram.

---

* The most important Russian revolutionary in Georgia then was tall, stooped, balding Victor Kurnatovsky, who had shared Lenin's Siberian exile and even met Plekhanov in Zurich. Many of the most active revolutionaries were not Caucasians but Russians. In the railway depot, Sergei Alliluyev was assisted by the affable, ginger-bearded Mikhail Kalinin, another railway worker of peasant origins whom Soso was to meet now: he would be Stalin's long-serving head of state. The other leaders were Georgians—Jordania, Jibladze, Mikha Tskhakaya and Philip Makharadze, all founders of the Third Group back in 1892.

He suddenly noticed through the tram window the studied nonchalance of plainclothes secret policemen—as easily recognizable as G-men in an American movie—in position around the observatory. He stayed on the tram, returning later to reconnoitre, but he could never live there again.

The raid changed his destiny: here ended any aspiration to a life of normality. He had played with the idea of becoming a teacher, earning extra cash by tutoring (though he normally tried to convert his pupils to Marxism), charging ten kopecks an hour. That was all over now. Henceforth he lived on others, expecting friends, sympathizers or the Party to fund his philanthropic revolutionary mission. He instantly entered what Trotsky called "that very serious game called revolutionary conspiracy"— a murky terrorist netherworld with its own special customs, fastidious etiquette and brutal rules.

As Soso entered this secret world, he pushed ahead with the plans for an aggressive May Day demonstration.

The governor-general of the Caucasus, Prince Golitsyn, marched Cossacks, Dragoons, artillery and infantry into Tiflis for a showdown. They bivouacked in the squares. On the morning of Sunday, 22 April 1901, some 3,000 workers and revolutionaries gathered outside the Soldiers Bazaar. The Cossacks had other ideas, but Soso was prepared. Sergei Alliluyev noticed that the activists were "unseasonably dressed in heavy overcoats and Caucasian sheepskin hats." When he asked why, a comrade answered: "Soso's orders."

"What for?"

"We'll be the first to receive the Cossack whips."

Indeed the Cossacks waited in every courtyard down Golovinsky Prospect. At noon, "the garrison gun boomed"; the demonstrators started to march up Golovinsky to Yerevan Square, where the seminarists were to join them, singing "The Marseillaise" and "The Warsawianka." The Cossacks galloped down on them, drawing sabres and brandishing their heavy *nagaika* whips that could kill a man. The *pharaohs*—the police— advanced, sabres drawn. A forty-five-minute pitched battle of "desperate encounters" broke out down the boulevard as the Cossacks charged any group larger than three people. The red banners—declaring DOWN WITH TYRANNY—were passed from hand to hand. Fourteen workers were seriously wounded and fifty arrested. Martial law was declared in Tiflis.[13]

This was Stalin's first success. While the genteel Jordania was arrested and imprisoned for a year, his *Kvali* closed, Stalin just fled to Gori for a few days. No wonder Jordania loathed this young hothead, but Stalin had just started. He and his allies were soon keen to intensify the "open struggle"—even if it cost "torrents of blood."

These young radicals discussed the murder of Captain Lavrov, the deputy chief of the Gendarmes in Tiflis, but the real action was in the railway depots where the railways director, Vedenev, energetically resisted Stalin's strikes.

Stalin now met another partner-in-crime, Stepan Shaumian, the well-off, highly educated son of an Armenian businessman. Shaumian, closely connected with the plutocracy of the Caucasus, was tutor to the children of the city's richest oil baron, Mantashev, and he soon married the daughter of a top oil executive.

"Tall, well built and very handsome with a pale face and light-blue eyes," Shaumian helped organize a solution to the problem of Vedenev: the railway boss was sitting in his office when a pistol, pointed through his window, shot him through the heart.

No one was caught.[14] But this shot marked the start of a new era in which "all tender feeling for family, friendship, love, gratitude and even honour, must," according to the much-read *Revolutionary Catechism* of the nihilist Nechaev, "be squashed by the sole passion for revolutionary work." The amoral rules—or rather the lack of them—were described by both sides as *konspiratsia,* the "world apart" that is vividly drawn in Dostoevsky's novel *The Devils.* Without understanding *konspiratsia,* it is impossible to understand the Soviet Union itself: Stalin never left this world. *Konspiratsia* became the ruling spirit of his Soviet state—and of his state of mind.

Henceforth, Stalin usually carried a pistol in his belt. Secret policemen and revolutionary terrorists now became professional secret fighters in the duel for the Russian Empire.*

---

* Going underground meant that Stalin also avoided conscription into the army in 1901. On his last arrest in 1913, he told the police he had been "exempted from conscription for family reasons in 1901." The Gori police officer Davrichewy helped provide the paperwork enabling him to escape military service, according to his son's memoirs, possibly by citing Stalin's family problems and also moving his birthday a year later to 21 December 1879. Stalin was not bothered by conscription again until 1916.

9

Stalin Goes Underground: *Konspiratsia*

J ust at this time, the Gori priest's son Kote Charkviani was arguing with a street-cleaner on a Tiflis backstreet when a familiar voice said: "Smash him up, Kote. Don't be afraid, he's the tamed street hound of the Gendarmes!" It was Soso, who could divine a traitor or a spy almost by instinct. He could not hang around to chat. The secret police were after him.

Then "he disappeared into the narrow curved street . . ." But that conspiratorial instinct was an essential quality in this game of mist, mirrors and shadows. The antagonists were locked in an intimate, desperate and amoral embrace in which agents, double-agents and treble-agents promised, betrayed, switched sides and betrayed again their allegiances.

In the 1870s, the rebels were middle-class populists, *narodniki*, who hoped that the liberal future lay with the pure peasantry. A faction of *narodniki* developed into the terrorist groups Land and Freedom and later People's Will, who believed that the murder of Emperor Alexander II would achieve revolution.

People's Will embraced the ideas of the small-time philosopher Nechaev whose amoral *Revolutionary Catechism* begot Lenin and Stalin. "Regroup this world of brigands into an indivisible destructive force," he suggested, killing police "in the most agonizing way." The anarchist Bakunin shared that dream of harnessing the "swashbuckling robber-world" to the Revolution. Lenin borrowed the disciplined organization, total dedication and the gangsterish brutality of the People's Will, qualities that Stalin personified.

Alexander II, faced with a terroristic cat-and-mouse game, started to create a modern security service as sophisticated as the terrorists themselves. He reorganized his father's Third Section into a plainclothed secret police, the Division for Protection of Order and Social Security, soon shortened to "Okhrana." Yet, throughout the reforms, the People's Will actually had an agent within the department. The police hunted down the terrorists, but it was too late. In 1881, they got their man, killing Alexander II on the streets of St. Petersburg.

His heir, Alexander III, created the double system that Stalin knew. Both the Okhrana and the prestigious semi-military Gendarmes, the "Tsar's eyes and ears," dressed in a fine blue white-trimmed uniform with boots and sabre, ran their own intelligence services.

At its elegant headquarters at 16 Fontanka by the Moika in Petersburg, the Okhrana Special Section meticulously collated labyrinthine charts and colour-coded files of terror groups. Their *bureaux noirs* practised *perlustratsia* (perlustration): 380,000 letters annually were being opened by 1882.* They had a reputation in Europe as the sinister organ of Autocracy but never even approached the brutal competence of Lenin's Cheka, let alone Stalin's NKVD. They wielded three punishments. The rope was rarely used, being reserved for assassins of Romanovs and ministers, but it had one decisive effect: the execution of Alexander Ulyanov, a young man on the edge of a conspiracy against the Tsar, helped radicalize his younger brother, Lenin. Next was *katorga*, hard labour, again quite rare. The most common punishment was "administrative exile," for periods of up to five years.

The mastermind of *konspiratsia*, Moscow Okhrana chief Zubatov, evolved a new system of surveillance. Detectives were employed, but their real tools were the *agentura*, the "external agent"—the *shpik*, or "spook," in revolutionary vernacular—who followed characters like Stalin. The Okhrana's most effective tactic was the *provokatsia*—the provocations of their "internal agents." The secret policeman should treat his *agent provocateur* like "a beloved woman with whom you have entered illicit rela-

---

* When Interior Minister Plehve was assassinated in 1904, his police director, Lopukhin, found forty of his own private letters in the dead man's safe: the Minister was perlustrating his own chief of police.

tions," explained Zubatov. "Look after her like the apple of your eye. One careless move and you dishonour her . . . Never reveal the name of your informer to anyone, even your director. Forget his name and remember only his pseudonym." The stakes were high: one side's *provokator* was the other's *predatel* (traitor), who faced death.

In return for sometimes huge salaries, these double-agents not only penetrated the "internal life of the revolutionary organizations" but also sometimes directed them. The Okhrana even set up their own revolutionary groups and trade unions. And their very existence was designed to inspire a cannibalistic frenzy of suspicion and paranoia among the revolutionaries. The craziness of Stalinist terror in the USSR shows how successful they were. Yet *konspiratsia* could be as dangerous for the authorities as for the terrorists.*

Russia faced a blossoming of conspiracies in this war on terror: the Okhrana had to foil not only the Social-Democrats, the Armenian nationalist Dashnaks and the Georgian Socialist-Federalists but Russia's most deadly terrorists, populist socialists called the Socialist-Revolutionaries, the SRs. In the best example of the danger of double-agents, the Okhrana recruited Evano Azef, head of the SR Fighting Brigade, which effectively used suicide bombers. During 1902–5, Azef received massive payments, but simultaneously he arranged the assassination of two Interior Ministers and a Grand Duke.

Yet overall, despite Okhrana-Gendarme rivalry and bureaucratic muddle, the secret-police suppression and infiltration of the revolutionaries was astonishingly subtle and successful: they were the best secret services of their day.† Indeed Lenin copied the Okhrana to organize "a few

---

* During the 1880s, Colonel G. P. Sudeikin of the Petersburg Okhrana cultivated a young People's Will terrorist named Degaev, a success that allowed the policeman to become "the master of revolution in Russia." But this had a price: the Colonel was even forced to order murders to conceal his double-agent. Then in 1883 Degaev lured him to a meeting and murdered him. Degaev ultimately disappeared. Years later, a mathematics professor in an obscure U.S. midwestern university was exposed as none other than Degaev, a story finely told in Richard Pipes's *Degaev Affair*. Such tactics are always a deadly gamble. In our times, the U.S. intelligence officers who set up the Afghan mujahideen to fight the Soviets and the Israeli intelligence officers who sponsored Islamic radicals on the West Bank to counteract the PLO learned similar lessons when their organizations developed into the Jihadist al-Qaeda and Hamas, respectively.

† The Okhrana could not afford to ignore the ingenuity of the SR assassins. In a foreshadowing of al-Qaeda and 9/11, the success of aeroplane flight suggested these new machines as weapons. SR terrorists considered flying a dynamite-packed biplane into the Winter Palace, so the Okhrana in 1909 ordered the monitoring of all flights as well as people learning to fly and members of aero-clubs. It is a mark of the Okhrana's excellence that

professionals as highly trained and experienced as the secret police with conspiratorial techniques at the highest level of perfection."

Stalin was precisely such a man; this "world apart" was his natural habitat. In the Caucasus, it was even harder to make sense of the game. A Georgian upbringing was the ideal training for the terrorist-gangster, based on sacred loyalty to family and friends, fighting skill, personal largesse and the art of vengeance, all punched into Stalin on Gori back-streets. The Caucasian secret police were more violent yet more venal. Stalin became eerily adept at corrupting them and at divining their spies.[1]

Stalin was constantly tailed by Okhrana spooks whom he became expert at foxing: "Those dolts," he laughed as he pulled off another serpentine escape in the backstreets of Tiflis. "Are we supposed to teach them how to do their own jobs?"[2] He avoided the arrests that followed his May Day bedlam, but he had close misses. Once he was singing Georgian songs in an illicit bookshop when the police surrounded the place: he walked right past the "dumb policemen." Another time at a revolutionary meeting, the police raided the house, but Stalin and his friends jumped out of the window into the rain without their galoshes, roaring with laughter.[3]

He changed names—he used the alias "David" at this time—and lodged in at least six apartments. When he was staying with his friend Mikha Bochoridze, the police raided the house (where Kamo would later take the money after the Tiflis heist). Stalin pretended to be a sick tenant, lying in bed, shrouded in sheets and bandages. The police searched the house but, having no orders about an invalid, they went to consult their officers. They were sent back to arrest the "patient," who meanwhile had made a swift recovery—and exit.[4]

Between escapes and meetings, Stalin was busy writing his first arti-cles in a catechismic, romantic and apocalyptic style. Lado had teamed up with Abel Yenukidze, a sandy-haired, genial ex-seminarist and woman-izer, to create a radical newspaper *Brdzola* (Struggle), which they printed on an illegal printing-press in Baku.[5]

The police spies hunted and sometimes even caught up with him: on 27 and 28 October 1901, they observed "Intellectual Josef Djugashvili lead-ing a meeting" at the Melani Tavern.

On 11 November, he was one of those running a city conference

---

in 1909 it was imaginative enough to envisage a crime that was beyond the scope of the FBI and CIA in the twenty-first century.

attended by about twenty-four Marxists. Here he was attacked by the moderates as a "slanderer." They would all have known of Jibladze's accusations against the "obnoxious" Soso, but they also recognized his energy, competence and ruthlessness. Stalin, following Lenin's vision of a militant sect of professional revolutionaries, warned of the dangers of electing ordinary workers to their Committee because "police agents would be elected." Instead the conference elected a committee of four workers and four intellectuals.

His many enemies surely demanded his expulsion, later claiming that he was driven out of Tiflis. This wishful thinking has been repeated by historians ever since. Fortunately, the Gendarme agents, who were better informed and whose reports were written that day, reveal that Soso was elected as the fourth intellectual. But perhaps this was part of a compromise that killed two birds with one stone. He was elected to the Committee, joining the leadership for the first time, but as the secret police were closing in, he was "rescued" (and his comrades rescued from his malevolent machinations) by being sent on "a propaganda mission"— conveniently far away from Tiflis.

The Gendarmes noticed that the newly elected, ever-present Stalin missed his Committee meeting on 25 November 1901—and, as ever like Macavity, T. S. Eliot's elusive cat, disappeared into thin air.

He was in fact on the train to Batumi, turbulent oil port of the Russian Empire, where he would spread blood and fire.[6]

10

"I'm Working for the Rothschilds!"—
Fire, Massacre and Arrest in Batumi

Comrade Soso brought his new merciless style to Batumi with a vengeance. Within three months of his move to the seaside boom-town, the Rothschilds' refinery had mysteriously caught fire. A militant strike had led to the storming of the prison and a Cossack massacre. The town was flooded with Marxist pamphlets; informers were being murdered, horses slaughtered, factory managers shot. Soso was in a feud with the old-style Georgian revolutionaries and was having an affair with a married girl while the secret police hunted him down.

He hit the ground running in Batumi. He rendezvoused at a tavern in the Turkish Bazaar with Constantine Kandelaki, a worker and Social-Democrat, who became his Batumi henchman. He ordered Kandelaki to call a series of meetings. "At an agreed knock, we opened the door," wrote one of the local workers, Porfiro Kuridze, who confronted "a slim young and energetic man, with black hair," worn very long.

"Nobody knew his name," records Domenti Vadachkoria, who held one of these meetings at his apartment. "It was just a young man in a black shirt, a long summer coat and a fedora." Already something of a veteran in *konspiratsia* and a believer in his own instinctive eye for traitors, Stalin ordered Vadachkoria to "invite seven workers to a meeting" but "asked me to show him the invited workers." He stood at the window while "I walked the invited workers one by one along the lane. Stalin asked me not to invite one of them. He was an amazing conspirator and knew human nature well. He could look at someone and see right through them. I told him a man wanted to work with us." The man's name was Karzkhiya.

"That guy's a spook," said Stalin. Shortly afterwards, continues Vadachkoria, "when Cossacks broke up a meeting, we saw that man in a policeman's uniform. It was decided to wipe him out. He was killed." Here is the first instance when Stalin sniffs out a traitor and has him killed, probably his first murder.* In any case, henceforth, he played rough in "the serious game of conspiracy." There would be other Karzkhiyas. But even then he left what he called the "black work"—the killing—to his henchmen.

At the meetings, Stalin announced that he was bringing a newly aggressive spirit to the Revolution in Batumi. Then he asked everyone there to "gather another seven at your factory and repeat this conversation."[1] Setting up his headquarters at Ali the Persian's Tavern in the bazaar, Comrade Soso moved around all the time in a frenzy of often nocturnal visits and lectures. He first lived with Simhovich, a Jewish watchmaker, then with an ex-brigand, now oil worker, Silvester Lomdzharia, who with his brother Porfiro became Stalin's bodyguards.

One day, Stalin rose early and disappeared without a word. Kandelaki arrived soon afterwards and waited nervously until he returned.

"Guess why I got up so early this morning?" asked Stalin exuberantly. "Today I got a job with the Rothschilds at their refinery storehouse. I'll be earning 6 abaz daily [1 rouble 20 kopecks]." The Franco-Jewish dynasty, who personified the power, glamour and cosmopolitanism of international capitalism, would not have been as amused as Stalin, but they never knew that they had employed the future supreme pontiff of international Marxism. Stalin started laughing, almost singing: *'I'm working for the Rothschilds!'*

"I hope," joked Kandelaki, "the Rothschilds will start to prosper from this moment onwards!"

---

* The dates of these memoirs are always important. In memoirs dictated in 1936, Vadachkoria implies that it was Stalin who ordered the murder, a naïve thing to record that year; an unthinkable thing to record a year later during the Great Terror, or afterwards. The story of Stalin just *suspecting* the police spy and being right about it was published as part of the cult of personality. The story of the sleuth being killed appears *only* in the archival original and is published here for the first time.

Stalin said nothing, but they understood one another: he would do what he could to ensure that the Rothschilds prospered.[2]

On New Year's Eve, Soso gathered together his top thirty rebels for a party-cum-meeting at Lomdzharia's house, serving cheese, sausage and wine—but he banned excessive boozing. His bloodcurdling and melodramatic speech ended: "We mustn't fear death! The sun is rising. Let's sacrifice our lives!"

"God forbid we die in our beds!" shouted the toastmaster. The workers cheered, inspired by Stalin's aggression—even if Batumi's moderate Marxists, led by Karlo Chkheidze, the local hospital manager, and teacher Isidore Ramishvili, were not. They ran a Sunday school for workers, a soppy approach anathema to Stalin. The "legals" initially helped fund his work, but friendly relations did not last long. Stalin was about to "turn Batumi upside down."

Batumi was a subtropical frontier-town on the Black Sea, dominated by the Empire's great financial-oil dynasties, the Nobels and the Rothschilds. Even twenty years later, the poet Osip Mandelstam called Batumi "a Russian-style California Goldrush city."

The Tsar had only gained this seaside nest of pirates from the Ottoman Padishah in 1878, but the oil boom in Baku, on the other side of the Caucasian isthmus, had presented the challenge of how to transport the black gold to the West. The Rothschilds and Nobels built a pipeline to Batumi, where they could refine the oil, then load it into the tankers moored in Naphtha Harbour. Suddenly Batumi, also the port of export for manganese, liquorice and tea, became a "door to Europe," Georgia's "only modern town."

Batumi now boasted 16,000 Persian, Turkish, Greek, Georgian, Armenian and Russian workers, almost a thousand of them at the refinery, controlled by Baron Eduard de Rothschild's Caspian and Black Sea Oil Company. The workers, often children, lived miserably in Oil City on reeking streets, with overflowing cesspools beside oozing refineries. Typhus killed many. But Batumi's millionaires and foreign executives, especially the English, turned this backwater into a pleasure town with a seaside boulevard, white Cuban-style mansions, sumptuous brothels, a casino, a cricket pitch and an English Yacht Club.[3]

On 4 January 1902, "As I was coming home," says Kandelaki, "I saw the fire!" Then Stalin returned, cheerfully boasting: "You know, man, your words came true!" The Rothschilds would indeed "prosper" with Stalin as an employee. "My warehouse caught fire!"*

Crowds watched a black mushroom of smoke rise over the port. The workers helped put out the fire, which meant they were due a bonus. Stalin joined a deputation to meet the Rothschilds' French manager, François Jeune, his first encounter with a European businessman. But there is evidence that Stalin was henceforth in secret contact with the Rothschilds management—the start of his murky but lucrative relationship with the oil barons. The Rothschilds surely knew that the fire was arson, and Jeune refused to pay the bonus. This was the provocation Stalin sought. He called a strike.

The authorities attempted to stop him; the Okhrana tried to hunt down Batumi's new agitator; the *pharaoh*s harassed the strikers; the police spies watched the Marxists; the Rothschilds worried about their oil shipments. But Stalin headed for Tiflis—eleven hours by train—to procure the printing-press, necessary to broaden the strike. Leaflets had to be published in both Georgian and Armenian, so the Committee put him in contact with Suren Spandarian, an affluent but ruthless Armenian who, despite a wife and children, was an unrestrained Lothario. Stalin printed his Armenian pamphlets on the presses of Spandarian's father, a newspaper editor. Spandarian became Stalin's best friend.[4]

Stalin, assisted by Kamo and bearing his printing-press, returned to find Batumi in uproar. Kamo and Kandelaki quickly set up the press, which was soon broadcasting Stalin's words to all the workers of Oil City.

On 17 February, the Rothschilds and Nobels capitulated and agreed to the workers' demands, including a 30 percent pay rise—a triumph for the young revolutionary. In Tiflis, Captain Lavrov's Gendarmes were breaking the Marxists with raids and arrests, but in Batumi, formerly so quiet, Gendarme captain Giorgi Jakeli admitted that he was worried by the "sudden increased restlessness." He intensified surveillance of the enigmatic "Comrade Soso."

---

* Kandelaki, in memoirs recorded in 1935, before the Terror, strongly implies that Stalin was the Rothschilds arsonist. The Stalinist histories, which quote Kandelaki, suppress any suggestion that the Leader had been an arsonist, killer, bank robber or seducer. Kandelaki's record is published here for the first time. Historians have often mistaken him for David Kandelaki, a young trade official in the 1930s whom Stalin used as his secret emissary to open negotiations with Hitler, a probe three years before the 1939 Molotov-Ribbentrop Pact. Stalin had David Kandelaki shot in 1937. But the latter was not Constantine—or Kotsia—Kandelaki of Batumi, later a Menshevik and Minister of Finance in the independent Georgian Democratic Republic of 1918–21.

Stalin had to move out of Lomdzharia's apartment. After staying in different flats, he settled in the workers' township of Barskhana in a little house belonging to Natasha Kirtava, aged twenty-two, a peasant beauty and SD sympathizer whose husband had disappeared. Judging by Batumi folklore, Kirtava's own memoirs and his own later proposals, Stalin enjoyed a love affair with the young woman, the first but not the last with his many landladies and conspiratorial comrades. In her memoirs, she talks of his "tender attention and thoughtfulness" and even records a loving moment* amid the Marxist struggle: "He turned to me, stroked the hair off my forehead, and kissed me."[5]

The Rothschilds, under their managers Jeune and von Stein, were determined to avenge Stalin's success. On 26 February, they dismissed 389 troublemaking workers. They went on strike, sending "a man to find Comrade Soso," but he was in Tiflis, where he frequently visited his protégés Svanidze and Kamo.

Soso hurried back to Batumi next day, inviting his followers to a meeting at Lomdzharia's place, where "he proposed a series of demands"—and an even more provocative strike to shut down the whole oil terminal. One of his helpers, Porfiro Kuridze, did not recognize him: he had shaved off his beard and moustaches. When Stalin was not in Ali the Persian's Tavern, he used the Souk-suk Cemetery as his macabre headquarters, holding midnight meetings among the graves to elect delegates. Once when police surprised a meeting there, he hid within the wide skirts of a female comrade. At another gathering, surrounded by Cossacks, Stalin pulled on a dress and escaped in drag.

The workers were impressed with the "intellectual," whom they dubbed "the Priest." He gave them a reading list. "He once left us a book," said Kuridze. " 'It's Gogol,' Stalin explained, teaching us about Gogol's life."

Comrade Soso, usually dressed in a dashing Circassian coat with his trademark black wide-brimmed fedora and a white Caucasian hood tossed over his shoulder, quickly gained an aggressive following, known as the "Sosoists," an early version of Stalinists. Chkheidze and the "legals" of the Sunday school invited him over to receive a reprimand, but he refused to go. "They're armchair strategists and avoid real political struggle,"

---

* This would have irritated Stalin—the sort of personal detail that more sophisticated interviewees in the 1930s left out of their memoirs. Natasha Kirtava recorded two sets of memoirs, one in 1934 and the other in 1937. Needless to say, the unpublished kissing episode appeared only in the first, before the Terror.

sneered Soso, who had to be in absolute control. "Djugashvili's despotism," reported Captain Lavrov of the Tiflis Gendarmerie, "alienated many" in the struggle "between the older Socialists and the younger Socialists." The strike spread. Blacklegs were threatened, their horses slaughtered. But the secret police were after Soso the Priest. The Cossacks were massing.[6]

General Smagin, governor of Kutaisi Province, which included Batumi, rushed into town to lead the suppression of the strike. Addressing the workers, his message was bleak: "Back to work or Siberia!" Overnight on 7 March, Smagin arrested Stalin's bodyguard Porfiro Lomdzharia and the strike leaders.

Next day, Stalin arranged demonstrations outside the police station where the prisoners were kept. The pressure worked. The Gendarmes nervously moved the prisoners to a transit prison. The governor promised to meet the demonstrators. This did not suit Soso. At that night's meeting, he proposed storming the prison. Vadachkoria preferred to negotiate. "You'll never be a revolutionary," sneered Soso the Priest. The Sosoists backed him. The next morning, Stalin led aggressive demonstrations. The day after that, much of the town joined him on the march to storm the prison. But a traitor had betrayed the plan. Cossacks took up positions. Troops under the tough Captain Antadze blocked the way to the transit prison. They fixed bayonets. The vast crowd hesitated before the roadblock.

"Don't run or they'll shoot," Stalin warned.

"Soso suggested we sing songs. We didn't know the revolutionary hymns then so we sang 'Ali-Pasha'!" said Porfiro Kuridze.

"The soldiers won't fire," Stalin called out over the crowd, "and don't be afraid of the officers. Beat 'em up and let's free our comrades." The mob lurched forward towards the prison.

Soso was surrounded by a guard of Sosoists, mainly Gurian peasant-workers, led by Kandelaki. "The Gurians were brave conspirators. They tried to stop me going to the front but I did," Stalin bragged later. "So they created seven circles round me and even the wounded were held in place so it was impossible to break the circle."

Just as the crowd outside the jail started to charge the soldiers, the prisoners inside overcame their guards. One of the prisoners, Porfiro Lomdzharia, heard the rioters: "We tried to get out. The gate was shattered. Some prisoners escaped." The Cossacks galloped at the marauding demonstrators, who tried to grab their rifles. The rebels fired shots in return and pelted the Cossacks with rocks. The soldiers beat them back with rifle-butts but were forced to retreat. Captain Antadze was hit by stones, his cuff pierced by a bullet. The soldiers fought back, shooting into the air—and retreated again. But this time they stood their ground. "Again the loud voice of Stalin called upon us not to disperse and to free the workers," recalled a demonstrator, Injerabian. The mob surged forward.

"Then a terrible sound!" Captain Antadze barked the order "Fire!" Volleys of shots rang out. People fell to the ground. Everyone was running and screaming. "It was panic, absolute hell. The deserted square was covered with dead and dying, groaning" under the eyes of the soldiers. The dying cried out "Water" or "Help!" Then "I remembered Soso," says Kandelaki. "We got separated. I was afraid, starting to search for his body among the dead." But Vera Lomdzharia, Porfiro's sister, noticed Stalin wandering around observing the mayhem he had unleashed. Looking for her brother among the corpses, she attacked a soldier, but he replied: "It was Antadze."

Soso picked up "one of the wounded" and got him into a phaeton. "He brought him to our flat," reports Illarion Darakhvelidze. "Soso wrapped bandages around the wounded," agrees Kandelaki. Natasha Kirtava and other women helped wounded comrades into carts that took them to hospital. There were thirteen dead, fifty-four wounded. That night at Darakhvelidze's house, "We were extremely agitated." But Soso was exhilarated.

"Today we advanced several years!" Stalin told Kachik Kazarian. Nothing else mattered. "We lost comrades but we won." As in many other bloody campaigns, the human cost was irrelevant, subordinate to its political value. "The whiplash and sabre render us a great service, hastening to revolutionize any innocent bystanders." Young Trotsky was impressed by the Batumi massacre: "It stirred the whole country."

Jordania and Chkheidze fumed about "this youngster who wanted to be a leader" but "lacked necessary understanding of affairs . . . and used rough language." They believed that the massacre played into the hands of the authorities: was Stalin an *agent provocateur*?

Stalin rushed to his printing-press hidden in the cottage of Despina Shapatava, a young Marxist. "Thank the mothers who raised such sons!" he boomed in his printed response to the massacre, distributed all over town by next morning. However, an informer betrayed the press, and policemen raided the house. But Despina blocked the way. "My children are sleeping," she shouted. The police laughed: neither the press nor Stalin were interrupted. But he was not only fighting with words: it seems that he ordered the assassination of the Rothschilds' manager von Stein. "We entrusted [a comrade] to assassinate him," recalls one of Stalin's henchmen. "When von Stein's carriage got closer," the hit man drew his revolver but bungled the hit. "Von Stein turned his carriage round, fled and left the town that night by ship."

The hunt was on for Stalin, who now had to move his invaluable press to a safer hideout. He "attached great importance to conspiracy," says Kuridze. "Often he'd arrive in a coach, then change his clothes and disappear again just as quickly." He would alter his appearance, suddenly swap coats with comrades, often sporting "a hood over his long hair."[7]

That night, Stalin loaded the press onto a carriage, hid it in the cemetery, then carried it to a shack, the home of an old Abkhazian highwayman named Hashimi Smirba, at Makhmudia, seven versts outside Batumi but right under the cannons of the garrison fortress (and therefore beyond suspicion). The retired brigand was delighted to hide the press because his friend Lomdzharia told him it would print counterfeit roubles. Smirba would get his share. Smirba's son Hamdi, whose memoirs do not appear in the cult literature, recounts how Stalin arrived in the middle of the night with four heavy boxes and sprang into action, unpacking and setting them up in a cellar. The typesetters, and probably Stalin too, arrived and left dressed as Muslim women in veils. Working day and night, he hired builders to construct another house for Smirba containing a secret compartment for the whirring press.

"What's that noise?" asked one of the builders.

"A cow with a worm in its horn," replied Smirba.

Soso almost moved into Smirba's wooden cottage, where the old Muslim footpad hassled the young Georgian rebel for his share of the scam.

"You've been printing for days," said Smirba. "When are you going to use the money?"

Soso handed Smirba one of his leaflets.

"What's this?" exclaimed the amazed Smirba.

"We're going to overthrow the Tsar, the Rothschilds and the Nobels," replied Stalin, to Smirba's puzzlement.

Each morning, he hid the pamphlets in peasant fruit baskets which Smirba loaded onto his cart. Meeting Lomdzharia in town, the two bandits took the fruit baskets around the factories, distributing the leaflets. If anyone tried to buy fruit, Smirba demanded a steep price or claimed it was a special order. When the printer was broken, Stalin told Kandelaki, "Let's go hunting." Identifying the right spare parts in a local printing-shop, he then said: "The bear's shot, now skin it"—and sent in his henchmen, who stole them and delivered them to him at his HQ, Ali the Persian's Tavern in the bazaar. Once some Cossacks galloped down the street just as little Hamdi was delivering a part. He tossed the bag into the house and leaped into a ditch. Afterwards, Stalin helped dry the boy, praising his courage.

Smirba's whole village now knew there was something afoot in the new wooden hut visited by so many burly and veiled women, whereupon Soso gathered twelve trusted peasants to explain his mission. "After that," remembers Hamdi Smirba, "they respected the house."

"You're a good man, Soso," said Smirba, puffing on his pipe. "Shame you're not Muslim. If you become Muslim, you'll get seven beautiful virgins. Don't you want to become Muslim?"

"I certainly do!" laughed Soso.[8]*

The dead workers were buried on 12 March, an opportunity for yet another demonstration, 7,000 strong, inspired by the fiery proclamation written and printed by Stalin. The procession was surrounded on every

---

* The Batumi demonstration and the Smirba story became seminal Stalinist legends. When the boss of Abkhazia, one of Stalin's favourite courtiers, Nestor Lakoba, wrote his *Stalin i Hashimi* (Stalin and Hashimi) in 1934, he reinforced the cult of personality which had begun in 1929. Stalin's secretary Ivan Tovstukha worried about the text, writing to Stalin's then deputy Lazar Kaganovich, "Had the Hashimi text . . . Still things to correct and rewrite . . . What to do? Should it be thrown out?" It was not. Its publication won Lakoba favour but not for long. A year later, his work was outstripped by the massive exaggeration of *History of the Bolshevik Organization in the Caucasus* by Beria. Stalin himself, according to Beria's son, amended the manuscript, "striking out names and replacing them with his own." A huge volume called *The Batumi Demonstration 1902* followed in 1937. Beria swiftly moved to destroy his rival Lakoba, poisoning him and then murdering and personally torturing his wife and children. See *Stalin: The Court of the Red Tsar* for the full story. As for Hashimi Smirba himself, he moved house in 1916, burying the printing-press in his garden. He died in 1922 aged eighty-one. In his seventies, Stalin chuckled about Smirba. He knew Lakoba's book was widely regarded as propaganda. After all, it claimed that Stalin was "the greatest man of a whole epoch, such as history gives to humanity only once in one or two hundred years." But Stalin insisted, "It's true as it was told in that book—that's really how it happened."

side by mounted Cossacks. Singing was banned. Comrade Soso quietly supervised the funerals. The Gendarmes prevented any speeches. As the crowd left, the Cossacks mocked them by singing the Death March.

The secret police now knew Stalin was one of the leaders of the Batumi disturbances. The organization "achieved some big successes after the arrival of Josef Djugashvili in autumn 1901," Captain Jakeli reported to the chief of the Kutaisi Gendarmerie. "I have ascertained that Josef Djugashvili was seen in the crowd during the 9 March disorders . . . All evidence points to the fact of his active role in the disorders." They were determined to track him down.

On 5 April, Despina Shapatova warned Stalin that he had been denounced. He moved that night's meeting twice and finally it met at Darakhvelidze's house. Suddenly Despina ran in: the Gendarmes were outside or, as the presiding officer, put it: "Yesterday at midnight, I surrounded the house where intelligence told us they were holding a meeting of the Mantashev Refinery workers . . ."

Soso the Priest rushed to the back window, but it was hopeless. The house was surrounded by blue-uniformed Gendarmes. This time there was no escape.[9]*

---

* In early 1939, the Moscow Arts Theatre commissioned the brilliant but under-employed writer Mikhail Bulgakov to write a romantic play about young Stalin in Batumi to celebrate the dictator's sixtieth birthday that December. Stalin must have signed off on the commission. He admired Bulgakov—like Chekhov, a practising doctor-turned-writer—particularly for his novel *The White Guard*. Its dramatized version *The Days of the Turbins* was Stalin's favourite play: he saw it fifteen times. Yet, as with Pasternak and Shostakovich, Stalin played a game of cat-and-mouse, personally phoning Bulgakov to assure him he would be given work, then tightening the screws on him again. Bulgakov, like Pasternak, was fascinated by his omnipotent persecutor and had toyed with the idea of this play since 1936, even though he knew "it's dangerous for me." Basing the play on the book *The Batumi Demonstration 1902* and presumably on conversations with witnesses, Bulgakov finished a draft in June 1939, first calling it *The Priest*, Stalin's nickname among the workers, then *It Happened in Batumi*, then just *Batumi*. The romantic play contains no love affairs but it implies Stalin's relationship with Natalia Kirtava, for his companion in the play is a Natasha, who is jointly based on Kirtava and Lomdzharia's sister. The cultural apparatchiks liked and approved the play. In August, Bulgakov, declaring that he wanted to interview witnesses and read the archives, set off by train for Batumi with his wife, Elena. But Stalin did not wish his status as statesman (he was just about to sign the Molotov-Ribbentrop Pact with Hitler) undermined by any revelations contained in these archives, many of which have been used in this book. The Bulgakovs were recalled by telegram: "Journey no longer necessary. Return to Moscow." Bulgakov fell ill. Stalin read the play. Visiting the Arts Theatre, he told the director that *Batumi* was a good piece but could not be staged, adding (hypocritically), "All young people are the same, so why write a play about the young Stalin?" The play was hackwork for Bulgakov, who secretly finished his anti-Stalin masterpiece *The Master and Margarita* before his death in 1940.

PART TWO

To the Moon

Move tirelessly
Do not hang your head
Scatter the mist of the clouds
The Lord's Providence is great.

Gently smile at the earth
Stretched out beneath you;
Sing a lullaby to the glacier
Strung down from the heavens.

Know for certain that once
Struck down to the ground, an oppressed man
Strives again to reach the pure mountain,
When exalted by hope.

So, lovely moon, as before
Glimmer through the clouds;
Pleasantly in the azure vault
Make your beams play.

But I shall undo my vest
And thrust out my chest to the moon,
With outstretched arms, I shall revere
The spreader of light upon the earth!

—SOSELO (Josef Stalin)

11

The Prisoner

Stalin was imprisoned in Batumi Prison, where he immediately distinguished himself by his surly swagger and arrogant audacity. Prison affected him deeply and remained with him. "I got used to loneliness in prison," he said much later, though in fact he was rarely alone there.

His fellow prisoners, whether enemies who later denounced him in exile or Stalinists who praised him in official books, agree that Stalin in prison was like a frigid sphinx: "scruffy, pockmarked, with a rough beard and long backcombed hair." His fellows were most struck by "his complete calmness." He "never laughed with an open mouth, only smiled coolly" and was "incapable of co-operating with anyone . . . He walked by himself. Always unruffled."[1] But initially he made a foolish mistake.

On 6 April 1902, he faced his first interrogation at the hands of Gendarme captain Jakeli. He denied he had even been in Batumi at the time of the massacre, claiming he had been with his mother in Gori. Two days later, he ordered another prisoner to throw two notes into the prison yard where friends and families of the prisoners gathered to deliver food and messages. But the guards retrieved the notes in Stalin's handwriting. The first sent a message "to tell the teacher . . . Josef Iremashvili that Soso Djugashvili's been arrested and ask him to tell his mother that when Gendarmes ask her 'When did your son leave Gori?,' she must reply, 'He was here in Gori all summer and winter until 15 March.' "

The other note summoned his former pupil Elisabedashvili to Batumi to take over his organization. Captain Jakeli had already consulted the Tiflis secret police, who revealed that Stalin had been a leading light on the Tiflis Committee. But now he also briefed Gori, who reported that two men had arrived there from Batumi and talked to Keke, her brother Giorgi Geladze (Stalin's uncle) and Iremashvili. All three were arrested and interrogated: not a happy day for Keke.[2]

The men from Batumi had come to collect Stalin's mother, but the clumsy note-tossing also implicated Elisabedashvili, who was living in Tiflis with Kamo and Svanidze. The Gendarmes arrested Kamo, who reluctantly led them to the Sololaki bathhouse, where they seized a disrobed Elisabedashvili. He was taken to meet the "famous Captain Lavrov," who handed him over to Captain Jakeli. As Elisabedashvili entered the Batumi prison yard, Stalin rushed past him, whispering: "You don't know me."

"I know," replied Elisabedashvili. "Hello from everyone!"

The next day, Elisabedashvili was interrogated by Captain Jakeli.

"Do you know Josef Djugashvili?"

"No."

"Nonsense! He says he knows you!"

"He might be insane."

"Insane?" laughed the captain. "How can such a person be mad? We had Marxists here before but they were quiet enough. This Djugashvili has turned the whole of Batumi upside down."

When Elisabedashvili was led past Stalin's cell, he caught a glimpse, through the bars, of "an outraged Soso cursing his cellmate and punching him. Next day, I learned that they had placed a stool-pigeon in his cell." Elisabedashvili was released—but soon returned, on Stalin's orders, to direct Batumi's Sosoists.[3]

As for Keke, she obeyed Soso's summons. Around 18 May, she set off from Gori and only returned on 16 June. She visited her son twice in Batumi Prison. On her way via Tiflis, she somehow bumped into Crazy Beso, drunk and angry.

"Stop or I'll kill you!" he shouted, denouncing his rebel son. "He wants to turn the world upside down. If you hadn't taken him to school, he'd be a craftsman—now he's in prison. I'll kill such a son with my own hands—he's disgraced me!" A crowd gathered. Keke slipped away, her last encounter with her husband.

Soso's rebellion was the ruin of Keke's ambition. She must, in her way, have worried as much as Beso. She applied for his release and probably delivered messages from his comrades. In his egocentricity, old Stalin acknowledged her suffering: "Was she happy? Come on! What happiness for Keke if her son was arrested? We didn't have much time for our mothers. Such was the fate of mothers!"*

Stalin was soon the kingpin of Batumi Prison, dominating his friends, terrorizing the intellectuals, suborning the guards and befriending the criminals.[4]

The Imperial prisons were a hidden civilization with their own customs and tricks, but Stalin, as ever, ignored the etiquette that did not suit him. The prisons, "like the country itself, combined barbarism with paternalism," says Trotsky. There was no consistency: sometimes political prisoners were placed in one big cell known as "the Church," where they would elect "Elders."

The revolutionaries lived by a set of chivalrous rules. Whenever comrades arrived or departed, it was traditional for the whole prison to sing "The Marseillaise" and wave a red flag. Revolutionaries, sacred intellectuals and self-appointed crusaders, were too elevated to socialize with mere criminals, but, "I preferred them [the criminals]," Stalin said, "because there were so many rats among the politicals." He loathed the duplicitous chatter of the intellectuals. "Rats" were killed.

If they were in solitary cells, the politicals communicated through a ponderous but simple code of knocks—"the prison alphabet." Sergei Alliluyev was in prison in the Metekhi Fortress of Tiflis but the tapping on his stove-pipe informed him: *"Bad news! Soso arrested!"* Then there was the impoverished jailhouse system of communication known as the "prison telegraph" by which prisoners delivered packages to each other by swinging them on strings from their windows whence they were hooked by another string with a stone on the end.

When the prisoners walked in the courtyards, discipline was lax: it was hard to keep any secrets there. Soso always seemed to know who was arriving, how prisoners were behaving. Like American Mafiosi running La Cosa Nostra from prison, Soso swiftly improved his communications with the outside world. "He continued to run things from prison."†

---

* "Happy?" Keke sardonically told an interviewer in 1935 when asked if she was happy to be Stalin's mother. "You ask me what kind of happiness I felt? The whole world is happy looking at my son and our country. So what should I feel as a mother?"
† Stalin swiftly developed his clandestine craft. A sympathetic worker in Batumi worked for the company that supplied wood to the prison. One day he was approached and told he

The authorities erred seriously when they allowed their revolutionaries to study in prison. These obsessive autodidacts studied hard there, none more so than Stalin, whose cellmate says, "He spent the whole day reading and writing . . . His prison day had a strict routine: he woke early in the morning, did morning exercises, then studied German and read economic literature. He never rested and he liked to recommend comrades what books to read . . ." Another prisoner said that Stalin made "prison into a university." He called it his "second school."

The prison guards were lenient, either because the revolutionaries were socially superior "gentlemen," or because they had been bribed or because they were sympathetic. One of Stalin's friends was put in a cell near to his and asked him about the *Communist Manifesto*: "We couldn't meet," reminisced Stalin, "but I read it aloud and he could hear it. Once during my reading, I heard some steps outside and stopped. Suddenly I heard the guard say: 'Please don't stop. Comrade, please continue.' "[5]

One article must have been doing the rounds of the "prison telegraph": in March 1902, the Marxist now using the alias "Lenin" published an essay "What Is to Be Done?: Burning Questions of Our Movement," which demanded a "new vanguard" of ruthless conspirators—a vision that immediately split the Party. "Give us an organization of revolutionaries," promised Lenin, "and we shall overturn the whole of Russia!"[6]*

Captain Jakeli rounded up Batumi's Sosoists, including Stalin's young landlady and girlfriend Natasha Kirtava. When she appeared in the jail-yard, Natasha was swiftly approached by an unknown prisoner: "Comrade Soso asks you to look up at his window."

Natasha was alarmed in case this prisoner was a stool-pigeon. "I don't know a Comrade Soso," she answered.

But when she was locked in her cell, Stalin appeared at her window. "So, comrades, are you bored?" he inquired grandly. She saw that Comrade Soso was still very much in command of the struggle inside and outside the prison. "The prisoners loved him because he took such cordial

---

was to help deliver the wood and must follow his instructions precisely. He delivered the logs, carried them into the courtyard and sure enough, at 3 p.m. sharp, the warders led out a single prisoner, Stalin, who gave him an urgent message to deliver in Batumi.

* Lenin encapsulated Stalin's dream of himself as a knight in a military-religious order. "Our Party is not a school of philosophers," he asserted revealingly, but "a fighting Party. Until now it resembled a hospitable patriarchal family. Now it must become like a fortress—its gates only opened for the worthy." Any other way was a "desecration of its Holy of Holies."

care of them." He certainly took good care of Natasha. Once she went to see him in his cell for a chat when one of the prison guards caught her and drove her away with the handle of his sabre. Stalin demanded the dismissal of the guard. His courage won him popularity among the prisoners but also respect from the authorities: he got his way.[7] It was not only Sosoists who admired him: another prisoner, who shared his cell, admitted that, although Soso later became a monster, he was "a very pleasant and gallant cellmate."[8]

The Prosecutor in Tiflis ruled there was not enough evidence to charge Stalin with leading the Batumi riot. Probably witnesses were too afraid to testify. He was off that hook but remained in prison because Captain Lavrov was investigating another case—Stalin's role on the Tiflis Committee. On 29 August, the Gendarmes indicted Stalin along with his old comrades on the Committee. Yet the bureaucracy muddled along slowly.[9]

He fell ill with his old chest sickness, which he sometimes claimed was his heart, at other times a shadow on the lung. During October, Soso managed to get the prison doctor to assign him and his sidekick Kandelaki to hospital.[10] Against revolutionary etiquette, he also appealed three times to Prince Golitsyn, the governor-general himself:

> *My worsening cough and the pitiful condition of my aged mother, who was left by her husband twelve years ago and of whom I am the only support, force me to apply for the second time for a humble discharge, under police surveillance. I beg you to heed my request and respond to my petition.*
>
> *J. Djugashvili. 23 November 1901*[11]

His sickness did not stop him making trouble. When the Exarch of the Georgian Church came to minister to his errant sons on 17 April 1903, the ex-seminarist led a violent protest that got him clapped in solitary confinement. The riot, not the first organized by Stalin, led to his transfer to the stricter Kutaisi Prison, in western Georgia.

Two days later, when the prisoners were mustered for their transfer, Stalin found that Natasha was being transferred with him. The warders started to handcuff him.

"We're not thieves to be handcuffed!" snapped Stalin. The officer took off the cuffs. The story shows Stalin's authority over prisoners and officers alike—the Tsarist police were biddable in a way unthinkable for the Soviet secret police. Then the prisoners were gathered for the march through Batumi. Stalin demanded a cart for their belongings and "a phaeton for me, the woman," recalls Natasha proudly. Incredibly Stalin, that master of the prison system, got his way here too.* Only the best for Stalin's girl: Natasha travelled to the station in a phaeton.

When their train arrived at nearby Kutaisi, Stalin held everyone back: "Let Natasha go in front so everyone can see that women also fight these dogs!"[12]

At Kutaisi, the authorities tried to force the prisoners to behave. The politicals were split up, but Stalin soon found a way to communicate and plan a counterattack. When Natasha Kirtava was moved out of the collective cell into solitary, "Emotion overcame me. I started crying." Stalin heard about this on the prison telegraph and had a note delivered to her that read: "What do your tears signify, she-eagle? Is it possible prison has defeated you?"

In the prison yard, Stalin met a moderate comrade, Grigol Uratadze, who hated him but almost admired his "glacial temperament: in six months, I never once saw him crying, angry or indignant—he always conducted himself with total composure" and his "smile was carefully calibrated to his emotions . . . We used to chat in the courtyard." But Stalin just "walked alone in strange little short steps . . . Everyone knew how surly he was," but he was also "absolutely imperturbable."

Stalin was hostile to the bumptious intellectuals, but, with the less elevated worker-revolutionaries, who did not arouse his inferiority complex, he played the teacher—the Priest. Soso "organized the reading of newspapers, books and magazines, and gave lectures to the prisoners." Meanwhile he confronted Kutaisi's more severe regime. The regional governor refused his demands. On 28 July, Soso gave a sign and the prisoners started a noisy protest, banging the steel doors so loudly that the whole town was alarmed. The governor called for troops, who surrounded the prison, but then he capitulated, agreeing to place all the politicals in one cell. Stalin won, but the governor got his revenge: it was the dreariest dungeon in the bowels of the jail.

---

* As Soviet leader, Stalin disdained Tsarist leniency, determined to avoid it in his own repressions. "The prisons resemble nothing so much as rest-homes," he wrote at the height of the Terror in 1937. "The prisoners are allowed to socialize, can write letters to each other at will, receive parcels . . . !"

When some of the prisoners were swiftly despatched to Siberian exile, Stalin suggested a group photograph. Just as he liked to set up the group photographs when he was in power, so now he directed everyone's position and placed himself in his favourite place—middle top row: "I'm also one of the soldiers of the Revolution so I'll stand here in the centre." There he is: long-haired and bearded, the self-appointed leader.

When his comrades were led out for their long journey, "Comrade Soso stood in the courtyard and raised a red flag . . . We sang the Marseillaise."[13]

The secret police now mislaid Stalin . . . in their own prison. The Gendarmes and the Okhrana in Tiflis both thought that "Chopura, the Pockmarked One," had long since been released. Captain Lavrov believed he was again leading the workers in Batumi "under special surveillance." Clearly the spooks were watching completely the wrong man. Batumi was not too sure either until Lieutenant Colonel Shabelsky settled the case of the lost Pockmarked One by informing everyone that "Djugashvili has been in prison for a whole year already (now in Kutaisi)."[14]

The grinding mechanisms of Tsarist justice, which sent cases like that of Stalin from local governors to Justice and Interior Ministries in Petersburg, generated a recommendation for three years' exile in eastern Siberia.* On 7 July 1903, the Justice Minister sent this recommendation to the Emperor, who approved Stalin's sentence with his Imperial stamp. Nicholas II was such a punctilious if unimaginative autocrat that he diligently read even the most trivial paper sent to his office. So there were several occasions when the fate of the future Red Tsar crossed the desk of the last Emperor.

Now the police managed to lose Stalin all over again. The governor of Tiflis thought he was in the Metekhi Fortress, but the prison replied that he had never been there. So the head of the Tiflis police declared:

---

* The Tsarist authorities recognized, due to the special challenges of evidence and secrecy, that terrorists and revolutionaries could not be tried by jury or judge: the local Gendarme officer recommended a sentence to the local governor-general who forwarded it on to the Special Commission—five Justice and Interior officials who passed sentence. The Interior Minister confirmed it; the Emperor signed off. Stalin was habitually sentenced this way. Between 1881 and 1904, only 11,879 were sentenced like this, while during Stalin's reign of the same approximate timespan, he presided over the deportation of an astonishing 28 million, several million of whom never returned. As for capital punishment under the Tsars, Catholic Poles and Jews in the western provinces were much more likely to be hanged than Orthodox Russians or Georgians.

"Location of Djugashvili so far unknown." The police appealed to the Gendarmes, who revealed that Stalin was back in Batumi Prison, which was well and good—except that he was still in Kutaisi Prison. It took a month and a half to find him: such confusion has fuelled the feverish imagination of conspiracy-theorists ever since. Were the Gendarmes or the Okhrana hiding him from one another because he was a double-agent? There is no evidence for this. The muddle might be suspicious if it applied only to Stalin, but it was almost universal. In the interlinked worlds of murderous conspiracy and sluggish pen-pushing, there was as much confusion as *konspiratsia*.

While he waited, he heard terrible news. On 17 August 1903, Soso's hero, Lado Ketskhoveli, who had been arrested in Baku and incarcerated in the Metekhi Fortress, was standing at his cell-window baiting the guards with shouts of "Down with Autocracy!" when one of them shot him through the heart. Such a fate could easily have befallen Stalin himself. He never forgot Lado.

On 8 October, Stalin finally learned that he was departing on a very long journey. His first stop would be a return to Batumi. He organized another group photograph. As he departed the prison, his comrades waved the flag, singing "The Marseillaise."

"I'm being exiled," Stalin wrote to the newly released Natasha Kirtava. "Meet me near the prison." She raised ten roubles and some food to help him on the cold journey into the Russian winter, but he left wearing just a light Georgian *chokha,* boots and no gloves. As he was marched onto the prison steamship in Batumi Harbour for the first leg of his journey via Novorossiisk and Rostov, the beautiful Natasha waited on the wharf: "I saw him off."

This voyage would take a Georgian, accustomed to the singsong, wine-flavoured lushness of Georgia, to another life in a frozen far-off country: Siberia.[15]

12

The Frozen Georgian: Siberian Exile

The journey to Siberia was often more deadly than the exile itself. Stalin experienced the full gamut of horrors of the dreaded *etap*, the slow stage-by-stage progress to the east, picking up other prisoners on the way. Stalin claimed that his ankles were sometimes shackled to iron balls and once said emotionally: "There's no better feeling than straightening your back after wearing shackles."

When he reached Rostov-on-Don, he was already out of money and telegraphed Batumi to ask for more. Kandelaki sent it. Somewhere not far out, he started to suffer agonizing toothache and consulted a doctor's assistant. "I'll give you medicine that'll cure your tooth for ever," he promised. "He put the medicine into my rotten tooth himself," Stalin recalled. "It was arsenic but he never told me you had to take it out of the tooth. So it stopped aching all right but a couple of teeth fell out altogether. He was right—those teeth never ached!" Toothache was just another of the many ailments that tormented Stalin throughout his life.

The farther from civilization they travelled, the more the prisoners were exposed to the extremes of Siberia, disease and violence. Somewhere in Siberia, one of the prisoners "was almost dying of gangrene," Stalin recounted in his seventies. The closest hospital was 1,000 kilometres away at least. The doctor's assistant was found and he decided to amputate. He poured spirit on the leg; asked several men to hold him down and started to operate. I couldn't bear to watch the operation and I sheltered in the barracks, but the man's bone was sawn without anaesthetic so you couldn't escape his screams. I can still clearly hear that scream!" En route, he also encountered scores of Gurian peasant-workers, arrested during his Batumi demonstration. Soso admitted a rare moment's guilt seeing these bewildered Georgians shivering on the road to Siberia—but they assured him of their gratitude.

The criminals were a real hazard. Usually they "respected our struggle," said Stalin's henchman Vyacheslav Molotov, who made a similar trip to Irkutsk, but they also terrorized the politicals. "During that *etap*," Stalin told one of his adopted sons, "it was my fate to come up against a psychotic safe-breaker, a giant of a man, almost two metres tall. I made some harmless remark to him about my tobacco pouch . . . The exchange ended in a fight. The idiot forced me to the ground, breaking several ribs. No one helped me." Stalin was knocked unconscious, but typically drew a political lesson: "As I was coming round, it occurred to me that politicians must always win over allies." In future, the psychopaths would be on his side.[1]

On arrival in Irkutsk, the distant capital of Siberia, Stalin was despatched westwards to a regional centre, Balagansk, seventy-five versts from the nearest railway station. Now they travelled by foot and cart: Stalin was absurdly underdressed for the Siberian freeze, still in his white Georgian *chokha* with its bullet pouches. He found seven exiles in Balagansk and stayed with Abram Gusinsky, a Jewish exile, trying to avoid being sent farther.[2] But he had been assigned to Novaya Uda. The local police recorded that "Josef Djugashvili, exiled by His Imperial Majesty's command of 9 July, arrived on 26 November and was taken under police supervision."

Novaya Uda, 70 versts from Balagansk and 120 from the closest station, thousands of versts from Moscow or Tiflis and his farthest exile, was a tiny town divided into two halves: the poor lived in shacks on a marshy promontory while the marginally better-off lived around a couple of shops, a church and a wooden fortress built to terrify into submission the local shamanistic Mongol tribe, the Buryats. There was little to do in Novaya Uda except read, argue, drink, fornicate and drink more—these were pastimes for locals and exiles alike. The settlement boasted five taverns.

Soso took to all these local pastimes, but he found his fellow exiles intolerable. There were three others in Novaya Uda, Jewish intellectuals who were either Bundists (followers of the Jewish Socialist Party) or SDs. Stalin had met few Jews in the Caucasus but henceforth he encountered many of the Jews who had embraced Marxism as a means of escaping the repression and prejudice of the Tsarist regime.

Stalin opted for the poor part of town, staying in "the beggarly ramshackle two-room house of a peasant, Martha Litvintseva." One room was a larder where the food was kept, the other, divided by a wooden partition, was the bedroom where the whole family lived and slept around a stove. Stalin slept on a trestle table in the larder on the other side of the partition: "At night, he lit a small lamp and read when the Litvintsevs were asleep."[3]

Siberian exile was regarded as one of the most terrible abuses of Tsarist tyranny. It was certainly boring and depressing, but once settled in some godforsaken village, the exiles, intellectuals who were often hereditary noblemen, were usually well treated. Such paternalistic sojourns more resembled dull reading-holidays than the living hell of Stalin's murderous Gulags. The exiles even received pocket-money from the Tsar—twelve roubles for a nobleman such as Lenin, eleven roubles for a school graduate such as Molotov, and eight for a peasant such as Stalin—with which to pay for clothes, food and rent. If they received too much money from home, they lost their allowance.

Wealthier revolutionaries could travel first-class. Lenin, who enjoyed a private income, financed his own trip to exile and behaved throughout like a nobleman on an eccentric naturalist's holiday. Trotsky, who was subsidized by his father, a rich farmer, mused pompously that Siberia was a "test of our civic sensibilities" where the exiles could live happily "like gods on Olympus." But there was a big gap between the well-off like Lenin and the penniless like Stalin.*

The behaviour of exiles was governed by a set of rules. Each settlement elected a committee which could try anyone who broke Party rules.

---

* When Lenin arrived, he reprimanded the stationmaster, availed himself of the local merchant's library, brought out his wife, Nadya Krupskaya, and his mother-in-law to care for him, and even employed a maid to clean the house. The Lenins patronized the peasants who, noted Krupskaya, "were generally clean in their habits." Lenin raved about the landscape of this "Siberian Italy," a pleasant environment for writing. "Generally," wrote Krupskaya, "exile didn't pass by so badly." The system favoured noblemen and Orthodox Russians and Georgians over Jews and Poles. Lenin and his friend Yuli Martov were arrested at the same time on the same charges but, while the noble Russian Lenin enjoyed his scenic reading-holiday, his fellow SD leader, the Jewish Martov, struggled to survive the desperate Arctic freeze of Turukhansk.

Books must be shared. If an exile died, his library was split between the survivors. No consorting with criminals. On departure, the exile was allowed to choose a gift from each fellow exile and should present a keepsake to his host family. Exiles divided the housework and the duty of collecting the mail. The arrival of the post was their happiest moment. "You remember how good it felt in exile to receive a letter from a friend?" recalled Yenukidze when he was in power.

Yet in the Wild East rules were hard to maintain: sexual adventures among the exiles were rife. "Like palms on a Diego Rivera landscape, love struggled towards the sun from under the heaviest boulders," declaimed Trotsky grandiloquently, "couples came together . . . in exile." When Golda Gorbman, who later married Stalin's lieutenant Klimenti Voroshilov, was in exile, she was seduced and impregnated by Yenukidze, the Georgian who was later one of Stalin's magnates. In power, the Politburo liked to reminisce about these scandals. Stalin himself never forgot the cheek of the exile Lezhnev, who bedded the local Prosecutor's lovely wife and was sent to the Arctic as punishment. Molotov quoted the story of the two exiles who fought a duel for a mistress—one was killed and the other got the girl.

Exiles had to rent rooms from local peasants: they found themselves living in cramped and noisy little rooms, irritated by screaming children and lack of privacy. "The worst thing [about exile] was the lack of separation from the hosts," wrote Yakov Sverdlov, later in exile with Stalin, but this sharing of rooms led also to more sexual temptation. Local custom banned affairs with exiles. But this was impossible to enforce: the local girls found the exiles exotic, educated, affluent and hard to resist—especially when they were often sharing the same bedroom.

Revolutionaries were naturally fractious, but their feuds in the isolation of exile had a malice all of their own. "Men bared themselves before you and showed themselves in their pettiness—there was no room to show decent features." The exiles behaved appallingly, but Stalin's conduct as reckless seducer, procreator of illegitimate children, serial feuder and compulsive troublemaker was one of the worst. No sooner had he arrived than Stalin started to break the rules.[4]

He cut his Jewish fellow exiles but embraced the local hobby: pub-crawls with the criminals. "There were some nice salt-of-the-earth fellows among them and too many rats among the politicals," he told Khrushchev and the rest of the Politburo at their dinners in the 1940s. "I hung around mostly with the criminals. We'd stop at the saloons in town, see if any of us had a rouble then we'd hold it up to the window, and drink up every kopeck we had. One day I'd pay, next day someone else." This consorting with criminals was considered beneath the dignity of the snobbish middle-class revolutionaries. "Once they organized a comrade's court," says Stalin, "and put me on trial for the offence of drinking with criminals." This was neither the first nor the last trial that the uncongenial Soso faced from his comrades.[5]

Yet he did not lose contact with the outside world or settle for a long stay. In December 1903, the mail brought a letter from Lenin. "I first met Lenin in 1903," said Stalin, "not a personal meeting, more a postal one. It wasn't a long letter but a bold and fearless critique of our Party." He exaggerated. This was not a personal letter—Lenin had not yet heard of Stalin—but a pamphlet: "A Letter to a Comrade on Organizational Tasks." Nonetheless its effect on Stalin was real enough. "That simple bold note reinforced my belief that in Lenin, the Party had a mountain eagle."

Stalin burned it afterwards but he soon learned that at the SD Party's Second Congress, held in both Brussels and London, Lenin and Martov had defeated their rivals the Jewish Bundists, who wanted to combine socialism with national territories for minorities. But then the victors had fallen out among themselves, Lenin demanding his exclusive sect of revolutionaries, Martov embracing a wider membership and mass worker participation. Lenin, who revelled in schismatic confrontations, split the Party, claiming that his group were the Majoritarians—Bolsheviki—and Martov's the Minoritarians—Mensheviki.*

Stalin claimed that he wrote immediately to his lame Goreli friend Davitashvili in Leipzig, who was in contact with Lenin—but this was one of his fibs. In fact he did not write for almost a year, but he was already a

---

* Even at this early date, Lenin and Stalin, soi-disant champions of the proletariat, were against the involvement of real workers. They believed in an oligarchy that would rule in the name of the workers, a concept that became the "dictatorship of the proletariat." Stalin was convinced that the election of workers to the Party committees would include too many amateur revolutionaries and more police agents. Leninists were also less sympathetic to the land aspirations of peasants. Most Georgian Social-Democrats believed in wide worker and peasant participation and land grants to peasants, so they became Mensheviks. The Georgian Mensheviks under firebrands like Jordania were very effective and increasingly popular; Georgian Mensheviks were much more violent than Russian Mensheviks. Jibladze and Noe Ramishvili were as enthusiastic about terror and expropriation as Stalin up to 1907. But ultimately Bolsheviks were much more disciplined, merciless and comfortable with terror and killing. To complicate matters, there were mild Bolsheviks such as Kamenev, just as there were extreme Mensheviks.

Leninist. Trotsky believed one could recognize a Bolshevik on sight. Stalin was, says Iremashvili, "an instant Bolshevik." In 1904, there was a strong sense that something world-shattering was stirring: the movement was flourishing. As Nicholas II blundered closer to "a victorious little war" with Japan in his quest for a Far Eastern empire, the Revolution was suddenly closer than it had ever been. This was no time to be in Novaya Uda.[6]

Soso had no sooner arrived than he started to plan his escape—which was as much part of the revolutionary experience as arrest and exile itself.

Escape was "not too difficult. Everyone tried to escape," wrote Trotsky. "The exile system was a sieve."

The escapee needed money to buy his "boots"—the false papers. Usually the full escape kit—"boots," food, clothes, train tickets, bribes—cost around one hundred roubles. Conspiracy-theorists ask naïvely how Stalin raised the cash: was he an agent for the Okhrana? Probably Egnatashvili, via Keke, and his Party comrades provided the money. But raising it was hardly unusual: between 1906 and 1909, over 18,000 obscure exiles out of a total of 32,000 somehow raised the money to escape.

Stalin made his record more suspicious by changing the number of his escapes and arrests in his own propaganda. Yet it turns out that he was arrested and escaped *more* often than he officially claimed. When he personally edited his *Short Course* biography in the 1930s, he signed off on eight arrests, seven exiles and six escapes, but when he re-edited the book in 1947, using his blue crayon, he reduced the numbers to seven arrests, six exiles and five escapes. In conversation, he claimed, "I escaped five times." Amazingly, Stalin was being modest or forgetful. There were in fact at least nine arrests, four short detentions and eight escapes.

The last word belongs to Alexander Ostrovsky, expert on Stalin's secret-police connections: "The fact of Stalin's frequent escapes might be seen as surprising only to a person who is completely unfamiliar with the specifics of the pre-revolutionary exile system."

Soso made his first, amateurish attempt after reading Lenin's pamphlet in December 1903: his landlady and children gave him some bread for the trip. "Initially," he told Anna Alliluyeva, "I didn't succeed because the police chief had an eye on me. The freeze set in and then I collected winter supplies and set off on foot. My face almost froze!" As he got older, these tales grew taller. "I fell into a frozen river, the ice gave way," he told his Soviet henchman Lavrenti Beria. "I was chilled to the bone. I knocked at a door, nobody invited me in. At the end of my strength, I had finally the luck to be welcomed by some poor people who lived in a miserable hut. They fed me, warmed me by the stove and gave me clothes to reach the next village."

He managed to make it to Abram Gusinsky's house in Balagansk, seventy versts away.

> One night, when there were terrible frosts of −30, we heard a knock.
> "Who's there?"
> "Unlock the door, Abram, it's me, Soso."
> Then an ice-coated Soso entered, dressed very flippantly for Siberian winter in a felt cloak, a fedora and a dandyish Caucasian hood. My wife and daughter so admired the white hood that Comrade Stalin with Caucasian generosity took it off and gave it to them.

He already had the "necessary documents." But he could go no farther.

"Suffering frostbite on his nose and ears," according to Sergei Alliluyev, "he couldn't get anywhere and returned to Novaya Uda." No doubt, his convict friends warmed him up in the boozing stews of the frontier-town while he planned his second attempt.

Soso wrote to Keke, and she "sewed the right clothes and sent them as soon as she could. Soso escaped wearing them." He had moved into another house belonging to Mitrofan Kungarov, who, on 4 January 1904, gave Stalin a lift out of Novaya Uda. Arming himself with a sabre, Stalin tricked Kungarov, claiming that he just wanted to reach nearby Zharkovo to complain about the police chief. Kungarov was probably the drunken sledge-driver who demanded to be paid in vodka at every stop. "We travelled in −40 temperatures," recalled Stalin. "I wrapped myself in furs. The coachman actually opened his coat while driving to let the bitter freezing wind blow against his almost naked belly. Apparently alcohol warmed his body: what healthy people!" But when the peasant realized that Stalin was escaping, he refused to help and stopped the sledge. "At that moment," said Stalin, "I opened my fur coat and showed my sword and ordered him to drive on . . . The peasant sighed and made the horses gallop!"*

---

* In 1934, the children who had provided the bread for the escape wrote to Stalin; he wrote back with a present for them—a radio and gramophone. In 1947, pensioner Kungarov wrote: "Generalissimo of the Soviet Union Comrade J. V. Stalin, I deeply apologize for

Soso was on his way. Coming up to Orthodox Epiphany, he was hoping the police would be distracted by their celebrations. "Exiled Josef Djugashvili has escaped! Appropriate measures are taken to recapture him!" telegraphed the local police. He made it to Tyret Station and may have gone to Irkutsk before heading back along the Trans-Siberian Railway.

The Siberian stations, even during holidays, were patrolled by uniformed Gendarmes and Okhrana spies, sometimes professionals, frequently informing freelancers, watching for escapees. But Stalin had procured not just the usual "boots" but the ID card of a police agent. In faraway Siberia (as in the Caucasus), any papers could be bought, but this was unusual. Stalin boasted that at one of the stations a real spook was on his tail, following him until the escapee approached a Gendarme, showed him his false ID and pointed out the police spy as an escaping exile. The policeman arrested the protesting spook while Stalin calmly boarded the train for the Caucasus. It is a story that demonstrates the layers of murkiness in which Stalin blossomed. If Soso really was a police spy, it is unlikely he would have told the story at all and, in any case, he might have invented it. But it certainly added to the mystique (and suspicion) of this ace of conspirators.[7]

Within ten days, he was back in Tiflis. When he burst into a friend's apartment, they barely knew who he was, as he had lost weight in Siberia.

"Don't you recognize me, you cowards!" he laughed, whereupon they greeted him and rented him a room.

Stalin's timing was impeccable. That January 1904, Russia stumbled into war. The Japanese attacked the Russian fleet at Port Arthur in the Far East. The Emperor and his ministers were convinced the primitive Japanese "monkeys" could not defeat civilized Russians. Yet Nicholas's army was antiquated, his peasant soldiers ill armed, his commanders hapless cronies.

"I remember," says Stalin's roommate, "that he was reading *History of the French Revolution*." He knew how war and revolution, those horses of the apocalypse, often gallop together.

---

bothering you but in 1903 you lived at my place and in 1904 I personally took you to Zharkovo on the way to the Tyret Station and when the police interrogated me I lied for you that I had taken you to Balagansk. For lying I was imprisoned and received ten lashes. I ask you to help me." It is highly unlikely that Kungarov would make this up, but Stalin read the letter and said he did not recall this, asking Kungarov to give more details. Possibly Stalin's memories of the first exile were less vivid, but more likely he nursed a grievance against Kungarov for refusing to help him escape.

. . .

Georgia was seething. "Georgians are such a political nation," reflected Stalin later, "I don't think there's a Georgian alive who isn't a member of some political party." Young Armenians joined the Dashnaks, Georgians joined the Socialist-Federalists, and many others joined the Mensheviks, Bolsheviks, Anarchists or the SRs—the latter were conducting a vicious terrorist campaign against the Tsar and his ministers. As the war strained the sinews of the Empire, the Okhrana tried to suppress the restlessness by arresting droves of revolutionaries.

Not every comrade was delighted at the return of the truculent, aggressive Soso, and his enemies devised a way to rid themselves of him. There was a problem with Stalin's Marxist orthodoxy: Lenin had defeated the Bundists because he believed in an internationalist party for all the peoples of the Empire. Even Jordania preached Marxism for the whole Caucasian region. Yet young Stalin, clinging to the romantic dreams of his poetry, insisted eccentrically on a Georgian SD Party. So his enemies accused him of Bundist tendencies, not a Marxist internationalist at all. At this time, Stalin adapted Marx to his own instincts. He quoted Marx, observed David Sagirashvili, "but always in his own peculiar way." Challenged at one meeting, Soso "wasn't in the least perturbed," simply saying, "Marx is the son of an ass. What he wrote should be written as I say!" With this, he stormed out.

Fortunately Stalin was vigorously defended by Georgia's first Bolshevik, Mikha Tskhakaya, one of the founders of Mesame Dasi, who now supported Lenin's radical approach. Stalin respected the energetic, older Tskhakaya, with his goatee-beard and ideological gravity. He later mocked him, but he was as grateful as a man could be who regarded "gratitude as a dogs' disease."

Tskhakaya pleaded for Stalin, saving him from expulsion, but he made him undergo a new introduction to Marxism. "I can't trust you with much," he lectured Soso. "You're still young and need a foundation of stable ideas—or you'll encounter difficulties."

Tskhakaya introduced him to a young Armenian intellectual named Danesh Shevardian to lecture him on the "new literature." Tskhakaya, Stalin laughed later, "began our instruction on the creation of the planets, life on earth, protein and protoplasm and after three hours, we finally reached slave-owning society. We couldn't stay awake and starting dozing off . . ."

Yet Stalin's anecdotes concealed the humiliating truth: Tskhakaya ordered him to write a *Credo* renouncing his heretical views. The Armenian read it and was satisfied. Seventy printed copies were distributed.* Stalin was forgiven, but Tskhakaya said he had to "rest" before he could receive a redemptive mission.[8]

Soso shamelessly sponged off his friends. "If he visited some guy's family," recalled Mikheil Monoselidze, ex-seminarist friend of Kamo and Svanidze, "he behaved as if he was a member of the family. If he noticed they had wine, fruit or sweets that he liked, he wasn't embarrassed to say, 'Well, someone said I was invited to drink wine and eat fruit,' and he'd open the cupboard and help himself . . ." He believed they literally owed him a living out of gratitude for his sacred mission.

He spent time with his well-off friend Spandarian, who took him to a circle run by Lev Rosenfeld, the future "Kamenev," Stalin's co-ruler after Lenin's death, and later his victim. Kamenev's father, a rich engineer who built the Batumi–Baku railway, subsidized his Marxist son. Younger than Stalin, though he looked years older, he was red-bearded and schoolmasterly with myopic, watery-blue eyes. He befriended, but always patronized, Stalin—until it was too late. Kamenev was a Bolshevik but a very moderate one, already in conflict with Stalin's hotheads.

"I often had fights with the intellectuals," remembers Kamo," and I had a quarrel with Kamenev who didn't want to attend a demonstration." At Kamenev's, Soso met another old friend—Josef Davrichewy, who had attended the poshest school in Tiflis, the gymnasium on Golovinsky Prospect, with Kamenev and Spandarian.

Davrichewy, flirting with Socialist-Federalism, was "delighted to see Soso for the first time since Gori." He resembled Stalin (and believed they were half brothers). "We talked for ages," reminisces Davrichewy, snobbishly adding that Stalin "knew no one in Tiflis."[9]

---

* The *Credo* was one of the important secrets of Stalin's past. It seriously undermined Stalin's Leninist credentials, putting him closer to the 1918 Mensheviks, who created an independent Georgia, and the Bolshevik "deviationalists" of 1921–22. In 1925, striving to succeed Lenin, Stalin started to seek out and destroy any copies. In 1934, he twice approached Shevardian (first via his boss in the Trade Commissariat, Stalinist magnate Anastas Mikoyan, then through an old Tiflis comrade, Malakia Toroshelidze, rector of Tiflis University). Shevardian buried his papers in his village. In the 1937 Terror, Mikoyan and Beria were despatched to Yerevan with a deathlist of 300 Armenian Bolsheviks. Mikoyan saved one of the 300, Shevardian, who was still arrested. His family destroyed the papers. Shevardian was shot by Beria on 24 October 1941, as the Germans advanced. Not all recipients of the *Credo* were shot: Tskhakaya remained a favourite.

· · ·

This was not quite true, for he now met up with many of the young revolutionaries who would rule the USSR with him—or at least share his life. One day, Sergei Alliluyev returned from Baku with some printing-press type, and delivered it to Babe Bochoridze's house, a favourite with the revolutionaries. "I looked round," wrote Alliluyev.

> A young man of twenty-three or -four entered the adjoining room.
>
> "He's one of us," said Babe.
>
> "One of us," the young man repeated, inviting me in. He sat me at the table and asked: "Well what good news have you to tell me?"

Even though he was ten years younger than Alliluyev, the haughty Soso presumed to command, giving orders on the transport of the press. They had already met as conspirators but now Alliluyev invited him into his home to meet his beautiful and notoriously promiscuous wife. Stalin later grumbled that the Alliluyev women "would never leave him alone," always "wanting to go to bed with him."

13

Bolshevik Temptress

The Alliluyevs would become family and travel with Stalin from this world of prisons, death and conspiracy to the peak of power—and then back to the world of prisons, death and conspiracy, at the hands of Stalin himself.

Sergei was a "fascinating adventuresome man like his Gypsy forefathers. He got into fights: if anyone ill treated the workers, he'd beat them up." His wife, Olga, *née* Fedorenko, "a real beauty with grey-green eyes and blonde hair," was a highly sexed Marxist temptress. Olga "often fell in love with men," wrote her granddaughter Svetlana.

Her parents, of German ancestry, were ambitious and hardworking with high hopes for Olga, but Sergei Alliluyev, then twenty-seven, was their lodger, a fitter of serf and Gypsy origins who had worked since he was twelve. Olga, just thirteen, was meant to marry a local sausage-maker but fell in love with the lodger. They eloped. Her father chased Sergei with a whip but it was too late. Sergei and Olga immersed themselves in revolutionary activism while raising a family of two daughters and two sons.

The youngest Alliluyev, Nadezhda, was still a baby, but the older children grew up with this unstable, nymphomaniac mother and a household devoted to the cause, abustle with an ever-changing cast of young conspirators—particularly those who were dark, mysterious and to their mother's taste. Georgians were her type. "On occasion, she had affairs with a Pole, then a Hungarian, then a Bulgarian, and even a Turkish man," says Svetlana. "She liked southern men and sometimes huffed 'Russian men are bumpkins.'"

Olga Alliluyeva favoured Lenin's brooding envoy Victor Kurnatovsky, now in Siberian exile—and Stalin. Her son Pavel Alliluyev supposedly complained that his mother "chased first Stalin then Kurnatovsky." It is claimed that Nadya said her mother had admitted sleeping with both. Her granddaughter Svetlana certainly writes that Olga "always had a soft spot for Stalin," but "the children came to terms with this, the affairs sooner or later ended, family life went on."*

The affair sounds likely; if so, it was typical of its time.

In the underground, the revolutionaries were, under a façade of prudishness, sexually liberal. Married comrades constantly found themselves thrown together in the fever of their revolutionary work.[1]

When he was not with the Alliluyevs, Soso was again in command of Kamo and his young Sosoist acolytes. If he wanted an order obeyed fast, he would say, "I'll spit now—and before it's dry, I want you back here!"

Kamo was rapidly becoming one of the Party's most useful thugs, expert in enforcement, setting up printing-presses and smuggling leaflets. He never wrote an article or gave a speech, but he was now teaching his craft to other young ruffians. In his tactless (and unpublished) memoirs, Kamo reveals much about how he and Stalin lived at this time. When distributing pamphlets, he worked out that the best place to hide was a brothel, "because there were no spooks there!" He was so short of cash that he virtually had to become a paid gigolo to survive. First there was the doctor's wife, who let him stay. "I often wondered why my landlady looked after me so diligently. Then I had intimate intercourse with her. I was utterly disgusted—but as I had no other secret apartment, I had to submit and I had to borrow money from her too."

Another woman, a Jewish nurse, also propositioned him. Kamo succumbed to her too: "Afterwards I went away and tried not to see her any

---

* The "affair" resurfaced when Stalin married Olga's youngest daughter, Nadya. The rumour spread that Stalin was her father. Both apparently heard the rumour, but she was already three when Stalin met the family. Meanwhile, in 1904, Soso had also been courting more traditionally a Georgian girl of a good family, Nina Gurgenidze, asking her to marry him. When she forsook him and married a dishevelled lawyer, Soso cursed: "How could you have married that scruff!" The lawyer husband was shot in 1937.

more!" He may not have been the only one reduced to living off women. One unsourced but sometimes well-informed biographer claims that Stalin started an affair with a certain Marie Arensberg, wife of a German businessman in Tiflis, who helped him with tips for extorting money from merchants.

Kamo's bosom pal was a young, dirt-poor nobleman named Grigory Ordzhonikidze, known as "Sergo." Trained as a male nurse, Sergo was notoriously pugnacious, tempestuous, handsome and exuberant—a cartoon Georgian with big brown eyes, an aquiline profile and extravagant moustaches.

"Become my assistant!" Kamo urged Sergo.

"Assistant of the prince or the laundrywoman?" bantered Sergo, referring to Kamo's disguises as a street pedlar with a basket on his head, a prince in Circassian uniform, a poor student or, his masterpiece, a laundrywoman with a bag of washing. Sergo became close to Stalin, an alliance that would take him to the Kremlin but ultimately destroy him.

The schoolboyish stunts of Stalin, Kamo and Sergo caught the town's attention. Sergo's cousin, Minadora Toroshelidze,* remembers seeing those three in the gallery of the Artistic Society Theatre, which was then presenting *Hamlet*. Just when Hamlet's dead father appeared, they threw hundreds of leaflets towards the chandelier, whence they wafted down into the laps of the aristocrats and bourgeoisie. The three then scarpered. At the State Theatre, they dropped the leaflets onto the deputy governor's head.[2]

Awaiting the Party's forgiveness, Soso was drawn back to Batumi, where his reception by the Mensheviks Jibladze and Isidore Ramishvili was glacial.

"I heard a knock on the door," says Natasha Kirtava. "Who is it?" she asked.

"Me! Soso!"

"Soso, man! I sent you a letter in Irkutsk—how did you manage to turn up here?"

---

*Minadora, *née* Ordzhonikidze, was a Menshevik married to the Bolshevik Malakia Toroshelidze, who was also close to Stalin. Minadora was the only woman to sign the Menshevik declaration of independence for Georgia in 1918. After Stalin and Sergo reconquered Georgia in 1921, she stayed in Tiflis with Toroshelidze, rector of Tiflis University, one of those who received a copy of the *Credo*. In 1937, they were both arrested. In a typical random irony of Stalin's Terror, she, the Menshevik, was released; he, the Bolshevik, was shot. But perhaps this was not coincidental: Stalin liked her. Minadora's memoirs are unpublished.

"I escaped!" She welcomed her lover, who was dressed in the military uniform he used as disguise. The Prussianized uniformed hierarchy of the Romanov Empire was one big fancy-dress shop of disguises for the revolutionaries. When Natasha told her comrades of Soso's return, "some were happy, some were sad." The Menshevik Ramishvili denounced Stalin to Natasha.

"Throw him out," he shouted, "or we'll expel you from the Party."

Stalin chivalrously left Natasha, but Ramishvili was spreading the rumour that there was something fishy about his escape: Stalin must be a police spy. After moving house eight times in his soldier's uniform, Soso was forced to return to Natasha, who loyally raised cash for his return to Tiflis.

"Where are you going, Soso, what will we do if you fail again?" she asked him. As she remembered later, he stroked her hair and kissed her, saying, "Don't be afraid!"

A railwayman lent him another uniform—"the peaked cap, tunic and torch of a train ticket-collector," recalls the railway conductor, who regularly gave Soso lifts between Tiflis and Batumi. But Stalin did not forget Natasha. Once he was in Tiflis, he wrote using pseudo-medical code to invite her to join him. "Sister Natasha, your local doctors are ridiculous; if your disease is complicated, come here where there are good doctors."

"I couldn't go," she says, "for family reasons." Was her husband back? Stalin was outraged.[3]

He and Philip Makharadze, an older Bolshevik and founder of the Third Group, were busy at this time editing and contributing to the Party's illegal Georgian newspaper, *Proletariatis Brdzola* (Proletarian Struggle), which was published at their secret press in Avlabar, the workers' district in Tiflis. But then he returned to Batumi for a month in April, another unhappy visit.

At a May Day celebration at the seaside, Stalin apparently got into a row with some locals, presumably Mensheviks, which led to a Marxist wine-lubricated factional brawl in which he was beaten up.

He encountered Natasha Kirtava, who had turned down his proposal to live together. "I rushed up to greet him," she writes. "But the angry Soso shouted at me: 'Get away from me!' "[4]*

---

* Kirtava became a Party official and avid Stalinist in Batumi. Her memoirs are written in the rigid hieroglyphic Bolshevik language, but even in the 1930s she dared record how she turned down Stalin—and how that infuriated him. The story has not been published until now.

Bruised and rejected in Batumi, hunted by the Gendarmes in Tiflis, Soso retreated to Gori, where he hid out with his uncle Giorgi Geladze and presumably saw Keke. Davrichewy says that he got new papers in Gori in the name of "Petrov," another of his many aliases.[5]

At the end of July, Tskhakaya despatched Stalin to western Georgia, the old principalities of Imeretia and Mingrelia, where he was to form the new Imeretian-Mingrelian Committee. He headed off to Kutaisi, a Georgian provincial town of 30,000 "chaise-drivers, policemen, tavern-owners, pale bureaucrats and idle petty-nobility." This was a vital task because the peasants of the west, especially in Guria, had been politicized like no others in the entire Empire. This remote landscape of "mountains, swampy valleys, and gently rolling hills covered by cornfields, vineyards and tea plantations" now buzzed with rebellion. Assisted by the Red Prince, Sasha Tsulukidze, and a new friend, an orotund and grandiloquent young actor named Budu "the Barrel" Mdivani, Stalin was to enjoy a run of luck as a revolutionary in the strangest of times: the Japanese war was bleeding away the lifeblood of the Empire. In July 1904, the terrorists of the SR Fighting Brigade blew to pieces the hardline Interior Minister Plehve, who was succeeded by an inexperienced aristocrat, Prince Sviatopolk-Mirsky. Strikes and unrest spread as Mirsky experimented haplessly with a thaw.

The villages of western Georgia were already alight. In the ensuing jacquerie, peasants attacked the nobility, seized land and drove out the Tsar's police. Stalin started to travel hectically across the Caucasus, leaving Tiflis more than ten times on trips to organize the Revolution and raise funds from Kutaisi to Vladikavkaz and Novorossiisk. The Okhrana noticed his return to Tiflis, writing in October: "Djugashvili escaped from exile and now is a leader of the Georgian worker's party." The Gendarmes tried to ambush him in Tiflis, but he was tipped off and escaped. Arrested again with Budu Mdivani and confined to Ortachala Prison in Tiflis, he and his new friend escaped. The police fired at them but Budu covered Soso with his body.

In western Georgia, he travelled with fishing-rods and tackle, and when arrested by the local police he convinced them he was just fishing. In September and December, he took the train for his first visit to Baku, the oil boomtown, where Bolshevik printing-presses mobilized workers to launch a December strike. The workers won.[6]

Just when the SDs should have been united, they were tearing themselves apart. While the Bolsheviks concentrated on their revolutionary vanguard, Jordania and the Mensheviks shrewdly appealed to the revolting Georgian peasants, offering them what they really wanted: land. Stalin conducted the feud in his base of Kutaisi with such feline use of slander, lies and intrigue that a local Menshevik wrote a rare letter to a member of the Committee that brilliantly reveals his character and style:

> Comrade Koba [Stalin] told you that we were against you and demanded your sacking from the Committee [wrote the Menshevik Noe Khomeriki] but I promise nothing of the sort happened and everything Koba told you is a malicious lie! Yes: a calumny to discredit us! I just wonder at the man's impudence. I know how worthless he is, but I didn't expect such "courage." But it turns out he'll use any means if the ends justify them. The end in this case—the ambition—is to present himself as a great man before the nation. But . . . God didn't grant him the right gifts so he had to resort to intrigues, lies and other "bagatelles." Such a filthy person wanted to pollute our sacred mission with sewage!

Stalin claimed he had the right to sack whomever he wanted from the Committee, even though he knew this was untrue. Khomeriki called him "Quixote Koba"—but, as so often, Stalin's shameless "impudence" won the day.*

Triumphant at winning control for Lenin, in September 1904 Stalin now wrote two letters to his Gori chum Davitashvili, in Leipzig, praising Lenin the "mountain eagle," attacking the Mensheviks and boasting that his "committee had been hesitating but I convinced them." Plekhanov, he wrote, "has either gone off his nut or is showing hatred and hostility," while Jordania was an "ass." This obscure Georgian was quite happy to

---

* Noe Khomeriki later served as Minister of Land in the independent Georgia of 1918–21 before leading the Menshevik rebellion of 1924 when he was captured and shot. His letter was confiscated in a Gendarme raid and then long lost in the archives. It is unusual because it is so specifically damning in its analysis of Stalin's methods and ambitions. In late 1950, Beria, then the Politburo grandee in charge of the nuclear project, was out of favour and feared his own destruction. We now know that he heard about this letter from Georgian circles and, gathering ammunition to use against Stalin if need be, he secretly and unofficially asked an archivist to trace it. But Beria did not find it. The letter resurfaced only in 1989.

denounce the international sages of Marxism. The letter worked: Lenin heard about Stalin for the first time. The "mountain eagle" acclaimed him as his "fiery Colchian."*

On New Year's Eve 1904, Soso ordered a small gang of railway workers to meet him outside the Nobleman's Club on Tiflis's Golovinsky Prospect. Noble liberals were then holding a so-called Banquet Campaign to canvass the Tsar for a constitution, but the Bolsheviks loathed such half-baked bourgeois liberalism. As soon as the chairman opened the banquet, Stalin, backed by his workers, burst in and demanded to speak. When the banqueters refused, Stalin sabotaged the evening by shouting, "Down with Autocracy," then led his workers out singing "The Marseillaise" and "The Warsawianka." On 2 January, the Tsar's chief Far Eastern port, Port Arthur, still stocked with troops and munitions, surrendered to the Japanese. So began 1905.[7]

On Sunday, 9 January, when Stalin was in Baku again, the revolutionary-cum-police-agent Father Gapon marched at the head of 150,000 hymn-singing workers to submit a Humble and Loyal Petition to the Tsar at the Winter Palace in Petersburg. Cossacks blocked the way. They fired two warning salvoes, but the workers continued to advance. The troops fired on the crowd, and then charged. Two hundred workers were killed, and hundreds more wounded. "There is no God any longer," murmured Father Gapon. "There is no Tsar."

Bloody Sunday shook the Empire, unleashing a tempest of demonstrations, ethnic massacres, killings and open revolution. Strikes mushroomed across the Empire. Peasants burned the palaces and libraries of their masters—3,000 manor houses were destroyed. The unrest spread to the army. "The Tsar's battalions," wrote Stalin in an article, "are dwindling, the Tsar's navy is perishing and now Port Arthur has shamefully surrendered—the senile decreptitude of the Autocracy is revealed again." But the Tsar still hoped for a miracle. In one of the most extraordinary naval ventures in history, he sent his leaky Baltic Fleet to almost circumnavigate the globe, via Africa, India, Singapore, to fight the Japanese. Had the gamble succeeded, Nicholas II's victory would have resounded down the ages.

The Tsar sacked his luckless Interior Minister and appointed a new one, who suggested that some political concessions might be necessary.

---

* Colchis, land of the Golden Fleece, was the ancient name of Georgia: hence Colchian.

Kamo, psychopath, childhood friend and cutthroat, wearing a Georgian *chokha* coat, was "an extraordinary man" who often begged Stalin: "Let me cut his throat!" Simpleton, lover, escapologist, bank robber, killer, and master of disguises—from washerwoman to prince—he led Stalin's Tiflis heist. When arrested, he feigned madness for years, undergoing such tortures that doctors concluded he was truly insane.

Conspiracy: During the 1905 Revolution, Stalin ran a Faginesque network of street children *(top)* who smuggled guns and ran errands as his private intelligence service. Meanwhile, Stalin was pursued and watched by the agents or "spooks" of the Tsarist secret police, the Okhrana, who pose *(left)* in their street costumes. Yet he became adept at tricking and infiltrating the secret police themselves.

Left: Vladimir Illich Lenin around the time he met Stalin, who revered him but always had his own opinions. Stalin, through his bank robberies and gangsterism became Lenin's main fund-raiser. *Centre:* Stalin, arrested 1906. *Right:* Leon Trotsky, the vain and brilliant Jewish intellectual and Chairman of the Petersburg Soviet was arrested in 1905. Meeting in London, Stalin hated him on sight.

Doomed. Stalin's first wife was a pretty dress-maker with noble connections. Kato Svanidze *(bottom left and right)*, with whom he had a son, Yakov.

The Daily Mirror

No. 1,105.   Registered at the G.P.O. as a Newspaper.   THURSDAY, MAY 16, 1907.   One Halfpenny.

RUSSIAN REVOLUTIONISTS MEET SECRETLY IN A CHURCH HALL.

Day after day Russian Labour delegates meet in a hall attached to the Brotherhood Church, Southgate-road, N., in order to plot against the Russian Government. The large photograph shows three of them entering the hall, and the inset the Brotherhood Church, where the meetings take place.—(*Daily Mirror* photograph.)

Harmless pedestrians who pass the delegates in the streets have no idea of their proximity to revolutionists who are plotting against a throne.—(*Daily Mirror* photograph.)

The entrance to the hall, showing three delegates going in to a meeting and a watchman at the door.—(*Daily Mirror* photograph.)

Stalin in London: On this trip, Lenin ordered Stalin's Tiflis bank robbery. Stalin was almost beaten up by English dockworkers and learned English by listening to church services. Newspapers were enthralled by terrorist radicals in London. The revolutionaries hid from their photographers (*facing page, top left*). When they ran out of money, Lenin had to borrow from Joseph Fels, an American soap millionaire who insisted every delegate sign the agreement (*below*). Everyone signed using aliases: "Vasily from Baku" (*right sheet, eight down on the left*) is probably Stalin.

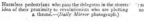

RAIN OF BOMBS.

Revolutionaries Hurl Destruction Among Large Crowds of People.

TIFLIS, Wednesday.—About ten bombs were hurled to-day, one after the other, in the square in the centre of the town, which was thronged with people at the time.

The bombs exploded with terrific force, many people being killed and injured.

Window-panes, doors, and chimneys were shattered over a large area.—Reuter.

TIFLIS, Later.—It now appears that the bomb outrage was connected with an attack on a Treasury van which was escorted by five Cossacks and two other soldiers.

The van, which was proceeding from the Post Office to the local branch of the Imperial Bank, contained a sum of £25,000. When the van reached the Erivan-square, a bomb was thrown, and an appalling explosion ensued, striking terror among the large number of people in the square, scattering them in all directions.

In order to increase the confusion the robbers threw bomb after bomb, which burst with deafening reports. Two employees of the Imperial Bank were hurled out of the van, which, together with the bags containing the money, disappeared without leaving any trace behind it.

The number of victims has not yet been ascertained, but it is known that two soldiers were killed and that the robbers got away with the sum of £25,000.—Reuter.

RUSSIAN REVOLUTIONISTS AFRAID OF THE CAMERA.

A band of Russian revolutionists entering the Brotherhood Church Hall, Southgate-road, N., where their meetings are being held.—(Park.)

Stalin masterminded the Tiflis bank robbery—bold, bloody, lucrative—that made global headlines *(top right)*. It seemed the perfect crime, but European police hunted the gangsters and the money. The fallout almost ruined Stalin. Murderous daredevil and chief bank robber Kamo was arrested in Berlin *(above)*. Poor nobleman Sergo Ordzhonikidze *(left)*, who later became a trusted but ultimately doomed Kremlin ally, was Stalin's protégé.

Baku, the lawless oil boom city filled with ostentatious millionaires, where Stalin embraced gangsterism, extortion and piracy to fund Lenin. A Baku oil fountain *(top left)* and hellish oilfields *(bottom left)*. *Top right:* The palace of Nageyev, a self-made tycoon possibly kidnapped on Stalin's orders. *Bottom right:* The Baku oil baron Mukhtarov (with his wife) who ordered Stalin to be beaten up or killed.

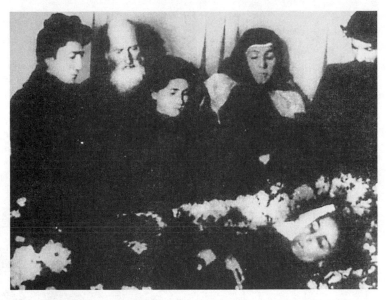

Kato, Stalin's wife, died a terrible death: He was heartbroken *(top, on the far right)*. The family blamed him. He said his tenderness died with her. He threw himself into the grave and then narrowly escaped arrest at her funeral, legging it over the cemetery wall. After Kato, Stalin enjoyed a string of love affairs with, amongst others, Alvasi Talakvadze *(below left)* and Ludmilla Stal *(below right)*, the experienced Russian Bolshevik who may have inspired his famous name.

Stalin thrived in the underworld, on the run, in and out of prison, hunting spies in his own Party and repeatedly escaping from Siberian exile. Here in police mugshots: *(top left)*, Stalin in Baku 1908, and *(bottom left and right)*, headed "Baku Gendarmerie," in 1910—his shorter left arm is visible. Times were harder: He is noticeably thinner.

"One would think you're afraid a revolution will break out," replied the Emperor.

"Your Majesty, the revolution has already begun"—the 1905 Revolution, which Trotsky later called the "Dress Rehearsal." At the time, it seemed like the real thing, a savage and exhilarating battle across the Empire, but especially in the Caucasus, where Stalin learned the methods that he would use throughout his life.[8] He found himself in his element, revelling in the bloodcurdling drama.

"WORKERS OF THE CAUCACUS! TIME FOR VENGEANCE!" he wrote. "They're asking us to forget the swish of the whips, the whiz of the bullets, the hundreds of our hero-comrades killed, and the hover of their glorious ghosts around us whispering: 'AVENGE US!' "[9]

14

1905: King of the Mountain

Nineteen-hundred-and-five began and ended with slaughter. It was the year of revolution in which young Stalin, for the first time, commanded armed men, tasted power, and embraced terror and gangsterism. On 6 February, he was in Baku when some Armenians shot a Tartar in the centre of the city. Azeri Turks—or "Tartars" as they were often called—retaliated. The news spread. The authorities, who had long resented Armenian wealth and success, encouraged the Muslim Azeri mobs to pour into the city.

For five long days, Azeri gangs killed every Armenian they could find, with the frenzied hatred that comes from religious tension, economic jealousy and neighbourly proximity. While anti-Semitic pogroms broke out across the Empire, Baku descended into an orgy of ethnic killing, burning, raping, shooting and throat-cutting. The governor, Prince Nakashidze, and his police chief did nothing. Cossacks handed over Orthodox Armenians to be slaughtered by Azeri mobs, armed by the police. One Armenian oil baron was besieged in his palace by an Azeri mob, whom he picked off with a Winchester rifle until he ran out of ammunition and was torn to pieces. Eventually, the Armenians, wealthier and better armed, started to fight back and massacre Azeris.

"They don't even know why they're killing each other," said the mayor. "Thousands of dead lay in the streets," wrote a witness of the Baku slaughters, "and covered the Christian and Mussulman cemeteries. The odour of corpses stifled us. Everywhere women with mad eyes sought their children, and husbands were moving heaps of rotting flesh." At least 2,000 died.

Stalin was there to see these infernal and apocalyptic sights. He had formed a small Bolshevik Battle Squad in Baku. Now he gathered this mainly Muslim gang and ordered them to divide the two communities wherever possible while simultaneously taking the opportunity to steal any useful printing equipment—and raise money for the Party by protection-rackets. Stalin, according to his first biographer, Essad Bey,* who grew up in Baku, "presented himself to the head of the [Armenian] household and gravely informed him that the time was near when the household would fall beneath the knives of the Muslims," but "after a donation to Bolshevik funds, Stalin conveyed the Armenian merchants to the countryside."[1]

Afterwards Soso hurried back to Tiflis, where there was every danger of an ethnic bloodbath between Georgians and Armenians or Christians and Muslims. The city was paralysed by strikes; the police arrested revolutionaries and Cossacks charged demonstrators on Golovinsky Prospect.

Stalin helped organize a demonstration of reconciliation to prevent a massacre and wrote a passionate pamphlet which, printed and distributed by Kamo, warned that the Tsar was using "pogroms against Jews and Armenians" to "buttress his despicable throne on the blood, the innocent blood of honest citizens, the groans of dying Armenians and Tartars."

Stalin led the demonstration on 13 February "to struggle against the devils sowing strife among us." He proudly reported that 3,000 of his own pamphlets had been distributed, and that "in the leading core [of the crowd] a banner-bearer was carried shoulder-high to deliver a strong speech"—himself no doubt.[2] But the bad blood between Bolsheviks and Mensheviks was now thoroughly poisonous.

Jordania, the aristocratic Menshevik leader, returned from exile. His towering authority and sensible pro-peasant policies won over the Geor-

---

* Essad Bey was one of the pseudonyms of Lev Nussimbaum, the son of a Jewish Baku oil baron, who wrote *Stalin: Career of a Fanatic.* He also wrote the classic love story *Ali and Nino* under the name Kurban Said, whose identity was a mystery until a new biography— *The Orientalist* by Tom Reiss—revealed Nussimbaum's bizarre life and ethnic transformation into a Muslim in Fascist Italy. A notorious fantasist is hardly an ideal historical source; his unsourced anecdotes were long regarded as myths yet they often turn out to be historically correct. Nussimbaum must have known exiles from Tiflis and Baku and recorded their stories, but his unreliable material has to be counter-checked.

gians, who overwhelmingly embraced Menshevism. At the Tiflis Committee, Isidore Ramishvili, who in Batumi had whispered about Stalin's suspicious escape, openly accused him of being a government agent, though he apparently had no proof of this. Emboldened by Jordania, Mensheviks and then Bolsheviks each elected their own Committees.[3]

In April, Stalin headed west, where armed gangs and elected Committees had taken control of government and justice, even though some of the peasants thought "Committee" was actually the name of a new sort of Tsar. Arson and assassination became routine in a "separate republic where police power could not enter." Stalin wrote frenziedly, and spoke at mass meetings against the Mensheviks in Batumi and Kutaisi. At one debate, "Comrade Koba performed strongly in a session that started at 10 p.m. and lasted until dawn." Then, dressed in black and grey with his moustache and beard shaved off for disguise, he was smuggled into the forest to hide until he could escape by night.

Stalin's Menshevik enemy was the charismatic firebrand Noe Ramishvili, "aged 25, tall, thin, with smiling eyes and energetic voice." Khariton Chavichvili, a Menshevik,* saw the duellists face one another like mythical champions. First Ramishvili arrived, then "the famous Soso, Comrade Koba, smaller than Ramishvili but just as thin. His look was calmer, deeper, his face coarser, perhaps due to the pockmarks. His style, manners were totally Georgian, yet there was something utterly original, something hard to fathom, both leonine and feline about him. Under an ordinary appearance, wasn't there something extraordinary?" Chavichvili was impressed too by the oratory—or lack of it: "He wasn't an orator" but "a master of the art of dissimulation." He spoke "with a light smile, eyes fixed . . . concisely, clearly, and was very persuasive" even though Ramishvili was the better speaker. Even when "the famous Soso" lost to the Mensheviks, which was often, the "workers kissed him with tears in their eyes."[4]

Yet an envious fury at the smug, often Jewish Mensheviks seethed beneath Soso's glacial calm. After one debate, he tore into the Mensheviks: "Lenin's outraged that God sent him such comrades as the Mensheviks! Who are these people anyway? Martov, Dan, Axelrod are

---

* Chavichvili's two volumes of memoirs are invaluable but rarely used by historians: they were only published in tiny editions in French. Chavichvili was a hostile witness who wrote in exile, yet he is half impressed, half appalled by Stalin's magnetism.

circumcised Yids. You can't go into a fight with them and you can't have a feast with them!"[5]

When Stalin was in Kutaisi, the miners of nearby Chiatura appealed to him. This mountain mining town was the only real Bolshevik stronghold in Georgia. With every intention of holding it, he now began to spend much of his time there. Astride snow-peaked mountains with precipitous cliffs and low clouds, Chiatura was growing fast: Russia's biggest manganese mine supplied around 60 percent of the world's production. Dominated by a lunar landscape of ore heaps, its 3,700 "black-skinned" workers toiled eighteen-hour days in choking dust for paltry salaries. Lacking baths or even housing, miners slept down in the mines. "Animals," wrote Kote Tsintsadze, a gunman who was Stalin's future bankrobbery supremo, "lived better than Chiatura workers."[6]

On a hot summer day, 2,000 miners, covered in dust like blackamoors in a minstrel show, listened to the Mensheviks and then to Stalin. Chavichvili saw how Soso "the ultimate tactician" let the Mensheviks speak first, boring the audience. When his turn came, he said he did not want to tire them and refused to perform. "The workers then begged him to speak," at which he talked for just fifteen minutes with "striking simplicity." Stalin "kept a stupefying sang-froid . . . he talked as if in a fresh and serene conversation . . . he seemed to see nothing but observed everything." He won the debate. His plain speaking outflanked the grand oratory of more flamboyant performers whom the workers distrusted. Years later, he worked the same trick with famous orators like Trotsky. He realized his own attraction, explaining to Chavichvili that the Menshevik speaker was a "great orator but your big cannon is no use here when you need to shoot short distances."

Stalin took control of Chiatura, says Chavichvili, which became "the Bolshevik fortress." Soso "was very powerful there: he surrounded himself with men twice as old, twice as cultured, but the admiration and affection with which he enveloped himself permitted him to impose his iron discipline on his troops." Known as "Famous Soso" or "Sergeant-Major Koba," he set up a printing-press with the help of the pretty young student Patsia Goldava, who later toted a revolver in the 1907 Tiflis bank robbery.[7]

The Famous Soso was the champion of armed resistance, founding, arming and commanding the Red Battle Squads, half-partisans, half-terrorists, across Georgia. "We must devote serious attention to setting up the Battle Squads," wrote Stalin, a superb military and terrorist organizer—but the experience gave him not just the taste for military command, but the delusion that he had a gift for it.

Even the Mensheviks were arming, appointing Stalin's rival Ramishvili to organize their Military Technical Commission and their bomb factories. By mid-1905, these militias were ruling the streets and villages of Georgia—in between raids by Cossacks. Sometimes Stalin and the Bolsheviks cooperated with the Mensheviks, sometimes not.

In Chiatura, Stalin armed miners and local gangsters, appointing Vano Kiasashvili as commander. "Comrade Soso used to arrive to give his orders and we launched the Red Squad," says Kiasashvili, who trained his partisans, stole guns and smuggled in ammunition over the hills. At Chiatura Station, Chavichvili watched Stalin giving orders to his other Battle Squad chieftain, Tsintsadze, the dashing, red-haired daredevil who recruited as gangsters a handful of female students, most of them in love with him. Tsintsadze's and Stalin's gunmen disarmed Russian troops, ambushed hated Cossacks, raided banks and murdered spooks and policemen "until nearly the whole province was in our hands." Chiatura, boasted Tsintsadze, "became a kind of preparatory military camp."[8]

Soso was constantly in and out of Chiatura to oversee this guerrilla war. Oddly, when he was there, the aristocratic manganese-mining tycoons hid and protected him. First he stayed at the mansion of Bartholome Kekelidze, then with the grander Prince Ivan Abashidze, deputy chairman of the Council of Manganese Industrialists, related to Princes Shervashidze, Amilakhvari and Prince David, alias Black Spot, the seminary teacher. (Prince Abashidze was also the great-grandfather of the present President of Georgia, Mikheil Saakashvili.) What was going on?

All the revolutionaries were funded at least partly by big business and the middle class, many of whom were alienated by the Tsarist regime and in any case excluded from any influence. In Russia itself, the plutocrats, such as the textile tycoon Savva Morozov, were the biggest Bolshevik contributors, while among lawyers, managers and accountants "it was a status symbol to give to the revolutionary parties." This was especially true in Georgia.

Yet there is more to this than just hospitality and philanthropy. Stalin had probably learned the lucrative art of protection-racketeering and extortion from his criminal acquaintances and from his dealings in Baku and Batumi. Now he offered security in return for money. If the tycoons did not pay, their mines might be blown up, their managers murdered; if they did pay, Stalin protected them.

Two of his fighters recall, in unpublished memoirs, how Stalin kept his side of the bargain, showing that he could really deal with the devil. When the tycoons were robbed, reports G. Vashadze, "it was not local citizens who organized the search for the 'criminals' but J. V. Stalin." Some "thieves robbed the manager of a German manganese company and stole 11,000 roubles," says N. Rukhadze. "Comrade Stalin commanded us to find the money and get it back. We did so."

It is not surprising that the tycoons preferred to have Stalin on their side: Chiatura crackled with assassinations. "The capitalists," wrote Tsintsadze, "were so afraid it didn't take them long to cough up." As for any policemen or spooks, "the Chiatura organization decided to get rid of them." They were hit one by one. Stalin, with his brigands riding shotgun through the hills, his newspapers pumping out his own articles, and his surprisingly impressive performances at mass meetings, became the king of the mountain. "Comrade Koba and [Prince] Sasha Tsulukidze," wrote a rich young Bolshevik lawyer, Baron Bibeneishvili, "were our big guns." But the Mensheviks were winning in the rest of the Caucasus.[9]

"I've had to travel all around the Caucasus taking part in debates, encouraging comrades," Soso recounted to Lenin, who was abroad. "The Mensheviks campaign everywhere and we've got to repel them. We've almost no people (and still too few, two or three times less than the Mensheviks) . . . Almost all of Tiflis has fallen into their hands. Half of Baku and Batumi. But the Bolsheviks have the other half of Baku, half of Batumi, some of Tiflis, and all of the Kutaisi Region with Chiatura (the manganese-mining district, 9,000–10,000 workers). Guria belongs to Conciliators who lean towards the Mensheviks."[10]

Stalin, wrote one of his Menshevik enemies, "was working very energetically, travelling around Guria, Imeretia, Chiatura, Baku, Tiflis, throwing himself to and fro, but all his work was mainly factional, trying to stamp the Mensheviks into the filth."* He fought the Mensheviks viciously—"Against them," he said, "any methods are fine."[11]

---

* He fought in print too. "Our Mensheviks are really too tiresome!" wrote Stalin in his pamphlet accusing them of Marxist phoniness. The article is interesting for its quaint phrases and parables: "One day a crow found a rose but that doesn't prove a crow is a nightingale." The Mensheviks "remind us of the thief who stole the money and shouted 'Stop thief!'" But he concluded, "It is well known that the tongue always turns to the aching tooth."

. . .

On 5 May 1905, a new—and liberal—viceroy stepped off the train at Tif-lis Station to "marching bands, plumed hats, golden epaulettes and bombastic speeches." Count Illarion Vorontsov-Dashkov, aged sixty-eight, was a "horsebreeder, oil investor, scion of great aristocratic families," married to a Princess Vorontsov who was descended from one of the famous nieces of Catherine the Great's partner, Prince Potemkin. Family friend and ex–Court Minister to the Emperor, he was open-minded and fair: one of his first acts was to appoint a liberal to govern Guria. But Count Vorontsov-Dashkov was too late and too inconsistent. In the brutal Battle of Mukden, in Manchuria, the Tsar's armies had lost tens of thousands of peasant-soldiers yet failed to defeat the Japanese. On 27 May, the Russian Baltic Fleet, after that quixotic round-the-world voyage during which it had succeeded only in sinking an English fishing-boat in the North Sea, was ignominiously routed by the Japanese at the Battle of Tsushima. Even its admiral was captured. These disasters rocked the Empire. Jews were slaughtered in pogroms. On 14 June, the crew of the battleship *Prince Potemkin of Taurida,* the showpiece of the Black Sea Fleet, mutinied.

Within days of his arrival, Count Vorontsov-Dashkov was faced by the collapse of his power, armed gangs in Tiflis, terrorism at the railway depot, and another bloodbath in Baku. The count could scarcely square his liberal instincts with the brutal reality as his generals and Cossacks launched murderous raids on radicals in Tiflis. He was soon faced with open warfare, wild terrorism and a rash of industrial action. "In 1905," writes one historian, "everyone from palm-readers to prostitutes went on strike."[12]

On 9 June, Sasha Tsulukidze, Stalin's beloved Red Prince, died of tuberculosis. The funeral at Kutaisi attracted 50,000 people, who followed the open coffin to Khoni singing "The Marseillaise." Even though he was a wanted man, Stalin delivered the funeral oration, a passionate speech that one spectator could still recite three decades later.*

The Famous Soso lived in a frenzy at this time—heading east to Tiflis, west to Batumi, thence to Kutaisi, commanding his Battle Squads.

---

* In October 1940, the celebrated Georgian writer Shalva Nutsubidze was suddenly freed from jail and brought to meet Stalin, who admired, edited and contributed to his translation of Rustaveli. At dinner in Stalin's mansion at Kuntsevo, Nutsubidze remembered the speech at Tsulukidze's funeral and proceeded to recite it. "Extraordinary talent goes hand in hand with extraordinary memory," exclaimed Stalin, who walked up to his guest and kissed him on the forehead. For the full story, see *Stalin: The Court of the Red Tsar.*

"Terrorism assumed gigantic proportions," said Baron Bibeneishvili, himself a Bolshevik terrorist. It seemed that every young revolutionary was tinkering with explosive devices, stealing guns and robbing banks. "Almost every day there was a 'political killing' or an attack on some representative of the old regime." Landowners, Gendarmes, officials, Cossacks, police spies and traitors were regularly murdered in broad daylight. In Tiflis, the ex–governor-general, Golitsyn, had survived an Armenian Dashnak assassination attempt only because he wore a chain-mail vest. Between February 1905 and May 1906, the viceroy reported to the Emperor that 136 officials had been assassinated, 72 wounded. Across the Empire, 3,600 officials were killed or wounded—these official figures are probably massive understatements. In Baku, the governor, Prince Nakashidze, was killed by the Dashnaks, his police chief by a Bolshevik hit man.

"There was much competition between the parties in their terroristic antics," explained Stalin's Gori friend Davrichewy. In Kutaisi, Soso ordered his Battle Squad there to obtain arms by raiding the Kutaisi Arsenal. They rented a house nearby and mined under it—but the tunnel collapsed.

After Bloody Sunday and a series of massacres in Tiflis, the Cossacks were especially hated. Stalin ordered Kamo and his terrorists to attack them. Between 22 and 25 June, the Tsar's horsemen were bombed five times.

In his white palace in Tiflis, the sexagenarian viceroy, his decent dreams in tatters, was on the edge of a nervous breakdown, while in the revolutionary bedlam far beneath him, Stalin flourished in a seething atmosphere of relentless struggle. Illiterate ruffians and cutthroats like Kamo always prosper in lawless times, but Stalin was unusual—as adept at debating, writing and organizing as he was at arranging hits and heists. The command, harnessing and provocation of turmoil were his gifts. The viceroy declared martial law and handed over power to his generals.[13]

One day a young priest in the village of Tseva, between Chiatura and the station at Jirual, was at the bazaar when he was greeted by an unknown man. "I am Koba from Gori," he said. "I'm not here to shop. I have private business with you." Taking Father Kasiane Gachechiladze aside,* Stalin

---

* Father Kasiane Gachechiladze's memoirs were written secretly during Stalin's lifetime and inherited by his grandson, who saw this author talking about this project on Georgian television and made contact. The account of his leading horses cross-country, his movements and his conversation all chime with other sources.

said he knew that the priest owned some donkeys and asked him how to get over the hills to Chiatura, adding, "No one knows this area better than you."

The priest realized that the sinister stranger knew a lot about him and his young family. He also noticed that the local Red Battle Squad's hit man and policemen-slayer was standing guard outside the bazaar. "There weren't police in Tseva then—the Red Squad was in charge there." "Koba of Gori," clearly a Red chieftain, courteously requested the use of the priest's donkeys and offered the considerable sum of fifty roubles to set up a route over the hills. The money eased the priest's anxiety.

Stalin insisted on taking the priest for a drink in the local tavern.

"They'll inform you in advance when I'm coming," he said before disappearing. "Father, do not be late: I want to make the journey there and back in a day. We're both young men."

Soon the priest got the word. Stalin returned with two henchmen who helped him load the donkeys with saddlebags containing money, printing-presses and probably ammunition. Stalin knew the trains to Chiatura were often searched, and had concluded that this was the safest way to reach his "Bolshevik fortress."

The priest and the ex-seminarist, precisely the same age, chatted as they trekked. Sometimes under a tree, Stalin rested his head on the priest's knee for a nap. During Stalin's dictatorship, Father Gachechiladze wished he had murdered his companion, but at the time "he impressed everyone. I even liked him—he was restrained, serious and decent. He even used to recite poetry to me," adding that they were his own compositions. He was still proud to be a poet.

"Some of my poems were even published in the newspapers," boasted Stalin, who rarely talked politics but claimed that "the police are after me because a friend of mine got into a fight in Chiatura over a girl—and I oversupported him." He displayed his stiff arm as evidence of this fight (yet another of his versions). Stalin recited the blessing before meals. "You see, I still remember it," he laughed. He sang as they walked. "Music has such power to relax the soul!" he reflected.

A peasant invited priest and revolutionary to a feast. The tipsy Stalin sang "with such velvet softness" that the peasants wanted to "marry him to their daughter."

The priest complimented him: "You'd have made a great priest."

"I the cobbler's son competed with noble children and I was superior to all of them," replied Stalin.

When they arrived in Chiatura, Stalin disappeared with the saddle-bags into the bazaar and returned with them empty: "Now at least I can rest my head on them on the train home," said Stalin.

This was Stalin's secret life in the revolutionary summer of 1905—an armed chieftain leading packhorses laden with saddlebags of smuggled guns and plundered banknotes over the baking hills to Chiatura.[14]

In Tiflis, the Cossacks and the terrorists fought for the streets. Thousands met in the City Hall on Yerevan Square every day, barracking the City Council and proposing ever more radical measures. On 29 August, a public meeting of students discussing Nicholas II's proposal of a compromise parliament named after Interior Minister Bulygin was raided brutally by the Cossacks, who entered the hall shooting. Sixty students were killed, 200 wounded.

Stalin rushed back to Tiflis to meet his ally Shaumian and plan a response, on paper and in dynamite. He wrote a leaflet, raced to Chiatura and back again in time to co-ordinate a spectacular vengeance, set for 25 September. "On Stalin's return," says Davrichewy, "the signal was given—a red lantern lit atop Holy Mountain. At about 8 p.m., the gangsters opened fire outside the main barracks . . . When the Cossacks galloped out, grenades were tossed among the child-slayers." Stalin's terrorists launched nine simultaneous attacks.

Bolshevik and Menshevik hit men and agitators were already cooperating on the streets. On 13 October, Stalin and the Bolsheviks met the Mensheviks and agreed to coordinate politics and terrorism to redouble the pressure on the Autocracy, which seemed on the verge of collapse. Across the Empire, workers and soldiers elected councils, or "soviets," the most famous being in Petersburg. The peasants rampaged in the countryside, while on 6 October a strike on the Moscow–Kazan railway escalated into a general stoppage across the Empire. It seemed that Tsardom was finished.

"The coming storm," wrote Soso, "will break over Russia any day in a mighty cleansing flood to sweep away all that is antiquated and rotten."

In St. Petersburg, even Nicholas II, whose political antennae were as sensitive as a stone, was forced to understand that he was about to lose his realm. He was ready to make peace with the Japanese, but political concessions went against his deepest convictions of holy Autocracy. He envied and hated his most able ministers, but his mother and uncles forced him to consult the brilliant ex–Finance Minister Sergei Witte. Before leaving to make peace with Japan at Portsmouth, New Hampshire, under the aegis of U.S. President Teddy Roosevelt, Witte forcefully told the Tsar, whom he despised, to concede a constitution. Nicholas II wavered, then asked his tall, soldierly cousin, Grand Duke Nikolai Nikolaievich, to become military dictator.

As Romanov Autocracy tottered, we have a rare glimpse of Stalin as gang leader dealing out death in the backstreets of Tiflis.[15]

15

1905: Fighters, Urchins and Dressmakers

One night in Tiflis in late 1905, Josef Davrichewy, Stalin's Goreli friend, who now headed the armed wing of the Georgian Socialist-Federalists, heard fighting in a backstreet at the foot of Holy Mountain. He found Kamo, Stalin's enforcer, threatening an unknown Armenian with his pistol.

"If you don't return the banknotes to the safebox you were meant to guard, you're a dead man!" Kamo was saying. "Think! I'll count to three. One . . . two . . . careful my friend . . . three!"

Davrichewy ran up and seized Kamo's arms. "Not here, you idiot. Not in this area. You know *we* run everything round here." Those streets were controlled by Davrichewy's militia. But the "overexcited" Kamo broke free and shot the other man three times.

"At the third blast," says Davrichewy, "both of us ran for it." The dying victim slid bleeding to the pavement.

"In God's name, why stick your nose in our business?" asked Kamo when they were safe. "Koba'll be furious—you know he's not always accommodating." Davrichewy was not happy either: "his" neighbourhood was soon crawling with policemen. But this was not the end of the affair.

Stalin sent Kamo to invite him for a powwow. When they met, Davrichewy "told him off for killing the Armenian in the neighbourhood where we maintain security."

"Listen," Stalin replied calmly. "Don't worry about us. Kamo did what was necessary and you should do the same. Now I have a proposal for you: come with us. Leave the Federalists. We're old Gorelis, I admire and remember our games. Come while there's still time? If not . . ."

"If not, what?" demanded Davrichewy.

Stalin "didn't answer but his eyes shrank and his expression became hard."[1]

Just at that time of world-shattering events, Stalin entered the life of the other family, apart from the Alliluyevs, whose fate would be intertwined with his. He asked his protégé Svanidze to find him somewhere to live.* Svanidze, intelligent, blue-eyed and blond, knew just the place. The apartment at the townhouse of 3 Freilinskaya Street was right behind the military headquarters, in the centre of Tiflis, near Yerevan Square. It had many advantages: first it was populated by lovely Georgian girls. Svanidze's three sisters, Alexandra (Sashiko), Maria (Mariko) and Ekaterina (Kato), ran Atelier Hervieu, a prosperous couture house named after its French couturier Madame Hervieu, making uniforms and dresses.

The girls were Rachvelians from Racha (in western Georgia), famous for its placid and loving beauties. Sashiko had recently married Mikheil Monoselidze, a Bolshevik who knew Stalin from the seminary, but the other two girls were single. The youngest was Kato, a curvaceous, "ravishingly pretty" brunette. Their atelier of young seamstresses made it a sunnily feminine place to be.

One day, Svanidze took Monoselidze aside and "said he wanted to bring Comrade Soso Djugashvili to stay at our place and told me not to say a word to his sisters. I agreed," says Monoselidze.

"So, in 1905, Alyosha invited to stay in our place a fellow whom everyone considered the leader of the Bolshevik faction," writes his wife, Sashiko. "He was poorly dressed, thin, with an olive complexion, his face slightly pockmarked, smaller than average: Soso Djugashvili."

"Our place," recalls Mikheil Monoselidze, "was above the suspicion of the police. While my fellows did illegal stuff in one room, my wife was fitting the dresses of generals' wives next door." The waiting-room was usu-

* Stalin did not only know the Svanidzes via Alyosha. Simon Svanidze, father of Alyosha and his three sisters, was a teacher in Kutaisi; the mother, Sipora, one of the noble Dvali clan. In Kutaisi, Sipora's cousin, a Dvali, was chief of police. Both the Svanidzes and Police Chief Dvali hid Stalin from the secret police, another example of how Georgian connections were more important than loyalty to the state.

ally full of counts, generals and police officers—the ideal home and head-quarters for an underworld boss. Indeed Stalin held many of his gangster and terrorist meetings at Madame Hervieu's atelier. He hid his secret papers in the bodies of her fashion mannequins.

"Soso," remembers Sashiko, "would sit and write for days preparing articles for *Brdzola* and the newspaper *Akhali Tskhovreba* [New Life], edited by Monoselidze. In the evenings, he would finish his work and dis-appear, not returning until two or three in the morning." Stalin's head-quarters was the Mikhailovsky Hospital on the banks of the Kura, where he ran a printing-press in the basement. In such dangerous times, Stalin was, Davrichewy notes, "always ready to draw his gun." But there was time too for flirtations and Stalin's cruel games.

When Pimen Dvali, a Bolshevik cousin of the Svanidzes, was staying, he slept all day.

"What can one do with him?" grumbled Stalin, shaking him. Dvali woke up. "Is anything disturbing you?" asked Stalin ironically.

"No, Soso dear," replied the sleepyhead, falling into another slumber. Stalin "went to him, rolled up cigarette-papers, stuck them between Pimen's toes—and lit them. Pimen's toes were burned and he leaped up. We laughed!"*

Stalin sat and read socialistic pamphlets or novels to the sisters and seamstresses, says Sashiko, "or he would tell jokes, play the fool or tease sleepy Pimen again." Once when the girls' parents were visiting from Kutaisi, "Stalin sang a romantic song with such powerful emotion that all were enchanted, even though they could see he was rough and devoted to revolution," says one of Kato's cousins. Being Stalin, he would play mis-chievous power games. One day, the seamstresses suddenly demanded higher salaries. "My wife and Kato were stunned," explains Monoselidze, "because these women were working in good conditions. But then every-thing became clear: Soso had put them up to it. We were very amused and so was Soso . . ."

Kato, the youngest and prettiest, was especially charmed.[2]

---

* The memoirs of Sashiko Svanidze and her husband, Monoselidze, are invaluable. Both were recorded in the early to mid-1930s when Stalin was already dictator, but they are nonetheless astonishingly honest. Sashiko's memoirs are unpublished; portions of Mono-selidze's memoirs were used in the cult literature, but most of their reminiscences were deemed unsuitable. At this time, 1905–6, Bolsheviks arriving from the provinces reported to Stalin at the hospital, but the leaders—Shaumian, Spandarian, Abel Yenukidze (another Rachvelian) and Budu "the Barrel" Mdivani—were regulars at the Svanidzes' along with Soso's hit men, Kamo and Tsintsadze.

· · ·

Far from Soso's Tiflis atelier, at the court of the Romanovs, Grand Duke Nicholas told the Emperor he would rather shoot himself than become military dictator. Nicholas II had few choices remaining to him. On 17 October, he bitterly agreed to grant Russia's first ever constitution, an elected parliament, the "Imperial Duma," and a free press. Nicholas soon regretted this generosity: his manifesto accelerated a haemorrhage of ecstatic turbulence and savage violence across the Empire.

The next day on the Caspian, the paraffin-fuelled tinderbox of Baku burst into flames, figurative and real. The Armenians, led by their well-armed Dashnaks, avenged the pogroms of February, heading into the countryside to massacre Azeri villages. Soon the oilfields were burning. In Russia itself, 3,000 Jews were slaughtered in an orgy of pogroms that climaxed on the streets of Odessa.

Stalin was in the boulevards of Tiflis: "Crowds of demonstrators, brandishing the flags of revolution and free Georgia thronged the streets. A huge crowd assembled before the Opera House and, under an emerald-green shining sky, sang songs of freedom," recalls Josef Iremashvili. The excitement was "so great," remembers another participant, "that one richly dressed woman took off her red skirt . . . and made an impromptu red flag." Iremashvili spotted his friend Stalin. "I saw him climbing on to the roof of a tram and gesticulating as he addressed the crowd." But Stalin's excitement was tempered by distrust of the Tsar's concession: if it was shoved a little harder, the rotten throne would surely come crashing down.

The Duma was "a negation of the people's revolution," wrote Stalin. "Smash this trap and wage a ruthless struggle against liberal enemies of the people." The Emperor had lost Russia—and to get it back, he would have to start again and "conquer boundless Russia for a second time."[3]

Stalin and his friends the Svanidzes and the Alliluyevs were living in special times: the viceroy only controlled central Tiflis and his garrisons. In the rest of the city, "Armed workers patrolled the streets as popular militias," says Anna Alliluyeva. "Their ranks were swollen by new friends who appeared on the outskirts of Tiflis on short lean little horses. We always stopped to admire these skilled horsemen in their cowls, enormous sheepskin coats and soft high leather boots . . . peasants and shepherds from the hills."[4] Soso gloried in the drama. "The thunder of revolution is roaring!" he wrote. "We hear the call of the brave . . . Life is seething!"[5]

In the streets, Jibladze led the Menshevik militias. Stalin, Tskhakaya and Budu Mdivani formed the Bolshevik high command. The factions were allies, each controlling their own working neighbourhoods.[6] "The Tiflis suburbs," wrote Trotsky, "were in the hands of armed workers." Didube and Nadzaladevi were so free they were nicknamed "Switzerland." Yet even a year after the *Credo,* Stalin was still deviating towards his Georgian version of Marxism, which was attacked at the Union Committee. The rambunctious Sergo Kavtaradze, one of his Kutaisi henchmen, lost his temper and called Stalin a "traitor."

"I don't intend to have a row about this. You do as you like!" answered Stalin calmly. Then he lit a cigarette and stared unblinkingly right into Kavtaradze's eyes. It was probably then, after the meeting, that the two came to blows. Kavtaradze threw a lamp at Stalin.[7]*

The Svanidze sisters hosted a theatrical fund-raiser for radical causes and proudly introduced Stalin to Minadora Toroshelidze, who was impressed by his speech. "Comrades," he said, "do you think we can defeat the Tsar with empty hands? Never! We need three things: one—guns, two—guns and three, again and again—guns!" He set about getting them. "One of his first coups—and the most insolent—was the pillage in broad daylight of three arms arsenals in Tiflis," says Davrichewy. "In those times, everyone was arming themselves no matter how or what the price!"[8]

The massacres in Baku and the pogroms in Odessa raised the tension in Georgia. Stalin rushed between Baku and Tiflis as mobs in both cities tried to storm the jails. The Revolution seemed on the verge of triumph. In Petersburg, the Soviet, led by Trotsky, defied the Tsar, brazenly promoting itself as a parallel government.† In Moscow, the Bolshevik militia fortified the cavernous factories of Presnaya. But the worm was about to turn: the Tsar, planning vengeance, backed the anti-Semitic Black Hundred nationalists who set up their own death squads to kill Jews and socialists all over Russia. Hardline generals were in the ascendant, troops massed. In Georgia, the Emperor ordered Major-General Alikhanov-Avarsky to crush the Gurian peasants and Chanturian miners: the Cossacks were coming.

On 22 October, seven Georgian schoolboys at the smart Tiflis Gym-

---

* Stalin's reaction to this insult was a surprising one, and he never forgot it. For Kavtaradze's fate, see the Epilogue. The Union Committee united both Bolsheviks and Mensheviks.

† Stalin, writes Trotsky, "spent 1905 in an unpretentious office writing dull comments on brilliant events." Most historians have followed Trotsky's line.

nasium were killed by Russian Black Hundreds. In the ensuing fighting, forty-one died with sixty-five wounded. Stalin's terrorists repeatedly retaliated against the Russian Cossacks and Black Hundreds.[9]

On 21 November, a firefight broke out in Tiflis's Armenian Bazaar between Armenians and Azeris. Twenty-five Muslims were killed. Stalin and the Social-Democrats fielded their gangs to keep the sides apart, believing that the strife was being fomented by the Okhrana. Tiflis was like a "seething cauldron," wrote Trotsky, on the edge of civil war. The desperate viceroy, acknowledging that he had lost control, offered Jibladze the Menshevik 500 rifles to keep the peace. The Battle Squads kept the two sides apart but refused to return the guns.

Davrichewy noticed that the Bolshevik gangsters did not take part because, without Stalin, Kamo could not decide what to do. "During the conflict, Stalin wasn't in Tiflis." Where was he?[10]

As Nicholas prepared to reconquer his turbulent Empire, as the tide of revolution reached its high-water mark, Stalin travelled to Finland to meet his "mountain eagle" for the first time: Lenin.

16

1905: The Mountain Eagle— Stalin Meets Lenin

I was happy to meet the mountain eagle of our Party, a great man, not only politically but also physically too," Stalin reflected, "because Lenin had taken shape in my imagination as a stately and imposing giant." On 26 November 1905, a Party meeting elected Stalin and two others to represent the Caucasus at a Bolshevik conference in St. Petersburg. On about 3 December, using the alias "Ivanovich," Stalin set off for the imperial capital—to meet Lenin.

As Soso and his fellow delegates travelled north by train, the Emperor unleashed his backlash: Trotsky and the Soviet were arrested. Stalin reported as instructed to the Petersburg offices of the SD newspaper, *Novaya Zhizn* (New Life)—but it had been raided. The Georgians wandered the streets until they met a friend on Nevsky Prospect. It is one of the remarkable features of this period that a stranger like Stalin could stroll along the capital's main boulevard and meet someone he knew. It happened repeatedly. But there was little time to see the sights. The friend put them up for two days until they found Lenin's wife, Krupskaya, who gave them money, code names and tickets for the new venue, Tammerfors in Finland, the Tsar's semi-autonomous grand duchy where the freedoms of 1905 survived an extra year.

Stalin and the other forty Bolshevik delegates, poorly disguised as teachers on a day trip, left Petersburg by train and arrived in Tammerfors (now Tampere) at 9:08 a.m. on 24 December, checking into the Hotel Bauer by the station: many of them shared rooms. "How enthusiastic everyone was!" remembers Krupskaya. "The Revolution was reaching its zenith and every comrade seized this with the utmost enthusiasm."

The next morning, Christmas Day, Lenin opened the conference in the People's Hall where the Finnish Red Guards—Bolshevik worker-militiamen—were headquartered.* Stalin waited to see his hero, expecting him to turn up late, having kept his followers in rapt anticipation: he believed this was the way a leader should behave. But instead he was amazed that Lenin was already there "early, chatting with the most ordinary delegates!" And was he a giant? "Imagine my disappointment when I saw the most ordinary man, below average height, in no way different from ordinary mortals."

Unimpressive in person but exceptional in personality, Vladimir Illich Ulyanov, known as Lenin, was small and stocky, prematurely bald with a bulging, intense forehead and piercing, slanted eyes. He was genial, his laughter was infectious, but his life was ruled by his fanatical dedication to Marxist revolution, to which he devoted his intelligence, his pitiless pragmatism and his aggressive political will. Back in Tiflis, Stalin told Davrichewy that it was Lenin's blend of intellectual force and total practicality that made him so remarkable "among all those chatterboxes."

A hereditary nobleman on both sides, Lenin was raised in a loving squire's family. His father was the inspector of schools in Simbirsk, his mother the daughter of a landowning doctor raised to the rank of state counsellor. Descended from Jews, Swedes and Tartar Kalmyks (to whom he owed his slanting eyes), Lenin possessed the domineering confidence of a nobleman:† as a young man he had even sued peasants for damaging his estates. This helps explain Lenin's contempt for old Russia—"Russian idiots" was a favourite curse. When criticized for his nobility, he replied: "What about me? I am the scion of landed gentry . . . I still haven't forgotten the pleasant aspects of life on our estate . . . So go on, put me to

---

* Still the Lenin Museum, one of the last shrines to Lenin in the Western world.
† There were embarrassments in his ancestry: his mother was the granddaughter of Moishe Blank, a Jewish merchant who married a Swede. The prominence of Jews among the Bolsheviks was always an issue in Soviet Russia. Indeed in 1932 Lenin's sister Anna wrote to Stalin about Lenin's Jewish background. "Absolutely not one word about this letter!" Stalin scrawled on it. It remained secret until the 1990s.

death! Am I unworthy to be a revolutionary?" He was certainly never embarrassed about living off the income from his estates.

The rustic idyll on the family estate ended in 1887 when his elder brother Alexander was executed—it changed everything. Lenin qualified as a lawyer at Kazan University, where he read Chernychevsky and Nechaev, imbibing the discipline of Russian revolutionary terrorists even before he embraced Marx. After arrest and Siberian exile, he moved to western Europe, where he wrote "What Is to Be Done?"

"Cunts," "bastards," "filth," "prostitutes," "useful idiots," "cretins" and "silly old maids" were just some of the insults Lenin heaped on his enemies. Revelling in the fight, he existed in an obsessional frenzy of political vibration, driven by an intense rage and a compulsion to dominate allies—and smash opposition.

He cared little for the arts or personal romance. Stern, bug-eyed Krupskaya was more manager and amanuensis than wife, but he did engage in a passionate romance with the wealthy, liberated and married beauty Inessa Armand. Once in power, Lenin indulged in little affairs with his secretaries, according to Stalin, who claimed that Krupskaya complained about them to the Politburo. But politics was everything to him.

Lenin was not a brilliant speaker. It was hard to hear his voice and he could not pronounce his *r*'s but "after a minute," wrote Gorky on first seeing Lenin at this time, "I, like everyone else, was absorbed . . . as I heard complicated political questions treated so simply." Stalin, watching Lenin speak, "was captivated by that irresistible force of logic which, though somewhat terse, thoroughly overpowered his audience, gradually electrified it and then carried it completely!"

Yet Stalin was not ever so lovestruck that he was afraid to contradict Lenin. He was unformed as a politician, but he was already distinguished by a haughty and truculent individuality. Once he had observed the "mountain eagle," he made himself known. Lenin invited him to report on the Caucasus, but when they discussed the elections to the Imperial Duma the two clashed. Lenin advocated participation in the elections, but young Stalin stood up and sharply attacked him. There was silence in the hall until Lenin unexpectedly gave way, proposing that Stalin draft the resolution.

"In intervals of the conference," writes Krupskaya, "we learned how to shoot" Mausers, Brownings and Winchesters. Indeed Stalin carried a pistol. After one debate, he supposedly stormed out and, in a fury, fired his gun into the air outside the hall, a Georgian hothead in the Finnish freeze. But the conference was already out of time: the Bolshevik militia in Moscow rose, too late, in open revolt. Now the delegates heard that the Tsar's Semyonovsky Guards were brutally storming Presnaya, the workers' redoubt. Blood flowed on the streets of Moscow.

Simultaneously in Tiflis, the tough commander of the Caucasus, General Fyodor Griiazanov, and General Alikhanov-Avarsky prepared to retake the Caucasus and destroy the Battle Squads. "The Reaction," said Trotsky, "was in full swing!" The conference broke up in disarray.

Stalin considered himself superior to all the other delegates* except Lenin. "Among all these chatterboxes," he boasted, "I was the only one who'd already organized and led men in combat."

Soso headed back to Tiflis in the midst of battle.[1]

The generals massed their Cossacks, surrounded the workers' districts, banned meetings, ordered shooting of rebels on sight and forbade anyone to wear Caucasian hoods or the cloaks that concealed weapons. On 18 January 1906, General Griiazanov began his assault. Jordania and Ramishvili ordered their partisans, who included Kamo and the Bolsheviks, to defend the Tiflis workers' district.

There was still fighting on the streets when Stalin reached the Svanidze apartment around four days later. Anna Alliluyeva now watched from her window as the Cossacks "moved forward, shooting into the night. By dawn, troops had broken into Didube and Cossacks' horses flashed by our windows, the streets ringed by Cossacks." Tiflis rocked from "uninterrupted shooting, the rattle of artillery fire and cavalry on the streets." Sixty rebels were killed, 250 wounded, 280 arrested. The woody hillsides, she recalls, were thick with dead bodies. She saw "two prisoners,

---

* The most important of these delegates was Leonid Krasin, brilliant engineer, ladies' man and Lenin's financial, terrorism and explosives expert, whom Stalin already knew from Baku. There, Krasin had invented the electrical generating system for oil on behalf of big business while creating an underground printing-press for the Bolsheviks. In 1905, he helped Lenin raise funds through his contacts with the plutocratic industrialists such as Savva Morozov and with the actress Kommissarzhevskaya, who had donated her box-office receipts, but his specialities were terror, bank robbery and bomb-making. At Tammerfors, Stalin also met Emelian Yaroslavsky, who became his chief propagandist in power; Yakov Sverdlov, who shared his exile, became Lenin's chief organizer and first Soviet head of state; and Solomon Lozovsky, Stalin's future Deputy Foreign Commissar, whom he tried and shot in 1952 during his anti-Semitic terror. Lozovsky was the only one of Stalin's victims who had the courage to defy the dictator openly in court: see *Stalin: The Court of the Red Tsar*.

one had blood on his face," and cried out as she recognized "the most courageous and beloved of Stalin's young pupils."

"Kamo!"

As Griiazanov crushed Tiflis, General Alikhanov-Avarsky savagely reconquered western Georgia. The Battle Squads tried to block the railway-tunnel to Kutaisi, but the Cossacks shot, looted, burned and hanged as they advanced. They took Kutaisi. Their "troops, killing anyone they recognized, set fire to the city, robbing the taverns and shops," remembers Tsintsadze. The west was reduced to "ashes and charcoal." Once all was lost, Stalin, travelling in the west, tried to persuade the peasants to disarm, rather than perish, but they would not listen to him: "I was impotent." Then Alikhanov-Avarsky moved eastwards to reconquer the lawless, scorched hinterland of Baku and the Tsar's burning oilfields.

Tsintsadze and his pretty comrade Patsia Goldava arranged a killing-spree of all suspected traitors, who were murdered before they could escape to Tiflis. The gunmen, whom the Cossacks were seeking in the provinces, found refuge in the capital. But the days of Stalin's Battle Squads were over. They returned to the underground where he re-formed them into a secret squad of assassins. He had a task for them already.[2]

Back in Tiflis, under the whip of the Cossacks, Stalin and the Mensheviks met to pass a death sentence. General Fyodor Griiazanov—nicknamed General Shitheap, a pun on his name—the nemesis of the Georgian Revolution, was the most hated man in the Caucasus. Stalin summoned chief assassin Tsintsadze. Soso and the Mensheviks, "working together," jointly ordered another of their hit men, Arsene Jorjiashvili, "who belonged to Stalin's gangsters," to kill the General with the assistance of Kamo. But Stalin also simultaneously commissioned Tsintsadze: "Prepare some good fellows, and if Jorjiashvili fails to do the job in a week, we entrust it to you." Tsintsadze and two of Soso's best hit men started to stalk the General while the other group raced to kill him first.[*]

Within a few days, there were two abortive assassinations, each cancelled because the General was with his wife. Meanwhile, Griiazanov oversaw yet another massacre on the streets of Tiflis.

On 16 February, the General, flanked by a formidable Cossack bodyguard, galloped out of the military headquarters, ignoring a few Georgian

---

[*] This management by competition was typical—it resembles the way Stalin would later order Marshals Zhukov and Konev to race each other to take Berlin in 1945.

workmen painting the railings around Alexander Gardens opposite the Viceroy's Palace. As his carriage passed, the workmen dropped their paints and threw "apples"—their homemade grenades—into his lap, tearing the Butcher of Tiflis to pieces. The Cossacks gave chase. The hit men scarpered, but the wounded Jorjiashvili was swiftly caught and executed, an instant hero in Tiflis.

Who else was on the hit-team? Historians used to agree that the Mensheviks carried out the hit, but actually it was a joint effort. Tsintsadze explains that Stalin and the Mensheviks at that time worked together "in the same organization." An Armenian terrorist said Stalin had commissioned the hit. Davrichewy specifies that the other hit man was Kamo. In the 1920s, two Bolshevik terrorists claimed a pension for killing Griiazanov, their notes recently surfacing in the Georgian archives. Stalin, it seems, commissioned both Menshevik and Bolshevik hit men.

A workman later claimed that he saw Stalin watching nearby, and this rings true because it seems he was injured by bomb fragments or in the rush to escape the Cossacks.

That night, says Sashiko, Stalin did not come home. The girls were worried: had he been arrested? Afterwards, he claimed he had run for a tram, pursued by police, but slipped, hurting himself so badly that Tskhakaya took him to Mikhailovsky Hospital and hid him at Babe Bochoridze's place, then at another safe house, using an old friend's passport. But after the assassination the city was under curfew, with checkpoints everywhere. Soldiers raided the apartment and found "Giorgi Berdzenoshvili" (Stalin) in bed with one bandage round his head, another over his right eye and cuts and bruises across his face.

The Russian soldiers were confused because their orders did not specify what action to take on finding a bandaged man in bed. But, as he looked too ill to move, they left to consult their superiors, sending back a cart to convey the suspicious-looking patient to prison. By then, the patient had disappeared into the night. This was neither the first nor the last time he used the mystery-man-in-bandages trick to escape the police.

In the darkness, a comrade smuggled Stalin, "head and face damaged and hidden in a hood and a big cloak," by phaeton to another safe house.

When Stalin turned up at home with the story of falling off the tram chased by *pharaoh*s, the Svanidze girls were relieved, especially Kato. Sashiko and her husband realized something was happening between the two of them. "Gradually," writes Monoselidze, "when Soso was living at our place, my wife and I noticed that Soso and Kato liked each other . . ."[3]

17

The Man in Grey:
Marriage, Mayhem (and Sweden)

On the initiative and orders of Stalin," said one of his top gangsters, Bachua Kupriashvili,* a permanent gang of brigands was now assembled. "Our tasks were procuring arms, organizing prison escapes, holding up banks and arsenals, and killing traitors." Stalin commissioned Tsintsadze to set up "the Technical Group or the Bolshevik Expropriators Club, it was soon known by another nickname—Druzhina, the Group, or just Outfit."

The "leader of the heists," said Stalin later, "was Kote Tsintsadze, together with Kamo." Stalin's boyhood friend, arrested in the storming of Didube, had been tortured horribly by the Cossacks, who almost sliced off his nose. But Kamo admitted nothing and was released. "He could bear any pain," marvelled Stalin, "an astonishing person."

Soso strained his ingenuity to raise cash for Lenin, travelling widely to Novorossiisk, on the Black Sea, and Vladikavkaz, in Ossetia. In Tiflis, he ordered schools and the seminary to deliver cash from their teachers while he discreetly prepared the Outfit for his gangster rackets.

---

* Bachua Kupriashvili, one of the leading brigands in the Tiflis bank robbery, recorded his memoirs during the Stalin years. He confirms Stalin's direct command of the Outfit but is careful not to link him directly to its heists. The memoirs have remained forgotten in the Georgian archives for sixty years.

Stalin would order the delivery of a letter to a businessman, illustrated with "bombs, a lacerated corpse and two crossed daggers," then come calling with a Mauser in his belt to collect the money, according to several sources. But Stalin's first biographer, Essad Bey, unreliable though often well informed, claims that "Soso obtained his information" about wealthy targets "through his mistress, Marie Arensberg, [a] German businessman's wife in Tiflis." But bank robbery was the fastest way to raise large sums.

"It was Stalin," says Davrichewy, the other notorious bank robber from Gori, "who really opened the age of bank heists in Georgia." The Outfit managed to pull off a spree of daring bank robberies in 1906 even though, as the Menshevik Tatiana Vulikh says, "Tiflis was at war; patrols day and night, cordoning off whole city-blocks."

First, Tsintsadze hit the city pawnshop, bursting in with revolvers blazing, and bagged a few thousand. "One day Stalin's gangsters hit, pistols firing, the Georgian Bank of Agriculture opposite the Viceroy's Palace in broad daylight in Tiflis," recalls Davrichewy. "Shouting 'Hands up!' they grabbed bundles of notes and disappeared firing into the air. Kamo was in command according to a plan devised by Stalin, a superb organizer."

The competition between the bank robbers intensified, but there was a comradeship too. "All the main bank-robbers," boasted Davrichewy, "were from Gori!" It was Davrichewy who pulled off the biggest heist so far, bagging over 100,000 roubles for the Socialist-Federalists in a robbery at Dusheti. Stalin, Tsintsadze and Kamo responded with robberies of ever increasing daring. They held up a train at Kars, though it went wrong and several of the gang were killed in the shootout. Then, in November 1906, Kote held up the Borzhomi stagecoach, but the Cossack outriders fought back. In the shootout, the stagecoach's horses bolted with the money.

Next they held up the Chiatura gold train, bearing wages for the mines. Stopping the train, the gangsters and the Cossack guards fought a two-hour gun-battle, killing a soldier and a Gendarme before the Outfit got away with 21,000 roubles, "of which we sent 15,000 to the Bolshevik faction [Lenin in Finland] and kept the rest for our group to plan for future expropriations," recalls Tsintsadze.

Presently, Stalin's highwaymen held up the Kadzhorskoe stagecoach, bagging another 20,000 roubles. Some was kept to fund Stalin's newspaper *Brdzola*, but most was sent to Lenin, hidden in bottles of Georgian wine.

. . .

"All of them were great friends and everyone loved them: sweet, kind, always cheerful . . . and ever ready to help anyone," remembers Tatiana Vulikh, who knew the gangsters well. The Outfit was about ten strong, including the gun-toting girls Patsia, Anneta and Alexandra. The gangsters lived in a couple of apartments, men in one room, women in another. None of them read much except two of the girls. Mostly consumptive, "They were so poor that they often had to stay in bed because there were not enough trousers to wear between them!"

Stalin socialized with Kamo and Tsintsadze, but he usually gave orders to the Outfit through a bodyguard whom he called his "Technical Assistant,"* though his comrades jokingly dubbed him "Soso's Adjutant." Thus that "great conspirator who rarely walked with other comrades" usually kept himself at least one remove from the ordinary gangsters. Behind the gunmen themselves, Stalin ran his own intelligence and courier network: the little boys at Tamamshev's Caravanserai and at various printing-houses ran errands, delivered pamphlets, gathered intelligence.

The gangsters were not stealing for themselves. The gunmen of other gangs spent the cash on clothes, girls and wine, but Stalin never showed any interest in money, always sharing what he had with his comrades. "Stalin dressed poorly," wrote Jordania, "was constantly in need of money and, in this way, he differed from other Bolshevik intellectuals who enjoyed the good life—such as Shaumian, Makharadze, Mdivani and Kavtaradze." Soso's gangsters shared his Marxist faith and asceticism. Their "gospel was Lenin's *What Is to Be Done?* They would follow Lenin even against the Party," says Vulikh. "Their simple-minded goal was to get 200,000–300,000 roubles and give them to Lenin saying, 'You can do whatever you want with this money.' "

The gangster glamour concealed psychotic Mafia-style brutality: stealing any loot meant death. Stalin ordered Kamo, as Davrichewy witnessed, to execute a comrade suspected of pilfering. The bigger the success, the more dangerous the temptations. After Davrichewy's 100,000-rouble heist at Dusheti, the Federalist gangsters fell out among themselves, killing to carve up the swag. One of their leaders stole a tranche of cash, trying to cover his tracks by blaming the peasants in

---

* The word "technical" was a Bolshevik euphemism for terrorism or killing—both Krasin and the Mensheviks called their bomb-making laboratories their "Technical Departments."

whose garden it had been initially buried. Showing the fraternity between bank robbers, the Federalist embezzler asked Stalin's gunman Eliso Lominadze to recover the proceeds. Lominadze tortured the peasants for an entire night before realizing they had not stolen the cash. "Afterwards he despaired that he'd been so cruel to innocents," says Vulikh. So he murdered the real culprit who had commissioned him. If he had found the cash, he probably would have stolen it for the Bolsheviks. In any case, the money was lost to the Socialist-Federalists: the Okhrana observed their leaders spending the rest of the booty in the casinos of the Côte d'Azur.

The secret police struggled to pin down the culprits of these heists: once they found out about Josef Davrichewy, they blamed him for most of them. But first they muddled him up with Stalin because they were both Goreli gangsters who shared the diminutive "Soso"—and then confused them both with Kamo and Tsintsadze. " 'Kamo' *is* Tsintsadze," reported the secret police, "who escaped from Batumi Prison and arrived in Tiflis where he co-operated with Josef Djugashvhili (whose alias must be 'Soso')."

In this world of swashbuckling heroics and sordid murders, Stalin evolved his stoical views on the value of human life: "When he heard that a comrade had been killed in an expropriation, Soso would say, 'What can we do? One can't pick a rose without pricking oneself on a thorn. Leaves fall from the trees in autumn—but fresh ones grow in the spring.' "[1]

Yet Soso's heists were a means to an end: the seizure of power. Now the boy, who had studied Napoleon even in the midst of raucous drinking parties, kidded himself that he "could seize Tiflis and wanted to take it in armed rebellion—he found a map somewhere." He liked to spread the map on the floor of his hideouts, deploying imaginary regiments in the shape of little tin soldiers. The son of one of his hosts ran to his father to tell him that "Uncle Soso" was "playing soldiers." When the incredulous host peered into the room, he found Stalin lying on the floor moving tin soldiers around the Tiflis map. Stalin looked up and boasted: "I've been appointed commander of the Party's headquarters to devise the plan." He presumably planned his bank robberies with similar diligence.[2]

The stories of deluded but ambitious military operations are revealing because Stalin, who bragged that he had now commanded in battle, always regarded himself as a "military man," a natural commander-in-chief, according to his daughter, Svetlana. One day "Uncle Soso" would play real soldiers with the ten-million-strong Soviet armies that took Berlin, but these tin soldiers were the nearest he ever came to military training.

The bank robberies funded Stalin's newspapers, which were expensively printed at the Party's secret Avlabar press. Stalin edited them, and contributed articles under the bylines "Besoshvili" (Son of Beso) and "Koba."

"I remember well," says Monoselidze, "how Soso entrusted Makharadze [his co-editor] to write two articles and bring them to the press at 9 a.m. but he didn't appear until midday the next day, saying he still hadn't written them . . . Soso came in and he asked why the paper was held up and I told him. He gritted his teeth, stuck a cigarette in his mouth and confronted Makharadze, condemning him . . . Then Soso took the articles from his own pocket and we printed them." Stalin had written them himself anyway.

Stalin "was a wonderful organizer," believed Monoselidze, "and hugely serious, but he'd very rarely lose his temper. Soso often didn't even have cash to buy cigarettes. Once at midnight Kato let him in. He showed me he had fresh vegetables, cucumbers, heads of boiled lamb and pig, and two bottles of red wine."

"Come on, man," exclaimed Stalin. "Let's have a feast! The Party gave me a salary of 10 roubles!"

At the haute couture–cum–terrorist headquarters, the Revolution affected the sweet-natured Kato too: She was in Yerevan Square the day the Cossacks massacred students and workers there. Her sisters, fearing that she was dead, found her helping the wounded in a scene that resembled a minor battlefield.

Stalin and Kato were falling for one another: even when he was on the run, he crept back for trysts in Madame Hervieu's salon. At one rendezvous in the atelier, Gendarme lieutenant Stroev approached the house with two man-hunting German dogs. Madame Hervieu rushed in and warned the lovers. Soso jumped out of the back window—though probably the Gendarme was innocently calling to order a new uniform. Stalin revelled in this sort of escapade. He so often visited his Menshevik friend Minadora Toroshelidze after dark that her mother-in-law started to grumble that her reputation would suffer.

"What can I do? If they see me by day they'll nab me," laughed Stalin. It was to Minadora that he liked to call himself "the Man in Grey."[3]

. . .

On 15 April, the Avlabar printing-press, the Party's most invaluable treasure, was betrayed and raided by the police. Stalin's Menshevik enemies accused him of turning double-agent, a story repeated as truth in most biographies. But did he really betray the printing-press?

In March 1906, Stalin attended a Party conference in Tiflis and Baku sporting "a great coat, and a beard on his sharp face—for he was all sharpness—and a many-coloured scarf in cross-stripes, resembling a Jewish prayer-shawl* plus a sort of bowler-hat." After the conference, Razhden Arsenidze, a Menshevik, claimed that Stalin was arrested but mysteriously released. "I witnessed," writes Arsenidze, "how Stalin was freed from the Gendarme Department and didn't appear at Metekhi Prison despite his stories of his triumphant appearance there to the applause of the other prisoners—that was just the fantasy of a self-enamoured storyteller. There were lots of rumours about his treachery . . ."

Stalin was surely arrested after the conference, possibly detained in another Tiflis prison such as Ortachala, and then released. Most likely, he used his ill-gotten gains to bribe Gendarmes, who were in any case confused about his identity. But he attracted, almost courted, such accusations because he was rude and arrogant, and he specialized professionally in sailing close to the wind. There is not the slightest evidence of this treachery—and there is a rather large hole in the story.

This arrest was said to be at the time of the Avlabar raid, but in fact by 15 April Stalin was on a long, well-documented journey, a thousand miles away, in Sweden.[4]

Around 4 April 1906, Stalin left for Stockholm to see Lenin again, and arrived after a comical journey that featured a shipwreck and an onboard factional punch-up.

He took the train to Petersburg and thence to Hangö in Finland with a hundred others who boarded the ship *Oihonna* for Stockholm. The passengers included Stalin, Krasin and a circus of clowns and performing-horses. The snobbish Mensheviks tried to spend their funds on first-class tickets, despatching the rougher Bolsheviks to third-class. The delegates drank too much and then got into a fistfight, though whether this

---

* This must be the scarf, resembling a Jewish prayer-shawl, that Stalin was wearing in the famous police mugshot (see this book's cover) taken during this mysterious arrest.

involved the clowns is not recorded. Sea air seems to have stimulated pugnacity in the revolutionaries.

Then to cap a truly bizarre scene, just outside the harbour, the *Oihonna* was shipwrecked and the rescue barge *Solid* was sent out but could do nothing. Stalin spent the night on a sinking ship wearing a life-jacket until rescued. They boarded another ship, the *Wellamo,* which finally conveyed them to Sweden.

On arrival in Stockholm, Stalin had to report to the police station, where he was interrogated by the walrus-moustached Superintendent Bertil Mogren of the Swedish Criminal Investigation Department, who frequently served as a bodyguard to King Oscar II. Stalin was, he noted, "small, thin, [with] black hair and beard, pockmarked, big nose, grey Ulster coat and leather cap." Stalin identified himself as "the journalist Ivan Ivanovich Vissarionovich wanted by the [Russian] police," using his father's name as his surname—"Son of Vissarion." He also gave Superintendent Mogren his new birthday—21 December 1879. He had one hundred roubles in his pocket and said he was staying for two weeks at the shabby Hotel Bristol (which no longer exists) near Stockholm Station before heading for Berlin.

The Fourth Congress, opening on 10 April, was a much more important meeting than the Finnish conference because its 156 delegates represented the union of Bolsheviks, Mensheviks, Polish Socialists and Jewish Bundists. Most of the Mensheviks were Georgians: the Bolsheviks were outnumbered. Jordania, Isidore Ramishvili and Uratadze from Kutaisi Prison were among the sixteen Georgians, of whom Stalin was the only Bolshevik.

In Stockholm, he met many of the men* who would be important in his own road to power: he shared his hotel room with a metalworker, mounted postman and working-class dandy (who favoured winged-collars and ballroom-dancing) named Klimenti Voroshilov, who would become his Defence Commissar, First Marshal and accomplice in the 1937 slaugh-

---

* Stalin here met for the first time the Polish socialist Felix Dzerzhinsky, who would become founder of the Soviet secret police, the Cheka, and his ally in the power struggles after Lenin's death; Grigory Radomyslsky, the Jewish milkman's son soon known as "Zinoviev," his triumvir after Lenin's death, whom Stalin liquidated with Kamenev in 1936; and Alexei Rykov, Lenin's successor as Premier, with whom Stalin would share power for a while and then liquidate in 1938. At the Congress, Stalin also met up with old friends Said Devdariani, from the seminary; Kalinin, his future Head of State, whom he knew through the Alliluyevs; and his Tiflis comrade Stepan Shaumian.

ter of the Soviet military. Blond, rosy-cheeked and blue-eyed Voroshilov, another choirboy, was charmed by the "jolly and zestful" Stalin, "a bundle of nervous energy" who liked to sit on his bed reciting poems by heart.

At the Congress, Stalin listened to the titans of Marxism, Plekhanov, Martov and Lenin, but remained proudly his own man on the two main issues: on the peasantry, Lenin proposed nationalization of the land, while the Mensheviks suggested municipalization. Stalin rejected both: the man who would one day oversee the deaths of 10 million peasants in his collectivization campaign, at this time proposed giving land to the peasants. Lenin was defeated with Stalin's help.

When the Congress debated whether to run in elections for the Imperial Duma, most Bolsheviks were against, but Lenin supported the idea and voted with the winning Mensheviks. Stalin abstained. The gathering optimistically called itself the Unity Congress, but the Bolsheviks were simply outvoted. Lenin and Krasin, his urbane money-laundering and terrorism maestro, made themselves scarce when the Congress passed a resolution to ban the bank robberies. Defeat, wrote Stalin, "transformed Lenin into a spring of compressed energy which inspired his followers." But Lenin had no intention of giving up his bank robbing—he needed the money.

Lenin and Krasin must have discussed more bank robberies with Stalin because he arranged for Kamo to travel north from Tiflis to collect guns and bombs from their Finnish villa. If so, this was the first time that Lenin observed Stalin's value as a ruthless underground operator as well as a forceful independent politician.[5]

On the way home, Soso met up in Berlin with Alyosha Svanidze, who was studying at Leipzig University, but he was in Tiflis by June.[6]

"When Soso returned," recalls Sashiko, "it was hard to recognize him. In Stockholm, the comrades had made him buy a suit, a felt hat and a pipe so he looked like a real European. It was the first time we saw him well dressed." Sashiko was not the only sister who was impressed.

"Soso and Kato declared their emotions to us," says Monoselidze. "We started to take the matter in hand."

On 15 July, Soso addressed a secret meeting at the Avlabar People's Theatre until the lookouts ran in to warn that the police were surrounding the building. The Bolsheviks burned their papers. But it was too late to vanish. "When the police asked for an explanation," writes Minadora Toroshelidze, "they all claimed they were 'rehearsing a play.'"

"I know very well what kind of actors you are!" replied the policemen—but let them go.

Outside Stalin greeted Minadora Toroshelidze, pulling her aside with his patron Tskhakaya. "Kato Svanidze and I are getting married tonight," he told them. "You're both invited to come to the party tonight at their house."

Kato "was very sweet and beautiful: she melted my heart," Stalin was to tell his daughter, Svetlana. He later confided in a girlfriend "how much he loved her. You can't imagine what beautiful dresses she used to make!"

A letter he wrote from Berlin, probably on his way home from Stockholm, shows that he respected her. "The news from here promises nothing good," he wrote, "but no use dwelling on it. Perhaps I'll find Alyosha and lead him down the 'wrong path.' Unless this would make Ekaterina Semyonovna [Kato] unhappy. Your friend Soso."

Kato worshipped Soso "like a demigod" but understood him. She "was fascinated by Stalin, and enchanted by his ideas. He was charming and she really adored him," but she knew he was devoted to the cause and that he had a rough temper. In old age, Stalin reminisced that "she was a Rachvelian you know," meaning that she was good-hearted, beautiful and devoted—but there was more to her too. Kato was educated and emancipated by Georgian standards, and socially superior to Stalin. She helped organize SD fund-raisers and was capable of rescuing and treating the wounded after a Cossack massacre. As her sister's memoirs make clear, Kato knew perfectly well that Stalin was organizing his bank robberies, including the Yerevan Square outrage.

She wanted a church wedding—and Soso agreed, even though he was an atheist. But most priests refused to marry him because Stalin, then using the name "Galiashvili," only had false papers. Finally, Monoselidze found Father Kita Tkhinvaleli, of a nearby church, who knew the groom from the seminary. The priest would marry them only at two in the morning.

On the night of 15–16 July, family and friends saw Kato and Soso married in the romantic flickering of candlelight in a small church with Tskhakaya as the groom's witness. The scruffy Stalin "wasn't dressed like a bridegroom," says Elisabedashvili, "and we all laughed throughout the ceremony especially Comrade Soso himself."

Afterwards, Sashiko arranged a wedding supper attended by the hit men Kamo and Tsintsadze, with whom Stalin was already beginning to plot the Yerevan Square bank robbery. Tskhakaya, the *tamada*—the Georgian toastmaster—told jokes; Stalin "sang sweet songs in his sweet voice," while Kamo laughed: "Where are the idiotic police? All their wanted men are here and they could come and trap us like goats!"

The couple were in love. "I was amazed how Soso, who was so severe in his work and to his comrades, could be so tender, affectionate and attentive to his wife," said Monoselidze. But within weeks,* Kato would learn how hard it was to be married to a man whose real wife and mistress was the Revolution.

She was soon pregnant. "All the time he was thinking how to please her," wrote Monoselidze, "when he had time . . . But when he was involved in his work, he forgot everything." Keke, always the realist, was delighted, but she confided in her niece Anna Geladze: "Soso got married. She's a little woman but what kind of family life is she supposed to conduct, I wonder?"[7]

There was no honeymoon. Stalin came alive at night, a risky, trigger-happy existence that stayed with him all his life. The Tsar's ruthless forces of reaction often killed suspects, no questions asked. "It's enough," Soso wrote to the Svanidzes, "just to stay alive and the rest will take care of itself."

Once, at 5 a.m., he and Monoselidze were locking up their secret printing-press when they were challenged as burglars by a policeman who reached for his revolver. But Stalin was quicker on the draw, pulling out his Berdana gun and shouting: "I'm going to shoot!"[8]

---

* According to Ketevan Gelovani, the granddaughter of Kato's mother's sister, whom this author interviewed in Tbilisi, Soso behaved gently towards her except for flashes of temper: "Soon after the wedding, he burned her hand with a cigarette in a fury, but she loved him and he was mostly so kind and tender to her." There is a legend in Finland that he took her on honeymoon to Karelia; however, there is no evidence that she accompanied him to Sweden, and besides they were not yet married.

18

Pirate and Father

S talin was about to open fire when his brother-in-law grabbed the gun. He recognized the terrified policeman who had been bribed not to interfere with their printing-press. Soso's edginess was understandable: the Cossacks had crushed the revolutionaries and the Okhrana was hunting him down, as he organized more heists for the Outfit in different parts of the Caucasus to fund the purchase of arms in Europe. Stalin was away from his new wife for weeks, oblivious to the fact that his life put her in real danger.

Around 9 September 1906, Stalin attended Jordania's SD conference in Tiflis, and then at a Baku hotel. Tsarist repression and Menshevik success had broken the Bolsheviks in Georgia. Besides, the Mensheviks had officially given up terrorism, regarding Stalin and his Outfit as embarrassing bandits. Out of the meagre forty-two delegates, only six, including Stalin, Shaumian and Tskhakaya, were Bolsheviks.

Stalin compensated for this by defiantly sneering at the Mensheviks, on whom he played sinister tricks. "He spent the whole conference smiling ironically," says Devdariani, his Menshevik seminary friend, "thinking 'Make whatever resolutions you like, they're irrelevant to the Revolution.' " Stalin was so "defiant, crude and sullen" that the Menshevik chairman, Arsenidze, accused him of "behaving indecently," like a whore, a "woman of the streets" who wears no knickers. Stalin "jauntily replied that he hadn't yet dropped his trousers." Then, grinning "spitefully from the left side of his mouth," he stalked out. "After a few minutes, we heard the agreed whistle warning us the police were coming. We scattered," says Arsenidze. "But there were no police anywhere. It was Koba's prank."

Yet Stalin had become "the main financier of the Russian Bolshevik Centre," according to the Menshevik, Uratadze, and he remained one of Lenin's chief funders for the next three years. After the conference, it seems likely that Stalin headed west to Sukhum on the Black Sea to open a new front in his campaign of robberies: piracy on the high seas.

On 20 September, the steamship *Tsarevich Giorgi*, 2,200 tons and 285 feet long, was on its way from Odessa to Batumi, carrying passengers and a considerable treasury. Unknown to the ship's captain, groups of Bolshevik gangsters, guns and grenades concealed under felt cloaks, boarded the ship when it stopped to deliver wages at Novorossiisk, Sukhum and New Athos.

At 1:15 a.m., as the sleeping ship passed Cape Kodori, the gang of twenty-five pirates, including "workers and intellectuals," drew Mausers, Berdanas and bombs from their cloaks and held up the ship. The chief gangster, described by the Gendarmes afterwards as a "short Georgian in his twenties with gingerish hair, and freckles," took over the bridge, training his Mauser on Captain Sinkevich. The duty officer, steersman and crew were held at gunpoint, though four sailors probably assisted the pirates as "inside men."

The chief pirate, reported the crew later, was glacially calm and courteous throughout the heist. "We're revolutionaries through and through, not criminals," he announced. "We need cash for the Revolution and we'll take only Treasury funds. Obey my commands and there'll be no bloodshed. But if you're thinking of resisting, we'll kill you all and blow up the ship."

"I submitted," Captain Sinkevich admitted in an interview with the *Tiflissky Listok* afterwards. The crew and passengers were gathered and warned "to see nothing." The captain showed the money to the chief gangster. The police announced officially that the Bolsheviks took 16,000 roubles, but the pirates probably bagged much more.

The gangster boss ordered Captain Sinkevich to lower the lifeboats. The pirates held some of the ship's officers hostage as they loaded the cash, after which they ordered the sailors to row them ashore. They were conveyed so efficiently that the pirate chief, "being touched by their extremely conscientious obedience to his orders, ordered each sailor to be given a 10-roubles tip." The *Tsarevich Giorgi* was free to sail for Batumi.

On raising the alarm seven hours later, Cossacks and Gendarmes hunted the Bolshevik pirates along the coast without finding a single trace of the gang or the loot. Stalin and two Russian Bolsheviks hid at the home of Stepan Kapba, one of the gang—as remembered by his sister years later. Then, the sister testified, they moved on to another safe house belonging to the Atum family, and finally on to the Gvaramia home. As an old man, Kamshish Gvaramia recalled how Stalin arrived at his house. His father was excited at being asked to "hide the pockmarked chieftain of the gang that held up the mail-ship off Cape Kodori who subsequently became leader of this great country."

Stalin and the gangsters moved westwards through Abkhazia, across the Enguri River, into Guria. Old men told the writer and compiler of Abkhazian history Fasil Iskander how Stalin ordered the murder of seven unreliable gangsters (including the four collaborating sailors) and then led a train of horses packed with cash across the hills, a carbine over his shoulder. Iskander tells the story in his classic *Sandro of Chegem*. After delivering the cash to henchmen in Kutaisi, Stalin caught the train to Tiflis, leaving the bodies to be "eaten by jackals."

Did Stalin really lead the pirate heist? The police description of the pirate chieftain fits Stalin in style, looks and speech: he too often insisted that he was "a revolutionary not a criminal." But the description is very vague. Most memoirs claim that he organized, but did not participate in, the robberies.[*]

Yet we know from the memoirs of the Svanidzes and Davrichewy that Stalin carried a gun and was not shy of using it at this time. The well-informed Menshevik Arsenidze explained that Stalin "did not participate" in the notorious Tiflis heist but added, "There were a whole bunch of expropriations." He heard that "even Stalin had participated" in one of them. Stalin had connections at the ports of Novorossiisk, New Athos and Sukhum, where the pirates boarded the ship—he had visited these places in 1905. Stalin's practise of leading packponies with saddlebags full of banknotes over the hills is confirmed by Father Gachechiladze's memoirs cited earlier.

---

[*] This was true especially after the 1907 London Congress banned expropriations and ordered expulsion from the Party for those who disobeyed. But this was September 1906—the London Congress was in the future.

This was not Stalin's only involvement in piracy. He later orchestrated the robbery of another mail ship and planned several others in Baku.* The Abkhazian historian Stanislav Lakoba, whose other researches are meticulous, followed the legend to its source and managed to interview, independently of each other, two aged witnesses before they died. They confirmed that he had led the attack and collected the cash.

The dates fit perfectly. Stalin was not at home. The Baku conference had ended. These few days are blank. The ship was robbed on 20 September and it would have taken Stalin a few days to reach Tiflis. As arranged with Lenin and Krasin in Stockholm, Kamo and two of Stalin's comrades were waiting in Tiflis to set off on a trip to buy weapons for the Party.

There is no documentary proof of Stalin's role, but his participation is at the very least highly plausible. It certainly looks as if the robbery was timed for a reason—and Kamo received the money.

Five days after the holdup, on 25 September, Kamo left Tiflis with enough cash to travel round Europe and buy arms.[†]

Kamo, accompanied by the loquacious actor-revolutionary Mdivani and Kavtaradze, who had thrown the lamp at Stalin, first took the train to St. Petersburg. They were met and given instructions by Krasin, who ran the "Bolshevik Centre," their clandestine headquarters in Finland, with Lenin and his ally Alexander Bogdanov, philosopher and organizer. This threesome were known as the "Small Trinity."

Krasin knew Stalin from Baku and Stockholm. Always in stiff white collars and sporting a well-tended Charles I beard, he lived a double life: on one hand, he was a socialite womanizer and friend of millionaires; on the other, his bomb factories provided murderous devices for the Bolsheviks and other terrorist groups.[†] "His dream," says Trotsky, "was to create a bomb the size of a walnut." He never accomplished the walnut-bomb.

Krasin was the first in a line of sophisticated worshippers of violence

---

* This piracy was quite common among the revolutionary bandits: Stalin's Gori alter ego, Davrichewy, chief of the military wing of the Socialist-Federalists, tells how he robbed a ship carrying funds at roughly the same time as the *Tsarevich Giorgi* heist. Meanwhile, off Odessa, revolutionaries seized a noble dinner-party on a pleasure ship, the *Sofia*, where they grabbed £5,000 in gold.
† At this time Krasin loaned his most advanced infernal device to the Maximalist-SR terrorists, who used it to blow up the house of the Tsar's brilliant Premier Stolypin. Many were killed in the inferno but Stolypin survived.

to "almost fall in love with Kamo," whom he put in contact with Meyer Wallach,* a worldly Jewish Bolshevik with spectacles and wavy fair hair.

Kamo and the two Georgians met Wallach in Paris. The Jewish fixer and the Armenian psychopath worked well together, travelling to Liège, in Belgium, Berlin, then Sofia, in Bulgaria, to buy arms, mainly Mausers, Mannlicher rifles and ammo. In Varna on the Black Sea, they bought a leaky yacht, the *Zara,* loaded it with arms, appointed as captain a revolutionary sailor from the battleship *Potemkin,* and hired four crew. Kamo volunteered as cook and enforcer, wiring up the boat to his berth so he could blow it up if Tsarist agents tried to board. In the Black Sea, a storm rocked the *Zara,* which sprang a leak, then ran aground. Kamo ignited his suicidal dynamite—but it failed to explode. The captain tried but failed to commit suicide. Seamen and cook were rescued, freezing, by a passing sailing-boat. The *Zara* sank, the spoils of Stalin's piracy returning to the waves.

Kamo made it back to Tiflis, where Stalin had a new idea for a colossal bank robbery. A few months earlier, in Tiflis, he had bumped into a certain Voznesensky who had studied with him at the Gori Church School and the Tiflis Seminary. Voznesensky told his school friend that he now worked in the Tiflis banking mail office with access to the invaluable, secret schedules of the cash stagecoaches. Stalin invited him for a cup of milk at the Adamia milkbar, where he was persuaded to help the Bolsheviks expropriate money that passed through the mail office. Voznesensky, who was interviewed by a secret Party investigation in 1908, confessed that he agreed to help "*only* for Koba" because "Koba wrote a poem on the death of Prince Eristavi of such revolutionary character: it impressed me so much." Only in Georgia could a terrorist receive the timing and tip for a robbery because he was such a fine poet!

Stalin introduced Voznesensky to the Outfit, keeping in contact and meeting his inside man every few months. He had last met Voznesensky in late 1906, so it seems the Okhrana was right that the robbery was originally planned for January or February 1907. But it had not happened. In his own surly and laconic answers to a cross-examination by a Menshevik Party inquiry, Stalin confirmed that he had been behind the world's most notorious heist, running the two "inside men," including the "one Comrade Koba knows from school," whom he had introduced to the Outfit.

---

* Later Stalin's People's Commissar for Foreign Affairs during the 1930s, Maxim Litvinov.

Stalin's other "inside man" was Grigory "Gigo" Kasradze, another Goreli, a cousin of Keke and Father Charkviani, who was interviewed by a different Party investigation committee. He too was groomed by Stalin for months before the robbery. Both were part of Stalin's own private intelligence network.

Kamo, after the sinking of the *Zara*, lacked the necessary armaments for these new operations so Stalin sent him back to see Krasin. A grand sympathizer, Prince Koki Dadiani, lent him his passport, allowing him to travel to the capital in style. At their Finnish hideout, Kamo met Lenin and Krupskaya. "He was a fearless fighter of limitless audacity and unbreakable willpower," Krupskaya observes, "but also exceedingly sensitive, somewhat naïve . . ." Lenin called him his "Caucasian bandit," thrilled that he always packed two pistols, which he regularly invited Krupskaya's noble mother to strap on. Lenin and Krupskaya, both brought up with privilege and culture, courted Kamo. They were always drawn to the glamour (and utility) of brutal cutthroats, following the sentiments of the anarchist Bakunin: for the Revolution to triumph, he wrote, "we must join with the swashbuckling robber-world, the true and only revolutionaries in Russia."

Entranced by Kamo's simple-eyed sweetness, the Lenins sensed that his strange tranquillity might, at any moment, be shattered by an act of insane violence. He once met the Lenins for lunch saying he had a present for them, which he slowly placed on the table wrapped in a napkin. "Everyone went silent. 'He's got a bomb!' they thought," recounts Krupskaya. "But it was a watermelon." Kamo returned to Tiflis with a shipment of grenades.[2]

Lenin, according to Stalin's gangster Kupriashvili, ordered Stalin to raise much-needed funds to pay for the coming London Congress. Stalin kept in contact with Kamo and his inside men in the banking system but also travelled back to Baku, where he was busy founding and editing the Russian newspaper *Bakinsky Proletary* (Baku Worker) with Shaumian and Spandarian. Involved in so much skulduggery, Soso seemed untouchable. But, while he was away, his wife was not so lucky.

During a raid on a Bolshevik in Moscow, the Okhrana found a note that read: "3 Freilinskaya Street, seamstress Svanidze, ask for Soso." Not long afterwards, Kamo asked the Svanidzes to host a "Moscow Jewish comrade" for two weeks. The sisters welcomed him but soon after his departure, on 13 November 1906, the Gendarmes raided the house asking for

Soso and Kato. The sisters realized that the "Moscow Jewish comrade" was a traitor. The Gendarmes fortunately did not find either Soso or his documents hidden inside the fashion mannequins. But Kato was arrested—along with her cousin, the bomb-maker Spiridon Dvali, who was sentenced to death. This was no joke for a girl already four months pregnant.

Sashiko Svanidze sprang into action to help Stalin's wife, calling in the favours of her clients, who included most of the Gendarme officers: "I went to see the wife of Gendarme Colonel Rechitsky (whose dress I was making at the time) and requested her to reduce Dvali's death penalty and to release the innocent Kato." The Colonel's wife did get Dvali's sentence reduced and helped the pregnant Kato even more by allowing her to await her release in a police station instead of prison. The sisters were also making the gowns for the wife of the police station chief, who immediately took Kato home with her and looked after her.

On Stalin's return after his frantic shuttling around the Caucasus, "He was deeply despondent about what had happened," notes Monoselidze. "He insisted on visiting Kato," so Sashiko went to see the wife of the police station chief and "told her our cousin from our village had come to visit Kato. The police officer's wife permitted it, so we took Soso to their apartment at night and they had a rendezvous there. Fortunately none of them knew Soso by sight. The police officer's wife demanded that Kato be allowed home for two hours every evening. Soso and Kato met every evening like that" until her release two months later.

Soon after her release, on 18 March 1907, Kato was delivered of a son, Yakov.* According to Kato's cousin Ketevan Gelovani, Soso was present for the birth along with his mother. Keke and "the little woman" Kato got on very well. Stalin was over the moon at being a father. "After the birth of the baby," Monoselidze observes, "his love for wife and child became ten times more." He nicknamed the baby "Patsana" (Laddie). Writing day and night, however, Stalin became "irritated when the baby's crying disturbed his work. But as soon as the mother fed it and the baby stopped crying, he kissed him, tickling his nose, fondling him."

Soso had much on his mind. That March 1907, Stalin's Outfit planned a heist on the Kutaisi stagecoach, but, just before the chosen day,

---

* Known as Yasha to the family, he was christened months later and registered years later—hence confusions about his birth. The name was probably a tribute to Stalin's protector, Yakov "Koba" Egnatashvili.

its chieftain, Tsintsadze, was arrested. Stalin appointed Kamo as his successor. Stalin's pet psychopath was more than capable of controlling the band of bandits, always tottering between simple enthusiasm and frenzied killing. When he heard a Bolshevik, probably Stalin, arguing theory with a Menshevik, he exclaimed: "What are you arguing with him for? Let me slit his throat." Kamo, with Tsintsadze's female gunslingers Anneta, Patsia and Alexandra, held up the Kutaisi stagecoach—but the Cossacks fired back. Kamo and the girls found themselves in the midst of a savage firefight, but when it was at its most intense the girls swooped in and grabbed the money-bags, which they then smuggled to Tiflis in their lingerie. "Anneta and I wrapped it around our bodies," recalls Alexandra Darakhelidze. Kamo hid the cash in wine-sacks and sent it to Lenin in Finland.

Stalin's inside men in the banking mail now informed the Outfit that a huge delivery was due in Tiflis—it might be as big as a million roubles, enough to fund Lenin's expensive organization for years. Stalin and Kamo prepared for a spectacular heist.

Barely a month later, Stalin, elected as non-voting delegate to the Fifth Congress, left Laddie and Kato in Tiflis, setting off on a long journey via Baku, St. Petersburg, Stockholm and Copenhagen. Stalin, travelling under the name "Ivanovich," was on his way to London.[3]

Around 24 April, when he was in Denmark, he took the train down to Berlin to meet Lenin. We know they met secretly on this trip and that Stalin visited Berlin. They had one subject to discuss: the imminent Tiflis bank robbery. If Lenin went to Berlin, writes Trotsky, "then it was not for theoretical conversation but was undoubtedly devoted to the impending expropriations and the means of forwarding the money." The secrecy was aimed as much at their comrades as at the Okhrana: the Party, now dominated by Mensheviks, had banned brigandage.

Lenin and Stalin then proceeded separately to London.[4]

19

Stalin in London

On 27 April/10 May 1907, after a tedious journey, Stalin and his companions Tskhakaya and Shaumian disembarked at Harwich, in England. Catching the train to London's Liverpool Street Station,* they were greeted by sensational headlines in the English press, thrilled to have exotic "Anarchists" loose in the capital, which, then as now, was a notorious refuge for murderous extremists.†

The delegates were met by an incongruous crew of English reporters and photographers, twelve Special Branch detectives and two Okhrana agents, as well as by local sympathizers who were either English socialists or Russian exiles.

"History is being made in London!" declared the *Daily Mirror*, which seemed to be most fascinated by the fact that some of the revolutionaries were "women burning with zeal for the great cause"—and by their lack of

---

* They were not meant to be in London at all: the original plan was to hold the Congress in Copenhagen, so Stalin travelled to St. Petersburg, then to Finland and on to Malmö in Sweden, whence he and his fellow delegates were ferried to Copenhagen. But the Danes expelled them to Sweden, which sent them back to Denmark, which despatched them to Esbjerg, where they caught a steamship to London.

† The other big news during these weeks was a plot against the life of the Tsar and a photo-portrait of the three-year-old Tsarevich Alexei headlined: TSAREVICH WEARS HIS FIRST PAIR OF KNICKERS; the wedding of the Tsar's cousin Grand Duke Nicholas to the daughter of the Prince of Montenegro; and the birth of a son to the English Queen of Spain, headlined AN ENGLISH BABE.

luggage in that age of stately travel. "There is not a man over forty and many little over twenty"—Stalin was twenty-nine, Lenin was thirty-seven (but "we always called him the Old Man," Stalin said later). "It was," concluded the *Daily Mirror*, "a most picturesque crowd."

As with the Soviet Union itself, the delegates were meant to be equal but some were more equal than others. Maxim Gorky, "the famous novelist," said the *Mirror*, "is in London but where he is staying, only his intimate friends know." Gorky resided with his actress-mistress in the comfort of the Hotel Imperial in Russell Square, where Lenin and Krupskaya joined them. It was wet and cold when they arrived. The domineering Lenin took charge, checked Gorky's sheets for dampness and ordered the gasfire lit to warm their wet underwear.

"There's going to be a right old scuffle here," Lenin told Gorky as the Leninist socks dried. The delegates with private incomes stayed in small hotels in Bloomsbury, though Lenin and Krupskaya took rooms in Kensington Square, whence he headed out every morning to pick up his favourite takeaway, fish and chips, outside King's Cross Station. However, money was extremely short for the poor delegates like Stalin.

Legend says he spent the first nights with Litvinov, whom he now met for the first time, in the Tower House hostel on Fieldgate Street, Stepney, which the novelist Jack London called the "monster dosshouse": it cost sixpence for a fortnight. Its conditions were so dire that Stalin supposedly led a mutiny and got everyone rehoused. He was settled into a cramped first-floor backroom at 77 Jubilee Street in Stepney, which he rented from a Jewish-Russian cobbler and shared with Tskhakaya and Shaumian.

Foggy and wet, London was an intimidating city for a visitor from Georgia. "At the outset I found London swallowed and suffocated me," wrote another Russian Communist visitor, Ivan Maisky, later Stalin's Ambassador to London. "I felt lonely and lost in its giant stone ocean . . . with its grim rows of little houses swallowed up in a black fog."

If London was foreign, Whitechapel, where Russian was commonly spoken, was more familiar. One hundred and twenty thousand Jewish refugees from the Russian pogroms, gangsters and socialists among them, lived in the East End. Lenin visited Rudolf Rocker's Anarchist Club, near Stalin's rooms in Stepney, where he ate Jewish gefilte fish. Stalin probably did so too. Soso also could hardly have missed the savage jungle of Slavic-Hebraic gang-warfare. The East End gangs, all from the Russian Empire, controlled so-called rookeries of "shootflyers" (gold-watch thieves) and "whizzers" (pickpockets). Three gangs vied for supremacy: the Bessarabian Tigers fought the Odessans, who fought the Aldgate Mob led by Darkie the Coon (a swarthy Jewish gangster named Bogard).

On arrival, Stalin and the others registered at the Polish Socialist Club on Fulbourne Street off the Whitechapel Road across from the London Hospital.* Observed by Special Branch detectives and excited journalists, they received their sparse allowance of two shillings a day, guidance on how to find the main Congress, and secret passwords to avoid Okhrana infiltration.

Meeting upstairs in "modest premises with little furniture belonging to a socialist club with tables and chairs and foreign autographs on the walls," the Bolsheviks started the political business with their own factional meeting at which they elected a secret committee, and like all good conferencers, "They studied the city map." But the *Daily Mirror* had no time for such mundane details. "The women are said to be conspicuous for their unflinching courage and nerve," the reporter revealed admiringly. "Revolver practise enters their daily exercise. They drill themselves constantly in front of the mirror by which they become adept in aiming and pulling the trigger . . . Most of these are young girls, one being eighteen wearing her long fair hair in a long coil down her back."

The eagle-eyed *Daily Express,* however, noticed "a sturdy resolute-looking man who . . . stood at the corner of Fulbourne Street, obviously a foreigner and equally obviously a person of some importance. Apparently unconcerned, he was taking a lively interest . . . This was Monsieur Seveff, one of Russia's secret police, and his duty is to keep watch on the Russian Socialists"—who, that paper added significantly, "had little luggage."

The delegates then proceeded to the SD Fifth Congress, taking the bus or walking to Islington, where they were amazed to find they were meeting in a church, the Brotherhood Church on Southgate Road: "down the dim and dirty streets of working-class quarters, it was like dozens of buildings, soot-grimed walls, high narrow windows, grimy roof with a short steeple." Inside, the delegates found "a simple bare room that could hold 300–400." Gorky was unimpressed by the church décor, "unadorned to the point of absurdity." The vicar, the Reverend F. R. Swan, whose flock included the future Labour Prime Minister Ramsay MacDonald, was a pacifist follower of William Morris.

---

* Now a furniture warehouse, a camera shop and a gentleman's outfitters.

On 30 April/13 May 1907, the father of Russian Marxism, Plekhanov, opened the Congress after delegates sang a funeral hymn for fallen comrades. Stalin watched how Lenin often sat with the tall, haunted and spectre-thin Gorky, international celebrity and Bolshevik fund-raiser who had once watched a hanging in Gori.* The Bolsheviks sat on one side, the Mensheviks on the other; every vote was "ultra tense."

There were 302 voting delegates representing 150,000 workers, but after the glory days of 1905 the Party was in dire straits, shattered by Nicholas II's repressions. There were 92 Bolsheviks, most of whom were determined to continue the armed struggle of 1905 and avoid participation in the Duma. They were outnumbered by 85 Mensheviks, 54 Jewish Bundists, 45 Polish-Lithuanians and 26 Letts who supported participation in the Duma elections. Lenin also wanted to adopt the strategy of gun and ballot-box favoured in our time by terrorists from the IRA, Hamas and Hezbollah. So he used Menshevik help to win that battle before turning on them again.

The entire Party was shrinking, but the Bolsheviks had been so routed in Georgia that Stalin, Tskhakaya and Shaumian were only consultative delegates without votes.

"Who is that?" Stalin supposedly asked Shaumian as a new orator took the podium.

"Don't you know him?" answered Shaumian. "It's Comrade Trotsky"— real name Lev Bronstein, the undoubted star in London, who had just pulled off an escape from Siberia by dashing 400 miles through the tundra on a reindeer-propelled sleigh. Here Stalin first saw (and probably shook hands with) Trotsky, who for his part did not recall meeting his nemesis until 1913.

While Stalin had been commanding his militias in Chiatura, Trotsky had been Chairman of the Petersburg Soviet. Effortlessly brilliant in writing, dizzyingly eloquent in performance, unmistakably Jewish in accent, and shamelessly vain, Trotsky, with his dandyish suits and plumage of mane-like tresses carefully bouffed, possessed the shine of international radical celebrity, light-years ahead of Stalin. Despite being a rich Jewish farmer's son from faraway Kherson Province, he was overweeningly arrogant, regarding Georgians as bumpkin "provincials."

Lenin, who had nicknamed him "the Pen" for his virtuoso journalism,

---

* Later in life, Gorky would become the dictator's friend, shameful apologist, pathetic trophy and possibly victim. See *Stalin: The Court of the Red Tsar*.

now complained that Trotsky was showing off. Stalin, whose gifts lurked in the shadows while Trotsky's glittered in the spotlight, hated him on sight: Trotsky was "pretty but useless," wrote Stalin on his return. Trotsky simply sneered that Stalin "never spoke."

It was true that Stalin did not speak during the entire Congress. He knew that the Mensheviks, who hated him for his truculence and banditry, were gunning for him as part of their campaign to ban bank robberies and score points off Lenin. When Lenin proposed the vote on credentials, Martov, the Russian Menshevik leader, prompted by Jordania, challenged the three nonvoters, Stalin, Tskhakaya and Shaumian.

"One can't vote without knowing who's involved. Who are these people?" asked Martov.

"I really don't know," replied Lenin insouciantly, though he had just met Stalin in Berlin. Martov lost his challenge.

"We protest!" shouted Jordania, but to no avail. Stalin henceforth loathed Martov, real name Tsederbaum, who was, like Trotsky, Jewish.

The Jewish presence irked Stalin, who decided that the Bolsheviks were "the true Russian faction" while the Mensheviks were the "Jewish faction." There must have been some grumbling about this in the pub after the sessions. "It wouldn't be a bad idea for us Bolsheviks," said the Bolshevik Alexinsky to Stalin "in jest," "to organize a pogrom in the Party." At a time when thousands of Jews had just been slaughtered in pogroms, it was a "jest" in poor taste.* Its resentment of Jewish intellectuals exposed Stalin's burning inferiority complex. But here too is the emer-

---

* Stalin slyly blamed this on Grigory Alexinsky in *Notes of a Delegate,* his account of the London Congress published under the name "Koba Ivanovich" in *Bakinsky Proletary.* He pointed out that the "majority of Mensheviks were Jews, then came Georgians and then Russians. On the other hand, the overwhelming majority of the Bolshevik group were Russians, then came Jews (not counting Poles and Letts of course), then Georgians . . ." Much has been made of the Jewish nature of the SDs, but Stalin's figures show how Georgian the Party was too. Arsenidze asserts that Stalin was "neutral" on the Jews, merely interested in what was useful politically. In his articles, he was sympathetic to their plight: "Groaning under the yoke are the eternally persecuted and humiliated Jews who lack even the miserably few rights enjoyed by other Russian subjects." On a related theme, he also attacked the Mensheviks for being "intellectuals" instead of workers and expressed amazement that the Mensheviks had attacked the Bolsheviks for containing too many intellectuals: "We explained the Menshevik shouts by the proverb: 'The tongue ever turns to the aching tooth.' " As we have seen, this was a favourite phrase. As for the challenge to his credentials, most histories retell this to diminish his importance and standing, but never mention that the respected Tskhakaya and Shaumian were challenged simultaneously. There was another reason for Lenin's insouciance. He had offered a merger deal to the Georgian Mensheviks: if Jordania did not interfere in Russian matters, he could become leader of a united Party in Georgia. Jordania never took up the offer.

gence of Stalin the Russian (for there was no anti-Semitism in Georgia, where Babylonian Jews had lived for two millennia without a single pogrom). Weary of Georgia's petty squabbles and Menshevik dominance, he was ready to concentrate on Baku and Russia herself. Henceforth he wrote in Russian, not Georgian.

Lenin got his way at the Congress. More Bolsheviks than Mensheviks were elected to the Central Committee, while he continued to keep his secret Bolshevik Centre. "Now," reflected Stalin later, "I got to see Lenin in triumph."

However the Mensheviks did achieve one resolution that affected Stalin: they passed a rigorous condemnation of bank robberies that decreed expulsion from the Party for anyone who broke the rules. They appointed the gay Menshevik aristocrat Georgi Chicherin (later the second Soviet People's Commissar for Foreign Affairs) to investigate all the bank robberies since the Stockholm Congress. "Stalin was very reserved during that meeting, mostly silent, keeping himself in the shadows," noticed Devdariani, his Menshevik friend. Trotsky later understood that Stalin was preoccupied with his bank robberies in May 1907: "Why did he bother to come to London? He must have had other tasks."

Outside, "Curious Englishmen gathered and just stared at us as if we were animals from faraway lands!" The press besieged the building while the early versions of paparazzi pushily photographed the shy revolutionaries, who begged them to desist. RUSSIAN REVOLUTIONISTS AFRAID OF CAMERA! headlined the *Daily Express*. "Do you realize that the reproduction of those portraits could mean death?" one Russian told the newspaper, not realizing that all the precautions were irrelevant.

The spooks were already inside the church. The Russian secret police—then as now—was irritated by the English tendency to grant asylum to Russian dissidents. "Because of London's liberalism, it'll be impossible to count on co-operation of local police forces," complained A. M. Garting, the director of the Okhrana Foreign Agency, based in Paris. Two agents followed the revolutionaries to England. Special Branch and the Russian secret policemen lurked in the street to the delight of the press, but the Okhrana did not need outside help—their double-agent Yakov Zhitomirsky, who received 2,000 francs a month, was one of two traitors inside the Congress. In the Okhrana archives, we find the speeches reported as tediously as in the official protocols.

Lenin was at his best in London. Inside the church, the delegates ate during sessions, but funds were dwindling. Lenin worried that his Bolsheviks were not eating enough, so he arranged for Gorky's mistress to distribute beer and sandwiches.

After sessions, Lenin chatted to delegates on the grass in the sunshine of Hyde Park, lectured them on English pronunciation, laughed with them unaffectedly, gave them tips on cheap accommodation and took them to his favourite pub, the Crown and Woolpack in Finsbury, where a Special Branch detective was said to have hidden in a cupboard to eavesdrop though he spoke no Russian. On 13 May, Stalin may have attended his only Chelsea soirée. In an early case of radical chic, the artist Felix Moscheles invited the Marxists to a reception filled with guests in evening dress at his house at 123 Old Church Street. There Ramsay Mac-Donald toasted the Russians; Plekhanov and Lenin responded. Their hosts expressed surprise that they were not kitted out in white tie.

Stalin was not in Chelsea most nights—he spent more of his time on the rough side of town. His experience was surely like that of Maisky: "I tramped along dreary streets, feebly lit by antiquated gas-lamps, crossed deserted bridges, seeing glimpses of dark shadowy canals beneath. I saw London's belly and heard the calls of prostitutes and brazen laughter of their drunken escorts. I nearly fell over homeless creatures sleeping on the steps of closed shops." At some point, in a pub, Stalin was almost beaten up by East End dockers. Litvinov supposedly rescued him. According to his daughter, Litvinov joked that this was the only reason Stalin later spared him, saying, "I haven't forgotten that time in London."

Back in Stepney, Mister Ivanovich (a.k.a. Stalin), who wore a tunic-style jacket, baggy trousers and high boots, spent much time in his room reading, but he also employed a youth named Arthur Bacon to run errands. "Stalin wrote a letter to someone a street or so away," recalled Bacon in an interview after the Second World War, "and wanted it taken round by hand. He couldn't write English so the cobbler's wife addressed the envelope." Bacon was usually paid a halfpenny per errand, but Stalin gave him two bob: "That was money then, you know," said Bacon. Stalin, either generous or ignorant, had paid him 4,800 percent above the going rate. "His favourite treat was toffee," added Bacon. "I bought him some every day."

While Stalin was living in East End penury, he probably saw little of London. The Bolsheviks were so politically obsessed and culturally parochial, they scarcely noticed either natural or cultural landmarks. To admire a city, wrote Trotsky, "you have to expend too much of yourself. I had my own sphere of activity which brooked no rival: Revolution." Soso was the same. He hardly had any money, but during the Second World War he confided in one of his young diplomats, Andrei Gromyko, later Soviet Foreign Minister and President, that he had spent his time "in churches listening to the sermons—the best way to learn English." Despatching Gromyko as Ambassador to Washington, he suggested he do the same.

Meanwhile the Congress had run out of cash to pay the sixty-five roubles for each delegate to get home. Something had to be done. The Russian-Jewish socialist Fyodor Rothstein, who had helped organize the Congress, appealed to the leftist journalist H. N. Brailsford of the *Daily News* and the Labour MP George Lansbury. They approached the tycoon Joseph Fels, American owner of the Fels-Naphtha Soap Company.

"Before I decide," replied the soap baron, "I want to see these people." Brailsford and Lansbury took Fels to the Brotherhood Church to watch a session. "How young they all are, how absorbed!" exclaimed the Philadelphian, who offered the Party £1,700. Fels's loan agreement stipulated, "We, the undersigned delegates" must repay him by 1 January 1908. Fels insisted it be signed by every delegate. Lenin agreed but then ordered the revolutionaries to use only aliases. They duly signed this extraordinary document in English, Russian or Georgian. Lenin probably just signed "Vladimir." It is believed Stalin used a favoured alias: "Vasily from Baku." Fels died before Lenin came to power, but his heirs were repaid in 1917.

When Churchill* met Stalin for the first time in 1942, they bonded, after a frosty start, in a nocturnal Kremlin drinking marathon at which the Prime Minister asked about this London visit.

"Lenin, Plekhanov, Gorky and others were there," Stalin answered.

"Trotsky?" asked Churchill about the enemy whom Stalin had had assassinated two years earlier.

"Yes, he was there," replied Stalin, "but went away a disappointed man not having been given any organization to represent such as the Battle Squads which Trotsky hoped for . . ." Even thirty years later and after murdering his great enemy, Stalin was still proud that he had commanded Battle Squads while the celebrated War Commissar Trotsky had not.

---

* Churchill, aged thirty-three, was living at his bachelor flat at Mount Street W1 while Stalin, twenty-nine, was staying as Koba Ivanovich in Stepney. Already Under-Secretary for the Colonies in the Liberal government of Sir Henry Campbell-Bannerman, he had just published his biography of his father, Lord Randolph. He was famous enough for a biography of himself to be published, the first. While Stalin was in England, Churchill travelled up to give a speech in Scotland which was reported in the papers.

"The London Congress is over," reported "Koba Ivanovich," Stalin's latest pseudonym, in the *Bakinsky Proletary,* "ending in the victory of Bolshevism."

However Stalin and Shaumian remained in London to nurse Tskhakaya, who had fallen sick. "I had a temperature of 39 or even more," recounts Tskhakaya, so Stalin and Shaumian stayed on "to care for me because we all lived in one room."

There is a legend among Welsh Communists that, after the Congress, Stalin forsook his nursing duties to visit the miners of the Valleys: after all, his 1905 stronghold, Chiatura, was a mining town. But despite a miraculous blossoming of sightings of "Stalin in Wales" among the Communists of the Rhondda during the Second World War, there is not the slightest evidence that he visited Wales.* Besides, he had not yet invented the name "Stalin." But he was also supposedly spotted on the docks of Liverpool, a Scouse version of his encounter with the London dockers. Sadly, "Stalin in Liverpool" belongs with "Stalin in Wales" in that fabulous realm of urban mythology, regional aspirational fantasia and leftist personality cult.[1]

After about three weeks in London, Soso spent a week in Paris. Then, borrowing the papers of a just-deceased Georgian, Simon Jvelaya, he arrived home in Tiflis on the eve of the big bank robbery.[2]

---

* "Stalin in Wales" persists: the Welsh writer John Summers "confirmed" it on a visit to the mining town founded by a Welshman, Hughesovska (now Donetsk) in the Soviet Union in the 1970s. A Welsh website still lists Stalin among "scary individuals who have spent quality-time in Wales," alongside the serial-killer Fred West, the magician Aleister Crowley, the Nazi Rudolf Hess and the Ugandan tyrant Idi Amin: "Stalin briefly visited the South Wales valleys to garner support and raise funds for the Russian Revolution." Of Stalin's helpers, Fyodor Rothstein, the Bolshevik fixer in London, became Soviet Ambassador to Persia, dying before the Terror. His son Andrew Rothstein enjoyed a strange career between the English Establishment and the Stalinist *nomenklatura,* he studied at Oxford University, then worked in the Marxism-Leninism Institute during the Terror and was fortunate to survive, later returning to London to become the sage of British Marxism. In one of his more bizarre reminiscences, Stalin told a group of British MPs during the Second World War that he had seen Benito Mussolini, then a socialist, at a Marxist meeting when he was in London. It is possible he did see Mussolini at some socialist conference in Germany, but the future Duce was not then in London. Stalin's English errand-boy Bacon became a hospital orderly at Beckenham Hospital. He gave an interview to the *Daily Express* in 1950 when he was fifty-six. "I wonder if Generalissimo Stalin, Father of all the Russias, remembers the tall boy who bought him toffee," concluded Bacon. The house on Jubilee Street no longer exists.

20

Kamo Goes Insane:
The Game of Bandits and Cossacks

On 10 May 1907, Kamo was setting the fuse on one of Krasin's bombs when it exploded in his face. He almost lost an eye, but he managed to get secret treatment and recover sufficiently to lead the Outfit on the big day that was getting closer. The other gangsters missed their arrested chief, Tsintsadze, considering Kamo a self-promoting attention-seeker. "Kamo was very pleased with himself," said Kupriashvili, "showing off his value to important comrades and bragging."

Stalin got home by 4 June, just after Nicholas II's energetic Premier, Peter Stolypin, launched his reactionary coup, resetting the Duma election rules to ensure a conservative majority and intensifying his harsh crackdown on the revolutionaries. Many were arrested, many deported to Siberia in prison-trains dubbed "Stolypin carriages," and so many hanged that the noose was nicknamed "Stolypin's necktie." There had been 86,000 political prisoners in 1905; by 1909 there were 170,000.

Kamo gathered a large team of Georgia's finest hoodlums and bank robbers, including the core of the Outfit and the five female shooters. They lived and waited in a small communal apartment while Kamo himself rented a grand residence, "living under cover as a prince." The Okhrana believed there were about sixty brigands involved in the heist, so it is likely that the Bolsheviks recruited help from the SRs and other top triggermen: the terrorists often cooperated, most recently when Krasin provided the SRs with the bombs to dynamite Premier Stolypin's home. If the SRs hoped for a cut of the booty, they were to be disappointed.

Stalin informed the Bolshevik Tiflis Committee of Lenin's orders given to him in Berlin; they approved the operation. He must have expected local outrage and international scandal: Kamo and the gunmen resigned temporarily from the Party, on Lenin's suggestion, thus technically liberating themselves from the London resolution. Stalin and Shaumian planned to move to Baku directly afterwards. The Bolsheviks were finished in Georgia, with as few as 500 supporters. Soso was consciously burning his Georgian bridges and starting afresh in a more ambitious enviroment.*

Early on 13 June, Kamo confirmed to Stalin and Shaumian that the heist would take place that day. The gangsters waited at the Tilipuchuri Tavern, where Stalin was supposedly seen early that morning.† Somewhere before 10 a.m., rigged up in his officer's uniform, swashbuckling his Circassian sabre, Kamo rode out into Yerevan Square; the gangster boys and girls took up their positions. It was a warm summer's day.

When the bombs shook the city, Kato Svanidze Djugashvili was cuddling Stalin's three-month-old baby, Laddie, on the balcony beside her sister, Sashiko. "We rushed inside, absolutely terrified," says Sashiko Svanidze. For the rest of the day, the wounded were treated in makeshift surgeries. Cossacks and Gendarmes galloped through the city, raiding houses, cordoning off boroughs and blocks in the hope of recovering the money before it left Tiflis.

"That night," reports Sashiko, "Soso came home and told us that Kamo and his gang had done it, stealing 250,000 roubles for the Party."

---

* The Bolshevik position in Georgia was undermined by the assassination of the hugely popular Prince Ilya Chavchavadze, who had published Soso's poems, in August 1907. The Bolsheviks had attacked his patriarchical version of Georgian culture and, it was widely believed, had decided to kill him; there is some evidence that Stalin's friend Sergo Ordzhonikidze organized or took part in the assassination. It may be that the SDs played no role in the murder at all. Stalin always praised Chavchavadze's poetry in his old age and there is no evidence that he ordered the hit, but he was very close to Sergo and he was certainly more than capable of separating literary merit from cruel necessity: politics always came first.

† Stalin himself later implied he was in the Tamamshev Caravanserai and saw Tsintsadze give the gangsters their pep talk, but Tsintsadze had just been arrested. Perhaps the old dictator was muddling this bank robbery with another, that of 1912 (see Chapter 29). In 1907 Kamo was presumably the pep talker.

He must have told the sisters about Kamo's playacting because they realized why he had just borrowed their father's sword. The Svanidze memoirs show that, far from being innocently oblivious of Stalin's double life, Kato was perfectly aware that she was married to the godfather of bank robberies in the Caucasus. But Stalin suddenly informed the family that his wife and baby were to leave imminently for Baku. The Svanidzes did not approve. They must have felt strongly, because even in the 1930s the family dared criticize Stalin for taking her on the thirteen-hour train ride "in such a hot summer" and with a baby. But it was to no avail: "Soso left for Baku and took Kato," grabbing 15,000 roubles for his future plans.

Kamo lay low. Before leaving, he graciously offered Stalin's "inside man" 10,000 roubles for his help. Voznesensky graciously accepted 5,000.

Now things again started to go wrong. The police announced that 100,000 roubles in 500 denomination notes were marked. Some gangsters wanted to burn the notes. Kamo refused. The rest of the cash was in smaller denominations.

All the hoodlums wanted to meet Lenin, but Kamo's eye needed foreign treatment, so it was he, bearing most of the money, who took the train via Baku to Lenin in Finland. Prince Koki Dadiani, whose family had once ruled Mingrelia, again lent Kamo his passport. Adding a new layer to this favourite disguise, Kamo now posed as the Prince accompanied by his new young bride (one of the female gangsters, ironically, but usefully, a policeman's daughter) on the day after his wedding. The Outfit's girls were already experienced in hiding money and dynamite on their persons: the dynamite gave off a harsh acidic stench especially when strapped to a sweating body, so the ladies had to douse themselves in scent. Money was easier, the swag travelled in the bride's lingerie and clothes. Venal policemen had probably been bribed to turn a blind eye.

Kamo delivered the equivalent of around £1.7 million ($3.4 million) in today's money to Lenin, enough to fund the faction for some time. Kamo spent the summer with his hero, planning a giant "spectacular." But the reaction soon caught up with Lenin, who fled to Geneva, where "the Swiss burghers," writes Krupskaya, "were frightened to death ... and could talk of nothing except the Russian expropriations." "Georgia" became a byword for gangsterism: when Tskhakaya visited them in a *chokha* coat, their landlady almost fainted with alarm and "with a shriek of fright, she slammed the door in his face."

This was far from the end of the story: the Tiflis bank robbery made

Kamo a legend,* but its repercussions would help shatter the Party and were still threatening to damage Stalin as late as 1918.[1]

As in every successful criminal enterprise, the hoodlums were soon fighting over the spoils. The police had published the serial numbers of 100,000 roubles of the notes. They would be very hard to cash, but Krasin's Technical Group forger, known as Fat Fanny, changed some of the numbers on the notes. Lenin and Krasin decided to proceed, particularly since the rest of the heist-money was clean. The money was instantly smuggled abroad. Some was laundered through the Credit Lyonnais Bank. Litvinov distributed the cash to his operatives to change the money in different cities.

Meanwhile the secret police frantically pulled out the stops to catch the culprits, but they could discover nothing concrete. Their Tiflis informers, particularly one code-named "the Fat Lady," revealed that SR gunmen had participated but had been robbed of their share of the spoils.

Their first suspect was the *other* Gori bank robber, Davrichewy, who was (according to Okhrana reports) "hiding in Lausanne under the name of Kamo."

The Okhrana knew that "Kamo sent all the money to Krasin and Lenin," but now the revolutionaries started to fall out. Lenin cashed at least 140,000 roubles from the proceeds of Kamo's robbery. But in 1908 he embarked on a vicious if esoteric feud that would again tear the Party in half. He broke with Bogdanov and Krasin,† who purloined about 40,000 roubles of the Tiflis money for themselves. Litvinov sent "two Georgian terrorists" to tell them that if they did not return it fast, the Georgians would "bump off" one of the Central Committee.

Lenin was soon short of money again. Bank robberies were not his only dubious source of funding. He ordered a pair of roguish Bolshevik con men to seduce two unprepossessing sisters who had inherited the

---

* The other gangsters, who had actually conducted many more heists, were jealous of Kamo's fame. "Our Outfit was called the Kamo Group," says Bachua Kupriashvili, "but it wasn't true. We accepted Kamo into the group over a year after it had been set up. He played his role in this big action after which everything was ascribed to him . . . But Kote Tsintsadze, Intskirveli, Eliso Lominadze . . . were not inferior and probably superior to Kamo."

† Lenin published an epistemological polemic, "Materialism and Empiricism," which attacked Alexander Bogdanov's mystical philosophical relativism, which he believed threatened Marxist materialism.

huge fortune of their uncle, Schmidt, the late industrialist. The double seductions were successful, though Lenin admitted that he would not have been able to do it himself. One of the seducers, Victor Taratuta, stole considerable sums of the inheritance to spend on high living before passing on the remainder to Lenin.

Kamo, now in Berlin, decided to help out by pulling off the biggest bank robbery of all, a 15-million-rouble heist "that would fund the Party for six years but cost at least 200 lives." Hoarding stocks of dynamite and using a passport in the name of Mirsky, an insurance agent, he travelled in August to Berlin to procure explosives. But Lenin's man in Berlin was Dr. Zhitomirsky, the double-agent who had informed the Okhrana about the London Congress. Zhitomirsky now betrayed Kamo.

On 27 October/9 November 1907, the German police raided Kamo's hotel room and found numbered banknotes and 200 dynamite fuses, twelve fulminates of mercury and twenty electric batteries. The Okhrana were excited but they still did not know the identity of "Mirsky." On 31 October/13 November, Garting, director of the Tsar's Foreign Intelligence Service, announced triumphantly that "Mirsky" was planning a "vast heist" and that he had some of the Tiflis banknotes, but there was no proof of his participation in the actual outrage. The Okhrana still believed that Davrichewy was "Kamo." So who was "Mirsky"?

Finally the Okhrana got lucky. On 1 March 1908, a former Bolshevik brigand in Kutaisi Prison, Arsen Karsidze, revealed that the chief bank robber was Simon Ter-Petrossian, known as Kamo, now held as "Mirsky" at Berlin's Alt-Moabit Prison. Another report confirmed that Davrichewy was in exile in Switzerland and was not Kamo after all.

The Tsar's government applied to extradite Kamo, who would face the death penalty. Krasin rushed to Berlin to orchestrate his defence and hired the German leftist attorney Oscar Kohn. Krasin advised Kamo to feign insanity, a role he was more qualified to play than most.

Kamo started to act like a madman in a way that only someone who had truly cracked could. He managed to maintain it for two whole years. First he started to bawl, cry, tear his clothes, beat the jailers. They moved him to a frozen dungeon where he was kept nude for nine days. He apparently did not sleep and spent the nights standing up for four months. Then he stopped eating; they force-fed him by tube. He pulled the hairs out of his head; tried to hang himself but was cut down; slit his wrists but was resuscitated. In May 1908, they moved him to Berlin's Bukh psychiatric hospital for diagnosis. He copied other patients and adopted that great cliché of madness: he pretended to be Napoleon. The doctors were still sceptical and decided to put him through a series of torments that would have broken anyone else. He was burned by a red-hot iron and needles were driven under his nails, but he withstood it all. At last the Germans accepted that he was insane and, washing their hands of the troublesome loon, handed him over to the Russians, who, regardless, put him on trial for the Tiflis "outrage" and its fifty casualties. In court, the shambling, raving Kamo suddenly pulled a bird, Petka the greenfinch, out of his sleeve during the trial and talked crazily to his avian friend instead of the lawyers.

Premier Stolypin and the viceroy, Vorontsov-Dashkov, were determined to hang him. But his lawyer, Kohn, orchestrated such a successful European publicity campaign against the execution of a lunatic that Stolypin reluctantly decided that hanging would "unfavourably affect Russian interests."

In tests, the Russian doctors found that Kamo's skin did not register pain. They stuck more needles under his fingernails, then electrocuted him. "The burned flesh," Kamo mused, "stung terribly." Those doctors too were convinced.

In September 1910, Kamo was declared insane and locked up forever in the Metekhi Fortress's unit for the criminally insane. The Bolsheviks acclaimed Kamo's heroism, but one doctor explained that "only a terribly ill patient in a state of madness behaves this way." Kamo, writes the historian Anna Geifman, was a creature of "unresolved passions and anxieties . . . unable to function normally . . . Feigning insanity, he actually was insane."

Meanwhile the police tracked the marked banknotes which started turning up all over Europe. In Paris Litvinov found a detective under his hotel bed: he was arrested with twelve marked banknotes but was deported to London. Krasin was picked up in Finland. Other money-changers were arrested in Munich, Zurich, Paris, Berlin and Stockholm.

"The Mensheviks did not get a penny [of the Tiflis heist cash]," reported the gleeful Okhrana, so "they demand on the basis of the resolutions of the London Congress to expel all these expropriators from the Party."

Stalin was in trouble.[2]

The outraged Mensheviks commissioned three different committees, operating over two years, to investigate who had organized the Tiflis bank robbery, one headed by Jordania in Tiflis, a second by Jibladze in Baku, and a third abroad, under Chicherin. The murderous heists damaged their reputation, but they also wanted to destroy Lenin, using Stalin and Kamo.

The Mensheviks managed to interrogate virtually all the key culprits, including Stalin himself, interviewed as "Comrade Koba" in Baku. Astonishingly, this survives in the archives, the first direct evidence of his involvement. The "inside men," Kasradze and Voznesensky, admitted everything, blaming Stalin. Lenin asserted his own innocence to Chicherin, since the heists "had been carried out by non-Party members." The Committees in Tiflis and Baku, according to Arsenidze and Uratadze, voted to expel Stalin. But the Party was already split, hence it is questionable if the Mensheviks had the power to expel a Bolshevik.

They nonetheless collected the evidence against Stalin to confront Lenin. In August 1908, they met in Geneva, where Martov lambasted Lenin. Noe Ramishvili named names—including the usual suspects Kamo and Tsintsadze—then declared that "all of these acted under the direction of Comrade Koba."

Lenin jumped up to interrupt. "Don't give the family name of this last," he snapped.

"I won't," smiled Ramishvili, "because we all know that he's well known as the Caucasian Lenin." Stalin would have been proud.

"You take responsibility that these names won't be divulged to the police?" insisted Lenin. The secrecy of Stalin's meetings with Lenin had paid off: the Mensheviks could nail Stalin but could not implicate Lenin. But if any proof were needed of their relationship as early as 1907–8, Lenin's protection of Stalin provides it.

It seems that Stalin was expelled, though surely not by the Central Committee but locally, in Tiflis and Baku. If proven, even this would have been a real blot on his revolutionary legitimacy.

When the Bolsheviks came to power with Stalin as one of Lenin's closest henchmen, the Mensheviks tried to undermine them by resuscitating the whole affair. Martov published an article in 1918 that listed three examples of Stalin's banditry—the Tiflis heist, the murder of a Baku worker, and the piratical holdup of another ship called the *Nicholas I* off Baku. Worse, Martov wrote that Stalin had been expelled from the Party in 1907. In 1918, Stalin needed the credentials of a long-serving Old Bolshevik and sensed danger in the expulsion story. So, somewhat hysterically, he attacked this "contemptible act of an unbalanced, defeated man" and sued Martov for "this filthy libel" before the Revolutionary Tribunal, one of the strangest trials in Soviet history.

Stalin neither denied nor admitted his role in the heists, but insisted, "Never in my life was I tried before any Party organization and expelled," which was probably literally true because the Committees in Tiflis and Baku were Menshevik, not Bolshevik, and any expulsion was informal. Witnesses were going to be summoned to Moscow, but it was hard to do so during the Civil War. The trial was cancelled, and Martov reprimanded, but Stalin had made his point.

"You're a wretched individual," he snarled at Martov, who went into exile.* When Stalin returned to Tiflis in 1921 as a conquering Bolshevik, he was booed at a meeting and openly called a "bandit" to his face: he stormed out. Stalin's brigandage and expulsion were never mentioned again during his reign.

Most important, Lenin did not take Stalin's local expulsions seriously: "Such expulsions are almost always based on errors, unverified reports or misunderstandings . . ." Of course he knew more about it than he let on, but he increasingly recognized that Stalin, terrorist, gangster and covert organizer, had the "right stuff."[3]

The uproar about the Georgian job had been spectactular, but the heists were not over yet. The game of "bandits and Cossacks" was rougher still in Baku, where the stakes were much higher than in Tiflis. They proved too high for Kato.

---

* After Lenin's death in 1924, Stalin's Bolshevik legitimacy became hugely important as he tried to prove himself worthy to become the heir. If Martov had proved Stalin's expulsion, he might have saved Russia from Stalinism.

21

The Tragedy of Kato: Stalin's Stony Heart

Stalin settled Kato and Laddie, their baby, in the apartment of an oil worker and plunged himself into a life of banditry, espionage, extortion and agitation, the murkiest years of his entire career. Probably again on the Rothschild payroll, he soon moved his little family outside Baku city into a "Tartar house with a low ceiling on the Bailov Peninsula which he rented from its Turkish owner," just above a cave, right on the seaside.

Kato, a born homemaker, made the shack cosy, with a wooden bed, curtains and her little sewing-machine in the corner. Visitors noticed the contrast between the sordid exterior and the tidiness inside—but Soso was not often there. Kato did not know many people, but Sergei Alliluyev visited them. He was now the manager of the local power plant and lived with Olga and the children in a villa by the sea. It was here in Baku that their youngest daughter, Nadezhda, wearing a pretty white dress, fell over the edge of their sunny yard into the Caspian Sea. Stalin jumped in and rescued her, a romantic tale, often retold as she grew up.

Always dressed in his trademark black fedora, Stalin gave a speech on 17 June 1907, the very day he arrived, and threw himself into his editing of the two Bolshevik newspapers, *Bakinsky Proletary* and *Gudok* (Whistle); he immediately set about dominating the Party there with his brand of aggressive politics, terrorist intimidation and gangster fund-raising.

Everywhere in Russia, "The reaction had triumphed, all liberties destroyed and revolutionary parties smashed," recalls Tatiana Vulikh, but Baku, ruled as much by the oil companies and corrupt policemen as by the Tsar's governors, followed its own rules. Stalin was on the run in Tiflis, but for a few months before Stolypin's next crackdown he could stroll the Baku streets. Tiflis, said Stalin contemptuously, had been a parochial "marsh" but Baku "was one of the revolutionary centres of Russia," its oil vital to the Tsar and the West, its workers a true proletariat, its streets violent and lawless. Baku, wrote Stalin, "would be my second baptism of fire."[1]

Baku was a city of "debauchery, despotism and extravagance," and a twilight zone of "smoke and gloom." Its own governor called it "the most dangerous place in Russia." For Stalin, it was the "Oil Kingdom."

Baku was created by one dynasty. Swedish by origin, Russian by opportunity and international by instinct, the Nobels made their first fortune selling land mines to Tsar Nicholas I, but in 1879, the year of Baku's first "fountain" of oil, the brothers Ludwig and Robert Nobel founded the Nobel Brothers Oil Company in the town known mainly for the ancient Zoroastrian temple where Magi priests tended their holy oil-fuelled flames.* The drilling had already started; entrepreneurs struck oil in spectacular gushers.

The Nobels started to buy up land particularly in what became the Black City. Another brother, Alfred, invented dynamite, but Ludwig's invention of the oil tanker was almost as important. The French Rothschilds followed the Nobels into Baku. By the 1880s, Baron Alphonse de Rothschild's Caspian Black Sea Oil Company was the second biggest producer—and its workers lived in the industrial township called the White City.† By 1901, Baku produced half the world's oil—and the Nobel Prize, established that year, was funded on its profits.

Its oil boom, like the Kimberley Diamond Fever or the California Gold Rush, turned peasants into millionaires overnight. A dusty, windy ex-Persian town, built on the edge of the Caspian around the walls and

---

* The Persian word for fire is *azer*—hence the name of the country, Azerbaijan.

† They were soon joined by an Englishman, Sir Marcus Samuel, later Viscount Bearsted, founder of Shell. In 1912, Eduard de Rothschild, Alphonse's son, sold most of the Rothschild interests in Baku to Royal Dutch Shell, then headed by Henri Deterding. The Rothschilds took most of their payment in Royal Dutch Shell shares. This proved a classically brilliant Rothschild deal. The Rothschilds eschewed oil investments in Russia for almost a century—making another fortune in the Russian oil boom of the twenty-first century. The ex-Rothschild palace is now Azerbaijan's Justice Ministry.

winding streets of a medieval fortress, was transformed into one of the most famous cities in the world.

Its "barbaric luxury" filled the newspapers of Europe, scintillated by instant riches, remarkable philanthropy and preposterous vulgarity. Every oil baron had to have a palace, many as big as a city block. Even the Rothschilds built one. The Nobels' palace was called Villa Petrolea, and was surrounded by a lush park. One oil baron insisted on building his palace out of gold but had to agree to cover it with goldplate because the gold would melt; another built his mansion like the body of a giant dragon with the entrance through its jaws; a third created his vast palace in the shape of a pack of cards emblazoned in golden letters: "Here live I, Isa-Bey of Gandji." A popular singer made his fortune when a performance was rewarded by some land on which oil was struck: his neo-classical palace is now the headquarters of Azerbaijan's state oil company.

Baku was a melting-pot of pitiful poverty and incredible wealth, its streets, observes Anna Alliluyeva, full of "red-bearded Muslims . . . street porters called *ambal*s bent under excessive loads . . . Tartar hawkers selling sweetmeats, strange figures in whispering silks whose fiery black eyes watched through slits, street barbers, everything seemed to take place in the streets," crowded with tribesmen in pleated coats with jewelled daggers, Persians in waistcoats and felt hats, Mountain Jews in fur hats, and Western millionaires in frock coats, their wives in French fashions. Stalin called its workforce of Turkish Azeris, Persians, Russians, Chechens and Armenians "a national kaleidoscope." The rich promenaded down the Seaside Esplanade shadowed by carriages of gun-toting bodyguards.

Yet the source of all this money, the derricks and the refineries, poisoned the city and corrupted the people. "The oil seeped everywhere," says Anna Alliluyeva. "Trees couldn't grow in this poisonous atmosphere." Sometimes it bubbled out of the sea and ignited, creating extraordinary waves of fire.

The Black and White Cities and other oil townships were polluted slums. The 48,000 workers toiled in terrible conditions, living and fighting each other in grimy streets "littered with decaying rubbish, disembowelled dogs, rotten meat, faeces." Their homes resembled "prehistoric dwellings." Life expectancy was just thirty. The oilfields seethed with "lawlessness, organized crime and xenophobia. Physical violence, rapes and bloodfeuds dominated workers' everyday lives."

Baku, states Stalin, was "irrepressible," its rootless proletariat ideal for the Bolsheviks. It was especially corrupt; its moral ambiguities and duplicitous opportunities suited Stalin's conspiratorial cynicism. It was said that there were only ten honest men in the entire city (a Swede—Mr. Nobel, of course—an Armenian and eight Tartars).

"Equal parts Dodge City, medieval Baghdad, industrial Pittsburgh and nineteenth-century Paris," Baku "was too Persian to be European but much too European to be Persian." Its police chiefs were notoriously venal; its Armenians and Azeris armed and vigilant; its plentiful gunmen, the *kochis*, either performed assassinations for three roubles a victim, guarded millionaires or became "Mauserists," gangsters always brandishing their Mausers. "Our city," writes Essad Bey, "not unlike the Wild West, was teeming with bandits and robbers."

In Baku, brashly taking on oil barons, and Menshevik and Bolshevik "rightists," Stalin prospered to become the revolutionary and criminal kingpin of the Oil Kingdom. It was through Baku* that he, belatedly, found a national Russian role, graduating from "an apprentice to a craftsman of the Revolution." Here he became the "second Lenin."[2]

In August 1907, when poor Kato was suffering grievously from the stifling, polluted heat of Baku, Stalin returned to Germany to attend the Congress of the Second International in Stuttgart. He met up with Alyosha Svanidze, still studying at Leipzig. Soso and his brother-in-law, writes Monoselidze, "went sightseeing, visiting meetings of German workers in restaurants, and cafés."

The Germans "are a queer people like sheep," Stalin later told the Yugoslav leader Milovan Djilas (he told Churchill the same story). "Wherever the ram went, they just followed." On the way to the conference, some German Communists felt unable to leave the station because there was no ticket-collector. They were so obedient to the rules that, Stalin said, "They actually missed the meeting for which they'd made the entire trip." He joked that a Russian comrade had shown them a "simple solution: leave the platform without handing in the tickets!"[3]

Soso was back in Baku in time for another outbreak of ethnic turbulence. On 19 September, an Azeri worker named Khanlar was murdered

---

* Stalin had "great knowledge of the oil industry," wrote his Georgian protégé Mgeladze. Baku became enormously important in 1942 when Hitler, in desperate need of oil, ordered his armies to push towards the oilfields. The result was the Battle of Stalingrad, which in effect was the battle for Baku. Stalin called in his Deputy Oil Commissar, Nikolai Baibakov: "Hitler wants the oil of the Caucasus. On pain of losing your head, you're responsible for ensuring no oil is left behind . . . Do you know Hitler has declared that without oil he'll lose the war?"

by Russian nationalists. In protest the workers went on strike. Stalin spoke at the funeral demonstration.

At a meeting soon afterwards, he and the Bolsheviks routed the Mensheviks and took control of the local organization: Baku became a Bolshevik city. Soso concentrated on his work, but, Monoselidze notes, "when he was involved, he forgot everything"—including Kato.

"Soso loved her so much," says Elisabedashvili, who joined him in Baku. "Wife, child, friend were only okay if they didn't hinder his work and saw things his way. You had to know Soso to understand his love."

"It was too hot in Baku" for Kato. "Soso would go early in the morning and return late at night while Kato sat at home with a tiny baby terrified that he would be arrested," remembers Monoselidze. "Bad diet, little sleep, the heat and stress weakened her and she fell ill. Surrounded by strangers, she had no friends around her. Soso was so busy he forgot his family!"

Stalin knew he was being a neglectful husband and father, but, like many who have suffered broken families, he could not change his behaviour. He must have talked about it with Elisabedashvili: "Soso regretted it and was angry at himself for having married in such circumstances."

Kato "prayed that Koba would turn away from his ideas and return to a peaceful homelife." But he had chosen a mission that in many ways let him off the normal responsibilities of a family man. Bolshevik wives knew this. "Am I a martyr?" Spandarian's much cuckolded wife, Olga, asked of her marriage to Stalin's friend—but she might have been describing Stalin too. "I make as much as I can of my life. My path is not covered with roses but I chose it . . . He's not for family life but that doesn't diminish his character. He carries out his mission . . . It's possible to love a man and forgive him everything for the sake of the good he has inside." Kato knew that Stalin, like Spandarian, had "sworn to remain for ever a true Knight of the Grail" of Marxism.*

The Svanidzes in Tiflis heard first that Kato "was very thin," recalls her sister Sashiko, who invited her to recuperate in their home village.

"How can I leave Soso?" replied Kato.

Soon the Svanidzes heard from Elisabedashvili that "she was sick and

---

* Trotsky too was neglectful: he abandoned his wife and two daughters in Siberia, blaming "Fate"—and later treated his children appallingly. Bolshevism and family were incompatible.

they wrote to ask Soso to bring her back." Kato begged him. Now she was really ill, "but he kept postponing the trip until she became weak and suddenly he realized he had to act immediately." In October, Stalin was sufficiently alarmed to escort her back to Tiflis. But the journey itself, more than thirteen hours, was debilitating: "It was too hot on the way and she drank bad water at a station." Afterwards, Soso hastened back to Baku, leaving her with her family.

Back at home, she deteriorated. Already weak, exhausted and malnourished, she had contracted typhus, which is usually accompanied by a fever and diarrhoea. Its speckled rash showed first red and then darkened ominously. Historians usually diagnose her illness as tuberculosis, but if so it had infected her innards. Family and friends, whose memoirs were not available to previous historians, agree on a diagnosis of typhus along with haemorrhagic colitis. Kato haemorrhaged blood and fluid in miserable spasms of dysentery.

Stalin rushed back again from Baku to find the mother of his Laddie dying. He "nursed her desperately and tenderly, suffering himself," but it was too late. She supposedly called for a priest to give her final sacraments and Stalin promised her an Orthodox burial. Two weeks after her return home, on 22 November 1907, Kato, aged just twenty-two, "died in his arms."* Stalin was poleaxed.[4]

---

* The family, who were there and know best, write that she suffered a stomach complaint, haemorrhagic colitis and typhus. Almost certainly Kato suffered intestinal or peritoneal TB (not always associated with pulmonary TB), which leads to weight loss, stomach pain, diarrhoea and bowel bleeding. Levan Shaumian, who grew up in Stalin's home in the 1920s, says she died of TB and pneumonia. Typhus is spread by infected water and food, typhoid by bedbugs and reduced resistance, but both flourish among the poor and malnourished—and both can lead to bleeding bowels and darkening rashes. There was no treatment until the 1950s. Katevan Gelovani, a close Svanidze relative interviewed in Tbilisi by this author, calls it "stomach cancer," which may be her explanation of the bleeding from the bowels. Mariam Svanidze, another cousin still alive in Tbilisi (aged 109) and interviewed by this author on 31 October 2005, remembers the death clearly. "I was then nine years old. Kato and my father got typhus at the same time. Books say Kato died of TB, but I can assure you it was typhus," says this sturdy and lucid centenarian wearing a floral dressing-gown in a Tbilisi old people's home. "Both got the red rash. We knew if the rash went black, they'd die. My father's rash stayed red. He lived, but I remember that Kato's turned black. Then all the family knew she'd die. And die she did."

22

Boss of the Black City: Plutocrats, Protection-Rackets and Piracy

Soso closed Kato's eyes himself. Stunned, he managed to stand beside his wife's body with the family for a photograph but then collapsed. "Nobody could believe Soso was so wounded," wrote Elisabedashvili. He sobbed that "he couldn't manage to make her happy."

Soso was in such despair that his friends were worried about leaving him with his Mauser. "I was so overcome with grief that my comrades took my gun away from me," he later told a girlfriend. "I realized how many things in life I hadn't appreciated. While my wife was alive, there were times I didn't return home at night. I told her when I left not to worry about me but when I got home, she'd be sitting there. She'd wait up all night."*

The death was announced in *Tskaro* newspaper;† and the funeral was

---

* Stalin's reaction to the death is very similar to his behaviour after the suicide of his second wife, Nadya Alliluyeva, in 1932, down to the suicide threat, self-pity and blaming himself for neglect.

† The announcement of the death read: "We notify our comrades, friends and family of the death of Ekaterina Semyonovna Svanidze Djugashvili, expressing the deepest sorrow on behalf of Josef, husband, Simon and Sepora, parents, and Alexandra, Alexander and Mariko, siblings." Mikheil Monoselidze adds, "In 1936, I buried my wife, Sashiko, next to Kato." Sashiko died of cancer, but it might have been a mercy. By the early 1930s, the Svanidzes were among Stalin's most intimate courtiers. But their fortunes would be sud-

held at 9 a.m. on 25 November 1907, at the Kulubanskaya Church, right next to the Svanidze home—where they had married. The body was then conveyed through the town and buried at St. Nina's Church in Kukia. The Orthodox funeral was both traumatic and farcical. Stalin, pale and tearful, "was very downcast yet greeted me in a friendly way like the old days," remembers Iremashvili. Soso took him aside. "This creature," he gestured at the open coffin, "softened my heart of stone. She died and with her died my last warm feelings for humanity." He placed his hand over his heart: "It's all so desolate here, so indescribably desolate."

At the burial, Soso's habitual control cracked. He threw himself into the grave with the coffin. The men had to haul him out. Kato was buried—but, just then, revolutionary *konspiratsia* disrupted family grief. Soso noticed some Okhrana agents sidling towards the funeral. He scarpered towards the back of the graveyard and vaulted over the fence, disappearing from his own wife's funeral—an ironic comment on his marital negligence.

For two months, Stalin vanishes from the record. "Soso sank into deep grief," says Monoselidze. "He barely spoke and nobody dared speak to him. All the time he blamed himself for not accepting our advice and for taking her to Baku in the heat." Perhaps sensing the subdued anger in the Svanidze household, Soso went home to his mother in Gori to grieve. When he met one of his school friends, "He cried like a brat, hard as he was."

"My personal life is shattered," sobbed Stalin. "Nothing attaches me to life except socialism. I'm going to dedicate my existence to that!" This was the sort of rationalization that he would use to explain ever more unspeakable tragedies which he himself arranged for his family and friends. In old age, he talked wistfully and tenderly about his Kato. He paid her a characteristic compliment. He signed his first articles in tribute to his father ("Besoshvili"), but now he chose a new byline: "K. Kato" (Koba Kato).

Even though his son was in Tiflis, he had no intention of moving back to that parochial "marsh" where he was already a political outcast. So he abandoned his son for more than ten years.

---

denly and terribly reversed: their story is told in the Epilogue. The Tiflis grave, with photographs of Kato and Sashiko, is still there; so is an old fence at the back of the cemetery, perhaps the one Stalin vaulted to escape the police. Among the gravediggers, there is a story that because Kato died of typhus, the authorities first tried to bury her in a mass "plague grave" but that the family recovered the body and buried her themselves.

"Kato died," says Monoselidze, "leaving eight-month-old Laddie to us." Kato's mother, Sepora, and the Monoselidzes raised the baby, whom Stalin barely even visited. Perhaps Laddie reminded him of the entire disaster.

This was not the Georgian way. The family, while awed by his conspiratorial competence, were appalled. In their memoirs, the Svanidzes and Elisabedashvili, writing thirty years later during Stalin's dictatorship, though before the Terror, courageously recorded their disapproval of his behaviour, making it clear they continued to blame his neglect for Kato's death.

"After that," Monoselidze concludes tellingly, "Soso went to Baku and I didn't see him until 1912, though we got a letter from exile asking for some wine and jam."[1]

When Stalin emerged from mourning at the end of 1907, he joined decadent Spandarian for a New Year's Eve dinner in a Baku restaurant. He was among old friends in the revolutionary capital of the Empire. The Bolsheviks there formed a cast reunion of Stalin's career so far: as the Bolsheviks dwindled in Russia itself, Russian and Caucasian revolutionaries flooded into Baku, often interfering with Stalin's work.* It was probably quite a party because Spandarian, who was "very close to Stalin in moral character," was also "an incredibly lazy and sybaritic ladies' man and lover of money." Spandarian's womanizing did not worry his wife, Olga, who said, "Suren never swore to be faithful to me, only to remain for ever the Knight of the Idea" of Bolshevism. But the Bolshevik playboy certainly shocked his comrades. "All the children in Baku," recalls Tatiana Vulikh, "who are up to three years old look like Spandarian!"

Soso threw himself into his work again, reassembling the Outfit. He and Spandarian immediately started to push for more radical strikes and agitation, calling on the often illiterate Azeri and Persian workers to support them. Most intellectuals were too snobbish to bother with these illiterates, but Soso packed meetings with the Muslims, who voted for him en masse. One of his important contributions was to promote and work with

* He met up again now with his comrades from Tiflis such as Sergo, Budu "the Barrel" Mdivani, Alliluyev, Kavtaradze, the gangster Tsintsadze, most of the Outfit—and the tall, blue-eyed Shaumian. Stalin's new friend Voroshilov and his old friend Yenukidze were soon joined by Lenin's special agent, the well-connected but severe noblewoman Elena Stasova ("Comrade Absolute"), Rozalia Zemliachka, Alexinsky and a girl named Ludmilla Stal. But there were also many Mensheviks from his past, such as Devdariani. It was a small world.

the radicals of Himmat (Energy), a Muslim Bolshevik group. The Muslims often hid Stalin in mosques when he was on the run. In a row with Mensheviks, one of Stalin's Muslim allies drew a dagger on Devdariani.

Through these Muslim connections, Stalin helped arm the Persian Revolution. He sent fighters and arms under Sergo to overthrow the Shah of Persia, Mohammed Ali, whom his Bolsheviks tried to assassinate. Stalin even crossed the border to Persia himself to organize his partisans, visiting Resht: the 1943 Teheran Conference was not his first time in Iran.

Shaumian was rattled by the crushing success of the Tsar's backlash. He and Yenukidze, who had just returned from exile, took a more "right-ist" moderate approach than Stalin, but could not break his dominance. Shaumian urged restraint. Stalin mocked his privileged existence, intriguing against him with his "closest friend and right-hand man, Spandarian." After Stalin's death, it was said he feuded with Shaumian, but this tension has been exaggerated. They worked well together—with mutual suspicion.[2]

Soon after his return, Stalin left on a secret trip to visit Lenin, who had now settled in Geneva. We know they met sometime in 1908, we know Stalin went to Switzerland. Stalin himself mentioned such a meeting in his reminiscences. He also met Plekhanov, who "exasperated" him. Stalin "was convinced he was a congenital aristocrat." What really turned him against the sage was the fact that "Plekhanov's daughter had aristocratic manners, dressed in the latest fashions, and wore boots with high heels!" Stalin was already at least partly a sanctimonious ascetic.[3]

Stalin and Lenin would have discussed money. Lenin was duelling with the Mensheviks while pursuing the fissiparous feud against Bogdanov and Krasin, who had stolen much of his Tiflis-heist booty, which in turn was being vigorously pursued by the European police. Thus the organization, now battered within by Lenin's schisms and without by Stolypin's victorious repression, was, explains Vulikh, "desperate for money."

Sure enough, says Kavtaradze, Stalin's henchman in Baku, "It was decided once again to get cash for the Party." When the "chief financier of the Bolshevik Centre" heard the word "money," he reached for his Mauser.

"In Baku," says Sagirashvili, who was there too, "Koba was on the lookout for the criminal types, the 'hotheads' as he called them, the cutthroats. In America, such men would be gangsters," but Stalin surrounded them "with the aura of revolutionary fighters." Stalin "suggested organizing the Bolshevik Battle Squad." Tsintsadze, Kupriashvili and some new faces joined Stalin's Outfit of so-called Mauserists.

Kavtaradze assisted Soso with the planning under the aegis of his portentously named Self-Defence Headquarters. Stalin's other sidekick was a red-haired lawyer, born in Odessa, son of a well-off Baku family with noble Polish antecedents: Andrei Vyshinsky, now twenty-three, a Menshevik, had given up the law, organized terrorist gangs and become a hit man in 1905. But Stalin, perhaps recognizing a usefully ruthless young rogue, relaxed his anti-Menshevik rigour. He commissioned Vyshinsky to procure arms and bombs.

"Politics is a dirty business," Stalin said later. "We all did dirty work for the Revolution." Stalin became the effective godfather of a small but useful fund-raising operation that really resembled a moderately success- ful Mafia family, conducting shakedowns, currency counterfeiting, extor- tion, bank robberies, piracy and protection-rackets—as well as political agitation and journalism.

Stalin's aim, says one of his Mauserists, Ivan Bokov,* was "to threaten the oil tycoons and Black Hundreds [the right-wing Russian nationalists who had their own armed groups]." He ordered the Mauserists to murder many of the Black Hundreds, according to Bokov. Then the Outfit planned to rob the Baku State Bank. Kavtaradze explains that "we learned that 4 million roubles for the Turkestan Region were being transported by ship via Baku and the Caspian Sea. Therefore at the start of 1908 we started to assemble in Baku." They would take the captain hostage— echoes of the *Tsarevich Giorgi*.

An act of piracy took place on a ship named the *Nicholas I* in Baku port: the Mensheviks investigated Stalin for this outrage, yet another infringement of Party rules. At the 1918 libel trial, Martov had enough evidence of Stalin's participation in the *Nicholas I* heist to call for wit- nesses. Later, the Trotskyite Victor Serge wrote that Vyshinsky, in a rash admission before the Bolsheviks came to power, had said, "Koba was deeply embroiled" in "the expropriation on the steamer *Nicholas I* in Baku harbour."

---

* Stalin's career in Baku is shadowy, but the memoirs of the Mauserists give us helpful clues. They could not be used in the Soviet era, especially during Stalin's dictatorship, and are mostly unpublished, but they remain in the archives.

Next, "Stalin thought up the idea" to raid the Baku naval arsenal. As ever, "He took the initiative to make us the [inside] connections with naval people," reminisced his gunman Bokov. "We organized a gang of comrades . . . and raided the arsenal," killing some of the guards. But Soso was also raising money day to day through "contributions from industrialists."

Many tycoons and middle-class professionals were sympathetic contributors to the Bolsheviks. Berta Nussimbaum, wife of an oil baron and mother of the writer Essad Bey, was a Bolshevik sympathizer. "My mother," Essad Bey says, "financed Stalin's illicit communist press with her diamonds." It remains astonishing how the Rothschilds and other oil barons, among the richest tycoons in Europe, funded the Bolsheviks, who would ultimately destroy their interests. Alliluyev remembered these Rothschild contributions.

The Rothschild managing director, David Landau, regularly contributed to Bolshevik funds, as recorded by the Okhrana—whose agents noted how, when Stalin was running the Baku Party, a Bolshevik clerk in one of the oil companies "was not active in operations but concentrated on collecting donations and got money from Landau of the Rothschilds." It is likely that Landau met Stalin personally. Another Rothschild executive, Dr. Felix Somary, a banker with the Austrian branch of the family and later a distinguished academic, claims he was sent to Baku to settle a strike. He paid Stalin the money. The strike ended.

Stalin regularly met another top businessman, Alexander Mancho, managing director of the Shibaev and Bibi-Eibat oil companies. "We often got money from Mancho for our organization," recalls Ivan Vatsek, one of Stalin's henchmen. "In such cases, Comrade Stalin came to me. Comrade Stalin also knew him well." Either Mancho was a committed sympathizer or Stalin was blackmailing him, because the businessman coughed up cash on request at even the shortest notice.

Stalin was also running protection-rackets and kidnappings. Many tycoons paid if they did not wish their oilfields to catch fire or "accidents" to befall their families. It is hard to differentiate donations from protection-money, because the felonies Stalin now unleashed on them included "robberies, assaults, extortion of rich families, and kidnapping their children on the streets of Baku in broad daylight and then demanding ransom in the name of some 'revolutionary committee,'" states Sagirashvili, who knew him in Baku. The "kidnapping of children was a routine matter at

the time," recalls Essad Bey, who as a boy never went out without a phalanx of three *kochi* bodyguards and a "fourth servant, mounted and armed,
who rode behind me."

Baku folklore claims that Stalin's most profitable kidnapping was that
of Musa Nageyev, the tenth richest oil baron, a notoriously stingy ex-
peasant who so admired the Palazzo Cantarini in Venice that he built his
own (bigger) copy—the majestic Venetian-Gothic Ismailiye Palace (now
the Academy of Sciences). Nageyev was actually kidnapped twice, but his
own accounts of these traumas were confused and murky. Neither case
was ever solved, but Bolshevik involvement was suspected. Years later,
Nageyev's granddaughter, Jilar-Khanum, claimed that Stalin jokingly sent
the oil baron thanks for his generous contributions to the Bolsheviks.*

It was said that the millionaires like Nageyev were keen to pay up
after a "ten-minute conversation" with Stalin. This was probably thanks to
his system of printing special forms that read:

> The Bolshevik Committee
> proposes that your firm
> should pay ___ roubles.

The form was delivered to oil companies and the cash was collected by
Soso's technical assistant—"a very tall man who was known as 'Stalin's
bodyguard,' visibly packing a pistol. Nobody refused to pay."

The Bolshevik boss befriended organized crime in Baku, their operations and those of the Mauserists often overlapping. One gang controlled
access to some wasteland in the Black City section. Stalin "made an agreement with the gang only to let through Bolsheviks, not Mensheviks. The
Bolsheviks had special passwords." In Russia's wildest city, both sides used

---

* In his first kidnapping, Nageyev's ransom was 10,000 gold roubles—or his kidnappers
threatened to cut him into pieces. "I can pay only 950 roubles," Nageyev replied. "Of course
you can slice me up, but then you won't get anything." He paid only the 950. Then in
December 1908, Nageyev was again kidnapped by gangsters led by "a Georgian with black
hair and unusual pockmarks." Nageyev supposedly paid 100,000 roubles. Stalin was at liberty in Baku for the first kidnapping, but in Baku Jail for the second. Had Stalin been at
liberty on the latter occasion, he would still not have participated directly. In any case, he
ran his criminal-terrorist organization from his cell: he could easily have ordered either or
both kidnappings. On the other hand, the story does not appear in any of the Bolshevik
memoirs, and in 1909 newspapers claimed the second gang of kidnappers were rogue
policemen linked to deputy city governor Colonel Shubinsky. Nonetheless Nageyev probably contributed to Bolshevik funds like the other oil barons. Like them, too, he lost his
fortune in the Revolution; he died in 1919.

violence: the oil tycoons employed Chechen ruffians as oilfield guards. One of the richest oil barons, Murtuza Mukhtarov, who resided in Baku's biggest palace based on a French Gothic château, ordered his *kochi*s to kill the young Stalin. Soso was badly beaten up by Chechens, probably on Mukhtarov's orders.*

Stalin's secrecy was so absolute that the Mauserist Bokov said, "It was sometimes so conspiratorial that we didn't even know where he was for six months! He had no permanent address and we only knew him as 'Koba.' If he had an appointment he never turned up on time; he turned up either a day early or a day later. He never changed his clothes, so he looked like an unemployed person." Soso's comrades noticed that he was different from the usual passionate Caucasian. "Sentiment was foreign to him," says one. "No matter how much he loved a fellow, he'd never forgive him even the tiniest spoiling of a Party matter—he'd skin him alive."

So again he succeeded in raising money and guns, but with him there was always a human cost. The traditional Bolsheviks like Alexinsky and Zemliachka were "very indignant at these expropriations" and killings. "Stalin blamed one member for provocation. There was no definite evidence, but that person was forced out of the city, 'judged,' condemned to death and shot."

Stalin prided himself on being what he called a *praktik*, a practical hard man, an expert on what he called "black work," rather than a chatty *intelligent*, but his gift was for being both. Lenin soon heard a storm of complaints about Stalin's banditry, but by now, writes Vulikh, Stalin "was the true boss in the Caucasus" with "a lot of supporters devoted to him who respected him as the second person in the Party after Lenin. Among the intelligentsia, he was less loved, but everybody recognized that he was the most energetic and indispensable person."

Soso had an "electrical effect" on his followers, of whom he took good care. He had a talent for political friendship that played a major role in his

---

* The beating-up was a humiliation that may have contributed to his brutal deportation of the entire Chechen race during the Second World War at the cost of hundreds of thousands of lives. Equally, he deported many other peoples during the war and victimized other races such as the Poles and Koreans with whom he had had no such experience. As for Mukhtarov, he refused to surrender his palace to the Bolsheviks when the Red Army took Baku in 1920. "As long as I am alive, no barbarian in army boots will enter my house!" In a shoot-out, he fired on the Bolsheviks until he was overcome, at which point he shot himself. His beautiful wife, Liza-Khanum, for whom his Baku château was built, lived on in the basement, then escaped to Turkey, where she lived until the 1950s. Mukhtarov's château is now the Baku Wedding Palace.

rise to power. His roommate from Stockholm, Voroshilov, the eager, fair-haired and dandyish lathe-turner,* joined him in Baku but fell ill. "He visited me every evening," said Voroshilov. "We joked a lot. He asked if I liked poetry and recited a whole Nekrasov poem by heart. Then we sang together. He really had a good voice and fine ear." "Poetry and music," Stalin told Voroshilov, "elevate the spirit!" When Alliluyev was arrested again, he worried about his family, so once released he came to consult Soso, who insisted he had to leave, giving him cash to move to Moscow. "Take the money, you've children, you must look after them."

The death of Kato was a grievous blow, but even in early 1908 the widower who signed his articles "Koba Kato" found time for partying, and never lacked female company.

---

* When Marshal Voroshilov was out of Stalin's favour in his last years, he used to plead: "But, Koba, we became friends in Baku in 1907." "I don't remember," Stalin replied. For his future life, see the Epilogue.

23

Louse Racing, Murder and Madness— Prison Games

Whenever the Outfit pulled off a heist, Stalin and Spandarian spent a little of it on a wild party. In a very Bolshevik in-joke on the Party's endless political schisms, Soso called these festivities *uklonenia*—deviations.

"When Stalin collected some extra pennies," reports A. D. Sakvarelidze, who ran Stalin's cash-counterfeiting operations, "we'd hold a 'deviational' meeting in a remote bistro or a private room at a gorgeous restaurant, often Svet Restaurant on Trading Street, where we'd have a feast, especially after celebrating the success of some deed. Spandarian especially liked 'deviations' where we'd talk frankly, eat deliciously and sing loudly, particularly Stalin." Wherever Spandarian went, girls usually followed.

A comrade from Batumi introduced his pretty sister, Alvasi Talakvadze, to Stalin. She was just eighteen, a self-confessed "spoilt child," brimming with revolutionary ardour. "Koba—the head of the Baku proletariat—used the backroom of my brother's flowerstall in the Bibi-Eibat oilfield as his base," she explains. So Stalin took Talakvadze under his wing, giving her the moniker "Comrade Plus" because of her enthusiasm. Even in absurdly turgid Stalinist jargon, the girl's memoirs record a close relationship: "Koba was enlightening me ideologically, conducting with me discussions on social-political subjects, and developing in me class-consciousness, introducing me to a faith in victory." One is tempted to read "developing class-consciousness" and "introducing faith in victory" as euphemisms, because Alvasi Talakvadze later let it be known she was Stalin's girlfriend in 1908.

His gift for conspiracy was ingenious, if sometimes macabre. This girlfriend became "adept at tricking the spooks, but Koba devised the most original tricks." One day, he ordered her to take some secret documents to the Balakhana oilfield in a coffin. "You must play the role of a mourning sister who is burying her dead baby brother with her bare hands," said Stalin, sending her to a cemetery and directing her performance like a playwright. "You'll loosen your hair, hold the coffin, sob, say you're left alone and blame yourself for his death. Don't bury it too deeply." He handed her a shovel. The "director" praised her performance, covertly observing her. "Even now," she mused later, "I don't know how he watched me so acutely."

Alvasi Talakvadze does not seem to have been his only relationship with a comrade. He also came to know Ludmilla Stal, "a famous activist among women" who was described later as "buxom but pretty." The daughter of the owner of a steel mill from south Ukraine, six years older than Soso, she was already a prison veteran. Soon afterwards, she went into exile in Paris. The affair was said to be intermittent, but it had an influence on the younger Stalin. They possibly met later during Stalin's visits abroad to see Lenin, with whom Ludmilla worked closely. They certainly met again in 1917. But nothing survives of their friendship—except one surprising lifelong relic: his renowned name.

The secret police had lost Stalin when he moved cities after the Tiflis spectacular. Now they were back on his case. When Stalin's hit man Bokov was arrested, "The Gendarme asked me: who was Stalin himself and in particular what was his role in the robbery of the [Baku port] arsenal?"

On 15 March 1908, the Gendarmes raided a Party meeting in the People's Hall. Stalin, Shaumian and Spandarian escaped, but the Gendarmes were on the trail of the Mauserists. Just as Tsintsadze and the Outfit set the date for the holdups of the State Bank and the gold ship, Cossacks and Gendarmes "attacked our safe house." In the shootout, several Cossacks were killed, but the Outfit lost its best Mauserist triggerman, Intskirveli, veteran of the Tiflis bank robbery. The plans were abandoned;

Kavtaradze left secret work and went to Petersburg University—but he remained in Stalin's life until the end.

On the night of 25 March, Baku's police chief raided "several dens of delinquents where certain criminal suspects were arrested including Gaioz Besoevich Nizheradze, bearing criminal papers, who I therefore placed at the disposal of the Gendarmerie." The man carried the passport of a nobleman named Nizheradze, but perhaps the patronymic "Son of Beso" was a better guide to the real identity of the most prominent Bolshevik in the Caucasus: "the second Lenin." After four years, the Okhrana had got Stalin.[1]

When the new prisoner arrived in Baku's Bailov Prison wearing a blue-satin smock and a dashing Caucasian hood, the other political prisoners passed the word to be careful. "This is secret," they whispered. "*That* is Koba!" They feared Stalin "more than the police."

The bogeyman did not disappoint. He had the "ability quietly to incite others while he himself remained on the sidelines. The sly schemer did not spurn any means necessary but managed to avoid public responsibility." In his seven months at the famous Bailovka, set amid the oilfields, Stalin dominated its power structures. He read, studied Esperanto, which he regarded as the language of the future,* and stirred up a series of witch hunts for traitors that often ended in death. His reign at the Bailovka was a microcosm of his dictatorship of Russia.

Soso was placed in Cell 3 with the mainly Bolshevik politicals (most Mensheviks were in Cell 7). The politicals were so organized in the Bailovka, they even had a Credentials Commission. In his cell, Stalin found his fellow Bolshevik *praktik* Sergo and his Menshevik henchman Vyshinsky. The latter was elected Elder in charge of food, which was a sensible appointment since he received regular hampers of delicacies from his prosperous wife and parents. He shared these hampers with Stalin, a prudent generosity that may have contributed to his survival in the Terror.

The Elders divided the days into hours for leisure, cleaning and discussion. Bedmates (Stalin shared with a Goreli named Ilia Nadiradze) and domestic chores were assigned by the Elders, including washing up dishes and emptying latrines, but typically, recalls Sakvarelidze, "Stalin was often released from such duties."

---

* In power, he persecuted and arrested Esperanto speakers.

One of his cellmates, Simon Vereshchak, a Menshevik, wrote a penetrating portrait of Stalin in the Bailovka. He hated him for his crude cunning yet, in spite of himself, was fascinated by Stalin's supreme confidence, vigilant intelligence, machine-like memory and sangfroid: "It was impossible to throw him off balance, nothing could get his goat!" Stalin was the only cellmate who slept soundly even when the prisoners could hear men being hanged in the courtyard.

Soso did not invent the death penalty for traitors. "In the Bailovka," explains Vereshchak, "*provocateurs* were usually killed"—but after investigation and trial. Stalin killed by proxy, and stealth. First, "Mitka the Greek stabbed a young worker for being a police spy. Koba had ordered the hit." Then "a young Georgian was beaten up in the corridor of the political building. The word spread, '*Provocateur!*' Everyone joined in, beating him with whatever they could, until the walls were spattered in blood. The bloody body was taken away on a stretcher. Later we learned that the rumour had started with Koba."

The politicals held debates that often turned sour. Stalin most disliked the Christian Socialists, who followed Leo Tolstoy. Sergo, who always hit first and thought afterwards, got into a fight with some SRs. "Sergo really punched but none of the SRs was strong enough to hit Sergo," Stalin later wrote to Voroshilov, protecting Ordzhonikidze's *amour propre* when the three of them were ruling the USSR. In fact, the SRs beat up Sergo.

Stalin dealt with political dilemmas by making himself "the best authority on Marx. Marxism was his element in which he was unconquerable. He knew how to substantiate anything with an appropriate formula from Marx" yet his style was "unpleasant, coarse, devoid of wit, dry and formal."*

Stalin still preferred rogues to revolutionaries. He was "always seen in the company of cutthroats, blackmailers, robbers and the gunslingers— the Mauserists." Sometimes the criminal prisoners raided the politicals, but the Georgian criminals, probably organized by Stalin, served as their bodyguards. In power, he shocked his comrades by promoting criminals in the NKVD, but he had used criminals all his life.

---

* Stalin found many of his Mauserist gangsters in the Bailovka (such as his cellmates the Sakvarelidze brothers). His Menshevik opponents, Devdariani from the seminary and Isidore Ramishvili from Batumi, were also in his crowded cell, but now the two factions were again forced to work together, and they turned a blind eye to his banditry.

These two species came together to bet on prison games such as wrestling competitions and louse racing. Stalin did not like chess but "he and Sergo Ordzhonikidze often played backgammon all night." The cruellest game was "Madness," in which a young prisoner was placed in the criminals' cell to be driven mad. Bets were taken on how long it would take for the youngster to crack up. Sometimes the victim really did go crazy.

The prison was overcrowded with victims of Stolypin's repressions: 1,500 shared cells built for 400. Stalin suffered from a shadow on his lung and found it hard to breathe in the heat. The sturdy "Barrel" Mdivani, who was at certain times in the same cell, lifted Soso onto his shoulders to let him breathe at the high window while the rest of the cell laughed and shouted: "Giddy-up, Barrel, giddy-up!" When the Barrel later visited Stalin in the Kremlin, he always greeted him: "Giddy-up, Soso!"

Stalin protested against the conditions and provoked the authorities, who sent a company of soldiers to beat up the politicals. Forced to run the gauntlet, "Koba walked, his head unbowed, under the blows of the riflebutts, a book in his hands," observed Vereshchak. In response, "He smashed the door of his cell with a slop-bucket, ignoring the threat of the bayonets."

It was impossible to move "without standing on someone's toe," but the overcrowding presented opportunities for shenanigans. Stalin's bedmate Nadiradze from Gori arranged for his wife to escort Keke on a visit to Baku. The two women visited son and husband. Stalin "greeted her so cordially. His mother burst into tears on seeing her only son," but he "calmed her saying the revolutionary couldn't do without prisons . . . We chatted gaily for two whole hours," says Nadiradze. Stalin got his mother to deliver secret notes to the Baku revolutionaries—which almost got her arrested.

The Outfit was planning Soso's escape. At night, he used a hacksaw, smuggled to him by a warder, to cut the bars of his cell. Outside the jail walls, his Mauserists waited on the appointed day with a phaeton to whisk him to freedom. But the plan must have been betrayed because at the last minute incorruptible Cossacks assumed guard duties. Stalin's escape attempt had to be cancelled.

The slow Tsarist system, creaking along with its usual confusion and leniency, took even longer than usual to sort out his identity and prosecute his case. Finally he was given a surprisingly lax sentence of just two years' exile in European Vologda Province instead of Asiatic Siberia.

Just before his departure, the disorder in the overcrowded Bailovka gave Stalin the chance to attempt a swap between himself and another prisoner. It seemed to go according to plan:* the substitute took his place; Soso kissed his fellow prisoners goodbye and was escorted from his cell.[2]

---

* In July 1937, at the height of the Great Terror, the man from Gori who arranged this swap, I. P. Nadiradze, wrote to another of his cellmates, Andrei Vyshinsky, Stalin's craven but dreaded Procurator-General, to ask him to confirm that he had served time for political murder and had helped arrange Stalin's swap and escape. Vyshinsky confirmed the former, but on the swap that sinister survivor sat on the fence: "As for the fact of organizing the replacement for Comrade Stalin . . . I cannot attest to this because I do not remember." Nadiradze was clearly under investigation in the Terror or he would not have appealed to the dangerous Vyshinsky on this sensitive subject at such a risky moment. But it is almost unthinkable that he would have written the letter were it not completely true as far as it goes.

24

"River Cock" and the Noblewoman

Yet somewhere the swap was unravelled. Stalin's attempted substitution must have been unmasked before he even left the Bailovka (betrayed by the same police spy who had informed on his planned escape or foiled by an underbribed guard) in time to be despatched to his place of exile. Vologda was much closer than Siberia, but the *etap* took over three months including a stay in Moscow's Butyrki Prison, where so many would perish in Stalin's Great Terror.

Soso again had no winter clothing and wrote to Shaumian in Baku for help. "We couldn't even get hold of a second-hand suit," wrote Shaumian, "but sent him 5 roubles." Stolypin had tightened up the more relaxed regime in Baku. The police were successfully smashing the Bolsheviks there, its membership withering away, its leaders arrested or killed. "No money," reported Shaumian. "Revolutionaries hungry and weak."

In Vologda Prison,* Stalin led a protest and defied the authorities. "He didn't really obey anyone," says a fellow prisoner. "He only retreated when they used force." On the way from Vologda town to his place of exile, he either fell sick with typhus or managed to persuade a doctor to

---

* The chief jailer there was named Serov, ironically the father of the future General Ivan Serov, one of Stalin's top secret policemen, deporter of the Chechens and other peoples, and first KGB Chairman.

park him in the comfort of Viatka Hospital. Finally, travelling by sleigh through frozen landscape, Stalin arrived in late February 1909 at the village of Solvychegodsk.

One of the first to welcome him to the Solvychegodsk community of about 450 exiles was an exiled girl, a teacher named Tatiana Sukhova, with whom it seems he conducted a love affair.

In his short time in Solvychegodsk, he was to find two mistresses among the small group of politicals. Even in these years of penniless obscurity he was never without at least one girlfriend, and often more. Indeed in exile he became almost libertine.

Stalin was "handsome" to women, Molotov recalled, despite his pockmarks and freckles. "Women must have been enamoured by him because he was successful with them. He had honey-coloured eyes. They were beautiful." Soso was "quite attractive," Zhenya Alliluyeva, future sister-in-law and probable mistress, told her daughter. "He was a thin man, strong and energetic [with] an incredible shock of hair and shining eyes." Everyone always mentions those "burning eyes."

Even his unattractive features had their charms. His enigmatic mien, his arrogance, ruthlessness, feline vigilance, obsessional studying and acute intelligence perhaps made him more compelling to women. His oddness could be seen as eccentric. Maybe his very lack of interest was somehow winning. Certainly, his apparent inability to look after himself—he was lonesome, skinny, scruffy—made women, throughout his life, wish to look after him. And then there was his nationality.

Georgians enjoyed a reputation for being passionate and romantic. When not being a surly brute, Stalin played the chivalrous Georgian suitor, singing songs and admiring girls' beautiful dresses while presenting them with silk handkerchiefs and flowers. Furthermore, he was sexually competitive, cuckolding his comrades when it suited him, especially in exile. Stalin the flirt, the boyfriend, even the husband, was sometimes tender and humorous. But if the ladies expected a traditional Georgian Casanova they must have been bitterly disappointed when they grew to know him better.

Strange, eccentric and lacking in empathy, he was riddled with complexes about his personality, family and physique. He was so sensitive about his webbed toes that when his feet were later being examined by his Kremlin doctors, he hid the rest of his body—and his face—under a blanket. He later had his pockmarks powdered by his bodyguards and covered in official photographs. He was shy about his own nudity even in the Russian bathhouse, the *banya,* and uneasy about his stiff arm, which later prevented him from slow-dancing with women: he admitted he "couldn't take a woman by the waist." As Kato learned during their marriage, he was impossibly distant and hard to know. His seething, egocentric energy sucked the air from every room and wore down the weak without giving them emotional nourishment. The tender moments could not compensate for the glacial detachment and morose oversensitivity. As Natasha Kirtava discovered, when crossed, he turned nasty.

Women ranked low on his list of priorities, far below revolution, egotism, intellectual pursuits and hard-drinking dinners with male friends. Combining coarse virility with Victorian prudery, he was certainly no sensualist, no epicurean. He rarely talked about his own sex-life, yet he was promiscuous—which may explain his lifelong tolerance of shameless womanizing in his companions. Spandarian in Baku was notorious. Later, as the rulers of Soviet Russia, Yenukidze and Beria were both debauched to the point of priapic degeneracy. Provided they were competent, hard-working and loyal, they were safe. In his own life, he regarded sex less as a moral question than as a security hazard.

On one hand he distrusted strong, clever women like his mother, despised pretentious women "with ideas," and disliked overscented glamourpusses who, like Plekhanov's daughter, wore "boots with high heels." He preferred young, malleable teenagers or buxom peasant women who would defer to him. On the other hand, even as late as the 1930s, he took some of his lovers from the ranks of educated, liberated female revolutionaries, his intellectual equals, sometimes even noblewomen, his social superiors. But the Marxist mission, and his own sense of separateness, always came first.

Women (and children if they inconveniently arrived) were expected to understand when the wandering Marxist crusader chose to vanish into thin air.

Tatiana Sukhova was sitting in her house with some other exiles when someone reported that "a new cluster of convicts had arrived and among them a comrade from Baku, Osip Koba, a professional, a key person." A little later, furnished with proper clothes by his fellow exiles, Osip (a Russian diminutive for Josef) entered their house "wearing high boots, black overcoat, black satin shirt and a high Astrakhan hat with a white hood around his shoulders in the Caucasian style."

It was spring in Solvychegodsk, a tiny medieval fur-trading outpost, 700 years old, with a dusty square, a wooden merchant's mansion, a post office and a beautiful sixteenth-century church. The river Vychegda flowed through the town. Ten of the exiles lived in a communal house—"a real salvation for us," says Tatiana Sukhova, "because it was a way to keep active. It was like a university—there were even lectures. Those who lived alone often started drinking."

The district police chief, Zivilev, nicknamed "the River Cock," was a petty, irascible but comical stickler with a falsetto voice. Known as "God and Tsar of Solvychegodsk," he banned any meetings of more than five exiles, amateur dramatics and even skating, rowing and mushroom-picking. When he spotted any transgression, he was given to chasing exiles along the riverbank like an irate cockerel, hence the nickname.

Stalin was "cruel, outspoken and disrespectful to superiors," according to the local policemen. River Cock had him locked up once for reading revolutionary literature aloud and fined him twenty-five kopecks for attending the theatre.* Yet there were covert if wild parties among the exiles and the inevitable flirtations. "We were singing—and I began to dance," remembers a girl, Shura Dobronravova. "Koba clapped his hands and suddenly I heard his voice saying, 'Shura is the joy of life!' I saw Koba looking at me with his mysterious smile." The sequel is not recorded.

Once the exiles went boating together, waving red flags and singing. The River Cock ran along the bank screeching, "Stop singing!" But he could not punish all of them, so they got away with it.

Stalin often organized these secret meetings of exiles, but he "watched every member of the group very carefully," recalls Alexander Dubrovin, "and demanded a report of every action." Dubrovin's memoir implies that Stalin hunted traitors and ordered their killing. "There was an exile called Mustafa. This Mustafa turned out to be a traitor. According to a comrade, he was drowned under the high bank of the Vychegda river."

"I often visited [Stalin] in his room," recalls Tatiana Sukhova, a woman of twenty-two, with light-brown hair and grey eyes. "He lived in poverty, sleeping on a wooden crate covered in planks and a bag of straw with a flannel blanket on top and a pink pillowcase." He was depressed—

---

* Soso befriended the post-office clerk who doubled as a jailer and whom he had met when he picked up his money orders. Soso liked to hunt alone in the forests during the summer and would meet the postman-jailer to pass him notes that he would deliver to the prisoners in the local prison. The local priest let Stalin use his library.

it was only months since the death of Kato. "I often found him half lying there even in daytime," but, as ever, books served as his comfort and castle: "Since he was very cold, he lay in his coat and surrounded himself with books." But she says she cheered him up. They spent more and more time together, laughing at the others and even going on boating dates. It seems the friendship turned into some kind of affair and Stalin remained fond of Sukhova into the 1930s.* He later wrote to her, begging forgiveness for never having kept in contact: "Contrary to my promises, which I remember were many, I've not even sent you a card! What a beast I am but it's a fact and if you want, I present my apologies . . . Keep in touch!" They did not meet again until 1912.

In June, the local police recorded that Soso attended a meeting with all the other exiles, including a girl named Stefania Petrovskaya, who enjoyed a love affair with Stalin sufficiently serious that he decided to marry her.

Stefania, a teacher aged twenty-three, was above Stalin on the social scale, an Odessan noblewoman whose Catholic father owned a house in the centre of the city. She had attended the elite gymnasium there before going into higher education. "Noblewoman Petrovskaya," as she appears in police reports, had been arrested in Moscow and given two years in Vologda exile, but she had just finished her sentence when she met Osip Koba. Stalin was not there for very long, but the relationship must have been intense because she hung around in godforsaken Solvychegodsk for no good reason—and then followed him back to the Caucasus.

Exiles were isolated from Party politics abroad, but they caught up on the latest schisms from battered back copies of journals that arrived from family and friends. Stalin was irritated by Lenin's feud with Bogdanov. "How do you like Bogdanov's new book?" Soso asked his friend Malakia Toroshelidze, in Geneva. "In my view, some of Illich's [Lenin's] individual blunders are significantly and correctly noted in it. He also notes that Illich's materialism is . . . different from Plekhanov's which . . . Illich tries to hide."

Stalin respected Lenin, but never completely uncritically. The deification only came after Lenin's death and with a clear political purpose. Now he regarded Lenin's schisms as the self-indulgence of spoiled émigrés. In Russia, where Bolshevism was in decay, the *praktiki* could not afford such nonsense. "The Party had as a whole ceased to exist," admitted Zinoviev.

* See the Epilogue.

It was so bad that some, the "Liquidators," proposed winding up the Party. Stalin on the other hand agreed with the so-called Conciliators that the Bolsheviks had to work with the Mensheviks—or disappear altogether.

He was sure the Party needed him and he had no intention of hanging around in Solvychegodsk: the more revolutionaries that Stolypin exiled, the more the system was overwhelmed. Escapes multiplied. Of 32,000 exiles in 1906–9, the authorities could never account for more than about 18,000 at any one time. Soso wrote to Alliluyev in St. Petersburg asking for his address and place of work, obviously planning on a trip to the capital. He started raising funds: some money orders arrived at the post office. The prisoners staged a fake gambling game in which Stalin "won the entire kitty of 70 roubles."

In late June, after River Cock's morning inspection, Sukhova helped Stalin don a *sarafan*, a long, sleeveless Russian dress. We do not know if he shaved his beard, but in full drag, he travelled, accompanied by Sukhova, by steamboat to the local centre, Kotlas. On parting, he managed a romantic flourish, unabashed by his transvestite garb, telling Sukhova: "One day I'll pay you back by giving you a silk handkerchief."

Then he caught the train to the Venice of the North.[1]

"Once, in the evening," recounts Sergei Alliluyev, still married to the libidinous Olga, "I was strolling along Liteinyi Boulevard [in St. Petersburg] when I suddenly saw Comrade Stalin coming in the opposite direction." The friends embraced.

Stalin had already visited the Alliluyev flat and workplace but had found no one home. Central Petersburg was a small world, however. Alliluyev recruited a concierge to hide Soso. These concierges were often Okhrana informers, so, if Bolshevik sympathizers, their places were ideal hideouts, never searched.

The concierge hid Stalin in the porters' lodge of the Horse Guards barracks on Potemkin Street right next to the Taurida Palace, once the home of Catherine the Great's political partner, Prince Potemkin, and now seat of the Duma. At the barracks, "Cabs would drop off court officials . . . while Stalin went into the city to visit friends," says Anna Alliluyeva. He "would stroll serenely by the guard at the barrack gates, holding the regimental rollcall under his arm."

Stalin, who was on a mission connected to "publishing a newspaper," made the necessary contacts and swiftly departed for the Caucasus.

In early July 1909, he re-emerged in Baku with yet another name—Oganez Totomiants, Armenian merchant. But the Okhrana noticed his return nonetheless: "The Social-Democrat escapee from Siberia has arrived— he's known as 'Koba' or 'Soso.' " Two Okhrana agents inside the Bolshevik Party, "Fikus" and "Mikheil," now informed regularly on Stalin, who gloried in the code name of "the Milkman,"* because he used a Baku milkbar as his base. He was intermittently watched, but the secret police took months to identify Soso and hunt him down. Why?

Here is one of the enduring mysteries of young Stalin: was the future Soviet dictator an agent of the Tsar's secret police?[2]

---

* The secret police adapted their own witty code names for their surveillance targets: a baker would be "Bun," a banker "Moneybags," the poet Sergei Esenin was "Typesetter," while a pretty girl might be "Gorgeous" or "Glamourpuss."

25

"The Milkman":
Was Stalin a Tsarist Agent?

In the Oil Kingdom of Baku, the Milkman tried to reinvigorate the shattered Bolsheviks, joining up with Spandarian, Sergo and Budu Mdivani. He rallied the remnants of the Outfit and "started to plan an attack on a mail ship," says the Mauserist Kupriashvili, to fund their newspaper *Bakinsky Proletary*.

Yet it was a dark time. "The Party is ailing," wrote Stalin. "There's nothing good to write. We've no workers," he complained to Tskhakaya, adding that he now believed in reuniting with the Mensheviks. Conciliation was anathema to Lenin, but dire circumstances had now forced Stalin to become a Conciliator. The tough *Komitetchiki*, the Committeemen inside Russia, were increasingly frustrated with Lenin and the bickering émigrés: "Why must these damned 'trends' split us . . . what useless skirmishes—both sides deserve a thrashing!" Stalin demanded the appointment of a Russian Bureau to run the Party inside the Empire and the creation of a national paper based in Russia, not in exile. "The Central Committee," Stalin complained in print, "is a fictitious centre."

Soso's ideas for the future of the Party reached the Central Committee in Paris, which, in January 1910, appointed him to the new Russian Bureau, a recognition of his energetic persistence and organizational talents. He had graduated from Caucasian activist to Russian Bolshevik leader—yet in Baku he was playing his own game against Shaumian.

"Stalin and Spandarian concentrated all the power in their hands," grumbled Shaumian's wife, Ekaterina, the oil executive's daughter. Faced with Stalin's dominance and Tsarist repression, Shaumian, like many others, took a regular job, even working for a sympathetic oil baron, Shibaev: he tried to withdraw from the underground. "Everyone has 'seen sense' and got private jobs," Soso told Tskhakaya. "Everyone except me, that is— I haven't 'seen sense.' The police are hunting me!" Stalin, that sea-green incorruptible, never "saw sense" and hated those that did, like Shaumian, "who gave up our work three months ago!" He tried to tempt Shaumian back into the fold. Alone after Kato, Stalin despised Shaumian's happy home,* blaming his wife, Ekaterina: "Like a doe, she thinks only of nurturing and was often hostile to me because I involved her Stepan in secret business that smelt of prison." Ekaterina Shaumian complained that Stalin "intrigued against Shaumian and behaved like a termagant."

Stalin made quick visits to Tiflis "concerned with financial matters," the euphemism for expropriations and protection-rackets. Unknown to him, his father died, probably while he was there. Beso, by now a dosshouse drunk, was admitted to Mikhailovsky Hospital. Medical records chart his decline from TB, colitis and chronic pneumonia. He died on 12 August, aged fifty-five. He had made no attempt to find Soso. Without relatives or money, he was buried in a pauper's grave.[1] For the Bolshevik who signed himself "Son of Beso," the father had died years before.[†]

Back on the Caspian, Stalin was now joined by his girlfriend from exile, Stefania Petrovskaya, soon described by the Okhrana as "mistress of well-known leader of local RSDWP." She must have been devoted to him

---

* Just as he was to despise the happy marriages of his grandees in power, after the suicide of his second wife in 1932. See *Stalin: The Court of the Red Tsar*.

† Until recently, historians repeated that Beso had died about 1890, perhaps in a bar brawl, but the new archives disprove this. Once in power, Stalin's henchmen and historians tried to find photographs of Beso and showed them to the dictator for identification: the Georgian Party archives contain piles of photographs of local cobblers and Beso candidates. One photograph probably is Beso for it was displayed in the cult museums, but Stalin himself refused to identify it. The local Party bosses also tried to find Beso's grave but failed there too. In the 1940s, Elisabedashvili, who survived the Terror, presented Stalin with a clock that he claimed had belonged to Beso. Stalin refused to accept it, implying that someone else, probably Egnatashvili, was his real father. He preferred this gap in his life to any hint of the man himself.

because, on her release from exile, she did not return to either Moscow or Odessa but followed Stalin to Baku.

He now gave her his ultimate compliment: he jettisoned the pen name "K. Kato" and became "K. Stefin," based on Stefania—and a step nearer "Stalin." The adoption of the names of lovers as pen names is a peculiarity in such a chauvinist. We have no letters between them. But the "K. Stefin" shows that Stefania was important to him. They moved in together—or, as the secret police noted, the Milkman "cohabited with his concubine."

There now started a farrago of bewildering scandals that revealed that Stalin's Party was riddled with Tsarist spies. Stalin reacted by unleashing a hysterical, murderous witch hunt for traitors which only succeeded in destroying the innocent—and drawing suspicion onto himself. It began in September 1909, when Stalin's own secret-police contacts warned him that his valuable printing-press had been betrayed by an Okhrana double-agent: it was about to be raided. The press had to be swiftly moved and secretly reassembled in new premises.

Stalin "rushed to me," recalls his henchman Vatsek, "and asked me to get cash. I got him 600 roubles from Mancho," the oil baron. But it was not enough. A little later, "Josef Vissarionovich Djugashvili came running with Budu Mdivani." The tycoon then gave Stalin another 300 roubles.

Stalin found the press a new secret location in the Baku old city, setting it up in the dark cellars and alleyways of the Persian Fortress. But he discovered that the married couple who actually ran the press had embezzled money. He sent his Mauserists after them. The husband got away. The wife was interrogated by Stalin's gunmen, but she somehow escaped before she could be liquidated.

In October 1909, the police raided a safe house to pick up Stalin's fellow Baku Bolshevik, Prokofi "Alyosha" Japaridze. The policemen were surprised to find Stalin and Sergo with Japaridze. The ranking detective, as ever incapable of independent thought, left some policemen on guard and went to consult his superiors. Stalin and Sergo bribed the policemen with ten roubles. Japaridze had to stay and face arrest, but Stalin and Sergo were allowed to escape.

Stalin, on a tip-off from another of his contacts in the Baku Okhrana, blamed these betrayals on the Secretary of the Bolshevik Oil Workers Union, Leontiev. Stalin decided that there were five Okhrana double-agents in the Party. He decided to kill Leontiev, but the latter called his bluff, reappearing and demanding a Party trial. Stalin refused to hold a trial since this would reveal his moles inside the Okhrana. Leontiev was let off, raising suspicions about Stalin's own relationship with the secret police.

"The betrayal of someone with whom you've shared everything," said Stalin later, "is so horrible, no actor or writer can express it—it's worse than the very bite of Death!" Stalin orchestrated a cannibalistic inquisition in Baku to find traitors, real and imagined, just as he would across the entire USSR in the 1930s. The difference is that in Baku the Party really was infested with police spies.

Stalin printed the names of the five "traitors," but secret-police archives reveal that only one was, in fact, a spy; all the others were innocent. The witch hunt gathered pace. When Baku was visited by a top Moscow Bolshevik named Chernomazov, "Comrade Koba stared disgustedly at him. 'You're a traitor!' he shouted." In this case, Stalin was right.

The disarray was reported to the gleeful Baku Okhrana by their real spies code named "Fikus" and "Mikheil," the traitors who really had infiltrated the Bolsheviks but were never identified by witchfinder-general Stalin. No doubt in Baku he ordered innocent people killed as traitors just as he would in the Terror.

It was a mess. Soso liked to fix such messes with quiet killings, but that did not work this time. He and another comrade accused each other of being spooks. Indeed the Mensheviks, and some Bolsheviks, suspected that Stalin himself, with his secret-police contacts, was the biggest traitor of the lot. So was he betraying the Party to the police? Here is the case against Stalin.

Stalin certainly cultivated shadowy Tsarist connections, receiving a stream of mysterious tip-offs from contacts in the secret police. Once Stalin was walking in Baku's streets with a comrade when an Okhrana officer approached him. "I know you're a revolutionary," he said. "Here's a list of all your comrades who will be arrested in the near future." On another occasion, a comrade arrived to meet Stalin at a Party safe house and was startled to pass a senior Gendarme officer on his way out. He challenged Stalin, who said the Gendarme was aiding the Bolsheviks.

In Tiflis, during a roundup of revolutionaries, Stalin was amazed to find a Menshevik, Artyom Gio, in a secret hideout. "I wasn't expecting it!" Stalin blurted out. "Haven't you been arrested?" Just then a stranger entered. "You can talk freely," Stalin reassured Gio. "He's a comrade of mine." This "comrade" turned out to be a police interpreter who then recited the list of comrades, including Sergei Alliluyev, who had been arrested that day—and warned Stalin that the police would arrest him that very night.*

The Okhrana's agent "Fikus" reported that an unknown Gendarme officer visited Stalin and Mdivani to warn them about the Gendarme raid on the printing-press. As we saw, they saved the press.

So what was Stalin's relationship with the secret police?

"Stalin was giving addresses of comrades disagreeable to him to the Gendarmes to get rid of them," insists Arsenidze. "His comrades decided to put him on Party trial . . . but, at the trial meeting, Gendarmes appeared and arrested the judges and Koba." In 1909, adds Uratadze, "the Baku Bolsheviks accused him of denouncing Shaumian to the police." Jordania claimed that Shaumian even told him, "Stalin denounced me—no one else knew the address of my safe house." All three of these accusers were Menshevik exiles whose stories have been widely accepted.

Then the secret police always seemed strangely confused about Stalin. The Gendarme chief in Baku, Colonel Martynov, only "discovered" that the Milkman was Soso Djugashvili in December 1909—almost six months after his escape. Was he being protected by his Tsarist controllers?

If one throws into this poisonous cauldron the accusations of betrayal against him as early as 1902, his secret-police contacts and his escapes from exile and prison, it might look plausible that he was a Tsarist agent.[2] Was the future supreme pontiff of international Marxism an unprincipled megalomaniac traitor? If Stalin was a phoney, was not the entire Soviet experiment a fraud too? And was everything he did, particularly the Great Terror, an attempt to cover up his guilt? It was a tempting theory—especially during the Cold War.

---

* Gio's memoirs are remarkable because they were published in the Soviet Union in 1925, just after Lenin's death but before Stalin had established his dictatorship—virtually the only moment in Soviet history when this could have happened. The book came out in Leningrad, then the fiefdom of Zinoviev, who presumably permitted this as a warning to Stalin, with whom he was competing for Lenin's throne. Gio reveals that the Georgian police interpreter betrayed the Tsarist state not because he was a Marxist but because he was a Georgian "nationalist." Gio also recounts how Stalin gave him code words to contact another comrade named Kornev, who turned out to be so suspicious that he was probably a police agent. Gio believed that this Kornev had tricked Stalin, but it is equally possible that Stalin was testing or sacrificing Gio, or that he was in the process of recruiting Kornev.

. . .

Yet the case against Stalin is actually a weak one. The Menshevik stories of Shaumian's betrayal do not stand up. There was tension but no feud with Shaumian: the two towering Bolshevik figures in the Caucasus were "friendly but with a shadow." During 1907–10, Shaumian was only arrested once, on 30 April 1909, when Stalin was still in Solvychegodsk. Shaumian was next arrested, on 30 September 1911, when Stalin was imprisoned in Petersburg. It is unlikely Stalin arranged either arrest.

Stalin was flexible and amoral. His Messiah-complex led him to believe that anyone opposed to him was an enemy of the cause—thus any compact was justified, no matter how Mephistophelian. Yet there is no proof that he betrayed any comrades or that he was tried by a Party court.

Stalin's secret-police contacts are not as suspicious as they seem. When he visited Tiflis for a short conference in November 1909, we know, ironically from "Fikus," the Okhrana agent within the Bolsheviks, that "Due to the efforts of Koba (Soso)—Josef Djugashvili, who came from Baku—the conference decided to arrange that Party members should infiltrate different state institutions and collect intelligence for the Party." So Stalin was in charge of the Party's intelligence/counterintelligence—the penetration of the secret police.

It was his job to groom Gendarme or Okhrana officers, to generate tip-offs about traitors and police raids, and to engineer quick releases for arrested comrades. If one reads them carefully, every one of the stories of Stalin's secret-police meetings, even the most hostile ones, reveals that he was actually *receiving* intelligence, not giving it. Some contacts, like the police interpreter, were sympathizers; most just wanted money.

The secret world is always a marketplace. The Caucasian police were particularly venal, and prices for releasing comrades were well known. The Bailov prison governor charged 150 roubles per prisoner to substitute a stand-in.* In Baku, the deputy head of the Gendarmerie, Captain Fyodor Zaitsev, was notorious. "Soon all our comrades were released," remembers Sergo, "by means of small payments to Captain Zaitsev, who readily accepted bribes." Shibaev, the Baku oil baron, paid Zaitsev 700

---

* Sometimes the police set the price too high. "My dear," wrote an unknown Bolshevik, "unfortunately I cannot help you. The official asks 800 roubles for cancellation abroad [this meant going abroad instead of into Siberian exile] for Yakov Mikhailovich [Sverdlov]. Where to get this sum?"

roubles to free Shaumian. Captain Zaitsev was almost certainly the senior Gendarme secretly meeting Stalin. In April 1910, Zaitsev's venality caught up with him, and he was dismissed.

The money flowed both ways. Virtually all Okhrana agents were paid, but Stalin received no such mysterious income. Even when he was flush with bank-robbery cash, he spent little on himself and was usually penniless, in marked contrast to the real Okhrana agents, who were lavishly rewarded bon viveurs.

The secret police also ensured that their agents were virtually always at liberty: they wanted value for money. Yet Stalin spent only one and a half years at liberty between his arrest in 1908 and 1917. After 1910, he was free for just ten months.

The muddle of the Tsarist secret police is a major plank in the case against Stalin, and the flimsiest. Such mistakes were universal, not restricted to Stalin. The security agencies had totally infiltrated the Bolsheviks, but no organization before computers could have digested their millions of reports and card indexes. Indeed the Okhrana were remarkably successful, emerging well from comparisons with, say, today's generously funded U.S. security agencies in the age of computers and electronic surveillance.

As for Stalin's many escapes from exile (and there are more to come), "Those who didn't escape," explained one secret policeman, "did not want to, for personal reasons." Stalin's covert craft, feline elusiveness, and use of intermediaries made him especially hard to catch; his ruthlessness discouraged witnesses.

Finally, the evidence, in the many surviving secret-police archives, is overwhelming that Stalin was not a Tsarist agent—unless this is overturned by some decisive document* lurking undiscovered in provincial

---

* A major piece of evidence that Stalin was an Okhrana agent was a probable forgery, the so-called Eremin Letter, that appeared in the 1920s and was published by *Life* magazine in the 1950s, forming the backbone of the conspiracy-theory books by I. D. Levine and E. E. Smith. Colonel Eremin was indeed the head of the Tiflis Okhrana from February 1908. The letter was clearly drafted by someone who knew a lot about Stalin and the Okhrana, but it contained a series of mistakes of detail. While appreciating Stalin's amorality, it also grasped his devotion to the cause, claiming that he was an unsatisfactory agent because in the end he was a fanatical Marxist. When the Eremin Letter was published in *Life* after Stalin's death, his successor, First Secretary Nikita Khrushchev, and the Politburo ordered the KGB Chairman, General Serov, to analyse its veracity. His investigations, recently found in the archives, also conclude that it was a forgery. As for the theory that the Great Terror was Stalin's effort to suppress evidence of his Okhrana links, *The Secret File of Joseph Stalin* by Roman Brackman (2001) puts the argument robustly.

Okhrana archives, missed by Stalin himself, his own secret police, his many enemies and the armies of historians who have searched in vain for a smoking gun for almost a century.

Stalin was supremely well qualified for this moral no-man's-land. On each of his nine or more arrests, the secret police would routinely have tried to turn him into *their* double-agent. Simultaneously, Stalin, that master of human frailty, would have been assiduously probing, seeking weak or venal policemen to become *his* agents.

When he did recruit an informer from the secret police, who was playing whom? It is likely that some of the secret policemen were double-crossing Stalin in the spirit of *konspiratsia,* passing him the names of innocent Bolsheviks as "traitors" in order to sow destructive paranoia within the Party—and protect their real agents. This explains why most of the Baku "traitors" named by Stalin were innocent, while the real Tsarist agents, "Fikus" and "Mikheil," remained unsuspected.

Yet ultimately Stalin was a devout Marxist "of semi-Islamic fervour," allowing no friend or family to stand between him and his mission. He regarded himself as an undiscovered but remarkable leader of the working class—a "Knight of the Grail," in Spandarian's phrase. As far as we know, he never wavered from this mission even in the worst of times—and in this he was almost unique.

Yet this cesspit of duplicity and espionage helps explain some of the craziness of Soviet history. Here is the origin of the paranoiac Soviet mind-set, the folly of Stalin's mistrust of the warnings of Hitler's invasion plans in 1941 and the bloody frenzy of his Terror.

The Okhrana may have failed to prevent the Russian Revolution, but they were so successful in poisoning revolutionary minds that, thirty years after the fall of the Tsars, the Bolsheviks were still killing each other in a witch hunt for nonexistent traitors.[3]

In the spring of 1910, the Milkman was such a master of evasion that the secret police could no longer cope. "The impossibility of his continued surveillance," reported the Baku Gendarme commander Colonel Martynov, "makes necessary his detention; all the agents have become known to him and even newly assigned agents failed, while the Milkman managed both to deceive the surveillance and to expose it to his comrades, thus spoiling the entire operation. The Milkman mainly lives with his concubine Stefania Petrovskaya."

On 23 March 1910, Colonel Martynov arrested the Milkman, now using the alias "Zakhar Melikiants," and "the noblewoman of Kherson Province, Stefania Petrovskaya." The couple were interrogated separately in Bailov Prison. The Milkman first denied having a relationship with Stefania. But he then requested permission to marry her. Soon Stalin was calling her "my wife."

PART THREE

When the luminary full moon
Drifts across the vault of the sky
And its light, shining out,
Begins to play on the azure horizon;

When the nightingale's whistling song
Starts to twitter softly in the air
When the yearning of the panpipe
Glides over the mountain peak;

When the mountain spring, dammed up,
Once more sweeps the path away and gushes,
And the forest, woken by the breeze,
Begins to toss and rustle;

When the man driven out by his enemy
Again becomes worthy of his oppressed country
And when the sick man, deprived of light,
Again begins to see sun and moon;

Then I too, oppressed, find the mist of sadness
Breaks and lifts and instantly recedes;
And hopes for the good life
Unfold in my unhappy heart!

And, carried away by this hope,
I find my soul rejoicing, my heart beats peacefully;
But is this hope genuine
That has been sent to me at these times?

—SOSELO (Josef Stalin)

26

Two Lost Fiancées
and a Pregnant Peasant

Stalin at first pretended he had never used the name Totomiants, and insisted that he could not have committed any crimes during the 1905 Revolution because he had been in London for a year—though he admitted his escape from exile. When Lieutenant Podolsky asked him about Stefania, Soso, now thirty, admitted meeting her in Solvychegodsk, but "I never cohabited with her," he said. Whether this was clandestine craft, caddish abandonment or chivalrous care for her reputation, he was capable of all three. But she did not deny him. Four days earlier, Stefania, aged twenty-four, had told Podolsky, "Yes, I know Djugashvili. I'm living with him."

Three months later, the Gendarmes decided to free her, but "in view of [Stalin's] tenacious participation in the revolutionary parties and his high position, despite all previous administrative punishments, and his two escapes from exile, I propose the extreme penalty of five years' Siberian exile." That was the maximum. Unfortunately, the corrupt Captain Zaitsev had just been dismissed and the new ranking officer was less flexible.

With Soso stuck in prison, his comrades procured the phlegm of a prisoner with TB and bribed a doctor to get him transferred to the prison hospital, whence he appealed to the governor of Baku with a romantic request:

> *In view of my diagnosed pulmonary tuberculosis . . . I humbly request Your Excellency to . . . examine my health, put me under less restraint and expedite the accomplishment of my case.*
>
> *I ask Your Excellency to allow me to marry Stefania Leandrovna Petrovskaya, resident of Baku.*
>
> *29 June 1910. Petitioner Djugashvili*

Stefania, now released, must have visited him in prison and received a proposal because the next day, Soso wrote again, this time calling her his "wife": "I have learned from my wife who visited the Gendarmes Department that Your Excellency considers it necessary to deport me to Yakutsk. I do not understand such a severe measure and wonder if insufficient knowledge of my case might have led to some misunderstanding . . ."

These appeals were against revolutionary rules, but Stalin's wheedling lies did not move Colonel Martynov, who still recommended five years. But the liberal viceroy's office in Tiflis watered down the punishment. On 13 September, Stalin was sentenced to complete his exile in Solvychegodsk and banned for five years from the Caucasus. Though he would return again to Baku, the Tsar's officials ironically forced Stalin to escape the periphery and concentrate on the greater stage of Russia itself.

On 31 August, the deputy prosecutor wrote to the Baku governor: "Jailed prisoner J. V. Djugashvili petitions to allow him to marry Baku resident Stefania Petrovskaya. Does Your Excellency have any objections to my allowing Djugashvili's request?" Whether out of sloppy paperwork, bureaucratic mistake or deliberate malice, it was only on 23 September that Bailov Prison's governor received this: "Prisoner Djugashvili is permitted to marry Stefania Petrovskaya: the prisoner is to be informed. The ceremony will be in the presence of the Governor in the Prison Church."

When the warders brought this joyous news to Stalin's cell, he was gone: on that very day, "23 September 1910, Josef Djugashvili was deported to Vologda Province." By the end of October, he was back in Solvychegodsk. Not only did he not marry his fiancée and unofficial wife, he never saw her again.[1]

. . .

Solvychegodsk* had not improved in his absence. There were fewer exiles and the police regime under the ridiculous River Cock was tighter than ever. There was even less to do. We do not know if Stalin ever thought again about his fiancée in Baku, but he was to console himself for the dreariness of exile with another bout of skirt-chasing that led to a forgotten semi-official marriage, and an illegitimate son.

"It was bad living in Solvychegodsk," recalls a fellow exile named Serafima Khoroshenina, then aged about twenty-two, a well-educated teacher's daughter from Perm Province. "The police surveillance was bearable but the exiles aren't alive—they've actually died. Everyone lives inside themselves . . . with nothing to say. There wasn't even common entertainment so the exiles drowned their sorrows in drink." She might have added that the other main pastime, after feuding with other exiles and hitting the bottle, was fornication. After the Second World War when the Soviet dictator was discussing a diplomatic sex scandal with the British Ambassador, Stalin laughed knowingly that "such questions arise from boredom."

He first stayed with the Grigorov family. While he was there, he started an affair with the young teacher Serafima Khoroshenina. They moved in together, staying in a single room in the house of a young widow, Maria Kuzakova.

Stalin was not the only one who found sexual adventure as a consolation. He spent much time with a flamboyant Menshevik in a white suit named Lezhnev, "who had been deported to this backwater from Vologda Town because he had seduced the Town Prosecutor's wife," according to their fellow exile Ivan Golubev. "He used to tell us about his Vologda adventures and it was impossible not to fall about with laughter—Stalin almost died laughing!"

However much he was carousing in the Kuzakova household, Soso's mind was elsewhere. Always green-fingered, he started to plant pine trees. And he read frantically, history books and more novels including those by Tolstoy, whose politics he loathed but whose literature he admired. But he

---

*Stalin's presence as an exile would return to haunt this region. In 1940, he ordered the construction of a giant steel-mill in Cherepovets because he remembered it from his Solvychegodsk exile, even though it was totally unsuitable: the nearest iron-ore and coal deposits were over 1,000 miles away. But his advisers were too frightened to tell him. The Second World War delayed construction, but building started in 1949. Due to its inconvenient location, it is still known as "Stalin's Belch."

was soon ready to escape, bored to tears and desperate to get news of developments from Lenin.

On 10 December, a letter arrived from the Bolshevik Centre. Stalin replied, sending "warm greetings to Lenin," whom he backed as "the only correct" one against the "Liquidationist trash" and "Trotsky's base lack of principle . . . Lenin's a shrewd fellow who knows a thing or two." But "the immediate task, which will stand no delay, is to organize a central [Russian] group which would command all illegal, semi-legal and legal work . . . Call it whatever you like. It doesn't matter. Yet it's as urgent as the bread of life itself. It would begin the Party's revival." As for himself, "I have six months left to serve. After that I'm at your service," but "if the need is urgent, I can weigh my anchor immediately . . ." He was ready to escape—but needed the funds.

Faced with the SD meltdown inside Russia, Lenin tried one last time to reunite with the Mensheviks. Stalin, half-Conciliator, half-Leninist, approved. When the wooing came to naught, Lenin returned to his natural state of exuberant feuding.

"Dressed in a beaverskin hat," Soso presided over secret meetings of the seven exiles in a dovecote. He was "often very cheerful, laughing and singing in his magical mountain voice," recalled Ivan Golubev, "but he despised toadies." Once, he revealed a truth about himself: "We must remain illegal until the Revolution because going legal would mean turning into a normal person." Stalin had no wish to be a "normal person." In normal life, his peculiarities would have been intolerable, but in the revolutionary underground (and later the idiosyncratic, paranoiac and conspiratorial Soviet leadership), they were virtues of a "Knight of the Grail."

"I'm suffocating here without active work, literally suffocating," he wrote on 24 January 1911, in another letter to a Moscow comrade, whom he hailed: "A Caucasian Soso is writing to you—remember me from Baku and Tiflis in 1904." The tedium was tormenting him. He talked constantly about escape. Seething about the factional time-wasting of the feuding émigrés, he vented his disdain for both sides, even Lenin: "Everybody heard about the storm in a teacup abroad: the bloc of Lenin-Plekhanov on one hand and the bloc of Trotsky-Martov-Bogdanov on the other. As far as I know, the workers favour the first bloc but generally they disdain those abroad . . ."

Stalin's outburst soon reached Lenin in exile: he was displeased. At the time, Lenin was holding a Party school at Longjumeau near Paris, and had invited Sergo to study there. Sergo talked up his ally Stalin. One day, Lenin and Sergo were strolling the boulevards.

"Sergo, do you recognize the phrase 'storm in a teacup'?"

"Vladimir Illich," replied Sergo, knowing that Lenin had somehow heard of Stalin's letter, "Koba's our friend. A lot of things connect us."

"I know," said Lenin. "I also remember him well. But the Revolution's not yet won. Its interests must come before personal likes and dislikes. You say Koba's our comrade as if you mean he's a Bolshevik and won't let us down. But do you close your eyes to inconsistency? Such nihilistic jokes . . . reveal Koba's immaturity as a Marxist."

Lenin fired a shot across Stalin's bows, but soon forgave "Soso of the Caucasus." Soon afterwards, the Menshevik Uratadze told Lenin about Stalin's expulsion in Baku. "It's not worth ascribing too much significance to such things," answered Lenin, laughing it off. That prompted Uratadze to sneak to him about Stalin's brutal outrages. "That," said Lenin, "is exactly the sort of person I need."

The escape funds—seventy roubles—arrived in Solvychegodsk, but they were almost instantly stolen from Stalin. The money was telegraphed to an exiled student in Vologda named Ivanian. It was usual to despatch such funds to a third party because otherwise exiles lost their allowances. But there was always the risk of theft.

In late January to mid-February, Stalin invented a medical appointment in order to get to the provincial capital, planning to drop by Ivanian's place, collect the money and catch the train to Petersburg. But the student had other ideas. When Stalin reached Vologda, Ivanian moved him to the house of another exile, Count Alexei Dorrer. First, however, according to Stalin, "Ivanian didn't pass me the money but just showed me the telegram about sending it (with various words obliterated . . .). He himself couldn't explain either the 'loss' of the money or the missing words in the telegram."

Soso, according to some accounts, nonetheless took the train to Petersburg, undeterred by the lost money. After walking around all day exhausted, he noticed a pharmacy bearing the Georgian name Lordkipanidze, staggered inside and confessed he was an escapee. The Georgian took pity on his compatriot, hiding and feeding him. Stalin was always amazed how complete strangers helped him.

But a fuming Stalin had to return to Solvychegodsk—and he never forgot Ivanian, "guffawing about the 'bandit who stole the money and when I met the rascal after the Revolution, he had the nerve to ask me for help.'" If Ivanian really did steal Stalin's money, it was an act of astonishing courage—and folly. Still protesting his innocence, he was shot in 1937.*

"I also used to hit the bottle," Serafima Khoroshenina writes laconically. Perhaps it was the drinking-bout to recover from this frustrating interlude that led Stalin to formalize his relations with her. Some time before 23 February, he and Serafima Khoroshenina registered as cohabiting partners, a sort of civil marriage (because only religious marriage existed in the Orthodox Empire). It is an alliance entirely lost or omitted from Stalin's biography.

The couple were not to enjoy their blissful honeymoon for long. "On 23 February, by order of the Governor of Vologda Province, Serafima Khoroshenina was despatched to serve her time in Nikolsk." Such were the caprices of Tsarist Autocracy—she was not even given time to bid goodbye to her partner. But she left Stalin a farewell note. To paraphrase Wilde: to lose one fiancée almost on the day of the wedding may be regarded as a misfortune but to lose a new "wife" a week afterwards looks like carelessness. Merry word had spread of this sudden alliance, regarded as a semi-marriage, because a Bolshevik named A. P. Smirnov cheekily probed him in a letter that inquired: "I've heard you got married again."

No sooner was Serafima out of his bed than his landlady, Maria Kuzakova, took her place. "He was a very polite lodger," she recalls. "Quiet and gentle. Always in his black fedora and autumn coat. He spent most of his time at home reading and writing, and I could hear the floor creaking at night because he liked to pace as he worked." One day she asked him his age.

"Guess," he said.

---

* In the early 1920s, Ivanian had the misfortune to literally bump into Stalin in Moscow and he apparently did ask for his help. On 7 June 1926, when he was already the dominant Soviet leader, Stalin was consulted on Ivanian, then an official with the Commissariat of Internal Trade. "In response to your inquiry, I notify you of the following facts that you need to know," Stalin wrote in his characteristic numbered paragraphs. Point Six concluded: "Later after I went abroad, I received all the Central Committee documents proving that 70 roubles had been sent to me . . . [and] the money was not lost but received by the addressee in Vologda." Ivanian was expelled from the Party but reinstated after Old Bolsheviks interceded for him. When Stalin unleashed the Terror, the Transcaucasian boss and secret policeman Beria pursued him. Ivanian wrote desperately to the dictator: "I still declare I had nothing to do with the 70 roubles . . . Please help clear my name." He was ironically exiled back to Vologda, then transported to Tiflis and executed.

"Forty?"

"No, I'm twenty-nine," he laughed. Kuzakova, whose husband had been killed in the Russo-Japanese War, had three marauding children. "Sometimes they made such an unbearable rumpus that he'd open the door smiling and he'd sing with them." It is hard to believe Soso was that good-tempered, but Maria became devoted to him, listening to his stories of the seminary.

River Cock, perhaps discovering his near escape, intensified his searches of Stalin's room, which infuriated Kuzakova. The police knocked on the windows in the middle of the night. This woke the children, who sobbed while Stalin watched with absolute calm. They confiscated some letters from Serafima, including her farewell note, but he continued to meet up for picnics and parties to discuss politics with the other exiles. This irked Zivilev, but Stalin got his revenge. "Once, among the prome-nading public," remembers Golubev, "Stalin gave him such a dressing-down that he became terrified of bumping into Stalin, who used to joke that he hardly saw him." Indeed Kuzakova says, "I'd never seen the police so afraid of one man."

Stalin was now so close to the end of his two-year sentence that there was no point in escaping, however much he was "suffocating." He was bored enough to attend the local theatre, for which he was fined twenty-five kopecks. Presumably, Maria Kuzakova was another consolation. By the time he left, it seems she was pregnant with his child. According to her family, she told him she was expecting. He claimed he could not marry but promised to send money, which of course he never did.

On 25 May, River Cock arrested Stalin for attending a meeting of other revolutionaries, sentencing him to three days in the local jail. But Soso had survived his full term. When he was released on 26 June, he never even returned to bid goodbye to his pregnant landlady. "She came home and found her tenant and his stuff gone and only the rent on the table under a napkin." This was the reason that locals were discouraged from having affairs with exiles: they tended to leave suddenly.*

On 6 July 1911, Soso travelled by steamer down the river to Kotlas and thence to Vologda, where he was ordered to reside for two months. He

---

* The son, Constantine, was born after Stalin's departure. Kuzakova left memoirs during the dictatorship that naturally did not contain a confession of their affair., but on balance, it seems that the baby was Stalin's son. The dates on the birth certificate do not tally, but, as with Yakov Djugashvili and indeed Stalin's own movable birthday, such documents were often pre-dated or forward-dated. Such events were in any case registered very casually in

was under Okhrana surveillance from the moment he settled at various addresses in Vologda. Now the police spies gave him a new code name— "the Caucasian."

His prolific skirt-chasing was not over. Under the eyes of the Okhrana's spooks, the Caucasian passed the time in the seduction of a saucy schoolgirl who was the mistress of one of his comrades. When it suited him, he borrowed both the man's girlfriend and his passport.[2]

---

those days, especially in tiny villages far from Petersburg. Soso made no attempt to meet the child, but, unusually, the boy was later brought to Moscow, given a favoured job in the Central Committee apparat, and protected. He had an interesting career. Given the mother's insistence, Stalin's acquiescence in the child's later career, and his wife Nadya Alliluyeva's knowledge of the affair, it seems probable the dictator knew Constantine was his son. See the Epilogue.

27

The Central Committee and "Glamourpuss" the Schoolgirl

I am ready. The rest is up to you," Stalin wrote to Lenin once he was settled in Vologda, but he wanted to make sure that henceforth he was assigned to the centre. "I want to work but I'd work only in Petersburg or Moscow. I'm free again!"

Stalin treated his own feuds with lethal seriousness, but still sneered at Lenin's émigré rows. "Koba wrote that he can't be bothered to bark at the Liquidators or Vperod [the factions of Krasin and Gorky respectively, both opposed to Lenin], because he'll only mock those who are barking," wrote one Bolshevik to his comrades in Paris—where Lenin probably heard about Stalin's latest "immaturity." Nonetheless, in Paris at the end of May, the Central Committee (CC) appointed a Russian Organizational Committee, with Sergo as a member and Stalin as a special travelling envoy, a promotion soon known to the Okhrana.

Sergo set off for Russia to brief the ragged Bolshevik organization on the new appointments. The Okhrana watched the Caucasian even more closely, but he was an expert dodger of police spies. In early August, he managed to slip out of Vologda and reach Petersburg on a flying visit to meet Sergo. "Sergo gave Stalin Lenin's directive . . . and Lenin's request that he come abroad to discuss Party activities." Here was another minor escape, but Stalin managed to return to Vologda without the spooks even realizing he had gone.

Vologda was a metropolis compared to Solvychegodsk, with 38,000 citizens, libraries, theatres, a cathedral dating from the 1580s, a house that had belonged to Peter the Great and a grand governor's mansion. Stalin spent a month gathering funds for a longer excursion, and he read voraciously, visiting the library seventeen times. "I'd have thought you'd been strolling some other city's streets," his fellow exile from Solvychegodsk, Ivan Golubev, wrote teasingly, "but I . . . learn you've not budged, wallowing in semi-exile conditions. That's sad if true. So what are you going to do now? Wait? You might go insane with idleness!"

Yet Stalin seemed to be indulging the sybarite hidden within his steely ascetic for perhaps the only time in his life. His Okhrana surveillance soon divined the reason: a runaway schoolgirl who was the live-in mistress of Stalin's fellow exile Peter Chizhikov. Aged just sixteen, she was Pelageya Onufrieva, a pupil at the Totma Gymnasium and daughter of a prosperous Solvychegodsk smallholder. She had embarked on an affair with Chizhikov when he was exiled to Totma and eloped with him to Vologda, where she met the Caucasian. Chizhikov, who had encountered Soso in prison a few years earlier, soon fell under his spell, running his errands and raising money for his next escape. He did not seem to mind when this friendship developed into a *ménage à trois* with Soso.

Pelageya was just a frivolous and rebellious schoolgirl, but she somehow managed to impress the Okhrana agents with her fine clothes. They code-named her "Nariadnaya"—the Well-Dressed One, or Glamourpuss. No wonder even the obsessionally ambitious and committed Stalin was happy to waste a month in her company. "I always knew him as Josef," she recalls. The serpent literally offered Eve the forbidden fruit: "In those days one wasn't supposed to eat in the street but there was a shady avenue lined with trees. I went there with Stalin who often invited me . . . Once we sat on a bench and he offered me the fruit: 'Eat some. No one will see you here . . .'"

His friend Chizhikov worked during the day at the Colonial Goods Store. As soon as he left his home to go to work at 9 a.m., the spooks watched Stalin turn up and disappear inside. "We were quite happy when we were at home," Glamourpuss recounts, "we'd read quietly. He knew I loved literature. We talked a lot about books. We used to have lunch together, walked around town for hours and visited the library and we joked a lot. I was silly but so young." Soso, ever the teacher, lectured her on Shakespeare (including literary criticisms of *The Tempest*) and the paintings of the Louvre (which he must have visited during his week in Paris). Most touchingly he poured out his heart about Kato: how he had loved her, how he had wanted to shoot himself after her death, how his friends had taken away his gun and what beautiful dresses she made—and he mentioned his son Yakov. Stalin "had lots of friends. He had good taste—despite being a man," jokes Glamourpuss. "He talked about southern landscapes, how beautiful were the gardens, how elegant the buildings. He'd often say to me, 'I know you'd love it in the south. Come and see it for yourself . . . You'll be treated as one of the family!' "

Glamourpuss was cheeky and intelligent. Stalin was attracted to strong women, but ultimately preferred submissive housekeepers or teenagers. He undoubtedly enjoyed adolescent and teenage girls, a taste that later was to get him into serious trouble with the police. Even though the rules in Tsarist Russia were much laxer than they are today, particularly far away from the capital, this must reveal, at least, a need to dominate and control on Stalin's part. But it was not an obsession—some of his girlfriends were older than him.

Pelageya seemed to have understood the Caucasian better than most. She was probably the only person in his life to have teased him about his strangeness; he opened up to her. Even this most thin-skinned and touchy of men enjoyed Glamourpuss's mischief. He nicknamed her "Polya"; she called him "Oddball Osip."

"It was a long hot summer," she reminisces, but when it was over she felt "she would never see him again." One senses that Stalin had women in every town at this point. He told Glamourpuss that he was engaged to another girl in St. Petersburg, later writing to her: "You know I travelled to St. Petersburg to get married, but finally I ended up in prison . . ." If Oddball Osip had another woman, Polya the Glamourpuss, at the centre of a *ménage à trois,* could hardly complain. But who was the woman in Petersburg?

Glamourpuss "always knew he was going to leave. I wanted to see him off but he wouldn't let me, saying he was being followed." But "just before he left, he came over that morning" for a tender parting.

"I want to give you this as a present," he said, handing her a book, "to remember me by. It'll interest you."

"It certainly will," said Glamourpuss.

"Give me something to remember you by," asked Oddball Osip.

She gave him as a keepsake the cross that hung around her neck, but he would not take it. Instead he accepted the chain and "hung it on his watch." She asked for a photograph of him, but Stalin, about to plunge again into his secret life, refused: "No one photographs me. Only in prison by force. One day, I'll send you my photograph, but for now, it would just get you into trouble."

The book he gave her was *A Study of Western Literature* by Kogan, a special present from an autodidactic bibliophile, dedicated:

To clever, fiery Polya
From Oddball Osip*

They never met again but he kept writing. His letters, reported Pelageya, "were always very witty—he knew how to be funny even in the difficult moments of life." But when he was exiled in 1913, "I lost contact with him for ever."

However delightful the Glamourpuss, Oddball Osip could linger no longer. At 3:45 p.m. on 6 September 1911, the Okhrana spies reported that, accompanied by Chizhikov, "the Caucasian arrived at the station with two pieces of luggage—a little trunk and a bundle, apparently of bedclothes, and boarded the train for Petersburg." The spooks noticed that Stalin twice checked all the carriages, pretending to miss his tails.

"Djugashvili went by train Number Three under observation of agent Ilchykov," the Vologda Okhrana telegraphed Petersburg. "I ask you to meet him. Captain Popel." Yet Soso outwitted the reception party at the station: when he arrived at 8:40 p.m., he had shaken off the agents.

"The provincial," sneers the snobbish Trotsky, "arrived in the territory of the capital." Stalin first searched for Sergei Alliluyev, but he was not home. So he just strolled up and down Nevsky Prospect until he bumped into Silva Todria, his Georgian printing expert.

Just before Stalin's arrival, Stolypin, the Russian Premier, was assassinated right in front of the Emperor's box at the theatre in Kiev. The assassin was a rogue secret-police informer, who again personified the dangers

---

* In 1944, the secret police confiscated her copy of this book along with postcards from Stalin. See the Epilogue.

of *konspiratsia*. The victim was the last great statesman of the Russian Empire.

"Dangerous times," Todria warned Soso. "After Stolypin's murder, the police are everywhere. Concierges check all papers."

"Let's find a boarding-house near by," suggested Soso. The boarding-house "Russia" accepted his Chizhikov passport.

At the Alliluyev home, the doorbell rang. "I was very happy to see our friend Silva Todria," writes Anna, "but he wasn't alone. Behind him stood a thin man named Soso in a black coat and fedora." They asked for Sergei Alliluyev, but he was not home—so they waited. Soso read the newspapers. When Alliluyev got home, they peered out of the window: the police spies had picked up his trail when he collected his luggage. Now they watched the street.

Alliluyev called in his daughters, Anna and Nadya: "Go outside into the courtyard and see if there are two spooks in bowler hats." The excited girls spotted one agent in the courtyard, another in the street and two more at the corner.

Stalin returned for the night to the Russia guesthouse. At 7:50 a.m. on 9 September, there was a banging on his door.

"Let me sleep!" shouted Soso, always the nocturnal creature. The police burst in and arrested him, finding maps, photographs, letters, a German phrasebook (suggesting he was hoping to travel to Lenin's imminent Prague Conference) and the passport of Chizhikov, who had thus lent Stalin not just his girlfriend but his name too.[1]

Locking him up in the Petersburg House of Detention to await sentence, the Okhrana took charge of the Caucasian, keeping him for three weeks, neither informing the local police department nor handing him over to the Gendarmes. Probably they were making the usual attempt to turn him into a double-agent, but on 2 October they eventually informed the Petersburg Gendarmerie, whose Colonel Sobelev thereupon recommended exile "to eastern Siberia . . . for five years."

The Interior Minister, A. A. Makarov, reduced the sentence to three years. Stalin was allowed to suggest Vologda as his place of residence and to travel by his own means, instead of in a cluster of convicts. The physical description on his file was so inconsistent it might have belonged to another man. Was this just another case of the Tsarist regime's lenient muddle? Had palms been greased in 16 Fontanka or at the Interior Ministry? Did Stalin make some duplicitous deal or was the Okhrana hoping he would unconsciously lead them to his comrades? We do not know—but, the moment he was released with his travel-pass back to Vologdan exile, he slipped his Okhrana tails and disappeared for ten days into the streets of Petersburg, technically escaping again.

He met up with his friends Sergo and Spandarian. "In December 1911, Stalin was hiding from the police on Petersburgskaya Storona in the apartment of the Tsimakov family," says Vera Shveitzer, Spandarian's chief mistress, "and we went to see him. He lived in a cold room in a wooden glass-roofed house in a courtyard." They got an exuberant reception: Stalin "ran up to us and took our hands and dragged us into the room, roaring with laughter; we laughed back."

"You know how to enjoy yourselves," he said.

"Yes, we'll dance to celebrate your release!" answered Spandarian.

Sergo and Spandarian were about to travel to Lenin's Prague Conference, which marked the formal birth of the Bolshevik Party—and the divorce from the Mensheviks. Stalin had been invited but, after his new sentence, he was unable to go. Sergo and Spandarian took his messages to Lenin. "There was a small meeting in my apartment," recalls Shveitzer, attended by the three Caucasians. Sergo gave Stalin fifty roubles. On the run, "Stalin spent every night in a different place."

On Christmas Day, he was back in Vologda. He walked the streets in black coat and fedora looking for lodgings. His new landlord was a retired Gendarme who "didn't like Josef Vissarionovich"—for paternal as well as political reasons. The old Gendarme and his wife had a divorced daughter named Maria Bogoslovskaya with three young children and a sixteen-year-old maid named Sophia Kryukova. Soso lived on a little bed behind the curtain next to the stove in the kitchen, but he evidently entered into another affair with the divorcee Maria. Even though she wrote her memoirs in 1936, when nothing explicit could be recorded about the private foibles of the Leader, Sophia the maid implies that the exile and the divorcee had a relationship. "He and Maria often used to argue and she used to cry. They shouted and were almost at each other's throats. During their rows, the names of other women could often be heard."

Stalin flirted with the maid while fending off the jealous Gendarme's daughter. "Once after a public holiday," says Sophia the maid, "I noticed Josef Vissarionovich was watching me from behind the curtain. I had long black hair and wore an attractive dress with a long skirt of flowered Japanese cloth."

"That dress really suits you," said Stalin. "In my homeland, Georgia, girls your age wear dresses like that." Sophia was sensible in 1936 not to reveal how well she knew Stalin, but they obviously spent some time together because she introduced him to her boozy father, who embarrassed her.

"Don't worry," Stalin comforted her, "my father was a drunkard too. Mother brought me up." He clearly enjoyed showing off about his education and foreign languages. When he read *Zvezda* (the Bolshevik *Star*) and foreign newspapers, he impressed her by translating passages into Russian. "It really made me laugh," she recalls.

Stalin usually came home late at night and was visited only by a tall dark man, possibly Shaumian or Yakov Sverdlov, a rising young Bolshevik. He met up again with his cuckolded friend Chizhikov. Their *ménage à trois* was not resuscitated because Glamourpuss had gone back to school. But she was on his mind. On arrival, he sent an erotic postcard of Aphrodite to his teenage Venus in Totma: "Well, fiery Polya, I'm stuck in Vologda and hugging your 'dear' 'nice' Petenka [Chizhikov]. So drink the health of your famous Oddball Osip."*

Romancing the landlord's daughter and her maid, Stalin was killing time while awaiting developments in Prague. There, the Conference of just eighteen delegates, a sign of how much the Party had shrunk, chose the first true Bolshevik Central Committee. Sergo and Spandarian were elected, but the rising star was a stirring, working-class orator named Roman Malinovsky. Lenin was thrilled by this genuine proletarian talent. "He makes an excellent impression," he exulted; "the soil is rich!" Malinovsky looked the part: "tall, strongly built and dressed almost fashionably" with "thick reddish hair and yellow eyes," his pockmarks gave him "a fierce expression as if he'd been through fire." But he had one serious drawback: when arrested some time earlier and convicted of rape and burglary, he was recruited by the Okhrana and code-named "Portnoi" (the Tailor). He was their highest-paid agent.

---

* His other, considerably less glamorous correspondent there was a stolid and bespectacled Bolshevik of just twenty-two who had been in exile in Solvychegodsk just before him. His name was Vyacheslav Scriabin, later "Molotov," who became his longtime political henchman. Molotov heard that Stalin was known as the "Caucasian Lenin." He was musical and could play the violin and mandolin. He earned one rouble a day by playing mandolin for rich merchants and their molls in the local restaurant and in the new cinema there. Stalin regarded this as beneath him as a Bolshevik. Later he taunted Molotov, "You performed for drunk merchants—they smeared your face in mustard!" Scriabin did not adopt his "industrial name" Molotov until 1914. At this time he was called Ryabin, Zvanov, Mikhailov and V.M., though the Okhrana called him "the Runner" because he walked so fast.

At the first Central Committee, Lenin and Zinoviev proposed the co-option of Stalin.* He had gained a new importance for Lenin as a nationalities expert. Lenin now recognized that Stalin was one of the few Bolsheviks who shared his keenness to formulate policies that would win followers amongst the non-Russian peoples of the Empire, but without promising them independence. The Tailor dutifully reported to his Okhrana paymasters that Stalin, Spandarian and Sergo "were elected to the Russian Bureau to be paid 50 roubles monthly wages." Unlike the Okhrana, Stalin took some time to find out about Prague and wrote to Krupskaya to learn more. "I got a letter from Ivanovich [Stalin's Party code name]," Krupskaya told Sergo, but "it's immediately obvious he's terribly cut off from everything, head in the clouds . . . What a pity he couldn't attend the Conference." In a coded letter, Stalin begged Shveitzer for news of Prague.

The isolation was about to end. Sergo was already on his way to Vologda.

On 18 February 1912, the Vologda police spies reported that the Caucasian met "an unknown man"—surely Sergo—who announced his promotion to the Central Committee, the highest organ of the Party, a status he would hold for the rest of his life, and handed over his salary, secret addresses and codes. It was probably now that Stalin agreed with Krupskaya, chief code maker as well as Lenin's wife, to use Gorky's poem "Oltenian Legend," as their code. His handwritten copy of the poem survives.

Meanwhile Lenin, back in Paris, panicked at the lack of news: "There's no word of Ivanovich. What's happened to him? Where is he now? How is he?" Sergo finally reported to Lenin that he had met Soso: "I made a final agreement with him. He is satisfied."

It was time to disappear again. Whenever he wanted to vanish from Vologda, Soso bribed the local police with five gold roubles and, according to Vera Shveitzer, escaped five times.

His landlady, Gavrilova, found him packing. "Are you going away?"

He hesitated: "Yes I am."

She said she would have to inform the police.

"Could you do it tomorrow?" he asked. She agreed.

---

* Stalin's associates from Tiflis and Baku, Kalinin and Shaumian, were elected candidate CC members—substitutes if full members were arrested. Elena Stasova became Secretary of the Russian Bureau.

At 2 a.m. on 29 February, his tails reported him boarding the train for Moscow without permission. But first he received a last letter from his schoolgirl. He bought another sensual postcard, showing a sculpture of a couple wildly kissing and wrote this to Glamourpuss:

> *Dear PG,*
>
> *I got your letter today . . . Don't write to the old address since none of us are there any more . . . I owe you a kiss for the kiss, passed on to me by Peter. Let me kiss you now. I'm not simply sending a kiss but am kiiissssing you passionately (it's not worth kissing any other way),*
>
> *Josef*

So, on the last night of February 1912, Stalin surreptitiously caught the train, via Moscow, to the capital. Lenin's new CC member was on the road.[2]

28

"Don't Forget That Name and Be Very Wary!"

O n one cold gloomy Petersburg winter day, I was studying when there was a knock at the door," says Kavtaradze, who was attending Petersburg University while giving maths lessons to the Alliluyev sisters. "Suddenly in came Stalin. I knew he'd been exiled. He was as friendly and merry as usual, wearing a light overcoat despite the biting frost but . . . he wouldn't take his coat off. 'I'll be here for a bit . . . I'll just rest a while. I came straight from Moscow and I noticed I was being tailed in Moscow and when I got off the train, I spotted the same spook . . . he's lurking right outside your place!"

"This was serious," notes Kavtaradze. The two Georgians waited until darkness. Kavtaradze decided that there was only one way to escape: Stalin would have to dress up in drag. Kavtaradze procured some dresses and Stalin modelled them—but the look just did not work. "I could get women's dresses," said Kavtaradze, "but it was impossible to make Stalin look like a woman."

The spook, reflected Stalin, "doesn't want to arrest me—he wants to observe. So I'll get some sleep."

"Yes, sleep: maybe he won't be able to take the frost. Like Napoleon's army," joked Kavtaradze.

"He will," replied Soso, who slept all day. But when they emerged onto the streets, the agent was still there. "Let's walk a little," said Soso.

He was hungry, so they ate at Fedorov's restaurant, but the spy reappeared. "Damn!" swore Stalin. "He pops up from nowhere!"

A cab clattered down the street. Stalin hailed the carriage and leaped on, but the spook hailed another. The galloping phaetons chased each other down Liteiny, but, realizing he was close to a safe house, Stalin jumped out of the moving cab into a snowdrift, which enveloped him completely. The spy's galloped past, following the now empty carriage.*

Stalin dressed up "in the uniform of the Army Medical College and went out." This was his favoured disguise in Petersburg that year. He stayed about a week. His new assignment was to convert the Bolshevik weekly *Zvezda* into a daily, *Pravda* (Truth).

Stalin was brought to the flat of Tatiana Slavatinskaya, aged thirty-three, a cultured and good-looking Bolshevik, an orphan who had educated herself and studied at the Conservatoire, becoming a fan of Chaliapin's singing. One of Lenin's covert operatives, Elena Stasova, trained her in code making. Married to a Jewish revolutionary named Lurye and mother of two children, Tatiana sheltered various Bolsheviks on the run, one of whom "brought a Caucasian with the codename 'Vasily' who lived with us for a while."

She did not much like "Vasily"—Stalin's latest alias. "Initially, he seemed too serious, too closed and shy, and his only concern was not to bother us. It was very hard to make him sleep in a bigger, more comfortable room, but on going out to work I always ordered the housemaid† to cook him dinner along with the children. He stayed a week and I ran his errands as messenger." Stalin appointed her his secretary for the Duma elections. Slavatinskaya seems to have been fairly liberated, in the style of these early feminists. He started an affair with his "dear darling Tatiana" that was "well known" among Soviet grandees during Stalin's rule.

Sometimes Stalin stayed with the Alliluyevs. The Venice of the North

---

* Kavtaradze was arrested by the Gendarmes the next day. When they showed him a photo of Stalin, he laughed because he looked "so tousled." "Do you know him?" asked the officer. "No, he looks crazy." "Do you know Djugashvili?" "Yes I know Soso Djugashvili, I just saw him." "Do you know he's a state criminal who's very dangerous and on the run?" "Well, you know we Georgians always know each other . . ." Kavtaradze was released.

† The housemaid was an Estonian girl who later married Kalinin, becoming the first lady of the USSR before being arrested during Stalin's Terror while her husband remained head of state. See *Stalin: The Court of the Red Tsar*.

was a picture of "frosts, snowdrifts, icy sledge paths," writes Anna Alliluyeva. "Its streets were filled with low Finnish sleighs decorated with ribbons and jingly bells" pulled by "stumpy little horses," bearing "loads of laughing passengers." Anna and her younger sister Nadya were glued to their windows longing for a ride—when Soso appeared: "Who'd like a sleigh-ride? Well, get dressed and hurry up, we're leaving straight away!" The girls were delighted. "We all jumped up shouting with excitement," recounts Anna. "Now we were invited"—and by none other than "Soso himself," whose articles they loyally read. The girls knew him better now: "Usually uncommunicative, he can also laugh and joke boyishly and tell amusing stories. He sees the funny side of people and imitates them to such perfection that everyone roars with laughter." But now he was in a hurry.

"Come on! Fedya [their brother Fyodor], Nadya! Get dressed"—and he ordered their maid, Fenya: "Get the fur coats!"

In the street, Soso called out to the driver: "How about giving us a ride!"

Stalin was in good spirits: "Every word . . . makes us laugh. Soso laughs with us all as the sleigh glides down Sampsonevsky Prospect past the station" with its "small steam trains." Suddenly, Soso jumped off the sleigh and back into his secret life: "Stop, I'll get off here, you can ride home"—and, just like that, the Bolshevik Macavity vanished into the station. Was he really having fun with the girls, or was the whole outing a cover to shake off a spook?

Soso disappeared again. The police spies lost him but guessed correctly that he would resurface in the Caucasus.[1]

On 16 March 1912, the Okhrana's double-agent "Fikus" reported that Stalin was back in Tiflis, where he was staying with a singing teacher who worked at the Teachers' Society School, directed by the severe Elena Stasova.* His

---

* Now known as "Comrade Zelma," Stasova was the granddaughter of the architect to the Emperors Alexander I and Nicholas I and daughter of a noble lawyer who worked in the Senate, a herald at Alexander II's coronation: she had much in common with those cultured nobles Lenin and Krupskaya. She knew Stalin from Baku and was a specialist in secret work, often involved in keeping Party funds. Stasova was so humourless and prissy that Stalin laughed at her. She later became one of Lenin's secretaries. After Lenin's death, when Krupskaya opposed him, Stalin half jokingly threatened to appoint Stasova as his widow instead. She did not seek high office after Lenin's death, almost disappearing, one of the very few Old Bolsheviks to survive the Terror. She emerged as a revered antique in Khrushchev's reign, living on into Brezhnev's, and dying in 1966.

hostess was told "not to ask the name of her visitor," but Stalin, perhaps missing home, sang Georgian songs with her.

Soso met up with his playboy friend and CC member Spandarian, and with Stasova. He visited his son, Yakov, whom the Svanidzes were bringing up "as their own with our own children." The Monoselidzes remained shocked by his callous neglect. "My nephew, having been left an orphan by his mother," complains Sashiko, "was also almost orphaned by his father." Soso did not stay long, rushing over to Batumi and then back to Baku.[2]

There he found another witch hunt for traitors: the Mensheviks were investigating Spandarian, hoping to prove that he had either falsified a Party stamp or that he was an Okhrana spy. Stalin defended his friend. The Mensheviks refused to let him attend their investigation but agreed to send an envoy to hear Stalin's side of the story. The envoy was Boris Nikolaevsky, the Menshevik who would, in sunny Californian exile, become the chronicler of the underground. Nikolaevsky consulted a Bolshevik, Abel Yenukidze, genial godfather to Nadya Alliluyeva, Svanidze friend and sceptical acquaintance of Stalin, who ultimately destroyed him.

"Have you ever heard the name 'Koba'?" Yenukidze asked Nikolaevsky, in a Baku café.

"No," replied Nikolaevsky.

"Koba," explained Yenukidze, "is a dangerous fellow who's capable of anything!" The Georgians were different from Russians: "We're a vengeful people."

Nikolaevsky laughed and asked in a mock-Caucasian accent: "Will he cut me with his dagger just a little bit?"

"Don't laugh," replied Yenukidze seriously. "He'll cut your throat if he believes it necessary. It's not Great Russia here: this is Old Asia. Don't forget that name and be very wary." Yenukidze would pay dearly for such outspokenness about his "dangerous" comrade.

Stalin was "waiting when I arrived, sitting in the shadows so he could easily observe me," recounts the wary Nikolaevsky. They may have cleared up the question of Spandarian, but while in Baku Stalin ordered his Mauserists to kill a former sailor of the battleship *Potemkin* whom he accused of being an Okhrana spy. "He was shot," notes Nikolaevsky, "and left for dead, but he regained consciousness and claimed rehabilitation."

The Mensheviks ordered Nikolaevsky, who now became "very interested in old Koba's deeds," to investigate. But Nikolaevsky was arrested. Stalin vanished again.[3]

. . .

"We need to send 'Ivanovich' [Stalin] to Petersburg immediately," Krup-skaya told Sergo, who was in Kiev. Stalin and Sergo, those two high-handed Georgians, who would later dominate the USSR together, revelled in their new CC eminence. Stasova grumbled that "Sergo and 'Ivanovich' keep giving orders but say nothing about what is happening around us." Days later, Spandarian was arrested.

Stalin rushed northwards, pausing for a quick chat with Spandarian's girlfriend, Vera Shveitzer, in the station buffet at Rostov-on-Don, to meet Sergo in Moscow,* where they visited Malinovsky. He betrayed them. As the Georgians left Moscow, they noticed their Okhrana tails. The agents saw them onto the train, but Stalin then jumped off outside the station. In Petersburg, it took the Okhrana six days to realize that Soso had never arrived.

The secret police, aided by Malinovsky and other double-agents, had decided to mop up the CC. On 14 April, Sergo was arrested too, but Soso the super-conspirator managed to outwit the spooks just a little longer, surrepticiously reaching the capital.

Suddenly the Revolution received a bloody boost. On 4 April, troops on the river Lena's Siberian goldfields fired on workers, killing 150. "The Lena shots broke the ice of silence," Stalin exulted in *Zvezda*, "and the river of popular resentment is flowing again. The ice has broken. It has started!" Strikes broke out across the Empire. Challenged in the Duma, Maklakov, the Interior Minister, arrogantly replied: "So it was. So it will be."

Stalin was beside himself with excitement. "We live!" he boomed in an article. "Our scarlet blood seethes with the fire of unspent strength!" Lenin declared that "the Revolution is resurgent."

In Petersburg, Stalin stayed with N. G. Poletaev, proletarian poet and Bolshevik Duma deputy, whose house enjoyed parliamentary immunity, and saw Tatiana Slavatinskaya, his assistant. From the "untouchable Pole-taev's house," Stalin "started to run the weekly *Zvezda*," writing a stream of passionate articles. Trotsky dismisses them as "the language of Tiflis

---

* The nine-year-old son of a Moscow Bolshevik remembered how a Caucasian came to visit his father. The father was out, so the Caucasian tenderly chatted to the child. As he was leaving, the Caucasian sharply slapped the boy's face then said, "Don't cry, little boy. Remember, today Stalin [or whichever name he was then using] talked to you!" When the boy told his parents, they were angry and baffled until they heard of this mountain custom in Georgia: when a prince visited a village family, the peasant would slap his son across the face and say, "Remember today this Prince visited our house."

Seminary homilectics," but they were stirring stuff, not at all like the leaden ideological claptrap of the future. The Alliluyev girls read them aloud to each other. Their favourite began: "The country lay in chains at the feet of its enslavers." With his "scarlet blood seething," Soso wrote a much admired May Day appeal that was a surprising hymn to his beloved Nature, the last throwback to his days as a romantic poet: "Nature is awakening from its winter dream. The forests and mountains are turning green. Flowers adorn meadows and pastures. The sun shines more warmly. We feel in the air the pleasure of new life and the world is beginning to dance for joy."*

"In April 1912," recalled Stalin, "we agreed on the *Pravda* platform and worked out the first issue." Founded in three little rooms, the first Bolshevik daily was legal—but its illegal editor-in-chief, Stalin, had to run it from the shadows. *Pravda* was funded by Victor Tikhomirnov, son of a Kazan tycoon who left him 300,000 roubles and whose childhood friend was Vyacheslav Scriabin—"Molotov." Tikhomirnov channelled thousands of roubles through Molotov, a founder of *Pravda*.

Stalin decided it was time to meet this young man. Molotov was told to wait in a courtyard behind a dentist's apartment near their printing-press. Stalin suddenly emerged, as if out of nowhere, from behind a pile of firewood. Soso liked to cultivate this mystery: his feline charisma certainly dazzled the ponderous but younger Molotov, who had never met a real CC member.

"I didn't see how he appeared, but he wore the uniform of a psychoneurology student. We introduced ourselves." Molotov noticed the pockmarks and the Georgian accent. "He discussed only the most important issues without wasting a second on anything unnecessary. He delivered some *Pravda* materials. No superfluous gestures. Then he vanished

---

* Stalin blasted the regime of "Nicholas the Last." The Emperor and Empress were already placing their trust in a Siberian healer and dissolute hierophant named Grigory Rasputin. Once Rasputin's intimacy with the monarchs was known, this created a growing scandal that alienated monarchists and Marxists alike. Few knew that the little heir, Tsarevich Alexei, suffered from haemophilia. Nicholas and Alexandra increasingly believed that Rasputin alone could staunch the bleeding and ease the child's pain. The ever-changing Interior Ministers and Okhrana directors now started using their agents to tail Rasputin and chronicle his orgies to discredit him with the Emperor. Increasingly the Empress judged her ministers by their attitude to Rasputin. Stalin wrote about him when he called the Tsar and his courtiers "destroyers of liberties, worshippers of gallows and firing-squads, thieving quartermasters, robber police, murderous secret policemen and dissolute Rasputins! . . . To complete the picture: the brutal shooting of toilers in the Lena goldfields."

just as suddenly as he had appeared. He climbed over the fence and all this was done with classic simplicity and grace."

The next day, Molotov, almost lovestruck, gushed to a friend: "He's astonishing, he possesses internal revolutionary beauty, a Bolshevik to the marrow, clever, cunning as conspirator . . ." When they met again, they talked all night. It was the beginning of a partnership that would last for the next forty-one years.

Soso's vigilance was sensible: he was virtually the last CC member at liberty. Sergo and Spandarian were behind bars. On 22 April 1912, the first *Pravda* was published. When Stalin strolled out of the parliamentary sanctuary of Poletaev's apartment, the Okhrana arrested him. By June, thanks to Malinovsky's betrayals, only one ineffectual CC member was at liberty. The organization was again in ruins. Stasova rushed up from Tiflis to repair some of the damage, but she too was arrested.

On 2 July, Stalin, sentenced to three years' exile, was despatched to Siberia.[4] His courtiers later flattered him with the nickname "the Doctor of Escapology." This was to be his shortest exile.

29

The Escapist: Kamo's Leap
and the Last Bank Robbery

On the way to Tomsk, somewhere near Vologda, Stalin encountered Boris Nikolaevsky, the Mensheviks' Baku investigator. Soso gave nothing away but borrowed Nikolaevsky's treasured blue tea mug, which he then pinched.

On 18 July 1912 he arrived in Tomsk and was placed on a steamship up the Ob to Kolpashevo, where he disembarked for a week and met Simon Vereshchak, his Menshevik cell mate in Bailov Prison. Stalin dined with Vereshchak and Simon Surin, a Menshevik and Okhrana agent, before boarding another steamer upriver to his destination, Narym, where he was welcomed by Yakov Sverdlov, another young CC member.

Narym could have been worse. A settlement of 1,000 people with 150 houses, it was just within the agricultural belt. Its forests teemed with life, but it was high summer and the marshy landscape swarmed with mosquitoes—and with too many exiles, who even ran their own café, butcher's shop and colonial goods store, plus, more important for Stalin, two escape bureaux.

"He arrived at my home," remembers his landlady Yefrosina Alexeyeva, "in a Russian embroidered open-necked white shirt which left his chest exposed." She tried to put him off because there were already two exiles living in her spare room, but "he went into the exiles' room, looked around, talked with his comrades, then moved in" with Sverdlov.

Son of a wealthy Jewish printer from Nizhny Novgorod, the twenty-seven-year-old Yakov Sverdlov sported round spectacles and "black luxuriant hair," but his most surprising feature was that out of this apparently meek figure of "remarkable gentleness" burst a "thunderous voice—the Devil knows how that monstrous voice could come from such a small man," laughed Molotov. "A Jericho trumpet!" He looked like the sort of Jewish intellectual that Stalin loathed, but actually Sverdlov was a ruthless and unpretentious organizer. The two most impressive Bolsheviks in Russia shared a room and irritated each other.

Stalin, always the lazy egotist, avoided his share of the housework. The meticulous Sverdlov ended up doing it himself. "I liked to creep out for the post on Sverdlov's day to do it," chuckled Stalin when he recounted memories to Sverdlov and the Alliluyev girls. "Sverdlov had to look after the house whether he liked it or not—keep the stove alight and do the cleaning . . . How many times I tried to trick you and get out of the housework. I used to wake up when it was my turn and lie still as if asleep."

"And do you think I didn't notice?" replied Sverdlov. "I noticed only too well."

The local Georgians, led by an exile known as "the Prince," had heard of Soso, "a great man," for whom they threw a Georgian feast. The guests sang in Russian and Georgian, dancing the *lesginka*. At the dance, a local housewife named Lukeria Tihomirova, aged twenty-five, bumped into "the Georgian in a double-breasted black coat," who introduced himself as Djugashvili. But this time he did not bother to flirt, just sitting with Lukeria's two-year-old niece on his knee, not even drinking.

"So young and already smoking a pipe," she said flirtatiously. But Soso did not take the bait. The CC member had much on his mind: *Pravda,* the Duma elections—and a big bank robbery. He did not intend to stay long.

Lenin and Krupskaya, who had moved from Paris to Cracow, encouraged Soso and Sverdlov to escape. Sverdlov set off first but was recaptured. Then it was Soso's turn.

"My sons took him by boat to the riverport," says his landlady Alexeyeva.

"I'm leaving my books for my comrades," Soso told her, doling out "apples and sugar and two bottles of good vodka from the parcel he'd received." Then he set out with Yakov and Agafon Alexeyev in their canoe. At "dusk on a dark overcast night, no moonlight," remembers Yakov Alexeyev, they paddled him to the river jetty, asking when he would return.

"Expect me," he replied, "when you see me." On 1 September, he caught the steamboat to Tomsk. Sverdlov followed and they travelled together. Stalin, always selfish and in command, posed as a commercial traveller on the train. So he bought a first-class ticket, mischievously forcing the diminutive Sverdlov to hide in his dirty laundry basket. They were confronted by a Gendarme, who, suspicious of the laundry, was just about to stab it with his bayonet when Sverdlov cried: "There's a man in here!" A grinning Stalin bribed the policeman just in time. They reached Petersburg.* The prolific escapist had spent just thirty-eight days in Narym.[1]

Around 12 September, an unkempt Stalin with "a long beard, crumpled cap, worn shoes and an old jacket with a black shirt" was again strolling up and down Nevsky Prospect, looking suspiciously like an escaped convict among the dapper boulevardiers and fashionable ladies, when he saw Kavtaradze.

"I've escaped from Narym," said Stalin. "I arrived safely but nobody is at the safe house . . . Just as well I at least met you." Kavtaradze was alarmed by this dishevelled Siberian vision—"his look was inappropriate for Nevsky Prospect"—but immediately led him to a new safe house belonging to "a certain Rear-Admiral's widow," probably Baroness Maria Shtakelberg, descendant of a Catherine the Great courtier, who rented rooms to Georgian students. Presently Stalin and Sverdlov moved in with the Alliluyevs.

Stalin visited the Stasova apartment, where he collected the CC treasury which Elena had left with her brother on her arrest. He then bumped into an old girlfriend.

"I was on my way to teach down Nevsky Prospect," says Tatiana Sukhova, "when suddenly I felt a man's hand on my shoulder. It made me

---

* Stalin told this story to Molotov on their way to the Teheran Conference in 1943 and to his son-in-law Yuri Zhdanov. Back in Narym, the district policeman found Stalin was missing the next day but waited to see if he would return from Tomsk. By the time the police reported his escape to the governor of Tomsk, who had issued an alert, it was 3 November and Stalin had been in Petersburg for weeks.

jump but a familiar voice addressed me: 'Don't be afraid, Comrade Tatiana, it's me!' And there was Comrade Osip Koba standing next to me." They arranged to meet at "some workers' meeting." Later they walked together and, "as we passed a café, Comrade Koba took a red carnation and gave it to me."

Days later, he arrived in Tiflis, where his Bolshevik gangsters were assembling. Kamo was out.[2]

Stalin had kept a distant eye on his demented brigand, Kamo. In Tiflis, Budu Mdivani and Tsintsadze were preparing to spring the prisoner from the Metekhi Fortress's Unit for the Criminally Insane, where a doctor recorded Kamo's bizarre behaviour: "Complains that mice bother him, though his building has no mice. Patient suffers from hallucinations. He hears strange voices, talks with someone, and is answered." The guard who watched him "noticed that Ter-Petrossian rises during the night, catches something in the air, crawls under the table, trying to find something . . . complains someone is throwing stones in the room and when asked who, replies, 'The devil's brother.' " In fact, Kamo was planning his escape.

Kamo's warder was a simpleton named Bragin whom he gradually charmed and then recruited as courier. Mdivani and Kamo's sisters met Bragin and gave him escape tools, saws and ropes, which he smuggled in to his patient. Kamo sawed through the bars, replacing them with paste made from his bread. It took him five days to sever his shackles, which he held in place with wire.

On 15 August 1912, Mdivani and Tsintsadze's Mauserists waved a handkerchief three times from the street. Kamo broke the shackles and bars and abseiled down the walls. The rope snapped and Kamo, who felt little pain, toppled into the Kura. Clambering out, he tossed his shackles into the river and walked to the nearest street, where he boarded a tram (to confuse search dogs) before making the rendezvous with the Mauserists.

One night, recalls Sashiko Svanidze, while police combed the city and the press sensationalized the escape, "Comrade Budu Mdivani came and told Misha [Monoselidze, her husband] that they'd sprung Kamo from the Mental Hospital the night before . . . They brought Kamo, who stayed for a month at our place." Sashiko, Stalin's son and her own children were then staying in the country, but Kamo looked after Monoselidze for a month by cooking him delicious meals. Kamo, in disguise, then escaped abroad via Batumi and Istanbul.

"Kamo came to us in Paris," recalls Krupskaya. "He suffered greatly from the split between Illich [Lenin] on one hand, and Bogdanov and Krasin* on the other," bewildered by the schism between the three heroes for whom he had performed his most outrageous bank robberies. Kamo wavered and Lenin "listened with great pity for this extremely daring but naïve man with a fiery soul." Lenin, like Stalin, knowing that concern and health care offered ways of controlling his political protégés, offered to pay for an operation on Kamo's damaged eye. After surgery in Brussels, Kamo set off to smuggle arms into Russia. He was arrested in Bulgaria and Istanbul, each time managing to charm his way to freedom. Back in Tiflis, Kamo assembled the Outfit. A mail coach with a huge sum of cash was expected to gallop down the main highway into the city. Around 22 September, Stalin, in charge of Party financial matters inside Russia, also arrived in Tiflis.

It was probably now that Tsintsadze, as Stalin recalled after the Second World War, gave the gangsters his pep talk in a private room at the Tamamshev Caravanserai on Yerevan Square before they rode up the Kadzhorskoe Highway.

On 24 September, Kamo and Tsintsadze, with Kupriashvili and about eighteen gunmen, ambushed the mail coach three miles outside Tiflis. The highwaymen tossed bombs at the police and Cossacks: three policemen and a postilion were killed. A fourth policeman was wounded but opened fire on the bank robbers. The holdup escalated into a brutal firefight. The gunmen failed to grab the money; the Cossacks rallied. When the Outfit eventually retreated, the Cossacks gave chase but Tsintsadze and Kupriashvili, both crack shots, covered their retreat, picking off seven Cossacks in a galloping battle down the Kadzhorskoe Highway.

It was the last bow of the Outfit. Kamo was tracked down to his hideout with eighteen of his gangsters. They were arrested. Kamo received four death sentences.

---

* Krasin finally left active politics, but Lenin welcomed his return to the Bolsheviks after the Revolution, appointing him People's Commissar for Trade, Industry and Transport, and later Ambassador to London. Krasin the engineer was one of the brains behind the refrigeration, embalming and displaying of the dead Lenin in 1924. He himself died in 1926.

"I'm resigned to death," Kamo wrote to Tsintsadze, "I'm absolutely calm. On my grave there should already be grass growing six feet high. One can't escape death for ever. One must die one day. But I'll try my luck once more and perhaps one day, we'll laugh at our enemies again . . ."[3] This seemed highly unlikely.*

Soso did not linger in Tiflis.

---

* Once again, Kamo cheated the noose, benefiting from the broad amnesty of Nicholas II on the three hundredth anniversary of the Romanov dynasty in 1913. Kamo remained in jail for five years but lived to meet up again with Stalin and play out the ultimate insane violence after the Revolution. See the Epilogue. Of the female gangsters, Anneta and Patsia died of TB, as did many of the others. By the end of the 1930s, only Alexandra Darakhvelidze and Bachua Kupriashvili survived to leave their memoirs.

30

Travels with the Mysterious Valentina

Stalin was back in Petersburg, editing *Pravda* and staying with Molotov and Tatiana Slavatinskaya, within days of the failed robbery. He poured out articles,* drafted the Manifesto and presided over the nomination for the Duma elections. After supervising the selection of the Bolshevik candidates in Petersburg in mid-October, he oversaw Malinovsky's nomination in Moscow.

Soso's life on the run was an exhausting series of "sleepless nights . . . He flitted from one place to another, crossing street after street to confuse the Okhrana, making his way through back alleys," explains Anna Alliluyeva. "If happening to pass a workman's café," he "would sit there over a cup of tea until 2 a.m.," or if noticed by a Gendarme, "he'd pretend to be tipsy and dive into a café, sitting it out until dawn with the cabdrivers amid the stench of cheap tobacco before coming to sleep in a friend's place"—especially the Alliluyev apartment with the sensual Olga and her lively daughters. Stalin often "dropped in," sitting on the sofa in their dining-room "looking very tired."

---

* His articles are revealing of his cynical view of diplomacy (he paraphrases Talleyrand) and his belief in doublespeak (long before Orwell coined the word): "When bourgeois diplomats prepare for war, they shout loudly about 'peace.' A diplomat's words must contradict his deeds—otherwise what sort of diplomat is he? Fine words are a mask to conceal shady deeds. A sincere diplomat is like dry water. Or wooden iron."

The girls were always delighted to see him; their mother, Olga, looked after him. "If you feel like taking a rest, Soso," said Olga, "go and lie on the bed. It's no good trying to catch a nap in this bedlam . . ." Reading between the lines of Anna's accounts, Soso still had a special relationship with Olga, at least in their devotion to the cause. When leaving their place, he would say to Olga, "Come out with me." Olga "didn't ask any questions. She put on her coat and went out with Stalin. Having plotted their course of action, they hired a cab and drove off. Stalin made a sign and Mother got out. He was evidently shaking the police off his tracks. Stalin continued his journey alone."

Stalin invited Olga to the Mariinsky Theatre: "Please, Olga, let's go to the Theatre immediately—you'll just be in time for the opening performance." But, just before the play, he added, "I did so want to see a play even just once, but I can't." Olga had to go on her own and deliver a message to a box at the Mariinsky.

On 25 October 1912, six Bolsheviks and six Mensheviks were elected to the Imperial Duma—not a bad result. Karlo Chkheidze, the Menshevik whom Stalin had outraged in Batumi in 1901, was elected Chairman of the SD faction with Malinovsky as his deputy. Among the "Bolshevik Six," the Okhrana had managed to get two agents elected to the Duma, quite an achievement of *konspiratsia*. They took the Okhrana right into Lenin's inner circle.

In *Pravda*, Stalin pushed for conciliation with the Mensheviks. When the Bolsheviks planned a demonstration outside the Duma, the Mensheviks persuaded them to abandon it. This alarmed Lenin, who bombarded Stalin with articles attacking his conciliatory policy. Remarkably, Stalin turned down forty-seven of Lenin's articles. Lenin, now in Cracow, summoned Stalin and the Six. "Comrade Stalin," remembered one of the Bolshevik Six, "immediatedly stated that the Bolshevik delegates had to visit Lenin abroad."

On 28 October, the spooks observed Stalin visiting his friend Kavtaradze. They followed them when they went to eat in Fedorov's restaurant, a favourite haunt, but after dinner the police agents realized that he had disappeared. They searched for Soso, but he had vanished.[1]

Lenin ordered Valentina Lobova, another of the liberated, capable girls of the Bolshevik generation, to accompany Stalin. She commissioned Lenin's "foreign minister" and secret fixer Alexander Shotman to get Stalin to Cracow "with maximum speed and absolute security. This is a directive from Lenin." Stalin "had arrived in Petersburg in the company of

Valentina Lobova," in Shotman's tactful words, "staying in a hotel as a Persian citizen with a good Persian passport in his pocket."

Shotman explained the covert routes to Cracow—the riskier southerly route via Abo, or the longer, safer route by foot across the Swedish border at Haparanda. Stalin chose the Abo route. Then Stalin set off with Valentina Lobova, smuggled out of Petersburg in a covered cart. They caught the train to Finland from Levashovo Station, using Russian passports. In Finland, Eino Rakhia, later Lenin's bodyguard, delivered a Finnish passport and accompanied the couple to the Abo steam-ferry. "Two policeman verified documents . . . Although Comrade Stalin . . . did not at all resemble a Finn, everything happily went off without a hitch." Stalin and Valentina boarded the ferry across the Baltic to Germany.

This was another of Soso's mysterious relationships. Valentina, code-named "Comrade Vera," was a beauty married to a Bolshevik who was yet another Okhrana mole: the Party had never been more riddled with traitors. We do not know if she was aware that her husband was a double-agent, but she was totally trusted by Lenin. Shotman's memoir shows that Soso (on Persian papers, name unknown) had been travelling with Valentina for some time. They first came to Helsinki, sharing a room in a guesthouse, in "late summer," possibly September, right after his escape from Narym. Shotman implies that they were together. Travelling hundreds of miles after September 1912, they were apparently lovers, one of those little affairs between comrades thrown together on dangerous missions. When Valentina's husband was later executed as a traitor, it must have contributed to Stalin's growing distrust of perfidious wives.*

The pair caught the train to Cracow in Galicia, a province of the Dual Monarchy of the Habsburg Emperor-King Franz-Josef.²

Lenin adored Cracow. The Galician capital was an ancient Polish city. The sarcophagi of the Polish kings lay in the Royal Castle. And it was here that the Jagellonian University had been founded in 1364.

Lenin, Krupskaya, and her mother shared an apartment at 49 Lubomirski Road with CC member Zinoviev, his wife and son, Stepan. Lenin and Zinoviev formed the Party's Foreign Bureau with Krupskaya as Secre-

---

* Her husband, journalist Alexander Lobov, was shot in 1918 as an Okhrana agent. She was cleared but died of TB in 1924. Shotman, who remained close to Lenin into the 1920s, was executed by Stalin in 1939.

tary. Cracow crackled with political intrigue, and reminded Lenin of home. "Unlike exile in Paris or Switzerland," said Krupskaya, "there was a close connection with Russia"—4,000 of its 150,000 inhabitants were exiles from the Russian Empire, mainly Poles. "Illich liked Cracow very much. It was almost Russia."

Lenin enjoyed himself ice-skating, while Krupskaya did the shopping in the ancient Jewish Quarter, where prices were lower. "Illich praised the Polish sourmilk and corn whisky." He played hide-and-seek with Zinoviev's son under the furniture. "Stop interfering, we're playing," he would say, dismissing interruptions—but he was eagerly awaiting Stalin and the Six.

Arriving in the first week of November, Stalin met up with the Lenins, sleeping on the sofa in their kitchen. Stalin, Malinovsky and another Duma deputy, Muranov, were charmed and berated by Lenin, who vigorously argued against any reunion or conciliation with the Mensheviks: his Bolsheviks had to remain a separate party.

Lenin may have been a highly educated nobleman but, with simple joviality and iron will, he was adept at handling tough men of action. He welcomed Stalin and put him at his ease: food brought them closer. Krupskaya served sausagey "German" food, which Stalin suffered for two days but then could not resist saying to Lenin: "I'm hungry—I crave shashlik!" Lenin agreed, "Me too, I'm ravenous, but I'm afraid of offending Nadya. Have you got money? Come on, let's go eat somewhere . . ." Yet they disagreed on tactics. It was one of the many occasions when Lenin was more hard-line than Stalin, who grumbled that "Illich recommends a hardline policy for the Six, a policy of threatening the majority of the faction [Mensheviks] but Illich will give way . . ."

After ten days, Stalin returned to Petersburg, probably on a *polupaska* pass, that allowed families with relatives over the border to cross back and forth. He thought Lenin clumsily out of touch and remained an obstinate Conciliator; Lenin considered removing Stalin from *Pravda*.[3] When the new Duma convened, Malinovsky read out a manifesto, probably written by Stalin, that was friendly to their estranged Menshevik brethren. In defiance of Lenin, Stalin even secretly met up with Jordania and Jibladze, those long-standing Menshevik enemies.*

Lenin bombarded Stalin with demands for another trip to Cracow to discuss the national question—and the *Pravda* problem. First Krupskaya

---

* This tryst with the arch-heretics would be concealed during the Soviet era.

tried to lure Stalin to Cracow to save him from arrest: "Kick Vasiliev [Stalin] out as soon as possible, otherwise we won't save him. We need him and he's already done his main job." Stalin wriggled out of the trip, citing his health.

"To K.St. Dear friend," Krupskaya wrote to Stalin, on 9/22 December, for the first time using an abbreviation of his new name, Koba Stalin. "It seems you aren't planning to come here . . . If so, we protest against your decision . . . We absolutely insist on your visit here . . . regardless of your health. We demand your presence categorically. You have no right to act differently." Stalin prepared his trip, again with Lobova. Lenin and Krupskaya were delighted: "We hope Vasia [Stalin] and Vera [Valentina] are coming soon with the children [the Duma Six]."

On 15 December, the Duma broke for Christmas.[4] Stalin and Valentina left for Cracow,* probably taking the most direct but riskier route. On the train westwards, two passengers were reading aloud from a nationalist newspaper. "Why do you read such rubbish!" Stalin shouted at them. He and Valentina disembarked at a Polish frontier-town on the Russian-Austrian border and prepared to cross on foot—like smugglers.

This was to be Stalin's longest ever trip abroad—and would bring him to Vienna, that crossroads of civilization, on the eve of the Great War.

---

* There has been much debate about Stalin's two journeys to Cracow: he himself told many stories about crossing the border. (The old tyrant told the story about the border-crossing and Lenin and the food to his favourite youngster, Yuri Zhdanov.) Was he just lying? In his personal anecdotes, he tended to exaggerate more than totally invent his stories, especially about such a well-known trip. When he lied outright, he did not tell the lie himself, simply inserting it into the information of his propagandists. Thus he probably used that route at least once. Shotman says he arranged the first trip; the other sources are mixed up about the two trips. So this author believes that the meetings with Shotman concerned the first trip for which there was plenty of time to plan. For the second trip, for which there was no such time, Stalin and Valentina probably took the risk of crossing the border by a smugglers' path.

31

Vienna, 1913: The Wonderful Georgian, the Austrian Artist and the Old Emperor

Stalin knew no one at the small frontier-town, but he was an expert at the art of riding the random. He walked the streets until a Polish cobbler asked him: "You're a stranger?"

"My father was a cobbler in Georgia," replied Stalin, knowing that the Georgians and Poles shared the chains of Russia's Prison of Nations. "I must cross the border." The Pole offered to take him, accepting no payment. Telling this story after the Revolution, Stalin paused, "as if trying to peer into the past," then added: "I'd like to know where that man is now and what happened to him. What a pity I forgot his name and can't trace him." Like many of those who helped Stalin in his youth, the cobbler may well have wished he had buried the Georgian in the forests between empires. Stalin never mentioned that he had a companion at the time, Valentina Lobova.

Across the border in Polish Galicia, Stalin was desperate to get to Lenin, but "I was terribly hungry." He went into the station restaurant in Trzebinia, where he soon made a mockery of himself. He summoned the Polish waiter in Russian. "The waiter carted around lots of food," but Stalin was ignored until he lost his temper: "This is scandalous! Everyone else has been served except me!" The Pole did not serve his soup; Stalin had to fetch it himself. "In my fury, I threw the plate on the floor, flung a rouble at the waiter, and flew out!" He was ravenous by the time he reached the Lenins.

> We'd hardly greeted each other when I burst out,
> "Lenin, give me something to eat at once. I'm half-dead. I've had nothing to eat since yesterday evening."
> "Why didn't you eat at Trzebinia? There's a good restaurant there."
> "The Poles wouldn't give me anything to eat," said Stalin.
> "What a fool you are, Stalin!" laughed Lenin. "Didn't you know Poles regard Russian as the language of oppression?"[1]

Lenin must have wondered at this blindness—or "greater Russian chauvinism"—in his supposed "expert" on nationalities, but Stalin would adopt a deeply Russian hostility to any sort of Polish independence.*

The two men bonded as never before. "They met me in such a hospitable manner," Stalin reported in old age. "He [Lenin] wouldn't let me go anywhere, he persuaded me to stay with his family; I had breakfast, lunch and supper there. I broke the established rule only twice: I warned Krupskaya that I'd be out for dinner and visited the old parts of Cracow where there were lots of cafés." Stalin's favourite restaurant was Hawelka, which still stands on the central Market Square. When Stalin dined out, Lenin was concerned.

"Listen, old chap, that's twice you've dined out—aren't we treating you right?"

"No, Comrade, I'm delighted with everything, but I feel uneasy that you provide everything."

"But you're our guest," insisted Lenin. "How was dinner in your restaurant?"

"The food was fine but the beer was excellent."

"Ah, now I understand," answered Lenin. "You miss your beer. Now you'll have beer at home too," and "he asked his mother-in-law to provide two or three bottles of beer for the guest every day." Stalin was again touched by Lenin's solicitude.

"Illich was very nervous about *Pravda*," recalls Krupskaya. Lenin was actually exasperated with Stalin's conciliatory editorials. "Stalin was also nervous. They were planning how to adjust matters." Lenin mulled over

---

* Stalin told this story to Stanislaw Kot, the Polish Ambassador, at a Kremlin banquet in December 1941.

his dual problems of asserting control over *Pravda,* creating a nationalities policy and promoting his valued henchman. He needed a Bolshevik expert on nationalities who was not Russian—and certainly not Jewish. Three years earlier, he had hailed Stalin as more of an expert on nationality than Jordania. Here was a solution that would kill two birds with one stone.

Lenin proposed that, instead of returning to Petersburg, Stalin stay on to write an essay laying out their new Bolshevik nationalities policy. Stalin accepted.

Around 28 December 1912, Lenin, Stalin and Zinoviev were joined by Malinovsky and two other Duma deputies, Stalin's friend Valentina Lobova and a wealthy Bolshevik couple who lived in Vienna, Alexander and Elena Troyanovsky, along with their child's Latvian nanny. "Koba didn't speak very loudly" but "in a deliberate measured manner . . . with indisputable logic," recalls the nineteen-year-old nanny, Olga Veiland. "Sometimes he went through to the other room so he could pace up and down listening to the speeches."

Stalin still resisted Lenin, who was now vociferously backed by Malinovsky—for the most dubious reasons. Lenin and the Okhrana shared their opposition to any SD reunification. Thus the secret police ordered Malinovsky to push this hard line, while Stalin still argued he could convert a few Mensheviks. He hoped Lenin would see that "it was better to co-operate and postpone hardline politics for a while." Besides, the Duma Six needed a real leader: himself, no doubt.

"There's an insufferable atmosphere here," Stalin grumbled in a letter to Petersburg. "Everyone's impossibly busy, goddamned busy, [but] my situation isn't actually too bad." He then wrote an almost loving letter to his old friend Kamenev: "I give you an Eskimo kiss on the nose. The Devil take me! I miss you—I swear it like a dog! There's no one, absolutely no one to have a heart-to-heart conversation with, damn you. Can't you somehow make it over here to Cracow?"

Yet Stalin did make a new friend in Cracow: Malinovsky. The convicted rapist and Okhrana traitor, two years older than Stalin, was now enjoying a lavish Okhrana salary of 8,000 roubles per annum—more than the director of Imperial Police, who got only 7,000.

"He was lively, resourceful, handsome," remembered Molotov, "and he looked a bit like Tito." Henceforth Stalin wrote to him warmly, sending love to "Stefania and the kids." Malinovsky slyly denounced other Bolsheviks as traitors to distract attention from himself, but the pressure of a double life was beginning to drive him to breakdown.

At the last meeting on New Year's Eve 1912, Stalin caved in to Lenin. *"All* decisions are being accepted *unanimously,"* enthused Lenin to Kamenev. "A huge success." But Stalin's retreat was far from bitter. The meeting, as Malinovsky reported to his Okhrana paymasters, reestablished the Bolshevik machine: a Foreign Bureau (Lenin and Zinoviev with Krupskaya as Secretary) alongside a Russian Bureau, dominated by Stalin and Sverdlov, now *Pravda's* chief editor, with Valentina Lobova as secretary.* Stalin was moved from *Pravda* yet emerged as the senior Bolshevik in Russia (salary: sixty roubles a month), on a prestigious mission to play the theoretician. Stalin was writing hard on the nationalities question, Lenin making suggestions. Stalin sent off his first draft to Petersburg.

Afterwards, Lenin and the Bolsheviks went out to the theatre to celebrate the New Year, "but the play was very bad," recalls Olga Veiland. "Vladimir Illich walked out with his wife." Lenin, Stalin and the others saw in the New Year 1913 in a private room at a restaurant. When she was an old lady, Veiland confided that Stalin had started to become flirtatious. "Lenin seemed very cheerful, joking and laughing. He started singing and even joined in the games we were playing."[2]

Soon afterwards, Stalin arrived at the apartment of the Troyanovskys in a frozen Vienna, shrouded in snow. Lenin called them "good people . . . They have money!" Alexander Troyanovsky was a handsome young nobleman and army officer: his service in the Russo-Japanese War had converted him to Marxism and now he edited and funded *Prosveshchenie* (Enlightenment)—which was to publish Soso's essay. Fluent in German and English, he lived with his beautiful noble-born wife, Elena Rozmirovich, in a large, comfortable apartment at 30 Schönbrunnerschloss Strasse,† the boulevard along which the old Emperor Franz-Josef travelled back and forth every day from his residence at the Schönbrunn Palace to his office at the Hofburg.

The antique, bewhiskered Habsburg Kaiser, who had reigned since 1848, travelled in a gilded carriage drawn by eight white horses, manned by postilions decked out in black-and-white-trimmed uniforms and white

---

* Stalin's friend from Tiflis, Kalinin, was not promoted to the CC because he was temporarily suspected of being an Okhrana double-agent: the Bolsheviks, even while being betrayed by Malinovsky at the very heart of the Party, suspected an innocent comrade.
† Now a boarding-house, the Pension Schönbrunn, which unusually still bears the blue plaque put up in 1949 that reads: J.V. STALIN RESIDED IN THIS HOUSE DURING JANUARY 1913. HE WROTE HIS IMPORTANT WORK "MARXISM AND THE NATIONAL QUESTION" HERE.

perukes, escorted by Hungarian horsemen with yellow-and-black panther furs over their shoulders. Stalin would not have been able to miss this vision of obsolescent magnificence—and he was not the only future dictator to see it: the cast of twentieth-century titans in Vienna that January 1913 belongs in a Tom Stoppard play.* In a men's dosshouse on Meldemannstrasse, in Brigettenau, another world from Stalin's somewhat grander address, lived a young Austrian who was a failed artist: Adolf Hitler, aged twenty-three.

Soso and Adolf shared one of the sights of Vienna: Hitler's best friend Kubizek recalls, "We often saw the old Emperor when he rode in his carriage from Schönbrunn to the Hofburg." But both future dictators were unmoved, even disdainful: Stalin never mentioned it and "Adolf did not make much ado of it for he wasn't interested in the Emperor, just the state which he represented."

In Vienna, both Hitler and Stalin were obsessed, in different ways, with race. In this city of antiquated courtiers, Jewish intellectuals and racist rabble-rousers, cafés, beer halls and palaces, only 8.6 percent were actually Jews but their cultural influence, personified by Freud, Mahler, Wittgenstein, Buber and Schnitzler, was much greater. Hitler was formulating the anti-Semitic *völkische* theories of racial supremacy that, as Führer, he would impose on his European empire; while Stalin, researching his nationalities article, was shaping a new idea for an internationalist empire with a central authority behind an autonomous façade, the prototype of the Soviet Union. Almost thirty years later, their ideological and state structures were to clash in the most savage conflict of human history.

The Jews did not fit into either of their visions. They repelled and titillated Hitler but irritated and confounded Stalin, who attacked their "mystical" nature. Too much of a race for Hitler, they were not enough of a nation for Stalin.

But the two nascent dictators shared a Viennese pastime: both liked to walk in the park around Franz-Josef's Schönbrunn Palace, close to where Stalin stayed. Even when they became allies in the 1939 Molotov–Ribbentrop Pact, they never met. Those walks were probably the closest they ever came.

"Those few weeks that Comrade Stalin spent with us were devoted entirely to the national question," says the Troyanovskys' nanny, Olga

---

* Josip Broz, the future Marshal Tito, was also working there as a mechanic.

Veiland. "He involved everyone around him. Some analysed Otto Bauer, others Karl Kautsky." Despite intermittent study, Stalin could not read German, so the nanny helped—as did another young Bolshevik whom he met now for the first time: Nikolai Bukharin, an intellectual pixie with sparkling eyes and a goatee beard. "Bukharin came to our apartment every day," says Olga Veiland, "as Stalin lived there too." While Stalin flirted hopefully with the nanny, she preferred the witty, puckish Bukharin. Besides, it was her job to clean Stalin's shirts and underwear, which, she complained after his death, was something of a challenge.

Stalin and Bukharin got on well. Stalin would write to him from exile, the start of an alliance that culminated in a political partnership in the late 1920s. But Soso came, suffocatingly, to adore and, fatally, to envy Bukharin. The friendship that began in Vienna ended in the 1930s with a bullet in Bukharin's head.

"I was sitting at the table beside the samovar in the apartment of Skobelev . . . in the ancient capital of the Habsburgs," reports Trotsky, also living in Vienna, "when suddenly the door opened with a knock and an unknown man entered. He was short . . . thin . . . his greyish-brown skin covered in pockmarks . . . I saw nothing in his eyes that resembled friendliness." It was Stalin, who "stopped at the samovar and made himself a cup of tea. Then as silently as he had come, he left, leaving a very depressing but unusual impression on me. Or perhaps later events cast a shadow over our first meeting."

Stalin already despised Trotsky, whom he had called a "noisy phoney champion with fake muscles." He never changed his view. Trotsky, for his part, was chilled by Stalin's yellow eyes: they "glinted with malice."

Stalin's stay with Troyanovsky was a revelation—it was his first and last experience of civilized European living, as he himself admitted. He lived in the room that overlooked the street and "worked there for entire days." At dusk, he would stroll around Schönbrunn Park with the Troyanovskys. At dinner, he sometimes talked about his past, reminiscing about Lado Ketskhoveli and how he was shot in prison. He was characteristically morose. "Hello, my friend," he wrote to Malinovsky, now back in Petersburg. "So far I'm living in Vienna and writing some rubbish. See you soon." But he improved. "Shy and solitary at first," says Olga Veiland, "he became more relaxed and fun." He did not feel uneasy with Troyanovsky's genteel style. On the contrary, he remained fond of him throughout his life.

Little Galina Troyanovskaya was a spirited child who got on well with Stalin. "She loved being in adult company," and Stalin played with her,

promising to bring her "mountains of green chocolate from the Caucasus." He "used to laugh very loudly" when she did not believe him. But
she often teased him back: "You're always talking about the nations!" she
groused. Stalin bought the child sweets in Schönbrunn Park. Once he
made a bet with her mother that if they both called to Galina, she would
go to Stalin for the sweets. They tested his theory: Galina ran to Soso,
confirming his cynical view of human nature.*

Stalin now asked Malinovsky to return the first draft of his article so
he could revise it, adding, "Tell me 1. How is *Pravda*? 2. How is your faction? 3. How is the group doing? . . . Yours Vasily." He rewrote the article
before he left Vienna forever.†

Lenin awaited him in Cracow; betrayal lurked in Petersburg.[3]

---

* In the incestuous world of Bolshevism, Elena later divorced Troyanovsky and then had
an affair with Malinovsky the traitor (according to Malinovsky). She married the Bolshevik grandee Nikolai Krylenko, a member of Lenin's first government, later Commander-
in-Chief of the Red Army, then Procurator-General, finally a brutal People's Commissar
for Justice who was himself shot in the Great Terror. Fortunately Krylenko left Elena in
the late 1920s, which probably saved her life, for she survived the Terror, working quietly in
the archives, dying naturally in 1953. The Troyanovskys' daughter Galina married another
Bolshevik magnate, Valerian Kuibyshev, Stalinist Politburo member, womanizer and
drinker who ill treated her. Stalin said he would have intervened if he had known of
Kuibyshev's drunken promiscuity. Kuibyshev's suspicious death from alcoholism in 1935
suited Stalin. The nanny Olga Veiland became a Party and Comintern apparatchik, retiring young and surviving into old age. The destiny of Troyanovsky—even though he turned
against the Bolsheviks—was very different: see the Epilogue.
† *Marxism and the National Question* was Stalin's most famous work: he himself never
stopped editing it during his long life. It was an answer to the Austrian socialists who proposed what Lenin called "an Austrian federation within the Party." As ever, Lenin was
being practical and farsighted, as well as ideological. He feared that the Jewish Bundists or
Georgian Mensheviks, who advocated variations on cultural autonomy or even national
separatism, would make the Party and ultimately the Russian Empire ungovernable under
Bolshevism. He needed a theory that offered the ideal of autonomy and the right of secession without necessarily having to grant either. Lenin and Stalin agreed that nothing
should stand in the way of a centralized state. Stalin defined the nation as a "historically
formed, stable community of people, united by community of language, territory, economic life and psychological make-up." On the Jews, Stalin asked: "What sort of nation is
a Jewish nation which consists of Georgian, Dagestani, Russian and American Jews who
don't understand each other, inhabit different parts of the globe . . . and never act
together in peace or war? They're being assimilated" for they have "no stable and large stra-
tum associated with the land . . ." He attacked "Austro-Marxism" and national autonomy,
but in the Caucasus accepted "regional autonomy." The right of secession was offered (in
theory) but should not be taken. This paper was not beautifully written, but it had a sort of
subtlety that turned into a reality when Stalin created the web of republics that became the
USSR. It remains relevant because the breakup of the Soviet Union in 1991 allowed the full
republics such as Ukraine, Estonia and Georgia to become independent but not the
autonomous republics such as Chechnya.

32

The Secret Policeman's Ball: Betrayal in Drag

I returned to Cracow to show Lenin," Stalin recounted. "Two days later, Lenin invited me over and I noticed the manuscript lying open on the desk. He asked me to sit next to him."

Lenin was impressed. "Is it you who really wrote this?" he asked Stalin, a little patronizingly.

"Yes, Comrade Lenin, I wrote it. Did I get something wrong?"

"No, on the contrary, it's really splendid!"

Lenin was determined to publish the piece as policy "The article is *very good*!" he told Kamenev. "It's a fighting issue and we won't surrender one iota of our principled opposition to the Bundist trash!" In a letter to Gorky, he acclaimed Stalin as his "wonderful Georgian."

Soso published the article in March 1913 under his new byline "K. Stalin," the second time he had used it. It had been evolving since 1910 when he started signing articles as "K.St.," then "K. Safin" and "K. Solin."

The conspiratorial life required a roster of aliases, often chosen at random. Ulyanov may have taken "Lenin" from the Siberian river Lena, but he used 160 aliases altogether. He kept "Lenin" because it happened to be his byline on the article, "What Is to Be Done?," made his name. Similarly Soso used "Stalin" when he published the article on nationalities that made his reputation, which was one reason that it stuck. If he had not been such a self-obsessed melodramatist, he might have been known to history as "Vasiliev" or "Ivanovich."

Its other attraction was the vague similarity to "Lenin" itself, but Stalin also fashioned aliases out of the names of his women: it is plausible that his girlfriend Ludmilla Stal helped inspire this one. He would never have admitted it. "My comrades gave me the name," he smugly told an interviewer. "They thought it suited me." Molotov knew this was not true, saying, "That's what he called himself." But this flint-hearted "industrial name," meaning Man of Steel, did suit his character—and was a symbol of everthing a Bolshevik should be.*

The name was Russian, though he never ceased to be Caucasian, combining the Georgian "Koba" with the Slavic "Stalin" (though his friends still called him "Soso"). Henceforth he adopted what the historian Robert Service calls a "bi-national persona." After 1917, he became quadri-national: Georgian by nationality, Russian by loyalty, internationalist by ideology, Soviet by citizenship.

It started as a byline—and ended as an empire and a religion. When he was dictator, Stalin shouted at his feckless son Vasily for exploiting their surname: "You're not Stalin and I'm not Stalin! Stalin *is* Soviet power!"

By mid-February 1913, the newly minted "Koba Stalin" was back in Petersburg, where the Bolsheviks, betrayed at every turn by Malinovsky, were on the run.[1]

"It's a total Bacchanalia of arrests, searches and raids," Stalin reported to the Troyanovskys in a letter opened by the Okhrana. He added that he had not forgotten his promise to six-year-old Galina: "I'll send the chocolate to Galochka."

Stalin, now empowered by Lenin, but beleaguered by vigorous

---

* "Solin" and "Safin," the earlier versions of his new name, may have been typos because *sol* means "salt" in Russian: "Man of Salt" does not quite have the metallic sheen of the final version. When they were typesetting *Zvezda* in April 1912, says Vera Shveitzer, "The editorial board once changed the signature arbitrarily. The next day when J. V. Stalin opened *Zvezda* and saw the signature 'Solin,' he smiled: 'I don't like meaningless borrowed bylines.' " He returned to "K.St." until January 1913. Stalin was not the only "industrial name": Rosenfeld became "Kamenev"—Man of Stone (though he remained much too fluffy for the moniker); and Scriabin became "Molotov"—Hammer Man. There was also a fashion for taking aliases from jailers: Bronstein borrowed the name "Trotsky" from one of his prison warders. Contrary to many claims in Western biographies, "Stalin" is not a Russianization of Djugashvili: *Djuga* does not mean "iron" or "steel" in either Georgian or Ossetian.

Okhrana action, did not even try to hide. He stayed on Shpalernaya Street in the town centre at the apartment of Duma deputies Badaev and Samoilov, attending meetings at the home of their fellow deputy Petrovsky. Stalin sighs, in another letter, "There aren't any competent people. I can hardly keep up with everything."

His first challenge was to defend his parliamentary star, Malinovsky, from a shocking accusation. An article identified Malinovsky as an Okhrana spy. Since the article was signed "Ts," the Bolsheviks believed that the libeller was a Menshevik, Martov (real name Tsederbaum), or his brother-in-law Fyodor Dan. "The Bolshevik Vasiliev [Stalin] came to my apartment (he was known as 'Ioska Koriavyi' [Joe Pox]) trying to stop the rumours about Malinovsky," said Fyodor Dan. Joe Pox warned Dan's wife, Lidia, that she would regret it if the Mensheviks tried to smear Malinovsky.

Yet, thanks to Malinovsky, Stalin's every move was now monitored by the Imperial Police director himself. On 10 February, Sverdlov was arrested, betrayed by Malinovsky. Now Stalin decided to appoint his Baku comrade Shaumian as *Pravda*'s editor, but Malinovsky persuaded Lenin that the Armenian would be too conciliatory, like Stalin himself. Lenin backed Malinovsky's candidate, Chernomazov, who, as Stalin had divined back in Baku, was another Okhrana double-agent.

By February 1913, Malinovsky had betrayed the whole CC in Russia, except Stalin and the ineffectual Petrovsky. The Okhrana were determined to stop any SD reunion: Stalin the Conciliator was next.

On Saturday night, 23 February, Bolshevik sympathizers held a fundraising concert and masquerade ball at the Kalashnikov Exchange, hardly Stalin's usual scene. But the Alliluyev girls were excited about it. Stalin and their maths tutor, Kavtaradze, talked about going.

That afternoon, Stalin visited Malinovsky. The double-agent demanded he come to the ball. Stalin—as he later told Tatiana Slavatinskaya—refused, saying, "He wasn't in the mood and didn't have the right clothes. But Malinovsky kept insisting," even reassuring him about security. The dapper traitor opened his dandyish wardrobe to Stalin, producing a stiff collar, dress shirt and silk cravat which he tied around Stalin's neck.

Malinovsky had come almost directly from a meeting with his Okhrana controller, Imperial Police director Beletsky, probably promising to deliver Stalin.

"Vasily [Stalin] and I went to the party," wrote his mistress, Tatiana Slavatinskaya, "and the party was nice." Stalin, in his fancy cravat, sat at a table with the Bolshevik Duma deputies. "I was really surprised to see . . . our dear Georgian boy . . . at such a crowded party," Demian Bedny, a proletarian bard, who in the 1920s became one of Stalin's closest courtiers, informed Lenin afterwards. "It was really impudent to go there—was it the devil's work or some fool who invited him? I told him, 'You won't escape.' " Bedny hinted that there was a traitor in their midst.

At about midnight, plainclothed Okhrana officers, backed by Gendarmes, took up positions at the back of the concert hall where the guests sat at tables. "Stalin was actually chatting to Malinovsky himself," noticed Tatiana, when "he spotted that he was being followed."

The detectives approached Stalin's table and asked his name. He denied he was Djugashvili. Comrades stood up around him and tried to smuggle him to safety behind the stage. "He went into the artists' dressing-room," says Slavatinskaya, "and asked them to get me." Once again, Stalin resorted to dressing up in drag, but he managed to tell Tatiana that he had "visited Malinovsky before the party and been followed from there." Stalin was made up and decked out in a long dress. As he was being led out through the dressing room, a secret policeman spotted his big shoes (and surely his moustache). The policeman "seized him with a yell."

"Djugashvili, we've finally got you!"

"I'm not Djugashvili. My name is Ivanov," replied Stalin.

"Tell those stories to y'grandmother!"

It was over.

"Two plain-clothed agents asked him to go with them. All was done quietly. The ball went on." Malinovsky hurried "after Comrade Stalin 'protesting' his arrest and promising to take measures to free him . . ."

Lenin innocently wrote to the traitor to "discuss how to forestall more arrests." Lenin and Krupskaya fretted that "Vasily" (Stalin) must be "well protected." It was too late: "Why is there no news of Vasily? What has happened to him? We're worried."

Stalin's arrest was regarded as enough of a success for Police Director Beletsky to inform Interior Minister Maklakov himself, who on 7 June 1913 confirmed the Special Committee's recommendation: J. V. Djugashvili was condemned to four years in Turukhansk, an obscure Siberian realm of frozen twilights, forgotten by civilization.[2]

PART FOUR

Over this land, like a ghost
He roamed from door to door;
In his hands, he clutched a lute
And sweetly made it tinkle;
In his dreamy melodies,
Like a beam of sunlight,
You could sense truth itself
And heavenly love.
The voice made many a man's heart
Beat, that had been turned to stone;
It enlightened many a man's mind
Which had been cast into uttermost darkness.
But instead of glorification,
Wherever the harp was plucked,
The mob set before the outcast
A vessel filled with poison . . .
And they said to him: "Drink this, o accursed,
This is your appointed lot!
We do not want your truth
Nor these heavenly tunes of yours!"

—SOSELO (Josef Stalin)

33

"Darling, I'm in Desperate Straits"

The steamer that slowly conveyed Stalin up the Yenisei River from Krasnoyarsk in mid-June 1913 revealed a Siberia of inconceivable remoteness and wild vastness. His destination, Turukhansk, was larger than Britain, France and Germany combined, yet contained just 12,000 people.

The Yenisei flowed through narrow valleys with high terraces until it widened so far that he could peer across its glistening flatness and see no land at all. The Siberian *taiga* was hilly and forested with dense larch climbing to ridges of flat alpine tundra. It was green and lush in summer, but severe and icily white in a winter that lasted nine months a year, sinking to temperatures as low as −60°. Between villages of peasants and convicts, the colossal spaces were only rarely dotted with the tents and reindeer of the shamanistic Tungus and Ostyak nomads.

The game of escape, capture and escape again was over. This was, as Robert Service puts it, "a landbound Devil's Island." This time, though Stalin did not yet realize it, the Autocracy meant business. From Petersburg it took just over a week to reach the regional capital, Krasnoyarsk, whence he was despatched northwards into Turukhansk. It was Stalin's home for four years but would enter his heart and never leave it.

After travelling for twenty-six days, he disembarked on 10 August at the village of Monastyrskoe,* the "capital" of Turukhansk Province. "As you see I'm in Turukhansk," he wrote to Zinoviev (and Lenin) in Cracow. "Did you get my letter sent on the way? I've fallen ill. I need to recover. Send me some money." He was already planning his escape: "If you need my help, let me know and I'll come immediately."

Lenin did need his help. On 27 July, he had held a CC meeting at which he had ordered that Stalin and Sverdlov be sprung from exile. Each was sent sixty roubles, but once again Malinovsky betrayed the plan to the Okhrana, which telegraphed Turukhansk police chief Ivan Kibirov, warning that Stalin was an escape-artist. The officers in such places were themselves effectively exiled: Kibirov, an Ossetian, had been removed from the Baku police and posted to Turukhansk for misdemeanours unknown. Possibly because of their shared Ossetian origins, he favoured Stalin.

Soso was assigned to stay in Miroedikha, a hamlet to the south where he soon made himself felt. An exile named Innokenti Dubrovinsky had drowned in the river that summer, leaving an impressive library. Exile etiquette decreed the sharing of the libraries of the dead, but typically Stalin "expropriated" the books, refused to share them and started to read them ravenously. The life of the exiles rotated around just this sort of petty quarrel which Stalin was so expert at provoking. The other exiles were outraged—they complained, and blackballed him. Philip Zakharov, a Bolshevik, confronted the book-thief, but Stalin treated his impertinent visitor "like a Tsarist General would receive a private soldier who had the insolence to appear before him with a request." Stalin behaved like the *Khoziain*, the Master, long before he was dictator of Russia—indeed he had done so since childhood.

After just two weeks, he had to be moved (no doubt with his new library) to another hamlet, Kostino. There he found four other exiles, and this pedagogue manqué spent his time teaching two Georgian criminals to read. Soon he learned that his old roommate Sverdlov was nearby in Selivanikha.[1]

Around 20 September, Stalin visited Sverdlov, who lived in a peasant bathhouse. Staying together in the converted *banya*, they dreamed of escape. "I've just bidden farewell to Vaska [Stalin], my guest here for a week," Sverdlov told Malinovsky, the last Bolshevik leader at liberty

---

* This trading centre boasted a large missionary monastery, which had baptized the local tribesmen and which was led by a Mikhail Suslov, the great-grandfather and namesake of the Soviet grandee who was favoured by Stalin after the Second World War and who became the *éminence grise* of the Brezhnev era.

inside Russia. "If you have money for me or 'Vaska' (they might have sent some), then send it . . . Last week, we wrote asking for some newspapers and magazines. Do what you can." Malinovsky was certainly doing what he could to betray the two hopeful escapees.

On 1 October, Lenin and the CC, reacting to Stalin's offer to Zinoviev, again proposed to spring him and Sverdlov, assigning one hundred roubles to the project. Within nineteen days, Stalin had "received an offer from a comrade in Petersburg to escape to the capital." Stalin and Sverdlov prepared for this challenging escape, spending all their money and credit. The Bolshevik manager of the Canadian fur-trading company Revelion provided flour, sugar, tea and tobacco; the local doctor donated medicines; others forged passports.

The "doctor of escapology" was almost ready, but now winter was descending on the *taiga*. It was harsher and more desolate than anything the Georgian had experienced before. He was soon at the lowest ebb of his life so far. Daily life in Turukhansk was meant to be a struggle. If most Tsarist exiles were like holidays, Turukhansk was a slow death: many exiles perished out there from the extremities of weather. By early November, it was −33°, heading for −50°. Saliva froze on the lips, breath crystallized. And the cold made living much more expensive. Stalin appealed to his girlfriend Tatiana Slavatinskaya. His panic is obvious:

Tatiana Alexandrovna, I feel rather ashamed to write this but I have no other choice—my need is urgent! I don't have a kopeck. All my supplies are gone. I had some money but everything was spent on warm clothes, shoes and food supplies which are very expensive here . . . By God, I don't know what's going to happen to me. Could you stir up some friends and raise 30 roubles? Maybe more later. It would be my salvation and the sooner the better since winter is in full swing (yesterday −33) . . . I hope you can do this. So, my dear, please get started. Otherwise "the Caucasian of Kalashnikov Exchange" is going to perish . . .

Tatiana not only sent him his old clothes but also bought him winter underwear. When it arrived, he was thrilled: "Darling dear Tatiana, I got your parcel. But I didn't ask for new clothes, just the old ones, yet you've spent your money on new ones. Dear darling, it's a shame because you're short of money, but I don't know how to thank you!" Even with his new clothes, Stalin begged Tatiana for money: "Darling, My need is more urgent with every passing hour. I'm in desperate straits: on top of everything, I got ill, a cough on the lungs. I need milk, money. I have none. My dear, if you find money, send it immediately. It's unbearable to wait any longer . . ."

He must have been sending out letters to all his friends, particularly Malinovsky, the very man who had put him in Siberia:

Hello, my friend

I feel a bit uncomfortable writing but needs must. I've never suffered such a terrible situation. All my money's gone, I've got a sinister cough along with sinking temperatures (−37), a general deterioration in my health; and I've no supplies, no bread, sugar, meat, kerosene. All my money's gone on living expenses and clothing and footwear . . . I need milk, I need firewood but . . . money, I'm out of money, friend. I don't know how I'll get through the winter . . . I have neither rich family nor friends, and I've no one to ask so I'm appealing to you . . .

Stalin suggested that Malinovsky appeal to the Menshevik Karlo Chkheidze, whom he had tormented in Batumi, "not only as my compatriot but as Chairman of the faction. I don't want to die out here without even writing you a letter. The matter is urgent because waiting means starving when I am already weak and sick." He had got "44 roubles from abroad," from Berne, Switzerland—and nothing else. He tried to raise money another way. Zinoviev claimed they were publishing his nationalities essay as a pamphlet:

Then I hope (have a right to hope) for a fee (money is the breath of life in this ill-fated place, where they have nothing but fish). I hope if that happens, you'll stand up for me and get me the fee . . . I embrace you, goddamn me . . . Do I really have to vegetate here for another four years?

Josef

Malinovsky replied in transparent code: "Dear brother, I'll sell the horse: I've asked 100 roubles for it."

Yet when the hundred-rouble escape fund arrived, it was sent to Sverdlov. Stalin took umbrage: did they only want Sverdlov and not him? But things looked up a little. Zinoviev replied that they were publishing Stalin's pamphlet. He got twenty-five roubles from Badaev, the Duma deputy, but he needed more. He must have written to Georgia, to his mother and the Svanidzes, because he received a parcel from Tiflis, and he appealed to the Alliluyevs too.

The books and money demanded from Zinoviev did not arrive. Stalin again became desperate: "You wrote that you'd be sending the 'debt' in small bits. Send it as soon as possible however small the bits. I terribly need the money. It would be fine without my damn illness which requires money . . . I'm waiting."

Stalin was writing another article entitled "Cultural-National Autonomy," which he sent, via Sergei Alliluyev, to Troyanovsky for his journal *Prosveshchenie*. But he became ever more irritated with Zinoviev, writing on 11 January 1914, referring to himself in the third person: "Why are you keeping silent, my friend? I haven't had a letter from you for three months. Stalin . . . hoped to get the relevant fee, and thus wouldn't need to ask anyone for money any more. I think he has a right to think like that." Stalin never forgot his treatment at the hands of Zinoviev, showy orator and supercilious Jewish émigré, things he despised.

In January 1914, after six months of anxiety and struggle, money started arriving: the policeman Kibirov reported to his superiors that Stalin had received 50 roubles from Petersburg, 10 roubles from Sashiko (Svanidze) Monoselidze in Tiflis, 25 from Badaev, plus another 55 from Petersburg, almost enough for an escapee's "boots."

The Imperial Police director, Beletsky, learned (probably from Malinovsky) that an escape was imminent. He telegraphed Turukhansk that Stalin and Sverdlov had each received another 50 roubles "to organize their escape." A local Okhrana informer confirmed that "Djugashvili and Sverdlov are thinking of escaping . . . on the very first steamboat down the Yenisei this summer." Beletsky ordered: "Take all measures to prevent this!" The Okhrana decided "to place Djugashvili and Sverdlov in a northern village where there are no other exiles and to attach two inspectors specially to watch them."

This was dire news. "Djugashvili and I are being moved 180 versts northwards, 80 versts north of the Arctic Circle," a downhearted Sverdlov told his sister Sara. "We're torn away even from the post office. The mail only comes once a month by foot and really only eight or nine times a year . . . The name of the place is Kureika."

Stalin was being moved to the very edge of the Arctic Circle.[2]*

---

* Sverdlov was wrong: there were two Kureikas. But their destination was just south of the Arctic Circle.

34

1914: Arctic Sex Comedy

I f Stalin called Kostino "an ill-fated place," Kureika was a freezing hell-hole, the sort of place where a man could believe himself utterly forgot-ten and even lose his sanity: its desolate solitude and obligatory self-containment were to remain with Stalin throughout his life. In March 1914, he and Sverdlov were transported northwards on a horse-drawn cart by their armed personal Gendarmes, Laletin and Popov.

They arrived to find that Kureika barely merited the name of hamlet, and it seemed that virtually all its inhabitants were related. Sixty-seven villagers, thirty-eight men and twenty-nine women, were packed into just eight ramshackle *izba*s, wooden peasant bungalows, more like huts than houses. Most of the citizens of this interbred settlement belonged to three families; these were the Taraseevs, the Saltykovs and the seven Pereprygin orphans.[1]

"One Monday, I was just boiling water for the washing," said Anfisa Taraseeva,* "when I saw a man—with thick dark beard and hair—come in

---

* In 1942, the First Secretary of Krasnoyarsk, Constantin Chernenko, who had risen in the Terror by denunciation and even participation in executions, commissioned the well-known historian M. A. Moskalev to interview Stalin's Turukhansk acquaintances for a sycophantic book, *Stalin in Siberian Exile*. Chernenko printed the book and sent it to Moscow for approval. After all, Politburo member and secret-police chief Beria had built

with a small case and some knotted bedding. 'Hello, *khoziaika* [house-wife], I'm staying with you,' he said. He put down his suitcase as if he'd always lived with us. He played with the children and . . . when the men came back, he said, 'I'm from Petersburg. My name is Josef Djugashvili.' "

Stalin and Sverdlov moved into the *izba* of Alexei and Anfisa Taraseev. At first all went well. The exiles got on easily with Taraseev, who agreed to receive their money orders. It was still cold there, but the ice was thawing. Life in Kureika was governed by the weather: when the Yenisei River froze, locals travelled on the icy river in sleighs, pulled by teams of reindeer and dogs. Then there was the "bad roads season" when the roads were so muddy that they were impassable. In May, the steamships started to ply the Yenisei for a few months; then the locals would boat downriver, tugged from the banks by dog-teams—until the freeze came.

Only the reindeer, snow-foxes and Tungus indigenous tribesmen could really function in deep midwinter. Everyone had to wear reindeer fur. The thirteen-year-old Lidia Pereprygina, one of the family of orphans, noticed that Stalin was underdressed with only a light coat. Soon he sported a full outfit—from boots to hat—of reindeer fur.

"In the new place, it's much harder to settle," Sverdlov wrote on 22 March. "It was bad enough I didn't have a room to myself." The two Bolshevik roommates were friendly enough at first: "We're two of us sharing. My old friend, the Georgian, Djugashvili, is here with me: we met before in earlier exiles. He's a good fellow but"—even after barely ten days together, there was a big "but"—"he is too much of an individualist* in everyday life."

Worse, the Taraseevs had a noisy brood of children. "Our room adjoins the hosts," complained Sverdlov in a letter, "we've no separate entrance. The children hang around the whole day, disturbing us." But

---

his career on overseeing a preposterously inflated history of Stalin's Caucasian career. But this time it did not work. Stalin was incensed by Chernenko's inquiries, though they are a blessing for us historians. The dictator was working long hours to win the war; he knew there was nothing glorious to reveal in Kureika, quite the contrary; he both craved his idolatrous cult and disdained it; and Moskalev was a Jew, a race Stalin increasingly distrusted. He phoned Chernenko and shouted at him. The book was withdrawn. Moskalev was arrested in the anti-Semitic, postwar Terror but survived as a top Soviet historian into the 1960s. Chernenko's career was frozen. However, his sycophancy found him another patron: he became Leonid Brezhnev's long-serving *chef de cabinet*, Politburo member and penultimate successor as Soviet leader in 1984: the short reign of this senile mediocrity symbolized the geriatric obsolescence of the Soviet Union. Chernenko died in 1985. His successor was the vigorous reformer Mikhail Gorbachev.

* "Individualist" was a Marxist insult because Bolsheviks were meant to submit the individual to the collective.

Sverdlov was also infuriated by the silent Tungus tribesmen, who visited the exiles. Dressed from head to food in reindeer furs, the Tunguses would become part of Stalin's life. They were tough, nomadic fishermen and herdsmen with Oriental features who lived in harmony with their reindeer, believing in a mixture of primitive Orthodoxy and ancient spiritualism, interpreted by shamans—indeed "shaman" is a Tungus word.

The Tunguses "sat down, and kept silent for half an hour before standing up and saying, 'Goodbye, we've got to go.' They come in the evening, the best time for studying," sighed Sverdlov. But Stalin befriended these men, as laconic as himself.

The tension was not just about children and housework. The touchy, vindictive Stalin brooded about the money sent to Sverdlov, and not to himself, as an escape fund. Days after his arrival, he had received neither the hundred roubles promised by Malinovsky nor the fees and the books from Zinoviev. Was Zinoviev disrespecting him? Was Sverdlov double-crossing him?

The Georgian and the Jew, the lost fulcrum of the Bolshevik Party in the Russian Empire, captive in their eight-shack village many time-zones from Europe, soon started to aggravate each other. On one side of their tiny dark room, Sverdlov scribbled about his roommate's egotism, while on the other Stalin, at his nitpicking, seething worst, wrote to Malinovsky demanding that he sort out what had happened to the hundred roubles:

> Five months ago, I received an invitation from a comrade in Petersburg to go there and to find the money for the trip. I answered four months ago but got no answer. Can you explain this misunderstanding to me? Then three months ago, I got a postcard from Kostya [Malinovsky himself offering to "sell the horse . . . for 100 roubles"]. I didn't understand it and haven't received the 100 roubles. Well, then Comrade Andrei [Sverdlov's alias] got this sum . . . but I suppose it's only for him. I've got no letters from Kostya ever since. I've received nothing from my sister Nadya [Krupskaya] for four months.

Stalin concluded that they had "chosen another man" to spring—Sverdlov. "Am I right, brother? I ask, dear friend, for a direct precise answer because I like clarity just as I hope you like clarity."[2]

No two men liked clarity less than Stalin and Malinovsky, expert conspirators and dissimulators. But while the former stewed in distant frustration, the latter's entire world was falling apart. There was a good reason Malinovsky had neither sold the "horse" nor answered Stalin's letters. Stalin's "dear friend Roman" was now an "hysterical" alcoholic double-agent swigging vodka out of a teapot—and on the verge of a nervous breakdown. Finally, a new Interior Minister and police director sacked Malinovsky, who resigned from the Duma on 8 May 1914. The Malinovsky case exploded very publicly in the faces of the government and police.

Malinovsky's strongest defenders in the Party had been Lenin—and Stalin. "Lenin must have known," Malinovsky said later, but he was wrong. Lenin would not believe the truth. But he weighed up the kudos won by Malinovsky in the Duma and his help in defeating (or removing, by arrest) the Conciliators (including Stalin) to conclude that "if he is a *provocateur,* the secret police gained less from it than our Party did."*

Stalin, paranoia personified, did not suspect the greatest traitor of his political career. The Malinovsky case played its role in making him—and his comrades—obsessively paranoid. Malinovsky entered the Bolshevik consciousness. Like Banquo's ghost, he haunted Soviet history. Henceforth, in the Bolshevik world of *konspiratsia,* nothing was too outlandish. If Malinovsky could be a traitor, why not the Soviet marshals, why not the entire General Staff, why not Zinoviev, Kamenev, Bukharin and most of the Central Committee, all shot as spies during the 1930s on Stalin's orders?[3]

On the Arctic Circle, Stalin tormented himself and his roommate about the missing hundred roubles. "There's a comrade [in Kureika]," reflected Sverdlov. "We know each other very well, but the saddest thing is that in exile a person appears bare, revealed in all his little idiosyncracies. The worst thing is that these 'little things' dominate a relationship. There's little chance to show one's better side."

---

* Like the Azef case, the revelations about Malinovsky, aired in the Duma, shook the political establishment and helped to undermine the credibility and competence not just of the Okhrana but also of the Duma, the Emperor and the state itself. One of Malinovsky's first accusers was Elena (Rozmirovich) Troyanovskaya, Stalin's hostess in Vienna, who had become Secretary to the Bolshevik Duma deputies. Yet the traitor dismissed this as the sour grapes of his ex-mistress. When Malinovsky was captured by the Germans during the war, Lenin sent him clothes, but after the Revolution, faced with the evidence, he changed his view: "What a swine: shooting's too good for him." Malinovsky was tried in November 1918, prosecuted, ironically, by Elena Rozmirovich's husband, Nikolai Krylenko, at a tribunal chaired by Elena herself. Malinovsky was shot.

As the winter thawed, the Okhrana again warned on 27 April 1914 that the Bolsheviks were going "to organize the escapes of well-known Party men, Sverdlov and Djugashvili." Stalin and Sverdlov frequently borrowed Fyodor Taraseev's boat, but now the Gendarmes banned river expeditions. In May, when the steamboats again plied the Yenisei, Kureika's tedium changed from an agony of cold to a plague of mosquitoes.

Soon Stalin "stopped talking to me," wrote Sverdlov, "and let me know that I had to leave him alone and live separately." Both moved out, Stalin temporarily finding refuge in Philip Saltykov's *izba*. Moving out did not end Stalin's Arctic sulk. "You know what nasty conditions I have in Kureika," Sverdlov told his wife, Klavidia, who was in exile nearby. "The companion . . . appears to have such a sense of his own personality that we don't talk and meet one another." Sverdlov's letters capture the stress, depression (and bland menu) of this aimless existence.

> *I eat fish. My landlady makes me pies. I have sturgeon, white salmon with battered potatoes and caviar, salted sturgeon, sometimes I eat them raw. I feel too energyless even to add vinegar. I've ended all regular life. I eat irregularly. I study nothing. I go to sleep at odd times. Sometimes I walk for the whole night, sometimes I sleep at 10 a.m.*

Stalin must have lived the same way: he never lost the nocturnal hours of Siberia.

In this eight-hut universe, the entire population must have been aware of this schism. "We just couldn't harmonize our characters," regretted Sverdlov. But there was probably another big but unspeakable reason for their fallout: a girl.[4]

No sooner had Stalin and Sverdlov settled with the Taraseevs than the Georgian must have noticed the youngest girl among the Pereprygin orphans. There were five brothers and two sisters, Natalia and Lidia. We know no details of how this developed. But some time in early 1914 Stalin, now thirty-four, embarked on an affair with Lidia, aged thirteen.

We catch a glimpse of Stalin and Lidia together staggering from drinking-bout to drinking-bout because we have her memoirs of their boozy carousals: "In his spare time, Stalin liked to go to evening dances—he could be very jolly too. He loved to sing and dance. He especially liked the song 'I'm guarding the gold, the gold . . . I'm burying the gold, burying the gold, Guess where, pure damsel with your golden hair' . . . He often joined birthday dinners." The memoirs of Stalin's thirteen-year-old mistress were recorded twenty years later at the height of his dictatorship while she remained a Siberian housewife. The official who recorded her reminiscences would not have dared record the seduction, but the memoirs are still tactless. "He often liked to drop in on some people," says Lidia, meaning herself. "And he also drank." Was this how he seduced her—or she him? Girls in places like Kureika matured early—and Lidia does not sound like a shrinking violet.

Sverdlov may have disapproved of Stalin's seduction of the thirteen-year-old, the latest in a line of adolescent girls romanced by the thirty-something Georgian. And Stalin may well have thrown him out in order to enjoy more privacy with his little mistress. But this was far from the end of the scandal.

The two Bolsheviks, now ignoring each other, were carefully watched by their own Gendarme inspectors, Laletin and Popov, whose sole job was to ensure that they did not escape. In cases of such close proximity, the policemen either became the companions, if not personal servants, of the exiles—or their mortal foes. The red-bearded, red-tempered Ivan Laletin soon became Stalin's enemy.

Once Stalin was going out hunting with his rifle when he was challenged by the Gendarme. He was allowed to handle hunting-rifles with permission, but he refused to surrender his gun to the policeman. In the ensuing fracas, "Gendarme Laletin swooped on Josef Vissarionovich and tried to disarm him." A fight started. The Gendarme "drew his sabre and managed to cut Stalin on the hand." Stalin reported Laletin to Captain Kibirov.

By early summer, no matter how furtive the creeping around the eight huts, almost everyone must have known about Stalin's little mistress. The sabre-rattling Gendarme surely saw his chance to nail the insolent Georgian.

"One day," recalls Fyodor Taraseev, the only villager who dared record the story, "Stalin was staying at home, working, and not leaving the house. The Gendarme found this suspicious and decided to check up on him. Without knocking on the door, he burst into the room."

Taraseev prudently claims that Stalin was just "working," yet the inspector found this oddly "suspicious." And Stalin was furious at being interrupted. The memoirs unanimously emphasize his calmness during searches: so was there something unusual about this one? After all, the policeman deliberately surprised him "without knocking." It sounds very much as if the policeman caught Stalin and Lidia *in flagrante delicto.*

Stalin attacked him. The policeman again drew his sabre. In the ensuing fight, Stalin was wounded in the neck by the sabre, which so inflamed his anger that "he kicked out the rogue!"

"We witnessed this scene," says Taraseev. "The Gendarme was running away towards the Yenisei river, cravenly waving his sabre in front of him while Comrade Stalin was pursuing him in a state of high excitement and fury, with his fists clenched."

If it was a secret, it was out. Even though local lore discouraged affairs with exiles, the local girls were bound to be attracted to these worldly, educated revolutionaries in their midst. This statutory rape was not rape by force but an old-fashioned seduction because, according to the later investigation by KGB Chairman Ivan Serov, "J. V. Stalin started living together with her." Presumably she was sharing his room, which is how the policeman had caught them together. In his report to Nikita Khrushchev and the Politburo in 1956, which remained secret until the twenty-first century, General Serov implied that the living together was almost as shocking as the seduction.*

Stalin moved into the Pereprygin *izba.* There were two rooms and a shed for cattle in winter. The seven siblings were crammed into one fuggy, cow-dungy room; Stalin rented the filthy second chamber that could only be reached through the cowshed and family room. It contained just a "table covered in newspapers, wooden trestle bed, and tangle of fishing and hunting nets, tackle and hooks, all made by Stalin himself." Everything was covered in soot from the black tin chimney in the middle of the room.

The glass in the windows was broken, so Stalin sealed the cracks with old newspapers or boarded them up. The only light in this Arctic twilight, where night often lasted throughout the day, was a lamp, but he often

---

* For decades there were rumours of Stalin's rape or seduction of a girl in Turukhansk and his fathering a child. This first appeared in Essad Bey's biography of 1931. Svetlana Alliluyeva says her aunts told her Stalin had a son in exile. The stories were repeated in biographies and sensational newspaper articles but seemed outlandish, presumably just anti-Stalin myths. But it is confirmed by the KGB in General Serov's 18 July 1956 memorandum to First Secretary Khrushchev and the Politburo. Serov, a brutal Stalinist secret policeman, had the sense to separate himself from Beria and attach himself to Khrushchev. After Stalin's death, he assisted Khrushchev in the arrest and execution of Beria, becoming the first Chairman of the KGB, the new version of the secret police. His memo was read in secrecy at a Politburo meeting and signed by all Stalin's old henchmen before being consigned to the top secret "Special File."

lacked kerosene. The lavatory was an outhouse. The Pereprygins were dirt poor, "one day eating *shchi* [cabbage broth], the next day the holy spirit [nothing], but they owned one cow."

At night, Lidia would creep into his room, recounts Stalin's first biographer, Essad Bey, who must have talked to fellow exiles. Certainly she was not shy about recalling what underwear he favoured—"He wore white underwear and a sailor-striped vest," she confided to her interviewer in 1952 when Stalin was almost worshipped as a demi-god.

The brothers were not happy about the seduction. There are hints of their disapproval: Stalin got his food and bread from his old landlady, not from the Pereprygins, though Lidia claimed that "this was because the girls were too young to cook." Yet as orphans the girls had cooked for their brothers from an early age. More likely, Soso and his moll were banned from family meals.

The affair might have remained tolerable, but there was worse to come: Lidia fell pregnant with Stalin's child. The Pereprygin brothers were angry, even though the exact law of consent was hardly enforced in distant communities in the Arctic Circle, where girls married and had children in their early teens. According to General Serov, Gendarme Laletin, despite having fled from the irate Stalin, threatened "to instigate criminal proceedings for living together with an underage girl. J. V. Stalin promised the Gendarme to marry Pereprygina when she came of age." So, once again, Stalin became engaged—and the family, whether gratefully or begrudgingly, accepted the relationship.* In return, Stalin "shared his fish with them" as one of the family. Indeed he treated Lidia almost as his young wife. When his friend the elderly Elizaveta Taraseeva visited, Stalin commanded: "Lidia, Lidia, *babushka*'s come to tea! Feed her well."

The policeman's interference was the final straw. Stalin complained to Captain Kibirov, who favoured his fellow Caucasian. Stalin had a village of witnesses to the hapless Gendarme drawing his sword on an exile and the ignominious chase along the riverbank. Yet it took considerable chutzpah for Stalin to complain about the policeman when he had impregnated an underaged girl. As so often with Stalin's self-righteous indignation, it worked.

---

* Fourteen was technically the age of consent in the Russian and European regions of the Tsarist Empire, but this was Siberia. Besides, there was no precise legal concept of statutory rape in Tsarist law: for the police, it was as much a crime "against female honour" as a violation of her father's chattels. The seducer's agreement to marry and then the exchange of marriage vows were seen as rectifying an untoward situation.

That summer of 1914, around June, Kibirov agreed to replace Laletin, telling his deputy, "All right, let's send Merzliakov to Kureika. Since Djugashvili is so keen to replace his inspector, let's get him out of harm's way." In a reversal of roles, Gendarme Laletin was afraid of his prisoner—and with good reason. His replacement, Mikhail Merzliakov, now arrived. Stalin immediately assumed the role of quasi-aristocratic master, while the Gendarme became a cross between valet, batman and bodyguard for the rest of his sentence.

Stalin kept studying the nationalities issue, and English and German. "Dear friend," a rather more cheerful Stalin wrote to Zinoviev on 20 May, "my warmest greetings to you . . . I'm waiting for the books . . . I also ask you to send me some English journals (an old or new issue doesn't matter—it's for reading since there's nothing in English here and I'm afraid I'm losing all my acquired English skills without any practice . . ."

Soso's engagement to Lidia, indeed the relationship itself, was a transitory amusement to be abandoned by the wayside of his revolutionary mission. The pregnancy was presumably an irritant. Yet the locals claim that Lidia was in love with Stalin. It was not her last pregnancy by him.[5]

In late summer, Sverdlov left Kureika and moved to Selivanikha, while Suren Spandarian, Stalin's best friend, arrived in nearby Monastyrskoe.

In late August 1914, Stalin took the boat downriver for a reunion with Spandarian—just as the Archduke Franz Ferdinand, heir to the Habsburg throne, was assassinated in Sarajevo, a shot that sent Russia and the Great Powers lurching into the Great War. "The bourgeois vampires of the belligerent countries plunged the world into a bloody shambles," wrote Stalin. "Wholesale slaughter, ruin, starvation and . . . savagery—so that a handful of crowned and uncrowned robbers may pillage foreign lands and rake in untold millions."

As the lights went out all over Europe, Stalin found himself irrelevant, forgotten, frustrated and engaged against his will to a pregnant adolescent peasant-girl, at the centre of nothing—except an Arctic sex scandal. Nineteen-fourteen was not his finest hour. As the Great Powers fought, the snows obscured the sun and the news from the outside world. Stalin disappeared into the Siberian winter.[6]

35

The Hunter

Now the only exile in ice-bound, twilighted Kureika, Stalin started to live closely with aboriginal Tunguses and Ostyaks. There was little to do, but survival was a struggle: tundra wolves howled at the edge of the village. When Stalin visited the outhouse lavatory, he fired a rifle to keep the wolves at bay. When he travelled, the sleigh "dashed along under the interminable howls of wolves." The wolf-packs of Kureika entered Stalin's consciousness, the enemies always circling his Siberian hut. He sketched them on documents during meetings, especially towards the end of his life as he orchestrated a last Terror campaign, the Doctors' Plot. In his last exile, he told visitors, "The peasants used to shoot mad wolves."

Yet somehow it suited Stalin: he began to enjoy Kureika. Strangely, it became one of the happiest times in his morose life. His favourite companions were a little dog called Stepan Timofeevich, or Tishka for short, which the locals gave him as a present, a Tungus fisherman named Martin Peterin, and his police inspector, Merzliakov. Lidia's pregnancy was increasingly visible. Siberia became more bearable because Stalin now began to receive regular money orders: during 1915–16, he received ten, worth more than one hundred roubles in all, so he could buy food and clothes and pay bribes where necessary.*

---

* The payments have attracted suspicion, but they are much too meagre for the wages of an Okhrana agent. They included some of his CC salary; and, as we have seen, Sverdlov

He became the solitary hunter, a role that suited his self-image as a man on a sacred mission, riding out into the snows with a rifle for company, but no attachments except his faith, lacking all bourgeois sentimentality but always displaying Arctic stoicism even when beset by tragedy. For the rest of his life, he regaled Alliluyevs or Politburo grandees with tales of his Siberian adventures. Even when he ruled Russia he was still that solitary hunter.

"Osip" or "Pockmarked Oska," as they called him, venturing out alone in a head-to-foot reindeer-fur outfit, became a skilled hunter and close companion of the tribesmen. Laletin did not permit him to own a rifle, so, one local remembers, "We took the rifle to the woods and left it on a pre-agreed tree so he'd find it." He shot Arctic foxes, partridges and ducks on long expeditions.

The villagers began to respect Pockmarked Oska, with his pipe and books. "The locals liked him," says Merzliakov. "They visited him and sat all night with him. He visited them too and attended their merry parties." They brought him fish and venison, which he purchased. He appreciated their laconic tranquillity and was amused by their respect for shamans and by their persistent belief, despite nominal Orthodoxy, in the masters and spirits who inhabited the spaces of Siberia. Above all, he studied and copied their fishing and hunting techniques.

Fish and reindeer were their staples. The reindeer, who are able to live on blankets of lichen, were treated with sacred respect by the tribesmen, providing transport (pulling sleighs), clothing (furs), investment (the wealthiest chiefs owned herds of 10,000) and food (boiled reindeer meat), all in one. Peterin, probably an Ostyak creole, taught his friend the art of

---

received far more. Yet during the Great Terror in 1938 Stalin's secret police chief, "poison dwarf" Nikolai Yezhov, who had become his closest henchman and was presiding over the slaughter of over a million innocent people, began to realize that he was dispensable. Yezhov, sinking into alcoholism and sexual debauchery under the terrible strain of killing and torturing, gathered materials to use as security or blackmail against his master and the rival magnates Beria, Georgi Malenkov and Khrushchev. He procured Stalin's ten money orders and kept them in his personal safe, but there is no smoking gun here. Three of them were money from Gori, probably from his mother or Egnatashvili. The other seven, from Moscow and Petersburg, adding up to 100 roubles, delivered 10 roubles here, 10 roubles there, though two were a more considerable 25 roubles each. They did not save Yezhov, who was dismissed in late 1938 and shot in 1940. Interestingly Stalin did not deign to destroy the money orders, just filing them in Yezhov's papers where they were found by Professor Arch Getty, who has generously shared them with me. For the full story of the rise and fall of Yezhov, see *Stalin: The Court of the Red Tsar.*

Yenisei fishing. Stalin made his own fishing-line and dug his own personal ice-hole, remembers Merzliakov, whose memoir, recorded in 1936, is the best account of his life in Kureika. According to Stalin's own somewhat Gothic account, he learned to fish with such dexterity at his ice-hole that the Ostyak whispered awestruck: "Thou ist possessed by the Word." Stalin enjoyed the fish diet: "There were lots of fish, but salt was as precious as gold, so they just threw the fish into their outhouse where in the −20° freeze they piled up like frozen pieces of wood. Then we'd break flakes off and let them melt in our mouths." He started to catch huge sturgeons.

"Once," he recounted, "a tempest caught me on the river. It seemed I was done for, but I made it to the bank." Another time, he was coming home with Ostyak friends with a good catch of sturgeon and sea-salmon when he got separated from the others. A *purga,* the blinding blizzard of the tundra, blew up suddenly. Kureika was far away, but he could not abandon his fish, sustenance for weeks, so he trudged on until he saw figures ahead. He called after them, but they disappeared: they were his companions but, seeing him embroidered from beard to feet in white ice, they believed him a demon spirit and fled. When he finally reached a hut and burst in, the Ostyaks cried out: "Is that you, Osip?"

"Of course it's me and I'm not a wood-spirit!" he retorted, before falling into a deep sleep for eighteen hours.

He was not imagining that he was in danger—the tribesmen were accustomed to losing men on their fishing expeditions. "I remember in spring at high water, thirty men went out fishing and in the evening when we came back, one was missing," Stalin recounted. They casually explained that their companion had "remained out there." Stalin was puzzled until one said that "He drowned." Their nonchalance perplexed Stalin, but they explained: "Why should we have pity for men? We can always make more of them, but a horse, try to make a horse!" Stalin used this in a 1935 speech to illustrate the value of human life, but actually it must have been another experience that taught him its cheapness.

"I went on a hunt one winter," Stalin told his magnates Khrushchev and Beria at one of his dinners after the Second World War, "took my gun, and crossed the Yenisei on skis for about 12 versts and saw some partridges on a tree. I had twelve rounds and there were twenty-four partridges. I killed twelve and the rest just sat there, so I thought I'd go back for twelve more rounds. When I came back they were still sitting there."

"Still sitting there?" prompted Khrushchev. Beria urged Stalin to continue.

"That's right," boasted Stalin, "so I killed the remaining twelve, tied them to my belt and dragged them home with me." By the time he told this to his son-in-law Yuri Zhdanov, he boasted he had shot *thirty* birds, the temperature was *–40°* and *another* wild storm forced him to abandon partridges and gun—and even hope. But luckily, the women (possibly Lidia) found him swooning in a snowdrift and rescued him—and he slept for thirty-six hours.*

Stalin amassed a little medicine cabinet and became the closest thing Kureika had to a doctor: "J. V. helped people with medicine, dressed wounds with iodine and gave drugs." He "taught the tribesmen to wash," says Merzliakov, "and I remember how he washed one of them with soap." He suffered from rheumatism, which he eased in the bathhouse, but the pain remained into old age, when he used to perch on the Kremlin's heaters during long meetings. He was good at playing with the Tungus children, singing and romping with them, sometimes telling them about his own unhappy childhood. Little Dasha Taraseeva "used to ride on his back, pulling his thick dark hair and crying, 'Neigh like a horse, uncle!' " When Fyodor Taraseev's cow sickened with colic, Stalin impressed him with the skills he had learned as a boy in Georgia: he "slaughtered the cow and carved the meat like a real master."

Stalin still enjoyed partying. "At the Taraseevs' place, the young gathered in a circle for a party—Stalin danced in the middle beating time, then he started singing," recalls a visitor to Kureika, Daria Ponamareva, " 'I'm burying the gold, burying the gold,' " always that favourite song. "He was expert in dancing," says Anfisa Taraseeva, "and taught the young."

Sometimes, the Georgian from the lush mountainous Caucasus peered out at the *taiga*. "In this damned land, nature is abominably barren—the river in summer, snow in winter, that's all that nature provides here," he

---

* Just before telling his henchmen this story, the ageing Stalin had suffered a similar accident to that of U.S. Vice President Dick Cheney in 2006: while showing off his shooting skills, he had misfired, closely missing Politburo grandee Anastas Mikoyan and peppering two of his guards. Already beginning to hate and scorn the ailing dictator in the postwar years, Beria and Khrushchev had heard this story of Stalin's exploit repeatedly. They did not believe it. "After dinner," writes Khrushchev, "we were spitting with scorn in the bathroom: 'So Stalin claimed to have skied 12 versts in winter, shot twelve partridges, skied back 12 versts and returned, another 12 versts, shot another twelve partridges and skied another 12 versts home—48 versts on skis!' " (48 versts equals 32 miles.) "Listen," exclaimed Beria, "how can a man from the Caucasus who never had the chance to ski, travel a distance like that? He's lying." Khrushchev agreed: "Of course, he was lying! I'd seen with my own eyes that Stalin couldn't shoot at all!" In fact, in the 1920s and early 1930s, Stalin enjoyed hunting on holiday, though he regarded it as a waste of time.

wrote poignantly to Olga Alliluyeva on 25 November 1915, "and I'm driven mad with longing for scenes of nature . . ."

He also spent much time alone, writing at night. "My dog Tishka was my companion," Stalin reminisced. "In winter nights, if I had kerosene and could read and write, he'd come in, press close to my legs and whimper as if he was talking to me. I leaned down patting his head, saying, 'Are you frozen, Tishka? Warm yourself up!' " He joked that he "liked to discuss international politics with the dog, Stepan Timofeevich," clearly the world's first canine pundit. For Stalin, pets had advantages over people: they provided selfless affection and passionate admiration yet never betrayed their masters (nor became pregnant by them), and yet they could be abandoned without guilt.

The inactivity, isolation from the political game and lack of reading materials sometimes depressed him bitterly, especially when he brooded about Lenin and Zinoviev. Had they forgotten him? Where was his latest article? And why had he not been paid? In the winter of 1915, he sarcastically asked them: "How am I? What am I doing? I'm not all right. I'm doing almost nothing. And what can I do with a complete lack of serious books? . . . In all my exiles, I've never had such a miserable life as here."

Even this fanatical Marxist, convinced that the progress of history would bring about revolution and dictatorship of the proletariat, must have sometimes doubted if he would ever return. Even Lenin doubted the Revolution, asking Krupskaya, "Will we ever live to see it?" Yet Stalin never seems to have lost faith. "The Russian Revolution is as inevitable as the rising of the sun," he had written back in 1905 and he had not changed his view. "Can you prevent the sun from rising?"

When he could get his hands on newspapers, the future Supreme Commander-in-Chief eagerly discussed "the ulcers of war" with Merzliakov. During the Second World War, he sometimes quoted examples from the battles of the First that he had followed in Kureika.* As the Tsar tottered from one bungled defeat to another, Stalin must have anticipated that this war would, like that of 1904, finally bring Revolution. Perhaps he was not just misleading the Okhrana when he told Petrovsky in Petersburg: "Someone spread a rumour that I wouldn't be staying for my whole

---

* After the débâcle of the 1942 Kharkov offensive, Stalin gave Khrushchev a dressing-down. "During the First World War," he said, "when one of the armies was encircled in East Prussia, the commander of the neighbouring army fled to the rear. He was put on trial—and hanged."

sentence. What nonsense! I swear and I'll be damned if I don't keep my word, that this won't happen. I'll remain in exile until my sentence ends [in 1917]. At times I've considered escaping but now I've finally rejected the idea." One senses his weariness: if Lenin and Zinoviev would not help him, then he would not help them.

Somewhere around December 1914, Lidia gave birth to a baby.[1]

36

The Robinson Crusoe of Siberia

The child died soon afterwards. Stalin made no comment about this, but he was definitely in Kureika at the time and the whole settlement must have been aware of it. Whether or not Lidia's brothers forgave their libidinous tenant, the relationship with Lidia continued.

Stalin's new policeman, Merzliakov, made his life much more pleasant. He did not spy on his charge, follow him or search him, and he allowed him to meet friends, go on long hunting expeditions and even disappear for weeks on end. "In the summer we went by boat . . . pulled by dogs and on return we rowed back. In winter we went on horseback," and the fur-clad, pipe-puffing Stalin would despatch the half-policeman, half-valet Merzliakov to collect his mail. Almost twenty years later, Stalin was still grateful to Merzliakov—and probably saved his life.*

---

* In 1930, Merzliakov was accused of being a kulak, one of the richer peasants, whom Stalin was determined to liquidate in his brutal war on the peasantry. He appealed to Stalin: "I think you won't have forgotten how I was." Stalin responded: "I knew Mikhail Merzliakov at the time of my exile in the village of Kureika where he was my guard 1914–16. He only had one order—to look after me (the only exile in Kureika at the time). It is clear I could not have 'friendly' relations with Merzliakov. But I have to testify that even if our relations were not 'friendly,' they were not hostile as usual between guard and exile. It seems to me this can be explained by Merzliakov's lip-service to his duties without the usual police zeal, he didn't spy on me, didn't persecute me . . . colluded in my long absences and often criticized his officers for his 'tedious' orders . . . So in 1914–16, Merzliakov distinguished himself from other policemen. It is my duty to testify this before you."

In February 1915, "during the months when it was always dark with no distinction between day and night," he was visited by Spandarian and his mistress Vera Shveitzer. They had driven 125 miles up the frozen Yenisei on sledges, propelled by dog-power, harrassed by wolves. At last they had seen the tiny settlement from afar and Soso's snow-covered *izba*, whence he emerged, smiling, to greet them. Most of the inhabitants and the Gendarme welcomed them too.

"We stayed at Josef Vissarionovich's place for two days." Vera noticed that Soso, suffering from arthritis, was "wearing a jacket but he had only one of his arms through the sleeve. Later I realized he likes to dress in such a way so as to keep his right arm free." Stalin, who was delighted to see them, went out to the river and proudly returned with an enormous three-pud sturgeon over his shoulder: "There are no small fish in my ice-hole."

Spandarian and Shveitzer came to discuss the trial in Petersburg of the five Bolshevik Duma deputies and *Pravda* editor Kamenev. Lenin had declared that he wished the Germans to defeat Russia, thereby accelerating the Revolution and a "European civil war." The Mensheviks supported Russia's patriotic war providing it was "defencist." In November 1914, Kamenev and the deputies were arrested for treason; during his trial Kamenev refused to follow Lenin's unpatriotic defeatism, but was still found guilty and exiled to Siberia.

Stalin and Spandarian were disgusted by Kamenev's behaviour. "That man's not trustworthy," declared Stalin, "he could betray the Revolution," whereupon, wrapped in tarpaulins, dressed head to foot in reindeer furs and guided by Tungus tribesmen, Spandarian and Vera took Stalin back with them to Monastyrskoe, the Northern Lights gorgeously illuminating the tundra. "Suddenly Stalin started singing," writes Shveitzer. "Suren joined in and it was so lovely to hear well-known melodies carrying me away" as the sleigh rushed for two days across the ice in that endless twilight.

Spandarian and Stalin wrote to Lenin. Stalin, the Bolshevik hunter, no longer whining about owed money and unsent books, struck the very pose of militant virility that would be the Bolshevik style in power:

My greetings to you, dear Vladimir Illich, the very warmest greetings. Greetings to Zinoviev, greetings to Nadezhda! How are things, how is your health? I live as before, I munch my bread and am getting through half my sentence. Boring—but what can you do? And how are things

with you? You must be having a jollier time . . . I've read a little article
by Plekhanov in Rech—*what an incorrigible blabbing old woman!*
Eh! . . . And the Liquidators with their [Duma] deputy-agents . . . ?
There's no one to give them a beating, the devil knows! Surely they won't
remain unpunished? Cheer us up and inform us there'll soon be an organ to
give them a right good punching straight in their gobs!

Lenin remembered his "fiery Colchian" in exile. "Koba is well," he
informed his comrades; then a few months later, he asked: "Big request—
find out last name of Koba (Josef Dj—? Have forgotten). It's important."

When Stalin's exeat was over, he returned to Kureika for the rest of
the long winter. The ice thawed on the Yenisei. In May 1915, the steamboats brought interesting companions upriver from Krasnoyarsk.
Kamenev arrived in Monastyrskoe with the Duma deputies. Sverdlov and
Spandarian were nearby. During July 1915, Stalin was summoned to a
meeting at the house shared by Kamenev and Petrovsky in Monastyrskoe.

The Bolsheviks enjoyed an idyllic summer reunion. They even took
group photographs.* But for the Bolsheviks even the picnics were political, involving denunciations and trials. Stalin and Spandarian supported
Lenin and decided to put Kamenev on trial in Monastyrskoe.

Kamenev gave Stalin *The Prince* by Machiavelli, perhaps an unwise
gift for someone who was already Machiavellian enough. At a boozy dinner, Kamenev asked everyone round the table to declare their greatest
pleasure in life. Some cited women, others earnestly replied that it was the
progress of dialectical materialism towards the workers' paradise. Then
Stalin answered: "My greatest pleasure is to choose one's victim, prepare
one's plans minutely, slake an implacable vengeance, and then go to bed.
There's nothing sweeter in the world."[†]

At Kamenev's "trial," Stalin had the casting vote. Slippery as ever and
always building new alliances, he attacked Kamenev and then departed
for Kureika before the final vote, thus saving the victim. Kamenev patronized the cruder Georgian, while Stalin found him congenial but disdained

---

* Stalin poses with his trademark black fedora at a rakish angle, in his usual position at the
centre in the back, flanked by Spandarian and Kamenev. Sverdlov also stands in the back
row, while at the front, sitting on the floor, is Sverdlov's little son Andrei, who later became
one of Stalin's top NKVD investigators and torturers.
† Stalin was to repeat this philosophy in the early 1920s. Kamenev called it "Stalin's Theory of Sweet Revenge" after his defeat by the dictator in the mid-1920s. But he did not
take it, or Stalin, seriously until it was too late.

him as a man and politician: "I saw Gradov [Kamenev] and company in the summer," he wrote to Zinoviev. "They all rather resemble wet hens. So these are our 'hawks' are they!"

Stalin returned to another long winter in Kureika. In early November, after the snows had descended, he got permission to see the doctor in Monastyrskoe. Arriving in full furs on a four-dog sleigh, he burst into Spandarian's house and kissed his friend on the cheeks—and Vera twice on the lips.

"Oh Koba!" she exclaimed, delighted to see him. "Oh Koba!"

Spandarian, consumptive and suffering from nervous tension, was "sometimes so frantic that a gnat bite would drive him to tear his clothes to shreds. Suren was depressed," but "Stalin was very cheerful," recalls a fellow exile, Boris Ivanov, "and his arrival always reinvigorated him."

Stalin collected a letter from Zinoviev, to which he replied sarcastically:

> *Dear friend!*
>
> *I've finally got your letter. I thought you'd completely forgotten me, a slave of God, and yet it turned out you did not . . . And what can I do with a complete lack of serious books? . . . I have lots of questions and subjects in my mind but no source-materials. I'm dying to write but I have nothing to study . . . You ask about my finances. And why do you ask about that? You probably have some money—aren't you thinking of sharing it with me? Go on then! I swear it'll come just in time!*
>
> *Yours Djugashvili*

On arrival, Stalin helped embitter a local feud, the sort that he always relished, both as mean-spirited sport and political stimulant. The Bolshevik exiles in Monastyrskoe, led by Spandarian, had found themselves so short of sugar and furs that winter that they robbed the local Revelion trading shop of its precious goodies. When the police investigated, an exile named Petukhov sneaked on the thieves. Isolated and paranoid in their Siberian time warp, exiles took sides with either the robbers or the informer. Spandarian wanted to punish Petukhov and try him at another Party trial. Sverdlov backed Petukhov and wanted to try Spandarian for the robbery itself. But Sverdlov himself had become too close to the local police, giving officers German lessons. Spandarian and his allies accused Sverdlov of being a "morally tainted" Okhrana spy.

Sverdlov boycotted the Party trial at which Spandarian, Vera and five others voted to condemn Petukhov. Stalin, who had himself faced expulsion at similar sittings, grandly sat on the fence, abstaining from the vote for Petukhov's expulsion, explaining that "they should expel both Petukhov and Sverdlov." The row became so heated that some of Sverdlov's group were beaten up.

"Exile is the worst," wrote Sverdlov, "there's no trace of community or comradeship: isolation and distance are infernal and murderous." Now Spandarian "fell seriously ill . . . starting to cough blood."[1]

"We spent a long time in the village," says Stalin's police-batman, Merzliakov. "I had no idea who he was seeing. J. V. [Stalin] eventually returned to the police station himself to say that we could go back."

In Kureika again, Stalin survived the winter of 1915–16 in his sooty room chez Pereprygin, continuing his sexual relationship with Lidia. He was delighted to receive a parcel from Olga Alliluyeva in Petersburg that inspired a rare sentimentality:

> *I'm so grateful to you, deeply respected Olga, for your good and pure feeling towards me! I shall never forget your caring attitude to me. I look forward to the moment when I'm freed from exile and can come to Petersburg and personally thank you and Sergei for everything. I've only got two years left. I got the parcel. Thanks. I only ask one thing— don't waste any more money on me; you yourselves need the money but—do send me postcards of scenes of nature . . .*

Anna and Nadya Alliluyeva, the latter now fourteen, also sent their exiled hero a new suit, and hid a little note to him in the pocket.

In March 1916, when it was possible to use the sledge on the Yenisei, Stalin headed back to see Spandarian in Monastyrskoe "to send his letters," recalls Vera. "By the way," he complained to a comrade on 25 February, "tell me please what is going on with an article by K. Stalin 'On Cultural-National Autonomy'—was it published or somehow lost? I've been trying to find out for more than a year and have found out nothing . . . What am I doing? Certainly I'm not wasting my time! Yours Josef." The article had been sent to Lenin via Alliluyev—but somewhere it was lost forever.

Stalin found Spandarian seriously ill with TB and heart failure: the Armenian petitioned to be moved from Turukhansk. Worried about

Spandarian, Stalin also petitioned the authorities. After a few days, he sledged back to Kureika. "That," says Vera Shveitzer, "was the last time he met Suren Spandarian."*

During the summer, the Georgian lodger impregnated Lidia for the second time—and then typically made himself scarce. Local exiles, wrote one of them, Ivanov, "got to know that [Stalin] had disappeared from Kureika—he escaped," for some months. Where was he? Merzliakov was not quite sure himself. He allowed "JV" to fish alone downstream on Polovinka Island in the Yenisei River "for the whole summer . . . I just followed the rumours that he hadn't escaped yet." The policeman did wonder what Stalin could be doing on this remote island. "It's an empty (uninhabited) place, this Polovinka. Just sand. Where was he fishing? There was nobody else there." But it turns out Stalin did spend time on the "empty Polovinka."

Only a few local hunters stayed on this remote island, which was rich in game. Stepanida Dubikova reveals that "Osip" spent much of the summer there. "We helped him build a small hut for just one person out of birch branches." Stepanida and her family, who built their own birch hut, were the only others on Polovinka. "Osip used to visit our hut and I'd cook him his favourite, grilled sterlet." Stalin spent weeks totally alone in this one-man hut, fishing for himself, content in the extreme solitude. But sometimes he was not on his island either.

"Stalin arrived to see us," reports Badaev, the Duma deputy, in Yeniseisk, "and we met there . . . Despite the secrecy of his visit, all the exiles got to hear Comrade Stalin was here and dropped in to see us." He must have visited Kostino too, because on his way back he called in at Miroedikha, where he partied with a Georgian exile, Nestor Rukhadze, who "played the accordion and balalaika." Stalin, in "long coat, hat with earflaps and red galoshes," joined the local youths who "spent the evenings talking, singing and dancing."

Merzliakov had not kept his Captain Kibirov informed of Stalin's summer disappearance. The news spread, but Kibirov, whether bribed or charmed, the latest in a line of policemen to be suborned by Stalin, did nothing until his superiors heard that the Georgian exile had vanished, whereupon he arrested Fyodor Taraseev. Taraseev got one and a half

---

* Spandarian was allowed to move to Krasnoyarsk in August, but it was too late. Stalin inquired after his friend but the letters went astray.

years in prison for aiding an escape by lending his boat. Stalin was not punished.*

What was Stalin doing in the summer of 1916? Most likely, his need to get out of Kureika was connected with Lidia's second pregnancy, hence Merzliakov's suspicious but tactful vagueness. The Pereprygin brothers may have been cross again: when Stalin returned in early autumn he moved out of the Pereprygins' into Alexei Taraseev's house before returning to the Pereprygins' again where Lidia, now aged fifteen, was heavily pregnant. He seems to have caroused and visited friends on his local tour as far as Yeniseisk and Krasnoyarsk, but locals claim that he was devising a way to avoid marrying his pregnant teenage mistress.[2] By 1916, the rot at the head of the Empire had reached its outlying limbs—the Siberian police were loosening their grip. "We managed to escape all police officers and guards," said Badaev.

The war was not going well. The Emperor had left Petersburg (renamed Petrograd to sound less Germanic) and taken command of his armies. In Petrograd, his foolish, neurotic and ham-handed Empress, Alexandra, dominated the government. Prompted by Rasputin and a mediocre crew of mountebanks and war-profiteers, she hired and fired her ever more corrupt and inept ministers. No one knew it, but three centuries of Romanov rule had only months to run.

---

* Fyodor was apparently not the only person punished for Stalin's absence. This author received a letter from Mrs. Eva Purins of Downham Market, Norfolk, who writes that her great-grandmother, an exile named Jefinia Nogornova, was imprisoned in Krasnoyarsk for "helping to hide Stalin." If true, it must have been on this occasion.

37

Stalin's Reindeer-Propelled Sleigh
and a Siberian Son

In October 1916, Stalin, a fanatical Marxist with a damaged arm, was conscripted with his fellow exiles. He had successfully dodged the draft for over a decade. The call-up of exiles shows the manpower shortage of the Romanov war machine, but both Stalin and local officials must have known that his arm would not pass the medical examination. Turukhansk locals claim that Stalin persuaded Kibirov to put his name on the conscription list with "a false certificate," a shenanigan he may have arranged on his long summer exeat. Had he volunteered in order to escape his marital obligations and last months of exile in Kureika?

"Police Chief Kibirov," recalls Vera Shveitzer, "formed the first group of nine exiles to be sent to Krasnoyarsk." Stalin did not hang around in Kureika. He quickly said goodbye, giving one lady who had looked after him the "present of a signed photograph and two overcoats." Then, "seen off like a real hero," he set out with Merzliakov for Monastyrskoe.

After he was gone, in roughly April 1917, Lidia gave birth to a son whom she named Alexander. She did not inform the father for a long time—and Stalin never contacted her. But somehow he heard: he told the Alliluyev sisters that he had fathered a Siberian son during his last exile. He was utterly unfettered by paternal feelings, or even sentimental curiosity.

Stalin abandoned his son, but Turukhansk somehow made him more of a Russian. Perhaps Siberia froze some of the Georgian exoticism out of him. He brought the self-reliance, vigilance, frigidity and solitude of the Siberian hunter with him to the Kremlin. Generalissimo Stalin told the truth when in 1947 he wrote to one of his Kureika fishing pals: "I have not forgotten you and my friends in Turukhansk. Probably I'll never forget you." Molotov put it best: "A little piece of Siberia remained lodged in Stalin for the rest of his life."*

Around 12 December 1916, Kibirov put together the two groups of exiles, twenty in all, for the trip to Krasnoyarsk—"Stalin," writes Sverdlov, "was among the comrades." Sverdlov was barred from the glory of almost certain death on some forgotten field of the Eastern Front because he was a Jew, one of the few benefits of Romanov anti-Semitism. The others begged Stalin to make up with Sverdlov and shake hands. Stalin refused.

The conscripts departed in a picturesque parade of bunting-emblazoned sleighs, pulled by reindeer. The exiles, waving mandolins and balalaikas, "were given a Siberian *sakun,* which was a fur coat, reindeer *bokari*—fur boots—and gloves and hats made of reindeer fur," remembers another passenger, Boris Ivanov. "Only one person travelled in each sledge in a kind of linen cradle," but the policemen accompanied them as they galloped down the frozen Yenisei, passing through twenty-five little settlements which were all ordered to provide "beds, plump feather pillows, milk, meat and fish. In some places we stayed for days."

Stalin, taking command, decided that "we had no reason to hurry. We were exhausted but why should we hurry to be drafted?" records a fellow

---

* Some of Stalin's Kureika fishing friends kept in contact: V. G. Solomin wrote to ask for help, reminiscing about a giant sturgeon he caught for Stalin and Sverdlov. "Comrade Solomin," answered Stalin on 5 March 1947, "I send you 6,000 roubles from my [Supreme Soviet] deputy's salary. This sum is not so big, but it'll be useful. J Stalin." Molotov recalled how Stalin continued into old age to eat frozen nuggets of fish just as he had in Turukhansk. In 1934, a Stalin museum was founded in Stalin's love nest, the Pereprygin *izba,* which was expanded on his official seventieth birthday in 1949 into a pillared pavilion with the hut preserved in a glass bell. A giant statue of Stalin was built. Upriver, Stalin developed the Norilsk nickel-mining and smelting plant into a vast Gulag prison-city. In 1949, he ordered the creation of an Arctic railway and port which he personally supervised: 200,000 prisoners worked in terrible conditions there with many dying, though the Railway of Death was never completed. In 1961, during de-Stalinization, the museum was destroyed, the statue pushed through a hole in the ice, the *izba* burned. The once deserted region is now dominated by a hydroelectric dam that powers Norilsk Nickel, which has become a multi-billion-dollar conglomerate controlled by one of Russia's new oligarchs. As for the fate of Stalin's Siberian mistress and son, see the Epilogue.

traveller. " 'There'll be plenty of time,' he said, 'for the Germans to make mincemeat of us.' "

The exiles sometimes had "a party on two or three nights" with Stalin leading the singing. The policemen complained and telegraphed Kibirov, who threatened to "send the Cossacks after us but we telegraphed back: 'We're ready for your Cossacks.' Stalin took part in wording the telegram." He had managed to turn the trip into an almost two-month reindeer-propelled debauch. Somewhere along the way, the carousing convicts celebrated the New Year: 1917.

Finally, around 9 February, the sleighs arrived in Krasnoyarsk. On their word of honour, the police let the exiles settle for a few days before reporting to the Military Command. Stalin moved into the apartment of Ivan Samoilov, a Bolshevik, then he summoned Vera Shveitzer over from Achinsk. She told him Spandarian was dead.

Stalin reported to the medical examiner, who found him "unfit for military service" because of his arm. This was convenient but embarrassing for a future Supreme Commander-in-Chief who in his own eyes was as much a soldier as a politician. When Anna Alliluyeva revealed he was "unfit" in memoirs published just after the Second World War, Stalin never forgave her.

On 16 February, he applied to the Yeniseisk governor to spend the last four months of his exile in nearby Achinsk, "a large village of 6,000 inhabitants, two churches, and one-storey cottages," further west along the Trans-Siberian Railway, where Vera Shveitzer and Kamenev were living.

On 21 February, he moved into Vera Shveitzer's Achinsk apartment—just as, thousands of miles to the west, the Empress Alexandra started to lose control of Petrograd. On the 23rd, crowds rioted in the capital as Stalin settled into one of Achinsk's cottages. "He had no stuff," recalls his landlady's daughter, "just wearing a black overcoat, grey Astrakhan hat. He left the house after lunch and returned late at night." But he was often visited by "a swarthy woman with a Greek nose and yellow jacket and they spent much time together—he used to see her to the door, closing the doors himself." The woman was Vera Shveitzer, from whom he was inseparable during these ten days: "She was staying with him." The memoirs imply that they were living together, but we do not know if they were anything other than roommates—though Shveitzer always greeted him with kisses on the lips: "Oh Koba! Oh Koba!"

On Sunday, 26 February, fifty people were killed in fighting between

Two Caucasian rogues: Stalin *(right)* with his best friend, Suren Spandarian, a well-educated Armenian playboy, merciless Bolshevik and ally in Baku—where Spandarian was said to have fathered half the children under three years old. Here the friends meet up in Siberia, 1915.

Astonishingly promiscuous in exile, Stalin seduced women and planned escapes. *Top left:* The happiest affair was with saucy schoolgirl Pelageya (code-named Glamourpuss by the Okhrana). He sent her passionate postcards illustrated with lovemaking couples *(top right)*. *Middle left:* His postcard to another mistress, the teacher Tatiana Sukhova. *Below:* His landlady-cum-mistress Maria Kuzakova in old age during the 1950s with Constantine, her son by Stalin, and his baby.

Stalin, now rising to the top of the Bolshevik Party, arrested again in 1911.

Left: Vienna, 1913—Stalin, Hitler, Trotsky and Tito lived in the same city. Stalin's luxurious apartment block, now a boardinghouse, bearing his plaque. *Right:* Cracow, 1912–13—Stalin stayed in Lenin's flat.

Betrayal, 1913: Roman Malinovsky, ex-burglar-cum-rapi and star Bolshevik was the Okhrana's highly paid doubl agent. Neither Stalin nor Lenin believed he was a traito But he arranged Stalin's arrest by luring him to a fun raising party.

Left: Stalin, Central Committee member, refused to go to the cocktail party but Malinovsky persuaded him, lending him this silk tie. He was arrested in it. *Right:* Tatiana Slavatinskaya, Stalin's mistress, and his date at the party where he was betrayed. Stalin tried to escape in drag.

Arctic sex comedy. Escape from Kureika *(above)* on the Arctic Circle was impossible. Stalin loved hunting and living with Ostyak tribesmen and their reindeer *(left)*.

In 1914, he consoled himself by seducing the thirteen-year-old Lidia Pereprygina with whom he was surprised by the local policeman wielding a sabre. Stalin was so outraged he chased the policeman around the village. *Below right:* Middle-aged Lidia after the Second World War. *Below left:* Stalin and Lidia's illegitimate son, Alexander.

Siberian summer, 1915: Bolshevik exiles meet up to drink, picnic and hold trials of their comrades. *Top:* At the back, standing, Stalin in his fedora *(third from the left)* is between Spandarian in cloth cap *(second from left)*, and Kamenev with moustache *(fourth from left)*, while Sverdlov in a white shirt and glasses is third from right. Spandarian's partner Vera Shveitzer sits in front. The child is Sverdlov's son Andrei, one of Stalin's future secret-police torturers.

Stalin met most of the Soviet grandees during his youth and he never forgot any slights or rows. During the 1930s, he unleashed the Great Terror to liquidate many of them, having so many of his companions killed that the picture had to be culled too. First, in 1936, Kamenev was shot and his place next to Stalin was blanked out *(bottom left)*. In 1937–38, Stalin had approximately 1.5 million people shot. The group in the picture was savagely cut too: another five people have vanished *(bottom right)*.

Top: Vera Shveitzer was Spandarian's girlfriend. After his death, she moved in with Stalin. After the fall of the Tsar, they caught the train together for Petrograd. *Left:* Stalin's seduction and impregnation of thirteen-year-old Lidia Pereprygina seemed so outrageous as to be legendary. In 1956, Khrushchev ordered KGB boss Serov to investigate: Here is his top secret memo that proves it all, signed by Khrushchev, Voroshilov and the Politburo. (Serov was also ordered to investigate Stalin's links to the Okhrana and the Eremin Letter, which he covers in the memo's first pages before moving on to the underaged affair.)

Дни революціи. 1917 г.
Предъявленіе пропуска при въѣздѣ
3928 впъ Таврическій дворецъ.

Revolution, February–March 1917: When Stalin arrived from Siberia in Petrograd, he walked excitedly to Potemkin's Taurida Palace *(top)*, the seethingly chaotic political centre, home of Soviet, Duma, government—and marauding soldiers *(bottom)*.

Petrograd crowds and Cossacks. Bloodshed emboldened the throng, and soldiers began to desert the Tsar. The next day, crowds stormed the Arsenal, seizing 150,000 guns, burning down police headquarters and lynching policemen. One was tossed from a fourth-storey window, before the mob, using sticks and rifle-butts, smashed him into a bloody pulp.

Achinsk was oblivious. Kamenev and his wife, Olga, who was Trotsky's sister, held a salon. "I used to spend the evenings at the Kamenevs'," reminisces Anatoly Baikalov, exiled son of a goldmining tycoon. "Djugashvili, or Osip as we called him, was a frequent guest at their home." Kamenev, a "brilliant speaker and accomplished conversationalist," overshadowed the "dull and dry Stalin, devoid of colour or witticisms." When he did say something, "Kamenev dismissed it with brief, almost contemptuous remarks." The "taciturn and morose" Stalin just puffed on his pipe while its "poisonous smoke irritated Kamenev's pretty but vain and capricious wife," who "coughed and implored Stalin to stop. But he never paid any attention to her."

In Petrograd, the Tsar no longer reigned. On 1 March, in the Taurida Palace, a Provisional Government was formed under a new Premier, Prince Georgi Lvov. In the same building, a Soviet of Workers and Soldiers elected an Executive Committee, chaired by the Georgian Menshevik Karlo Chkheidze. These two parallel institutions took power. The Emperor, isolated, ill-informed, depressed, belatedly tried to return to the capital. But as the imperial train was stranded at Pskov, he haemorrhaged the support of his generals.

On 2 March, Nicholas II, declaring that "he was firmly convinced he had been born for unhappiness and that he had brought unhappiness to Russia," abdicated in favour not of his haemophiliac son, Alexei, but of his brother Grand Duke Michael, who succeeded as Michael II. But only technically.

The new Justice Minister, Alexander Kerensky, telegraphed Achinsk to order the release of the exiled Duma deputies: "All is in the hands of the people. Prisons are empty, ministers arrested, Empress guarded by our people." By that night, Achinsk knew that the Revolution had come at last—"but everyone spoke in whispers."

"The day we received the telegram, it was market-day and I decided that the local peasants shouldn't leave the market unawares . . . so I ran to tell them . . . there was no Tsar any more," recalls a Bolshevik librarian named Alexandra Pomerantseva, who shared Stalin's house. "On my way, I met Comrade Stalin" who "looked at my excited face."

"Where are you running?" he asked.

"I'm running to the market to tell peasants about the Revolution."

Stalin "approved of this"—and she headed for the marketplace.

On 3 March, Michael II abdicated when the government could not guarantee his safety. On the fourteenth, the Achinsk mayor opened a town meeting at which Kamenev proposed to send a telegram acclaiming Grand Duke Michael for his civic decency. Kamenev would live to regret his un-Bolshevik instinct for thanking Romanovs. "The next morning," Stalin, who was away in Krasnoyarsk that day, recalled in the 1920s, "I got to hear about it from Comrade Kamenev himself who came to tell me that he had done a foolish thing." Kamenev denied signing it and accused Stalin of lying.

Stalin telegraphed the Alliluyevs in Petrograd: he was on his way. He spent his last evening in Achinsk with Shveitzer. On 7 March, carriages took Kamenev, Shveitzer and Stalin to the station, whence they jubilantly departed. The trip took four days. At every station, the homecoming Bolsheviks competed with excited local orators to address crowds. Kamenev gave speeches; Stalin watched. He laughed at these speakers, later mimicking their overenthusiastic naïvety: "Holy revolution, long-awaited, dear revolution has finally arrived!"

On the morning of 12 March 1917, Stalin, wearing the suit he had worn for that party in July 1913, and *valenki* (long padded Russian boots), and carrying just a small wicker suitcase and a typewriter, arrived in Petrograd.[1]

PART FIVE

To Raphael Eristavi

When the laments of the toiling peasants
Had moved you to tears of pity,
You groaned to the heavens, oh Bard,
Placed at the head of the people's heads;
When the people's welfare
Had pleasantly exalted you,
You made your strings sweetly sound,
Like a man sent forth by heaven;
When you sang hymns to the motherland,
That was your love,
For her your harp brought forth
A heart-enrapturing twang . . .
Then oh Bard, a Georgian
Would listen to you as to a heavenly monument
And for your labours and woes of the past
Has crowned you with the present.
Your words have in his heart
Now put down roots;
Reap, grey-haired saint,
What you sowed in your youth;
For a sickle, use the people's
Heartfelt cry in the air:
"Hurray for Raphael! May there be many
Sons like thee in the fatherland!!"

—SOSELO (Josef Stalin)

38

1917 Spring: Floundering Leader

S oft fluffy snow was falling," says Vera Shveitzer. "As soon as we stepped off the train, we felt a gust of the political and revolutionary gale in the capital." Stalin, CC member, was back, his lifelong dreams come true. Yet there was no welcome party at the Nicholas Station. Soso and Vera let the excitement carry them into the streets: "Flowing together with the city crowd, we walked along Nevsky Prospect."

Stalin no longer needed to fear arrest or search for an old acquaintance to rescue him as he strolled the boulevards. The shooting, rioting and exhilaration of the February Revolution had completely changed the capital: it was now almost the freest city in Europe. Limousines, including requisitioned grand ducal Rolls-Royces, and armoured cars, raced around the city, honking horns, filled with workers, barely dressed girls and soldiers, waving flags and brandishing guns. Presses poured out newspapers to represent every political view while pamphlets of explicit pornography recounted the lubricious lesbian nymphomania of the fallen Empress and her orgies with Rasputin. The hated police—the *pharaohs*—were gone; the double-headed eagles had been smashed, but the class struggle had not truly started. The swaggering armed workers of the great factories threatened a nervous bourgeois, the *burzois,* yet the theatres still played—Lermontov's *Masquerade* was on at the Alexandrinsky—and the smart restaurants were opening in the wake of the streetfighting.

"There were meetings* and speeches everywhere," remembered Molotov, "the first experience of freedom in the full sense." Even the whores and thieves held meetings and elected soviets. Everything was reversed: soldiers had their caps on back to front and wore a fancy-dress shop of uniforms; women borrowed military headgear and breeches. People felt suddenly unrestrained in this febrile carnival: "Sexual acts, from kissing and fondling to full intercourse," writes Orlando Figes, were "openly performed on the streets in the euphoria."[1]

Stalin and Vera headed directly to the centre of power. "While chatting with us, Comrade Stalin without realizing it reached the Taurida Palace," where they bumped into Elena Stasova and Molotov. That night, Stalin, Molotov, Vera Shveitzer, Stasova and the Russian Bureau discussed the situation. No one was sure about the next move.

"Russia *was* an Empire" but "what is she now?" The political system they discovered functioning at the palace was, wrote Duma deputy Vasily Shulgin, "neither a republic nor a monarchy—a state formation without a name." Prince Lvov, the decent Premier, presided over a cabinet of conservatives and liberal "Kadets," Constitutional-Democrats. The Soviet, led by Chkheidze and containing Mensheviks, Bolsheviks and SRs, was as powerful as the government. Kerensky alone straddled both Soviet and government: "Only Kerensky knew how to dance upon the revolutionary quagmire." But actually he did not know how; so far, no one did.

When the Tsar abdicated, the big beasts of the SD jungle were abroad—Trotsky and Bukharin in New York, Lenin and Martov in Switzerland. The bewildered Bolsheviks in Petrograd were led by the junior Alexander Shlyapnikov, a worker aged thirty-three, and the twenty-seven-year-old Molotov.† There were fewer than 25,000 Bolsheviks in the whole of Russia and only about 1,000 veteran activists.

Days earlier Lenin had confessed that the Revolution "might not happen in our lifetime." When they heard, Krupskaya wondered, "Per-

---

* There were so many meetings, day and night, on every street corner that the ever adaptable Russian language coined the verb *miningovat*—to make meetings—just as during another revolution, in 1991, Russian created the word *khappening*—a happening—to describe the bizarre events of the new freedom.

† On 26 February, Shlyapnikov declared, "There is no and will be no revolution," but once it developed, he and Molotov managed to relaunch *Pravda*. When Molotov joined the Soviet Executive Committee, he wrote, "I had to speak against Kerensky. Lenin was far away. We had to decide everything ourselves."

haps it's another hoax." "It's staggering," exclaimed Lenin. "Such a surprise!" He started to send instructions to Molotov and Shlyapnikov: the war must be stopped; the Provisional Government opposed. But now, at the meeting of the Bureau, Stalin, aged thirty-eight, and Kamenev, just thirty-four, wished to take control and overrule Lenin, temporarily willing to support the Provisional Government provided it fought a defensive war and established essential civic liberties.

There was a "row." The Bureau totally rejected Kamenev, demanding an explanation for his betrayals, and only agreed to co-opt Stalin "in an advisory role . . . in the light of certain personal features which are basic to him." His egotism, rudeness (and possibly his sexual adventures) were notorious.[2]

When Anna Alliluyeva came home to the family apartment, now in the suburbs, reachable only by a small suburban train, she found some comrades talking there (Yenukidze had been an early arrival), but "I looked at the hat-stand and didn't recognize the black coat and long striped scarf on the table."

"Who's here?" she asked.

"Stalin's back," said one. "From exile. Just arrived!" She ran in to greet him—"We were expecting him!" He was pacing up and down. Anna was amazed how he had changed. "The clothes were the same—the black suit and blue shirt," but "his face had changed, not only was he tired, thin, hollow-cheeked, but he seemed older. Only the eyes were the same, that mocking smile."

"See! I found you!" said Stalin. "I got the train and I thought I'd never find you! How are you? How's Olga, Sergei, Pavel, Fedya? And where is Nadya?" Sergei managed a power station; Olga worked as a nurse; Pavel was at the front; Fyodor was studying; Nadya at a music lesson.

"Are you hungry?" asked Anna, lighting the samovar—just as their father got home. The men exchanged news in "agitated voices." Then Nadya, black-eyed, intense and exuberant, appeared in coat and hat. "Josef is here." The parents and children greeted and surrounded Stalin, who found himself the hero of a cosy Chekhovian family living in middle-class comfort, something he had never known.

"Everyone was laughing" as "Stalin mimicked the provincial orators speaking at stations on his return from exile." Anna and Nadya laid the table as he dashingly recounted his adventures in exile. He agreed to spend the night, bedding down in the dining-room beside Sergei.

"What time do we get up in the morning? Tomorrow morning I've got to go to *Pravda*."

"We wake up early," said Olga. "We'll wake you." Olga and her daughters retired next door, but they could not sleep—especially when Nadya started repeating Soso's stories about the speakers. "It was so funny we burst out laughing," said Anna. "We tried to stop but couldn't help ourselves, laughing louder and louder."

"Shut up, you youngsters!" called their father.

"Leave them, Sergei," intervened Stalin. "They're young, let them laugh!"

In the morning, they caught the train for the city, telling Soso they were inspecting a new apartment on Tenth Rozhdestvensky Street. As he jumped off the tram, Stalin called: "That's good—but make sure you keep a room for me . . ."[3]

Stalin staked his claim to leadership, not at the Taurida Palace but at the Bolshevik headquarters, which now occupied the sin-drenched mansion of "that Tsarist concubine" Mathilde Kseshinskaya.* "This den of luxury, spurs and diamonds located opposite the Winter Palace," in Trotsky's words, was strategically vital, close to the Peter and Paul Fortress as well as the Vyborg factories.

In the ballerina's boudoirs and ballrooms, Stalin reasserted himself, overturning the whippersnapper Molotov and the Russian Bureau. On 15 March, Stalin and Kamenev assumed control of *Pravda* and joined the Presidium of the Bureau. "I was thrown out," said Molotov. "Stalin and Kamenev delicately but skilfully expelled me because they had more authority and were ten years older, so I didn't resist." Appointed as a Bolshevik representative to the Executive Committee of the Soviet, Stalin was

---

* She was the lissom Polish ballerina who became Nicholas II's first and only real mistress while he was heir to the throne. He had been in love with her, but when he fell for Alix of Hesse, who became Empress Alexandra, he continued to back Kseshinskaya's rise to become the dominant prima ballerina of the Mariinsky. Afterwards, she entered an imperial *ménage à trôis* with her two Romanov lovers, Grand Dukes Sergei and Andrei. Between the sheets with the Emperor and the Grand Dukes and on stage in a stellar career built on imperial favour, Kseshinskaya gathered a collection of diamonds and residences that culminated in her building of the mansion. Its modernist style boasted parquet floors, crystal chandeliers, huge mirrors. A white hall had marble consoles and sofas inlaid with ormolu; its walls were covered in damask silk; its curtains were velvet. There was a small Louis XVI drawing-room with yellow silk walls—and the ballerina's bathroom, in white marble with walls of inlaid blue and silver mosaic, and a sunken bath, "resembled a Greek bathing pool." As a popular verse bawdily put it, she had "without sparing her legs, danced her way to a palace." The mansion is today the Museum of Modern Russian History.

welcomed at the Taurida Palace by his fellow Georgians Chkheidze and Irakli Tsereteli, its star orator. Stalin was exhilarated by the new politics, but even in those dizzy days he saw life as a Manichean struggle between light and darkness. "The chariot of the Russian Revolution," declared Stalin, "is advancing with lightning speed," but "glance around and you will see the sinister work of dark forces going on incessantly." He was quiet and vigilant. "In the work of the Soviet," recalls the Menshevik diarist Nikolai Sukhanov, "the impression made on me . . . was that of a grey blur."

In faraway Switzerland, Lenin was vainly attacking the Provisional Government and demanding immediate peace with Germany, but in Petrograd, Stalin and Kamenev swung rightwards towards mild conciliation, hoping to lure radical, internationalist Mensheviks into the Party—hardly a foolish idea, especially since they insisted on a radical foreign policy.* But they "created confusion and indignation among Party members," grumbled Shlyapnikov. Molotov relished being correct in opposing "their defensist line, a big mistake, Stalin's mistake." Kamenev and Stalin, sneered Trotsky, had turned the Bolsheviks into "a behind-the-scenes parliamentary group for putting pressure on the bourgeoisie."

Yet Stalin's critics exaggerated his folly. He was certainly cautious and colourless during those ten days, but his policies were sensible, realistic and tactical in their moderation. Trotsky admits that Stalin "had been giving expression to the hidden convictions of many Old Bolsheviks"—and of most Mensheviks. Even Krupskaya, on hearing Lenin's extremist ranting, muttered, "It seems Illich is out of his mind." The Bolsheviks then had no hope of overthrowing the Provisional Government—Lenin was audacious but out of touch. Besides, Lenin himself did not stick to his radical programme: he immediately made retreats and compromises before returning to it at the end of the year.

In Swiss exile, Lenin exploded while reading a speech by Chkheidze about conciliation with the Bolsheviks. "It's simply shit!" he shouted.

---

* On 17 March, in his article "The War," Stalin merely called for "pressure on the Provisional Government" about ending the war, while Lenin was already demanding its "overthrow." He did not attack the Mensheviks but only wanted alliance with those who backed his belief in a defensist war. He wanted the Soviet to keep mastery over the Provisional Government and he demanded the urgent calling of a Constituent Assembly. On one hand, he only proposed "pressure" on the government; on the other, when the Mensheviks and Bolsheviks held a joint debate on the Provisional Government, he damned it as the organ of "the elites" who simply substituted "one Tsar for another." He was still a Conciliator, as he explained at a Party conference at the end of March, held in the mansion and then in the Taurida.

"Vladimir, what language!" replied Krupskaya.

"I repeat: shit!"

Lenin started to scribble out his *Letters from Afar* to correct Kamenev's and Stalin's folly. Stalin's articles were being published almost daily.

Then on 18 March, Stalin stopped writing for a week, perhaps to reassess his policies: Lenin was coming.[4]

39

1917 Summer: Sailors on the Streets

On 27 March 1917, Lenin, Krupskaya, Zinoviev and Stalin's Georgian patron Tskhakaya boarded their famous Sealed Train. Almost a month after the February Revolution, Lenin had finally found a way to return to Russia. In the interim, he had entertained fantasies of taking a train pretending to be a deaf-and-dumb Swede or hitching a ride on a rickety biplane across central Europe. "We must get home," he said. "But how?" Fortunately, the German High Command believed that the clinical insertion of Lenin and his revolutionary bacillus might infect Russia with the virus of pacifism, thereby knocking her out of the war.[1]

Lenin dominated the Sealed Train as he would Russia herself: he would have approved the smoking-bans of our era and insisted on dictating the smoking rules and lavatorial visitation rights of the entire train—in preparation, the Bolshevik Karl Radek joked, "for assuming the leadership of the Revolutionary Government." Smokers were allowed to light up only in the lavatory, whereas non-smokers were issued with special "first-class" lavatory passes that gave them priority access.

On 3 April, they stopped at the Beloostrov Station on the Finnish-Russian border in what Krupskaya grandly called "those dear wretched little third-class railroad cars." Stalin's friend Ludmilla Stal welcomed Krupskaya with a delegation of women. Kamenev blithely climbed aboard to greet Lenin, but got a shock.

"What the hell have you been writing?" barked Lenin. "We've read a few issues of *Pravda* and we cursed you roundly."

The train steamed into Petrograd's Finland Station. Stalin boarded the carriage to greet "the Old Man," who was still only forty-six. With his Homburg hat, tweed suit and bourgeois umbrella, this bald little man was a stranger to Russia, new and old. Yet this was an angrier Lenin, more violent, merciless and impatient than the man who had gone into exile a decade earlier: if he lacked Soso's vindictive personal malice, he more resembled Stalin than the gentle fatherly image later peddled by Soviet propaganda. "I can't listen to music too often," he said after hearing Beethoven's Appassionata Sonata. "It makes me want to say kind stupid things and pat the heads of people. But now you have to beat them on the head, beat them without mercy." Lenin was buzzing with this next battle. "One fighting campaign after another," as he told his sometime mistress Inessa Armand. "That's my life." Stalin would have said the same things. Hailing from such different worlds—one with the manners of a nobleman, the other those of a peasant—they shared the same sentiments and favoured identical methods.

We do not know what Lenin said to him in the carriage,* but virtually as soon as they met, Stalin abandoned the "flabby" Kamenev and backed the Old Man.

Just before midnight, Lenin "alighted from the carriage with Stalin," observed Molotov, who was present. The famous yet mysterious Lenin found Finland Station in revolutionary fiesta. A military band burst into "The Marseillaise"; searchlights scanned the avid crowds. Lenin reviewed an honour guard of revolutionary sailors from the Kronstadt Base, 2,000 Putilov plant workers, a crowd waving red banners and an array of armoured cars.

A phalanx of Red Guards—armed Bolshevik workers—escorted Lenin into the station's Imperial Lounge, where he was greeted by the Soviet chairman, Chkheidze. But Lenin bounded onto an armoured car, telling the crowd (including Molotov, Voroshilov and Alliluyev) that the Provisional Government, with their "sweet speeches and great promises,

---

* The seductive Bolshevik Alexandra Kollontai had just delivered Lenin's furious *Letters from Afar* to the defiant Stalin and Kamenev. Even as the Old Man approached, Stalin had shortened or refused to publish Lenin's articles, which he criticized as "unsatisfactory . . . a sketch with no facts." Lenin called for immediate power seizure but did not deign to explain how he had decided to jump the first formal stage of Marxist development and jump straight to the second—"the transition to socialism."

are deceiving you just as they are deceiving the entire Russian people." The speech, writes one witness, "shook and astonished the Faithful . . . like a clap of thunder." The Bolsheviks must overthrow the government, end the "predatory imperialist war" and immediately transfer power to the soviets.

Many thought the Old Man was mad and out of touch. "Lenin is a has-been," the Menshevik Skobelev told Prince Lvov. Yet even his opponents could only marvel at his raging certainty: "Lenin," says Sukhanov, "displayed such amazing force, such superhuman power of attack."

Lenin rode his armoured car through the streets, surrounded by the blaring band, and the workers and soldiers, towards the Kseshinskaya Mansion, where, in the ballerina's white-columned drawing-room, he harangued incredulous Bolsheviks. The next morning, he addressed them in Room 13 of the Taurida Palace. "Everyone was dumbfounded," said Molotov. At first, only Alexandra Kollontai supported him unreservedly. The Bolsheviks, said Trotsky, "were as unprepared for Lenin as they had been for the February Revolution."

Lenin's *tour de force* won over Stalin, who confessed: "Many things became clearer." The people longed for peace and land, but the well-intentioned government insisted on honouring the Tsar's promises to fight on against Germany and foolishly delayed settling the land question until the election of a Constituent Assembly, months away. Lenin alone grasped that this interval was his unique opportunity to seize Russia. After 6 April, Lenin and Stalin started working closely together at *Pravda*.[2]

On 18 April, Lenin was helped by the blunder of Foreign Minister Milyukov, who issued a diplomatic note informing Britain and France that Russia intended to annex Ottoman territories, an imperial war without an emperor. The Soviet had backed the Provisional Government only providing it waged a defensive war. A wave of revulsion shattered the fragile ministry. Prince Lvov formed a new coalition with Kerensky as Minister of War.

Radical Bolsheviks called for an armed uprising. Lenin, in the first of many such retreats after arriving with all ideological guns blazing, had to restrain his own hotheads: the uprising was "incorrect . . . at present." When the Bolshevik Conference started on 24 April in Kseshinskaya's ballroom, Lenin "entered like an inspector coming into a classroom." Until Lenin's arrival, thought Ludmilla Stal, "all comrades wandered in the darkness." Stalin was firmly out of the darkness. When Kamenev attacked Lenin, Stalin mocked his erstwhile ally. He was a Leninist again—but that did not mean they agreed on everything.*

Stalin gave the report on the national question. He won the debate, but he was still best known for Caucasian banditry, and needed Lenin's support. "We've known Comrade Koba for very many years," Lenin declared. "We used to see him in Cracow where we had our Bureau. His activity in the Caucasus was important. He's a good worker in all sorts of responsible work." Molotov remembered Lenin explaining the essence of Stalin's attraction for him: he was a "commanding figure—you could assign Stalin any task."

On 29 April, Stalin came third with ninety-seven votes in the CC elections, just after Lenin and Zinoviev, a result that showed his standing in the Party. Stalin now spent most of his time at the Soviet, editing *Pravda* or working at the Central Committee with Lenin. The Central Committee chose Lenin, Stalin, Kamenev and Zinoviev as a decision-making Bureau for the first time, a precursor of the all-powerful Politburo.³

On 4 May, Trotsky finally arrived from America and immediately dazzled Petrograd, speaking almost nightly at the "packed-out" Cirque Moderne, where "he was often carried to the stage" by the crowd. He was, noticed Sukhanov, "intoxicated with his popularity."

Lenin recognized Trotsky's worth and courted him, inviting him to join the Bolsheviks a week later. The only thing that divided them, said Lenin, was "ambition." Stalin must have resented the return of this revolutionary star. He was to write more than sixty articles in 1917, but Trotsky sneered that he just produced "dull comments on brilliant events." When Lenin appointed a delegation to negotiate with Trotsky, Stalin was understandably left out.

Unlike Trotsky, Stalin did not make his mark in 1917. He put it best himself: "Before the Revolution, our Party led an underground existence—a secret Party. Now circumstances have changed"—and they did not really suit him. He flourished in the shadows.

Nineteen-seventeen was really Stalin's only experience of open democratic politics, hardly the ideal environment for someone trained in the

---

* Lenin's retreat from his extremism had brought him much closer to Stalin's often-denounced policies. Stalin felt that Lenin's insistence on "European civil war" was over the top, talk of "dictatorship" impolitic, and demands for "land nationalization" insensitive to peasant hopes. Lenin, attuning himself to the real demands of Russian politics, gradually altered these policies in public.

cutthroat clan intrigues of the Caucasus. He spoke quietly with a comical Georgian accent. "I didn't make out much of what he said," reports a witness, "but one thing I noticed: all of Stalin's sentences were sharp and crisp statements distinguished by clarity of formulation." A worker who saw him speak thought that "what he said sounded all right, understandable and simple, but somehow one couldn't remember his speech afterwards." He "avoided making speeches at mass meetings," but the plain, modest delivery of his anti-oratory proved to be surprisingly impressive and convincing for the many who distrusted showy intellectuals.

When Lenin seized power and, beleaguered on all sides, ran his government like a conspiratorial camarilla, Stalin was again in his element.

On 3 June, Soso's young fans Anna and Nadya Alliluyeva came to admire their hero at the First Congress of the Soviets in the Military School on Vasilevsky Island. "Stalin and Sverdlov attended the opening sessions—they were the first to arrive with Lenin. I saw the three of them enter the empty hall," reports Anna Alliluyeva, who was working for the Party. "We had not seen Stalin for many days and his room in the flat stood empty."

"We must call on him," whispered the schoolgirl Nadya. "Perhaps he's changed his mind about coming to live in our apartment." Next day, they witnessed the most dramatic moment of the Congress.

"There's no party in Russia that dares say, 'Just place power in our hands,' " boomed the Menshevik Tsereteli.

At this, Lenin leaped out of his chair and shouted: "There *is* such a party!"

Vereshchak, Stalin's Bailovka cell mate, noticed that "Lenin, Zinoviev and Kamenev were the main speakers" but "Sverdlov and Stalin silently directed the Bolshevik Faction—the first time I realized the full significance of the man."

Stalin impressed Trotsky, whose description reveals why he lost their struggle for power. "Stalin was very valuable behind the scenes," he wrote. "He did have the knack of convincing the average run of leaders, especially the provincials." He "wasn't regarded as the official leader of the Party," says Sagirashvili, another Georgian Menshevik in Petrograd throughout 1917, but "everyone listened to what he had to say, including Lenin—he was a representative of the rank and file, one who expressed its real views and moods," which were unknown to émigrés like Trotsky. Soso was the "unquestioned leader" of the Caucasians. Lenin, says Sagirashvili, "felt that behind him stood countless leaders from the provinces."* While Trotsky was prancing on the stage at the Circus, Stalin was finding new allies such as the young man he had unceremoniously kicked off the Buro, Molotov.[4]

Stalin moved in with Molotov, who lived at a spacious flat on Shirokaya Street, across the Neva on the Petrograd side, with three other comrades. "It was like a kind of commune," said Molotov. Stalin, unusually, apologized to Molotov for what the latter called "Stalin's big mistake." "You were the nearest of all to Lenin in the initial stage in April," confessed Stalin. The two became friends. Besides, Molotov, who had not been elected to the Central Committee in April, was in need of a patron. They were opposites: the sturdy, stammering and bespectacled Molotov was ponderous, correct, rather bourgeois. But they shared Marxist fanaticism, a head for boozing, a Robespierrean belief in Terror, a vindictive inferiority-complex—and a belief in Stalin's mastery.

Stalin had been constantly moving home, working at night and then grabbing sleep at friends' places. He often slept where he worked at the Kseshinskaya Mansion. Tatiana Slavatinskaya worked there as an assistant at the Central Committee under Sverdlov and Stasova. Ludmilla Stal helped edit *Rabotnitsa* (Working Woman) and manage relations with the Kronstadt sailors: they must have seen each other. It was said that Stalin reheated his romance with Stal. If so, she was not the only one.

Stalin did not just avail himself of Molotov's political fidelity and domestic residence. "He stole my girl, Marusya," Molotov laughed. Marusya was not the last woman whom Molotov would sacrifice to Stalin's will.

Early one evening, Anna and Nadya Alliluyeva arrived at *Pravda* to

---

* These "provincials" were the tough Committeemen who loathed Trotsky and would become the Stalinists of the future, many of them friends from the Caucasus. Such Bolshevik *praktiki* certainly knew Stalin's faults but they had much more in common with him than with Zinoviev or Trotsky. There was the excitable Sergo, the handsome Shaumian, the blond playboy Yenukidze, the easygoing ex-butler Kalinin and Voroshilov. Yet many Caucasians, especially the Mensheviks, hated Stalin. And he also had his Bolshevik critics from the Caucasus. Makharadze and Japaridze, old comrades from Tiflis and Baku, attacked Stalin's approach to the Caucasian peoples at the April Conference, as did the Pole Felix Dzerzhinsky. Yet Stalin befriended Dzerzhinsky, founder of the secret police, perhaps because Poles and Georgians identified with one another as proud peoples colonized by Russia. Both men studied for the priesthood, wrote poetry, were obsessed with loyalty and betrayal. Both were skilled practitioners of secret-police work. Both were dominated by powerful mothers and suffered from dour fathers. Both were terrible parents; both fanatical and solitary creatures. Surprisingly for two so similar, they became allies.

see him. "The offices were crowded and filled with cigarette smoke." An aide told them that "Stalin was busy," says Anna, so "we sent a message saying we'd like to see him and he came out to meet us."

"Well, hello," said Soso, smiling affectionately, "I'm glad you've come. How are things at home?"

"Your room's waiting for you," said the girls.

"How kind, but I'm terribly busy," he said. "But keep that room for me."

Then "someone came up to him and Stalin hurriedly shook hands with us"—and rushed back to work.[5]

Nineteen-seventeen was, to paraphrase Lenin, a game of two steps forward, one step back. During June, the radicals in the armed wing of the Bolshevik Party—the Military Organization, which now claimed the allegiance of 60,000 troops—demanded an armed demonstration. The date was set for this accidental revolution: 10 June. At a Party meeting, Lenin supported them. It was "wrong to force matters, equally wrong to let the opportunity slip," opined Stalin, who helped plan the demonstration and wrote its proclamation: "At the sight of armed workers, the bourgeois will take cover." Zinoviev and Kamenev opposed it.

On 9 June at the Soviet, the Mensheviks read out Stalin's appeal and Tsereteli railed against "the Bolshevik conspiracy to seize power." Lenin needed Soviet support—he hoped to use its legitimacy as cover for his Bolshevik coup. Instead the Soviet banned the demonstration. After hours of panic, Lenin agreed to call it off: "One wrong move on our part can wreck everything." He now became as cautious as Kamenev and Stalin had been in March. On the eleventh, Stalin, criticizing this "intolerable wavering," threatened to resign.

The Soviet defiantly held its own demonstration on 18 June, but the Bolsheviks hijacked it, with Stalin publishing his proclamation in *Pravda*. It was a propaganda triumph. "Bright sunny day," reported Stalin the next day, "the column of demonstrators is endless. From morn to eve, the procession files towards the Field of Mars, a forest of banners . . . a steady roar from the crowd . . . the Marseillaise and Internationale gave place to 'You Have Fallen Victims.' " There were "cries of 'All power to the Soviets!' . . . but not a single regiment or factory displayed 'Confidence in the Provisional Government!' " Meanwhile in the continuing war against Imperial Germany, Kerensky, War Minister, ordered an offensive that he hoped would bolster the government. The offensive, Russia's last of the war, was a disaster.[6]

Lenin was exhausted; suffering headaches, he retreated to sunbathe at a lakeside villa in Finland. Then the government faltered again: Kerensky's offensive ground to a halt while Finland and Ukraine moved towards independence. The Kadet ministers resigned in protest.

In Lenin's absence, his Military Organization* decided to seize power. The "night sky was lit up so brightly by the Aurora Borealis," writes Sagirashvili, "that one could read a newspaper outdoors. Men didn't sleep and some unknown force drew them out of doors to roam the streets. They could raise their eyes to this heavenly spectacle. A grandiose struggle of Darkness and Light."

On 3 July, masses of soldiers, sailors and workers, toting machine-guns with bandoliers of ammo criss-crossing their chests, marched on the Taurida Palace, the Bolshevik First Machine-Gun Regiment in the vanguard. Cars were held up at gunpoint and requisitioned. As armoured cars and trucks full of gunmen raced around the streets, some of the troops started firing haphazardly at *burzoi* shoppers on Nevsky Prospect. Gunfights broke out. Out at the Kronstadt naval base, Bolshevik sailors rose up, murdered 120 officers, including their admiral, and then demanded that Lenin, Zinoviev and Kamenev give them their orders to take the capital. When they received no answers, they telephoned Stalin, sitting at his *Pravda* desk with the Bolshevik bard Demian Bedny: should they march with their guns?

"Rifles?" replied Stalin. "You comrades know best . . . As for we scribblers, we always take our guns, our pencils, everywhere with us, [but] as for you and your arms, you know best!" Stalin had half encouraged this semi-accidental coup, asking, "Did the Party have the right to wash its hands and stand apart?" Trotsky was probably right that Stalin was one of the organizers of the July uprising: "Wherever a fight started, whether on a square in Tiflis, in Baku Prison, on a Petrograd street, he always strove to make it as sharp as possible."

The gun-toting mob seethed around the Taurida Palace, expecting the Soviet to seize power as in Lenin's slogan: "All Power to the Soviets." But inside, Chkheidze and the Soviet, discussing the formation of a new

---

* The Bolshevik Military Organization ignored Lenin's caution, showing that the Bolsheviks were still far from a disciplined force under a single leader. On the contrary, they remained insubordinate and fractious. The slavish monolith of the Party of Stalin was still years in the future.

ministry, did not want power. They feared it. The mob was inflamed by the Soviet's reluctance. Meanwhile Stalin's ambiguous answer had worked: the Kronstadt sailors were on their way.

At the Kseshinskaya Mansion, Stalin and the Central Committee suddenly lost their nerve and summoned Lenin back from holiday. "We could have seized power," Stalin said, "but against us would have risen the fronts, the provinces, the Soviets." Stalin rushed to the Taurida to reassure Chkheidze and the Soviet—but the genie was out of the bottle.

Lenin was on the train bound for Petrograd when Stalin heard that Justice Minister Pavel Pereverzev was about to accuse the Bolshevik leader of treason, revealing that he had been funded by Imperial Germany. This was partly true, but Stalin returned to the Taurida Palace and appealed to his Georgian compatriot Chkheidze to suppress the story. Chkheidze agreed, but it was too late.

In the early hours of 4 July, Lenin rushed to the mansion. "You should be thrashed for this!" he yelled at the Bolshevik hotheads.

In the overcast morning, 400,000 workers and soldiers ruled the deserted streets, soon joined by 20,000 heavily armed sailors who landed in a flotilla of boats. They had no plan: the cock-of-the-walk sailors with brass bands playing were more interested in parading their girlfriends through the boulevards and terrorizing the *burzois*: "Sailors with scantily dressed and high-heeled ladies were seen everywhere." The streets, recalled Stalin, "were scenes of jubilation." The sailors gathered outside the Kseshinskaya Mansion to demand some leadership: where was Lenin? He tried to hide in the mansion before emerging sheepishly to give a short speech that settled nothing.

The sailors, boosted by another 20,000 Putilov workers, headed for the Taurida Palace to sort out the diffident Soviet whose members had disappointed them. There were ugly scenes*—but at 5 p.m. the heavens opened: rain doused the accidental revolution. The crowds dispersed. The loyal Izmailovsky Guards relieved the besieged Soviet, now exposed as a toothless talking-shop. Lenin and the dispirited Bolshevik Central Committee retreated pathetically. The July Days were over.

The government, strengthened by Kerensky's growing popularity,

---

* Some broke into the palace where the Soviet sat under siege, refusing to take power. The mob seized Chernov, the frail SR leader, and started to lynch him until, in a virtuoso performance, Trotsky intervened, leaped onto a limousine, addressed the sailors and rescued the terrified politician.

decided to destroy the Bolsheviks. Despite Stalin's pleading, Justice Minister Pereverzev published evidence of Lenin's German financial backing. Many of the soldiers were swayed by this talk of treason.

At dawn on 5 July, government troops raided *Pravda,* just missing Lenin who was smuggled out by Stalin only minutes earlier. Overnight, howitzers and eight armoured cars took up positions to storm the Kseshinskaya Mansion, but the Bolsheviks had no will to defend their strongholds. Stalin speeded to the Bolshevik stronghold, the Peter and Paul Fortress, "where I managed to persuade the sailors not to accept battle"; shuttled between the soldiers and the Kseshinskaya Mansion to avoid a massacre; then asked Chkheidze and Tsereteli at the Taurida Palace for a guarantee of no bloodshed if the Bolsheviks surrendered the mansion and the fortress. Tsereteli agreed: "Stalin gave me a puzzled look and left." On 6 July, the 500 Bolsheviks inside the ballerina's mansion gave themselves up. Then Stalin returned to the Peter and Paul Fortress to oversee its surrender.

Lenin appreciated Stalin's tireless troubleshooting. But, "as a result of their disastrous failure," wrote John Reed, a socialist journalist from Portland, Oregon, "public opinion turned against them. Their leaderless hordes slunk back into the Vyborg Quarter, followed by a savage hunt of the Bolsheviki."

The thirty-five-year-old Kerensky, the only man who could unite left and right, assumed the premiership. Ironically the son of Lenin's headmaster in Simbirsk, he was a speaker of "burning intensity"—"the sudden fits and starts, the twitching of lips and the somnambulistic deliberation of his gestures make him like one possessed." Kerensky's Justice Minister ordered Lenin's arrest.*

The Bolsheviks were on the verge of destruction. Lenin was on the run. Stalin took charge of his safety.[7]

---

* Stalin's Menshevik henchman from Baku, Vyshinsky, was head of Moscow's Arbat region militia under Kerensky and signed arrest warrants for top Bolsheviks, including Lenin. After October, he joined the Bolsheviks. His shameful obedience to Kerensky ensured canine submission to Stalin to whose whim he owed his very survival.

1917 Autumn: Soso and Nadya

S talin moved Lenin five times in three days as Kerensky hunted down the Old Man. Trotsky and Kamenev were arrested, but Lenin, escorted by Stalin, returned to the underground. The police raided the house of Lenin's sister. Krupskaya hastened to Stalin's and Molotov's place on Shirokaya Street to learn where Lenin was.

On the night of 6 July, Stalin rustled Lenin to his fifth hiding-place, the Alliluyevs' smart new apartment, at Tenth Rozhdestvenskaya Street, where they had a uniformed doorman and a maid.

"Show me all the exits and entrances," said Lenin on arrival, even checking the attic. "We gave him Stalin's room," said Olga. Lenin was surprisingly cheerful, staying for four tense days. Anna Alliluyeva came home to find her apartment full of unknown, nervous people. "I immediately recognized the person to whom I was first introduced." Lenin sat on the sofa "in his shirtsleeves, wearing a waistcoat and a light-coloured shirt with a tie." In the "unbearably stuffy" room, Lenin cross-examined her: what had she seen on the streets?

"They are saying you've run off to Kronstadt and you were hiding on a minesweeper."

"Ha-ha-ha!" laughed Lenin with "infectious gaiety." Then he asked Stalin and the others: "What do you think, comrades?"

Lenin spent his days writing. Stalin visited daily. He quietly took the political pulse at the Taurida Palace, where he bumped into Sergo Ordzhonikidze. Both were worried that "many prominent Bolsheviks took the view that Lenin shouldn't hide but should appear [to stand trial]. Together," wrote Sergo, "we went to see Lenin." The government demanded Lenin's surrender. At the Alliluyevs', Lenin, Stalin, Sergo, Krupskaya and Lenin's sister Maria debated what to do.

Lenin at first favoured surrender. Stalin disagreed. He initially believed that Lenin and Zinoviev should wait and hand themselves in only when their safety could be guaranteed, but his visit to the Taurida convinced him that this was impossible. "The Junkers* want to take you to prison," he warned, "but they'll kill you on the way." Stasova arrived to report that more evidence of Lenin's treason was being published. "A strong shudder ran over his face and [Lenin] declared with the utmost determination that he would have to go to jail" to clear his name at a trial.

"Let's say goodbye," Lenin said to Krupskaya. "We may never see each other again."

Stalin and Sergo were despatched back to the Taurida Palace to seek a "guarantee that Illich wouldn't be lynched by the Junkers." The Mensheviks, Stalin reported back, "replied that they couldn't say what will happen."

Stalin and Sergo were now sure that Lenin would be murdered if he surrendered. "Stalin and the others urged Illich not to appear," says Krupskaya. "Stalin convinced him and . . . saved his life." Stalin was right: an ex–Duma member, V. N. Polovtiev, encountered the officer assigned to arrest Lenin. "How should I deliver this gentleman, Lenin?" the officer asked. "Whole or in pieces?"

The debate went back and forth. Suddenly Sergo drew an imaginary dagger and shouted like a Georgian bandit: "I'll slice up anyone who wants Illich to be arrested!"

That seemed to clinch it. Lenin had to be smuggled out of Petrograd: Stalin "undertook to organize Lenin's departure." A worker named Emelianov† agreed to hide Lenin in his shack in Razliv, to the north of Petrograd.

---

* Just as the police were known as *pharaoh*s so any military officers were nicknamed "Junkers" after the Prussian noble military class.

† Emelianov was arrested in the Great Terror. Krupskaya supposedly interceded on his behalf and he, along with his entire family, was kept in confinement until Stalin's death.

Olga and Anna Alliluyeva bustled around their guests, making sure that Lenin and Stalin were eating properly.

"What are you feeding Stalin?" asked Lenin. "Please, Olga, you must watch him, he's losing weight."

Stalin meanwhile checked that Lenin was being fed properly: "Well, how's the situation with provisions? Is Illich eating? Do the best you can for him." Sometimes Stalin turned up with extra food.

Lenin and Stalin cautiously studied the escape plans. On 11 July, "Stalin arrived before the departure and everyone gathered in Lenin's room to devise ways of disguising him." Olga tried bandaging Lenin's head, but that did not work. No one suggested drag.

"Wouldn't it be better if I shaved," suggested Lenin. "A moment later, Lenin sat with his face covered in soap" in front of the round shaving-mirror next to the portrait of Tolstoy in Stalin's bedroom. Soso personally "acted as barber," shaving off Lenin's beard and moustache.

"It's very good now." Lenin admired himself in the mirror. "I look just like a Finnish peasant, and there's hardly anyone who'll recognize me."

On the 12th, Stalin and Alliluyev escorted Lenin to Primorsky Station for his disappearing act: he hid at Razliv before moving to a barn in Finland. Travelling back and forth, Stalin became his main contact with Petrograd. "One of my sons used to bring Stalin to the shack [where Lenin was hiding] by boat," remembered Emelianov.

In a barrage of articles, Stalin denounced Kerensky's "new Dreyfus Affair," the "vile calumnies against the Leader of our Party," and the "pen pirates of the venal press." He specially mocked the Menshevik "blind fools" for acting as patsies. Kerensky, he wrote, would drown them "like flies in milk."

Hand over the Bolsheviks? he had the Mensheviks asking Kerensky in a rare example of Stalinist satire. "At your service, Messieurs the Intelligence Service." Disarm the Revolution? "With the greatest of pleasure, Messieurs Landowners and Capitalists."

Stalin acted as Bolshevik leader—and moved house: it was to change his life.[1]

"No one's watching the building," Olga Alliluyeva reassured him when he dropped in one day. "You'd better live with us, rest and sleep properly."

Stalin moved out of Molotov's apartment and into the Alliluyevs'. The rooms were airy, light and comfortable; the kitchen, the bathroom, even the shower, were modern and state of the art; the maid, living in a tiny room, cooked the meals. Stalin took Fyodor's bedroom (formerly Lenin's), which boasted a real bed, a round mirror on a wooden shaving-table, an ornate desk and a portrait of Lord Byron. At breakfast next day, he said he had not slept so well for a long time.

Soso was often alone with Olga. Sergei ran his power station; Nadya was on summer holiday in Moscow; Anna worked for the Party. Olga looked after him: she bought him a new suit. He asked her to sew in some thermal pads, two high vertical velvet collars and buttons up to the neck because his sore throat made a collar and tie uncomfortable.*

Soso's life remained chaotic: he would buy his food on the way home—a loaf of bread and some fish or sausage from a street kiosk. He worked tirelessly editing *Pravda*, writing so much at his desk with a golden bear standing on the pen set that he developed calluses on his fingers. Some-times he came home, sometimes not, once sufficiently exhausted to fall asleep in bed with a lit pipe, almost burning the place down.

In late July, he moved out again during the Sixth Congress, covertly held in a monastic building on Sampsonevsky Boulevard, in case of a police crackdown.[2] As acting leader, Stalin gave the main report, exhort-ing the 300 delegates to concentrate on the future: "We must be prepared for anything." After delivering another report "on the political situation," he insisted that Russia create her own revolution and stop believing "that only Europe can show us the way," a precurser of his famous slogan, "Socialism in One Country." Stalin's second report was probably written by Lenin or at least drafted with him, but his real partner in rebuilding the Party was Sverdlov, with whom he was finally reconciled.

"The report of Comrade Stalin has fully illuminated the activity of the CC," declared Sverdlov. "There remains for me to limit myself to the narrow sphere of the CC's organizational activity."

Stalin was chosen chief editor of the Party press and member of the Constituent Assembly, but when the Cental Committee was elected he appeared below Kamenev and Trotsky. The Bolsheviks were still at a low ebb, but Stalin predicted that the Provisional Government's "peaceful period is over. Times will be turbulent, crisis will follow crisis."[3]

---

* Thus Stalin designed his first semi-military tunic, a look probably copied from Kerensky, who now regarded himself as a Russian Napoleon: the vain Premier already lived in his own military uniform, boots and tunic despite having no military experience whatsoever. Stalin would wear this tunic for the rest of his life, often with a worker's cap. Lenin had now ceased to wear his Homburg hat and favoured workers' brimmed caps. In the Civil War, the so-called Party tunic, leather cap, coat, boots and Mauser became almost the Bol-shevik uniform and symbolized the military nature of the Bolshevik.

He returned to the Alliluyevs'. Nadya's summer holidays were over. She came home, ready for school.

That summer, Stalin lay low with the two sisters in the Alliluyev apartment, where he became the life and soul of the party. "Sometimes Soso did not come for days," writes Anna Alliluyeva. Then he suddenly arrived in the middle of the night to find the girls asleep, and bounded into their room. They were living in intimate proximity: Stalin's bedroom and Nadya's were linked by a door. From his bed or desk, he could see her dressing-table.

"What? Are you in bed already?" he roused the girls. "Get up you sleepy-heads! I've bought you roach and bread!" The girls jumped up and skipped into Soso's bedroom, which "immediately became carefree and noisy. Stalin cracked jokes and caricatured all the persons he met that day, sometimes in a kindly way, sometimes maliciously."

The autodidact seminarist and the well-educated teenagers discussed literature. He was playful and funny with their friends. He entertained them with stories of his adventures in exile, of Tishka the Siberian dog. He read them his favourite books—Pushkin, Gorky and Chekhov, particularly the latter's stories "The Chameleon" and "Unter Prisibeev," but he especially adored "Dushenka," which he "knew off by heart." He would often talk about women. "She's a real Dushenka," he would say of feather-headed women who lived only for their lovers with no independent existence. He teased their servant, the country girl Panya, and he gave them all nicknames. "When he was in a particularly good mood," says Anna, "he addressed us as 'Yepifani-Mitrofani,' " a joke on the name of his landlord in exile. "Well, Yepifani, what's new?" he greeted the girls. "Oh you're a Mitrofani, you are!" Sometimes he called them "Tishka," after the dog.

He talked politics with Sergei and the girls: they were members of the Bolshevik family. Nadya was so proud to be a Bolshevik that she was teased about it at school. Her godfather Yenukidze, Kalinin, Sergo and Sverdlov were already like uncles. Lenin had hidden in their home.

In September, recounts Anna, "Stalin brought home a Caucasian comrade . . . squarely built with smooth black hair and a pale lustreless face . . . who shook hands with us all shyly, smiling with his large kind eyes." "This is Kamo," said Stalin. "Listen to him—he's got plenty of interesting stories!" The girls were rapt: *This* was Kamo," who regaled them with "his half-fantastical life." The psychopathic daredevil had been in Kharkov Prison for five years, released by the Revolution. He had planned to escape, like the Count of Monte Cristo, as a dead man in a coffin until he discovered that the jailers smashed the skulls of every cadaver taken out of the prison with a hammer—just in case. "Kamo spoke a lot about Stalin and then his calm, quiet voice became exalted." Kamo had come to Petrograd looking for a new mission, but his connection with the Alliluyevs would lead to tragedy.

The day after Nadya returned, she started to clean the apartment, shoving around the chairs so loudly that Stalin, working on some article, stormed out of his room. "What's happening here?" asked Soso. "What's all the commotion? Oh it's you! Now I can see that a real housewife has got down to work!"

"What's up? Is that a bad thing?" retorted the highly strung teenager.

"Definitely not," answered an amused Soso. "It's a good thing! Bring some order, go ahead . . . Just show the rest of them!"

Nadya the schoolgirl was, observed her sister, Anna, "very vivacious, open, spontaneous and high spirited." Yet her upbringing in this nomadic and bohemian family, disrupted by constant visitors and by her mother's promiscuity, had caused her to develop a serious and puritanical streak, a craving for order and security.

"Papa and Mama are muddling along as usual," Nadya wrote to a friend. She came to despise her mother's dependence on fleeting sexual affairs. "We children are grown up," she wrote a little later, "and want to do and think what we please. The fact is she [Olga] has no life of her own and she's still a healthy young woman. So I've had to take over the housework." Perhaps she regarded her mother as a "Dushenka" like the heroine of Chekhov's story.

Gradually, in the course of that long, eventful summer, Stalin and Nadya became closer: she already admired him as the family's Georgian friend and Bolshevik hero. "They spent the whole summer of 1917 shut together in one apartment. Sometimes alone," says Nadya's niece, Kira Alliluyeva. "Nadya saw the romantic revolutionary in Josef. And my mother said he was very attractive. Of course Nadya fell in love with him." He nicknamed her "Tatka"; she called him Soso, or Josef.

Stalin, only child of a driven single mother, must have missed the laughter, playfulness and flirtation of family life. He had enjoyed this in exile, and it was now a decade since his marriage to Kato Svanidze. He had always liked the sort of girl who could cook, tidy and look after him like Kato—and his mother. Indeed, the Svanidzes said that Stalin fell for Nadya because she reminded him of Kato.

"Slowly Stalin fell in love with her," says Kira Alliluyeva. "A real love match." Soso could have been her father—his enemies would claim he actually was. The dates do not fit, but Nadya must have known that Soso had probably had an affair with her oversexed mother in the past. Was there competition between mother and daughter for their Georgian lodger?

"Olga always had a soft spot for Stalin," wrote Nadya's and Stalin's daughter, Svetlana. But Olga "disapproved" of Nadya's relationship, "doing her best to talk her out of it and calling her 'silly fool.' She could never accept that alliance." Was it because she knew Soso's nature or because she had had an affair with him herself—or both? However, "silly fool" Nadya was already in love with Soso. A few months later, she proudly told a confidante: "I've lost so much weight people say I must be in love."

Stalin later talked about how he chose Nadya over her elder sister: "Anna was somewhat pedantic and tiresomely talkative," while Nadya was "mature for her age in her thinking" and "stood with both feet on the ground. She understood him better." He was right about Anna, who was to irritate him for the rest of his life, but he had missed something about Nadya.

The teenager was, in her way, as neurotic, damaged and dark as he, perhaps darker. Nadya's strictness appealed to Stalin, but it would later clash disastrously with his own bedouin informality and wilful egotism. Worse, her sincere intensity masked the family's mental instability, a bipolar disorder that would ultimately make her anything but the placid homemaker. "But he got a taste of her difficult character," says Kira Alliluyeva. "She answered back and even put him in his place." The defiance of this pretty, devoted schoolgirl with the flashing Gypsy eyes must have then seemed attractive to Stalin. But ultimately theirs would be a fatal and ill-fated combination.

We do not know exactly when they became lovers. They became a public couple ten months later. But the relationship probably started at this time.[4]

The Bolsheviks were on the verge of a surprising recovery: its architect was not Lenin or Stalin, but a right-wing would-be military dictator. Kerensky promoted a new Commander-in-Chief, General Lavr Kornilov, a Siberian Cossack with slanting Tartar eyes, a shaven pate and a winged moustache, who emerged as a potential Russian "man on a white horse" to purge Petrograd of Bolsheviks and restore order. But Kornilov was as vain as Kerensky—he had a special bodyguard of scarlet-clad, sabre-rattling Turkomans—and not as clever: he was said to have "the heart of a lion, the brains of a sheep." Nonetheless Kornilov seemed the man of the moment, and he started reading books on Napoleon, always a bad sign in men of the moment.

Kerensky tried to regain the momentum, holding an all-party Moscow conference, away from the turbulent capital. "Petrograd," wrote Stalin in one of his religious metaphors, "is dangerous; they flee from it . . . like the devil from holy water." He was right: in Moscow, the General stole Kerensky's limelight. But the two men agreed that Kornilov should march front-line troops to Petrograd to restore order. Then Kerensky, who also fancied himself as the Russian Bonaparte, suspected the General of planning a coup. There was a dangerous surplus of Napoleons. Kerensky dismissed the General, who decided to march on Petrograd anyway.

The capital waited anxiously. Kerensky, appointing himself Commander-in-Chief, found he was without military support and was forced to rely on the Soviet, which remobilized the Bolshevik Red Guards. The General was arrested, but the Cabinet fell apart. Kerensky thereupon anointed himself the dictator of a five-man Directory. He had survived but, like Mikhail Gorbachev after the August coup of 1991, as a busted flush. Sustained by cocaine and morphia, he reigned, but no longer ruled, from the splendour of Alexander III's suite in the Winter Palace.

"We have at last a 'new' (brand new!) five-man Government," joked Stalin on 3 September, "chosen by Kerensky, endorsed by Kerensky, responsible to Kerensky." Bolshevik strength surged in the factories, and among soldiers and Kronstadt sailors. "The army that rose against Kornilov," wrote Trotsky, "was the army-to-be of the October Revolution."[5]

Stalin's short reign as Bolshevik leader revealed the overbearing arrogance that had always been his trademark. The Central Committee brought the Military Organization under firm control. Stalin rudely appropriated their funds and took over their newspaper *Soldat* in an "unprincipled style, violating the most elementary principles of party democracy." They appealed to the Central Committee. In an early description of Stalinism, they criticized his "outright system of persecution and repression of an extremely strange character." Stalin hauled the Military Organization before a Party trial.* His allies Sverdlov and Dzerzhinsky cleared up his mess.[6] But Trotsky, Zinoviev and Kamenev now reemerged from hiding and prison. On 4 September, Trotsky joined Stalin on the Central Executive Committee of the Congress of Soviets and on *Pravda*. Stalin was again overshadowed. The limelight belonged to Trotsky.

Stalin often bumped into his old Menshevik acquaintance David Sagirashvili in the corridors of the Smolny Institute.† When Sagirashvili accused him of propagating anti-Menshevik lies in his *Pravda*, "he would grin in a seemingly good-natured way" and explain, in a pre-Orwellian dictum, that a "lie always has a stronger effect than the truth. The main thing is to obtain one's objective." As Stalin later told Molotov, "Truth is protected by a battalion of lies."

At last, both the Petrograd and Moscow Soviets fell into Lenin's hands, but the Bolsheviks were still divided on what to do next. It was Lenin, by sheer force of will, who drove them to the October Revolution: sometimes one individual does change the course of history. Yet Kamenev now threatened to reroute history himself—the mild Bolshevik offered a completely different path. On 14 September, he began trying to negotiate a coalition with the Mensheviks and SRs at the Democratic State Conference in the Alexandrinsky Theatre.

The Old Man, hiding in Helsinki, was appalled and frustrated. On 15 September, he sent the Central Committee a letter ordering them to seize power on behalf of the Bolsheviks alone.

"History will not forgive us if we do not assume power now!" wrote Lenin. But Kamenev and Zinoviev feared losing everything. It was April all over again: they were not the only ones who thought Lenin was wildly misguided. "We were aghast!" admitted Bukharin. At the ensuing CC, attended by Trotsky, Kamenev, Sverdlov and Shaumian, up from the Caucasus, Stalin backed Lenin and proposed that the letter be distributed secretly to key Party organizations. The Central Committee refused by a

---

* That summer, the other intriguing Party scandal was that Kamenev was accused of having been an Okhrana agent: the Central Committee asked Stalin to inform the Soviet Executive Committee. There was an investigation. Kamenev was cleared on 30 August.
† After its humiliation in the July Days, the Soviet was moved out of the Taurida Palace into another neo-classical edifice next door, the Smolny Institute, built by Catherine the Great as a boarding-school for noble girls, where all the parties, including the Bolsheviks, now set up their offices. It was from the Smolny that Zinoviev and then, after his downfall in 1926, Sergei Kirov, a young protégé of Stalin's, ruled Leningrad. Here, in 1934, Kirov was assassinated, a crime which, whether or not it was organized by Stalin, provided the excuse for the Great Terror. During the Siege of Leningrad, the city was ruled from the Smolny. Today, it houses the office of the mayor of St. Petersburg.

vote of six to four, an extraordinary result just a month before the October Revolution that reveals the popularity of Kamenev's way. Yet the two ultra-radicals, Stalin and Trotsky, seeing no need for any Menshevik alliance, supported Lenin. At the CC on 21 September, Stalin and Trotsky demanded a boycott of the coming pre-parliament, where Kamenev hoped to continue his coalition-building, but they were again decisively defeated. Lenin ranted that Kamenev and Zinoviev were "miserable traitors!"

On 25 September, the Bolsheviks took control of the Soviet Executive Committee. Trotsky, returning as Soviet chairman after thirteen years of arrest, exile and emigration, started to assert Soviet command of the military. He and his Inter-Borough Party had only just joined the Bolsheviks but, while Lenin remained in hiding, Trotsky continued to perform nightly at the packed Cirque Moderne.

Lenin bombarded Kamenev and the Bolsheviks with a barrage of articles and secret letters, arguing that time was short, with Kerensky starting another crackdown, and that the second Congress of Soviets had been summoned to Petrograd. Thus they must seize power first—or they would have to share power in a coalition, "and cover themselves with eternal *shame* and *destroy themselves* as a Party!"

Lenin secretly moved back from Finland to hide in the comfortable apartment of Margarita Fofanova in Vyborg, whence he continued to spew forth his radical bile. "The success of the Russian and world revolutions just depends on two or three days' fighting," he declared, fearing that Kamenev's view could prevail. "Better to die a man than let the enemy pass!" When the Central Committee recoiled, he submitted his resignation. These letters were "written with extraordinary force," wrote Bukharin, "and threatened us with all sorts of punishments." In his brilliant rage, Lenin was beginning to sound almost deranged. Indeed Stalin, editor of the Party newspaper *Rabochii Put* (Workers' Way), actually censored Lenin's more outrageous ravings, publishing instead an earlier, more moderate piece.

Sometimes the ranting prophet broke free of his confinement. "One morning just before the October Revolution," recalls Anna Alliluyeva, "there was a ring at the door. I saw a smallish man dressed in a black overcoat and a Finnish cap on the threshold."

"Is Stalin at home?" he asked politely.

"Good Lord, you look just like a Finn, Vladimir Illich," Anna exclaimed to Lenin. "After a brief conversation, Stalin and he left together . . ."

Just days later, these scruffy, diminutive figures, who now walked the streets of Petrograd disguised and unrecognized, seized the Russian Empire. They formed the world's first Marxist government, remained at the peak of the state for the rest of their days, sacrificed millions of lives at the pitiless altar of their utopian ideology, and ruled the imperium, between them, for the next thirty-six years.[7]

41

1917 Winter: The Countdown

Petrograd in October 1917 seemed calm, but beneath the glossy surface the city danced in a trance of last pleasures. "Gambling clubs functioned hectically from dusk till dawn," reported John Reed, "with champagne flowing and stakes of 20,000 roubles. In the centre of the city at night, prostitutes in jewels and expensive furs walked up and down and crowded the cafés . . . Hold-ups increased to such an extent that it was dangerous to walk the streets." Russia, wrote Ilya Ehrenburg, later one of Stalin's favoured writers, "lived as if on a railway platform, waiting for the guard's whistle." Aristocrats sold priceless treasures on the streets, the food shortages worsened, queues lengthened, while the rich still dined at Donon's and Constant's, the two smartest restaurants, and the bourgeois vied for tickets to hear Chaliapin sing.

"Mysterious individuals circulating around the shivering women in lines for bread and milk, whispering that the Jews had cornered the food supply . . . Monarchist plots, German spies, smugglers hatching schemes," observed Reed. "And, in the rain, the bitter chill, the great throbbing city under grey skies rushing faster and faster toward . . . what?" Trotsky answered Reed's question, responding to the baying crowd at the Cirque Moderne: "The time for words has passed. The hour has come for a duel to the death between revolution and counter-revolution!" In the lonely magnificence of the Winter Palace, Kerensky waited, wasting the embers of his power in tokes of morphia and cocaine.

At 10 p.m. on the dark, drizzly night of 10 October 1917, Lenin seized his chance to convince the Central Committee: the eleven high Bolsheviks slipped one by one out of the Smolny to rendezvous at 32 Karpovka Embankment, a street-level apartment in the Petrograd District. It belonged to Galina Flakserman, the Bolshevik wife of the Menshevik scribe Sukhanov. "Oh the novel jokes of the merry muse of History," he reflected. "This supreme and decisive session took place in my home . . . but without my knowledge."

Some of the eleven were in disguise: a clean-shaven Lenin, who, Krupskaya thought, "looked every bit like a Lutheran priest," sported an ill-fitting curly wig that kept sliding off his bald pate. As Lenin started to address Stalin, Trotsky, Sverdlov, Zinoviev, Kamenev and Dzerzhinsky in a hot room with a blanket covering the window, Galina Flakserman provided salami, cheese and black bread, brewing up the samovar in the corridor. But no one ate yet.

"The political situation is fully ripe for the transfer of power," declared Lenin, but even then the Bolsheviks argued against him. Minutes were not taken, but we know that Stalin and Trotsky backed Lenin from the start. Kamenev and Zinoviev, who had grown a beard and cropped his locks as his disguise, remained unconvinced. The argument was "intense and passionate," but Trotsky wrote that no one could match Lenin's "thought, will, confidence, courage." Gradually Lenin overcame "the wavering and the doubtful," who now felt a "surge of strength and resolve." In the early hours, there was a loud banging on the door. Was it Kerensky's police? It was Galina Flakserman's brother Yury, come to help serve the sausages and man the samovar. The Central Committee voted on a vague resolution for an uprising. "No practical plan of insurrection, even tentative, was sketched out that night," recalls Trotsky. Nine supported Lenin against Zinoviev and Kamenev, who were "deeply convinced that to proclaim an armed uprising now means to gamble, not only with the fate of our Party, but with that of the Russian and international revolution."

Ravenous and punch-drunk, the winners fell upon the sausages, and teased Zinoviev and Kamenev.[1]

Five days later, on 16 October, at another secret meeting at the Lesnoi

District Duma on the northern outskirts, Lenin, backed by Stalin and Sverdlov (Trotsky being absent at the Soviet), again berated the doubters. "History will never forgive us if we don't take power now!" he cried, resetting his precarious wig.

"We don't have the right to take the risk and gamble everything at once," retorted Zinoviev.

Stalin stood with Lenin: "The date must be chosen expediently." The Central Committee must, said the former seminarist who saw his Marxism as a quasi-religion, have "more faith . . . There are two lines here: one holds a course for victory of revolution . . . the other doesn't believe in revolution and counts merely on staying as an opposition . . . Kamenev's and Zinoviev's proposals . . . give the counter-revolution the chance to get organized," Stalin warned. "We'll go on endless retreat and lose the entire revolution."

Lenin won ten votes to two. The Central Committee elected Stalin, Sverdlov, Dzerzhinsky and two others to a Military-Revolutionary Centre "to become part" of Trotsky's Military-Revolutionary Committee at the Soviet. The organ that would seize power had not yet been decided. The bewigged Lenin scuttled back into hiding as Kerensky sensed danger and raised the stakes: Petrograd was in danger from the advancing Germans. He announced the recall of loyal regiments from the front. There was no time to lose.

Then on 18 October Kamenev published an attack on the "ruinous step" of an uprising in Maxim Gorky's journal, *Novaya Zhizn*. It is an irony of 1917 that, for all Lenin's iron will, Kamenev, always "sodden with sentimentality," in Trotsky's words, was the only truly consistent Bolshevik. "Kamenev and Zinoviev have betrayed the CC!" Lenin exploded. "I demand the expulsion of both the strike-breakers." But Zinoviev insisted, in a letter, on continuing the debate in secret. Stalin, as chief editor of *Rabochii Put*, published the letter.*

At a confrontational CC meeting on 20 October, Trotsky attacked Stalin for this. Stalin sulkily offered his resignation. It was refused, but this marked the first clash between the two Bolshevik titans. Trotsky called for the expulsion of the "strike-breakers"; Stalin countered by proposing that they "be required to submit but kept in the CC." Kamenev

---

* Another conciliatory gesture to Kamenev that shows Stalin's instinct for maintaining some balance between Lenin and Trotsky, on the one hand, and the moderates on the other, in the Party. This was to pay rich dividends in the struggle to succeed Lenin.

tried to resign from the Central Committee, but was merely removed from the leadership. Stalin prepared the public for the rising in an article that declared: "The Bolsheviks have issued the call: be ready!"*

The Bolsheviks were getting ready themselves. In a third-floor office of the Smolny, Trotsky and Sverdlov held the first organizational meeting of the Military-Revolutionary Committee (MRC): it was secretly Bolshevik but had the advantage of operating under the aegis of the Soviet. This, not Stalin's Centre, would be the uprising's headquarters: he was not a member.†

On the twenty-first, the MRC declared itself the legitimate authority over the Petrograd garrison. Stalin, at the political centre of the Party, drafted the agenda for the second Congress of Soviets, assigning himself to speak on "nationalities," Lenin on "land war and power," and Trotsky on "the current situation."² On the twenty-third, the MRC took command of the Peter and Paul Fortress. Everything was ready: even myopic Molotov practised pistol-shooting in his Smolny office. "The existing government of landlords and capitalists," reported Stalin that day, "must be replaced by a new government of workers and peasants . . . If all of you act solidly and staunchly, nobody will dare to resist the will of the people."

At dawn on Tuesday, 24 October, Kerensky raided Stalin's newspapers at the Trud Press. As Stalin watched, the troops smashed the presses, seized machinery and set guards over the offices. He now had to prise the Bolshevik press machine back into operation: just as modern coups always seize the television station, in 1917 a revolution without newspapers was unthinkable. Stalin called Red units for reinforcements while he managed

---

* In this rarely quoted article of 20 October, biblically entitled "The Strong Bulls of Bashan Have Beset Me Round!," Stalin warned how he and the Party would regard intellectuals and artistic celebrities in their new Russia. Maxim Gorky, despite being a long-time supporter and funder of the Bolsheviks, now had severe reservations, declaring, "I cannot keep silent." Stalin mocked such "terrified neurasthenics . . . verily 'strong bulls of Bashan have beset me round,' threatening and imploring. Here's our reply!" Stalin warned that "there is a general croaking in the marsh of our bewildered intellectuals. The Revolution has not cringed before celebrities but has taken them into our service or, if they refused to learn, has consigned them to oblivion."

† Trotsky preferred to use his own new recruits to the Bolshevik Party, such as Antonov-Ovseenko, as his top operatives on the MRC, which had existed since 9 October. Sverdlov, Molotov and Dzerzhinsky were members. Why not Stalin? It is possible Stalin's confrontation with the Military Organization in August or just his general truculence inhibited Sverdlov from inviting him to join. But it is more likely Stalin was simply busy with his press responsibilities and communications with Lenin, both vital. As for the Centre, on which Stalin served, it never met, even though his propagandists claimed that it was the real centre of the Revolution.

to circulate the already printed papers. The Volkynia Regiment sent a company. By midday, Stalin had regained control of his presses. Later that day, he said the newspapers were "being set up again." But he had missed the CC meeting where the tasks were handed out for the coup. Trotsky accused him of "dropping out of the game" because he was not on one of the lists of assignments:

Bubnov: railways
Dzerzhinsky: post and telegraph
Milyutin: food supplies
Podvoisky [changed to Sverdlov]: surveillance of the Provisional
    Government
Kamenev and Vinter: negotiations with Left SRs [the radical
    wing of the Socialist-Revolutionaries]
Lomov and Nogin: information to Moscow

This list of second-raters proves nothing: Lenin, in hiding, and Trotsky, who also missed the meeting, were not even mentioned, while the "strike-breaker" Kamenev is included. Historians habitually follow Trotsky's (totally prejudiced but superbly written) version of events in asserting that Stalin "missed the Revolution," but this does not stand up to scrutiny. He was not the star of the day, but he missed a military assignment because he had his hands full at the raided newspapers, not because he was politically insignificant. Far from it: even Trotsky admits that "contact with Lenin was mainly through Stalin," hardly an unimportant role (though he cannot resist adding, "because he was the person of least interest to the police").

Stalin's "missing the Revolution" was no more than a few daytime hours of the twenty-fourth, while the coup actually stretched over two days. He was at the newspapers all morning. Then he was summoned by Lenin: Margarita Fofanova reveals that Stalin intended to give a speech that day at the Polytechnical Institute but suddenly "we had to hand him a note from VI." Lenin was twitching with fury at the Fofanova apartment. If Stalin had rushed to him, he would have found him ranting, "The Government is tottering! It must be *given the deathblow* at all costs . . . We mustn't wait! We may lose everything!"

Stalin arrived at the Smolny Institute, where he, along with Trotsky, addressed the Bolshevik delegates, just arrived for the Congress of Soviets, presenting the coup as a reaction to the government suppression of the Bolsheviks, not as an uprising.* "At the front they're coming over to us," Stalin explained. "The Provisional Government's wavering. The [cruiser] *Aurora* has been asked to fire on the bridges—in any case the bridges will be ours. There are mutinies among Junkers and troops. *Rabochii Put* is being set up again. The telephone system's not ours yet. The Post Office is ours . . ." Red Guards and Bolshevik troops were on their way.

"I met Stalin on the eve of the Revolution at midnight in the Smolny," reports Sagirashvili. Stalin was so excited that, "contrary to his usual solemnity and secrecy, he revealed the die had been cast." That night, the eve of Glorious October, Stalin popped home to the Alliluyevs. "Yes, everything's ready," he told the girls. "We take action tomorrow. We've got all the city districts in our hands. We'll seize power."[3]

Stalin kept Lenin informed. The Old Man sent almost hourly notes to the MRC to energize them before the Congress opened. It was set for the next day but Lenin insisted it be brought forward. "What are they afraid of?" he wrote in one note. "Just ask if they have a hundred trustworthy soldiers or Red Guards with rifles. That's all I need!"

It is no wonder that Lenin was frustrated. The October Revolution would become one of the iconic events of the twentieth century, mythologized by Soviet propaganda, romanticized in John Reed's *Ten Days That Shook the World*, immortalized by Eisenstein's cinematic masterpiece *October* and made ridiculous by Stalin's vainglorious exaggerations. But the reality of October was more farce than glory. Tragically, the real Revolution, pitiless and bloody, started the moment this comedy ended.

Still stuck at Fofanova's apartment, Lenin could not understand the delay. "Everything now hangs by a thread," he wrote that night. "The matter must be decided without fail this evening!" He paced the floor. Fofanova begged him not to emerge and risk arrest. Finally at 10:50 p.m., Lenin could stand it no longer.

---

* "Within the Military-Revolutionary Committee, there are two points of view," said Stalin. "The first is that we organize an uprising at once and the second is that we consolidate our forces. The CC has sided with the second view."

42

Glorious October 1917:
The Bungled Uprising

I have gone where you didn't want me to go," Lenin scribbled to Fofanova. "Illich asked for Stalin to be fetched," recorded Lenin's bodyguard, Rakhia. "Then he realized this would waste time." He glued on his curly wig, set a worker's cap on his head, wrapped a bandage around his face and put on some giant spectacles. Then he and Rakhia set off into the night.

Lenin boarded a tram. He was so tense that he breathlessly cross-examined the bemused ticket-collector before giving her a lecture on revolutionary strategy. It is unclear if she ever discovered the identity of this bewigged, bandaged, bespectacled loon, but there were probably many madmen loose in the city that night. Near the Bolshevik headquarters at the Smolny, a mounted government patrol actually stopped him, but released him as a harmless drunk. He was sober—but far from harmless.

At around midnight, Lenin reached "great Smolny"—"bright with lights," says Reed, it "hummed like a gigantic hive." Red Guards, "a huddled group of boys in workmen's clothes, carrying guns with bayonets, talking nervously together," warmed their hands round giant bonfires; the motors of armoured cars whirred, motorcycles revved, but no one recognized Lenin. He had no papers, so the Red Guards at the gates refused to allow him access.

"What a mess!" shouted Rakhia. "I'm a delegate [for the Congress] and they won't let me through." The crowd supported him and pushed the two of them inside: "Lenin came in last, laughing!" But when he doffed his cap, his glue-stiffened wig came off too.*

The Smolny was a campsite. While the Soviet met in the splendid ballroom, newspapers, fag-ends and bedding covered the floors. Soldiers snored in the corridors. The reek of smoke, sweat and urine blended with the aroma of boiled cabbage from the refectory downstairs. Lenin hastened through the corridors, holding on to his wig, trying to hide his identity. But the Menshevik, Dan, spotted him.

"The rotters have recognized me," muttered Lenin.

In the early hours of Wednesday, 25 October, Stalin, donning his leather jacket and cap, joined Lenin in Room 36 at the Smolny for an emergency CC meeting. Even Zinoviev and Kamenev were invited. Lenin insisted on accelerating the revolt. The Congress delegates were gathering in the very same building.

Lenin began to draft the key decrees on land and peace—still in disguise, "rather a strange sight," mused Trotsky. The coup was in motion. The Central Committee remained in constant session for two days in a "tiny room round a badly lit table with overcoats thrown on the floor," remembers a Bolshevik assistant, Sara Ravich. "People were continually knocking at the door, bringing news of the uprising's latest successes. Among those present were Lenin, Trotsky, Zinoviev, Kamenev and Stalin." Messengers arrived; orders were sent from the MRC in Room 10 and Lenin and the Central Committee in Room 36; both "worked at furious speed, engulfing and spitting out panting couriers, despatching commissars with power of life and death, amidst the buzz of telegraphs."

Stalin "hurried from one room to another," observed Sagirashvili, who was in the Smolny. "I'd never seen him in such a state before. Such haste and feverish work were very unusual for him." Gunfire crackled over the capital, but there was no fighting. The electric power station, the main post office and the Nicholas Station were won. They secured all the bridges except the Nicholas Bridge beside the Winter Palace. At 6 a.m.

---

* Earlier John Reed witnessed Trotsky himself being refused entry.
  "You know me. My name is Trotsky."
  "You can't go in. Names mean nothing to me!"
  "But I'm the Chairman of the Soviet!"
  "If you're as important a fellow as that, you must have at least one bit of paper!" retorted the guard, who summoned an equally bemused officer:
  "Trotsky! I've heard the name somewhere. I guess it's alright . . ."

the State Bank fell, at 7 a.m. the Central Telephone Exchange, at 8 a.m. the Warsaw Station.* But the vital Baltic sailors were late. The government continued to function—or at least survive—throughout the day.

Kerensky was at General Staff HQ absorbing the bad news. At 9 a.m., he finally realized that only the troops at the front could save Petrograd, and that only he could rally them. But he could not find a car until his men requisitioned a Renault from the American Embassy and a bulky Pierce Arrow touring limousine. Leaving his government in emergency session in the Winter Palace, Kerensky raced out of the city.

At the Smolny, the Congress prepared to open—but the Winter Palace had not yet fallen or even been surrounded. The palace remained the seat of government, guarded by 400 adolescent military cadets, a Women's Shock Battalion and some squadrons of Cossacks. A photographer persuaded some of these women to pose on their barricade. "It all had an operatic air and a comic one at that," said the American Louise Bryant, one of many journalists who were spectating that day. Outside, with surprising slowness, the Bolsheviks gathered their forces. Inside, the ministers were, sensed Justice Minister Maliantovich, "doomed men abandoned by everyone, roaming around inside a giant mousetrap."

Lenin, Trotsky, Stalin, Yenukidze and young Molotov, among others, began to discuss the new government after the formal CC meeting: first they had to decide what to call it. Lenin wanted to avoid the taint of capitalistic "ministries"—"a foul, worn-out term." He suggested "commissars."

"We've too many commissars already," said Trotsky. "How about 'People's Commissars'? A 'Council of People's Commissars' with a Chairman instead of a Premier."†

"That's wonderful!" exclaimed Lenin. "It has the awesome smell of revolution!"

Even at this moment, there were games of tactical modesty, ascetic denial being part of the Bolshevik culture. Lenin proposed Trotsky as

---

* The junior leaders such as Molotov and Dzerzhinsky were sent out on missions: Molotov, accompanied by a detachment of Red Guards, was ordered to arrest the editors of the SR newspaper and then a counter-revolutionary group of Mensheviks meeting at the Holy Synod.

† The Soviet Union became an empire of acronyms: the People's Commissars became "Narkoms"; the Council of People's Commissars was known as Sovnarkom; and its president (the effective Premier, successively Lenin, Rykov, Molotov, then Stalin) was Predsovnarkom. These lasted until Stalin reintroduced ministers at the end of the Second World War.

Premier. But a Jew could not be Premier of Russia. Trotsky refused, insisting it be Lenin. It was probably Lenin who proposed Stalin as People's Commissar of Nationalities. He, too, modestly refused, insisting he had no experience and was too busy at the Central Committee, happy just to be a Party worker, Yenukidze later told Sagirashvili. Perhaps it was to Stalin that Lenin replied with peals of laughter: "Do you think any of us has experience in this?" Lenin persisted, whereupon Stalin accepted his first real job since his days as a weatherman at the Tiflis Observatory seventeen years before. It did not seem real: some of the CC members treated this Cabinet making as a bit of a joke.

When the doors of the Bolshevik headquarters opened, "a blast of stale air and cigarette smoke rushed out" and John Reed "caught a glimpse of dishevelled men bending over a map in the glare of a shaded electric-light . . ." But the palace was still not taken.[1]

Lenin was beside himself. Trotsky and the MRC ordered the Peter and Paul Fortress to prepare to bombard the Winter Palace, just across the Neva, but found there were only six guns available. Five had not been cleaned for months; only one was operative. The officers told the Bolsheviks that the guns were broken. The commissars, not realizing that the guns just needed a clean, ordered the sailors to drag some small 3-inch training guns into position, but then discovered that there were no 3-inch shells, and that the guns lacked sights. It was late afternoon before they worked out that the original guns merely needed cleaning.

Back at the Smolny, Lenin, as usual, was raging. The building's "massive façade [was] blazing with lights . . . An enormous elephant-coloured armoured automobile, with two red flags flying from the turret, lumbered out with a screaming siren . . . The long barely illuminated corridors roared with the thunder of feet, calling, shouting," soldiers "in rough dirt-coloured coats," armed workmen "in black blouses." Occasionally, a leader such as Kamenev was spotted bustling down the staircases.

Kerensky's Cabinet still reigned at the Winter Palace, but Lenin could no longer delay his first appearance at the Soviet. At 3 p.m. Trotsky introduced him. Lenin claimed power. When he returned to Room 36, the palace still had not fallen.

Lenin paced his small office "like a lion in a cage. V. I. [Lenin] scolded, he screamed. He needed the Winter Palace at any cost," recalls Nikolai Podvoisky of the MRC; "he was ready to shoot us!" When some military officers were captured, "certain comrades in the Smolny," almost certainly Lenin, wanted to shoot them in order to discourage the others. He was always eager to start the bloodletting.

By 6 p.m. that evening, inside the palace, the military cadets, who had not eaten all day, decided to abandon ship to find some dinner. The Cossacks left too, disgusted by the "Jews and wenches" inside. Some of the Women's Shock Battalion floated away.

The comedy of Bolshevik errors had not run its course: the signal for the storming of the palace was a red lantern hoisted to the top of the flagpole of the Peter and Paul Fortress, but now that the big moment had come, no one could raise such a lantern because no one could find one. A Bolshevik commissar had to go out in search of this rare item. He eventually discovered a lamp, but it was the wrong colour. Worse, he then became disorientated in the darkness and fell into a bog. When he emerged, he could not raise the lantern, red or otherwise. The signal was never given.

Finally at 6:30 p.m. on the twenty-fifth, the Bolsheviks ordered the cruisers *Aurora* and *Amur* to steam upriver. They sent in an ultimatum: "Government and troops to capitulate. This ultimatum expires at 7:10 after which we will immediately open fire." The ultimatum duly ran out.

Nothing happened. The storming was delayed by a quixotic bid to stop the Bolshevik Revolution, despite the frenzied orders of Lenin and Trotsky.

The mayor of Petrograd, the white-bearded Grigory Shreider, who had been debating at the City Council how to prevent the bombardment of the palace, suddenly pledged to defend the government himself. The city councillors backed him. Thus it was that the venerable mayor, the councillors and the minister of food, Prokopovich, well-dressed bourgeoisie wearing velvet-collared cloaks, frock coats and fob-watches, marched out, four abreast like penguins on parade. Each was unarmed except for an umbrella, a lantern and a salami—dinner for the defenders of the palace. First they proceeded to the Smolny, where they were received by Kamenev, who seconded Molotov to accompany them to the Winter Palace. This parade of salamis and umbrellas, accompanied by the ponderous Molotov, headed down Nevsky Prospect singing "The Marseillaise," until they were stopped by a Red checkpoint outside Kazan Station.

The mayor demanded that the Red Guards make way, or shoot unarmed citizens, according to John Reed, who recorded the dialogue.

"No, we won't shoot unarmed Russian people," said the commander of the checkpoint.

"We will go forward! What can you do!" Prokopovich and Shreider insisted. "What can you do?"

"We can't let you pass," mused the soldier. "We will do something."

Then a laughing sailor thought of something. *"We will spank you!"* he roared, destroying the dignified aura with which the marchers had surrounded themselves. "We will spank you."

The rescue attempt ended in guffaws, but still the palace held out, even though its defenders were becoming increasingly drunk on the contents of the Tsar's superb wine-cellar. Meanwhile cars were crossing the bridges, trams rumbling along the streets, and that night Chaliapin was singing in *Don Carlos* at the Narodny Dom. "Up the Nevsky the entire world seemed to be promenading." The hookers, who, like rats on a ship or canaries in a coal mine, were the test of imminent danger, still silkily patrolled the Prospect. "The streets," says Sagirashvili, "were overflowing with all sorts of riffraff."

Finally at 9:40 p.m., the *Aurora* fired a blank shell: signal for the assault. Inside the palace, the Women's Shock Battalion were so alarmed by the boom that many of them went into the wrong sort of shock and had to be calmed down in a backroom. Outside the palace, the Bolshevik commanders, Podvoisky and Vladimir Antonov-Ovseenko, whom Lenin had wanted to shoot for their ineptitude, had amassed overwhelming force.

The gunners at the Peter and Paul Fortress managed a barrage of three dozen 6-inch shells. Only two hit the palace, but they succeeded in terrifying the defenders. Armoured cars raked the walls with machine-gun fire and small groups of sailors and Red Guards discovered that the palace was not only undefended but that the doors were not even locked. "The attack," admits Antonov-Ovseenko, "had a completely disorganized character." At about 2 a.m., they entered and started to work their way through the rooms.

In the Smolny's chandeliered hall, pervaded by a "foul blue cloud of smoke" and the "stifling heat of unwashed human bodies," the opening of the Congress, comprised (in Sukhanov's words) of "primitive . . . dark provincial" Bolsheviks, could not be delayed any longer. But the Kerensky ministry still reigned in the palace, so Lenin could not yet appear. Instead Trotsky took the stage for the Bolsheviks. When Martov and the Mensheviks attacked Lenin's "insane and criminal action," Trotsky, "his thin pointed face positively mephistophelean in its malicious irony," replied with one of history's most crushing dismissals: "You are pathetic bankrupts! Go where you belong. Into the dustbin of history!"

"Then we'll leave," retorted Martov. The Mensheviks foolishly walked out of the hall—and into history: they never returned to the portals of power. Sagirashvili, a Menshevik who "didn't agree with the boycott," despondently roamed the Smolny corridors until "Stalin put his hand over my shoulder in the most friendly manner and started to talk to me in Georgian," trying to recruit him to the Bolsheviks. Sagirashvili refused, but various ex-Mensheviks like Vyshinsky were to become some of Stalin's most loyal retainers.*

On the boulevards and bridges near the palace, the thunder of the big guns finally dispersed the promenading thrill-seekers. "Even the prostitutes," Sagirashvili noted, "disappeared from Nevsky Prospect where they once flocked like birds."

Kerensky's ministers, at their baize table in the gold and malachite room with crimson brocade hangings where Nicholas II and his family had dined before 1905, still debated whom to appoint as "Dictator." Suddenly they gave up the charade and decided to surrender.

Just then the door opened.

---

* Sagirashvili was not the only Menshevik whom Stalin was courting. A Bolshevik-turned-Menshevik, Alexander Troyanovsky, the noble officer with whom Stalin had stayed in Vienna, was walking in the streets when a pair of hands covered his eyes. "Are you with us or against us?" asked Stalin.

43

Power: Stalin Out of the Shadows

A little man flew into the room, like a chip washed up by a wave under the pressure of the crowd that poured in behind him . . . He had long rust-coloured hair and glasses, a short trimmed reddish moustache and a small beard," reported Maliantovich, Justice Minister. "His collar, shirt, cuffs and hands were those of a very dirty man."

"The Provisional Government is here," said Deputy Premier Konovalov. "What is your pleasure?"

"In the name of the Military-Revolutionary Committee," replied Antonov-Ovseenko, "I declare all of you . . . under arrest."

It was about 1:50 a.m. on 26 October. The new masters of the Winter Palace started to pillage, "pulling out carpets, curtains, linen, porcelain, plates." One soldier stuck some ostrich feathers in his cap, while the old palace retainers, still in their blue, red and gold uniforms, tried to restrain the looters. There was no storming of the Winter Palace: more people were hurt filming the storming scene in Eisenstein's movie. "The Neva," Sagirashvili observed, "washed away Kerensky's government."

As the ministers were carted off to the Peter and Paul Fortress, Antonov-Ovseenko lost all control inside the palace, and some of the girls of the Women's Shock Battalion were raped. "The matter of the winecellars became especially critical," he recounts. Nicholas II's cellars boasted Tokay from the age of Catherine the Great and stocks of Château d'Yquem 1847, the Emperor's favourite, but:

> the Preobrazhensky Regiment . . . got totally drunk. The Pavlovsky, our revolutionary buttress, also couldn't resist. We sent guards from other picked units—all got utterly drunk. We posted guards from the Regimental Committees—they succumbed as well. We despatched armoured cars to drive away the crowd, but after a while they also began to weave suspiciously. When evening came, a violent bacchanalia overflowed.

Exasperated, Antonov-Ovseenko called the Petrograd Fire Brigade. "We tried flooding the cellars with water—but the firemen . . . got drunk instead." The Commissars started smashing the bottles in Palace Square, but "the crowd drank from the gutters. The drunken ecstasy infected the entire city."

Finally Lenin's Council of People's Commissars appointed a special Commissar of the Winter Palace with the highest authority, but, Antonov-Ovseenko notes drily, "This person also turned out not to be very reliable."

At the Congress of Soviets, it was Kamenev, who, in spite of himself, announced that the Winter Palace had finally fallen. It was only then that Lenin removed his wig, washed off his makeup and emerged as the leader of Russia.[1]

Meanwhile Anna and Nadya Alliluyeva, keen to see the opening of the Congress, had walked to the Smolny and slipped into the great hall itself: "Judging by the excitement and cheers, we guessed something important had happened and there suddenly, in the crowd streaming towards us, we saw Stalin," who beckoned them over.

"Oh it's you! Delighted you're here. Have you heard the news? The Winter Palace has fallen and our men are inside!"

The Bolsheviks almost collapsed with exhaustion. "At the time of the October [uprising]," explains Fyodor Alliluyev, Anna's and Nadya's eldest brother and Soso's new assistant, "Comrade Stalin didn't sleep for five days." Sometimes they ate, sometimes they grabbed a catnap on the floor.

"The city was quiet, probably never so quiet in its history," wrote John Reed. As the news arrived at Smolny that the city was finally in Bolshevik hands, Lenin began to relax, cracking jokes (at Kamenev's expense) and reclining on newspapers on the floor. "The corridors were still full of hurrying men, hollow-eyed and dirty," but in committee-rooms "people lay sleeping on the floor, guns beside them."

The Bolshevik high command slept where they sat or bedded down on the floors of their Smolny offices. "Crushed by tiredness," Stalin stayed awake drafting the Appeal to the People, until "he finally fell asleep while sitting in a chair behind his table," says Fyodor Alliluyev. "The enraptured Lunarcharsky [People's Commissar of Culture] tiptoed up to him as he slept and planted a kiss on his forehead. Comrade Stalin woke up and jovially laughed at A. V. Lunarcharsky for a long time."

Lenin and Trotsky bedded down beside one another on a pile of newspapers. "You know," sighed Lenin to Trotsky, "it makes one's head spin to pass so quickly from persecutions and living-in-hiding to power!"[2]

At 6 a.m. on 26 October, as "a faint unearthly pallor [was] stealing over the silent streets, dimming the watchfires, the shadow of a terrible dawn greyrising over Russia," the "day broke on a city in the wildest excitement and confusion." The streets quickly returned to normal. "The bourgeoisie," notes Shlyapnikov, "from Guards officers to prostitutes," reemerged onto the streets. As the Congress was supposed to meet at 1 p.m., the delegates started gathering first thing, but by 7 p.m. Lenin had still not appeared.

Finally, at 8:40 p.m., he arrived to uproarious applause—"this short stocky figure with a big head set down in his shoulders, bald and bulging, little eyes, a snubbish nose, a wide generous mouth, a strange popular leader," reported Reed, "a leader purely by virtue of intellect, colourless—humourless, uncompromising and detached."

"We shall now proceed to construct the socialist order!" declared Lenin simply. He spoke with one foot characteristically off the floor. "I noticed a hole in his shoe," reports Molotov.

At 2:30 a.m., Kamenev* read out the new government on the stage of the Congress of Soviets. Soso appeared on the list as "J. V. Djugashvili-Stalin." He was still not well known to the public nor admired by the Bolsheviks who had been in emigration. His obscurity in 1917 would always remain an embarrassing bruise on a very thin-skinned man, and he tried

---

* Surprisingly, Lenin chose Kamenev to be the effective first Bolshevik head of state as Chairman of the Soviet Executive Committee, though he lasted only a few days. Sverdlov succeeded him.

to correct it by a mendacious cult of personality. But in fact Lenin and an array of high Bolsheviks had long appreciated his ruthless competence.

"In those days," says Fyodor Alliluyev, with such candour that his memoirs were never published, "Comrade Stalin was genuinely known only to the small circle of people who had come across him . . . in the political underground or had succeeded . . . in distinguishing real work and real devotion from chatter, noise [and] meaningless babble."

The entire Soviet government now worked round the clock, in one room, at one table. "After the victory Stalin moved into the Smolny," recalls Fyodor Alliluyev. "For the first three days, we didn't leave," says Molotov. "There was me, Zinoviev and Trotsky, then opposite were Stalin and Kamenev. We tried by fits and starts to picture the new life." When Kamenev and Trotsky decided they wanted to abolish capital punishment in the army, recalled Stalin later, Lenin overheard them. "What nonsense!" he barked. "How can you have a revolution without shooting people?" Lenin meant it.

The coup had been surprisingly easy, but the life-and-death struggle to keep power started immediately. Lenin did not wish to share his government with the Mensheviks and SRs, but Kamenev insisted on opening negotiations to do just that. When these failed, he resigned. Meanwhile, Kerensky rallied Cossack forces on the Pulkovo Heights outside the city and the Menshevik-led railwaymen went on strike, demanding a coalition. Stalin, along with Sverdlov, Sergo and Dzerzhinsky, organized the defence of Petrograd.

Lenin, Trotsky and Stalin formed an inseparable troika in those first months in power. Besieged from outside and within, undermined by compromisers, bunglers and windbags inside his own Party, Lenin divided his grandees into "men of action" versus "tea-drinkers." There were too many "tea-drinkers." Had the Soviet Republic settled into peaceful stability, the tea-drinking tendency, represented by men like Kamenev and Bukharin, might have given it a very different direction. But it was not to be. Lenin spent almost every hour together with his grittiest henchmen. In these first hours, Lenin dictated an undated decree that reveals Stalin's and Trotsky's special place as follows:

Instructions to the guards at the reception of Sovnarkom
No one is permitted to enter without specific invitation except for:
President of Sovnarkom Lenin . . .

Then before the typed names of Lenin's personal assistants is written in handwriting that is probably that of Lenin himself:

Narkom Foreign Affairs Trotsky
Narkom Nationalities Stalin

"Lenin could not get along without Stalin for even a single day," wrote Stanislaw Pestkovsky, the Polish Bolshevik who now became Stalin's chief assistant at the Commissariat of Nationalities. Lenin sometimes asked Stalin to countersign his Sovnarkom decrees. "Our Smolny office was under Lenin's wing. In the course of the day, he'd call Stalin an endless number of times and would appear in our office and lead him away." Once, Pestkovsky found both men up ladders examining maps together.

Stalin's two Caucasian gangsters, Kamo and Tsintsadze, came to Petrograd. "I found Stalin alone in a room," says Tsintsadze. "We were so happy to see one another." But just then, Lenin wandered into the room.

"Meet Kote Tsintsadze," Stalin said to Lenin (who already knew Kamo), "the old bank robber–terrorist of the Caucasus."

Yet Stalin communicated with his assistant Pestkovsky only in "grunts," and was too moody and taciturn to gossip with him, unlike the other loquacious Bolshevik magnates.*

On 29 November 1917 the Central Committee created the core leadership Bureau—the Chetverka, the Foursome, with Lenin, Stalin, Trotsky and Sverdlov as the most powerful men in Russia, authorized "to decide all emergency questions." But Sverdlov, who became nominal head of state (Chairman of the Central Executive Committee of the Soviet), spent his time running the Party Secretariat. As a result, as Trotsky recalls, "The Four became a troika."

Lenin drove ahead with his radical and repressive measures: "Peace, Land, Bread!" He opened peace talks with Kaiserine Germany. When Trotsky, People's Commissar for Foreign Affairs, reported on progress, Lenin replied: "I'll consult with Stalin and give you my answer." On 27 October, opposition press was banned. At the Central Committee on 2 November, Lenin effectively created the dictatorship of the Bolshevik oligarchs. On the fourth, Sovnarkom gave itself the power to rule with-

---

* Pestkovsky's first memoirs, when published in 1922, contained Stalin's grunts and moodiness. Naturally, when these were republished in 1930 the grunts were gone.

out the Soviets. The MRC initially acted as Lenin's enforcers, but on 7 December he created an All-Russian Extraordinary Commission for the Struggle Against Counter-revolution and Sabotage, known by its acronym "Cheka," with Dzerzhinsky as Chairman. The Cheka, precursor of the OGPU, NKVD, KGB and today's FSB, had absolute supralegal power over life and death.

"In that case why should we bother with a People's Commissar for Justice?" Isaak Shteinberg, a Left-SR, challenged Lenin. "Let's honestly call it the Commissariat of Social Annihilation!"

"Well said!" replied Lenin. "That's exactly how it's going to be!"

He told another acquaintance: "We're engaged in annihilation. Don't you recall what Pisarev said: 'Break, beat up everything, beat and destroy! Everything that's being broken is rubbish and has no right to life! What survives is good.'" Lenin's handwritten notes demanded the shooting, killing, hanging of "bloodsuckers . . . spiders . . . leeches." He asked, "How can you make a revolution without firing-squads? If we can't shoot White Guard saboteurs, what kind of revolution is this? Nothing but talk and a bowl of mush!" He demanded they "find tougher people." But Stalin and Trotsky were tough enough. "We must put an end once and for all," said Trotsky, "to the Papist-Quaker babble about the sanctity of human life." Stalin showed a similar taste for Terror. When Estonian Bolsheviks proposed liquidating "traitors" in the earliest days of the Revolution, he replied swiftly: "The idea of a concentration camp is excellent."

He "began to feel more sure of himself," writes Trotsky. "I soon noticed Lenin was 'advancing' Stalin, valuing his firmness, grit, stubbornness and slyness as qualities necessary in the struggle."* Molotov, who loathed Trotsky, judges that "it was not without reason that Lenin recognized Stalin and Trotsky as the leaders who stood out from the rest as the most talented." Soon even Sukhanov understood that Stalin "holds in his hands the fate of the Revolution and state." The Georgian, says Trotsky, "became accustomed to power."

Yet Stalin was never inevitable. The brains, confidence, intellectual intensity, political talents, faith in and experience of violence, touchiness,

---

* It is still widely believed that Stalinism was a distortion of Leninism. But this is contradicted by the fact that in the months after October they were inseparable. Indeed for the next five years Lenin promoted Stalin wherever possible. Lenin single-handedly pushed the Bolsheviks to frenzied bloodletting on orders that have recently been revealed in the archives and published in Richard Pipes's *Unknown Lenin*. He knew what he was doing with Stalin, even though he realized that "that chef will cook up some spicy dishes." Stalinism was not a distortion but a development of Leninism.

vindictiveness, charm, sensitivity, ruthlessness, lack of empathy, the sheer weird singularity of the man, were in place—but lacking a forum. In 1917, he found the forum.

He could not have risen to power at any other time in history: it required the synchronicity of man and moment. His unlikely rise as a Georgian who could rule Russia was only made possible by the internationalist character of Marxism. His tyranny was made possible by the beleaguered circumstances of Soviet Russia, the utopian fanaticism of its quasi-religious ideology, the merciless Bolshevik machismo, the slaughterous spirit of the Great War, and Lenin's homicidal vision of a "dictatorship of the proletariat." Stalin would not have been possible if Lenin had not, in the first days of the regime, defeated Kamenev's milder way to create the machinery for so boundless and absolute a power. That was the forum for which Stalin was superbly equipped. Now Stalin could become Stalin.

Within months of October, Lenin and his magnates used that power to fight the Civil War. It was then that Stalin, along with his cohorts, experienced that unrestrained power to wage war and change society by random killing. Like boys on their first foxhunt, they were blooded by the exhilaration and swagger. Stalin's character, damaged yet gifted, was qualified for, and fatally attracted to, such pitiless predations. Afterwards, the machine of repression, the flinthearted, paranoid psychology of perpetual conspiracy and the taste for extreme bloody solutions to all challenges, were not just ascendant but glamorized, institutionalized and raised to an amoral Bolshevik faith with messianic fervour. In a colossal bureaucracy run like a nepotistic village, Stalin showed himself a master of personal politics.* He was the patron of these brutal tendencies but also their personification: he was right when he blasphemously declared in 1929 that "the Party has made me in its own image." He and the Party had developed together, but this creature of covert but boundless extremism and brooding, malevolent darkness could always go further still.

He grew up in the clannish Caucasus; he had spent his entire maturity

---

* Trotsky later claimed that Stalin amassed power as a bureaucratic mediocrity, but it was actually Yakov Sverdlov, assisted by Elena Stasova, who ran the Party machine. Stalin was not a born bureaucrat at all. He was a hard worker utterly dedicated to politics; indeed everything with Stalin was political, but he worked in an eccentric, structureless, unbureaucratic, almost bohemian, style that would not have succeeded in any other government, then or now. Lenin's trust was won in the bank robberies and intrigues of the early years and, later, on the battlefields of the Civil War: Stalin was hardly in his office before 1920.

in the conspiratorial underground, that peculiar milieu where violence, fanaticism and loyalty were the main coinage; he flourished in the jungle of constant struggle, drama and stress; he came to power as that rare thing—both man of violence and of ideas, an expert in gangsterism, as well as a devout Marxist; but, above all, he believed in himself and in his own ruthless leadership as the only way to govern a country in crisis and to promote a mere ideal to a real utopia.

In a limitless government run as a giant conspiracy of bloodletting and clan patronage, who was the most qualified to prosper?

The dance of power between Trotsky and Stalin started at the very beginning, at the first meeting of the new government, a historic occasion at which the personal peccadilloes and political wheeler-dealering clashed with the sanctity of dialectical materialism.

The first Cabinet—the Sovnarkom in Bolshevik acronym—was held in Lenin's office in the Smolny, which was still so makeshift and amateurish that the only link with his new empire was a "cubby-hole for his telephone girl and typist" behind an unpainted wooden partition. It was surely no coincidence that Lenin's two outstanding magnates, "Stalin and I," writes Trotsky, "were the first to arrive."

Then, from behind the wooden partition, the two of them overheard seductive and affectionate sighs: "a conversation of a rather tender nature" in the "thick basso of [People's Commissar of the Navy] Dybenko, a blackbearded sailor, twenty-nine years old, a jolly and self-confident giant" who had recently "become intimate with Alexandra Kollontai, a woman of aristocratic antecedents approaching her forty-sixth year." At this epoch-making moment, Stalin and Trotsky found themselves eavesdropping on Kollontai's latest scandalous affair, about which "there'd been much gossip in Party circles."

Trotsky and Stalin, two arrogant self-annointed Marxist messiahs, two magnificent administrators, deep thinkers, murderous enforcers, rank outsiders, a Jew and a Georgian, looked at each other. Stalin was amused, but Trotsky was shocked. "Stalin came up to me with a kind of unexpected jauntiness and pointing his shoulder towards the partition said, smirking: 'That's him with Kollontai, with Kollontai!' "* Trotsky was not amused:

---

* Alexandra Kollontai always treated Stalin with old-world courtesy: she served as his Swedish Ambassador and died naturally. Dybenko was shot in the Great Terror.

"His gesture and laughter seemed to me out of place and unendurably vulgar especially on that occasion and in that place."

"That's their affair!" snapped Trotsky, at which "Stalin sensed he'd made a mistake."

The amazing and unthinkable had happened: Stalin, the Georgian cobbler's son, was close to the peak of a Russian oligarchical government, and almost instantly Trotsky was his natural rival.

Stalin, says Trotsky, "never again tried to engage me in conversation of a personal nature. Stalin's face changed. His yellow eyes flashed with the glint of malice."[3]

Epilogue

Old Ninika

Our Ninika has grown old
His hero's shoulders have failed him . . .
How did this desolate grey hair
Break an iron strength?

Oh mother! Many a time
With his "hyena" sickle swinging,
Bare-chested, at the end of the cornfield
He must have suddenly burst out with a roar.

He must have piled up mountains
Of sheaves side by side,
And on his face governed by dripping sweat
Fire and smoke must have poured out.

But now he can longer move his knees,
Scythed down by old age.
He lies down or he dreams or he tells
His children's children of the past.

From time to time he catches the sound
Of singing in the nearby cornfields
And his heart that was once so tough
Begins to beat with pleasure.

He drags himself out, trembling.
He takes a few steps on his shepherd's crook
And, when he catches sight of the lads,
He smiles with relief.

—SOSELO (Josef Stalin)

An Old Tyrant—in Remembrance
of Things Past

O n the lush hills above Gagra on the Black Sea coast, an old Georgian man, small, squat, paunchy, with thinning grey hair and a moustache, wearing a grey tunic and baggy trousers, sat on the verandah of a clifftop mansion, a fortified eyrie, with panoramic views, and talked to his elderly guests about how they grew up together . . .

The *mtsvadi* kebabs and spicy vegetable dishes of a Georgian *supra* were spread around the table with bottles of local red wine as the men talked in Georgian about their boyhoods in Gori and Tiflis, their seminary studies and their youthful radicalism. It did not matter that they had parted and followed their different paths, because the host "had never forgotten his schoolmates and fellow seminarists."

In the years before his death, Generalissimo Stalin, Premier of the Soviet government and General Secretary of the Communist Party, conqueror of Berlin and supreme pontiff of world Marxism, the old Soso, exhausted by more than fifty years of conspiracy, thirty years of government, four years of total war, would retire for many months to his favourite seaside villa on the semi-tropical Black Sea of his homeland, to spend the days gardening, conspiring and reading—and the warm evenings talking in remembrance of things past.

Sometimes he talked to his magnates Molotov or Voroshilov, sometimes to his younger Georgian viceroys and protégés, but often "Stalin invited Georgian houseguests whom he'd known in his youth. When he had time," recalls Candide Charkviani, First Secretary of the Georgian Party, whose name reminded Stalin of his patron, Father Kote Charkviani of Gori, "he kept in touch with his schoolmates. Stalin used to tell stories of his childhood and then remember his friends and decide he wanted to see them. So it was arranged to invite them to the house in Gagra." Stalin enjoyed planning this dinner-party: "Let's invite Peter Kapanadze and Vaso Egnatashvili . . . I wonder how Tseradze is? He was a famous wrestler . . . It would be good to get him along and . . ."

Whereupon Kapanadze, Egnatashvili and the other old men were gathered and driven from Tiflis to the Black Sea up into the hills, along the precipitous drive, through the steel gates and the drive-through guardhouse, to Stalin's secret and heavily guarded mansion, Coldstream.

There, the guards brought them to Stalin, who was often clipping roses or weeding around his lemon-trees, reading on the verandah, writing in the wooden summerhouse that was balanced on the edge of the cliff or playing billiards. Dinner would be laid by almost invisible ladies in aprons who then disappeared. Stalin opened the Georgian wine. Everyone helped themselves to food, set out as a buffet.

"The guests had a good time," says Charkviani. Stalin was friendly and nostalgic—but there were also flashes of dictatorial fury. "During the dinner, there was an unpleasant moment when Stalin noticed a pack of Georgian cigarettes with an illustration of a saucily posed girl." Abruptly, he lost his temper: "When have you ever seen a decent woman in such a pose? This is unacceptable!"

Charkviani and the other apparatchiks promised to redesign the cigarettes. Stalin calmed down. Mostly, Soso and the old friends "talked about theatre, art, literature and partially about politics." He poignantly remembered his two wives, Kato and Nadya; he talked about the problems of his children—and Peter Kapanadze walked solemnly round the table to whisper his condolences for the death of Stalin's son Yakov. Stalin nodded sadly: "Many families lost sons." Then he recounted his father's drinking, the Gori wrestling bouts, his adventures in 1905, the antics of Kamo, Tsintsadze and his bank robbers, and his increasingly Herculean exploits in exile. But always the fearsome shadow of the Terror, the shameful human cost of the Revolution and the wicked price of Stalin's lust for power hung over them all.

"Stalin recalled the lives of other Old Bolsheviks and told anecdotes about them." He mentioned names that made the guests shiver slightly, for they were people whom Stalin himself had wantonly murdered. Sometimes he mused that they had been wrongly executed—on his orders. "I was surprised," says Charkviani, "that when he mentioned people who were unjustly liquidated, he talked with the calm detachment of a historian, showing neither sorrow nor rage—but speaking without rancour, with just a tone of light humour . . ." The only time Stalin explained this sentiment was, much earlier, in a letter to his mother: "You know the saying: 'While I live, I'll enjoy my violets, when I die the graveyard worms can rejoice.' "

Looking back into his secret past, the old dictator reflected: "Historians are the sort of people who'll discover not only facts that are buried underground but even those at the very bottom of the ocean—and reveal them to the world." He asked, almost to himself: "Can you keep a secret?"

Stalin casually looked through a glass darkly as he remembered the lives of his family, friends and acquaintances whose mixed destinies form a microcosm of the colossal tragedy of his reign.[1]

Stalin "was a bad and neglectful son, as he was father and husband," writes his daughter, Svetlana Alliluyeva Stalin. "He devoted his whole being to something else, to politics and struggle. And so people who weren't personally close were always more important to him than those who were." But, worse, he permitted, indeed encouraged, his politics to destroy and consume his loved ones.

By 1918, most of the Alliluyev children were working for Soso. When Stalin was sent down to Tsaritsyn (Stalingrad) in 1918 during the Civil War, he took his girlfriend Nadya Alliluyeva and her brother Fyodor on his armoured train as his assistants. When they returned, Nadya was effectively his wife, moving into his apartment in the Kremlin and blessing him with two children, a son, Vasily,* and a daughter, Svetlana. After the Civil War, Nadya worked for a while as one of Lenin's secretaries.

Anna Alliluyeva also got married during the Civil War. She accompanied Stalin and Dzerzhinsky on their mission to investigate the fall of Perm, where she fell in love with Dzerzhinsky's Polish assistant, Stanislas Redens, who became a senior secret policeman and a member of Stalin's court. Their brother Pavel served as a diplomat and military commissar

---

* Since he used Vasily as his Party alias, he in some ways named his son after himself.

in the Defence Commissariat. All flourished in Stalin's entourage. Yet Stalin's effect on the family was nothing short of apocalyptic.

The first tragedy was that of the clever but fragile Fyodor. During the Civil War, he was recruited into special forces being trained by Kamo. The psychotic former bank robber was obsessed with tests of loyalty under fire. To this end, he devised a plan to simulate his unit's capture by enemy Whites. "At night he would seize the comrades and lead them out to be shot. If any began to beg for mercy and turn traitor, he would shoot them . . . 'That way,' said Kamo, 'you could be absolutely sure they wouldn't let you down.'" One revealed himself—and was shot on the spot. Then came the ultimate test: he cut open the chest and tore out the heart. "Here," he told Fyodor, "is the heart of your officer!"

Fyodor lost his mind. "He sat in silence for a number of years in hospital," said his niece Svetlana. "Slowly speech came back and he became a human being again." He never worked, but he outlived Stalin.

The marriage to Nadya was at first quite happy. Members of the Alliluyev family moved into Stalin's apartment and his country house, Zubalovo, ironically the former home of a Baku oil baron. Nadya seemed content to be a housewife and mother but soon craved a serious career. The pressure of Stalin's personality, the political stress of the war on the peasantry, the strain of raising two children and studying for a degree, as well as her manic jealousy of his habitual flirting, broke Nadya. Suffering from depression, she committed suicide in November 1932.

Stalin's parents-in-law, Sergei and Olga, lived on in the Kremlin and the dacha even as he decimated their family. After Nadya's death, a heart-broken Stalin became close to Zhenya Alliluyeva, the wife of Pavel, and this may have led to an affair. If so, it was over by the time Stalin unleashed the Great Terror.

Stanislas Redens was arrested and shot despite the pleas of his wife, Anna. Pavel Alliluyev died in suspicious circumstances. After the Second World War, Stalin's sisters-in-law Anna and Zhenya irritated him by interfering in family and political matters, and becoming too close to various Jews under investigation. With Stalin's permission, Anna wrote her memoirs, but they turned out to be characteristically tactless, especially about his stiff arm. He ordered the arrest of the two women. When they were released on his death, both were convinced that Stalin had freed them, refusing to believe that he himself had been responsible for their misery. Anna lost her mind in jail, but she lived until 1964.[2]

· · ·

Stalin's other family, the Svanidzes, were just as unfortunate. His son Yakov did not see his father again until 1921 when his uncle, Alyosha Svanidze, and Kamo's sister brought him to Moscow. He moved into Stalin's and Nadya's household, but his slow Georgian ways infuriated his father. When Yakov bungled a suicide, more of a cry for help, Stalin laughed that "he could not even shoot straight."

Alyosha Svanidze, who married a beautiful Jewish soprano, remained an intimate friend. He and Soso were "like brothers." He served abroad, then returned in the early 1930s as Deputy Chairman of the Soviet State Bank. After Nadya's suicide, the Svanidzes, including Kato's sisters, became even closer to Stalin: Mariko worked in Moscow as Abel Yenukidze's secretary, while Sashiko Svanidze Monoselidze frequently stayed with Stalin.

Alyosha's wife, Maria, and his sister Sashiko competed with the Alliluyev women, Anna and Zhenya, to care for Stalin. In the early 1930s, they virtually lived with him, but their competition irked the dictator.

In 1935, Sashiko's husband, Monoselidze, asked Stalin for financial help, and he replied:

> *I've given 5,000 roubles to Sasha [Sashiko]. For the moment this will be enough for both of you. I have no more money or I'd send it. These are royalties I get for my speeches and articles . . . But this should remain between ourselves (you, me and Sasha). No one else should get to know about it, otherwise my other relatives and acquaintances will begin to pursue me and will never leave me alone. So this is how it must be.*
>
> *Misha! Live happily a thousand years! Give my greetings to our friends!*

> *Yours*
> *Soso*
> *19 February 1935*

> *P.S. If you meet my mother, give her my greetings*

Sashiko died of cancer in 1936, but her sister Mariko was arrested in the case against her boss, Yenukidze. The next year, Stalin ordered the arrest of Alyosha Svanidze and his wife. He told the NKVD to demand that Alyosha confess to being a German spy in return for his life. Alyosha refused defiantly. "Such aristocratic pride," said Stalin. Alyosha, his wife, Maria, and his sister Mariko were executed in 1941 as the Germans advanced. During the Terror, Stalin liked to excuse the arrest of other leading families: "What can I do? My own family is in jail!"

Stalin's son Yakov, by Kato Svanidze, married during the 1930s and had a daughter, Galina, who is still alive. During the German invasion, he was captured by the Nazis. His father believed he had betrayed him and had his wife arrested. But Yakov committed suicide without breaking. Afterwards, Stalin regretfully admitted the boy had been "a real man."[3]

As for the women in his life, their fates are often mysterious, but they received little favour when their lover became the Soviet leader.

"Glamourpuss," the schoolgirl Pelageya Onufrieva, became a teacher, but in 1917 left her profession and married a mechanic named Fomin. Her father and brothers were targeted as kulaks during Stalin's war on the peasantry in the early 1930s, and were exiled to Siberia. In 1937, her husband was arrested and held as a potential saboteur. As a result her son lost a scholarship to study at Leningrad University, whereupon she wrote to Stalin. The scholarship was restored. However, her husband was again arrested in 1947 and sentenced to ten years in prison as an Enemy of the People.

When she was interviewed in 1944 about the Leader, a secret policeman demanded the postcards and book given by Stalin. "But my life has been hard and nomadic," she retorted, "I had a big family and I couldn't keep everything, but I kept the book. So it's a shame to give it to you because it's my only memory, not so much of Stalin but of the man named Josef. That's what I called him. I would say we were friends. The book's precious to me and you can take it when I'm dead." The apparatchik confiscated the book.

Ludmilla Stal worked for many years in the Central Committee, was decorated and helped edit Stalin's works, dying before the Second World War. Tatiana Slavatinskaya prospered in the CC Secret Department, becoming a member of the Central Control Commission. But in 1937 her son-in-law, a general, was shot, her daughter and son arrested and exiled for eight years. She and her grandchildren were expelled from the House on the Embankment, where many of the elite lived. One grandson, Yury Trifonov, the writer, chronicled the experience in his novella *House on the Embankment*.

As far as we know, Stalin met up with only one of his girlfriends.* "In 1925," recalls his companion in Solvychegodsk, Tatiana Sukhova, "I moved to Moscow and wanted to see Comrade Stalin very much. I wrote to him. I was very surprised to hear his voice on the phone that very evening." Next day they met at his office on Old Square: "We talked about my work, our mutual friends and Solvychegodsk."

In 1929, when Stalin was taking the waters in Matsesta, in the south, Sukhova, a teacher, contacted him again. "Three young men in white suits came and collected me" and took her to his villa, where she was welcomed by Nadya Alliluyeva and Stalin. They reminisced over supper. Nadya asked her about young Stalin in exile: "I described his appearance and said that Comrade Stalin was never parted from his white hood." Nadya laughed, "saying she never imagined he was such a dandy!" Then Stalin proudly showed her his tomatoes in his vegetable garden and took her to a firing-range beside the house, where he hit a bull's-eye with a rifle. He let her fire a "small English Montecristo" pistol—but she missed. "How will you defend yourself?" Stalin asked her. When she told him that she was badly treated at her resthouse, he muttered, "They must be reprimanded."

But the next year Sukhova was implicated in Stalin's trial of Ramzin and others. She appealed to him and he received her. "Is this the first time you've got into a scrape?" he asked, adding, "I'm always getting into trouble myself." He then phoned her institute and protected her. "Henceforth you must fight for yourself." They never met again.[4]

Stalin left at least two illegitimate children in his wake. Neither received any direct help from their father.

Constantine Kuzakov, the son of Stalin's Solvychegodsk landlady, Maria, had the most interesting career of the two. When Kuzakova saw Stalin's appointment to the government in 1917, she wrote to him asking for help. When she received no reply, she approached Lenin's office, where Stalin's, wife Nadya, still worked. Without telling Stalin, she

---

* Sukhova's later memoirs are unpublished. Natasha Kirtava and Alvasi Talakvadze became Party workers in Batumi and lived into old age, revered for their early association with Stalin. Stefania Petrovskaya, his fiancée in Baku, remained a Party member and was implicated in the Slepkov Case of 1932–33. Slepkov himself was spared in 1932, then shot in 1937, but her fate is unknown. Serafima Khoroshenina, Stalin's partner in Vologda, was alive in the 1930s and recorded her memoirs, but her fate is likewise unknown.

increased Kuzakova's benefits payments, but she informed the father afterwards.

Stalin must have helped get the boy into Leningrad University. In 1932, the NKVD made him sign a statement promising never to discuss his "origin."

He taught philosophy at the Leningrad Military Mechanical Institute, and was promoted to work in the CC *apparat* in Moscow by Andrei Zhdanov, the magnate closest to Stalin. Constantine later said that Zhdanov knew his "origin." He never met his father, though "once Stalin stopped and looked at me and I felt he wanted to tell me something. I wanted to rush to him, but something stopped me. He waved his pipe and moved on." During the Second World War, Constantine was a decorated colonel, but his mother died of starvation in the Siege of Leningrad.

In the summer of 1947, Kuzakov was called into Zhdanov's office where he found the fearsome but flashy secret-police chief Victor Abakumov. They accused Kuzakov's deputy of being an American spy, and Kuzakov was implicated. Stalin would not sanction his arrest, but Kuzakov was tried by a court of honour and dismissed from the Party. He had three children, but could not even get a job as a janitor.

After Stalin's death and Beria's arrest, he rejoined the Party and rose to become the longtime director of Soviet television in the Culture Ministry, dying in 1996.

Stalin left Lidia Pereprygina with a son, Alexander, probably born early in 1917. She then married a peasant fisherman, Yakov Davydov, who adopted Alexander as his own. Lidia became a hairdresser in Igarka and had eight more children. "Stalin never helped her," reported KGB chief General Serov. Alexander "was told [the truth] by his mother Lidia years after her affair with Stalin," says his son Yury. They "kept quiet about it and only the few locals in Kureika knew whose son he really was."

Alexander became a postman and Komsomol instructor, but in 1935 the NKVD called him to Krasnoyarsk to sign a promise, similar to Kuzakov's, never to talk about his origins. Then it was suggested he might move to Moscow, but he refused, "always scared of what could happen to him." Alexander Davydov served in the Second World War as a private, was wounded thrice, then promoted to major after World War II. He ran the canteen in the mining-town Novokuznetsk, where he married and had three children, dying in 1987. "My father told me I was Stalin's grandson," says Yury, who lives with his family in Novosibirsk.[5]

1917–1918

Stalin and Lenin spent spring 1917 working at Bolshevik headquaters, the modernist palace of notorious ballerina and Romanov mistress Kseshinskaya, where Lenin addressed the crowds in April.

Lenin, after demanding immediate revolution, tried to restrain Bolshevik hotheads but the abortive July Days coup, encouraged by Stalin, almost lost them the Revolution.

Love in Revolution: Stalin had known Nadya Alliluyeva since she was a child *(top left)* but when they met again in the summer of 1917, she was sixteen, a schoolgirl *(top right and at left)*. She worshipped the heroic Georgian who entertained her with jokes, readings and mimicry.

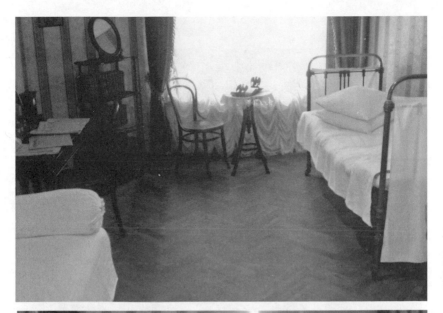

Stalin spent the summer hiding in the Alliluyev apartment, doted on by Nadya. *Top:* Stalin's bed with the mirror where he shaved Lenin. From his bed, he could see into Nadya's bedroom—through an adjoining door *(above)*. That summer they fell in love.

Lenin, in real danger, placed his safety in the hands of Stalin, his underworld expert, who moved him into the Alliluyev apartment, shaved and bewigged him, then smuggled him to Finland.

Top: Lenin called his government the Council of People's Commissars. Here is Lenin *(centre)* as Chairman, Stalin *(top left)*, Trotsky *(third row, right)* and, amongst others, Lunarcharsky *(second row, right)*, Dybenko *(bottom row, right)* and Antonov-Ovseenko, who commanded the storming of the Winter Palace *(bottom row, centre)*. The latter two were shot during the Great Terror on Stalin's orders. *Bottom:* Uprising. As Bolshevik forces seized the Winter Palace, an exhausted and impatient Lenin, Trotsky and Stalin formed a new government at their headquarters, the Smolny, the former girls' school patronised by Tsarina Alexandra. Afterwards Lenin and Trotsky slept on newspapers on the floor. Stalin fell asleep in a chair; Lunarcharsky, the new People's Commissar for Culture, kissed him on the forehead; Stalin awoke laughing.

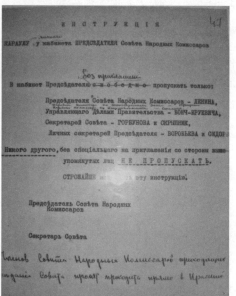

Stalin immediately became, with Trotsky, Lenin's inseparable troubleshooter. At the first meeting of the new government *(top)* a blurred Stalin hovers right behind Lenin. *Left:* Lenin's orders to his guards on access to his office. Lenin's writing below line three specifies that only Stalin and Trotsky could enter without an appointment.

Power at last. After eighteen years in the underground, Josef Djugashvili-Stalin, aged thirty-eight, is People's Commissar of Nationalities.

The sexually liberated feminist Bolshevik, Alexandra Kollontai, and her younger lover, strapping sailor Pavel Dybenko. At the first government meeting, Stalin sniggered to Trotsky about their passionate whisperings behind a screen. Trotsky rebuked him. They never made small talk again.

Stalin goes to war: When Lenin's government fought for survival in a savage civil war and brutal terror, Stalin blossomed. His paranoid bloodlust became the ruling genius of the Soviet Empire.

· · ·

Until Stalin organized the reconquest of Georgia in 1921,* his mother lived in a different country. Afterwards, Soso was reunited with Keke during his bitter visit to Tiflis, where he found himself hated as a bloody conqueror and former bandit.

Stalin wrote Keke regular letters, but kept his distance. "Lively and chatty," she was the only person in Stalin's world who dared ask: "I wonder why my son was not able to share power with Trotsky?" Stalin could never tolerate such independence.

Keke came on a short visit to Moscow and met Nadya. "This woman is my wife," Stalin warned Keke. "Try not to give her any trouble." She preferred to live in a two-room apartment in the old Viceroy's Palace on Golovinsky Prospect in Tiflis. Nadya sent her letters with news and photographs of the children. When Stalin was climbing to power, his letters were short:

My Mama, Live 10,000 years!

> *Yours,*
> *Kiss*
> *Soso*
> *1 January 1923*

Keke grumbled that he did not pay her enough attention: "Mama, I know you're disappointed in me but what can I do? I'm very busy and can't write too often. Day and night I'm up to my neck in it. Yours. Kiss. Soso, 25 January 1925." Or she ignored him and went on with her own life: "Mama, How are you? You didn't write for a long time. Maybe you're

---

* Georgia caused Stalin's schism with Lenin. Menshevik Georgia became independent in 1918. The Old Man was content to leave Georgia, but in 1921 Stalin and Sergo Ordzhonikidze arranged a successful invasion. The dashing, merciless Sergo rode triumphantly into Tiflis on a white horse, but he soon earned the nicknamed "Stalin's Ass" for his brutal suppression of the country. When it came time to define the status of Georgia, Stalin insisted that it join a Transcaucasian Federation, but the local Bolsheviks, led by the flamboyant Mdivani and the ideologue Makharadze, both associates of Stalin's for decades, demanded a separate Georgian republic. In the ensuing row between the Stalinists and the so-called deviationists, Sergo punched one of their opponents. This outraged Lenin, who now supported the Georgians against Stalin and Sergo. This led to Stalin's insulting Lenin's wife, Krupskaya. Lenin wrote his Testament, which demanded Stalin's removal from the General Secretaryship. But it was too late. Lenin suffered another stroke. Stalin survived.

annoyed with me. But what to do? I'm so busy. I sent you 150 roubles, I can't send more. If you need more, tell me how much. Yr Soso."

Their lack of intimacy was clearer after Nadya's suicide:

Greetings Mother dear

I got the jam, the ginger and the chukhcheli *[Georgian candy]. The children are very pleased and send you their thanks. I am well, so don't worry about me. I can endure my destiny. I don't know whether or not you need money. I'm sending you 500 roubles just in case. I'm sending also a photograph of me and the children . . .*

Keep well dear Mother and keep your spirits up. A kiss.

> *Your son*
> *Soso*
> *24 March 1934*

P.S. The children bow to you. After Nadya's death, my private life has been very hard, but a strong man must always be valiant.

When he visited her for the last time in 1936, she said she wished he had become a priest. This half-amused Stalin. He sent her medicines and clothes. When she deteriorated, he encouraged her. "Glad your health is good," he wrote in 1937. "Evidently our clan is strong!" She died soon afterwards amid the Great Terror. Stalin did not attend her funeral, but his wreath read: "Dear and beloved mother. From her son Josef Djugashvili." She was buried splendidly in the church on Holy Mountain.[6]

Stalin kept in contact with old friends from Gori and Tiflis. Sometimes he wrote them a note or just sent them money out of the blue. If they appealed to him, he liked to help. In 1933, he wrote to Kapanadze:

Hi Peta, as you see . . . I'm sending you 2,000 roubles. I haven't got more now. This money is a publishing royalty and we don't accept many royalties, but your needs are a special occasion for me . . . Apart from this money, you'll be given a 3,000-rouble loan. I've told Beria about this . . .

> *Live long and be happy*
> *Beso*

During the war, Kapanadze and Glurjidze, both ex-priests, and Tser-adze, his wrestling friend, got even luckier. On 9 May 1944, Stalin noticed the cash piling up in his safe (from his salaries as Party Secretary-General, Premier, Supreme Commander-in-Chief, People's Commissar of Defence and Supreme Soviet deputy). He could not spend the money so he scrawled this note:

1. To my friend Peter Kapanadze—40,000 roubles;
2. 30,000 roubles to Grisha Glurjidze;
3. 30,000 roubles to Mikhail Tseradze.

The note to Glurjidze read: "Grisha! Accept this small gift from me. Your Soso." He was indulgent to those who never dabbled in politics but it is unlikely he would have spared Iremashvili and Davrichewy. They opposed him politically.*

When Stalin seized Georgia in 1921, Iremashvili attended the funerals of those who fell in battle and found himself standing next to Keke Dju-gashvili. "Keke, it's your son who is to blame for this," said Iremashvili, who knew her well from Gori. "Write to him in Moscow: he's no longer my friend!" When Stalin visited Tiflis later that year, Iremashvili was arrested, but his sister appealed to Stalin, "who showed benevolent kind-ness to her: 'What a pity! It hurts me greatly for him. Hopefully [Ire-mashvili] will find his way back to me!' " Stalin ordered him to be freed and then invited him over. Iremashvili refused. He was arrested again and found himself under the control of Tsintsadze, Stalin's gangster, now a senior secret policeman. Stalin had him expelled to Germany, where he flirted with Fascism and wrote his hostile memoirs.

The colourful Davrichewy, Gori police officer's son and fellow bank robber, escaped to Paris. Under the name "Jean Violan," he became a famous First World War pilot and served as a French spy. Some accounts

---

* The Mensheviks enjoyed a strange trajectory: Karlo Chkheidze, as we saw, became the most powerful man in the early 1917 Revolution as Chairman of the Petrograd Soviet, while his fellow Georgian Menshevik Irakli Tsereteli became a powerful Russian minister during the summer of 1917. But when the Bolsheviks seized power, Chkheidze, Jordania, Tsereteli and Noe Ramishvili became the leaders of the independent Georgia. When the Bolsheviks invaded, they managed to flee into exile. Chkheidze committed suicide in 1926, Ramishvili was murdered in Paris in 1930. Jordania, Uratadze, Arsenidze, Sagirashvili and Nikolaevsky all survived in exile and wrote their memoirs. Sukhanov, who called Stalin a "grey blur," was shot in the Great Terror.

claim that he had an affair with the notorious courtesan Mata Hari, executed as a traitor in 1917, but the real story of his sexual espionage is no less dramatic. The French secret service suspected a beautiful young adventuress and aviatrix, Marthe Richard, of being a German spy. They enrolled the flying ace Davrichewy to watch her. She fell in love with "Zozo" Davrichewy and they started an affair so passionate that he threatened to kill himself if she was arrested. He managed to prove her innocence; she joined French intelligence and was despatched to Madrid, where she seduced the septuagenarian German intelligence chief.

In 1936, Stalin contacted Davrichewy and invited him to return. Wisely, Davrichewy stayed in Paris. Just after Stalin's death, Davrichewy declared in an interview: "I am Stalin's half brother." He himself died in 1975 after a life described in an obituary as "astonishing—revolutionary, aviator, spy, author." His remarkable memoirs were obscurely published in French in 1979.[7]

Kamo remained a Bolshevik hero, despite his macabre behaviour with Fyodor Alliluyev. But this dangerous simpleton was unsuited to peacetime work. He became a Chekist but his cruelty was too deranged even for them. By 1922, he was back in Tiflis employed in the customs service. When Lenin considered a Caucasian holiday, Kamo insisted on accompanying him: Lenin never came. According to Tiflis legend, Kamo drank too much, chattering about Stalin's role in the Tiflis bank robbery, a sensitive subject.* He was bicycling home after starting his memoirs when he was run over by a truck. It was said Stalin had him killed: after all, went the joke, it seemed a bit of a coincidence that the only bicycle in Tiflis should be hit by the only truck.

Kamo was buried in the Pushkin Gardens outside the Tilipuchuri Tavern in Yerevan Square, scene of his notorious exploit. His statue replaced that of Pushkin. Later Stalin ordered the removal of his monument. Kamo was reburied elsewhere.[8]

Egnatashvili, Soso's protector and possibly father, educated his two surviving sons, Sasha and Vaso, at a private school in Moscow. The family were restaurant entrepreneurs and soon expanded outside Gori.

---

* Tsintsadze joined the Georgian Cheka in 1921, and he too wrote his memoirs, at the same time as Kamo—but he was considerably more tactful. He joined the Georgian "deviationists" opposition to Stalin and was dismissed. Arrested as a Trotskyite, he died of TB in prison in 1930.

Egnatashvili and his sons established restaurants in Baku, while Vaso qualified from Kharkov University, becoming a history teacher.

Old Egnatashvili died in 1929, "very close to Stalin until his last day." Sasha Egnatashvili ran five restaurants in Tiflis until about 1929. In the early 1930s, both brothers were arrested. Sasha contacted Yenukidze, who had him released and brought to Moscow, where he was received by Stalin. Vaso was also released immediately. Stalin enrolled Sasha in the NKVD, and appointed him to run a Politburo dacha in the Crimea before promoting him to his own Guards Department. Sasha, the former capitalist restaurateur, was made chief of Stalin's catering department, known as the Base, a trusted position for a paranoid dictator who used poison on others and feared it himself. Egnatashvili became the dictator's food-taster, hence his nickname in the NKVD: "the Rabbit." Within the NKVD, he was quietly known as "Stalin's relative" or "brother," even by General Vlasik, who knew the dictator better than anyone. (One of Sasha's underlings was a cook who had contrived, in an astonishing culinary career hidden in the catering shadows of the NKVD universe, to serve not only Rasputin in his early days but also Lenin and Stalin: this world-historical chef was the grandfather of President Vladimir Putin.)

Vaso, who had been a Socialist-Federalist, not even a Menshevik, was promoted to editor of a Tiflis newspaper, then to Secretary of the Georgian Supreme Soviet, Stalin's eyes and ears in Georgia.

Sasha the Rabbit lived near Stalin's Kuntsevo mansion, his main residence, and often attended his dinners. When Vaso visited Moscow, he always stayed with Stalin. They remained close to Keke. Sasha Egnatashvili's letter to Stalin's mother on her birthday in 1934 reveals their special relationship: "My dear spiritual mother, Yesterday I visited Soso and we talked a long time . . . He's put on weight . . . Over the last four years, I've never seen him so healthy. More handsome than you can imagine. He was joking a lot. Who says he's older? He's younger than four years ago—no one thinks he's more than forty-seven!"

In 1940, Stalin remembered his father's old cobbling apprentice Dato Gasitashvili, who had been very kind to him as a boy. "Is Dato still alive?" he suddenly asked Sasha. "I haven't seen him for ages." Egnatashvili summoned Dato, still a Gori cobbler, to Moscow.

One day Stalin, his chief of personal security, Vlasik, and Beria arrived at the Egnatashvilis' for a Georgian feast: Stalin was reunited with Dato. When Stalin teased him, the old cobbler fearlessly replied: "Do you think you're Stalin to me as you are to others? To me you are the same little boy I held in my arms. And if you carry on, I'll pull down your trousers and spank your bottom until it's redder than your flag!" Stalin laughed. But, ominously, he noticed Sasha's wife: the Rabbit had happily but dangerously married an ethnic German ex-wife of a Jewish-Armenian businessman: their daughter lived in America.

"Your wife's in a bad mood," Stalin said. "Is she offended with me?"

Sasha explained that, being German, she was afraid for herself and for her daughter in America.

"We've an agreement with Germany but it doesn't mean anything," Stalin reassured her, according to Sasha's grandson, Guram Ratishvili. "War is inevitable. America and Britain will be our allies."

When the Germans invaded in 1941, Egnatashvili's wife was arrested and shot. "She just disappeared and never returned," says Sasha's grandson, "but Sasha never mentioned this to Stalin." Egnatashvili knew the rules of Stalin's court.

During the war, Egnatashvili, now a general, accompanied Stalin to Teheran and Yalta. "A Georgian chef in charge of supplying wine and shashlik was made lieutenant-general!" carps Khrushchev in his memoirs. "Whenever I came back from the front, I noticed he'd been awarded one or two more medals! And I remember Stalin once even gave me a dressing-down in front of this Lieutenant-General for provisions: he even got drunk with Stalin and the rest of us." Stalin the Russian warlord was sensitive to such attitudes—and he also learned from Beria about the corruption* in his households, transferring Egnatashvili to be director of the

---

* The Egnatashvilis had known Beria since 1918 in Baku, where he was a Bolshevik double-agent in the Azeri Musavist Party—or vice-versa. When Beria fell ill, the Egnatashvilis nursed their fellow Georgian. When Beria became Caucasian viceroy, then NKVD boss, he tried to keep a monopoly of information and influence in the Caucasus. Yet the Egnatashvilis were independent of Beria. Furthermore Sasha Egnatashvili served in Stalin's Guards Department under chief bodyguard General Vlasik, which was also outside Beria's power, a situation that Beria constantly tried to remedy. After the Second World War, Beria accused Vlasik of corruption in selling the gigantic quantities of food for Stalin prepared at the Base. Vlasik counteraccused Beria of corruption and managed to survive, but Egnatashvili, who ran the Base, would probably have been implicated. The duel between Beria and Vlasik for control of the guards lasted until Stalin's death. This is the first time that the story of General Egnatashvili and his wife has been told. It fits into a pattern. After the suicide of his wife, Nadya, Stalin distrusted the spouses of his courtiers. The pretty young wives of Alexander Poskrebyshev, his *chef de cabinet,* and Marshal Kulik, his military crony, were shot; the wives of the head of state, Kalinin, and Foreign Minister, Molotov, were arrested. Yet all these men continued to serve him devotedly without a word. See *Stalin: The Court of the Red Tsar.*

State Dachas in the Crimea to prepare the Big Three Yalta Conference. But afterwards he left Egnatashvili behind.

The Rabbit died of diabetes in 1948. Vaso Egnatashvili remained close to Stalin, attending those dinners of old Gori friends. But on Stalin's death Beria fired Vaso and jailed him. When Beria fell, Vaso was released, dying in 1956.[9]

The fate of Stalin's Bolshevik comrades was tragic, never mind the fate of the Soviet people. Kamenev and Zinoviev were shot in 1936, Bukharin in 1938; Trotsky was murdered with an icepick in 1940—all on Stalin's orders. During 1937–38, around one and a half million people were shot. Stalin personally signed deathlists for almost 39,000 people, many of them old acquaintances. Georgia, where Stalin's rising magnate Beria was in charge, was hit especially severely: 10 percent of the Communist Party were purged; 425 out of the 644 delegates to the Tenth Georgian Party Congress were shot.

The star victim was Stalin's old friend, Budu "the Barrel" Mdivani, who had several times saved his life in earlier days. But Mdivani had resisted Stalin in 1921 and the loquacious ex-actor irreverently joked that Beria should put an armed guard around Keke's house—not for her protection, but so she never gave birth to another Stalin. Stalin was reconciled with Budu in the 1920s. When he was in Moscow, Budu usually stayed with him. Stalin often visited the Mdivanis in Georgia—even becoming godfather to their son. But Stalin had not forgotten Mdivani's opposition. In 1937, he was arrested for plotting to kill Stalin and shot soon afterwards, along with most of his family.

The case of three of Soso's closest Georgian acquaintances reveals how differently things could turn out in the universe of diabolical randomness. Sunny, genial, hedonistic and conciliatory, Abel Yenukidze, Nadya Stalin's godfather, became Secretary of the Central Executive Committee, in charge of the Kremlin, the Party villas and the Bolshoi Ballet, which he used as his own private dating agency, becoming notorious for his taste for teenage ballerinas (and their mothers).

Uncle Abel was close friends with Stalin, but always preserved his own opinion. In his memoirs about the Baku printing-presses, he refused to praise Stalin for things he had not done. "Koba wants me to tell him he's a genius but I won't do it," he complained. He was sceptical of the growing repression, priding himself on sheltering persecuted Georgian comrades. Yet he and Stalin often holidayed together, sending each other affectionate notes. However, in 1936 Stalin selected Yenukidze as the first of his inner circle to be liquidated, even though he had never been a member of any formal opposition. He was arrested and shot in 1937.

Kavtaradze, on the other hand, had been a member of every opposition from the 1920s onwards. He not only threw a lantern at Stalin but later backed first Mdivani, then the Trotskyites. Yet each time Stalin saved, helped and promoted him.

In 1937, Kavtaradze was arrested (again) as a member of Mdivani's "conspiracy" and sentenced to death for planning to murder Stalin. The others were all killed, but the dictator spared Kavtaradze by placing a dash next to his name on the deathlist. In 1940 Stalin, deciding that he missed him, freed him and invited him to dinner the same night. They got on well, even though Stalin teased him, "To think you wanted to kill me." A few days later, he and Beria dined at Kavtaradze's apartment: their host was made head of the State Publishing House, then Deputy Foreign Minister and Ambassador to Rumania. He survived Stalin, dying in 1961.

Sergo Ordzhonikidze was, by the 1930s, the last Old Bolshevik with the prestige to challenge Stalin. As Stalin's enforcer he conquered the Caucasus in 1920–21, helped defeat the oppositions in the 1920s and ran heavy industry in the Five Year Plan into the 1930s. He and Stalin were inseparable, living in the same building, writing each other cosy notes, holidaying together. But in 1937 they clashed. Sergo committed suicide in the Kremlin.

Yet some of the earlier comrades survived.* Kalinin served from 1919 until his death in 1946 as head of state (Chairman of the Supreme Soviet). Marshal Voroshilov served as Defence Commissar, a vicious henchman during the Terror, and an inept bungler in the Finnish and Great Patriotic Wars. Stalin tormented Voroshilov with being "an English agent." Yet he outlived his master to become Soviet head of state until 1960.

---

* Mikha Tskhakaya, the greybeard who had promoted and protected Stalin in the early years before turning against Lenin and retiring to Genevan exile, survived to die in 1950 in his bed, an honoured Old Bolshevik. Inexplicably, Makharadze was allowed to survive the Terror. Stepan Shaumian, Stalin's roommate in London and junior partner in the Tiflis bank robbery and then Baku, was the brutal master of the Baku Commune in 1918 when he oversaw the murder of around 15,000 Azeris. He was then overthrown and shot by the Whites and the British as one of the legendary Twenty-six Commissars. Stalin then adopted Shaumian's son, Levan, and brought him up in his own household. Stalin's Siberian roommate and Soviet head of state Yakov Sverdlov died of influenza in 1919.

Meyer Wallach became Maxim Litvinov, People's Commissar for Foreign Affairs during the 1930s, later Soviet Ambassador in Washington. He was outspoken in his criticisms of Stalin, who planned a fatal car crash for him yet allowed him to survive, perhaps because he remembered Litvinov saving him from the dockers in London but more likely because of his international prestige. Stalin promoted his host in Vienna, Troyanovsky, making him the first Soviet Ambassador to the United States, and allowed him to live, even though he and Litvinov privately criticized him.

When he met Stalin again in 1918, Vyshinsky was clever enough neither to hide his unreliable political past nor to try to remind Stalin of the favours he had done him in Bailov Prison: he just formally, politely offered his services. As rebarbative, bloodthirsty and terrifying as he was cowardly and terrorized, he became the Soviet Procurator-General, the star inquisitor of the 1930s show-trials, and, in 1949, Stalin's last Foreign Minister. He died in 1954.

Molotov served as Premier from 1930 to 1941 and Foreign Commissar from 1939 until 1949. Stalin started to view him as a potential successor and, in 1952, viciously denounced his old partner. Chosen for liquidation,* Molotov was saved by Stalin's death but remained devoted to him. He became Foreign Minister again but failed to overthrow Khrushchev in 1957. Exiled as Ambassador to Mongolia, he lived until 1985, still seeing Stalin in his dreams.[10]

Until his last day, Stalin never ceased trying to glorify his past and conceal his early mistakes. The cult served his shameless vainglory and contributed to his political potency, yet he liked to assume a becoming modesty in front of colleagues. At heart, he was too intelligent not to appreciate that many of the paeans to his youth were ridiculous. When he saw Georgian writer Gamsakhurdia's *Youth of the Leader,* he wrote: "I ask you to prohibit publication of Gamsakhurdia's book in Russian. J. Stalin."

He was even more outraged by Fedorov's *Kartvelian Novelties,* published in 1940, scribbling in green pencil: "Comrade Pospelov was idiotic and tactless to approve Fedorov's book about me without my agreement

---

* His Jewish wife, Polina, was equally devoted to Stalin and became a Deputy Commissar in her own right, but her strident feminism irritated Stalin, while her friendship with Nadya made him uneasy. He almost destroyed her in 1939, considered having her murdered in a car crash and finally forced Molotov to vote for her arrest in 1949. The full story is in *Stalin: The Court of the Red Tsar.*

and knowledge. Fedorov's book must be pulped—and Pospelov must be punished. Stalin."

When Samoilova, an Old Bolshevik acquaintance from Baku days, asked if she could exhibit proofs of Stalin's earlier books and articles in her museum, she received this handwritten note: "I never thought you'd be so stupid in your old age! If the book's published in millions, why'd you need the manuscript? I *burned* all the manuscripts!" When a book was compiled of memoirs from 1905, Soso wrote three words: "Don't publish! Stalin."[11]

At dinner in his seaside villa, the ageing Stalin told stories to his old friends about these people from the past, some of whom had perished in their beds, many of whom had died in his dungeons with a bullet in the back of the head.

The old men had their say too. "They complained," observes Molotov, "about bribery and corruption everywhere." Another of these old Georgians "of whom Stalin was particularly fond," says Khrushchev, "told Stalin about the bad situation among youngsters in Georgia." Stalin was incensed and launched a purge of his homeland.

Presently the old men, several of whom had sung with Soso in the Gori and seminary choirs in white surplices, started to sing. "Georgian songs were heard late at night wafting from the Coldstream villa, sometimes accompanied by the host—a good old singer with a sweet voice . . ."

Soso was old, sclerotic and forgetful, yet until his death aged seventy-four, on 5 March 1953, the ageing choirboy remained the peerless politician, paranoid megalomaniac and aberrant master of human misery on a scale only paralleled by Hitlerite Germany. Responsible for the deaths of around 20 to 25 million people, Stalin imagined he was a political, military, scientific and literary genius, a people's monarch, a red Tsar.

Perhaps the young Stalin should have the last word. In August 1905, Soso, aged twenty-seven, mocked just such a deluded megalomaniac in a rarely read but weirdly self-prophesying article for *Proletariatis Brdzola*. "Before your eyes," he writes, "rises the hero of Gogol's story who, in a state of aberration, imagined he was the King of Spain. Such," concluded the young Stalin, "is the fate of all megalomaniacs."[12]

Stalin's Names, Nicknames, Bylines and Aliases

Josef Vissarionovich
   Djugashvili
Soso
Soselo
Beso
Koba
Petrov
Ivanovich
Koba Ivanovich
Besoshvili
Ivan Ivanovich Vissarionovich
Galiashvili
Simon Jvelaya
K. Kato
Gaios Besovich Nizheradze
Organez Totomiants
Zakhar Melikiants
Peter Chizhikov
Vasily, Vasiliev, Vasya, Vaska
Oddball Osip
Osip Koba

Ivanov
Pockmarked Oska
The Caucasian
The Milkman
The Pockmarked One
The Loper (Geza)
The Staggerer (Kunkula)
Pockmarked (Chopura)
David
The Priest
Father Koba
Giorgi Berdzenoshvili
K. Stefin
Ioska Koriavyi (Joe Pox)
K. St.
K. Safin
K. Solin
Koba Stalin
J. Djugashvili-Stalin
J. V. Stalin

Acknowledgements

I have been helped in my work on Stalin by many people in many countries and cities including my publishers all over the world, but especially in places visited by my subject. All have been extraordinarily generous to me in terms of time and knowledge. Needless to say, all the mistakes in this book are mine alone.

I must first thank my godfathers in the writing of Russian history, who have checked my work, improved on it and hopefully taught me how to write better: Isabel de Madariaga was and remains my first historical patroness and my books still, I pray, show the benefits of her strict but benign supervision of my first book on Catherine the Great and Prince Potemkin.

In this book, I have been hugely fortunate that two titans of Soviet history, Robert Conquest and Professor Robert Service, have kindly read the text for errors. I owe much to the professor of Russian and Eurasian Studies at Mt. Holyoke College, Stephen Jones, the chief authority on Georgian socialism, who shared his work with me, answered my questions and diligently corrected the text. Dr. David Anderson, senior lecturer in Arctic Anthropology, University of Aberdeen, corrected my Siberian sections with great generosity and patience. Dr. Piers Vitebsky, head of Anthropology and Russian Northern Studies at the Scott Polar Research Institute, Cambridge, advised me on Siberian anthropology and allowed me to use one of his photographs. I must also thank Professor Donald Rayfield, who has generously shared with me his wide knowledge of

Russian literature, Georgian culture and Bolshevik political history, as well as his contacts in Georgia, and has allowed me to quote his superb translations of Stalin's poetry in full.

I am very grateful to Professor George Hewitt for his kind help with the languages of the Caucasus and his contacts in Abkhazia, which have been invaluable. I cannot sufficiently thank Dr. Claire Mouradian, based in Paris, who, even though we have never met, placed at my disposal her encyclopaedic knowledge of Caucasian history and her wide contacts with the Georgian/Armenian émigré families, interviewed old witnesses and guided me to new sources.

The bulk of the new material in this work comes from the Caucasus. In Georgia, I must first thank the President and First Lady, Mikheil and Sandra Saakashvili. Tragically the archives of the Georgian Filial Institute of Marxism-Leninism (GF IML) have fallen into disrepair and only the personal decree of the President allowed me access to the sources that form the heart of this book. Natalia Kancheli, a senior aide to the President, and a great supporter, helped make this possible and I am eternally grateful. Gela Charkviani, an old friend and veteran of modern Georgian politics as well as the son of one of Stalin's confidants, started helping me when I was a war correspondent in early 1990s Caucasia but also gave me access to the manuscript of his father's memoirs, and found me all my helpers in Georgia. His niece Nestan Charkviani, herself a distinguished historian of Stalinism, helped me enormously in the archives, which she knows well, and in finding new sources and memoirs and interviewing new witnesses; she also read and corrected the text. I owe much to Nino Kereselidze, a fine historian, an industrious researcher and an impressive translator from Georgian. Thanks also to the GF IML's chief archivist, Vazha Ebanoidze.

Many others helped me in Georgia: Peter Mamradze, another old friend from the turbulence of recent politics, found me new witnesses and shared his knowledge of the Stalin folklore in Georgia. My friend Professor Zakro Megrilishvili again helped me access the unpublished Kavtaradze manuscript, his stepfather's memoirs, and work out the Tiflis bank robbery. Thanks too to Professor Nugzar Surgoladze. I am deeply grateful to another friend, George Tarkhan-Mouravi, who helped me out of pure friendship and a spirit of curiosity and offered me his contacts, his vast knowledge of sources and his family anecdotes. Professor Vahtang Guruli shared his unique archival research with me. Gia Sulkanishvili helped in small and big matters, and as ever I owe him much. Nick

Tabatadze, the head of Rustavi-2, the Georgian television station, gave encouragement and help; his station's TV report helped me find more witnesses and sources. Thanks to Tamara Megrilishvili, who let me advertise for sources/witnesses in her bookshop, Prospero's Books, the best between Moscow and Jerusalem; to Leka Basilieia; in Gori, to the director of the Stalin Museum, Gaioz Makhniashvili.

In the archives of Batumi, Adjaria, Memed Jikhashvili, an excellent historian of Transcaucasia but also a piece of history himself, as the nephew of Nestor Lakoba, Stalin's Abkhazian viceroy, helped me find new sources and pictures that were immensely important for the book.

In Abkhazia, I must thank Slava Lakoba, outstanding historian of Bolshevism, Abkhazia and Caucasia, who was extremely generous in sharing his work and above all his sources. George Hewitt and Donald Rayfield both helped me in this quest, as did Dr. Rachel Clogg.

In Baku, Azerbaijan, thanks to Fuad Akhundov, another old friend and expert on the oil boom and millionaires; to Fikret Aliev and Zimma Babaeva, director and deputy director of the Azeri State Archive (GIA AR and GA AR); and to Memed Jikhashvili too.

In Berlin and Baku, I owe much to Professor Jorg Baberowski, the chief expert on Baku and the violent culture of the Caucasus, who was very generous to me with his knowledge; and to Alexander Freese, for translating from German.

In Vienna, thanks to HSH Prince Karel Schwarzenberg, Peter and Lila Morgan, and Georg Hamann. Lisa Train visited the flat where Stalin stayed and took fine photographs. In Finland, thanks to my editor for his help with Tampere research, Aleksi Siltala; to Vuokko Tarpila; to the writer Aarno Laitinen; and to the Finnish expert on Lenin, Stalin and Finland Antti Kujola. In Sweden, thanks to Per Faustino and all my editors at Norstedts/Prisma, to Martin Stugart of *Dagens Nyheter*, to researcher Jenny Lankjaer, to Karen Altenberg, to Per Mogren. In Holland, thanks to two distinguished Dutch Stalin scholars, Erik van Ree and Marc Jansen, for their sharing of research. In Cracow, Poland, thanks to the London filmmaker Wanda Koscia and her friend Marta Szostkiewicz for her help.

In Russia, neither of my books on Stalin would have been possible without the generosity, help, encouragement and knowledge of Oleg Khlevniuk, the doyen of Stalin historians, senior researcher at the State Archive of the Russian Federation (GARF), and Alexander Kamenskii, professor of Early and Early-Modern Russian History at Moscow's Russian State University for Humanities. The chief Russian source for both my Stalin books is the Presidential Archive of the Russian State Archive of Social and Political History (RGASPI): so my gratitude to the director Dr. Kirill M. Anderson, the deputy director Dr. Oleg V. Naumov and the head of section and expert on Stalin's papers/handwriting, Larisa A. Rogovaya, is limitless. But I owe the biggest thanks to Dr. Galina Babkova, a distinguished lecturer on eighteenth-century history at Moscow University, who has helped me as much on this book as she did on its predecessors.

The following helped me in Russia: Vladimir Grigoriev, publisher and politician, Anatoly Cherekmasov and Zoia Belyakova in St. Petersburg, Dmitri Yakushkin, Eduard Radzinsky, Roy and Zhores Medvedev, Boris Ilizarov, Arkady Vaksberg, Larissa Vasilieva, Masha Slonim, Dmitri Khankin, Anastasia Webster, Tom Wilson, David Campbell, Marc and Rachel Polonsky and Dr. Luba Vinogradova. I am grateful to the director of the Smolny Institute Museum and Svetlana Osipova of the Alliluyev Museum in Petersburg. In Achinsk, I thank the director of the Achinsk Regional Museum; in Vologda, thanks to the director of VOANPI (Archive of Modern History of the Vologda Region) and to the director of GAVO (State Archive of the Vologda Region).

In America, thanks to Professor J. Arch Getty of UCLA for his generous sharing of Yezhov's dossier; to Professor Ron Suny; to Dr. Charles King of Georgetown; and to Roman Brackman, for kindly sharing some of his original sources with me. I am also very grateful to Prince David Chavchavadze and Princess Marusya Chavchavadze, to Redjeb Jordania and Nicole Jordania, to Musa Train Klebnikov, and her husband, the late, unique, much missed Paul Klebnikov, who encouraged me so much; and to Prince and Princess Constantine and Ann Sidamon-Eristoff.

In Stanford, California, thanks to Carol A. Leadenham and Irina Zaytseva, for their help with the Okhrana and Boris Nikolaevsky archives; to Alex Doran and Dr. Boris Orlov in Israel; and in Paris, thanks to Dr. George Mamoulia.

Perhaps the most exciting witness interviewed was Mariam Svanidze, aged 109, a relative of Stalin's wife who still remembers her death in 1907. For their interviews, memoirs, and family anecdotes, thanks to Sandra Roelofs Saakashvili (whose book tells the story of how her husband's family sheltered Stalin), Eteri Ordzhonikidze (daughter of Sergo), General Artem Sergeev (Stalin's adopted son), Galina Djugashvili (Stalin's granddaughter), Stalin's nephews and niece Leonid Redens, Kira Alliluyev and Vladimir Alliluyev (Redens), General Stepan Mikoyan (son of Anastas) and his daughter Ashken Mikoyan, Stalin's son-in-law Yuri Zhdanov (son of Andrei), Izolda Mdivani (widow of Budu's son), Susanna Toroshelidze (daughter of Malakia and Minadora), Zakro Megrilishvili (stepson of Shalva Nutsubidze), Martha Peshkova (daughter-in-law of Beria, granddaughter of Gorky), Vyacheslav Nikonov (grandson and biographer of Molotov), the late Maya Kavtaradze (daughter of Sergei Kavtaradze), the late Oleg Troyanovsky (son of Alexander), Katevan Gelovani (cousin of the Svanidzes), Memed Jikhashvili (nephew of Nestor Lakoba), Redjeb Jordania (son of Noe), Tanya Litvinova (daughter of Maxim), Guram Ratishvili (grandson of Sasha Egnatashvili), Gia Tarkhan-Mouravi, Tina Egnatashvili, Vajha Okujava, Shalva Gachechiladze (grandson of Father Ksiane), Serge Chaverdian (Shaverdian), Thamaz Naskidachvili, Irakli de Davrichewy, Alexandre de Davrichewy and Annick Davrichachvili (two grandsons and wife of another grandson of Josef "Soso" Davrichewy) and Julian Z. Starosteck.

In Britain, Dr. John Callow, director of the Marx Memorial Library (www.marx-memorial-library.org) and the ruling expert on Lenin in London, helped me greatly on 1907 and Stalin's Welsh tourism, as did Andy Brooks, General Secretary of the New Communist Party; Francis King of the Socialist History Society; Tony Atienza; Paul Barratt and Duncan Higgitt of the *Western Mail*.

In Britain and France, Sir Evelyn de Rothschild placed the Rothschild archives at my disposal, where Melanie Asprey investigated Stalin connections for me: thanks to both.

Thanks for help in small or large ways to Andrew Roberts; Ronald Harwood; John Witherow, editor of the *Sunday Times*; and to the *Sunday Times* picture editor, Ray Wells; Miklos Kun; Len Blavatnik; Clare and Raymond (Viscount) Asquith; John and Victoria Hyman; David King; Andrew Cook, for his inquiries into Special Branch; Rair and Tatiana Simonyan; Geoffrey Elliott; Dr. Dan Healey, expert on sex and crime in Tsarist/Stalinist Russia; Rosamond Richardson; Dr. Catherine Merridale, on Kamenev; Mark Franchetti; Sergei Degtiarev-Foster; Nata Galogre; Jon Halliday; Ingaborga Dapkunaite; Laurence Kelly; Lady Alexandra Gordon-Lennox; David Stewart-Hewitt; Lord Bruce Dundas; Hon. Olga Polizzi; Antony Beevor; Stephen Nash, HM's first Ambassador to Georgia; Andrew Meier; Donald Maclaren, HM Ambassador to

Georgia, and his wife, Maida; and my trainer Stewart Taylor of www
.bodyarchitecture.co.uk, who keeps me sane. Thanks as ever to Charles
and Patty Palmer-Tomkinson for their support and encouragement.

Special gratitude is due to my Russian teacher, Galina Oleksiuk.

I wish to thank my English editor, Ion Trewin of Weidenfeld &
Nicolson, who has genially, wisely edited all my history books; editorial
assistants Anna Hervé and Bea Hemming; Alan Samson, publishing
director; the brilliant king of copy editors, Peter James; the index by
Douglas Matthews and maps by David Hoxley. Thanks also to my paperback editor, Susan Lamb of Phoenix. In New York, I would like to thank
my American editor, the peerless Sonny Mehta, and his senior colleague,
Jonathan Segal, at Alfred A. Knopf.

My agent, Georgina Capel of Capel & Land, remains tirelessly exuberant and highly effective. I owe special thanks to Lord and Lady Weidenfeld, and to Anthony Cheetham, for their wisdom, support and
friendship over many years.

I must as ever thank my parents, Dr. Stephen and April Sebag-
Montefiore, first for their subtle medical and psychological analysis of
Stalin; second for judicious (if ruthless) editing skills; lastly for being the
most wonderful friends and tender parents anyone could wish for.

This book is dedicated to my son, Sasha, but I must mention the
other shining light in my life, my daughter, Lily. Both, I am ashamed to
say, were able to recognize Stalin's portrait before that of Thomas the
Tank Engine. My children's delightful nanny, Jayne Roe, made working at
home a pleasure.

Last but first, my darling wife, Santa, enjoyed the romantic *ménage à
quatre* with those brilliant charmers Catherine the Great and Prince
Potemkin but has found the blood-soaked presence of Stalin in our
marriage a trial of endurance. As we finally enter our own period of de-
Stalinization, I must thank Santa for her sunny encouragement, serene
charm and golden bounty of creativity, laughter and love.

Source Notes

A NOTE ON SOURCES

This book is based overwhelmingly on archival research, mainly in the Stalin archives of the Communist Party's Marxism-Leninism Institute, the archives of RGASPI in Moscow, Russia, and of GF IML in Tbilisi, the Republic of Georgia, as well as the GARF State Archive in Moscow, the archive of the Stalin Museum in Gori, the archives in Batumi, the State Archive in Baku of the Republic of Azerbaijan, and the Nikolaevsky archives and those of the Paris Office of the Okhrana, both at Stanford University, California.

I have been hugely fortunate in finding new sources, often unpublished or partly unpublished and barely used previously by historians. Archival sources are more reliable than oral history, but of course they too have their dangers and must be analysed carefully. But the anti-Stalinist histories often turn out to be just as unreliable.

Many of the archives used in this book, for example, were recorded by official Party historians during the period of Stalin's rise to power, cult of personality and Terror, from the 1920s to the 1950s. Those recorded in the 1930s were presumably collected in Georgia by apparatchiks working under Stalin's terrifying Transcaucasian First Secretary Lavrenti Beria. Therefore one must be constantly aware that they are recorded under massive pressure to present Stalin in a good light. At all times, one has to be aware of the circumstances and try to penetrate the Bolshevik language to see what the witnesses are really trying to tell us.

Yet those recorded before the Terror in 1937 are often astonishingly frank, tactless or derogatory about Stalin: a derogatory story about Stalin in an official memoir is almost certainly true. Many of the witnesses were so naive or honest that their memoirs were unusable at the time, or only usable in small sections. Such memoirs were not destroyed but were simply preserved in the archives. Many were edited, then copied and sent to Stalin's Moscow archive, so there are differences between versions. But the originals usually survived in the local archive.

Many witnesses were interviewed several times, so that we have sometimes three versions by the same witness with important differences. Almost always, the first version is the most revealing. Certain witnesses were tactful yet pointed in their criticisms: the Svanidze memoirs, which as far as I know remain mainly unpublished (except for the diaries of Maria Svanidze, Alyosha's wife, but they cover the 1930s) are amazingly critical of Stalin even though he was already dictator and they themselves were in his inner circle.

A word on the killings of traitors and the bank robberies: Stalin was keen to suppress these details. He sued Yuli Martov in 1918 to stop their publication and continued to suppress them once he was in power. Yet throughout the memoirs, despite official discouragement, we find details of Stalin's role that confirm the importance of this "black work" in his early life. When he finds a traitor, the memoirs usually state that the traitor was killed without specifying that anyone ordered the killing. But it is clear that the order involved Stalin. The same is true of cases of arson.

Many ordinary folk were unconsciously revealing, particularly Stalin's girlfriends, who could not be open about their personal connections with the Leader even when they had borne his children.

Many of these tales of childhood, exile, revolutionary battle and bank robberies are, I hope, useful finds for historians. Keke's memoir is especially telling. One senses that Stalin would have hated the memoir, which, again as far as I know, was not copied to Moscow and has not been published in Russian or English. I guess that Stalin was never informed that it had been set down. But there is also a wealth of other materials that tell us much about young Stalin.

In Georgia, I managed to unearth various unpublished memoirs from private family archives. Again all the usual rules must apply, particularly guarding against the vainglory of those who claim intimacy with the great and famous. But some were written secretly without direct intimidation. In the case of the Minadora Ordzhonikidze Toroshelidze memoirs, she and her husband were arrested in 1937—he was shot, she released—whereupon she cut sixteen pages out of the manuscript.

In Georgia and to a lesser extent Russia, one can still interview rare witnesses: in a Tbilisi old people's home, I interviewed Mariam Svanidze, a relation of Stalin's wife Kato, aged 109; I also spoke to other relations such as Ketevan Gelovani, who provided useful memories. Similarly, Stalin's granddaughter, Galina "Gulia" Djugashvili, supplied helpful pieces of the jigsaw puzzle, as did the daughters of Ordzhonikidze and Litvinov, among others. The most valuable was Guram Ratishvili, the delightful grandson of General Sasha Egnatashvili, who was able at last to fill in the gaps that have appeared in their family story in every Stalin history book (including my own) up to now.

There are also many published memoirs, particularly from the 1920s, which Stalin could not yet control. Thus the memoirs of Kote Tsintsadze, for example, were highly embarrassing. Though they are restrained and circumspect, they did reveal that Stalin ordered killings and bank robberies at a time when he was desperately trying to prove his heroic legitimacy, political and ideological, to succeed Lenin. When he assumed absolute power after 1929, Stalin, together with Beria, managed to pulp many copies of Tsintsadze's memoirs. Another example is the memoirs of Stalin's 1917 assistant Pestkovsky: the first rather irreverent version was published in 1922, but when they were republished in 1930 they had been cleansed. The same applies to Yenukidze, Makharadze, Shotman and many others.

But even the official cult literature has its uses. Lakoba's Smirba book, the collections on the Batumi demonstration and Stalin's schooldays, and Beria's "history" book are all works of propaganda, full of lies and exaggerations, but the quotations from the memoirs are accurate though selectively edited. I have tried to cross-check between books and originals.

One has to be just as careful with the anti-Stalin literature of exiles such as Iremashvili, Nikolaevsky, Vulikh, Uratadze, Vereshchak, Arsenidze and many others. Trotsky and Sukhanov are the two that have dominated Western histories of Stalin. They were anti-Stalin, so they were presumed to be right. Now, on closer analysis, one finds often that they contain errors that we can expose and prejudiced guesses that we can discount—but still they remain very useful.

I have been very fortunate to find less well-known exiled sources too, such as Josef Davrichewy, Khariton Chavichvili and David Sagirashvili, all of whom knew Stalin quite well, each leaving prejudiced, sometimes unreliable, but invaluable sources. One senses that these three, though anti-Stalin, tried to be evenhanded. The Okhrana/Gendarme files, some published by the Bolsheviks, some unpublished in archives, and those of the Paris office resting at Stanford, are very valuable but, based as they are on their own dubious surveillance and intelligence, they are often completely wrong.

Some memoirs and biographies have more value than one might expect. John Reed's *Ten Days That Shook the World* is very sympathetic to the Bolshevik legend and knows little of what was happening within the Party, yet it is a superb piece of reportage. So are David Sagirashvili's diaries. The earliest Stalin biographies are often surprisingly well informed: Boris Souvarine knew many of the players and had access to those witnesses in exile. More surprising is *Stalin: Career of a Fanatic* by Essad Bey, the first real Stalin biography, used with obvious reservations.

The memoirs of Khrushchev, Molotov, Mikoyan, Yuri Zhdanov (just published) and others are useful—but with reservations.

I have unapologetically used many published works widely and in detail and have tried to be punctilious in attributing the source. But some books are so outstanding that I would like to list them as my basic sources used throughout the book: Alexander Ostrovsky's *Kto stoyal za spinoi Stalina?* is the best scholarly work on Stalin's connections with the Okhrana and big business: it is unlikely to be bettered; Stephen Jones's *Socialism in Georgian Colors* is superb, essential reading; Professor Ronald Suny's masterly essays *Journeyman for the Revolution* and *Beyond Psychohistory*; Miklos Kun's *Stalin: An Unknown Portrait* overlaps with both my books on Stalin and is an amazing feat of research and understanding; Robert Conquest's *Great Terror* and his *Stalin: Breaker of Nations* are seminal works that still define Stalin today; Boris Ilizarov's *Tainaya zhizn Stalina* is full of the author's remarkable archival discoveries; on Stalin's poetry, I depend totally on Donald Rayfield's authoritative criticism and translation; on the secret police, I have used the excellent Jonathan W. Daly's *Autocracy under Siege: Security Police and Opposition in Russia, 1866–1905* and *The Watchful State: Security Police and Opposition in Russia, 1906–17*; Anna Geifman's brilliant introduction, *Russia under the Last Tsar: Opposition and Subversion, 1894–1917*, explains the different psychologies of the revolutionary, while her outstanding *Thou Shalt Kill: Revolutionary Terrorism in Russia, 1894–1917* was my basic source on terrorism; Robert Service's recent biographies on Lenin and Stalin are magisterial yet readable; on Baku, Jorg Baberowski's groundbreaking, important *Der Feind ist überall: Stalinismus im Kaukasus* is the only work that explains the culture of Caucasian violence. On the Revolutions, I used: Abraham Ascher's admirable *1905*; Orlando Figes's magnificent *A People's Tragedy*; Richard Pipes's many outstanding works including *The Russian Revolution*, *The Degaev Affair* and *The Unknown Lenin*; and Alexander Rabinowitch's excellent *The Bolsheviks Come to Power*.

ARCHIVES AND MUSEUMS

RGASPI Rossiiskii Gosudarstvennyi Arkhiv Sotsialno Politicheskoi Istorii, Moscow, Russia

GARF Gosudarstvennyi Arkhiv Rossiiskoi Federatsii, Moscow, Russia

GF IML Georgian State Filial of Institute of Marxism-Leninism, Tbilisi, Georgia

ABM Achinsky Oblastnoi Muzei, Achinsk, Russia

MSIR Musei Sovremennoi Istorii Rossii, Moscow, Russia

VOANPI Vologdsky Oblastnoi Arkhiv Noveishei Politicheskoi Istorii, Vologda, Russia

GAVO Gosudarstvenny Arkhiv Vologodskoi Oblasti, Vologda, Russia

GIAG Georgian State Historical Archive, Tbilisi, Georgia (Sakartvelos Sakhelmtsipo Saistorio Arkivi)

Archives of the Hoover Institution on War, Revolution and Peace, Stanford, California

GDMS Gosudarstvennyi Dom-Muzei I. V. Stalina, Gori, Georgia

Gosudarstvennyi Istoriko-Memorialny St-Peterburgsky Muzei "Smolny," St. Petersburg, Russia

Muzei Alliluyeva, St. Petersburg, Russia

GTsMSIR Gosudarstvennyi Tsentralnyi Muzei Sovremennoi Istorii Rossii, Kseshinskaya Mansion, St. Petersburg, Russia

GMIKA Khariton Akhvlediani State Museum, Batumi, Georgia

TsGAA Central State Archive of Adjaria, Batumi, Georgia

DMS Stalin House-Museum (former house of Watchmaker Simhovich), Batumi, Georgia

GK Guram Kahidze's private museum, Batumi, Georgia

KTA private archive of Konstantin Ter-Akopova, Batumi, Georgia

GIAA Gosudardvennyi Istoricheskiy Arkhiv Azerbaijana, Baku, Azerbaijan

Stockholm City Archives, Sweden

Office of the Governor of Stockholm, Sweden

PRO Public Records Office, London

Lenin Museum, Tampere, Finland

VIDEO

Baku, City of Dreams, produced, written and directed by Fuad Akhundov

INTRODUCTION

1. Historians will find out: A. Mgeladze, *Stalin kakim ya ego znal* (henceforth Mgeladze), pp. 240–41. RGASPI 558.11.787.2 Stalin to Zhdanov and Pospelov, 24 Sept. 1940—ban this book. All children alike: E. Radzinsky, *Stalin,* p. 11. All childhoods are the same, burn this: D. Volkogonov, *Stalin: Triumph and Tragedy,* p. 241. Boris Ilizarov, *Tainaya zhizn Stalina* (henceforth Ilizarov), p. 99.

PROLOGUE · THE BANK ROBBERY

1. This account of the Tiflis expropriation is based on the many sources listed in this note. On her role and that of others: GF IML 8.2.2.64, Alexandra Darakhvelidze-Margvelashvili, recorded 21 Feb. 1959. On his role, on cowardly comrades, who did what: GF IML 8.2.1.624.1–26, Bachua Kupriashvili. Kote Tsintsadze, *Rogor vibrdzolot proletariatis diktaturistvis: chemi mogonebani* (henceforth Tsintsadze), pp. 40–49. GF IML 8.5.384.3–10, Autobiographical notes by Kamo; GF IML 8.5.380.5–6, Personal File and Questionnaire, filled in by Kamo on day of his death. GF IML 8.2.1.50.239–55, D. A. Khutulashvili (sister of Kamo). The gang; Eliso hides; Stalin head of that organization: Archives of the Hoover Institution of War, Revolution and Peace, Stanford (henceforth Stanford), Boris Nikolaevsky Collection (henceforth Nikolaevsky), box 207, folder 207–10, letter from Tatiana Vulikh; folder 207–11. Tiflis Committee approves robbery: Razhden Arsenidze, interviews nos. 1–3, 103–4, Nikolaevsky box 667, series 279, folder 4-5, Inter-University Project on History of Menshevik Movement.

On Okhrana investigation/suspicions of coming robbery in Caucasus; 14 and 18 Jan. 1908: Stanford, Paris Okhrana archives, box 209, folder XXB.2, letter on suspects, 13 Feb. 1907. Arrest of Kamo and full biography, 31 Oct./13 Nov. and 27/14 Nov. 1908; and 14 Nov./21 Oct. 1907: Suspect in Tiflis expropriation—Josef/Soso Davrichewy: Stanford, Okhrana box 209, folder XXB.1.

Letter, R. Arsenidze to Boris Nikolaevsky, 8 Jan. 1957, on investigation by Silvester Jibladze and fights with Menshevik about Kvirili expropriation money: Nikolaevsky box 472, folder 2.

Grigory Uratadze, *Vospominaniya* (henceforth Uratadze), pp. 163–66—Stalin, the main financier of the Bolshevik centre, did not participate personally; pp. 71–72 on giving expro money to Shaumian.

On Kamo's role: I. M. Dubinsky-Mukhadze, *Kamo,* pp. 71–84; David Shub, "Kamo." Obeying Stalin from Gendarme report, R. Imnaishvili, *Kamo,* section 1, pp. 52–55; the expropriation, p. 59; betrayal of Kamo by Arsen Karsidze, p. 34. Account of expropriation as told by Kamo to his wife: S. F. Medvedeva-Ter-Petrossian, "Tovarish Kamo." Jacques Baynac, *Kamo,* pp. 90–100. Anna Geifman, *Thou Shalt Kill,* pp. 112–16, 212 and 299, including Kamo killing for Stalin. On psychology of Kamo and terrorists: "Introduction" in Anna Geifman (ed.), *Russia under the Last Tsar,* pp. 1–14. Jonathan Daly, *The Watchful State,* p. 67. Radzinsky, *Stalin,* p. 61. Robert C. Williams, *The Other Bolsheviks* (henceforth Williams), pp. 113–15.

Pretty girls, Stalin's iron discipline: Khariton Chavichvili, *Patrie, prison, exil,* p. 145. Lenin under attack from Mensheviks: Khariton Chavichvili, *Révolutionnaires russes à Genève en 1908,* pp. 80–83. Stalin and Shaumian in London, permission for expropriation, morning meeting, division of spoils: G. S. Akopian, *Stepan Shaumian,* pp. 44, 64. Vahtang Guruli, *Svodnaya Gruzia* no. 152 (225), 24 Sept. 1994, p. 4: SR theory and also Kamo accompanied by daughter of deputy police chief of Shorapani. On Okhrana informer reports that SRs conducted Tiflis expropriation and money stolen by Kamo, Tiflis Okhrana agents "N" and "Bolshaya" on 2 July and 15 July 1907: Vahtang Guruli, *Josef Stalin Materials for the Biography,* pp. 9–11, in Central Georgian State Historical Archive 95.1.82.15, 21, 23.

Lenin and Krasin create the "Technical Group," bombs and money: L. B. Krasin, "Bolshevistskaya partiianaya tekhnika," pp. 8–13.

Lenin and Krasin fight for the money under Menshevik attack: Boris Nikolaevsky, "Bolshevistskiy Tsentre," *Rodina* no. 2, 1992, pp. 33–35, and no. 5, pp. 25–31. Kamo on train with girl, policeman's daughter: Baron Bibineishvili, *Za chetvet veka* (henceforth Bibineishvili), pp. 92–94. Memoir of boys working for Stalin and other comrades by D. Chachanidze: GF IML 8.1.2.4. Joint operations and assassinations with Anarchists and no mention of arrest at time of expropriation: Tsintsadze, p. III. Kamo confides in Davrichewy that Stalin in charge, viceroy furious, Stalin's operations; Stalin opens era of the holdup, Gori connection, Kamo kills for Stalin: Josef Davrichewy, *Ah! Ce qu'on rigolait bien avec mon copain Staline* (henceforth Davrichewy), pp. 237–39, 174–77, 188–89. Stalin in Tiflis engaged in preparations, in Baku by 17 June, quote from L. D. Trotsky, Stalin on roof by G. Besedovsky, expulsion from Caucasus Regional Committee but supported by Lenin and CC: Alexander Ostrovsky, *Kto stoyal za spinoi Stalina?* (henceforth Ostrovsky), pp. 259–62. The other insider in bank/mail, G. Kasradze introduced to Kamo and Kasradze later interrogated by N. Jordania and admitted role in expropriation thanks to Stalin: GF IML 8.2.1.22.

That day on Yerevan Square: Roy Stanley De Lon, *Stalin and Social Democracy, 1905–1922: The Political Diaries of David A. Sagirashvili* (henceforth Sagirashvili), pp. 183–86. Candide Charkviani, "Memoirs," p. 15, on Kamo and Kote. Robert Service, *Stalin,* p. 163. Okhrana on Kamo spending all July with Lenin at dacha: Edward Ellis Smith, *The Young Stalin* (henceforth Smith), pp. 200–206. Boris Souvarine, *Staline,* pp. 93–110. Essad Bey, *Stalin* (henceforth Essad Bey), p. 82. L. D. Trotsky, *Stalin,* pp. 96–100. Miklos Kun, *Stalin: An Unknown Portrait* (henceforth Kun), pp. 73–75.

On Tiflis: Stephen F. Jones, *Socialism in Georgian Colors* (henceforth Jones), pp. 160–67. Razhden Arsenidze, "Iz vospominaniya o Staline" (henceforth Arsenidze). Boris Bazhanov, *Stalin,* p. 107. A. V. Baikaloff, *I Knew Stalin,* p. 20. Arrest of Djugashvili, known as teacher of workers and said to be always holding himself apart: GMIKA 116, Report of Chief of Kutaisi Province Gendarmerie to the Police Department, 9 Apr. 1902. *Armenian Review* no. 2 (3), 7 Sept. 1949, p. 114. Martov libel case: RGASPI 558.2.42. Kun, pp. 81–84; *Pravda,* 1 April 1918; *Vperod,* 31 March 1918. Stalin's role: interviews with Voznesensky, 20 Sept. 1907, and 10 June 1908, and with Comrade Koba (J. Stalin), 19 Mar. 1908: RGASPI 332.1.53: 15 (2) O2. 23 (10), 1905–1910, TSL Organized Committee to Investigate Tiflis Expropriation. Stalin on the bank robbery: GDMS 87.1955-368.11–13, Alexandra "Sashiko" Svanidze-Monoselidze: Kamo's sword. The other inside man: GF IML 8.2.1.54.214–15, Kote Charkviani, in which the memoirist, recording his memoirs in 1936, specifies how Stalin and Kamo groomed Gigo Kasradze, who was the brother-in-law of the priest's son Kote Charkviani. International newspapers: *Moskovskie Vedomosti,* 14, 15, 16, 17, 21 June 1907. *Isari,* 14 July 1907. *Le Temps,* 27 June 1907. *Daily Mirror,* 27 June 1907. *The Times,* 27 and 29 June 1907.

2. Berlin: Ostrovsky, pp. 256–59. I. V. Stalin, *Sochineniya,* 13:122 Stalin to Ludwig; also Smith, pp. 198–99. Trotsky, *Stalin,* pp. 96–107.

3. Arsenidze, p. 220—young men followed Stalin. GF IML 8.5.384.3–10, Autobiographical notes by Kamo. Stalin's magnetism by Kamo's sister Dzhavaira Khutulashvili: Kun, p. 75. Kamo's face: Sergei Alliluyev and Anna Alliluyeva, *Alliluyev Memoirs,* pp. 220–21. Role of girls, etc.: GF IML 8.2.1.624.1–26, Bachua Kupriashvili.

4. GDMS 87.1955-368.11–13: Alexandra "Sashiko" Svanidze-Monoselidze.

5. Davrichewy, pp. 174–77, 188–89, 237–39. Charkviani, "Memoirs," p. 15—Kamo truly amazing.

6. On the balcony as the bombs explode: GDMS 87.1955-368.11–13, Alexandra "Sashiko" Svanidze-Monoselidze.

7. Kun, p. 69, quoting Shaumian's son Levan—interview with Kun. Dirty business: Stalin to Yuri Zhdanov, see S. Montefiore, *Stalin: The Court of the Red Tsar* (henceforth Montefiore), p. 507.

8. Stalin's knowledge of the bank robbery before and after: GDMS 87.1955-368.11–13, Alexandra "Sashiko" Svanidze-Monoselidze. Souvarine, *Staline,* p. 100, quoting Tsintsadze. Charkviani, "Memoirs"—the fanatic Marxist. Minadora Ordzhonikidze-Toroshelidze, "Memoirs"—"man in grey," possibly a reference to Leonid Andreyev's play *Life of Man.*

9. Davrichewy, pp. 237–39, 174–77, 188–89.

10. RGASPI 558.4.647—Stalin carries Mauser: see Kun, p. 117. Arsenidze interviews, Nikolaevsky box 667, series 279, folder 4-5. See chapter 18, note 1.

11. RGASPI 332.1.53: 15 (2) O2. 23 (10), 1905–1910, TSK Organized Committee to Investigate Tiflis Expropriation. GDMS 87.1955-368.11–13: Alexandra "Sashiko" Svanidze-Monoselidze. GF IML 8.2.1.54.214–15, Kote Charkviani. GF IML 8.2.1.22, memoirs of G. Kasradze quoted by Ostrovsky, pp. 259–67. Razhden Arsenidze, interviews nos. 1–3, 103–4, Nikolaevsky box 667, series 279, folder 4-5. GF IML 8.2.1.624.1–26, Bachua Kupriashvili.

12. GF IML 8.2.1.624.1–26, Bachua Kupriashvili. Trotsky, *Stalin,* p. 104, quoting Bessedovsky on Sumbatov. Baikaloff, *I Knew Stalin,* p. 20. Radzinsky, *Stalin,* p. 61, quotes P. A. Pavlenko. Arsenidze, interviews nos. 1–3, 103–4, Nikolaevsky box 667, series 279, folder 4-5.

13. Report of Chief of Kutaisi Gendarmerie Maj.-Gen. Shopchansky: *Batumskaya Demonstratsia 1902 goda* (henceforth *Batumskaya*), pp. 235–36.

14. Handwritten account by Raphael Bagratuni of the memoirs of his relation the Okhrana officer Alexander Bagratuni/Bagratov sent to Isaac Don Levine: thanks to Roman Brackman private collection. This source is highly dubious yet its claims are well informed on details that have only recently surfaced in the Okhrana files in Tiflis and Stanford, such as the fact that the Okhrana expected the expropriation earlier in the year and the involvement of the SRs of Tiflis. His reference to a mansion perhaps has the same source as the Trotsky-Bessedovsky tale of Prince Sumbatov's house. Tbilisi folklore: Dr. Peter Mamradze interview on stories of Kamo's drunken claims in early 1920s.

15. Arsenidze, interviews nos. 1–3, 103–4, Nikolaevsky box 667, series 279, folder 4-5.

16. GF IML 8.2.1.624.1–26, Bachua Kupriashvili. Dubinsky-Mukhadze, *Kamo,* pp. 71–84. GF IML 8.2.1.5. RGASPI 558.6.658; Ostrovsky, p. 454; Niall Ferguson, *The World's Banker: History of the House of Rothschild,* pp. 1034–36, Appendix One, "Prices and Purchasing Power." A scholar of Imperial Russia, Greg King, simply converts Romanov-era roubles into today's U.S.$ by multiplying by ten, which turns 341,000 roubles into $3.4 million (one halves that dollar figure to convert into today's pounds sterling). None of these figures, however, gives the real value of the rouble in 1907; see Note on "Money." Contemporaries reckoned that the Emperor of Russia's private fortune of land, art, palaces, jewels and mineral wealth was about 14 million roubles. In today's money, that is only about £70 million ($140 million). One simply has to conclude that the bank robbery scored a very substantial amount of money. Greg King's *The Court of the Last Tsar,* pp. 231–39. GDMS 87.1955-368.11–13: Alexandra "Sashiko" Svanidze-Monoselidze. Capt. Zubov bribed: Ostrovsky, pp. 545–47.

17. Nadezhda Krupskaya, *Memoirs of Lenin* (henceforth Krupskaya), pp. 40 and 151–52. Radzinsky, *Alexander II*, p. 227, on Bakunin. Frank Owen, *Three Dictators*, pp. 114–15.
18. Uratadze, p. 234. Kun, p. 127. Davrichewy, pp. 237–39, 174–77, 188–89. GDMS 87.1955-368.11–13: Alexandra "Sashiko" Svanidze Monoselidze. Owen, *Three Dictators*, pp. 114–15. GF IML 8.2.1.624.1–26. Dubinsky-Mukhadze, *Kamo*, pp. 71–84. Akopian, *Shaumian*, p. 64. GF IML 8.2.1.5. RGASPI 558.6.658. Ostrovsky, p. 454.

1 · KEKE'S MIRACLE: SOSO

1. Beso-Keke marriage. The main source of this chapter, unless otherwise stated, is Keke herself in her memoirs, GF IML 8.2.15.2-15, E. G. Djugashvili, recorded on 23, 25, 27 Aug. 1935 by L. Kasradze (henceforth Keke). Marriage records: GF IML 8.5.213 and RGASPI 558.4.1.1, *Zaria Vostoka*, 8 June 1937, and RGASPI 558.4.665, M. K. Abramidze-Tsikhatatrishvili. Keke's chestnut hair, slender, large eyes: GF IML 8.2.1.1.143–6, M. K. Abramidze-Tsikhatatrishvili. Keke pretty, Beso a runt: Davrichewy, p. 26. Beso's originality: GF IML 8.2.1.48, N. Tlashadze. Gori weddings: D. Suliashvili, *Uchenichesky gody* (henceforth Suliashvili), p. 24. Sources quoted from: V. Kaminsky and I. Vereshchagin, "Detstvo i yunost vozhdya" (henceforth Kaminsky-Vereshchagin). The home: V. Vishnevsky, "Domik v Gori," *Zaria Vostoka*, 27 Dec. 1937, pp. 27–28.

    Georgian behaviour ritualized: D. Rayfield, *Stalin and the Hangmen*, p. 15. Singing on way to market: Kun, p. 227.
2. Ossetia: Kun, p. 19. *Genealogichesky Zhurnal* no. 1, 2001, pp. 39–40. Stalin, *Works*, 2: 363.
3. Beso's own account of his origins: Keke, pp. 2–15. Davrichewy, p. 26. The best review of the evidence is by Ostrovsky, pp. 76–82. Zaza: M. Lobanov, *Stalin: v vospominaniyakh sovremennikov i dokumentov epokhi* (henceforth Lobanov), p. 13. Beso's death, registered as "Ossetian": GF IML 8.14.160.1–8.
4. Geladze family: Ostrovsky, pp. 82–84. Keke, pp. 2–15. Kaminsky-Vereshchagin, pp. 22–101, especially G. I. Elisabedashvili (p. 25) and Maria Abramidze-Tsikhatatrishvili.
5. Davrichewy, p. 26. GF IML 8.2.1.48, N. Tlashadze. GF IML 8.2.1.49.185.210, Kote Khakhanashvili. GF IML 8.2.1.9, Ivan Geldiashvili.
6. Births: GF IML 8.5.213.41–53. RGASPI 71.10.275.24/558.4.2.1. RGASPI 558.4.2.2. New dates: Kun, p. 8; Ostrovsky, p. 83. "Kogda rodilsa I. V. Stalin," *Izvestiya TSK KPSS* no. 1, 1990, p. 132. Stalin looked more and more like Beso: GF IML 8.2.1.53, Alexander M. Tsikhatatrishvili.
7. GF IML 8.2.1.53, Alexander M. Tsikhatatrishvili. Author's interview with Gulia (Galina) Djugashvili, daughter of Yakov Djugashvili.
8. Nikita Khrushchev, *Khrushchev Remembers*, 1:301–2 (henceforth Khrushchev). Stalin speech to generals of VVS RKKA and government on 22 Mar. 1938, quoted in Ostrovsky, p. 55. Dato: GF IML 8.2.1.8, Dato Gasitashvili. Kamo: GF IML 8.2.1.50.239–55, Dzhavaira Khutulashvili, *née* Ter-Petrossian, Kamo's sister.
9. Suliashvili, p. 8. Charkviani, "Memoirs," pp. 1–2. Keke GF IML 8.2.1.53, Alexander M. Tsikhatatrishvili. Author's interview with Gulia (Galina) Djugashvili. Baedeker, p. 446.
10. Davrichewy, pp. 26–28. Keke.

11. Paternal candidates: author's interviews with Koba Egnatashvili's grandson Guram Ratishvili, son of Sasha Egnatashvili, about the family house, Koba's wrestling and businesses, attitude to Stalin, substitute father, great affection and later destiny of Egnatashvili boys Vaso and Sasha. There are huge inaccuracies in most accounts of the Egnatashvili connection, but Stalin was very close to Sasha Egnatashvili. Within NKVD, attitudes to Stalin's relationship with Egnatashvili: GARF 7523.107.127.1–6, General N. Vlasik and other interrogations. Guram Ratishvili is by far the most revealing and intelligent of the family witnesses. On genetic connection: author's interview with Tina Egnatashvili, great-niece. Davrichewy, pp. 26–28, and see also Davrichewy, "Je suis le demi-frère de Staline," where Gori mayor Jourouli is quoted as saying, "As far as I know, Soso was the natural son of *pristav* Damian Petrovich Davrichewy, my friend . . . Everyone knew about the liaison with the pretty mother of Soso, Kato [Keke]. Besides, the armed attack on *pristav* Davrichewy is the proof." Stalin's fondness for Father Charkviani, and closeness to Egnatashvili family: Charkviani, "Memoirs." Stalin's comment about priest as father—"Comrade Liapidevsky, your father was a priest—mine was a priest too"—quoted in Robert Tucker, *Stalin in Power*, p. 627. Mgeladze, p. 242. V. Sukhodeev, *Stalin v zhiznin i legandaakh*, pp. 19–20, on rumours that Stalin said that Egnatashvili was his father and that Egnatashvili married Beso to Keke to hide his sin. Prince Amilakhvari: Davrichewy, p. 69. Stalin and Beso: GF IML 8.2.1.1.143–6, M. K. Abramidze-Tsikhatatrishvili. GF IML 8.2.1.53, Alexander M. Tsikhatatrishvili.

12. Sergo Beria, *Beria My Father* (henceforth Beria), p. 21. Keke.

13. Mgeladze, p. 242—"I got the impression Stalin was illicit son of Egnatashvili." Author's interviews: Guram Ratishvili; and Galina "Gulia" Djugashvili adds another variant that Stalin and the Egnatashvili children were both suckled by the same wet nurse: they were "milk brothers." Davrichewy, pp. 26–28; Mayor Jourouli in Davrichewy, "Je suis le demi-frère de Staline." Tucker, *Stalin in Power*, p. 627. Within NKVD, on Egnatashvili relationship to Stalin: GARF 7523.107.126.1–6, General N. Vlasik interrogation.

14. Pride in father: RGASPI 558.4.663, Fyodor Alliluyev. Khrushchev, 1:301–2. Dreams clipped: "Anarchism or Socialism," in Stalin, *Works*, 1:296–372. Three cobblers—Stalin, Kaganovich and Mgeladze: Mgeladze, p. 237. RGASPI 558.11.1549.45, valiant son: Stalin to Keke, 24 Mar. 1934. Beso tells stories of bandit-heroes: RGASPI 558.4.665, G. Elisabedashvili.

15. Mgeladze, p. 242. The three sons of Egnatashvili who died of smallpox were born around the same time as Stalin; the two surviving sons, Vano and Sasha, were born later. Tucker, *Stalin in Power*, p. 627. Keke.

16. GF IML 8.2.1.53, Alexander M. Tsikhatatrishvili. Lobanov, pp. 13–14: memoir of David Papiashvili.

2 · CRAZY BESO

1. Khrushchev, 1:301–2. Keke. Charkviani, "Memoirs."

2. Keke. Moving house nine times: Ostrovsky, pp. 88–89. Violence: Kun, p. 12. Misery: Merzliakov in *Molodaya Gvardiya* no. 12, 1939, p. 37. Cossack's whips: Stalin, *Works*, 1: 25–27. Josef Iremashvili, *Stalin und die Tragödie Georgiens* (henceforth Iremashvili), pp. 5–6, 9–12. Beso's violence: N. Kipshidze. Keke's violence: Hana Moshiashvili—

quoted in Radzinsky, *Stalin*, p. 24. Svetlana on knife throwing, beatings by Keke quoted in Service, *Stalin*, p. 20. Beating: G.K. Zhukov, *Vospominaniya i razmyshleniniya* (henceforth Zhukov), 3:215. Chased with whip, strangling Keke, Stalin cut, treated like a dog, "Help! Come quickly!": Davrichewy, pp. 30–35.

3. Keke. R. G. Suny, "Beyond Psychohistory: The Young Stalin in Georgia." Stalin teaches Charkviani children to read: Charkviani, "Memoirs." Davrichewy, pp. 30–31. GF IML 8.2.1.10.23–47, Simon Gogchilidze. Lessons in secret, Beso drags by ears, my sister: GF IML 8.2.1.54.202–15, Kote Charkviani. Stalin speech, VVS RKKA and government on 22 March 1938: Ostrovsky, p. 55. Barber-quack; too much reading; coat to hide Soso to school: GF IML 8.2.1.9, Anna Nikitin-Geladze.

4. Keke. Davrichewy, pp. 26–31. Davrichewy, "Je suis le demi-frère de Staline," including Gori mayor Jourouli quotation.

5. Zhukov, 3:215. Svetlana Alliluyeva tapes: Stalin on mother, "He loved her," etc.—see Rosamund Richardson, *The Long Shadow*, p. 93. Svetlana Alliluyeva, *Twenty Letters to a Friend*, pp. 153–54, 204. Iremashvili, pp. 5–7. Beria, pp. 20–21. RGASPI 558.4.664, P. Kapanadze. Haughty, proud, Keke works for her family and Kulijanav sisters, Koba accuses Chernomazov; 1906 recruits Nato to newspaper: GF IML 8.2.1.15.266–72, Natalia Dondarov (Azarian). Keke.

6. First day of school: GF IML 8.2.1.24, V. Ketskhoveli; GF IML 8.2.1.41, I. Razmadze; RGASPI 558.4.665, S. P. Gogchilidze. Chintz bag: *Molodaya Gvardiya* no. 12, 1939, pp. 35–37. Iremashvili, pp. 4–7. Keke.

7. Keke. Versions of carriage accident: Ostrovsky, p. 89. Game of carriage chicken: Suliashvili, p. 9. Quack: *Alliluyev Memoirs*, p. 189. Stalin jumping: RGASPI 558.4.665, Peter Kapanadze. GF IML 8.2.1.10.23–47, Simon Gogchilidze. GF IML 8.2.1.9, Anna Nikitin-Geladze. Blue coat, red scarf, freckles: GF IML 8.2.1.9, Grisha Glurjidze.

8. GF IML 8.2.1.54, Kote Charkviani. Keke.

3 · BRAWLERS, WRESTLERS AND CHOIRBOYS

1. Stalin's home: Iremashvili, pp. 8–10. Plank bed: GF IML 8.2.1.10.23–47, Simon Gogchilidze. GF IML 8.2.1.15.266–72, Natalia Dondarov (Azarian). Keke.

2. Picturesque and savage: Imam Raguza, *Stalin*, p. 23. Ostrovsky, p. 90. Davrichewy, pp. 78–79.

3. Street culture: Raguza, *Stalin*, p. 23. Suliashvili, pp. 42–46. Z. Gulisov, *Materialy dela opisany mestnostey i plemen kavkazy*, Tiflis 1886. Stalin's participation, B. Ivanter and A. Khakhonov, quoted in Kaminsky-Vereshchagin, pp. 29–32, 48–50. Keenoba: GF IML 8.2.1.49.185–210, Kote Khakhanashvili.

4. How aristocrats lived: Simon Sidamon-Eristoff, *For My Grandchildren*, pp. 21–23. Prince Amilakhvari teaches Stalin swimming: Davrichewy, p. 70. Damage to aristocracy in Caucasus; 6 percent of population in Georgia as opposed to 1.4 percent in European Russia: Jones, pp. 1–29. Wrestling bouts, Stalin, Egnatashvilis: Charkviani, "Memoirs," p. 3.

5. Street fighter: GDMS 2.1955-148.1–11, Comrade Stalin in Gori Church School by Sandro Elisabedashvili (cousin of G. Elisabedashvili).

6. Stalin gang and schoolboys. Catapulting the cows, naughty, running: RGASPI 558.4.665.14, G. Elisabedashvili, and fuller versions GDMS 1955-146.1–11, "My

Memories of Comrade Stalin" by G. Elisabedashvili. Gangfights, Gorijvari, singing Suliko, calm and brutal, push to extremes: Davrichewy, pp. 82–84, 72–76, 45–49, 60–61. Amilakhvari's gardens: Raguza, *Stalin*, pp. 34–35. Gori days, Eristavi's gardens and swimming: David Papitashvili and commander and stone slinging, sultan and ministers and Georgian stories of Saakadze and others, A. M. Tsikhatatrashvili, all in Kaminsky-Vereshchagin, pp. 3–32. Wrestling schoolboys at castle: Suliashvili, p. 12. Kamo: Kamo's sister Dzhavaira Khutulashvili, quoted in Kun, p. 75. Tough school of swimming: GDMS 2.1955-148.1–11, Sandro Elisabedashvili (cousin of G. Elisabedashvili). Like a fish: GF IML 8.2.1.49.185–210, Kote Khakhanashvili. Wounded arm, beaten up, when Soso grows up to be a priest: GF IML 8.2.1.10.23–47, Simon Gogchilidze. Stalin beats up sneak, devoted friend: GF IML 8.2.1.54.202–15, Kote Charkviani. Explosions and catapults: GF IML 8.2.1.226–39, Petre Adamashvili. Wrestling with Tito: Montefiore, p. 470.

7. School: Stalin gains a year: RGASPI 558.4.669, P. Kapanadze. Keke. Strong will, always with a book, painting, Greek, improve yourself: GF IML 8.2.1.226–39, Petre Adamashvili. A. Gogebashvili, in charge of Psalms, and Gendarme, quoted in Ostrovsky, pp. 91–99. Stalin best pupil: Suliashvili, p. 13; and Lavrov in uniform, Russian language, pp. 16–23. Kaminsky-Vereshchagin, pp. 35, 42, 51–58. Poems at Gori: GDMS 3(1).1955-146.1–20, "My Memories of Comrade Stalin," by G. Elisabedashvili. Stalin threatens Lavrov with death: GDMS 2.1955-148.9–11, "Comrade Stalin at Gori Church School," by Sandro Elisabedashvili. Beautiful alto and Shakespearean comedy: GF IML 8.2.1.49.185–210, Kote Khakhanashvili. Psalm prize, people attend weddings just to hear Stalin, grand manner, protest: GF IML 8.2.1.10.23–47, Simon Gogchilidze. GF IML 8.2.1.54.202–15, Kote Charkviani. Books in belt: GF IML 8.2.1.9, Ivan Geldiashvili. Be prepared: RGASPI 558.11.778.45, Stalin to Ordzhonikidze.

4 · A HANGING IN GORI

1. Keke. RGASPI 558.4.662. Kun, p. 11. "Don't worry, Mummy": Kaminsky–Vereshchagin, p. 37. Accident: GF IML 8.2.1.10 S. P. Gogchilidze. "Detskie i scholy gody Iosefa Vissarionovicha Dzhugashvili": GF IML 8.2.6.306. "Sore legs"—J. Djugashvili to rector of seminary, 15 Nov. 1897: RGASPI 558.4.32. Geza: RGASPI 558.4.665, G. Elisabedashvili; also GDMS.

2. Adelkhanov incident in Tiflis: Keke, and also interview with *Pravda*, 27 Oct. 1935. RGASPI 558.4.655, S. P. Gogchilidze. See also *Molodaya Gvardiya* no. 12, 1939, pp. 43–45: Beso's words recalled by S. P. Gogchilidze and Masho Abramidze—how Egnatashvili tried to persuade Beso. The Adelkhanov factory: Service, *Stalin*, p. 24. Stink: M. Isaev in Kaminsky-Vereshchagin, p. 45. The seminal moment, "If Beso had prevailed, no Stalin": the phrase is that of Service, *Stalin*, p. 25. Letters mention me: GF IML 8.2.1.10.23–47, Simon Gogchilidze. Year off: GF IML 8.6.306.

3. House on Sobornaya Street; Stalin's rebellion: Iremashvili, pp. 7–10. Work for Beliaev: RGASPI 71.10.273. Joins Kulijanav sisters: Keke. Expulsion from school, scholarship, high marks: RGASPI 71.10.275. See also RGASPI 558.4.655, G. Elisabedashvili, and RGASPI 558.4.243, S. P. Gogchilidze. Scholarship: Ostrovsky, pp. 96–97. Pneumonia and scholarship doubled: GDMS 89, A. Gogebashvili. Reading, books, writing: Suliashvili, p. 15. Memoirs of Mikha Davitashvili, G. Parkadze and

Grisha Glurjidze: RGASPI 558.4.651 and GF IML 8.2.1.9. Influence of Z. Davi-tashvili: letter, E. Djugashvili to Z. Davitashvili, 15 Sept. 1927, quoted in Ostrovsky, p. 93. Social improvement ambitions and influence of father's stories of bandits like Arsene Odzelashvili: RGASPI 558.4.655, G. Elisabedashvili. Reading all night and influence of Lado Ketskhoveli, book subscription, Darwin, doubts about God: memoirs of G. Glurjidze, P. Kapanadze, G. Elisabedashvili and Demna Shengelaya, quoted in Kaminsky-Vereshchagin, pp. 50–54.

4. Charkviani girl in love: GDMS 3(1).1955-146.1–20, "My Memories of Comrade Stalin," by G. Elisabedashvili. Stalin on the sister—she was thirteen and he may have been much younger than her: Charkviani, "Memoirs."

5. Hanging: Grigory Razmadze, Suliashvili, p. 20. G. Glebov, "Ocherk A. M. Gorkogo o Gori," *Zaria Vostoka* no. 223, quoting Peter Kapanadze on 28 Sept. 1939, and article from *Novoe Obrezrenie*, 15 Feb. 1892; Kaminsky-Vereshchagin, pp. 48–50. A. M. Gorky, *Nejegorodsky Listok,* 26 Nov. 1896.

6. This account of Stalin's enrolment at the seminary is based on Keke, GF IML 8.2.15.2–15. Exam results at church school: RGASPI 71.10.275. Keke's efforts, exams, offers, fees: GF IML 8.2.1.10 and RGASPI 558.4.665, S. P. Gogchelidze. RGASPI 558.4.61. On fees of 140 roubles per annum: Ostrovsky, pp. 108–10. On entrance enrolment: RGASPI 558.4.10. Tucker, *Stalin as Revolutionary* (henceforth Tucker), pp. 80–82. Encouraged to denounce other students: see Smith, p. 37. Help from Egnatashvili: author's interview with Guram Ratishvili, grandson, Tbilisi. Help with "famous Princess Baratov" and fees from Davrichewy: Davrichewy, p. 31.

5 · THE POET AND THE PRIESTHOOD

1. Keke. Routine: Domentii Gogokhia, *Molodya Gvardiya* no. 12, 1939, p. 65. RGASPI 558.4.665, G. Parkadze. Jones, pp. 51–52. Kun, pp. 21–31. Philip Makharadze, *Ocherki revoliutsionnogo dvizheniya v Zakavkazi,* pp. 57–58. Tucker, pp. 82–83. Service, *Stalin,* pp. 33–37. Marks: RGASPI 558.4.17, 558.4.48, 558.4.665, 558.1.4326, 558.3.25. Trotsky, *Stalin,* p. 10. Stalin changed, pensive: V. Ketskhoveli in *Literaturnii Kritik* no. 12, 1939, pp. 103–5. Calm: GF IML 8.2.1.12, Said Devdariani.

2. Father: Charkviani, "Memoirs." Choir: RGASPI 71.10.404. Father sees rector and Stalin's attitude: GDMS 3(1).1955-146.1–20, "My Memories of Comrade Stalin," by G. Elisabedashvili. Keke at seminary: GF IML 8.6.306.

3. Humiliating, ransacking of boxes: Stalin to Ludwig in Stalin, *Sochineniya,* 3:113–14. Good marks: RGASPI 558.4.30 and 37. Atheist in first year, Simon Natroshvili story, five roubles for singing in choir: Charkviani, "Memoirs." Poet, burning eyes: Lev Kotyukov, "The Forgotten Poet Josef Djugashvili," *Zavtra* no. 41 (46), 1994.

6 · THE "YOUNG MAN WITH THE BURNING EYES"

1. Analysis and quotations of Stalin's poetry are based on Donald Rayfield's transla-tions and criticism in *PN Review,* vol. 44, 1984, pp. 45–47. I must also thank Profes-sor Rayfield for his personal guidance. Giving up poetry: Stalin to Levan Shaumian, Kun, p. 4. Stalin welcomed by cultural elite: Service, *Stalin,* p. 40. Kotyukov, "The Forgotten Poet Josef Djugashvili." Mandelstam, Pasternak: Montefiore, pp. 117–18.

2. Tiflis, porridge of peoples: Jones, pp. 159–63. Lima and Bombay: Jones's description, p. 81. Tiflis: *Baedeker*, pp. 465–71. Founding of Mesame Dasi, *Kvali*: Jones, pp. 49–50, 66–70. GF IML 8.2.1.9, Anna Nikitin-Geladze.
3. Books: GF IML 8.2.1.9, G. Glurjidze. From Stalin, Tolstoy, etc., G. Glurjidze, G. Parkadze, G. Glenov, quoted in Kaminsky-Vereshchagin, pp. 66–71. Stole from bookshop: M. Chaureli in *Vstrechi s tov. Stalinym*, pp. 156–57. Hugo's *1893* hero and *Vanity Fair*, see Tucker, pp. 85–87, 132. Nekrasov and Chernyshevsky: Radzinsky, *Alexander II*, pp. 91 and 157–60. Dostoevsky: Rayfield, *Stalin and the Hangmen*, p. 22. Gogol, Saltykov, Shakespeare, Maupassant, etc.: A. A. Gromyko, *Memoirs*, p. 101. Beria, p. 143. Stalin, Gogol: Stalin, *Works*, 1:151. By heart: K. Voroshilov, *Rasskazy o zhizhni*, p. 247. Seminary reading, woodpile, inquisitor Abashidze, reading at night in church: Iremashvili, pp. 19–21. Punishments: RGASPI 558.4.48, 665 and 53. GF IML 8.2.1.12.176–83, Said Devdariani.
4. Iremashvili, pp. 17–19.
5. *Das Kapital*: Service, *Stalin*, p. 41.
6. *Sochineniya*, 13:113–14. RGASPI 558.4.30 and 37. Charkviani, "Memoirs." Practical Marxism versus academic: GF IML 8.2.1.12.176–83, Said Devdariani. Laughing at peasants and urinating on icons: GDMS 3(1).1955-146.11–19, "My Memories of Comrade Stalin," by G. Elisabedashvili, and RGASPI 558.4.665.29. Marx books: GF IML 8.2.1.49.185–210, Kote Khakhanashvili. English books: GF IML 8.2.1.12.176–83, Said Devdariani.
7. G. Ninua, *Zaria Vostoka*, 17 July 1939. A. Okuashvili, *Zaria Vostoka*, 18 Sept. 1935. Stalin's account: Stalin, *Sochineniya* 8 (1948): 174. More practical Marxism: GF IML 8.2.1.12.176–83, Said Devdariani. Visit to Jordania: N. Vakar, "Stalin po vospominaniyom N. N. Jordania," *Posledniya Novosti*, 16 Dec. 1936, p. 2. Jordania: Uratadze, p. 11. Room on Mt. David, journal: D. Gogokhiya in Kaminsky-Vereshchagin, p. 72. Views evolving: Suny, "Beyond Psychohistory," p. 55. Lado, Jordania and Jibladze return and *Kvali*: Ostrovsky, pp. 121–23. Avoiding mother: Keke. Iremashvili, pp. 20–23. *Kvali* letter refused: GDMS 1955-146.17, G. Elisabedashvili. Home bedbugs: GF IML 8.2.1.12.176–83, Said Devdariani.
8. *Alliluyev Memoirs*, p. 44.
9. Charkviani, "Memoirs." Davrichewy, p. 174. Marxism: Stalin, *Works*, 1:296–372 "Anarchism or Socialism?" and 1:4. *Brdzola* issue 1. L. Trotsky, *My Life*, pp. 129–30. Tucker, pp. 88–93. Stalin version of Marxism, see Service, *Stalin*, pp. 48–53. *Credo*: Ilizarov, p. 227. Sergo Kavtaradze, "Memoirs."

7 · BATTLE OF THE DORMITORIES: SOSO VERSUS FATHER "BLACK SPOT"

1. Inquisitor Abashidze: Iremashvili, pp. 19–21. Punishments: RGASPI 558.4.48, 665 and 53.
2. GDMS 3(1).1955-146.11–19, G. Elisabedashvili, also RGASPI 558.4.665.29. GF IML 8.2.1.49.185–210, Kote Khakhanashvili. GF IML 8.2.1.12.176–83, Said Devdariani.
3. Abashidze stories: D. Gogokhiya, Simon Natroshvili, P. Talakvadze and Black Spot, G. Elisabedashvili, Kaminsky-Vereshchagin, pp. 66–67, 84–87. Renan's *Life of Jesus Christ*: RGASPI 558.4.676. *Molodaya Gvardiya* no. 12, 1939: P. Talakvadze, pp. 84–85. Marks, letter to Serafim, reprimands: RGASPI 558.4.48, 558.4.665, 558.1.4326, 71.1275. Refusal to cut hair: Kun, pp. 27–28. Punishments: RGASPI 558.4.53, 558.4.665,

558.4.53, 558.4.663, 558.4.60. Keke visits: Keke. Beso last meetings: GF IML 8.2.1.54.202–15, Kote Charkviani. GF IML 8.2.1.9, Anna Nikitin-Geladze. No more embracing: GF IML 8.2.1.9, Grisha Glurjidze. Teacher in Metekhi: RGASPI 558.11.76.113, Stalin to Beria, 19 Sept. 1931.

4. Debauches: Kun quoting A. Avtorkhanov, p. 30. Lessons in secret, Beso drags by ear; my sister: GF IML 8.2.1.54.202–15, Kote Charkviani. Lisa Akopova: RGASPI 558.1.721. RGASPI 558.11.775.10–13, letter about Praskovia Pasha Mikhailovskaya, fathered by Stalin in 1899. Ilizarov, pp. 284–86. Rayfield, *Stalin and the Hangmen*, pp. 13–14. Stalin reading Napoleon: memoir of Nikolai Popkhadze, seminarist and cousin of Svanidzes, told to Peter Mamradze. Kote Charkviani's sister: see G. Elisabedashvili, RGASPI 558.4.665 and GDMS 3(1)1955-146.1–20, Charkviani, "Memoirs."

5. Expulsion?: RGASPI 558.1.635, Stalin interrogation, Baku, 26 Mar. 1910: unexpectedly charged twenty-five roubles. Failure to pay fees: RGASPI 71.10.275, Yelena Tskhakaya. Old friends: RGASPI 558.1.5378, P. Kapanadze. Kun, pp. 7–34. Smith, pp. 52–53. Illness: Keke Djugashvili to H. Knickerbocker: *New York Post*, 1 Dec. 1930. Money to Kapanadze: RGASPI 558.1.5978 and 5080. Betrayed forty students: Simon Vereshchak, "Stalin v tyurme," *Dni*, 22 Jan. 1928. "I was expelled for Marxist propaganda": E. Yaroslavsky, *Landmarks in the Life of Stalin*, 1939, p. 14; also RGASPI 558.4.4349. Lack of funds: RGASPI 558.4.214. Church offer to be teacher: RGASPI 558.4.65. Expulsions: Kaminsky-Vereshchagin, p. 88. Yenukidze, quoted by Trotsky, *Stalin*, p. 21. Davrichewy, p. 67. Ostrovsky, pp. 153–55. On God: Molotov, *Molotov Remembers* (henceforth *Molotov Remembers*), p. 212. Priests teach how to understand people, and remark to Churchill—past belongs to God: Stalin to Marshal Vasilevsky in Volkogonov, *Stalin*, pp. 470 and 228. To Harriman—only God can forgive and may God help this enterprise: see A. Harriman and Elie Abel, *Special Envoy to Churchill and Stalin* (New York, 1975), p. 154. Meeting with Patriarch Sergei and Metropolitans Nikon and Alexei, 4 Sept. 1943: Dmitri Pospielovsky, *The Russian Church under the Soviet Regime*, 1:200. For a fuller account: V. Alexeev, "Neofizialny dialog (o vstreche Stalina s rukovodstvom pravoslavnoi zerkvi)," *Agitator* no. 6, 1989. See also Michael Burleigh, *Sacred Causes*, p. 236. GIAG 440.2.12, 440.2.64, and RGASPI 558.4.53. Lack of funds: RGASPI 558.4.214. School results on the Svidetelstvo Certificate: GF IML 8.1.414. Executor of God's will: letter from Stalin to Kosygin, 22 Oct. 1946: displayed at TsMSIR. Stalin did return to the seminary to raise funds for the Party during 1904–5, terrorizing the teachers.

6. Leaving the seminary: Keke. Frances Perkins, *The Roosevelt I Knew*, p. 142. Christian gent: Conrad Black, *FDR: Champion of Freedom*, p. 1080. Stalin and Tulin (Lenin): RGASPI 558.4.669, Peter Kapanadze. If no Lenin: Mgeladze, p. 82. Hiding out: Maria Makhstoblidze in Ostrovsky, p. 144. Criticism of Jordania: RGASPI 558.4.665, D. Kalandarashvili. James Moore, *Gurdjieff*, pp. 368–69.

8 · THE WEATHERMAN: PARTIES AND PRINCES

1. Weatherman: GF IML 8.2.1.5, V. F. Berdzenoshvili. Pay: RGASPI 558.4.66. Observatory: *Istoricheskie mesta Tbilisi*, pp. 30–34.

2. Keke. RGASPI 558.4.665 G. Elisabedashvili. GF IML 8.14.160, Vano Ketskhoveli.

3. Jones, chapters 3 and 4. Service, *Stalin*, pp. 52–53. Kun, pp. 53–54. *Alliluyev Memoirs*, pp. 23–25.

4. GDMS 1955-146.16–31, G. Elisabedashvili. Look: Iremashvili and Trotsky, quoted in Radzinsky, *Stalin,* p. 47.
5. Workers' circles: M. A. Moskalev, *Bolshevistsky organizatsii Zakavkazya periode pervoi russkoi revolyutsii,* p. 17. *Molodaya Gvardiya,* vol. 12, 1939, p. 101: 10 June 1926.
6. Early Christians: Trotsky, *My Life,* p. 137. Committees: Trotsky, *Stalin,* pp. 53–54. *Alliluyev Memoirs,* pp. 23–34.
7. Gendarme reports, Capt. V. B. Lavrov to Col. E. P. Debil: GIAG 153.2.302, GARF 124.11.1902.127, GARF 102.7.1902.175. GF IML 8.14.160.3, Matiorz Grikurov: Stalin and Beso at Adelkhanov shoe factory. *Alliluyev Memoirs,* pp. 23–34.
8. Stalin worships Lado Kestkhoveli and Sasha Tsulukidze: A. Yenukidze, *Nashi podpolnye tipografii na Kavkaze,* p. 24. Tsulukidze in Tskhakaya's words: *Voprosy Istorii KPSS,* no. 5, 1965. I. Dubinsky-Mukhadze, "Mikhail G. Tskhakaya," pp. 111–12. "Friend of Illich—Mikho," *Literaturanaya Gruzia,* no. 1, 1965, pp. 15–20. Anna Alliluyeva in *Alliluyev Memoirs,* pp. 24–27, 36–40, 47–48. Kun, pp. 192–98. Richardson, *Long Shadow,* p. 117. Beria, p. 150. L. Vasileva, *Kremlin Wives,* pp. 55 and 70. Svetlana Alliluyeva, *Dalyokaya muzika,* pp. 251–52, and *Dvadtsaty pisem k drugu,* pp. 39–47. See L. P. Beria, *Lado Ketskhoveli,* pp. 5–65. Also: Beria, p. 308.
9. Svanidzes: GF IML 8.2.1.34.343–51, Mikheil Monaselidze. Kamo: no decent people, enthralled—see Dzhavaira Khutulashvili in Kun, p. 75. Radzinsky, *Stalin,* p. 60. Stalin reading Napoleon: memoir of Nikolai Popkhadze, seminarist and cousin of Svanidzes told to Peter Mamradze. GDMS 1955-146.16–31, G. Elisabedashvili. "Soso's gramophone" and teaching mentally limited Kamo, giving nickname: GF IML 8.2.1.7.64–84, G. F. Vardoyan. GF IML 8.5.384.3–10, Autobiographical notes by Kamo, GF IML 8.5.380.5–6, Personal File and Questionnaire, filled in by Kamo on day of his death.
10. GDMS 1955-146.16–31, G. Elisabedashvili. Memoir Nikolai Popkhadze to Peter Mamradze. Sagirashvili, pp. 168–77.
11. SD split: Jones, chapters 3 and 4. Service, *Stalin,* pp. 52–53. Kun, pp. 53–54. Arsenidze, quoted in Kun p. 54. Muddled young: S. T. Arkomed (Grigol Karadzhian), *Rabochee dvizhenie,* pp. 55–56. Iremashvili, pp. 21–22. RGASPI 558.4.665, G. Elisabedashvili. Davrichewy, pp. 124–25. N. Vakar, "Stalin po vospominaniia N. N. Zhordania," *Poslednye Novosti,* 16 Dec. 1936.
12. Gendarme reports, Capt. V. B. Lavrov to Col. E. P. Debil: GIAG 153.2.302, GARF 124.11.1902.127, GARF 102.7.1902.175. GF IML 8.14.160.3, Matiorz Grikurov. *Alliluyev Memoirs,* pp. 24–27, 47–48.
13. Teacher: Raguza, *Stalin,* p. 65. Mochalov in Service, *Stalin,* p. 51. April 1901 riot: *Alliluyev Memoirs,* pp. 49–51. *Istoricheskie mesta Tbilisi,* pp. 68–73. Conscription: Davrichewy, p. 31. Police interrogation including "exempted from conscription 1901 due to family matters": RGASPI 558.4.214.
14. Shaumian, Vedenev murder, Lelashvili: Ostrovsky, pp. 585–89. Memoir of Nikolai Popkhadze, seminarist and cousin of Svanidzes, told to Peter Mamradze. Shaumian: Anastas Mikoyan, *Memoirs,* 1:72.

9 · STALIN GOES UNDERGROUND: *KONSPIRATSIA*

1. *Konspiratsia* and the secret world is based closely on the following sources: Richard Pipes, *The Degaev Affair,* pp. 26, 87, master of the revolution. Jonathan Daly, *Autocracy under Siege,* pp. 6, 9, 21–37, 38–44, 87–96; who learned from whom?, pp. 95–131.

Radzinsky, *Alexander II*, pp. 91, 153–62, 217–22, 340. Perlustration, creation of Okhrana, code names, danger of flying suicide bombers: Charles A. Ruud and Sergei A. Stepanov, *Fontanka 16: The Tsar's Secret Police*, pp. 54–56 and 69–79. On flying suicide bombers: Iain Lauchlan, *Russian Hide-and-Seek*, p. 361. Poles and Jews more hanged: Rayfield, *Stalin and the Hangmen*, p. 31. Yard keepers and Georgian cult of loyalty and violence: Jones, p. 99. Yenukidze on vengeance: Nikolaevsky box 207, folder 207-15, BN letter to T. Vulikh, 8 Aug. 1949. Stalin and spook: GF IML 8.2.1.54.202–15, Kote Charkviani. Davrichewy, p. 31. RGASPI 558.4.214.

2. Avoiding spies and laughing at them: GDMS 1955-146.16–31, G. Elisabedashvili.

3. "Neopublikovannye materialy iz biografii t. Stalina," *Antireligioznik*, vol. 12, 1939, pp. 17–21: memoir of bookshop owner Ambako Chelaidze.

4. GDMS 1955-146.16–31, G. Elisabedashvili. Ostrovsky, pp. 166–67.

5. Iremashvili, pp. 21-22. RGASPI 558.4.665, G. Elisabedashvili. Davrichewy, pp. 124–25. Vakar, "Stalin po vospominaniia N. N. Zhordania." Jones, pp. 72–74.

6. November meetings, Gendarme reports: GIAG 153.2.302/102.00.1898.5-52/153.1.3431/2. GARF 102.00.1898.5.52.B. List of twenty-four delegates to the Conference: GDMS 93.3, M. Gureshidze. Ostrovsky's version is the most convincing: Ostrovsky, pp. 167–70. Slanderer sent to Batumi: Uratadze, pp. 66–67. Muddled youngster: Arkomed, *Rabochee dvizhenie*, pp. 55–56. Iremashvili, pp. 21–22. RGASPI 558.4.665, G. Elisabedashvili. Davrichewy, pp. 124–25. Vakar, "Stalin po vospominaniia N. N. Zhordania." S. Talakvadze, *K istorii Kommunisticheskoi partii Gruzii*, 1: 59–63. Jones, pp. 106–7.

10 · "I'M WORKING FOR THE ROTHSCHILDS!"—FIRE,
MASSACRE AND ARREST IN BATUMI

1. GF IML 8.2.1.20.155–222, Kotsia Kandelaki. RGASPI 558.4.537, D. A. Vadachkoria. Porfiro Kuridze in *Batumskaya*, pp. 63–70. *Chernomorskii Vestnik*, 5 Jan. 1902.

2. GF IML 8.2.1.20.155–222, Kotsia Kandelaki. Throughout this chapter I have drawn on *Batumskaya*: Kote Kalandarov, pp. 36–40; Porfiro Lomdzharia, pp. 41–49; Gerasim Kaladze, pp. 49–55; Illarion Darakhvelidze, pp. 55–63; Porfiro Kuridze, pp. 63–70; Khachik Kazarian, pp. 75–78; G. Chkaidze, p. 124; Hashimi Smirba pp. 150–71. GF IML 8.2.1.20, K. Kandelaki. RGASPI 558.4.537, D. A. Vadachkoria (official version *Batumskaya*, pp. 106–12). Porfiro Kuridze, *Bakinsky Rabochyi*, 12 Jan. 1937. *Chernomorskii Vestnik*, 5 Jan. 1902.

3. New Year's Eve: GF IML 8.2.1.20.155–222, Kotsia Kandelaki. Lomdzharia bandit, visits to Tiflis: GDMS 1955-146.29–44, G. Elisabedashvili. GMIKA 18.50, Kote Kalandarov. GMIKA 26.104.33–42, Porfiro Kuridze. Batumi: *Annals of the Working Collective Batumi*, p. 315. Jones, pp. 28 (Mandelstam quote) and 87–88. Ostrovsky, pp. 170–71. Robert W. Tolf, *The Russian Rockefellers: The Saga of the Nobel Family and the Russian Oil Industry*, pp. 87–90.

4. When Porfiro Lomdzharia came out of prison, Jeune gave him 400 roubles for his brother Silvester's funeral and the substantial sum of 3,000 roubles. Since the Lomdzharia brothers were Stalin's enforcers with whom he often stayed, it is likely that he was involved. Later, Stalin raised money using protection-rackets, by threatening the families of businessmen or by demanding money in return for not striking. Perhaps the 3,000 roubles was to prevent any more fires at the refinery. RGASPI 161.1.11. GF IML 8.2.1.20.155–222, Kotsia Kandelaki, including Armenian help with printing from

Spandarian. Spandarian lover: Nikolaevsky Vulikh in box 207–9. Spandarian, a womanizer and fate of wife of Bolshevik: Olga Spandarian letter to Shaumian in *Vestnik Archivov Armenii*, no. 1, 1996 "Suren Spandarian in Siberian exile." RGASPI 558.4.537, D. A. Vadachkoria and official version *Batumskaya*, pp. 106–12. *Bakinsky Rabochyi*, 12 Jan. 1937. Porfiro Kuridze. François Jeune: Otar Gogolishvili in interview with Ostrovsky, pp. 586–87. Payments to and from Lomdzharia: GARF 102.1900.4871. I. S. Chulek, *Ocherki istorii Batumskoi kommunisteskoi organizatsis*, Batumi 1970, pp. 90–91.

5. Kirtava: GF IML 8.2.1.26.22–6 (1934) and 8.2.1.26.36–9 (1937), Natalia Kirtava-Sikharulidze memoirs. GMIKA 19.51: Natalia Kirtava-Sikharulidze memoirs. GF IML 8.2.1.43. GARF 3.1905.272.

6. GF IML 8.2.1.20.155–222, Kotsia Kandelaki. GMIKA 18.50, Kote Kalandarov. GMIKA 26.104, Porfiro Kuridze memoirs, pp. 33–42. *Batumskaya*, pp. 36–78, 124. Stalin's despotism: Lavrov in GARF 102.00.1898.5-52-V. Hiding in skirts: interview with Suren Levonian on mother Terun Levonian story.

7. 9 March: GF IML 8.2.1.20.155–222, Kotsia Kandelaki. GMIKA 26.104, Porfiro Kuridze memoirs, pp. 33–42. *Batumskaya*, pp. 36–78, 124, 203–27. GMIKA 105, 106, 154, Despina Shapatava. Rothschilds manager, Wanstein hit: GF IML 8.2.1.9, Theofile Gogiberidze. Changing clothes and wearing hoods: GM IML 8.2.1.15.174–81, I. Doborjinidze. Hooded Koba: see K. Kalandarov in *Batumskaya*, p. 70; you'll never be revolutionary, Vadachkoria, p. 86; conspiracy and mystery, P. Kuridze, p. 96; no moustaches or beard, p. 99; hooded and riot and Stalin puts on plays, Vera Lomdzharia, p. 102; demonstration, I. Darakhvelidze, pp. 116–17; Stalin calm, K. Kandelaki, pp. 118–26; Stalin helps wounded, p. 157. GF IML 8.2.1.20.155–222, Kotsia Kandelaki.

8. Hashimi Smirba: GF IML 8.2.1.20.155–222, Kotsia Kandelaki. GMIKA 21.57, Hamdi Smirba memoirs, p. 16, and 22.58, Hashimi Smirba, pp. 1–9. GMIKA 26.104.33–42, Porfiro Kuridze. *Batumskaya*, pp. 150–71. Stalin in women's dresses: Suren Levonian interview on mother Terun Levonian in Batumi. On truth of Smirba story: Stalin in Charkviani, "Memoirs." On Nestor Lakoba, see Montefiore, pp. 179–80. Jordania's reaction: Zhordania, "Stalin," p. 2. Trotsky, *Stalin*, pp. 31–32. Stalin, *Works*, 1.25. Stalin on his Gurian bodyguards and on losing people but winning: Mgeladze, p. 77. Stalin amends Beria's book: Beria, p. 18.

9. Funerals, arrest: police officer report, 6 Apr. 1902, *Batumskaya*, p. 177, and report of Jakeli, p. 178. GMIKA 115, Capt. Jakeli report on arrest of Stalin, involvement on 9 March. Letters to mother and Iremashvili; report of chief of Kutaisi Province Gendarmerie to the Police Department, 9 Apr. 1902, arrest of Djugashvili known as teacher of workers and said to be always holding himself apart, keeping himself secret: GMIKA 116, Illarion. On Stalin and Bulgakov: M. Bulgakov, *Batum*, Radzinsky, *Stalin*, pp. 9–11, quotes Elena Bulgakova; and Elena Bulgakova's diaries, 1939; also account of V. I. Nemirovich-Danchenko, Arts Theatre director. See: itlitbatum.ru. GF IML 8.2.1.20.155–222, Kotsia Kandelaki.

II · THE PRISONER

1. Uratadze, pp. 66–69, 208–10. GF IML 8.2.1.20.155–222, Kotsia Kandelaki.

2. Gendarme inquiries and Stalin's notes: RGASPI 558.4.80, 81 and 83. *Batumskaya*, pp. 233–35. Reports of Capt. Jakeli, 9 Apr. 1902, Maj.-Gen. Shopchansky, 9 Apr. 1902, Report of Gendarme Department Tiflis (Stalin member of Tiflis Committee), 1 May 1902, arrest report of Policeman Chkhikvadze, 6 Apr. 1902, report of Police-

man Gogoria in Gori (Iremashvili interrogated, two men come to meet Keke and take her to Batumi), 16 June 1902; Jakeli, 16 Oct. 1905, on great success in 1901; Col. Lavrov on great discord between juniors and old socialists, 9 Feb. 1903; GMIKA 153, 116, 118, Stalin, 1 May 1902, 119, 120, Eremov, 121, 125, Chopura and Mohevi. GF IML 8.2.1.20.155–222, Kotsia Kandelaki.

3. GDMS 1955-146.33–40, G. Elisabedashvili.

4. Keke: Mgeladze, pp. 154–55. Police reports and Keke's requests: RGASPI 71.10.401 and 404. RGASPI 558.4.405. Trip to Batumi: Keke. Visit again to Batumi spring 1903: see Keke's obituary, *Zaria Vostoka*, 1937. Kun, p. 42. On Keke's interview 1935, R. W. Davies, O. V. Khlevnuik, E. A. Rees (eds.), *Stalin-Kaganovich Correspondence*, p. 295.

5. Prison culture: GMIKA 19(51), N. Kirtadze (Kirtava-Sikharulidze), pp. 39(1)–42(4); Stalin gives message, p. 32(128); Gerasim Kaladze, pp. 42(1)–50(9); V. Chaidze, p. 96; V. Kalandze, p. 136. Stalin and the sympathetic guard: Chaureli in *Vstrechi s vozhdem narodov/Vstrechi s tov. Stalinym*, p. 154. How to communicate: Bibineishvili, pp. 59–63. Leniency: Rayfield, *Stalin and the Hangmen*, p. 31. Stalin prefers convicts: Khrushchev, 1:301. Stalin lonely: Oleg Troyanovsky, *Cherez gody*, p. 162. Studying and prisons barbarous/paternalist: Trotsky, *My Life*, pp. 35, 147 and 180. Second school: Stalin, *Works*, 2:28–32. Ordzhonikidze's reading, Stalin's memo on prison, 1937: Volkogonov, *Stalin*, p. 9. Prison culture, news of Soso's arrest, arguments in jail: *Alliluyev Memoirs*, pp. 43–45, 55–64; prison visits, pp. 33–35. Stalin's prison routine: Kalandadze, quoted in Trotsky, *Stalin*, p.35.

6. Lenin and "What Is to Be Done?": Tucker, pp. 23–31. Stalin, *Works*, 1:63–74.

7. GMIKA 19(51), N. Kirtadze (Kirtava-Sikharulidze), pp. 39(1)–42(4).

8. Story of Christofore Imnaichvili told to author by Tamaz Naskidashvili, letter, 20 Oct. 2005.

9. Innocent in Batumi, guilty in Tiflis and lost in prison system: RGASPI 558.4.79, 558.4.90; GARF 102.00.1898.5-52-V, 102.00.1902.825-16, 102.00.1898.5-59-A. GF IML 8.1.772, 5.268. Ostrovsky, pp. 185–96. *Batumskaya*, pp. 171–74.

10. Hospital: GF IML 8.2.1.20.

11. RGASPI 558.4.619, Stalin to Prince G. S. Golitsyn.

12. Exarch: Ostrovsky, p. 195. Transfer to Kutaisi: GMIKA 19(51) N. Kirtadze (Kirtava-Sikharulidze), pp. 39(1)–42(4).

13. At Kutaisi prison: GMIKA 19(51), N. Kirtadze (Kirtava-Sikharulidze), pp. 39(1)–42(4). Group photograph and 28 July protest: *Batumskaya*, pp. 95–99, 137–38: Dzuku Lolua and Varden Chaidze. Uratadze, pp. 66–69, 208–10.

14. RGASPI 558.4.79, 558.4.90; GARF 102.00.1898.5-52-V, 102.00.1902.825-16, 102.00. 1898.5-59-A. GF IML 8.1.772, 5.268. Ostrovsky, pp. 185–96. *Batumskaya*, pp. 171–74.

15. Sentencing: RGASPI 558.4.619, GARF 102.7d.1902.175; RGIA 1405.521.482. Finding Stalin: GIAG 13.27.5451 and 5461; 84.2.1960 and 1272; GIAG 17.2.1272; GF IML 8.5.204. *Batumskaya*, pp. 257–65. Ostrovsky, pp. 197–200. GMIKA 19(51).39(1)–42(4) N. Kirtadze (Kirtava-Sikharulidze). Money: GF IML 8.2.1.13, memoirs L. Janelidze. 28 million: A. Applebaum, *Gulag*, p. 518.

12 · THE FROZEN GEORGIAN: SIBERIAN EXILE

1. *Etap*: tooth arsenic and amputation: Charkviani, "Memoirs." Beaten up, and shackles: Kun, pp. 60–61. Racing the train: Smith, p. 112. Criminals: *Molotov Remembers*, pp. 145–46.

2. RGASPI 558.11.1494, Abram Gusinsky. Peasants: Charkviani, "Memoirs."

3. *Vstrechi s vozhdem*, p. 28—memoirs of grandson of Martha Litvintseva and Mikhail Gulkin. B. Ivanov, "V Novoi Ude," *Pravda*, 25 Dec. 1939.

4. Exile: allowance—see *Molotov Remembers*, p. 133. Charkviani, "Memoirs." Trotsky on Olympus in Volkogonov, *Trotsky*, p. 11. Krupskaya, p. 33. Lenin in exile: Service, *Lenin*, p. 110. Joy of letters Yenukidze to Voroshilov: RGASPI 71.2.41. Women, and duel: *Molotov Remembers*, p. 128. Lezhnev: Kun, p. 112. Voroshilov, Yenukidze, women: Vasileva, *Kremlin Wives*, p. 80. Love under boulders: Trotsky, *My Life*, p. 85. Sverdlov in Tucker, p. 158. Exile, Jews: Davrichewy, p. 129.

5. Khrushchev, 1:301. Khrushchev mentions "first exile" and "Vologda," which was Stalin's second exile, but it seems to belong to this first exile.

6. Lenin, letter to Stalin and Second Congress: Stalin, *Works*, 6:52–54. Tucker, p. 122. Service, *Stalin*, pp. 50–55. Iremashvili, pp. 212–13. Uratadze, p. 67. Bibeneishvili, pp. 80–83.

7. Two escapes: RGASPI 558.4.659 (also Sergei Alliluyev, *Proidennyi put*, p. 109). RGASPI 558.1.14. RGASPI 558.11.1494, A. Gusinsky. RGASPI 558.4.655, M. I. Kungarov letter. K. Chernenko, *I. V. Stalin v sibirskoi ssilke*, pp. 22–25, 32–37. Drink for driver: GF IML 8.5.205. Stalin boasts of tricking peasant driver of sledge and showing sword, as told by Stalin in 1910 to Ivan Kukulava: GF IML 8.2.1.27.202–10. Police spy ID: GF IML 8.2.1.7, D. Vadachkoria. I. Petrov, "Pervye shagi revolyutsionoi deatelnosti tov Stalina," *Molodoi Bolshevik*, vol. 21, 1939, p. 25. Sieve: Trotsky, *My Life*, p. 37. Trotsky in Volkogonov, *Trotsky*, pp. 44–45. Boots and Sergei Alliluyev's many escapes: Radzinsky, *Stalin*, p. 76. Police card: Kun, pp. 62–64. Police: GARF 102.00.1904.6.313, RGASPI 558.4.92. GF IML 8.2.1.9, Anna Nikitin-Geladze. Tsarist agent and escapes: I am indebted in this section, unless specifically attributed, to the researches of Ostrovsky, especially on timing of escape, p. 212; also pp. 431–62 and his analyses of Okhrana and Gendarme archives, 1900–10; on escapes from exile, pp. 431–36; Ostrovsky quote, pp. 436–38; quotation by police official L. A. Rataev, p. 437; money for agents, pp. 438–39; corruption of police Dvali, p. 515, Zubov and Zaitsev, pp. 545–47; Fikus report on intelligence gathering by Stalin, p. 578, on 800-rouble bribe, Y. Sverdlov, *Izbrannye proizvedeniya*, p. 595. Stalin's five escapes: Charkviani, "Memoirs." RGASPI 671.1.287, Turukhansk money receipts, 1913–15, collected by NKVD boss N. I. Yezhov and found in his safe. Ordzhonikidze and Zaitsev: RGASPI 558.4.258. P. A. Japaridze, *Vospominaniya o P. A. Japaridze*, pp. 61–62. GARF 110.19.119. Stalin meets police official on street and Gendarme tip-offs: GDMS 167, G. Varshamian. GARF 102.00.5-61-A. Tucker, pp. 109–10, quoting Roy Medvedev on story of E. P. Frolov. Roy Medvedev, *Let History Judge*, pp. 314–24. Service, *Stalin*, p. 74. For discussion of Eremin letter: Eric Lee, "Eremin Letter: Documentary Proof That Stalin Was Okhrana Spy?" Eremin text in Smith, p. 306. General Ivan Serov memo to First Secretary N. S. Khrushchev and Politburo: RGASPI 558.11.1288, 4 June 1956. Stalin and Spandarian versus Shaumian by Ekaterina Shaumian: Mikoyan, *Memoirs*, p. 72. Shaumian tensions, Tartars in meetings, Stalin's protection-rackets, killing informers, Spandarian debauchery, Stalin true boss, gangsterism: Tatiana Vulikh to Boris Nikolaevsky, Nikolaevsky box 207, folder ID 207–9. Uratadze, p. 67. Arsenidze, pp. 72 and 224. Jordania, "Stalin," in which Jordania quotes Shaumian. Olga Shatunovskaya: RGASPI 558.4.671. Shaumian's jobs; buy-out from arrest to Capt. Zaitsev: Akopian, *Shaumian*, pp. 64–76. Prison director Vachiev, 150 roubles each to free prisoners: *Iz proshlogo nashei partii: Stati i vospominaniya iz istorii Bakinskoi organizatsii*, pp. 146–47. B. Kaptelov and

Z. Peregudova, "Byl li Stalin agentom Okhranki?," *Rodina*, no. 5, 1989, pp. 67–69. B. Slavin, "Stalin i Okhranka," *Alternativy*, no. 1, 1998, pp. 78–81. Okhrana surveillance, 1908–13: *Krasny Arkhiv*, no. 2 (105), 1941, pp. 4–31. Stalin on betrayal, death: GF IML 8.6.312, D. Chekheidze (Turdospireli). Stalin edits his own *Short Course* biography including number of arrests: "I. V. Stalin sam o sebe: redakzionnaya pravka sobstennoy biografii," *Izvestiya TsK KPSS*, no. 9, 1990.

8. You cowards and French Revolution book: GF IML 8.2.1.11.125–7, Dmitri Gurgenidze. Stalin's nationalist views, Batumi, Gori and the *Credo:* RGASPI 157.1.54, M. Tskhakaya. Service, *Stalin*, p. 55. S. Kavtaradze unpublished mss—thanks to his daughter Maya Kavtaradze and Zakro Megrilishvili. GF IML 8.2.1.19, S. Kavtaradze. Beaten up and apartments: Ostrovsky, pp. 214–17. Bibineishvili, pp. 79–83. Georgian political nation and Tskhakaya stories by Stalin: Charkviani, "Memoirs." Marx son of an ass: Sagirashvili, p. 181. For Toroshelidze: Minadora Toroshelidze mss—thanks to Susanna Toroshelidze and Nestan Charkviani. For Shevardian story, see handwritten memoir by Sergei Danielovich Shevardian (Chaverdian): thanks to Claire Mouradian for recording and sharing this source with me.

9. GF IML 8.2.1.34, Mikheil Monoselidze. Davrichewy, pp. 118.19, 124–25. Catherine Merridale, "The Making of a Moderate Bolshevik." GF IML 8.5.384.3–10, Autobiographical notes by Kamo. GF IML 8.5.380.5–6, Personal File and Questionnaire, filled in by Kamo on day of his death. GF IML 8.2.1.34.332–4.

13 · BOLSHEVIK TEMPTRESS

1. Yenukidze, *Nashi podpolnye tipografii na Kavkaze*, p. 24. *Alliluyev Memoirs*, pp. 24–27, 36–40, 47–48, 65. Kun, pp. 192–98. Richardson, *Long Shadow*, p. 117. Beria, p. 150. Pavel Alliluyev on Stalin and Kurnatovsky; and Nadya on mother: Vasileva, *Kremlin Wives*, pp. 55 and 74. Svetlana Alliluyeva, *Dalyokaya muzika*, pp. 251–52, and *Dvadtsaty pisem*, pp. 39–47. Thanks to Gia Tarkhan-Mouravi for this family story in the footnote.

2. GF IML 8.5.384.3–10, Autobiographical notes by Kamo. GF IML 8.5.380.5–6, Personal File and Questionnaire, filled in by Kamo on day of his death. GF IML 8.2.1.50.239–55, Dzhavaira Khutulashvili *née* Ter-Petrossian, Kamo's sister. I. M. Dubinsky-Mukhadze, *Ordzhonikidze*, pp. 19–21, and *Kamo*, p. 19. Theatrical stunt: Susanna Toroshelidze's interview on her mother, Minadora Ordzhonikidze-Toroshelidze. Newspaper with Makharadze: Jones, p. 109. Marie Arensberg: Essad Bey, p. 94.

3. GF IML 8.2.1.26.22–6 (1934) and 8.2.1.26.36–9 (1937), Natalia Kirtava-Sikharulidze memoirs. GF IML 8.2.1.43, N. Kirtava-Sikharulidze. GF IML 8.2.1.31, V. Lomdzharia-Javakikidze: soldier's uniform. GF IML 8.2.1.34, I. Mshvidabadze: railway uniform—also RGASPI 558.4.655. GF IML 2913.2.4, F. Makharadze—suspicions of Stalin as police agent.

4. Stalin's nationalist views, Batumi, Gori, the *Credo:* RGASPI 157.1.54, M. Tskhakaya. Service, *Stalin*, p. 55. S. Kavtaradze unpublished mss. GF IML 8.2.1.19, S. Kavtaradze. Ostrovsky, pp. 214–17. Bibineishvili, pp. 79–83. Kirtava turns down Stalin: GF IML 8.2.1.26.22–6 (1934) and 8.2.1.26.36–9 (1937), Natalia Kirtava-Sikharulidze. GF IML 8.2.1.43, N. Kirtava-Sikharulidze. Beaten up: Ostrovsky, pp. 214–17. Kun, p. 66.

5. GF IML 8.2.1.25, V. Ketskhoveli. Davrichewy, p. 35—papers in name of Petrov/ Pavlov. Ostrovsky, pp. 216–17.
6. Imeret-Mingrel Committee: RGASPI 157.1.54, M. Tskhakaya. GF IML 8.2.1.19, S. Kavtaradze. Bibineishvili, pp. 80–82. Arrests, escapes and house moves: GF IML 8.2.1.5, G. F. Berdzenovshvili. Union Committee: RGASPI 558.4.658, Ts. Zelikson. Fishing: GF IML 8.2.1.34, I. Mshvidabadze: railway uniform—also RGASPI 558.4.655. Makharadze, *Ocherki*, p. 76. Tucker, p. 98. Baku: RGASPI 558.4.93. Kun, p. 92. Leader: GF IML 8.5.320. Kutaisi description and quote by P. Makharadze: Jones, pp. 88–89; Guria and Kutaisi landscape: "mountains, swampy valleys"—this is a direct quote from Jones, p. 133. Ten trips, etc.: Ostrovsky, pp. 576–77. Escapes, Budu and Stalin stories: interview with Izolda Mdivani (widow of Budu's son Vahtang) and Mdivani family in Tbilisi, Georgia, 2006.
7. Stalin's behaviour in Kutaisi. "Poliziya i soratniki ob I. V. Staline—A tsel ta chtoby pokazatsya narodu velikim chelovekom," *Otechestvenyye Arkhiv*, no. 4, 1995, pp. 77–80. The archivist whom Beria asked to find the letter was X. Serova, sister of one of his secret policemen, I. A. Serov. Stalin to Davitishvili in Leipzig and Lenin's reaction: Stalin, *Works*, 1:55–58. Influence of Jordania: Jones, p. 127. New Year's Eve, 1904, disturbing banquet: GF IML 8.2.1.11, Alexei Zakhomildin.
8. Baku, Jan. 1905: RGASPI 71.10.189. The Revolution, bloody Sunday: Orlando Figes, *A People's Tragedy* (henceforth Figes), pp. 173–86. Stalin, *Works* 1:75. Makharadze and Stalin editors: Jones, p. 109.
9. Stalin, *Works*, 1:75.

14 · 1905: KING OF THE MOUNTAIN

1. Baku: RGASPI 558.4.583, Mamed Mamediarov, Muktar Gadzhiev. Essad Bey, p. 69. Baku: Tolf, *The Russian Rockefellers*, pp. 151–58. Jorg Baberowski, *Der Feind ist über-all*, pp. 77–79.
2. Stalin, *Works*, 1:82–84 and 85–89. Thousands of dead: Armen Ohanian quoted in Tom Reiss, *The Orientalist*, p. 14.
3. S. Talakvadze, *K istorii Kommunisticheskoi partii Gruzii*, 1:118.
4. Chavichvili, *Patrie, prisons, exil*, p. 70. Stalin, *Works*, 1:422–23. Guria: Jones, p. 149. Victor Taratuta quote on separate republic. Committee as Tsar: Bibineishvili, p. 119. Debate with Isidore Ramishvili, Comrade Koba in Tskhratskaro, escape, clean-shaven, meeting in Gotsadze's father's house: GF IML 8.2.1.11.30–3, Davit Gotsadze. It is possible that this was one occasion when he was hidden in the nearby mansion of Chiatura manganese tycoon Prince Jibo Abashidze, ancestor of President Mikhail Saakashvili: see Sandra Roelofs Saakashvili, *Story of an Idealist*, pp. 37–38.
5. Circumcised Yids: Arsenidze, p. 221.
6. Chiatura: Jones, p. 91. Chavichvili, *Patrie, prisons, exil*, pp. 70, 72–87, 112–17. Also *Cahiers d'Histoire Sociale*, no. 26, Automne/hiver, 2005, pp. 133–44. Guria: Jones, p. 149. Bibineishvili, p. 119.
7. Printing-press: RGASPI 558.4.651, M. Beliashvili. Chavichvili, *Patrie, prisons, exil*, pp. 70–87, 112–17.
8. Menshevik armed detachments: Noe Ramishvili in Jones, p. 180. Stalin, *Works*, 1: 133–39 "Armed Insurrection and Our Tactics," *Proletariat Struggle*, 15 July 1905.

Chiatura armed: GF IML 8.2.1.25.261–87, Vano Kiasashvili. Kote Tsintsadze, "Chemi Mogonebani," *Revolyutsiis Matiane*, no. 2, pp. 117–22; no. 3, pp. 68–79. G. Parkadze, *Boevye Bolshevistkie druziny v Chiaturakh v 1905*, in *Rasskazy o Velikom, Staline* (Tbilisi, 1941), pp. 46–50; RGASPI 558.4.665. Sergo Kavtaradze, *Kak tov Stalin gromil Menshikov*, pp. 56–59 in *Rasskazy o Velikom Staline* (Tbilisi, 1941). Bibineishvili, pp. 88–90, 119. Stalin in the West, as speaker, tactician, style: Chavichvili, *Patrie, prisons, exil*, pp. 70–87, 112–17.

9. Chiatura tycoons: RGASPI 558.4.665, B. Kekelidze. GF IML 8.2.1.93–4, V. Bakradze. Saakashvili, *Story of an Idealist*, pp. 37–45. Bibineishvili, pp. 88–90, 119. Chavichvili, *Patrie, prisons, exil*, pp. 70–87, 112–17. Status symbol: Krasin in Williams, p. 59. Protection-rackets and Stalin defends tycoons: GF IML 8.2.1.7 G and GF IML 8.2.1.4.1.

10. *Perepiska V. I. Lenina i rukovodimykh im uchrezhdenii RSDRP s mestnymi partiinymi organizatsiami 1905–7*, vol. 2, part 1, p. 294.

11. Arsenidze in Smith, pp. 139–41. Comrade Koba in Tskhratskaro, debate, escape, clean-shaven, meeting in Gotsadze's father's house: GF IML 8.2.1.11.30–3, Davit Gotsadze. Roelofs Saakashvili, *Story of an Idealist*, pp. 37–38. Simon Vereshchak, *Dni*, 24 Jan. 1928.

12. Viceroy: the description of the viceroy's character and arrival are direct quotes from Jones, pp. 172–75; and prostitutes and palm readings, p. 186.

13. Speech at Khoni: Nutsubidze: Montefiore, p. 286. Stalin, *Works*, 1:90–132 "Briefly about Disagreements in the Party." Murders in Georgia: Jones, pp. 184–87. Stalin opens the era of bank robberies: Davrichewy, p. 175, and competitiveness, p. 181. Bibineishvili, p. 85. Bomb-making Bolsheviks: Vano Jejilava, "My Memoirs," *Revolyutsiis Matiane* (henceforth *RM*), no. 3, 1923, p. 135. Stalin orders bomb attacks on Cossacks: Davrichewy, p. 219. Terror: Daly, *Watchful State*, pp. 16–20. 3,600 wounded: Geifman, *Thou Shalt Kill*, p. 21. Svanidze cousin Dvali blows himself up: GF IML 8.2.1.34.327–37, Mikheil Misha Monoselidze. GDMS 87.1955-368.1–16, Alexandra "Sashiko" Svanidze-Monoselidze.

14. Unpublished memoirs of Kasiane Gachechiladze: thanks to his grandson Shalva Gachechiladze.

15. Jones, pp. 188–89. Stalin's Cossack attacks: Davrichewy, p. 200. Stalin, *Works*, 1:133–39 "Armed Insurrection and Our Tactics." Baberowski, *Der Feind*, p. 79.

15 · 1905: FIGHTERS, URCHINS AND DRESSMAKERS

1. Kamo kills, Stalin offers: Davrichewy, pp. 188–90.

2. Svanidzes: GF IML 8.2.1.34.327–37, Mikheil Misha Monoselidze. GDMS 87.1955-368.1–16, Alexandra "Sashiko" Svanidze-Monoselidze. Ravishing girl: Davrichewy, p. 228; pistol, p. 160. Koba at hospital: GDMS 3(1).1955-146.45–6, G. Elisabedashvili. Author's interview with Kato's cousin Katevan Gelovani, Tbilisi, 2005: Stalin hidden in Kutaisi by Svanidze parents and police chief Dvali. Author interview with Mariam Svanidze (aged 109) in Tbilisi, 2005.

3. Iremashvili, pp. 32–35. Skirtless woman: Jones, p. 189. Stalin, *Works*, 1:178–86. Jones, pp. 188–89. Stalin's Cossack attacks: Davrichewy, p. 200. Stalin, *Works*, 1:133–39. Baberowski, *Der Feind*, p. 79. Trotsky, *Stalin*, pp. 67 and 79.

4. *Alliluyev Memoirs*, pp. 101–2.

5. Stalin, *Works*, 1:191, "To All Workers," 19 Oct. 1905.
6. Talakvadze, *K istorii Kommunisticheksoi partii Gruzii*, 1:143.
7. Service, *Stalin*, p. 59. Kavtaradze Memoirs. Story of lamp-throwing: memoirs of Maya Kavtaradze.
8. Minadora Ordzhonikidze-Toroshelidze unpublished memoirs. Davrichewy, pp. 174–76 and 181.
9. Massacres in Tiflis and armed SDs: Jones, pp. 189–94. Davrichewy, pp. 194–95. Trotsky, *Stalin*, p. 67.
10. Jones, pp. 189–95. Davrichewy, pp. 194–96. Seething cauldron: Trotsky, *Stalin*, p. 79.

16 · 1905: THE MOUNTAIN EAGLE—STALIN MEETS LENIN

1. Tammerfors: best account of the Finnish angle is Antii Kujala et al., *Lenin Ja Suomi*. Portrait of Lenin is based on: Figes, pp. 141–51, 385–98; Service, *Lenin*, pp. 255–73; Service, *Stalin*, pp. 129 and 179; Tucker, p. 103. Stalin on Lenin: Stalin, *Works*, 6: 53–55. Davrichewy on Lenin and on Stalin as only fighter, shooting, pp. 160, 212–13. Krupskaya, pp. 128–29. Trotsky, *Stalin*, p. 69. Timing of Stalin's travels: Ostrovsky, pp. 242–43. Smith, p. 150. E. Yaroslavsky, "Tri vstrechi," *Pravda*, 23 Dec. 1939.
2. Jones, pp. 194–96. *Alliluyeva Memoirs*, pp. 101–7. Blocking the tunnel, crushing of Guria, terrorists to Tiflis, assassination of traitors, etc.: Kote Tsintsadze, *RM*, no. 2, 1923, pp. 79–85. Stalin regathers squad in Tiflis and conquest of west: GDMS 3(2).1955-146.68–72, G. Elisabedashvili. Stalin negotiates with peasants: Chaureli, "Vstrechi s vozhdem narodov," in *Vstrechi s tov. Stalinym*, p. 156. Formation of the Outfit on Stalin's orders: GF IML 8.2.1.624.1–26, Bachua Kupriashvili.
3. Griiazonov: Tsintsadze, pp. 40–41. Davrichewy, pp. 216–17. Stalin in charge according to Armenian terrorist: Kun, p. 79. Essad Bey, p. 72. Jones, p. 197. Geifman, *Thou Shalt Kill*, pp. 99–100. Boris Souvarine, *Staline*, pp. 98–100. Smith, p. 156. GF IML 8.2.1.34.327–37, Mikheil Misha Monoselidze. GDMS 87.1955-368.1–16, Alexandra "Sashiko" Svanidze-Monoselidze. GF IML 8.2.1.5, G. F. Berdzenoshvili. GF IML 8.2.1.3, N. Akhmeteli. RGASPI 558.4.658, B. Loshadze-Bochoridze. GOAG 153.1.764. Hiding wounded Stalin: Ostrovsky, p. 247. *RM*, no. 4, 1923, memoirs of A. Magriabiants. Uratadze, pp. 130–32. GF IML Bolshevik killers of Griiazanov: Chumburidze; the other assassin was Alexander Vashakidze. Hiding wounded Stalin, dreaming of seizing Tiflis on map: GF IML 8.2.1.3.291–310, Niko Akhmeteli.

17 · THE MAN IN GREY: MARRIAGE, MAYHEM (AND SWEDEN)

1. The gangsters, holdups, girls, pawnshop, Chiatura gold train: GF IML 8.2.1.624.1–26, Bachua Kupriashvili. Davrichewy, pp. 178–84, 226, 174–76. The gang: Nikolaevsky box 207, folders 207–10 and 207–11, Tatiana Vulikh to Boris Nikolaevsky. Uratadze, pp. 163–66. Dubinsky-Mukhadze, *Kamo*, pp. 45–58. Kutaisi and girls: Alexandra Darakhelidze-Margvelashvili. Urchins: GF IML 8.1.2.4. GARF 102.1906.206. Stalin on death: GF IML 8.2.1.34.317–54, Mikheil Misha Monoselidze. Griiazanov, expropriation, Druzhina, pawnshop, competition and cooperation with Mensheviks, robberies recounted including Chiatura train, Kutaisi

treasury and Tiflis: Tsintsadze, pp. 40–49. Stalin's technical assistant (Niko's brother Mate): GF IML 8.2.1.3.291–310, Niko Akhmeteli. Money raising by rackets in Tiflis: Essad Bey, pp. 90–95. Stalin on Tsintsadze and Kamo: see Charkviani, "Memoirs." Stalin's austerity: Jordania, "Stalin."

2. Hiding wounded Stalin, dreaming of seizing Tiflis on map: GF IML 8.2.1.3.291–310, Niko Akhmeteli. GDMS 278 A. N. Mikaberikdze. GDMS 118 Ruben Dashtoian.

3. GF IML 8.2.1.34.317–54, Mikheil Misha Monoselidze. GDMS 87.1955-368.1–16, Alexandra "Sashiko" Svanidze-Monoselidze. Escape out of the window: Service, *Stalin*, pp. 65–66. Man in grey: Minadora Ordzhonikidze-Toroshelidze unpublished mss. 1906 recruits, Nato to newspaper: GF IML 8.2.1.15.266–72, Natalia Dondarov (Azarian).

4. Avlabar arrest: Arsenidze, pp. 218–36. Stalin in scarf: GF IML 8.2.1.37, Raisa Okinshevich. Ostrovsky, pp. 248–52. For conspiracy theory, see Isaac Don Levine, *Stalin's Great Secret*, p. 90.

5. Stockholm: Voroshilov, *Rasskazy o zhizni*, 1:247. Shipwreck: see Kujala et al., *Lenin Ja Suomi*. Hans Bjorkegren, *Ryska Posten*, pp. 43–56. Thanks to the investigations of Martin Stugard of *Dagens Nyheter* and also to the help of the grandson of Inspector Mogren, Per Mogren. Williams, p. 75, Michael Futrell, *Northern Underground*, p. 47. Service, *Lenin*, p. 179. Service, *Stalin*, pp. 62–64. Tucker, pp. 41, 127 and 146. Smith, p. 175: shipwreck, quoting S. G. Strumenko. Trotsky, *Stalin*, pp. 72–73. Dzerzhinsky: Rayfield, *Stalin and the Hangmen*, pp. 56–57. GF IML 8.2.1.12.176–83, Said Devdariani. Report on Stockholm by Comrade K: Stalin, *Works*, 1:261–77. On agrarian question: Stalin, *Works*, 1:238–40 and 217–39. Shaumian also challenged by Mensheviks: Akopian, *Shaumian*, p. 44. Berlin: RGASPI 558.1.5095, Stalin to Monoselidze.

6. RGASPI 558.1.5095.

7. Minadora Ordzhonikidze-Toroshelidze unpublished mss. GF IML 8.2.1.34.317–54, Mikheil Misha Monoselidze. GDMS 87.1955-368.1–16, Alexandra "Sashiko" Svanidze-Monoselidze. Kato Rachvelian: Mgeladze, p. 199. Letter about Alyosha and Kato: RGASPI 558.1.5095, quoted in Kun, pp. 341–42. Loved her so much: RGASPI 558.4.647, Pelageya Onufrieva. Soso as demigod: Iremashvili, pp. 30, 39–40. Very beautiful, melted my heart: Svetlana Alliluyeva tapes—thanks to Rosamund Richardson. Ravishing: Davrichewy, p. 228. Katovan Gelovani interview with author: Stalin hid with teacher father of Svanidzes in Kutaisi, Kato and Alyosha enchanted, fascinated by Stalin. Mariam Svanidze, interview with author, Tbilisi, 2005. Stalin laughing and scruffy: GDMS 1955-146.51–6, G. Elisabedashvili. Marriage, little woman, what kind of family life: GF IML 8.2.1.9, Anna Nikitin-Geladze.

8. Shooting policeman: GF IML 8.2.1.34.317–54, Mikheil Misha Monoselidze.

18 · PIRATE AND FATHER

1. *Tsarevich Giorgi*: S. Lakoba et al. (eds.), *Istoria Abkhazia*, p. 219. S. Lakoba, *Boeviki Abkhazii v revolyutsii 1905–7*, pp. 65–68. S. Lakoba, "Legendarnoe nacholo veka." Thanks to S. Z. Lakoba for access to his interviews with T. Kapba-Arshba and Kamshisi Gvaramia. For legend of Stalin leading horses with money from the ship: Fasil Iskander, *Sandro of Chegem*, pp. 202–4. Davrichewy's piracy, p. 236. *Tiflissky Listok*, 22 and 24 Sept. 1906; *Kavkaz*, 24 Sept. 1906; *Kavkazskaya Zhizn*, 29 Sept. and 6 Oct. 1906; *Chernomorsky Vestnik*, 22 and 23 Sept. 1906. For the mules of Chiatura, see memoirs of Father Gachechiladze; for Stalin's horse riding, see his attempt to

ride in the 1945 Victory Parade, in Montefiore; for shooting, see earlier memoirs of M. Monoselidze and J. Davrichewy; for robbery of ship *Nikolai I*, see later chapters on Baku. Koba prank: Arsenidze, p. 220. Stalin greater involvement in robbery: Razhden Arsenidze, interviews nos. 1–3, 103–4, Nikolaevsky box 667, series 279, folder 4–5. Baku Tiflis Conference: GF IML 8.2.1.12.176–83, Said Devdariani. Uratadze, pp. 66–69.

2.   Kamo's adventures: Imnaishvili, *Kamo*, pp. 47–51. *Russian Review*, vol. 19, no. 3, July 1960, pp. 227–47. Williams, pp. 75, 185. Kun, p. 75. Geifman, *Thou Shalt Kill*, pp. 85–95 and 167. Krasin, "Bolshevistskaya partiinaya tekhnika," p. 813. B. Nikolaevsky, "Bolshevistky zentr," *Rodina*, nos. 2 and 5, 1992: no. 2, pp. 13–36. Krasin and Bogdanov: Stanford, Paris Okhrana, box 200, folder ID XVII n4a and folder XVII m 1. Tsintsadze on Chiatura railway heist—21,000 roubles in Souvarine, *Staline*, p. 100. Arsenidze, p. 232. Bombs and Krasin: Williams, pp. 61–63, 112. Radzinsky, *Stalin*, p. 59. Baikaloff, *I Knew Stalin*, pp. 20–21. Litvinov's arms buying: see *Istorichesty Arkhiv*, no. 4, 1960, pp. 95–110. Hugh D. Phillips, *Between the Revolution and the West: A Political Biography of Maxim M. Litvinov*, pp. 9–11. "From Bolshevik to British Subject—the Early Years of M. Litvinov," *Slavic Review* 48, no. 3, Fall 1989, pp. 388–98. Kamo's visit to Lenin: Krupskaya quoted in Trotsky, *Stalin*, p. 105. Bibineishvili, pp. 116–30. S. F. Medvedeva-Ter-Petrossian, "Tovarish Kamo." RGASPI 332.1.53: 15 (2) O2. 23 (10), 1905–1910, TSK Organized Committee to Investigate Tiflis Expropriation: abroad led by Y. Tychko and A. Ornatsky (Chicherin); in Tiflis led by Tigranov, Angreevsky, Nadejdin; it conducted interviews with Voznesensky, 20 Sept. 1907, and 10 June 1908 and in Baku with Comrade Koba (J. Stalin), 19 Mar. 1908. GDMS 87.1955-368.11–13, Alexandra "Sashiko" Svanidze-Monoselidze. The other inside man: GF IML 8.2.1.54.214–15, Kote Charkviani. GF IML 8.2.1.22, G. Kasradze, quoted by Ostrovsky, pp. 259–67. Tiflis Committee including Stalin and Philip Makharadze approve robbery: Arsenidze, interviews nos. 1–3, 103–4, Nikolaevsky box 667, series 279, folder 4–5. On Gigo Kasradze: GF IML 8.2.1.624.1–26, Bachua Kupriashvili.

3.   Arrest of Kato: GF IML 8.2.1.34.317–54, Mikheil Misha Monoselidze. GDMS 87.1955-368.1–16, Alexandra "Sashiko" Svanidze-Monoselidze. Note from Moscow police. GIAG 153.1.3440. *Bakinsky Rabochyn*, 25 Apr. 1931, and 21 Apr. 1936. November 1906 heist: Kote Tsintsadze in Souvarine, *Staline*, pp. 99–100. Baikaloff, *I Knew Stalin*, pp. 20–21. Arsenidze, p. 232. Kutaisi: Tsintsadze, pp. 41–49. Dubinsky-Mukhadze, *Kamo*, pp. 61–80. Kutaisi Kamo, and girls: GF IML 8.2.2.64, Alexandra Darakhvelidze-Margvelashvili. Geifman, *Thou Shalt Kill*, p. 115.

4.   Berlin: Smith, pp. 194–96, Krupskaya on Berlin. V. I. Lenin, *Polnoe Sobranie Sochineniya* (henceforth Lenin *PSS*), 15:571. Stalin on Berlin: Milovan Djilas, *Conversations with Stalin*, p. 79. W. S. Churchill, *Second World War* (London, 1951), 6:601. Stalin, *Works*, 2:408–9. RGASPI 71.0.406 and 558.4.583. Kun, pp. 85–87. Ostrovsky, pp. 256–59. H. Barbusse, *Stalin: A New World through One Man*, p. 53. Stalin, *Sochineniya*, 13:122, Stalin to Ludwig. Voroshilov, *Rasskazy o zhizni*, 1:336. V. I. Lenin, *Biograficheskaya khronika*, 2:223.

19 · STALIN IN LONDON

1.   Ultra tense, like animals: RGASPI 337.1.44, description of anonymous delegate. Tskhakaya nursed: RGASPI 157.1.18. GF IML 8.2.1.12.176–83, Said Devdariani.

Stanford, Paris Okhrana, box 195.16c, folder 1, on paying agent 1,500 roubles and Zhitomirsky, etc. Andrew Rothstein, *Lenin in Britain*, pp. 21–29. I. Muravyova and I. Sivolap-Kaftanova, *Lenin in London*, pp. 165–68. Ivan Maisky, *Journey into the Past* (henceforth Maisky), pp. 54, pp. 137–44. Volkogonov, *Trotsky*, p. 47. Williams, pp. 82–83. Service, *Stalin*, pp. 67 and 78–79. Service, *Lenin*, pp. 170 and 181–82. For Congress, Jews, Trotsky pretty but useless and numbers of delegates, see "On Notes of a Delegate": Stalin, *Works*, 2:47–80. Sympathetic to Jews: Stalin, *Works*, 1:20. *I. V. Stalin o Lenine*, quoted in Smith, p. 188. Radzinsky, *Stalin*, pp. 54–55. Smith, pp. 183–84. Trotsky, *My Life*, pp. 88–91. Akopian, *Shaumian*, p. 44. Maxim Gorky, *Days with Lenin* (London, n.d.), pp. 5–7. Stalin and Churchill, 15–16 Aug. 1942: RGASPI 45.1.282. Gromyko, *Memoirs*, p. 31. W. J. Fishman, *Streets of East End*, pp. 76–114. Alan Palmer, *The East End*, p. 111. George Lansbury, *My Life*, p. 246. J. Carswell, *The Exile: The Life of Ivy Litvinov*, pp. 63–70. Medvedev, *Let History Judge*, p. 309. W. J. Fishman, *East End Jewish Radicals*, p. 264. See also: *London Landmarks: A Guide with Maps and Places Where Marx, Engels and Lenin Lived and Worked. Piaty (Londonsky) syezd Protokoly*, pp. 121, 241, 349, 350. Voroshilov, *Rasskazy o zhizni*, 1:336. Tskhakaya ill and Ivanovich signs loan agreement: Dubinsky-Mukhadze, "Mikhail G. Tskhakaya," pp. 111–12. "Friend of Illich—Mikho," *Literaturnaya Gruzia*, no. 1, 1965, pp. 15–20. Tower House: *Observer*, 24 Oct. 2004; Mussolini: *Evening Standard*, 14 Oct. 2004. Bacon: *Daily Express*, 5 Jan. 1950. Congress: *Daily Mail*, 10, 11, 13, 20, 21 May 1907; *The Times*, 13, 17 May 1907; *Daily Mirror*, 22 May 1907 and 10, 11, 13, 14, 15, 16, 17, 18, 22 May 1907; *Daily Express*, 10 May 1907. Who is that, Stalin asked Shumian: Yves Delbars, *The Real Stalin*, pp. 53–55. I am especially grateful to Dr. John Callow, director and researcher of the Marx Memorial Library, London, who is the expert on this subject and gave me generous guidance as well as his own memories of the "Stalin in Wales/Liverpool" urban myths, heard at the *Morning Star* bazaar and Profile Books in Liverpool during the 1980s, respectively.

2. Paris: GF IML 8.2.1.56, G. I. Chochia. For travel timing and dates: Ostrovsky, pp. 255–59.

20 · KAMO GOES INSANE: THE GAME OF BANDITS AND COSSACKS

1. Tiflis expropriation: see the notes to the Prologue. GF IML 8.2.1.624.1–26, Bachua Kupriashvili. GF IML 8.2.1.50.239–55, Dzhavaira Khutulashvili. Chavchavadze killing: Ordzhonikidze; see V. M. Gurgenidze, quoted in Geifman, *Thou Shalt Kill*, pp. 92–96. Stolypin: Williams, p. 85. Service, *Stalin*, p. 69. Arsenidze, interviews nos. 1–3, 103–4, Nikolaevsky box 667, series 279, folder 4–5. Tsintsadze, pp. 40–49. Charkviani, "Memoirs." Thirteen Hours Tiflis–Baku: *Baedeker*, p. 471. Krupskaya, pp. 40 and 151–52. Radzinsky, *Alexander II*, p. 227, on Bakunin. Capt. Zubov bribed: Ostrovsky, pp. 545–47. Fanny: Futrell, p. 60.

2. GF IML 8.2.1.624.1–26, Bachua Kupriashvili. Kamo: Bibineishvili, pp. 94–110. Imnaishvili, *Kamo*, pp. 47–51. Dubinsky-Mukhadze, *Kamo*, pp. 12–86. *Russian Review*, vol. 19, no. 3, July 1960, pp. 227–47. Williams, pp. 74, 104, 114–23, 185. Kun, p. 75. Geifman, *Thou Shalt Kill*, pp. 38, 85–92, 116–18, 167, 190, 201. Krasin, "Bolshevistskaya partiinaya tekhnika," p. 813. Nikolaevsky, "Bolshevistky zentr." Stanford, Paris Okhrana, box 200, folder ID XVII n4a and folder XVII m 1. Tsintsadze on Chiatura railway heist—21,000 roubles in Souvarine, *Staline*, p. 100. Arsenidze,

p. 232. Bombs and Krasin: Williams, pp. 61–63, 112. Radzinsky, *Stalin*, p. 59. Baikaloff, pp. 20–21. Litvinov's arms buying: see *Istorichesky Arkhiv*, no. 4, 1960, pp. 95–110. Phillips, *Between the Revolution and the West*, pp. 9–11. "From Bolshevik to British Subject," *Slavic Review*, 48, no. 3, Fall 1989, pp. 388–98. Krupskaya quoted in Trotsky, *Stalin*, p. 105. Bibineishvili, pp. 116–30. Medvedeva-Ter-Petrossian, "Tovarish Kamo." RGASPI 332.1.53: TSK organized committee to investigate Tiflis expropriation. Stanford, Paris Okhrana, 209 folder XXb, folder 2; 209 XXb folder 1; folder XVII L folder 2, XX.328, XXb, XXVII C, XXVc folder 1, XXVIIc folder I, XXVIIc on Wallach and Kamo from the chief of the Intelligence Service Paris (including claim that sixty-three people took part in heist). On Okhrana informer reports that SRs conducted Tiflis expropriation and money stolen by Kamo: Vahtang Guruli, *Materials for Stalin's Biography*, pp. 9–11, and Tiflis Okhrana agents "N" and "Bolshaya" on 15 July and 2 July 1907. GIAG 95.1.82.15, 21, 23. Carswell, *The Exile*, p. 55. Credit Lyonnais: see Ostrovsky, pp. 499–500. Lenin versus Bogdanov: Service, *Lenin*, p. 98.

3. Chavichvili, *Révolutionnaires russes à Genève*, pp. 74–91. RGASPI 332.1.53: TSK organized committee to investigate Tiflis expropriation. Expelled: Arsenidze, p. 232. Y. Martov on Stalin's expulsion: *Vperod*, 31 Mar. 1918. Y. Martov, *Spasiteli il uprazdniteli? Kto i kak razrushal RSDRP?*, Paris, 1911, p. 23. Martov case: Service, *Stalin*, p. 164. Revolutionary Tribunal: 5 Apr. 1918—RGASPI 558.2.42, quoted in Kun, pp. 79–84; exactly the sort of person Lenin needs, expulsions not serious, p. 127. *Pravda*, 1 April 1918. Trotsky, *Stalin*, pp. 101–9. GF IML 8.2.1.624.1–26, Bachua Kupriashvili.

21 · THE TRAGEDY OF KATO: STALIN'S STONY HEART

1. Stalin's house: *Alliluyev Memoirs*, pp. 52–54, 137; Nadya falls into sea, p. 110, though Anna says their brother rescued Nadya. Home: GDMS 1955-146.51–6, G. Elisabedashvili. RGASPI 558.4.663, Sergei Alliluyev. Tidiness—Sergei Alliluyev quoted in Lily Marcou, *Staline: Vie privée* (henceforth Marcou), p. 53. Kun, p. 38. Tiflis a marsh: Stalin, *Works*, 2:188, and 8:174–75. Service, *Stalin*, p. 70. Suny, "A Journeyman for the Revolution," pp. 373–94. Spandarian's women: Vulikh in Kun, pp. 129–30. Tucker, p. 105. Starts in Russian: Stalin, *Works*, 2:42–46. Rothschilds: Smith, p. 399. Police laxer: RGASPI 124.1.2035, M. Frumkin. Fighting squads and arsenal, ship heists, Vyshinsky: GDMS 49, I. Bokov. RGASPI 558.4.583, I. Bokov. GF IML 8.2.1.19, S. Kavtaradze. GF IML 8.2.1.624.1–26, Bachua Kupriashvili. Ostrovsky, pp. 259–67. Pushing for strikes: see Sergo Ordzhonikidze and others in A. Rokhlin, *Dvadtsat piat let Bakinskoi organizatsii bolshevistikov*. GF IML 8.2.1.35, I. P. Nadiradze. Anastas Mikoyan, *Tak bylo*, pp. 347–48. Shaumian and filth of Baku: Mikoyan, *Memoirs*, pp. 72–74. Shaumian tensions, Tartars in meetings, Stalin's protection-rackets, killing informers, Spandarian debauchery, Stalin true boss, gangsterism: Tatiana Vulikh to Boris Nikolaevsky, in Nikolaevsky, box 207, folder ID 207-9. Persia: RGASPI 558.4.583 Mir Bashir Kasumov. Stalin's relations with Muslims in Baku: "History of the Working Turkic Proletariat" by Effendiev, "Istoriya rabochego," p. 53.

2. Baku too Persian, Nobel story, Rothschilds, wages, stories of tycoons Mantashev, etc.: Tolf, *Russian Rockefellers*, pp. 87–100, 139–41, 151–58, 182. Anna Alliluyeva in *Alliluyev Memoirs*, pp. 52–55, 84–86. Giving to Bolsheviks: Krasin in Williams, p. 59. Tiflis a marsh, Baku a centre: Stalin, *Works*, 2:188; second baptism of fire: Stalin,

Works, 8: 174–75. Suny, "A Journeyman for the Revolution," pp. 373–94. Assassinations, etc.: Geifman, *Thou Shalt Kill,* p. 414. Smoky and gloomy: Trotsky, *Stalin,* p. 4. Essad Bey, pp. 123–37. Mikoyan, *Tak bylo,* pp. 347–48. Shaumian and filth of Baku, Mikoyan, *Memoirs,* pp. 72–74. Kaleidoscope: Stalin, *Works,* 2:378. Baku irrepressible: Stalin, *Works,* 2:141. Oil kingdom: Stalin, *Works,* 2:141. On Baku, hit men and strikes: Stalin, *Works,* 2:81–83. Revolutionary centre: Stalin, *Works,* 1:189. Reiss, *The Orientalist,* pp. 9–15, including p. 12, "Dodge City" quotation, and Stalin connection with mother and Krasin, pp. 20–21; Essad Bey quotes, "my mother financed Stalin's press with her diamonds," p. 21; our city like Wild West, p. 32. Most dangerous place, rootless, physical violence, rapes, prehistoric, Gorky, life expectancy, disembowelled dogs: Baberowski, *Der Feind,* pp. 62–67. Nikita Dastakian, *Il venait de la Ville Noire*: Mauserists. Stalin expert on oil industry: Mgeladze, p. 28. For tales of Baku oil barons, Nobels, the palaces: Faud Akhundov's series "Legacy of the Oil Barons," parts 1–4, in *Azerbaijan International Magazine,* 1994. Farid Alakbarov, "Baku's Old City: Memories of How It Used to Be," *Azerbaijan International Magazine,* Autumn 2002. Also see Manaf Suleymanov's classic *Eskitdiklarim, Okhuduglarim, Gorduklarim* (What I Saw, What I Read, What I Heard).

3. Berlin, August 1907: RGASPI 558.15095. Kun, pp. 85–87, 341. W. S. Churchill, *Second World War,* 6:601. Stalin, *Works,* 2:48; 13:121, 388. Djilas, *Conversations with Stalin,* p. 79. Smith, pp. 194–96.

4. Spandarian a womanizer and fate of wife of Bolshevik: see Olga Spandarian letter to Shaumian in "Suren Spandarian in Siberian Exile," *Vestnik Archivov Armenii,* no. 1, 1966. Haemorrhagic colitis: GF IML 8.2.1.34.317–54, Mikheil Misha Monoselidze. GDMS 87.1955-368.1–16, Alexandra "Sashiko" Svanidze-Monoselidze. Typhus rash: author's interview with Svanidze cousin Mariam Svanidze, aged 109, Tbilisi, 2005. GDMS 1955-146.51–6, G. Elisabedashvili. Nursing her: author's interview with Svanidze cousin Katevan Gelovani, Tbilisi, 2005. Volkogonov, *Trotsky,* p. 11. TB and pneumonia, closed eyes: Levon Shaumian in Kun, p. 342. Sacraments: Delbars, *The Real Stalin,* pp. 52–53.

22 · BOSS OF THE BLACK CITY:
PLUTOCRATS, PROTECTION-RACKETS AND PIRACY

1. GDMS 1955-146.51–6, G. Elisabedashvili. GF IML 8.2.1.34.317–54, Mikheil Misha Monoselidze. GDMS 87.1955-368.1–16, Alexandra "Sashiko" Svanidze-Monoselidze. Gori: Davrichewy, p. 35. Iremashvili, pp. 30–40. Stalin in grave: author interview with Svanidze cousin Katevan Gelovani. Announcement: RGASPI 558.4.97. How he loved, overcome with grief, gun, failed to appreciate: RGASPI 558.4.647 Pelageya Onufrieva. Kun, pp. 117 and 341; farce at the funeral, p. 342.

2. *Alliluyev Memoirs,* pp. 52–54, 137, 110. Home: GDMS 1955-146.51–6, G. Elisabedashvili. RGASPI 558.4.663, Sergei Alliluyev. Marcou, p. 53. Kun, p. 38. Stalin, *Works,* 2:42–46 and 188; 8:174–75. Service, *Stalin,* p. 70. Suny, "A Journeyman for the Revolution," pp. 373–94. Vulikh in Kun, pp. 129–30. Tucker, p. 105. Smith, pp. 214 and 399. RGASPI 124.1.2035, M. Frumkin. Vyshinsky: GDMS 49, I. Bokov. Ostrovsky, pp. 259–67. RGASPI 558.4.583, I. Bokov. GF IML 8.2.1.19, S. Kavtaradze. GF IML 8.2.1.624.1–26, Bachua Kupriashvili. Sergo Ordzhonikidze in Rokhlin, *Dvadtsat piat*

let Bakinskoi organizatsii bolshevistikov. GF IML 8.2.1.35, I. P. Nadiradze. Shaumian: Mikoyan, *Tak bylo,* pp. 347–48. Shaumian and filth of Baku: Mikoyan, *Memoirs,* pp. 72–74. Tatiana Vulikh to Boris Nikolaevsky, Nikolaevsky, box 207, folder ID 207-9. Olga Spandarian letter in "Suren Spandarian in Siberian Exile." Persia: RGASPI 558.4.583, Mir Bashir Kasumov. Abel Yenukidze, "Iz proshlogo nashei partei," p. 18; Effendiev, "Istoriya rabochego," pp. 14–53. Muslim connections with Nariman Narimanov and Mammad Amin Rasulzade, see Rais Rasulzade, "Rasulzade: Founding Father of the First Republic," *Azerbaijan International Magazine,* 1999. Rasulzade enjoyed a fascinating career, founding the Azeri SDs (hiding Stalin on the run), then the Musavat Party, then helping create the independent Azerbaijan of 1918–21 before being rescued and taken to Moscow by Stalin, who let him go into exile (where Hitler tried to recruit him as a leader of a German-sponsored Caucasus).

3. Stalin in Switzerland: Ostrovsky, p. 265. Plekhanov and daughter in Switzerland: GF IML 8.2.1.3.291–310, Niko Akhmeteli.

23 · LOUSE RACING, MURDER AND MADNESS—PRISON GAMES

1. Raids in Baku and arrest: fighting squads and arsenal, ship heists, Vyshinsky, electric, almost too conspiratorial, killing opponents, plan to spring Stalin from jail: GF IML 8.2.1.6.183–203, Ivan Bokov. GDMS 49. I. Bokov quoted in Ostrovsky, pp. 259–67. RGASPI 558.4.583, I. Bokov. Vyshinsky on *Nicholas I* ship heist: Victor Serge, *Portraite de Staline,* p. 29. Vyshinsky, family in Odessa and Baku, in 1905–7, Bailovka, and in 1917–18: A. Vaksberg, *Stalin's Prosecutor,* pp. 13–27. GF IML 8.2.1.19, S. Kavtaradze. GF IML 8.2.1.624.1–26, Bachua Kupriashvili. RGASPI 558.4.523 and 627. RGASPI 4.84. RGASPI 4.107. S. Vereshchak, "Stalin vy tyurme," *Dni,* 24 Jan. 1928. Sagirashvili, pp. 182–83. Service, *Stalin,* pp. 78–79. Marcou, pp. 55–57. For K. Kato pseudonym: Stalin, *Works,* 2:125–31. Baku girlfriend: GMIKA 24(80).114, Alvasi Talakvadze. Yenukidze, "Iz proshlogo nashei partei," p. 18. Voroshilov: RGASPI 74.2.130 and 240. Ludmilla Stal, Tatiana Slavatinskaya: F. Chuev, *Kaganovich,* pp. 160–62. A. Daushvili, *Story of Soso Djugashvili,* pp. 239 and 252. Stal and Krupskaya in Paris, 1911: Krupskaya, p. 196. Maisky, p. 45. Marcou, p. 66; Ludmilla Stal biography: "Istoki podviga," *Ural,* no. 3, 1979. Stalin-Spandarian parties/deviations: GF IML 8.2.1.42, A. D. Sakvarelidze. Sentiment, skinning alive: GF IML 8.2.1.27.202–10, Ivliane Kukulava. Money from Mancho, Rothschilds, Landau, oil companies: RGASPI 124.1.325; RGASPI 71.15.213; RGASPI 558.4.659, Sergei Alliluyev. A. Rokhlin, *25 let Bakinskoi organizatsii bolsheviistikov,* pp. 81–83. Ostrovsky is the best historian of the relationship between Stalin and big business, pp. 473–75, 587–89, 593–94. Reiss, *The Orientalist,* pp. 9–21 and 32. Thanks to Prince Karol Schwarzenberg for Dr. Felix Somary story: it was told to him by Somary himself as an old man. Chechen guards beat up Stalin: I am grateful to Professor Jorg Baberowski for this story. Musa Nageyev kidnapping: Farid Alakbarov, "Baku's Old City: Memories of How It Used to Be." Mukhtarov and Stalin, tales of Baku oil barons, Nobels, the palaces, etc.: see Akhundov, "Legacy of the Oil Barons," parts 1–4. Memoirs of Manaf Suleymanov, *Eskitdiklarim*; see azeribook.com/history/ manaf_suleymanov. For Nageyev, also see Jilar Khanum, granddaughter, and Stalin's ten-minute chats quoted on echo-az.com/archive/2004_09/911/kultura02.shtml.

2. Bailov: GF IML 8.2.1.35.35–49, Ilya P. Nadiradze—swap, visit of Keke, hacksaw plan. Vereshchak, "Stalin v tyurme." Essad Bey, pp. 141–42. Smith, pp. 214–20. Service, *Stalin*, pp. 79–81. Trotsky, *Stalin*, p. 120. Sentencing: Ostrovsky, p. 281; Vyshinsky letter, p. 285. Vyshinsky, family in Odessa and Baku, in 1905–7, Bailovka, and in 1917–18: Vaksberg, *Stalin's Prosecutor*, pp. 13–27. Trip, Butyrki Prison, Viatka hospital, etc.: RGASPI 558.4.629 and 71.10.276. Louse racing, madness, wrestling, backgammon, Sergo fight versus SRs: GF IML 8.2.1.42, A. D. Sakvarelidze. Plan to spring Stalin from jail: GF IML 8.2.1.6.183–203, Ivan Bokov. Sergo and SRs, Stalin to Voroshilov: RGASPI 73.2.38. Giddy-up, escapes, Budu and Stalin stories: author's interview with Izolda Mdivani (widow of Budu's son Vahtang) and Mdivani family, Tbilisi, Georgia, 2006. Dirty politics: author's interview with Yuri Zhdanov. Dirty for the revolution: Beria, p. 18.

24 · "RIVER COCK" AND THE NOBLEWOMAN

1. Solvychegodsk: GAVO 108.1.5058.1–29. RGASPI 157.916 Stepan Shaumian to M. Tskhakaya. RGASPI 558.4.647—various memoirs in this font include Tatiana Sukhova; F. I. Blinov and Vologda transit jail; Stepan Belyakov, post office/jailer; Alexandra Dobronravova (dancing), A. Dubrovin (Mustafa drowned); M. Krapina on singing and River Cock and escape; priest's library. On Sukhova and Petrovskaya: GAVO 108.2.3992 and GAVO 108.1.2372. Stalin to Sukhova: RGASPI 558.1.4372. Details of Petrovskaya: office of Baku Governor, J. Djugashvili file including Baku interrogation of S. Petrovskaya and Stalin, RGASPI 558.1.635.1–95. Information from local Vologda archives, train times, etc.—Ostrovsky, pp. 290–92. Service, *Stalin*, p. 70. Smith, pp. 222–32. Escapes: Daly, *Watchful State*, p. 72. Sergei Alliluyev, *Pravda*, 22 Dec. 1939. *Alliluyev Memoirs*, pp. 136–37. Trotsky in Kun, pp. 96–97. V. Nikonov, *Molotov Molodost*, pp. 75–90. Georgian stranger helps: Charkviani, "Memoirs." Stalin to Malakia Toroshelidze: Dubinsky-Mukharadze, *Shaumian*, p. 156. Bolshevik collapse: Tucker, pp. 147–50. Service, *Lenin*, pp. 195–98. Lenin on porn quoted in Lauchlan, *Russian Hide-and-Seek*, p. 245. Stalin and the women: *Molotov Remembers*, pp. 164 and 174. Silk handkerchief, flower, T. Sukhova: RGASPI 558.4.647. Problems with dancing arm, can't take women by the waist: Montefiore, p. 260. Kun, p. 216—Kira Alliluyeva interview, quoting her mother, Zhenya. Author's interviews with Kira Alliluyeva, Moscow. Foot: Service, p. 571.

2. Sergei Alliluyev, *Pravda*, 22 Dec. 1939. *Alliluyev Memoirs*, pp. 136–37. E. D. Stasova, *Stranitsy zhizhn i borby*, p. 49. RGASPI 558.2.564 and 565, K. Savchenko. RGASPI 161.1.20. Milkman Okhrana reports: GARF 102.00.1909.5-3-A. Milkbar address: RGASPI 558.1.4516, Stalin to Tskhakaya.

25 · "THE MILKMAN": WAS STALIN A TSARIST AGENT?

1. Stalin's activities, Okhrana "Fikus" reports: GARF 102.00.1909.5-5-A. Death of Beso: RGASPI 71.1.275. Beso death and burial: GF IML 8.14.160.1–8. Financial matters: S. M. Levidova and E. G. Salita, *E. D. Stasova: biografichesky ocherk*, p. 173.

GF IML 8.2.1.624.1–26, Bachua Kupriashvili, on mail-ship piracy. Stalin, *Works*, 2: 150–62. RGASPI 558.1.26. RGASPI 558.1.4516. Service, *Lenin*, pp. 195–98.

2. Williams, pp. 154–55. RGASPI 558.1.4516, Soso Stalin to Tskhakaya. Service, *Lenin*, pp. 195–98. Tucker, pp. 147–49. Suny, "A Journeyman for the Revolution," pp. 373–94. RGASPI 124.1.325; RGASPI 71.15.213; RGASPI 558.4.659, Sergei Alliluyev. Rokhlin, *25 let Bakinskoi organizatsii bolshevistikov*, pp. 81–83. Ostrovsky, pp. 473–75, 587–89, 593–94. Stalin and Mdivani (Bochka) tipped off by Gendarmes: *Krasnyi Arkhiv*, no. 2 (105), 1941, p. 7. Traitor witch hunt: *Krasnyi Arkhiv*, no. 2 (105), 1941, pp. 7–8. Case of couple A. Prussakov and E. Kozlovskaya plus Leontiev: RGASPI 558.4.649, A. Khumarian. Leontiev case: *Zaria Vostoka*, 28 Apr. 1928, S. Yakubov. Okhrana agent: GARF 102.00.1909.5-3-A. Near arrest of Stalin, Sergo: Japaridze, *Vospominaniya*, p. 61. Stalin writes to editors of *Bakinsky Proletary* journal on provocations: RGASPI 558.1.26. Visit of Chernomazov and accusation of Koberidze: Ostrovsky, pp. 304–6. Stalin and Kuzma accuse each other: B. Kaptelov and Z. I. Peregudov, "Byl li Stalin agentom Okhranki?," *Rodina*, no. 5, 1989, p. 68. Russian Bureau appointed: *Proletarskaya Revolyutsiya*, no. 5, 1922, pp. 231–32. I. P. Vatsek: RGASPI 71.15.213. Shaumian: Mikoyan, *Tak bylo*, pp. 347–48. Mikoyan, *Memoirs*, pp. 72–74. Uratadze, p. 67. Arsenidze, pp. 72 and 224. Jordania, "Stalin." Olga Shatunovskaya: RGASPI 558.4.671. Tatiana Vulikh to Boris Nikolaevsky, Nikolaevsky, box 207, folder ID 207-9. How Okhrana recruited: *Alliluyev Memoirs*, pp. 43–45. Agents in Bolsheviks and how Okhrana spread suspicion deliberately: Daly, *Watchful State*, pp. 95, 106 and 117; killing informants the duty of honest person says Lenin, p. 37. Stefania Petrovskaya: K. Stefin in Stalin, *Works*, 2:179–201. Stalin accuses Chernomazov witnessed by GF IML 8.2.1.15.266–72, Natalia Dondarov (Azarian). Petrovskaya: GF IML 8.5.212, Col. Leontiev of Okhrana report, 28 Apr. 1914.

3. Tsarist agent: I am indebted in this section, unless specifically attributed, to Ostrovsky, pp. 431–62; on escapes from exile, pp. 431–39; on police corruption, pp. 515 and 545–47; on "Fikus" report on intelligence gathering by Stalin, p. 578; on 800-rouble bribe Sverdlov, p. 595. Stalin's five escapes: Charkviani, "Memoirs." RGASPI 671.1.287, Turukhansk money receipts, 1913–15. Ordzhonikidze and Zaitsev: RGASPI 558.4.258. Japaridze, *Vospominaniya*, pp. 61–62. GARF 110.19.119. Stalin meets police official on street and gendarme tip-offs: GDMS 167, G. Varshamian; GARF 102.00.5-61-A. Medvedev, *Let History Judge*, pp. 314–24. Service, *Stalin*, p. 74. Eremin letter: Lee, "Eremin Letter." Eremin text in Smith, p. 306. General Ivan Serov memo to First Secretary N. S. Khrushchev and Politburo: RGASPI 558.11.1288, 4 June 1956. Vulikh to Nikolaevsky, Nikolaevsky, box 207, folder ID 207-9. Uratadze, p. 67. Arsenidze, pp. 72 and 224. Jordania, "Stalin." Olga Shatunovskaya: RGASPI 558.4.671. Shaumian's jobs, buyout from arrest, Capt. Zaitsev: Akopian, *Shaumian*, pp. 64–76. Prison director Vachiev, 150 roubles each to free prisoners: "Iz proshlogo nashei partei," pp. 146–47. B. Kaptelov and Z. Peregudova, "Byl li Stalin agentom Okhranki?," *Rodina*, no. 5, 1989, pp. 67–69. Artyom Gio, *Zhizn podpolnika*, pp. 67–73. B. Slavin, "Stalin i Okhranka," *Alternativy*, no. 1, 1998, pp. 78–81, including Martynov report on Prague Conference, 1912, and Stalin's meeting with agent Tailor (Malinovsky), plan to visit Lenin and work on *Pravda*. Details of Okhrana surveillance, 1908–13: *Krasny Arkhiv*, no. 2 (105), 1941, pp. 4–31. Stalin on betrayal as bite of death: GF IML 8.6.312, D. Chkheidze (Turdospireli). Stalin edits his own *Short Course* biography including number of arrests: "I. V. Stalin sam o sebe: redakzionnaya pravka sobstennoy biografii," *Izvestiya TsK KPSS*, no. 9, 1990.

26 · TWO LOST FIANCÉES AND A PREGNANT PEASANT

1. RGASPI 558.1.628 and 635.1–95, office of Baku Governor—J. Djugashvili file including Baku interrogation of S. Petrovskaya and Stalin. RGASPI 558.11.1290 and RGASPI 558.4.130 and 208. Stalin arrests with Petrovskaya: State Historical Archive of Azerbaijan, 46.3.90.430, 46.1.324.165, 46.3.22.52, 46.3.348.10; and on Shaumian, Stalin and Petrovskaya, 1.1.479.12, 46.3.348.6, 7, 8, 156.1.51.66; ban from Caucasus 498.1.666.8–10, 46.3.495.103a, 498.1.176.73–4, 498.1.176.73–4, 498.1.175.38, 498.1.176.75–7, 81.1.27, 498.1.550.156. Hospital: GF IML 8.5.208, E. Esaian. Martynov: GARF 102.00.1910.5-6-B. Petrovskaya: GF IML 8.5.212, Col. Leontiev of Okhrana report, 28 Apr. 1914. On Stefania later: Ilizarov, p. 288; A. L. Litvin and others (ed.), *Genrikh Yagoda Narkom Vnutrennikh* (Kazan, 1997), p. 197.

2. RGASPI 558.4.628, various memoirs. Maria Kuzakova memoirs and others including Kryukova: RGASPI 558.4.647. Letters and contacts with abroad, 31 Dec. 1910, and Jan. 1911: Stalin, *Works*, 2:209–18. *Zaria Vostoka*, 23 Dec. 1925. Ivanian: RGASPI 558.1.5097. S. V. Malyshev, "Moia rabota v Pravde," *Bolshevistkaya Pechat*, vol. 4, 1937, p. 22. To Petersburg?: Kun, p. 109. Serafima Khoroshina, Kuzakova memoirs and local records—GAVO 108.1.4670 and 5058, 108.2.235; GAVO 18.2.4988 and PAVO 108.1.4670 3837.5.27, 3837.5.27 and 3837.5.2, and PAVO 859.10.43. Thanks to the directors of the two Vologda archives for their help. Ostrovsky, pp. 321–28: my account of the Serafima marriage is based on Ostrovsky's researches in Party Archive of Archangel Region (PAVO 859.10.21.1–2). Y. Sukhotin, "Bastard krasnogo vozhda." GARF 102.00.1910.5. Books, policemen, cheerful, singing, laughing, fiction and history books, jail time: RGASPI 558.4.540 Ivan Golubev. *Vstrechi s vozhdem: Rasskazy krestyan s Kureiki o tov. Staline*, pp. 32–36. Nikonov, *Molotov Molodost*, pp. 75–90. Sex and boredom: meeting of the British Ambassador Sir David Kelly and Stalin, 28 June 1949, cipher report, no. 548: thanks to Laurence Kelly and PRO 77618. Aram Ivanian: Kun, pp. 110–19; RGASPI 558.1.5097; Beria, p. 135. Lenin's anger: Dubinsky-Mukharadze, *Ordzhonikidze*, pp. 75–76. Planting pine trees: Mgeladze, pp. 54–55. Guy Chazan, "East-West Alloy Reviving Stalin's Belch," *Wall Street Journal*, 9 June 2004: thanks to Guy Chazan for this story. Lordkipanidze: Charkviani, "Memoirs."

27 · THE CENTRAL COMMITTEE AND "GLAMOURPUSS" THE SCHOOLGIRL

1. Vologda: RGASPI 71.10.276. RGASPI 71.10.647. RGASPI 558.1.4333. GARF 111.1.1110a. RGASPI 558.1.30. RGASPI 558.1.5377. RGASPI 558.1.647. P. G. Fomina-Onufrieva. Also: *Izvestiya TsK*, no. 10, 1989, p. 190. RGASPI 55.4.647 Sophia Kryukova. Life of Onufrieva: Kun, pp. 113–18. GARF 102.00.1911.5–83 and 102.7d.1911.2093. GAVO 108.1.5058. Ostrovsky, p. 331. *Krasnyi Arkhiv*, no. 8, 1937, pp. 165–97. *Krasnyi Arkhiv*, no. 2 (105), 1941, pp. 19–20. Details of Okhrana surveillance, 1908–13: *Krasnyi Arkhiv*, no. 2 (105), 1941, pp. 4–31. Stalin meets Sergo in Petersburg: RGASPI 161.1.20, V. L. Shveitzer. S. Alliluyev, "Vstrechi s Stalym," *Pravda*, 22 Dec. 1939. RGASPI 558.4.148 and 166. Spandarian to Krupskaya on Sergo giving Koba 50 roubles, Sept. 1911, in S. Shaumian, *Izbrannye proizvedeniya*, no. 1, pp. 346–7. A. S. Alliluyeva, *Vospominaniya*, pp. 38–40, on Todria, etc. Trotsky, *Stalin*, p. 134. "Serov" by M. Parrish in *Slavic Military Studies*, Sept. 1997, p. 127. General Ivan Serov memo to First Secretary N. S. Khrushchev and Politburo: RGASPI 558.11.1288, 4 June 1956.

2. GARF 7d.1911.2093 and 102.00.1912.5-14-V. RGASPI 558.4.166. On police, Gendarme, Okhrana and movements: Ostrovsky, pp. 336–42. RGASPI 558.2.75 and 76. Five escapes, five-rouble bribes, reunion with Spandarian, strict conspiracy, letter about Prague, Rostov meeting, jumping out of train: RGASPI 161.1.20, V. L. Shveitzer. RGASPI 558.2.75. RGASPI 17.4.647. *Molotov, Poluderzhavnyi,* p. 297. *Izvestiya TsK,* no. 5, 1989, p. 185. *Kommunist,* vol. 8–9, 1988. B. Slavin, "Stalin i Okhranka," *Alternativy,* no. 1, 1998, pp. 78–81. Code: Kun, p. 139. Prague: Ordzhonikidze, quoted in Kun, p. 129. Malinovsky: Ralph Carter Ellman, *Roman Malinovsky,* pp. 15–26, 31–33, 40–41, including quote on appearance, Lenin quote, hysterical, resigned, shot, pp. 58–66. Krupskaya, pp. 211 and 225. Radzinsky, *Stalin,* pp. 82–86 including Lenin and Malinovsky quotes. *Krasnyi Arkhiv,* no. 8, 1937, pp. 165–97. *Krasnyi Arkhiv,* no. 2, (105) 1941, pp. 19–20. Details of Okhrana surveillance, 1908–13: *Krasnyi Arkhiv,* no. 2, (105) 1941, pp. 4–31.

28 · "DON'T FORGET THAT NAME AND BE VERY WARY!"

1. S. Kavtaradze, *Iz vospominanii o tov. Staline,* pp. 3–17. Slavatinskaya: RGASPI 124.1.1782; Stalin letters to Slavatinskaya: RGASPI 558.1.5392. Yury Trifonov, *Otblesk kostra,* pp. 33–40. Relationship known: Ludmilla Stal/Tatiana Slavatinskaya: Chuev, *Kaganovich,* pp. 160–62. Sledding: *Alliluyev Memoirs,* pp. 138–41. RGASPI 161.1.20 V. L. Shveitzer.

2. Tiflis: RGASPI 558.4.534, M. Agayan. GF IML 8.2.1.34.317–54, Mikheil Monoselidze. GDMS 87.1955-368.1–16, Alexandra "Sashiko" Svanidze-Monoselidze. RGASPI 161.1.20, V. Shveitzer. GARF 102.00.1912.5-7-b. GARF 102.265.540. V. S. Emuksuzian, *Suren Spandarian,* pp. 26–29. *Istorichesky Zapisky,* no. 30, p. 80. Ostrovsky, p. 349. Visits to Tiflis and Baku: RGASPI 558.4.665; GFI ML 8.2.1.42. G. Haupt, *Les Bolsheviks par eux-même* (Makers of the Russian Revolution), pp. 268–73.

3. Baku: Nikolaevsky, box 207, folder 207-15, B. N. letter to T. Vulikh, 8 Aug. 1949. Rostov: RGASPI 161.1.20, Vera Shveitzer. *Krasnyi Arkhiv,* no. 2 (105), 1941, p. 26. Moscow leap out of train: Ostrovsky, pp. 350–51.

4. *Zvezda* and *Pravda:* Nikonov, *Molotov Molodost,* pp. 50–56; Molotov meetings with Stalin, pp. 113–15. RGASPI 161.1.20. Stalin, *Works,* 2:225–47, and 5:130. *Alliluyev Memoirs,* pp. 148–49. *Enziklopedichesky slovar Russkogo biographicheskogo instituta granat,* vol. 41, 2.62–63. Arrest: RGASPI 4.186. Stasova: RGASPI 71.10.407. May Day: Stalin, *Works,* 2:219. Daly, *Watchful State,* pp. 130-32. Trotsky, *Stalin,* p. 126; quoting Stalin and Lenin, p. 137. Service, *Stalin,* pp. 86–87. Malinovsky: Service, *Lenin,* p. 206. Slapping boy's face: Medvedev, *Let History Judge,* p. 337. RGASPI 161.1.20, V. Shveitzer.

29 · THE ESCAPIST: KAMO'S LEAP AND THE LAST BANK ROBBERY

1. Narym: RGASPI 4.186. RGASPI 558.4.647. GARF 102.00.1912.5-57-b. *Krasnyi Arkhiv,* no. 2 (105), 1941, pp. 26–27. RGASPI 161.1.20, Vera Shveitzer. Stalin and Sverdlov in Kolpashevo: Simon Vereshchak, *Dni,* 24 Jan. 1928. E. Pesikina, *Pravda,*

26 Dec. 1939: "V. Naryme"—including quote from Y. Alexeyev. RGASPI 4.647 and 558.4.190. Nikolaevsky's teacup: Kun, pp. 132–37. Kettle: Smith, p. 256. Memoirs: Chernenko, *Stalin*, pp. 74–79. Service, *Stalin*, pp. 88–89. A. S. Alliluyeva, *Vospominaniya*, p. 115. Sverdlov—hair, eyes, kind, gentle, Stalin and Sverdlov compare notes about exile: *Alliluyev Memoirs*, p. 141. Escape, thunderous voice: *Molotov Remembers*, pp. 141–44. Haupt, *Les Bolsheviks*, pp. 76–82. Escape: *Komsomolsky Pravda*, 10 Jan. 2007, Yuri Zhdanov memoirs.

2. Petersburg, *Pravda*, funds, election: Kavtaradze, *Iz vospominanii o tov. Staline*, pp. 3–17. *Oktyabre*, no. 11, 1942, pp. 100–103. Collects funds from Stasova: Stasova, *Stranitsy zhizhni i borby*, p. 101. A. E. Badaev, "O Staline," *Pravda*, 19 Dec. 1939. Visits to Tiflis and Baku: RGASPI 558.4.665. GF IML 8.2.1.42. RGASPI 558.4.647, Tatiana Sukhova. Slavatinskaya: RGASPI 124.1.1782. RGASPI 558.1.5392. Trifonov, *Otblesk kostra*, pp. 33–40. A. S. Alliluyeva, *Vospominaniya*, pp. 113–61. Doctor of escapology: Levon Shaumian quoted in Kun, p. 109. RGASPI 161.1.20, V. L. Shveitzer.

3. GF IML 8.2.1.624.1–26, Bachua Kupriashvili. Kamo and robbery: David Shub, "Kamo: The Legendary Old Bolshevik of the Caucasus," *Russian Review*, vol. 19, no. 3, July 1960, pp. 227–47. Imnaishvili, *Kamo*, section 1, pp. 74–88. Medvedeva-Ter-Petrossian, "Tovarish Kamo." Jacques Baynac, *Kamo: L'homme de main de Lénine*, pp. 90–100. Kamo's mental illness: Geifman, *Thou Shalt Kill*, pp. 167–70 and 323; Geifman, *Russia under the Last Tsar*, pp. 1–14. Kun, p. 75. Escape with help of Kote Tsintsadze and shootout on Kadzhorskoe Highway: Souvarine, *Staline*, pp. 101–3. Visits to Tiflis and Baku: RGASPI 558.4.665. GF IML 8.2.1.42.

30 · TRAVELS WITH THE MYSTERIOUS VALENTINA

1. RGASPI 124.1.1782; RGASPI 558.1.5392. Trifonov, *Otblesk kostra*, pp. 33–40. A. E. Badaev, *Bolsheviki v gosudarstvennoi Dume*, pp. 35–40. "Delo Malinovskogo," *Rech* 17 June 1917. GARF 102.00.1912.5–58b. RGASPI 558.4.157/193. Lenin, *Biograficheskaya khronika* 3:55. Elections: Service, *Stalin*, p. 90. A. S. Alliluyeva, *Vospominaniya*, pp. 113–16. Stalin's election articles including Trotsky as fake champion with fake muscles: Stalin, *Works*, 2:257–59 and 262–94. RGASPI 161.1.20, V. L. Shveitzer.

2. Route to Cracow, first trip: Alexander Shotman, "Kak iz iskry vosgorelos plamya," pp. 166–76. Smith, pp. 263–66, 270–76 and 300–303. Valentina Lobova: Kun, pp. 145–50. On meeting with Kalinin, Shotman, etc., and different theory of the journeys to Cracow: Ostrovsky, pp. 364–66 and 369–70. Slavatinskaya: RGASPI 124.1.1782; RGASPI 558.1.5392; Trifonov, *Otblesk kostra*, pp. 35–40. *Molotov Remembers*, p. 297. Badaev, *Bolsheviki v gosudarstvennoi Dume*, pp. 35–40. GARF 102.00.1912.5–58b. RGASPI 558.4.157 and 193. A. S. Alliluyeva, "Vospominaniya," *Roman-gazeta*, no. 1 (13), 1947, p. 38. Election of SD Duma leadership: G. I. Petrovsky, "Vospominaniya o Pravde," *Pravda*, 5 May 1922.

3. With Lenin in Cracow, first trip: RGASPI 558.1.5170. Lenin, *Biograficheskaya khronika* 3:50–55. GARF 102.265.531. Cracow, Lenin background: Krupskaya, pp. 204–5, including Stalin crossing border on transit pass. Service, *Lenin*, pp. 209–15. Lenin as Stalin's host, and beer: Charkviani "Memoirs." Food: *Komsomolsky Pravda*, 10 Jan. 2007, Yuri Zhdanov memoirs.

4. Back to Petersburg, Lenin summons Stalin back and election: Petrovsky, *Pravda*, 5 May 1922. Badaev, *Bolsheviki v gosudarstvennoi Dume*, pp. 35–40. Todria meeting

with Jordania: RGASPI 558.4.647. Letters from Cracow: GARF 102.265.532 (including 9/22 Dec. 1912 letter from Krupskaya to K.St.). RGASPI 558.4.560. GARF 102.00.1912.5–58b. Krupskaya letters Nov.–Dec. 1912 and Stalin letters from Cracow to Petersburg Dec. 1912–Jan. 1913: "Iz perepiski TSK RSDRP s mestnymi partinymi orgnizatsiyam," *Istorichesky Arkhiv*, no. 2, 1960, pp. 17–25. Lenin, *PSS*, 48:162–69.

31 · VIENNA, 1913: THE WONDERFUL GEORGIAN, THE AUSTRIAN ARTIST AND THE OLD EMPEROR

1. Second trip to Cracow: A. S. Alliluyeva, "Vospominaniya," *Roman-gazeta*, no. 1 (13), 1947, p. 38. Shotman, "Kak iz iskry vozgorelos plamya," pp. 166–76. Smith, pp. 263–66, 270–76 and 300–303. Kun, pp. 145–50. On meeting with Kalinin, Shotman, etc. and different theory of trips to Cracow, see Ostrovsky, pp. 364–66 and 369–70. Crossing and no food, fool Stalin: A. S. Alliluyeva, *Vospominaniya*, pp. 19–20. Stanislas Kot quoted in Smith, p. 405. RGASPI 124.1.233, Olga Veiland. Krupskaya letters: "Iz perepiski TSK RSDRP s mestnymi partinymi organizatsiyam," *Istorichesky Arkhiv*, no. 2, 1960, pp. 17–25. RGASPI 4.3.42. GARF 102.00.1913.5–46b. Kalinin suspected: Ostrovsky, p. 371. Kamenev Eskimo letter: RGASPI 71.10.189. Kun, including interview with Olga Veiland, pp. 150–55. Service, *Stalin*, pp. 91–92. Krupskaya, pp. 204–5. Lenin as Stalin's host and beer: Charkviani, "Memoirs." Lenin, *PSS*, 48: 162–69. Border crossing/food: *Komosomolsky Pravda*, 10 Jan. 2007, Yuri Zhdanov memoirs.

2. Second stay in Cracow Dec. 1912–Jan. 1913: RGASPI 71.10.189 and 558.1.4899. Malinovsky report on meetings: Stanford, Paris Okhrana, box 195, folder XVIc, 1 Mar. 1913. Illich nervous: Trotsky, *Stalin*, p. 149. Kun, p. 149. RGASPI 558.1.47 Stalin to Malinovsky, 2 Feb. 1913. *Molotov Remembers*, p. 101.

3. Vienna: RGASPI 558.4.647.418–20 and 431–4, Stalin in Vienna including Olga Veiland. RGASPI 124.1.233, Olga Veiland. RGASPI 558.1.47, Stalin to Malinovsky. RGASPI 558.1.47. RGASPI 30.1.3. Brigitte Hamann and Thomas Thornton, *Hitler's Vienna: A Dictator's Apprenticeship*, pp. 92 and 183. J. Sydney James, *Hitler in Vienna*, pp. 7–10, 107–10; Trotsky, *Hitler*, p. 143; Trotsky, p. 165. A. Kubizek, *The Young Hitler I Knew*, p. 83. Bruce Thompson, *Schnitzler's Vienna*, pp. 2, 7, 25. Bruce Thompson, *Hitler's Vienna*, pp. 246–61, on balls, winter, Tito, Trotsky, Hitler. Carl E. Schorske, *Fin de Siècle Vienna*, p. 119. Service, *Stalin*, pp. 92–93. Author's interview with Oleg Troyanovsky in Moscow. Troyanovsky, *Cherez gody*, pp. 24–25 and 161–62. Kun, including background of Troyanovsky, p. 153. Krylenko, Elena Rozmirovich: Vaksberg, *Stalin's Prosecutor*, pp. 33 and 328. Trotsky, *Stalin*, pp. 159–60 and 243. Smith, pp. 276–79. Stalin, *Works*, 2:257–59 and 262–94. Stalin asks for Bukharin's address from exile: RGASPI 558.1.5169. Wonderful Georgian: Lenin, *PSS*, 48:162–9. GARF 102.265.882.

32 · THE SECRET POLICEMAN'S BALL: BETRAYAL IN DRAG

1. Return from Vienna via meeting with Lenin, Cracow, Feb. 1913, and new name; Lenin approves: Charkviani, "Memoirs." Stalin, *Works*, 2:300–381. *Marxism and the*

National Question. Stalin and Lenin's view of nation: Service, *Stalin,* pp. 87 and 99–105. Van Ree, "Stalin and the National Question." GARF 102.265.532 (including 9/22 Dec. 1912 letter from Krupskaya to K.St.). Stalin name: Stalin, *Works,* 2:192, 254, 294 (12 Jan. 1913, first Stalin byline). Duranty quoted in Kun, pp. 158–59. Name: RGASPI 17.4.647, V. Shveitzer. *Molotov Remembers,* p. 164. Ludmilla Stal/Tatiana Slavatinskaya: Chuev, *Kaganovich,* pp. 160–62. Daushvili, *Story of Soso Djugashvili,* pp. 239 and 252. Stal and Krupskaya in Paris, 1911: Krupskaya, p. 196. Maisky, p. 45; Marcou, p. 66. Ludmilla Stal biography: "Istoki podviga," *Ural,* no. 3, 1979.

2. Arrest: police interrogation: RGASPI 558.4.214. Service, *Lenin,* p. 214. Makeup, drag, big shoes: Nikonov, *Molotov Molodost,* pp. 128–33. Slavatinskaya: RGASPI 124.1.1782; RGASPI 558.1.5392; Trifonov, *Otblesk kostra,* pp. 33–40. *Luch,* 26 Feb. 1913. Shotman, "Kak iz iskry vozgorelos plamya," pp. 175, 166. Badaev, *Bolsheviki,* pp. 155–66. Woman's mantle: Trotsky, *Stalin,* pp. 157–61. A. S. Alliluyeva, *Vospominaniya,* pp. 44–45. Stalin letters on Dan/Malinovsky, shortage of people, chocolate for Galochka, Malinovsky planting suspicions about others are recent discoveries by Ostrovsky, and also details of sentencing including informing of Minister of Interior: Ostrovsky, pp. 374–80. Georgian boy: GARF 102.265.882. GARF 102.00.1913.307. Vissarionov: GARF 102.00.1913.5–57V. *Iz arkhiva L. O. Dan,* p. 101. RGASPI 558.4.659 F. N. Samoilov. *Delo provokatora Malinovskogo,* p. 216— Malinovsky meets S. P. Beletsky. Ellman, *Roman Malinovsky,* pp. 15–26, 31–33, 40–41, 58–66. Krupskaya, pp. 211 and 225. Radzinsky, *Stalin,* pp. 82–86, including Lenin and Malinovsky quotes. RGASPI 558.1.47, Stalin to Malinovsky. RGASPI 558.1.48. Lenin's worries: Smith, pp. 300–303. Urals mission: Kun, p. 163.

33 · "DARLING, I'M IN DESPERATE STRAITS"

1. Yenisei: Service, *Stalin,* pp. 107–9. *Istoricheski Arkhiv,* no. 5, 1956, p. 116. GARF 5449.1.63: B. Ivanov, *Stalin i Sverdlov v Turukhanskoi ssylke.* V. Zavialov, "Tov. Stalin v Turuskanske," *Krasnoiarsky Rabochyi,* 21 Dec. 1939. Trotsky, *Stalin,* p. 170. Lenin, *Biograficheskaya khronika,* 3:125–50. Ostrovsky, pp. 387–88. Dubrovinsky's library: Trifonov, *Otblesk kostra,* pp. 35–37. A. V. Antonov-Ovseenko, *Stalin bez maski,* p. 383. F. Zakharov story quoted in Kun, p. 164.

2. RGASPI 558.4.220. Slavatinskaya: RGASPI 124.1.1782 Lenin, *Biograficheskaya khronika,* 3:125–50. RGASPI 558.1.52. RGASPI 55.1.49. RGASPI 558.1.89. RGASPI 558.1.659. GARF 102.00.1914.5–25b. RGASPI 558.1.4234. Also: Trifonov, *Otblesk kostra,* pp. 559–65. RGASPI 5581.1.5168. Bathhouse with Sverdlov: Kun, pp. 163–65. Escape suspicions: Zavialov, "Tov. Stalin." RGASPI 558.1.4235. Money received, 135 roubles: Ostrovsky, p. 395. Move to north: RGASPI 558.1.51. RGASPI 558.4.234. K. T. Sverdlova, *Y. M. Sverdlov,* pp. 175–77. Sverdlov and Stalin, week together, escape plans: E. Gorodetsky and Y. Sharapov, *Sverdlov,* pp. 95–100.

34 · 1914: ARCTIC SEX COMEDY

1. Kureika: Chernenko, *I. V. Stalin v sibirskoi ssylke,* pp. 140–42. I. M. and A. S. Taraseev and other memoirs: RGASPI 4.662 and 581. Money orders: Ostrovsky, p. 397. Mali-

novsky Case: RGASPI 558.1.52. Yakov Sverdlov, *Izbrannye,* pp. 267–80. Gorodetsky and Sharapov, *Sverdlov,* pp. 99–101. Vera Shveitzer, *Stalin v turukhanskoi ssylke,* including visit to Stalin in Kureika and his room, singing, Kamenev, pp. 30–32 and 47–50.

2. Ostrovsky, p. 397. Malinovsky: RGASPI 558.1.52. Sverdlov, *Izbrannye,* pp. 266–80, letters to Sara Sverdlova, L. I. Besser, D. F. Petrovskaya, wife Klavidia Novogorodzeva (depression, June 1914), p. 321, L. Dilevskaya (no trace of comradeship or community). Gorodetsky and Sharapov, *Sverdlov,* pp. 99–103. Shveitzer, *Stalin v turukhanskoi ssylke,* pp. 30–32 and 47–50. Ilizarov, pp. 291–93.

3. Malinovsky case: Ellman, *Roman Malinovsky,* pp. 31–66. Radzinsky, *Stalin,* quotes Lenin, p. 86. *Molotov Remembers,* p. 101. Smith, p. 249. Daly, *Watchful State,* pp. 150–53. Krylenko, Elena Rozmirovich: Vaksberg, *Stalin's Prosecutor,* pp. 33 and 328.

4. Sverdlov feud: Sverdlov, *Izbrannye,* pp. 266–80, 321. Gorodetsky and Sharapov, *Sverdlov,* pp. 99–103. GARF 5449.1.63 and 75, B. I. Ivanov. A. M., A. S. and F. A. Taraseev memoirs: RGASPI 558.4.581, 667 and 662. On movements from house to house in Kureika: Ostrovsky, pp. 397–99. Antonov-Ovseenko, *Stalin bez maski,* pp. 380–90. Ostrovsky believes there may have been an escape attempt: Ostrovsky, pp. 402–3. Kun, pp. 169–75.

5. Lidia and Laletin: RGASPI 558.4.662, L. P. Pereprygina-Davydova and F. A. Taraseev. RGASPI 558.4.667, M. A. Merzliakov. RGASPI 558.1.5169. A. Kolesnik, *Khronika zhizni semia Stalina,* pp. 58–62. Sukhotin, "Bastardy krasnogo vozhdia." A. Rokhlin, "Gde pryatali nezakonnnorojdennogo syna Stalina?," *Moskovsky Komsomolets,* 22 June 1996. Ivan Serov memo to Politburo: RGASPI 558.11.1288. *Izvestiya,* 8 Dec. 2000. Antonov-Ovseenko, *Stalin bez maski,* pp. 380–90. Pereprygin household, first Laletin sabre incident: Chernenko, *I. V. Stalin v sibirskoy ssylke,* pp. 140–49. *Vstrechi s vozhdem: Rasskazy krestyan s Kureiki o tov. Staline,* pp. 21–23 Anfisa Taraseeva—Stalin arrives; daughter Dasha on his back; songs; taught dancing; rubbed ointment versus rheumatism; Tishka dog; pp. 23–25 Ivan Saltykov on children, reading; writing more; making hut on Polovinsky Island, living there for weeks; hiding the rifles for Stalin; games out hunting; Pereprygins very poor. Elizaveta Taraseeva quoted in Ilizarov, pp. 308–9; Ilizarov quotes Merzliakov, pp. 300–305, and Lidia Pereprygina, pp. 310–11. Lidia in love: http://memorial.krsk.ru/Work/Konkurs/4/Panteon_stalina/00.htm. Kun, pp. 169–75. Svetlana Alliluyeva, *Only One Year,* pp. 381–82. Woman and child in exile. I. D. Perfilev in Volkogonov, *Stalin,* p. 8. Siberian girl steals into bed at night: Essad Bey, p. 191. Mark Franchetti, "Stalin's Secret Son by Girl 14," *Sunday Times,* 2001.

6. Spandarian arrives: Suren Spandarian, *Statii, pisma dokumenty,* pp. 340–41. RGASPI 161.1.10, V. L. Shveitzer. Shveitzer, *Stalin v Turukhanskoi ssylke,* pp. 18–31. Kun, p. 129. Dr. Dan Healy advised on the Tsarist age of consent and concept of statutory rape. Stalin on the First World War: Stalin, *Works,* 3:39–40.

35 · THE HUNTER

1. Winter, 1914–15. Turukhansk money receipts, 1913–15 collected by NKVD boss N. I. Yezhov and found in his safe: thanks to Professor J. Arch Getty for sharing this: RGASPI 671.1.287. Postal orders, letters to Alliluyevs, etc.: RGASPI 558.1.55 and 558.1.53. Visit to Stalin in Kureika and his room, singing, Kamenev: Shveitzer, *Stalin*

v turukhanskoi ssylke, pp. 30–32 and 47–50. Memoirs of Stalin in Kureika by Lidia Pereprygina, Daria Ponamareva and others: RGASPI 558.4.662. Stalin on Merzliakov: RGASPI 558.11.773. Extracts from Merzliakov and Lidia Pereprygina: Ilizarov, pp. 300–305 and 310–11. Kun, pp. 169–75. *Vstrechi s vozhdem: Rasskazy krestyan s Kureiki o tov. Staline*, pp. 21–23 and 23–25. Sverdlov gets fifty roubles per month salary in exile: Sverdlov, *Izbrannye*. Eating frozen fish flakes: Charkviani, "Memoirs." Lost in the blizzard, fishing, wood goblin and Tishka my companion, unfit for military service: A. S. Alliluyeva, *Vospominaniya*, pp. 55 and 62–63. Dog and hunting story: *Komsomolsky Pravda*, 10 Jan. 2007, Yuri Zhdanov memoirs. Stalin and Spandarian to Lenin, quoted in Service, *Lenin*, p. 112. Lenin to Zinoviev, do you remember last name of Koba, to V. A. Karpinsky, Koba sends regards, big request: Lenin, *PSS*, 48:101, 131, 161. Radzinsky, *Stalin*, p. 84. Pockmarked Joe: *Molotov Remembers*, p. 165. Shooting twelve partridges, skiing 48 versts and First World War: *Khrushchev Remembers* 1:302 and 385. Ulcers of war: Stalin, *Works*, 3:61.

36 · THE ROBINSON CRUSOE OF SIBERIA

1.   Summer–Winter 1915. Visits to Monastyrskoe, Party trial, Spandarian. F. Samoilov, "Bolshevistskaya fraktsiya IV Gosudarstvennoy Dumy v yeniseiskoi ssylke pered fevralskoie revolyutsiey." Spandarian to Lenin, 20 Aug.: Josef sends you all his warmest regards; 28 Sept.: Josef 150 versts away but . . . we'll see each other: Spandarian, *Statii, pisma, dokumenty*, p. 284. Last meeting: RGASPI 558.4.582 and 558.4.662 V. Shveitzer. Stalin and Spandarian: RGASPI 558.4.662, B. Ivanov. G. Petrovsky—Bolshevik meeting: RGASPI 558.4.662. Also GARF 5449.1.75. Money, I thought forgotten, Kamenev wet hens: RGASPI 558.4.54. Writing big articles—Stalin to Kamenev, send this to Lenin: RGASPI 558.1.56. I've found out nothing: RGASPI 558.4.662. Robbery and trial, Sverdlov accused: GARF 5449.1.75. RGASPI 558.4.662. A. E. Badaev, "O Staline," *Pravda*, 19 Dec. 1939. Sverdlov, *Izbrannye*, pp. 266–80, 321. Gorodetsky and Sharapov, *Sverdlov*, pp. 84–86 and 99–103. Ostrovsky, p. 408. RGASPI 558.11.1288. Spandarian ill: Ostrovsky, p. 409. Stalin inquires after Spandarian: S. Alliluyev, *Pravda*, 22 Dec. 1939. Vera Shveitzer: RGASPI 558.4.662. Condemnation of Kamenev: Merridale, "The Making of a Moderate Bolshevik," pp. 31–33, including Trotsky quote. Service, *Stalin*, pp. 109–10. Stalin noncommittal at Kamenev trial: Robert M. Slusser, *Stalin in October: The Man Who Missed the Revolution* (henceforth Slusser), pp. 13–14. Merzliakov and Lidia Pereprygina: Ilizarov, pp. 300–305 and 310–11. Revolution inevitable: Stalin, *Works*, 1:79. Kamenev and Stalin friends: Mikoyan, *Tak bylo*, p. 352. Kamenev gives Stalin Machiavelli: Rayfield, *Stalin and the Hangmen*, p. 22. Sweet revenge: Robert Conquest, *Stalin: Breaker of Nations*, p. 107.

2.   A. Lazebnikov, "Linii sudby," *Sovetskaya Kultura*, 16 July 1988. Merzliakov/Badaev, etc.: RGASPI 558.4.662. Moving house again, boat borrowed: RGASPI 86.1.112. RGASPI 558.4.54. Writing big articles—Stalin to Kamenev, send this to Lenin: RGASPI 558.1.56. I've found out nothing: RGASPI 558.4.662. Ostrovsky believes this was a full escape: pp. 409–13. F. Samoilov, *Po sledam minuvshego*, pp. 523–35. Pregnancy confirmed by General I. Serov: RGASPI 558.11.1288. Stalin drops in on Rukhadze: RGASPI 558.4.662, Kuzma Gavrilenko—Stalin on way from Kostino to Kureika via Miroedikha. Letter to author from Eva Purins,

9 Nov. 2000. Note in suit pocket: A. S. Alliluyeva, *Vospominaniya*, pp. 44–45. Spandarian: "Suren Spandarian in Siberian Exile."

37 · STALIN'S REINDEER-PROPELLED SLEIGH AND A SIBERIAN SON

1. Conscripted. Stalin volunteered: Ilizarov, pp. 311–12. Sleighs used first dogs, then reindeer, then horses; Stalin on go-slow: Shveitzer, *Stalin v Turukhanskoi ssylke*, pp. 43–51. Reindeer: *Alliluyev Memoirs*, pp. 189–90. RGASPI 558.4.218. Merzliakov, I. M. Taraseev, Arsenii Ivanov—present to mother: RGASPI 558.4.662. Sverdlov, *Izbrannye*, p. 99. Boris Ivanov: RGASPI 558.4.662 and GARF 5449.1.74. Kureika, memoirs of locals and history, conscription and hero's departure: http://memorial .krsk.ru/Work/Konkurs/4/Panteon_stalina/00.htm. I. D. Perfilev in Volkogonov, *Stalin*, p. 8. Svetlana Alliluyeva, *Only One Year*, pp. 381–82.

    V. G. Solomin to Stalin and Stalin reply, 5 Mar. 1947: RGASPI 559.11.804. The journey: Ilizarov, p. 313. Newspaper *Yeniseisk Krai* quoted by Ostrovsky, p. 416. Unfit for military service and trip to Petersburg with orators, etc.: A. S. Alliluyeva, *Vospominaniya*, pp. 55 55, 62–63, 165–69. Piece of Siberia: *Molotov Remembers*, p. 256. Achinsk: V. Shveitzer, "V Achinskoi ssilke," *Izvestiya*, 12 Mar. 1937. Stalin stays in Achinsk: RGASPI 558.4.218, 124.2.1549, 558.4.662, 649 and 667 (V. Shveitzer, V. P. Filipova, A. Pomerantseva) and RGASPI 4.649 (M. Muranov). Baikaloff, *I Knew Stalin*, pp. 27–30. Whispers: *Yeniseisk Krai* in Ostrovsky, p. 420. Trains and Stalin's movements: Ostrovsky, pp. 422–23. Petersburg: RGASPI 161.1.16. A. Shlyapnikov, *Semnadtsatyi god*, 2:443–47. Stalin stays with Baroness Maria Shtakelberg: Ostrovsky, p. 423. Grand Duke Michael telegram: Volkogonov, *Stalin*, p. 14.

38 · 1917 SPRING: FLOUNDERING LEADER

1. The account of 1917 from February to October is based on the following: Orlando Figes, *A People's Tragedy*; Richard Pipes, *The Russian Revolution*; Alexander Rabinowitch, *The Bolsheviks Come to Power*; Robert Service, *Stalin* and *Lenin*; Adam Ulam, *Lenin and the Bolsheviks*; W. Bruce Lincoln, *Passage through Armageddon: The Russians in War and Revolution* (henceforth Lincoln), Bernard Pares, *The Fall of the Russian Monarchy*; plus Leon Trotsky, *Stalin* and *My Life*; Nikolai Sukhanov, *The Russian Revolution*; and John Reed, *Ten Days That Shook the World* (henceforth Reed). Unless otherwise stated, Central Committee protocols are quoted from *Protokoly Tsentralnogo Komiteta RSDRP(b)*. On Petersburg, Feb.–Mar. 1917: *Molotov Remembers*, p. 133. Service, *Stalin*, p. 122. Lincoln, pp. 346–73. Figes, pp. 307–52.
2. Lenin doubts: *Molotov Remembers*, pp. 89–90 and 125. Service, *Stalin*, p. 122–25. Slusser, pp. 16–29. Sukhanov, *Russian Revolution*, p. 230. Bolshevik membership: Ostrovsky, p. 580.
3. Alliluyevs: Service, *Stalin*, p. 124. Vasileva, *Kremlin Wives*, p. 56—Yenukidze arrival and Nadya to Anna Radchenko. *Alliluyev Memoirs*, pp. 212, 184–91.
4. Coryne Hall, *Imperial Dancer: Mathilde Kschessinskaya and the Romanovs*, pp. 102–3 and 178–79. Stalin in charge and mistakes: "Protokoly i resolutsii Buro TSK RSDRPb Mart 1917g," *Voprosy istorii KPSS*, no. 3, 1963, pp. 134, 143–49, no. 5,

pp. 111–47, and no. 6, pp. 139–40. The war: Stalin, *Works,* 3:4–9. Volkogonov, *Stalin,* p. 20. Slusser, pp. 29–30, 43, 59–64. Service, *Stalin,* pp. 125–27. Radzinsky, *Stalin,* pp. 92–93. Service, *Lenin,* p. 263. Trotsky, *Stalin,* pp. 185–87 and 203. Shit and Krupskaya's view of Lenin's April Theses: Robert H. McNeal, *Bride of the Revolution,* pp. 167 and 171. Tucker, p. 165. Chariot: Stalin, *Works,* 3:1–3. Sergo: Dubinsky-Mukhadze, *Ordzhonikidze,* p. 131. Figes, pp. 354–84.

39 · 1917 SUMMER: SAILORS ON THE STREETS

1. Service, *Lenin,* p. 255. Slusser, pp. 16–30. Volkogonov, *Stalin,* pp. 15–20. Service, *Stalin,* pp. 125–27. Lincoln, pp. 362–65. Figes, pp. 141–54 and 385–98.
2. Krupskaya, pp. 294–96. Service, *Lenin,* pp. 255–73. Voroshilov: Vasileva, *Kremlin Wives,* p. 81. Williams, p. 176. Service, *Stalin,* p. 129. Volkogonov, *Stalin,* pp. 21–23. Trotsky, *Stalin,* p. 195. On Lenin: Lincoln, pp. 362–65; and Figes, pp. 385–98.
3. April, May: "Protokolyi resolutsii Buro TSK RSDRPb Mart 1917g," *Voprosy istorii KPSS,* no. 3, 1963, pp. 134, 143–49, no. 5, pp. 111–47, and no. 6, pp. 139–40. At April meeting—you could assign Stalin any task: *Molotov Remembers,* p. 137. April Conference: see *Sedmaya aprelskaya vserossiiskaya konferentsia RSDRPb, Protokoly.* Stalin, *Works,* 3:42, 51–60. Service, *Stalin,* pp. 125–28. Tucker, p. 165. Lenin as schoolmaster and Ludmilla Stal: Trotsky, *My Life,* p. 195. On Bureau elected by CC, on April Conference: Slusser, pp. 59–70 and 89–98. Figes, pp. 423–48.
4. Stalin, *Works,* 3:67–69. Speaker: A. I. Kobzov quoted in Volkogonov, *Stalin,* p. 21. Trotsky's return: Slusser, pp. 108–14, quoting Vereshchak and Trotsky on Congress of Soviets. Trotsky on stage: Sukhanov, *Zapiski o russkoi revolyutsii,* 7:44. Dull comments: Trotsky, *Stalin,* pp. 67 and 206–9 quoting Pestkovsky on speaking. Stalin avoided speaking: Service, *Stalin,* p. 126. Lenin, Shaumian and Yenukidze: Krupskaya, p. 304. Dzerzhinsky: Rayfield, *Stalin and the Hangmen,* pp. 56–57.
5. Move in with Molotov and Marusya; apology and a kind of commune: *Molotov Remembers,* pp. 37, 93, 122–23. Ludmilla Stal/Tatiana Slavatinskaya: Chuev, *Kaganovich,* pp. 160–62. Daushvili, *Story of Soso Djugashvili,* pp. 239 and 252. Stal and Krupskaya in Paris, 1911: Krupskaya, p. 196; Maisky, p. 45; Marcou, p. 66; Ludmilla Stal biography: "Istoki podviga," *Ural,* no. 3, 1979. Slavatinskaya at secretariat with Stasova: Stasova, *Stranitsy zhizhni i borby,* p. 84. Molotov: Slusser, p. 101. Alliluyevs visit Stalin: *Alliluyev Memoirs,* pp. 195–96.
6. June: Stalin, *Works,* 3:67–69; on demo, 3:92–94 and 105–9. Volkogonov, *Stalin,* p. 21. S. Pestkovsky, "Vospominaniya," *Proletarskaya Revolyutsiya,* no. 6, 1930, and *Proletarskaya Revolyutsiya,* no. 10, 1922, pp. 93–103. Role in Party: Sagirashvili, pp. 197–98. Trotsky's return: Slusser, pp. 108–18 and 125–39. Lincoln, pp. 387–90. Sukhanov, *Zapiski o russkoi revolyutsii,* 7:44. Trotsky, *Stalin,* p. 67. *Alliluyev Memoirs,* pp. 194–95. Figes, pp. 423–38.
7. 2–4 July: Stalin, *Works,* 3:110–33, 138–41 and 166–200. Slusser, pp. 139–50. Rabinowitch, *The Bolsheviks Come to Power,* pp. 1–16. Service, *Lenin,* pp. 283–85. Lenin, *PSS,* 21:9–10. I. G. Tsereteli, *Vospominaniya o fevralskoi revoliutsii,* p. 344. Krupskaya, p. 311. Trotsky, *Stalin,* pp. 206–11, quoting Ordzhonikidze. Radzinsky, *Stalin,* pp. 102–4. Service, *Stalin,* pp. 140–43. Dreyfus: Stalin, *Works,* 3:266. Bedny story: Slusser, pp. 155–60. Figes, pp. 427–38.

40 · 1917 AUTUMN: SOSO AND NADYA

1. Backlash and Lenin in hiding at Alliluyevs: A. S. Alliluyeva, *Vospominaniya*, pp. 181–90. Volkogonov, *Stalin*, pp. 24–26, quoting S. Alliluyev and V. N. Polovtiev on officer sent to kill Lenin. Dubinsky-Mukhadze, *Ordzhonikidze*, p. 178. Rabinowitch, *The Bolsheviks Come to Power*, pp. 17–38. Slusser, pp. 162–78 and 139–50. Service, *Lenin*, pp. 283–91. Trotsky, *Stalin*, pp. 206–11. Lincoln, pp. 392–96. Figes, pp. 427–38. Vyshinsky: Vaksberg, *Stalin's Prosecutor*, pp. 13–27.

2. Move into Alliluyevs, Olga makes coat, etc.: A. S. Alliluyeva, *Vospominaniya*, pp. 183–91. Service, *Stalin*, p. 141. Author's visit to the Alliluyev House Museum.

3. Sixth Congress and contact with Lenin: *Shestoi sezd RSDRPb, Avgust 1917 goda*. Service, *Lenin*, pp. 288–92. Radzinsky, *Stalin*, p. 108. Tucker, pp. 172–74. Service, *Stalin*, p. 143. Slusser, pp. 200–14. Trotsky, *Stalin*, pp. 213–21. *Molotov Remembers*, p. 165. Smith, p. 337. Rabinowitch, *The Bolsheviks Come to Power*, pp. 51–70 and 83–93. Figes, pp. 427–38. Stalin, *Works*, 3:110–33, 138–41 and 166–200.

4. Nadya Alliluyeva: letters to Anna Radchenko see Vasileva, *Kremlin Wives*, pp. 56–58, and quote from Svetlana, *Only One Year*. Author's interviews with Kira Alliluyeva, Moscow, 2001–2. A. S. Alliluyeva, *Vospominaniya*, pp. 183–91. On Nadya and Anna: Kun, pp. 211–15, quoting Vladimir Antonov-Saratovsky and interview with Kira Alliluyeva. Author's visit to the Alliluyev Museum.

5. Kornilov: Stalin, *Works*, 3:214 and 296–300. Sagirashvili, pp. 237–38. Rabinowitch, *The Bolsheviks Come to Power*, pp. 94–128. Lincoln, pp. 412–25. Figes, pp. 438–53.

6. Kamenev accused, Stalin uses repression against *Soldat*: Slusser, pp. 210–14. Rabinowitch, *The Bolsheviks Come to Power*, pp. 71–76. Figes, pp. 453–74.

7. September: Stalin, *Works*, 3:214, 271–76, 277–82, 296–300. *Alliluyev Memoirs*, p. 223. Rabinowitch, *The Bolsheviks Come to Power*, pp. 129–90. Lincoln, pp. 426–53. Figes, pp. 453–74. Sagirashvili, pp. 193–94.

41 · 1917 WINTER: THE COUNTDOWN

1. October. 10 Oct. CC: *CC Protocols*, pp. 83–100. Slusser, pp. 226–36. Tucker, pp. 44–46. Service, *Stalin*, pp. 148–50. Volkogonov, *Stalin*, p. 27.

2. 16–20 Oct.: *Protokoly Tsentralnogo Komiteta RSDRP(b). Avgust 1917–Fevral 1918* (henceforth *Protokoly TSK*), pp. 32–55. Stalin at CC: Stalin, *Works*, 3:407–8. Strong Bulls of Bashan Have Beset Me Round: Stalin, *Works*, 3:409–13. Trotsky, *Stalin*, pp. 228–34. Slusser, pp. 226–36. Service, *Lenin*, pp. 306–7. Stalin in contact with Lenin: Radzinsky, *Stalin*, pp. 110–14. Figes, pp. 475–81. Tucker, pp. 179–80. Lincoln, pp. 426–38. Rabinowitch, *The Bolsheviks Come to Power*, pp. 218–25, 231–42. Trotsky Mephisto: Reed, p. 85.

3. 20–24 October. "What Do We Need?": Stalin, *Works*, 3:414–17. Trotsky, *Stalin*, pp. 228–34. Slusser, pp. 234–45. Service, *Stalin*, pp. 151–53. Service, *Lenin*, pp. 306–22. *Molotov Remembers*, p. 162. *Protokoly TSK*, pp. 32–55 and 99–117. Volkogonov, *Trotsky*, p. 82. RGASPI 558.4.668 and 663, Fyodor Alliluyev. A. S. Alliluyeva, *Vospominaniya*, p. 61. Volkogonov, *Stalin*, p. 30. Radzinsky, *Stalin*, pp. 110–14, including Fofanova and Trotsky quotes on liaison with Lenin. Sagirashvili, pp. 198–200. Y. Lutsky, *Voprosy Istorii KPSS*, no. 11, 1986, pp. 81–90. Stalin's talk with Trotsky and Congress

delegates: "Pismo M. Zhakov k Vasilchenskoe," *Proletarskaya Revolyutsiya*, no. 10, 1922, pp. 88–93, including clue on his work earlier at *Rabochyi Put. CC Protocols,* pp. 119–20. Rabinowitch, *The Bolsheviks Come to Power,* pp. 242–61. Lincoln, pp. 438–46.

42 · GLORIOUS OCTOBER 1917: THE BUNGLED UPRISING

1. Lenin and Stalin to the Smolny 24–25 Oct.: Trotsky, *Stalin,* pp. 228–34. Service, *Lenin,* pp. 310–22. Recognized by rotters: Trotsky in Radzinsky, *Stalin,* p. 115. Sagirashvili, pp. 198–200, including Stalin's attempts to refuse Narkom, heard from Yenukidze and Karakhan. CC sittings: Y. Lutsky, *Voprosy Istorii KPSS,* no. 11, 1986, pp. 81–90. Rakhia and Ravich quoted in Radzinsky, *Stalin,* pp. 115–16. Molotov's role, government formed: *Molotov Remembers,* pp. 94–96. Figes, pp. 473–76, 483–85. Slusser, pp. 244–47. Rabinowitch, *The Bolsheviks Come to Power,* pp. 265–68, 271–72, 306. Lincoln, pp. 445–47. Smolny: Reed, pp. 87, 96; glimpse of MRC at work, p. 104.

43 · POWER: STALIN OUT OF THE SHADOWS

1. Fall of the Winter Palace: Trotsky, *Stalin,* pp. 228–34. Radzinsky, *Stalin,* pp. 115–19, rapes and Lenin takes off makeup. CC sittings: Y. Lutsky, *Voprosy Istorii KPSS,* no. 11, 1986, pp. 81–90. Rabinowitch, *The Bolsheviks Come to Power,* pp. 269–70, 276–92, including red lantern, faulty cannons, drinking, delays and bungles. Lincoln, pp. 446–57, including drinking at palace. Figes, pp. 485–95. Theatres, etc.: Reed, p. 95; Congress of Soviets, pp. 98–99; Trotsky, p. 104; spank you, pp. 106–7; looting, servants, pp. 108–10. Sagirashvili, pp. 193–200, 203–4, 238, 248–52.

2. Sleep, 25–26 Oct.: Trotsky, *Stalin,* pp. 228–34. CC sittings: Y. Lutsky, *Voprosy Istorii KPSS,* no. 11, 1986, pp. 81–90. Lincoln, pp. 452–55. Rabinowitch, *The Bolsheviks Come to Power,* pp. 303–4. Reed, pp. 112–13; dawn, pp. 116–17, 125; Lenin speaks, pp. 128–29; Kamenev, p. 138. Ulam, *Lenin and the Bolsheviks,* pp. 482–96.

3. 25 Oct. 1917 and after. 29 Nov. 1917, Chetverka Bureau: see Slusser, pp. 94–97. *Protokoly TSK,* p. 134, co-signed order of 3 Nov. 1917—thanks to Service, *Stalin,* p. 622. RGASPI 558.4.668 and 663, Fyodor Alliluyev. S. Pestkovsky, "Vospominaniya," *Proletarskaya Revolyutsiya,* no. 6, 1930, and *Proletarskaya Revolyutsiya,* no. 10, 1922, pp. 93–103. Trotsky, *Stalin,* pp. 228–47. Figes, pp. 496–512. Early days, revolution without shooting, Molotov quote, instructions on Lenin's office access, 22 Jan. 1918: Radzinsky, *Stalin,* pp. 118–23 and 137. Tucker, p. 182. Trotsky and Stalin most talented, tea-drinkers: *Molotov Remembers,* pp. 96, 141 and 148. Israel Getzler, *Sukhanov: Chronicler of the Russian Revolution,* p. 85. Sagirashvili, pp. 193–200, 203–4, 238. Lenin walks in: Tsintsadze, "Chemi Mogonebani," pp. 220–25. Stalin major role in defending Petrograd versus Krasnov revolt, Nov. 1917 with Dzerzhinsky, Sverdlov, Ordzhonikidze, and orders to CinC, 9 Nov., with Stalin and Lenin: Volkogonov, *Stalin,* p. 43. "The Four," 9 Nov. 1917: Trotsky, *Stalin,* pp. 240–43; encounter at first Cabinet meeting. Volkogonov, *Stalin,* p. 43. First days in power and founding of Cheka: Service, *Lenin,* pp. 309–11. Concentration camp: Service, *Stalin,* p. 158. Lincoln, pp. 457–68. Ulam, *Lenin and the Bolsheviks,* pp. 482–96, including Shlyapnikov and prostitutes. Lenin adds Stalin and Trotsky as the only two leaders permitted

access to his office without invitation (copy on display at Smolny Institute museum): RGASPI 5.1.1802.47. For Lenin's notes, see Pipes, *Unknown Lenin,* and quotes from Lenin and Trotsky in N. Ferguson, *War of the World,* pp. 148–51.

EPILOGUE · AN OLD TYRANT—IN REMEMBRANCE OF THINGS PAST

1. Charkviani, "Memoirs." *Molotov Remembers,* p. 212. Rayfield, *Stalin and the Hangmen,* pp. 8–10. *Khrushchev Remembers,* 1:305. Keke, Soso and Sasha Egnatashvili: RGASPI 558.11.1549.1–69. Svetlana quoted in Zhores Medvedev and Roy Medvedev, *Unknown Stalin,* p. 297. Historians will find out: Mgeladze, pp. 240–41.

2. Alliluyevs: Richardson, *Long Shadow,* pp. 73–75. Author's interviews with Vladimir Alliluyev (Redens), Leonid Redens, Kira Alliluyeva, Moscow, 2001–3. Kamo and Fyodor: Mikoyan, *Memoirs,* pp. 431–33. See Montefiore for full family story.

3. Svanidzes: Kun, p. 6. See Montefiore for full story. RGASPI 558.1.5099, Stalin to M. Monoselidze. GF IML 8.2.1.50.239–55, Dzhavaira Khutulashvili. Author's interviews with K. Gelovani and M. Svanidze, Tbilisi, 2005.

4. Women; Slavatinskaya: RGASPI 124.1.1782; Trifonov, *Otblesk kostra,* pp. 33–40. Kun, pp. 41 and 46. Marcou, p. 76. Petrovskaya: Ilizarov, p. 288; and possible case against a Sofia Petrovskaya in A. L. Litvin, *Genrikh Yagoda Narkom,* Kazan 1997, p. 197—it is not clear if this is the same Petrovskaya and in any case her destiny is unknown. Onufrieva: Kun, p. 116. On Stal and Slavatinskaya: Chuev, *Kaganovich,* p. 219. RGASPI 558.4.647, P. Onufrieva Fomina. RGASPI 558.4.647, Tatiana Sukhova.

5. RGASPI 558.4.662, L. P. Pereprygina-Davydova and F. A. Taraseev. RGASPI 558.4.667, M. A. Merzliakov. RGASPI 558.1.5169. Kolesnik, *Khronika zhizni semia Stalina,* pp. 58–62. Sukhotin, "Bastard krasnogo vozhdia." Rokhlin, "Gde pryatali nesakonnorojdennogo syna Stalina?" Ivan Serov memo to Politburo: RGASPI 558.11.1288. *Izvestiya,* 8 Dec. 2000. Antonov-Ovseenko, *Stalin bez maski,* pp. 380–90. Pereprygin household, first Laletin sabre incident: Chernenko, *I. V. Stalin v sibirskoy ssylke,* pp. 140–49. *Vstrechi s vozhdem,* pp. 21–25. Ilizarov, pp. 288–92, 300–15. Lidia in love: *http://memorial.krsk.ru/Work/Konkurs/4/Panteon_stalina/00.htm.* Kun, pp. 169–75. Svetlana Alliluyeva, *Only One Year,* pp. 381–82. Volkogonov, *Stalin,* p. 8. Essad Bey, p. 191. Mark Francherti, "Stalin's Secret Son by Girl 14," *Sunday Times* (London), March 2001.

6. Keke, Soso and Sasha Egnatashvili: RGASPI 558.11.1549.1–69. (45.1.1549). Medvedev and Medvedev, *Unknown Stalin,* p. 297. Beria, pp. 20–21.

7. Money to Kapanadze: RGASPI 558.1.5978 and 5080. Iremashvili, pp. 36, 59–61 and 77. Davrichewy, pp. 36, 244 and 160. Letter to author from Iralki de Davrichewy 23 Aug. 2006. For Mata Hari and Marthe Richard stories, see Francis Lacassin, "Mata Hari ou la romance interrompue," *Magazine Littéraire,* no. 43, Aug. 1970. Davrichewy, "Je suis le demi-frère de Staline," pp. 25–30.

8. Kamo: *Russian Review,* vol. 19, no. 3, July 1960, pp. 227–47. Kamo and Lenin: Ulam, *Lenin and the Bolsheviks,* p. 723.

9. Author's interview with Alexander Egnatashvili's grandson Guram Ratishvili, Tbilisi 2005. Kun, pp. 6–7. Loginov, p. 14. GARF 7523.107.127.1–6, General N. Vlasik interrogation. Roman Brackman, *Israel at Noon* (New York, 2006), p. 5. Putin grandfather, see Montefiore, *Court of the Red Tsar,* p. 293 (U.S. paperback).

10. Old Bolsheviks, Ordzhonikidze, Molotov, etc.: see Montefiore. Sergo versus Molo-

tov fight: *Molotov Remembers*, p. 113. Terror Deaths: 1937–38, see Service, *History of Twentieth-Century Russia*, p. 222. Georgian terror statistics: Amy Knight, *Beria*, pp. 79–84. Author's interview with Izolda Mdivani (widow of Budu's son Vahtang) and Mdivani family in Tbilisi, Georgia, 2006. Vyshinsky: Vaksberg, *Stalin's Prosecutor*, pp. 13–37.

11. Stalin stops publication: RGASPI 45.1.803.1, 558.11.730, 558.11.787, 558.11.1496, 558.11.730, 558.11.787.2.

12. Dinners in old age: Charkviani, "Memoirs." Megalomaniacs: "Provisional Revolutionary Government and Social Democracy," *Proletariatis Brdzola*, 15 Aug. 1905: Stalin, *Works*, 1:140–61. 20–25 million deaths: A. N. Yakovlev, *A Century of Violence in Soviet Russia* (New Haven, 2000), p. 234.

Select Bibliography

PRIMARY

Alexandrov, G. F., et al. (eds.), *Iosif Vissarionovich Stalin, Kratkaya biografiya*, Moscow 1946.
Alliluyeva, A. S., *Vospominaniya*, Moscow 1946 [Also: "Vospominaniya," *Roman-gazeta*, 1947].
Alliluyev, Sergei, "Vstrechi s tov. Stalinym," *Proletarskaya Revolyutsiya*, no. 8, 1937.
Alliluyev, Sergei, *Proidennyi put*, Moscow 1946.
Alliluyev, Sergei, and Alliluyeva, Anna, *The Alliluyev Memoirs*, ed. David Tutaev, London 1968.
Alliluyeva, Svetlana, *Twenty Letters to a Friend*, London 1967.
Alliluyeva, Svetlana, *Tolko odin god*, New York 1969.
Alliluyeva, Svetlana, *Only One Year*, London 1971.
Alliluyeva, Svetlana, *Dvadtsaty pisem k drugu*, Moscow 1981.
Alliluyeva, Svetlana, *Dalyokaya muzika*, New York 1988.
Alliluyev, V. F., *Khronika odnoi semi*, Moscow 2002.
Anninsky, L., et al. (eds.), *Stalin v vospominaniyakh sovremennikov i dokumentov epokhi*, Moscow 2002.
"Arkhivnye materaly o revolyutsionnoy delayatelnosti I. V. Stalina," *Krasny Arkhiv*, no. 2 (105), 1941.
Arkomed, S. T., *Robochee dvizhenie i sotsial-demokratiya na Kavkaze*, Moscow-Petrograd 1923.
Arsenidze, R., "Iz vospominanii o Staline," *Novy Zhurnal*, no. 72, June 1963.
Artyom: see F. A. Sergeev.
Badaev (Badayev), A., *The Bolsheviks in the Tsarist Duma*, London 1929.
Badaev, A., *Bolsheviki v gosudarstvennoi Dume, Vospominaniya*, Moscow 1954.
Bagirov, M., *Iz istorii bolshevistskoi organizatsii Baku i Azerbaijana*, Moscow 1948.
Baikaloff, A. V., "Turukhanskie bunt politicheskikh ssylnykh," *Sibirskie Arkhiv*, no. 2, Prague 1929.

Baikaloff, A. V., *I Knew Stalin*, London 1940.

Barbusse, H., *Stalin: A New World through One Man*, New York 1935.

Batumskaya Demonstratsia 1902 goda, Moscow 1940.

Bazhanov, B., *Bazhanov and the Damnation of Stalin*, Athens, Ohio 1990.

Beria, L. P., *K voprusu ob istorii bolshevistskikh organizatsiyakh v Zakavkaze*, Moscow 1935.

Beria, L. P., *Lado Ketskhoveli*, Moscow 1938.

Beria, S., *Beria My Father: Inside Stalin's Kremlin*, London 2001.

Bessedovsky, G., *Revelations of a Soviet Diplomat*, London 1931.

Bibineishvili, V. (Baron), *Za chetvet veka*, Moscow 1931.

The Bolsheviks and the October Revolution: The Minutes of the Central Committee of the Russian Social-Democratic Party (Bolsheviks), August 1917–February 1918, London 1974.

Bukharin, N., *How It All Began*, New York 1998.

Bulgakov, Mikhail, *Batum*, Moscow 2004.

Charkviani, Candide, "Memoirs" (mss).

Chavichvili, Khariton, *Patrie, prisons, exil—Staline et nous*, Paris 1946.

Chavichvili, Khariton, *Révolutionnaires russes à Genève en 1908*, Geneva 1974.

Chernenko, K. (and Moskalev, M. A.), *I. V., Stalin v sibirskoi ssilke*, Krasnoyarsk 1942.

Chetvertyi (obedinitelnyi) sezd RSDRP, Moscow 1949.

Chetvertyi (obedinitelnyi) sezd RSDRP. Protokoly. Aprel–Mai 1906, Moscow 1959.

Dan, F., *Proiskhozhendenie bolshevizma*, New York 1946.

Dan, Lydia, "Bukharin o Staline," *Novy Zhurnal*, no. 75, March 1964.

Dan, L. O., *Iz arkhiva L. O. Dan*, Amsterdam 1987.

Dastakian, Nikita, *Il venait de la Ville Noire: souvenirs d'un Arménien du Caucase*, Paris 1998.

Davrichewy, Josef, "Je suis le demi-frère de Staline," *Miroir de l'Histoire*, December 1967.

Davrichewy, Josef, *Ah! Ce qu'on rigolait bien avec mon copain Staline*, Paris 1979.

Djilas, Milovan, *Conversations with Stalin*, New York 1962.

Djugashvili, Galina (Gulia), "Ded, papa, mama i drugie," *Druzhba Naradov*, no. 6, 1993.

Effendiev, "Istoriya rabochego dvizheniya turetskogo proletariata," in *Iz prochlogo. Stati i vospominaniya iz istorii bakinskoi organizatsii*, Baku 1923.

Elwood, R. C. (ed.), *Vserossiyskaya Konferentsiya Rossiiskoi Sotsial-Demokraticheskoi Rabochei Partii 1912 goda*, London 1982.

Gachechiladze, S., "Memoirs" (mss, Tbilisi).

Gio, Artyom, *Zhizn podpolshika*, Leningrad 1925.

Gogebashvili, Y. (ed.), *Deda Ena*, Tiflis 1912 and 1916.

Gorky, Maxim, *Days with Lenin*, London n.d..

Gromyko, A. A., *Memoirs*, London 1989.

Iosif Vissarionovich Stalin, Kratkaya biografia, Moscow 1938–47.

Iremaschwili, *Stalin und die Tragödie Georgiens*, Berlin 1932.

Iskander, Fasil, *Sandro of Chegem*, London 1979.

Istoricheskie mesta Tbilisi. Putevoditel po mestam, svyazannym s zhiznyu i deyatelnostyu I. V. Stalina, ed. Georgian Filial of the Institute of Marx–Engels–Lenin, Tbilisi 1944.

Ivanov, B. I., *Vospominaniya rabochego bolshevika*, Moscow 1972.

Jordania, Noe: see Zhordania.

Kaganovich L. M., *Tak govoril Kaganovich*, ed. F. Chuev, Moscow 2002.

Kaminsky, V., and Vereshchagin, I., "Detstvo i yunost vozhdya. Dokumenty, zapiski, rasskazy," *Molodaya Gvardiya*, no. 12, 1939.

Kavtaradze, S., *Iz vospominanii o tov. Staline*, Voroshilovgrad 1936.

Kavtaradze, S., "Iz vospominanii," *Oktyabre*, no. 11, 1942.

Kavtaradze, S., "Memoirs" (mss in Georgian).

Kennan, G., *Siberia and the Exile System*, London 1891.

Khatissian, Alexander, "Memoirs of a Mayor," *Armenian Review* 2 (3), September 1949.

Khrushchev, N. S., *Khrushchev Remembers*, London 1971.

Khrushchev, N. S., *Khrushchev Remembers: The Glasnost Tapes*, London 1990.

Kollontai, A., *Iz moey zhizhni i raboty*, Moscow 1974.

Krasin, L. B., "Bolshevistskaya partiinaya tekhnika," in *Tekhnika bolshevistkogo podpolya, Sbornik statei i vospominanii*, Moscow 1925.

Krupskaya, N., *Vospominaniya o Lenine*, Moscow 1968.

Krupskaya, N., *Memoirs of Lenin*, London 1970.

Kvashonkin, A. V., Khlevnyuk, O. V., Kosheleva, L. P. and Rogavaya, L. A. (eds.), *Bolshevistkoe rukovodstvo. Perepiska 1912–27*, Moscow 1996.

Lado Ketskhoveli. Sbornik dokumentov i materialov, Tbilisi 1969.

Lakoba, Nestor, *Stalin i Hashimi 1901–2*, Sukhum 1934.

Lansbury, George, *My Life*, London 1928.

Lenin, V. I., *Polnoe sobranie sochineniyi*, Moscow 1958–65.

Lenin, V. I., *Biograficheskaya khronika*, 12 vols., Moscow 1970–82.

Lenin, V. I., *Perepiska V. I. Lenina i rukovodimykh im uchrezhdenii RSDRP s mestnymi partiinymi organizatsiyami 1905–7*, Moscow 1982.

Lobanov, M. (ed.), *Stalin: v vospominaniyakh sovremenikov i dokumentov epokhi*, Moscow 2002.

Ludwig, Emil, *Stalin*, New York 1942.

Lunacharsky, A., *Revolutionary Silhouettes*, New York 1968.

Makharadze, F., *Ocherki revoliutsionnogo dvizheniya v Kavkazi*, Tiflis 1927.

Makharadze, F., and Khachapuridze, G. V., *Ocherki po istorii rabochego i krestyanskogo dvizheniya v Gruzii*, Moscow 1932.

Medvedeva-Ter-Petrossian, S. F., "Tovarish Kamo," *Proletarskaya Revolyutsiya*, no. 8/9, 1924.

Meshcheryakov, N. L., *Kak my zhili v ssylke*, Leningrad 1929.

Mgeladze, A., *Stalin kakim ya ego znal*, Tbilisi 2001.

Mikoyan, A. I., *The Memoirs of Anastas Mikoyan*, vol. 1: *The Path of Struggle*, Madison, Connecticut 1988.

Mikoyan, A. I., *Tak hylo*, Moscow 1999.

Molotov, V. M., *Sto Sorok Besed s Molotovym*, ed. F. Chuev, Moscow 1991.

Molotov, V. M., *Molotov Remembers*, ed. F. Chuev, Chicago 1993.

Molotov, V. M., *Poluderzhavnyi vlastelin*, Moscow 1999.

Nikolaevsky, Boris, *Power and the Soviet Elite: The Letter of an Old Bolshevik and Other Essays*, New York 1965.

Nutsubidze, Ketevan, and Shalva Nutsubidze, *Nakaduli*, Tbilisi 1993.

Orlov, Alexander, *Secret History of Stalin's Crimes*, London 1954.

O Stepane Shaumiane, Vospominaniya, ocherki, stati, sovremennikov, Moscow 1988.

Perkins, Frances, *The Roosevelt I Knew*, New York 1946.

Pestkovsky, S. "Vospominaniya o rabote v Narkomnatse 1917–1919," *Proletarskaya revolutyutsiya*, no. 6, 1930.

Pestkovsky, S., "Ob oktiabrskikh druakh v Pitere," *Proletarskaya revolutyutsiya*, no. 10, 1922.

Protokoly Tsentralnogo Komiteta RSDRP(b). Avgust 1917–Fevral 1918, Moscow 1958.

"Protokoly Vserossiiskogo (martovskogo) soveshchaniya partiinykh rabotnikov 27 marta–2 aprelya 1917 goda," *VIKPSS*, no. 6, 1962.

Pyati (londonskii) sezd RSDRP, Protokoly, Aprel–Mai 1907 goda, Moscow 1963.

Raskolnikov, F. F., "Priezd tov. Lenina v Rossiyu," *Proletarskaya Revolyutsiya*, no. 1, 1923.

Rasskazy o velikom Staline, Tbilisi 1941.

Rasskazy starikh robochikh Zakavkazya o velikom Staline, Moscow 1937.

Reed, John, *Ten Days That Shook the World*, London 1982.

Revolyutsiya 1905 goda v Zakavkaze. Istpartotdel TsK KP (b) Gruzii, Tiflis 1926.

Roelofs, see Saakashvili.

Rokhlin, A. (ed.), *Dvadtsat piat let Bakinskoi organizatsii bolshevistikov*, Baku 1924–25.

Saakashvili, Sandra Roelofs, *Story of an Idealist*, Tbilisi 2005.

Sagirashvili, David, "Stalin iz vospominanii i rasmyshlennii," *Vestnik instituta po izuchenii istorii i kultury SSR*, no. 9, March–April 1954.

Sagirashvili, David, "Stalin and Social Democracy: The Political Diaries of David A. Sagirashvili," up. dissertation by Roy Stanley De Lon, Georgetown University, Washington, D.C. 1974.

Samoilov, F., "Bolshevistskaya fraktsiya IV Gosudarstvennoy Dumy v Yeniseiskoi ssylke pered fevralskoie revolyutsiey," *Proletarskaya Revolyutsiya*, no. 2/3, February–March 1927.

Samoilov, F., *Po sledam minuvshego. Vospominaniya starogo bolshevika*, Moscow 1934.

Schlyapnikov, A. G., *Semnadtsatyi god*, Moscow-Petrograd 1923.

Sedmaya (aprelskaya) vserossiiskaya konferentsiya RSDRP (bolshevikov). Petrogradskaya konferentsiya obshchegorodskaya konferentsiya RSDRP (bolshevikov), Aprel 1917 goda, Moscow 1958.

Serge, Victor, *Portraite de Staline*, Paris 1940.

Sergeev, F. A., *Statii, rechi, pisma*, Moscow 1983.

Shaumian, S., *Izbrannye proizvedeniya*, Moscow 1957 and 1978.

Shestoi sezd RSDRP(b), Avgust 1917 goda. Protokoly, Moscow 1958.

Shotman, A. V., "Kak iz iskry vozgorelos plamya," *Molodaya Gvardiya*, 1935.

Shveitzer, Vera, *Stalin v turukhanskoi ssylke. Vospominaniya podpolshchika*, Moscow 1940.

Sidamon-Eristoff, Prince Simon C., *For My Grandchildren: The Memoirs of Colonel Prince Simon C. Sidamon-Eristoff*, privately published.

Souvarine, Boris, *Staline*, Paris 1935.

Spandarian, S. (Timofei), *Stati, pisma, dokumenty 1882–1916*, Yerevan 1940 and 1958.

Stal, Ludmilla, "Rabotnitsa v Oktyabre," *Proletarskaya Revolyutsiya*, no. 10, 1922.

Stalin v vospominaniyakh sovremenikov i dokumentakh epokhi, ed. M. Lobanov, Moscow 2002.

Stalin, I. V. (K.), "K natsionalnomu voprusu: evreiskaya burzhuaznaya i bundovskaya kulturno-natsionalnaya avtonomiya," *Prosveshchenie*, no. 6, June 1913.

Stalin, I. V., *Sochineniya 1–13*, Moscow 1952–54.

Stalin, I. V., *Works 1–13*, Moscow-London 1953.

Stalin, I. V., "Sam o sebe, redakzionnaya pravka sobstevennoy biografii," *Izvestiya TsK KPSS*, no. 9, 1990.

Stalin, I. V., *Iosef Stalin v obyatiyakh semi: iz lichnogo arkhiva*, ed. Y. Murin and V. Denisov, Istochnik 1993 and Moscow 1993.

Stalin, I. V., *Slovo tov. Staliny*, ed. R. Kosolapov, Moscow 2002.

Stalin-Kaganovich Correspondence 1931–1936, ed. R. W. Davies, Oleg Khevnuik and E. A. Rees, New Haven 2003.

Stasova, E. D., *Stranitsy zhizhni i borby*, Moscow 1957.

Stasova, E. D., "Partiinaia robota v ssylke i v Petrograde," in *V gody podpolya: sbornik vospominii 1910g-fevral 1917*, Moscow 1964.

Stopani, A., *Iz proshlogo. Stati i vospominania iz istorii bakinskoi organizatsii i rabochego dvizheniia v Baku*, Baku 1923.

Sukhanov, N., *Zapiskie o russkoi revolyutsii*, Berlin 1922–23.

Sukhanov, N., *The Russian Revolution 1917: A Personal Record*, Oxford 1955.

Suliashvili, D., *Uchenicheskie gody*, Tbilisi 1942.

Sverdlov, Y., *Izbrannye proizvedeniya*, Moscow 1957.

Sverdlova, K. T., *Yakov Mikhailovich Sverdlov*, Moscow 1957.

Talakvadze, S., *K istorii Kommunisticheskoi partii Gruzii*, Tiflis 1925.

Toroshelidze, Minadora Ordzhonikidze, "Memoirs" (mss, Tbilisi).

Tovstukha, I. P., *Iosif Vissarionovich Stalin, Kratkaya biografiia*, Moscow and Leningrad 1927.

Trifonov, Y., *Otblesk kostra. Ischeznovenie*, Moscow 1988.

Trotsky, L. D., *Moya Zhizn*, Berlin 1930.

Trotsky, L. D., *Stalin*, London 1968.

Trotsky, L. D., *My Life*, London 2004.

Troyanovsky, Oleg, *Cherez godi i rasstoyaniya*, Moscow 1997.

Tsereteli, I. G., *Vospominaniya o fevralskoi revoliutsii*, Paris 1963.

Tsintsadze, Kote, "Chemi Mogonebani (My Memoirs 1903–1920)," *Revolyutsiis Matiane*, nos 2–3, Tiflis 1923–24.

Tsintsadze, Kote, *Rogor vibrdzolot proletariatis diktaturistvis, chemi mogonebani* (How to Struggle for the Dictatorship of the Proletariat: My Memoirs from 1903 to 1920), Tiflis 1927.

Uratadze, G., *Vospominaniya Gruzinskogo sotsial-demokrata*, Stanford 1968.

Vazek, I., *V gody podpolya* in *Rasskazy starykh rabochikh Zakavakazya o velikom Staline*, Moscow 1939.

Vereshchak, S., "Stalin v tyurme," *Dni*, 22 and 24 January 1928.

Voroshilov, K. E., *Stalin i Krasnaya Armiya*, Moscow 1937.

Voroshilov, K. E., *Rasskazy o zhizni*, Moscow 1968.

Vstrechi s tov. Stalinym, Moscow 1939.

Vstrechi s vozhdem. Sbornik vospominanii o vstrechakh s tov. Stalinym, Saransk 1940.

Yaroslavsky, E., *Landmarks in the Life of Stalin*, London 1942.

Yaroslavsky, E., "Tri vstrechi," *Pravda*, 23 December 1939.

Yenukidze, Abel, *Istoriya organizatsiya i raboty nelegalnykh tipografii RSDRP na Kavkaze za vremya ot 1900 po 1906g*, in Tekhnika bolshevistskogo podpolya, Moscow 1925.

Yenukidze, Abel, "Iz proshlogo nashei partei," in *Iz proshlogo. Stati i vospominaniya iz istorii bakinskoi organizatsii*, Baku 1923.

Yenukidze, Abel, *Nashi podpolnye tipografii na Kavkaze*, Moscow 1925.

Zhdanov, Yuri, memoirs of Stalin, *Komsomolsky Pravda*, 10 January 2007.

Zhordania, N. (interview by N. Vakar), "Stalin po vospominanyam N. V. Zhordania," *Poslednie Novosti*, 16 December 1936.

Zhordania, N., *Moya Zhizn*, Stanford 1968.

Zhukov, G. K., *Vospominaniya i razmyshleniya*, Moscow 1995.

SECONDARY

Abramov, A. N., *Nachalo revolyutsionnoi deyatelnosti I. V. Stalina*, Leningrad 1939.

Agursky, M., "Stalin's Ecclesiastical Background," *Survey*, no. 4, 1984.

Akopian, G. S., *Stepan Shaumian*, Moscow 1973.

Antonov-Ovseenko, A., *The Time of Stalin: Portrait of Tyranny*, New York 1980.

Antonov-Ovseenko, A., *Stalin bez Maski*, Moscow 1990.

Applebaum, Anne, *Gulag: A History*, London 2003.

Ascher, Abraham, *The Revolution of 1905—Russia in Disarray*, Stanford 1988.

Ascher, Abraham, *The Revolution of 1905—Authority Restored*, Stanford 1992.

Avtorkhanov, A., *Stalin and the Soviet Communist Party*, London 1959.

Baberowski, Jorg, *Der Feind is überall: Stalinismus im Kaukasus*, Munich 2003.

Baedeker, Karl, *Baedeker's Russia*, London 1914.

Baynac, J., *Kamo: L'homme de main de Lénine*, Paris 1972.

Bezirgani, G., "Koba i Kamo," *Perspektivi*, no. 6, 1991.

Biagi, E., *Svetlana: The Inside Story*, London 1967.

Black, Conrad, *FDR, Champion of Freedom*, London 2003.

Bjorkegren, Hans, *Ryska Posten: de ryska revolutionarerna i norden 1906–17*, Stockholm 1985.

Brackman, Roman, *Israel at Noon*, New York 2006.

Brackman, Roman, *The Secret File of Joseph Stalin: A Hidden Life*, London 2001.

Burleigh, Michael, *Sacred Causes: Religion and Politics from the European Dictators to Al Qaeda*, London 2006.

Carswell, John, *The Exile: The Life of Ivy Litvinov*, London 1980.

Charroux, Robert, "Révélations sur l'enfance de Staline," *Miroir de l'Histoire*, October 1963.

Clements, Barbara Evans, *Bolshevik Feminist: The Life of Alexandra Kollontai*, Bloomington, Indiana 1979.

Clements, Barbara Evans, *Bolshevik Women*, Cambridge 1997.

Cohen, S. F., *Bukharin and the Russian Revolution: A Political Biography*, London 1974.

Conquest, Robert, *The Great Terror: Stalin's Purge of the Thirties*, London 1973.

Conquest, Robert, *Stalin: Breaker of Nations*, London 1993.

Cooper, Julian, Maureen Perrie, and E. A. Rees (eds.), *Soviet History, 1917–53: Essays in Honour of R. W. Davies*, London 1995.

Dadiani, S., *Stalin v Chiaturu*, Tbilisi 1940.

Daly, Jonathan W., *Autocracy under Siege: Security Police and Opposition in Russia, 1866–1905*, DeKalb, Illinois 1998.

Daly, Jonathan W., *The Watchful State: Security Police and Opposition in Russia 1906–17*, DeKalb, Illinois 2004.

Daushvili, A., *Story of Soso Djugashvili*, Tbilisi 2000.

Delbars, Yves, *The Real Stalin*, London 1953.

De Lon, Roy Stanley, "Stalin and Social Democracy: The Political Diaries of David A Sagirishvili," unpublished dissertation, Georgetown University, Washington, D.C. 1974.

Delo provokatora Malinovskovo, Moscow 1992.

Deutscher, I., *Stalin: A Political Biography*, London 1966.

Dubinsky-Mukhadze, I. M., *Ordzhonikidze*, Moscow 1963.

Dubinsky-Mukhadze, I. M., *Shaumian*, Moscow 1965.

Dubinsky-Mukhadze, I. M., "Mikhail G. Tskhakaya (Tsakhaya)," *Voprosy Istorii KPSS*, no. 5, 1965.

Dubinsky-Mukhadze, I. M., *Kamo*, Moscow 1974.

Elliott, Geoffrey, *From Siberia with Love*, London 2004.

Elwood, R., *Roman Malinovsky: A Life without a Cause*, Newtonville 1977.

Emelianov, Y., *Stalin Put k Vlasti*, Moscow 2003.

Emuksuzian, V. S., *Suren Spandarian*, Moscow 1982.

Essad Bey, *Stalin: The Career of a Fanatic*, London 1932.

Essaiashvili, V. G. (ed.), *Orcherki istorii Kommunist Partii Gruzii,* Tbilisi 1957.

Ettinger, Elzbieta, *Rosa Luxemburg: A Life,* London 1988.

Farnsworth, Beatrice, *Alexandra Kollontai: Socialism, Feminism and the Bolshevik Revolution,* Stanford 1980.

Felstinsky, Y., *Bil li Stalin agentom Okhranki? Sbornik statei, materialov i dokumentov,* Moscow 1999.

Ferguson, Niall, *The World's Banker: The History of the House of Rothschild,* London 1998.

Ferguson, Niall, *The War of the World,* New York 2006.

Figes, Orlando, *A People's Tragedy: The Russian Revolution, 1891–1924,* London 1996.

Fishman, W. J., *East End Jewish Radicals,* London 1975.

Fishman, W. J., *Streets of the East End,* London 1979.

Fishman, W. J., *East End, 1888: A Year in a London Borough among the Labouring Poor,* London 1988.

Fuller, William C., Jr., *The Foe Within: Fantasies of Treason and the End of Imperial Russia,* Ithaca, New York 2006.

Futrell, Michael, *Northern Underground,* London 1963.

Geifman, Anna (ed.), *Russia under the Last Tsar: Opposition and Subversion, 1894–1917,* Oxford 1999.

Geifman, Anna, *Thou Shalt Kill: Revolutionary Terrorism in Russia, 1894–1917,* Princeton 1993.

Getzler, I., *Martov: A Political Biography of a Russian Social Democrat,* London 1967.

Getzler, I., *Nikolai Sukhanov: Chronicler of the Russian Revolution,* London 2002.

Gorodetsky, E., and Y. Sharapov, *Sverdlov,* Moscow 1971.

Guruli, Vakhtang, *Materials for Stalin's Biography,* Tbilisi 1998.

Hall, Coryne, *Imperial Dancer: Mathilde Kschessinskaya and the Romanovs,* London 2005.

Hamann, Brigitte, and Thomas Thorton, *Hitler's Vienna: A Dictator's Apprenticeship,* Oxford 1999.

Haupt, Georges (ed.), *Les Bolsheviks par eux-même* (Makers of the Russian Revolution), Paris 1969.

Hosking, G., *Rulers and Victims,* London 2006.

Ilizarov, B. S., *Tainaya zhizn Stalina. Po materialam ego bibliotek i archiva. K istoriografii stalinizma,* Moscow 2002.

Imnaishvili, R., *Kamo,* Tbilisi 1955.

Ivanova, L. (ed.), *Stranitsy slavnoi istorii. Vospominania o Pravde 1912–17g,* Moscow 1962.

Jones, J. Sydney, *Hitler in Vienna,* London 1983.

Jones, Stephen F., *Socialism in Georgian Colors: The European Road to Social Democracy, 1883–1917,* Cambridge, Massachusetts 2005.

Kaptelov, B., and Z. Peregudova, "Byl li Stalin agentom Okhranki?," *Rodina,* no. 5, 1989.

Kennan, George, *Historiography of the Early Political Career of Stalin,* American Philosophical Society, no. 3, 1971.

Kershaw, Ian, *Hitler 1889–1936: Hubris,* London 1998.

Khlevniuk, Oleg, *In Stalin's Shadow: The Career of Sergo Ordzhonikidze,* New York 1993.

King, Greg, *The Court of the Last Tsar,* London 2006.

Klier, J., and S. Lambroze, *Pogroms: Anti-Jewish Violence in Modern Russian History,* Cambridge 1992.

Knight, Amy, *Beria: Stalin's First Lieutenant,* Princeton 1993.

Kolesnik, A., *Khronika zhizni semia Stalina,* Kharkov 1990.

Kujala, Antti, "Russian Revolutionary Movement and the Finnish Opposition, 1905," *Scandinavian Journal of History,* no. 5, 1980.

Kujala, Antti, "Finnish Radicals and the Russian Revolutionary Movement, 1899–1907," *Revolutionary Russia* 5, December 1992.

Kujala, Antti, et al., *Lenin Ja Suomi,* Helsinki 1987.

Kun, Miklos, *Stalin: An Unknown Portrait,* Budapest 2003.

Lakoba, S., "Legendarnoe nacholo veka," *Sovetskaya Abkhazia,* no. 145, 28 July 1982.

Lakoba, S., *Boeviki Abkhazii v revolyutsii 1905–7 godov,* Sukhum 1984.

Lakoba, S., *Ocherki politecheskoi istorii Abkhazii,* Sukhum 1990.

Lakoba, S., *Otvet istorikam iz Tbilisi,* Sukhum 2001.

Lakoba, S., et al. (eds.), *Istoria Abkhazia,* Gadaut 1993.

Lang, D. M., *Modern History of Georgia,* London 1962.

Lauchlan, Iain, *Russian Hide-and-Seek: The Tsarist Secret Police in St. Petersburg, 1906–14,* Helsinki 2002.

Lee, Eric, "Eremin Letter: Documentary Proof That Stalin Was Okhrana Spy?," *Revolutionary Russia* 6, June 1993.

Levine, Isaac Don, *Stalin's Great Secret,* New York 1956.

Lieven, D., *Russia's Rulers under the Old Regime,* New Haven 1989.

Lieven, D., *Nicholas II: Emperor of All the Russias,* London 1993.

Lincoln, W. Bruce, *Passage through Armageddon: The Russians in War and Revolution, 1914–18,* New York 1986.

Loginov, V., *Taini Stalina,* Moscow 1991.

London Landmarks: A Guide with Maps to Places Where Marx, Engels and Lenin Lived and Worked, London 1963.

Ludwig, E., *Stalin,* New York 1942.

McNeal, R., *Bride of the Revolution: Krupskaya and Lenin,* London 1973.

McNeal, R., *Stalin: Man and Ruler,* London 1985.

Maisky, Ivan, *Journey into the Past,* London 1962.

Marcou, Lily, *Staline: Vie privée,* Paris 1996.

Maskulia, A. V., *Mikhail Tskhakaya,* Moscow 1968.

Medvedev, Roy A., *Let History Judge: The Origins and Consequences of Stalinism,* London 1971.

Medvedev, Zhores A., and Roy A. Medvedev, *The Unknown Stalin,* London 2003.

Merridale, Catherine, "The Making of a Moderate Bolshevik: An Introduction to L. B. Kamenev's Political Biography," in Julian Cooper, Maureen Perrie and E. A. Rees (eds.), *Soviet History, 1917–53,* London 1995.

Montefiore, Simon Sebag, *Stalin: The Court of the Red Tsar,* London 2003.

Moore, James, *Gurdjieff,* Shaftesbury, Dorset 1991.

Moskalev, M. A., *Bolshevistskie organizatsii Zakavkazya periode pervoi russkoi revolyutsii,* Moscow 1940 (See also Chernenko).

Muravyova, L., and I. Sivolap-Kaftanova, *Lenin in London,* Moscow 1981.

Nikolaevsky, Boris, "Bolshevistsky Tsentre," *Rodina,* no. 3/5, 1992.

Nikolaysen, H., *SD Networks in Transcaucasia and Stalin: The Rise of a Regional Party Functionary, 1887–1902,* Stanford 1991.

Nikonov, V., *Molotov Molodost,* Moscow 2005.

Obolenskaya, R., *Kamo: The Life of a Great Revolutionist,* London n.d.

Ostrovsky, Alexander, *Kto stoyal za spinoi Stalina?,* St. Petersburg 2002.

Owen, Frank, *Three Dictators,* London 1940.

Palmer, Alan, *The East End: Centuries of London Life,* London 1982.

Pares, Bernard, *The Fall of the Russian Monarchy,* London 1939.

Pearson, Michael, *Inessa: Lenin's Mistress,* London 2001.

Phillips, Hugh D., *Between the Revolution and the West: A Political Biography of Maxim M. Litvinov*, Boulder, Colorado 1992.

Pipes, Richard, *Formation of the Soviet Union: Communism and Nationalism, 1917–23*, Cambridge, Massachusetts 1964.

Pipes, Richard, *Revolutionary Russia*, Cambridge, Massachusetts 1968.

Pipes, Richard, *Russia under the Old Regime*, London 1982.

Pipes, Richard, *The Russian Revolution, 1899–1919*, London 1990.

Pipes, Richard, *The Unknown Lenin*, New Haven 1996.

Pipes, Richard, *The Degaev Affair*, New Haven 2003.

Pope, Arthur Upham, *Maxim Litvinov*, London 1943.

Porter, Cathy, *Alexandra Kollontai*, London 1980.

Pospielovsky, Dmitri, *The Russian Church under the Soviet Regime, 1917–82*, New York 1983.

Rabinowitch, A., *Prelude to Bolshevism: The Petrograd Bolsheviks and the July 1917 Uprising*, Bloomington, Indiana 1968.

Rabinowitch, A., *The Bolsheviks Come to Power: The Revolution of 1917 in Petrograd*, Chicago 2004.

Radzinsky, E., *Stalin*, London 1996.

Radzinsky, E., *Alexander II*, New York 2005.

Raguza, Imam, *La Vie de Staline*, Paris 1938.

Rayfield, D., *Stalin and the Hangmen: An Authoritative Portrait of a Tyrant and Those Who Served Him*, London 2004.

Rayfield, D., "Stalin the Poet," *PN Review* 44, Manchester 1984.

Reiss, Tom, *The Orientalist*, New York 2005.

Richardson, R., *The Long Shadow*, London 1993.

Rieber, A., "Stalin: Man of the Borderlands," *American History Review*, no. 5, 2001.

Robbins, Richard G., *The Tsar's Viceroys*, Ithaca 1987.

Rokhlin, A., "Gde pryatali nezakonnorojdennogo syna Stalina?," *Moskovsky Komsomolets*, no. 114, 22 June 1996.

Roobol, W. H., *Tsereteli: A Democrat in the Russian Revolution: A Political Biography*, The Hague 1976.

Rothstein, Andrew, *Lenin in Britain*, London 1970.

Ruud, Charles A., and Sergei A. Stepanov, *Fontanka 16: The Tsar's Secret Police*, Quebec 1999.

Schorske, Carl E., *Fin de Siècle Vienna*, London 1961.

Service, R., *The Bolshevik Party in Revolution: A Study in Organizational Change*, London 1979.

Service, R., "Joseph Stalin: The Making of a Stalinist," in John Channon (ed.), *Politics, Society and Stalinism in the USSR*, London 1998.

Service, R., *Lenin: A Biography*, London 2000.

Service, R., *A History of Modern Russia from Nicholas II to Putin*, London 2003.

Service, R., *Stalin: A Biography*, London 2004.

Seton-Watson, H., *The Russian Empire, 1801–1917*, Oxford 1967.

Sheinis, Z., *Maxim Maximovich Litvinov*, Moscow 1989.

Shub, David, "Kamo: Legendary Old Bolshevik of the Caucasus," *Russian Review*, 19 July 1960.

Slavin, B., "Stalin i Okhranka," *Alternativy*, no. 1, 1990.

Slusser, R., *Stalin in October: The Man Who Missed the Revolution*, Baltimore 1987.

Smith, E. E., *The Young Stalin*, New York 1967.

Stugart, M. (readers' queries), *Dagens Nyheter*, Stockholm, 22 March 2004.

Sukhodeev, V., *Stalin v zhizn i legendakh*, Moscow 2003.

Sukhotin, Y., "Bastard krasnogo vozhda," *Chas Pik*, no. 189, 21 October 1995.

Suleymanov, Manaf, *Eskitdiklarim, Okhuduglarim, Gorduklarim* [What I Saw, What I Read, What I Heard; Russian title *Dni Minuvshie*], Baku 1996.

Suliashvili, D., *Uchenichesky gody*, Tiflis 1942.

Suny, R. G., "A Journeyman for the Revolution: Stalin and the Labour Movement in Baku, June 1907–May 1908," *Soviet Studies*, no. 3, 1972.

Suny, R. G., *The Making of the Georgian Nation*, London 1989.

Suny, R. G., "Beyond Psychohistory: The Young Stalin in Georgia," *Slavic Review* 50, Spring 1991.

Thompson, Bruce, *Hitler's Vienna*, London 1983.

Thompson, Bruce, *Schnitzler's Vienna*, London 1990.

Tolf, Robert W., *The Russian Rockefellers: The Saga of the Nobel Family and the Russian Oil Industry*, Stanford 1976.

Tucker, R. C., *Stalin as Revolutionary, 1879–1929: A Study in History and Personality*, London 1974.

Tucker, R. C., *Stalin in Power: The Revolution from Above, 1929–41*, New York and London 1990.

Ulam, Adam, *Lenin and the Bolsheviks*, London 1966.

Vakar, N.: see Zhordania.

Vaksberg, Arkady, *Stalin's Prosecutor: The Life of Andrei Vyshinsky*, New York 1990.

Van Ree, Erik, "Stalin and the National Question," *Revolutionary Russia* 7, December 1994.

Van Ree, Erik, "Stalin's Bolshevism: The First Decade," *International Review of Social History* 39, 1994.

Van Ree, Erik, "Stalin's Bolshevism: The Year of Revolution," *Revolutionary Russia* 13, June 2000.

Vasileva, L., *Kremlin Wives*, London 1994.

Vasileva, L., *Deti Kremlya*, Moscow 2001.

Vitebsky, Piers, *Reindeer People*, London 2005.

Volkogonov, D., *Stalin: Triumph and Tragedy*, New York 1988.

Volkogonov, D., *Lenin: Life and Legacy*, London 1995.

Williams, Robert C., *The Other Bolsheviks: Lenin and his Critics, 1904–14*, Bloomington, Indiana 1986.

Yagubov, S., *Stalin byl voxhdem rabochego dvizheniya v Baku*, Moscow 1947.

Yergin, Daniel, *The Prize*, London 1991.

Zhukov, Y., "Gori-Tbilisi," *Novy Mir*, 12 December 1939.

Index

*"Biography in the grand tradition. . . . The story is riveting,
the main character a hero, and the author a gifted storyteller
with an impressive command of his subject."*
—The Washington Post Book World

POTEMKIN
Catherine the Great's Imperial Partner

As a young guardsman, Grigory Potemkin caught the eye of
Catherine the Great with a theatrical act of gallantry during the
coup that placed her on the throne. Over the next thirty years he
would become her lover, co-ruler, and husband in a secret marriage that left room for both to satisfy their sexual appetites.
Potemkin proved to be one of the most brilliant statesmen of the
eighteenth century, helping Catherine expand the Russian
empire and deftly manipulating allies and adversaries from
Constantinople to London. This acclaimed biography vividly
re-creates Potemkin's outsized character and accomplishments
and restores him to his rightful place as a colossus of the eighteenth century. It chronicles the tempestuous relationship
between Potemkin and Catherine, a remarkable love affair
between two strong personalities that helped shape the course of
history. As he brings these characters to life, Montefiore also
tells the story of the creation of the Russian empire. This is biography as it is meant to be: both intimate and panoramic, and
bursting with life.

Biography/978-1-4000-7717-5